WINSTON S. CHURCHILL
1874–1965

WINSTON S. CHURCHILL

by

RANDOLPH S. CHURCHILL

VOLUME II
Companion
Part 1
1901–1907

HEINEMANN : LONDON

William Heinemann Ltd

LONDON MELBOURNE TORONTO
JOHANNESBURG AUCKLAND

434 13008 7
First published 1969
© 1969 C & T Publications Limited
All rights reserved

Printed in Great Britain by
Butler & Tanner Ltd, Frome and London

Contents

PART 2

PART 3

Preface

WHEN MR RANDOLPH CHURCHILL died in
June 1968 this book was already in its final stages of
production. For over six years, under Mr Churchill's close
supervision, the documents were assembled and annotated by
his research assistants. In October 1968 the Churchill Trustees
asked me to complete Sir Winston's Official Biography, and I
undertook as my first task the final revision of these pages.

The majority of the documents in the three parts of this
Companion Volume come from the Chartwell papers, and have
not been published before. Mr Churchill also searched for
further unpublished documents in a large number of private
archives. In addition to these two principal sources of material,
Mr Churchill included a number of unpublished official documents, particularly in the later part of the volume which concerns the years during which his father held office. Quotations
from newspapers, parliamentary debates, and other published
sources have been kept to a minimum; but Mr Churchill did
not hesitate to include these where they provided an important
link or commentary for the other, previously unpublished,
documentation.

As in the first Companion Volume, which covered the years
1874 to 1900, it was Mr Churchill's aim in this volume to publish the bulk of the relevant letters which his father wrote and
received between 1900 and 1914, together with correspondence
concerning him which passed between other people. He made
every effort, with varying degrees of success, to track down
missing links, and in particular to find his father's answers to
letters which are in the Chartwell papers.

The sections of this Companion Volume follow in general the

chapter divisions of the main volume. The material has been
grouped according to subject rather than chronology. Some
explanatory headings and introductory material have been
added, in order that the reader may more easily find his way
through the documents. Mr Churchill was always conscious
of the need to present this large mass of unpublished material
in a way which would be serviceable to general readers and
historians alike.

Although these Companion Volumes contain nearly two
thousand pages of documents, they constitute no more than a
careful selection from a much larger mass of material which was
at Mr Churchill's disposal. He had to be particularly selective
when dealing with his father's activities at the Colonial Office,
the Board of Trade, the Home Office and the Admiralty. The
official files for each of these Departments of State are copious;
and complete volumes of unpublished material could easily
have been assembled for each one of them. But these archives,
although as yet largely unpublished, are now open to the
scrutiny of all historians, and Mr Churchill therefore set as his
objective when dealing with the public records the searching
out and publishing of what he judged to be the material of
widest significance. As the total bulk of this Companion Volume
exceeds by nearly three times the main volume to which it
relates, the reader will realize the extent to which the majority
of documents published here appear in print for the first
time.

Because several years elapsed between the preparation of the
main Volume Two and the final proof of this Companion
Volume, a large number of documents are published here which
were not available to Mr Churchill when he wrote the main
volume. These add significant new material for a number of
important and controversial periods in Churchill's career. In
particular the documents for 1903 and 1904 cast a new and
revealing light, not only upon Churchill's own rejection of
conservatism in those years, but also upon the political struggles
which hastened the end of A. J. Balfour's Conservative administration. Similarly, in the Home Office and Admiralty sections
there is much new material on Churchill's lesser known efforts

as a social reformer, and on the reaction of the Liberal Government to the social and industrial unrest of 1911 and 1912.

As with all the previous volumes of this work, Mr Churchill wished to acknowledge his indebtedness to Her Majesty the Queen, who graciously gave permission for him to have access to the Royal Archives, and to use documents which are her copyright. Mr Robin Mackworth-Young, Librarian at Windsor Castle, gave valuable help in the selection of this material. Lady Spencer-Churchill kindly gave permission for the publication of letters which are in her possession, and are indicated in the text as 'CSC Papers'. All Crown Copyright material, covering official documents and State papers, is reproduced here with the permission of the Controller of Her Majesty's Stationery Office. Important help was also given by Bodley's Librarian, and by the Librarians of the Beaverbrook Library, the Birmingham University Library, the British Museum, the Public Record Office and the National Library of Scotland. Mr Churchill also wished to express his thanks to all those who made the papers in their charge available to him and to all who granted copyright permission. In some cases it has unfortunately not been possible either for Mr Churchill, or for me, to trace the holders of copyright, and I beg them to accept sincere apologies.

During the period of over six years throughout which work on these volumes was in progress, Mr Churchill was helped by a number of research assistants. The initial research was planned and directed by Mr Michael Wolff, assisted by Mr Michael Molian, Mr Martin Mauthner and myself. Subsequent research, particularly in the British Museum and the Public Record Office, was undertaken by Mr Robert Taylor and Mr Alan Thompson. The documents were then examined and revised by Mr Cameron Hazlehurst. Mr Paul Addison made the revision of the documents covering the years 1910 to 1914; and both Mr Hazlehurst and Mr Addison added new material from the Chartwell and other archives. Mr Churchill also appreciated the help given at various times by Mr Frank Gannon, Mr George Thayer and Mrs José Harris. During these six years Mr Andrew Kerr, and later Mr Tom Hartman, prepared the majority of the footnotes, and were responsible for collating the work as it was done, and preparing each section for the printers. The final page proofs were scrutinized by Mr G. Norman Knight as well as by Mr Churchill's principal research assistants. The index was compiled by Wing Commander Roger F. Pemberton.

As one who was associated with the work of research and compilation on these volumes for several years, I believe I may, on Mr Churchill's behalf, pay tribute to what he himself described as the 'intricate as well as laborious task' carried out by all those associated with these volumes. Thanks should also go to Miss Eileen Harryman, archivist; and to Mrs Trevor Adams, Mrs Margaret Bentley, Mrs Margaret Burt, Miss Ida Depere, Miss Alice Golding, Mrs Richard von Goetz, Mrs Cameron Hazlehurst, Mrs Martin Mauthner, Miss Lynette Parker, Miss Barbara Twigg and Mrs Bettye Verran for their secretarial assistance. I myself should like to thank Miss Sarah Graham for helping to ensure that these volumes went to press so promptly.

Merton College   MARTIN GILBERT
Oxford
24 January 1969

Short Biographies

of the

PRINCIPAL CHARACTERS

to be brought before the reader in this volume

ASKWITH George Ranken (1861–1942); Controller-General, commercial, labour and statistical department, Board of Trade 1909–11; Chief Industrial Commissioner 1911–19; KCB 1911. Created Baron 1919.

ASQUITH Herbert Henry (1852–1928); Liberal MP for East Fife 1886–1918, for Paisley 1920–4; Home Secretary 1892–5; Liberal Imperialist during Boer War; Chancellor of Exchequer 1905–8; Prime Minister 1908–16. Succeeded by Lloyd George 1916; resigned Liberal leadership 1926. Created Earl of Oxford and Asquith 1925. Married first 1877 Helen, daughter of F. Melland, died 1891; 2nd 1894 Margaret (Margot), youngest daughter of Sir Charles Tennant, 1st baronet.

BALFOUR Arthur James (1848–1930); Conservative MP for Hertford 1874–85, for East Manchester 1885–1906, for City of London 1906–22; associated with Lord Randolph in the Fourth Party; entered Cabinet 1886; Conservative leader in Commons 1891–2, 1895–1902. As Prime Minister 1902–5 sought to keep Party together during tariff reform controversy; set up Committee of Imperial Defence 1902. Resigned Party leadership November 1911. Succeeded WSC as First Lord of the Admiralty 1915. Foreign Secretary 1916–19. KG 1922. Created Earl 1922. Died unmarried.

BECKETT Ernest William (1856–1917); Conservative MP for Whitby 1885–1905. Formerly a partner in the Banking firm of Beckett & Co in Leeds. Succeeded his uncle as 2nd Baron Grimthorpe in 1905.

BERESFORD Charles William de la Poer (1846–1919); 2nd son of 4th Marquess of Waterford. Rear-Admiral Mediterranean 1900–2; Conservative MP for York 1897–1900; for Woolwich 1902. Commanded

Channel Squadron 1903–5; C-in-C Mediterranean Fleet 1905–7,
Channel Fleet 1907–9; retired as Admiral 1911. Unionist MP for
Portsmouth 1910–16. His younger brother William married 1895 Lilian,
widow of the 8th Duke of Marlborough.

BOTHA Louis (1862–1919); Commandant-General of Boer forces 1900;
carried on guerrilla warfare 1900–2; surrendered May 1902; visited
Britain 1902; founded Het Volk party which won first elections under
responsible government 1907. As first Prime Minister of Union of
South Africa 1910–19 supported Britain in the First World War.

BRODRICK William St John Fremantle (1856–1942); Conservative MP
for Surrey 1880–1906; Secretary of State for India 1903–5; for War
1900–3. Succeeded as Viscount Midleton 1907. Created 1st Earl of
Midleton 1920.

BURNS John Elliot (1858–1943); trade union leader and agitator; elected
Independent Labour MP for Battersea 1892. President of Local
Government Board and Cabinet member 1905 (first artisan to reach
that rank). Opposed the Webbs' plan to reform the Poor Law. Twice
re-elected at Battersea as a Liberal in 1910 elections. President of Board
of Trade 1914, resigning at outbreak of war.

BUXTON Sydney Charles (1853–1934); Radical MP for Poplar 1886–1914;
Postmaster-General 1905–10; succeeded WSC as President of the Board
of Trade 1910–14; responsible for the Copyright Act of 1911 and the
Bankruptcy Act of 1913; High Commissioner and Governor-General
of South Africa 1914–20. GCMG 1914. Created Viscount 1914. Created
Earl 1920.

CAMPBELL-BANNERMAN Sir Henry (1836–1908); Liberal MP for the
Stirling Burghs 1868–1908; succeeded as Liberal leader in House of
Commons 1899; denounced British 'methods of barbarism' in South
Africa. Prime Minister December 1905 to April 1908; established
responsible government in Transvaal and Orange River Colony. His
wife Charlotte died 1906.

CARSON Sir Edward Henry (1854–1935); Conservative MP for Dublin
University 1892–1918, for Duncairn (Belfast) 1918–21; became leading
advocate after Oscar Wilde's libel action against Marquess of Queens-
berry 1895. Solicitor-General 1900–5; as leader of Irish Unionists in

Commons 1910–21 successfully ensured the exclusion of Ulster from Irish Home Rule. Attorney-General in Asquith's coalition government May 1915 to October 1916; First Lord of the Admiralty under Lloyd George December 1916 to July 1917; Member of the War Cabinet until January 1918. Lord of Appeal 1921–9. Knighted 1900. Created Life Baron 1921.

CASSEL Sir Ernest Joseph (1852–1921); naturalized international financier and philanthropist of German-Jewish origin. Racing enthusiast; close friend of King Edward VII, and of WSC, skilfully guiding both in their financial activities. Gave about £2 million to charities. Knighted 1899.

CECIL Lord Hugh Richard Heathcote Gascoyne ('Linky') (1869–1956); 5th son of 3rd Marquess of Salisbury and brother of Lord Robert Cecil. Conservative MP for Greenwich 1895–1906, Oxford University 1910–37. Created Baron Quickswood 1941. Until WSC crossed the floor, Hugh Cecil was his closest political friend, giving his name to the 'Hughligans', and fighting ardently both in defence of the Church of England and against Joseph Chamberlain's tariff policy.

CHAMBERLAIN (Joseph) Austen (1865–1937); son of Joseph, and half-brother of Neville Chamberlain; Liberal Unionist MP for East Worcestershire 1892–1914; Financial Secretary to Treasury 1900–2; Postmaster-General 1902–3; Chancellor of Exchequer 1903–5 and 1919–21; Foreign Secretary 1924–9; First Lord of the Admiralty, very briefly, in 1931; supported his father's views on tariff reform. After Balfour's resignation 1911 he and Walter Long, as rivals for Conservative Party leadership, stood down in favour of Bonar Law. KG 1925.

CHAMBERLAIN Joseph (1836–1914); member of Birmingham screw manufacturing firm; as Mayor 1873–5 improved the city's housing and sanitation. MP for West Birmingham 1885–1914. Broke with Liberal Party over Home Rule 1886; joined Salisbury's third Cabinet as Colonial Secretary 1895 and sought to further the cause of British imperialism; resigned 1903 over tariff reform, for which he campaigned until 1906, when ill health forced him to withdraw from public life. Three times married; his sons included Austen and Neville. Despite their differences over the tariff issue, he and WSC remained good friends.

CHURCHILL John Strange Spencer- ('Jack') (1880–1947); younger brother of WSC. Born in Dublin 4 February 1880; educated at Harrow; served in the South African War 1889–1900, where he was wounded and mentioned in despatches, and in First World War at Gallipoli. By profession a stockbroker. He married in 1908 Lady Gwendeline 'Goonie' Bertie (1885–1941), daughter of 7th Earl of Abingdon.

CHURCHILL Lady Randolph Spencer ('Jennie') (1854–1921); mother of WSC. Widow of Lord Randolph, who died in 1895. Married, as her second husband, in 1900, Captain George Cornwallis-West (whom she divorced 1913); thirdly, in 1919 Montagu Porch. She was the Proprietor and Editor of *The Anglo-Saxon Review*, 1899–1902. Published *The Reminiscences of Lady Randolph Churchill*, 1908; two plays, 1909 and 1912; and *Small Talks on Big Subjects*, 1916.

CURZON George Nathaniel (1859–1925); MP for Southport 1886–98; Viceroy and Governor-General of India 1898–1905; Lord Privy Seal 1915–16; Lord President of the Council 1916–19; Secretary of State for Foreign Affairs 1919–24; Leader of the House of Lords 1916–25. Created Baron Curzon 1898 (Irish peerage); Earl Curzon of Kedleston 1911; Marquess 1921. Succeeded as 5th Baron Scarsdale 1916. His first wife, Mary Victoria, died 18 July 1906.

DEVONSHIRE Spencer Compton, 8th Duke of (1833–1908). Conservative MP 1857–91. As Lord Hartington founded, with Chamberlain, Liberal Unionist Party which broke up Gladstone's administration 1886; joined Lord Salisbury's coalition government as President of the Council 1895–1902; held same office under Balfour 1902–3. Strongly opposed Chamberlain's tariff schemes and resigned 1903 due to Balfour's equivocal pronouncements on tariff. A respected leader of Victorian society. Succeeded as 8th Duke 1891; married 1892 Countess Louise Fredericke Auguste, widow of 7th Duke of Manchester.

ELGIN Victor Alexander Bruce, 9th Earl of (1849–1917); Colonial Secretary 1905–8 while WSC was Under-Secretary of State for Colonies. Married first in 1876 Constance Carnegie, daughter of the ninth Earl of Southesk by whom he had six sons and five daughters; she was ill for some years before her death in 1909. He married secondly in 1913 Gertrude Lilian, widow of Captain Frederick Charles Ashley Ogilvy.

FISHER John Arbuthnot ('Jackie') (1841–1920); entered Navy 1854; First Sea Lord 1904–10; organized redistribution of fleet to meet growing German threat; advocated Dreadnought battleships; issued programme of eight battleships 1909–10; reappointed First Sea Lord by WSC October 1914, resigning over Dardanelles May 1915. Knighted 1894. Created Baron December 1909.

GLADSTONE Herbert John (1854–1930); youngest son of W. E. Gladstone; MP for West Leeds 1880–1910; Liberal Chief Whip 1899–1905; Home Secretary 1905–10; first Governor-General of South Africa 1910–14. Created Viscount 1910.

GREY Sir Edward, third baronet (1862–1933). Liberal MP for Berwick on Tweed 1885–1916. Supported Boer War. Like Asquith vice-president of Liberal League led by Lord Rosebery. As Foreign Secretary 1905–16 upheld Anglo-French *entente* against German pressure. Created Viscount Grey of Fallodon 1916. His first wife, Dorothy, died after carriage accident 4 February 1906. Married 2nd widow of 1st Baron Glenconner 1922.

GUEST Frederick Edward (1875–1937); younger son of 1st Baron Wimborne, and WSC's cousin; Liberal MP 1910–22 and 1923–9; Conservative MP 1931–7. Helped promote aviation in Britain. Married, 28 June 1905, Amy Phipps of Pittsburgh, USA.

GUEST Ivor Churchill (1873–1939); son of 1st Baron Wimborne and Lord Randolph's sister, Lady Cornelia; WSC's cousin; Conservative MP for Plymouth 1900–6; Liberal MP for Cardiff 1906–10; Paymaster-General 1910–12. Created Baron Ashby St Ledger 1910; succeeded his father as 2nd Baron Wimborne 1914; created Viscount Wimborne 1918. Married, 10 February 1902, Hon Alice Katherine Sibell Grosvenor, daughter of 2nd Baron Ebury.

HALDANE Richard Burdon (1856–1928); Liberal MP for Haddingtonshire 1885–1911; QC 1890; Secretary of State for War 1905–12; Lord Chancellor 1912–15 and 1924; Member of the Judicial Committee of the Privy Council; author of several volumes of philosophical writing. Created Viscount Haldane of Cloan 1911; PC 1902; FRS 1906; KT 1913; OM 1915. Died unmarried.

HAMILTON Ian Standish Monteith (1853–1947); served as soldier in India where he met WSC; commanded mounted infantry division in advance on Pretoria 1900 (in which WSC took part). Military Secretary at War Office 1900–3; Quartermaster-General 1903–4; headed military mission with Japanese during Russo-Japanese war 1904–5; GOC-in-C Southern Command 1905–9; General 1907; Adjutant-General 1909–10; GOC-in-C Mediterranean command 1910–14; commanded Anglo-French army at Dardanelles 1915. Knighted 1900.

HARCOURT Lewis (1863–1922); son of Sir William Harcourt; Liberal MP for Rossendale 1904–17; First Commissioner of Works 1905–10 and 1915–17; Secretary of State for the Colonies 1910–15; PC 1905. Created Viscount 1916. Known as 'Lou-lou'.

HICKS-BEACH Michael (1837–1916); eldest son of 8th Baronet, whom he succeeded 1854. Conservative MP for East Gloucestershire 1864–85, for Bristol West 1885–1906. Twice Chief Secretary for Ireland 1874–8 and 1886–7, twice Chancellor of the Exchequer 1885–6 and 1895–1902. Created Viscount St Aldwyn 1905, Earl 1914.

HOZIER Clementine (1885–   ); daughter of Lady Blanche and Colonel Sir Henry Montagu Hozier; brought up by her mother following her parents' separation; educated at Berkhampstead School, where she became head girl, and at the Sorbonne; befriended by her great-aunt Lady St Helier who introduced her to London society; first introduced to WSC at a dance given by Lady Crewe in 1904; married WSC 12 September 1908; they had five children: Diana, born 1909; Randolph, born 1911; Sarah, born 1914; Marigold, born 1918; and Mary, born 1922.

HOPWOOD Sir Francis John Stephens (1860–1947). Appointed a member of the Commission to South Africa to advise on the Constitution for the Transvaal and Orange River Colonies. Permanent Secretary Board of Trade 1901–7; Permanent Under-Secretary of State for Colonies 1907–11; a Civil Lord of the Admiralty 1912–17. Knighted 1901; Privy Councillor 1912. Created Baron Southborough 1917.

JAMES Henry (1828–1911); lawyer and politician, befriended Lord and Lady Randolph and later WSC. Liberal MP for Taunton 1869–85, for Bury 1885–6. Twice Attorney-General under Gladstone 1873–4, 1880–5. Privy Councillor 1885. With Chamberlain and Hartington left Liberal Party and became Liberal Unionist (MP for Bury 1886–95). Chancellor of Duchy of Lancaster 1895–1902. Knighted 1873. Created Baron James of Hereford 1895.

LAW Andrew Bonar (1858–1923); Conservative MP for Blackfriars (Glasgow) 1900–6, Dulwich 1906–10, Bootle 1911–18, Glasgow Central 1918–22; an iron merchant before entering politics, he rose rapidly to the front rank of the Conservative Party; as a compromise candidate, with the skilful aid of Sir Max Aitken, succeeded Balfour as leader of the Conservatives in the House of Commons 1911; Secretary of State for the Colonies in Asquith's coalition government 1915–16; Chancellor of the Exchequer under Lloyd George 1916–18; Lord Privy Seal 1919–1921; Leader of the House of Commons 1916–21; Prime Minister and First Lord of the Treasury 1922–3.

LLOYD GEORGE David (1863–1945); Liberal MP for Carnarvon Boroughs 1890–1945. Opposed Boer War and Balfour's policy of rate-aid to voluntary schools. President of Board of Trade 1905–8 (when succeeded by WSC). As Chancellor of Exchequer 1908–14 introduced 'People's' Budget 1909 which led to constitutional crisis over House of Lords' veto. With WSC responsible for introducing far-reaching social reforms on which welfare state based. Succeeded Asquith as Prime Minister 1916, resigning 1922. Created Earl 1945.

LOREBURN Robert Threshie Reid (1846–1923); called to Bar 1871; entered Parliament as Liberal 1880; Solicitor-General and knighted 1894; Attorney-General 1895. Supported Boers during Boer War. As Lord Chancellor December 1905 to June 1912 established Court of Criminal Appeal 1907. Created Earl 1911.

LYTTELTON Alfred (1857–1913); son of 4th Baron; barrister 1881–1903; Liberal Unionist MP 1895–1913. Succeeded Chamberlain as Colonial Secretary September 1903–5; introduced Chinese labourers on Rand goldfields 1904; drew up (abortive) plan for granting representative government to Transvaal 1905. Father of 1st Viscount Chandos.

McKENNA Reginald (1863–1943); Liberal MP for Monmouthshire North 1895–1918; Financial Secretary to the Treasury 1905–9; President of Board of Education 1907–8; First Lord of the Admiralty 1908–11, when he exchanged offices with WSC; Home Secretary 1911–15; Chancellor of the Exchequer 1915–16; retired from politics 1919 when he became Chairman of the Midland Bank.

MALCOLM Ian Zachary (1868–1944); one of the 'Hughligans'. Conservative MP for Stowmarket 1895–1906; Croydon 1910–19; Parliamentary

Private Secretary to Chief Secretary for Ireland, George Wyndham, 1901–3. Married, 30 June 1902, Jeanne Marie Langtry, daughter of Lady de Bathe (Lily Langtry, the actress). Private Secretary to A. J. Balfour 1919. Created Baronet 1919.

MARLBOROUGH Charles Richard John, Duke of (1871–1934); known as 'Sunny'; succeeded his father 1892 as 9th Duke of Marlborough. Became close friend of his cousin WSC. Served with Queen's Own Oxfordshire Hussars, staff captain with Imperial Yeomanry in South Africa. Paymaster-General of the Forces 1899–1902; Under-Secretary of State for the Colonies 1903–5; Joint Parliamentary Secretary to the Board of Agriculture and Fisheries 1917–18. Married (1) 1895 Consuelo, daughter of Commodore William Vanderbilt of New York (marriage dissolved 1921), (2) 1921 Gladys, daughter of Edward Parke Deacon of Boston, USA.

MARSH Edward Howard (1872–1953); son of Professor Howard Marsh, Master of Downing College, Cambridge. 2nd Class Clerk, Colonial Office 1896; Assistant Private Secretary to Joseph Chamberlain 1900–3 and to Alfred Lyttelton 1903–5; 1st Class Clerk 1905. Private Secretary to WSC 1905–15, 1917–22 and 1924–9; accompanied WSC on tour of East Africa 1907–8; Private Secretary to J. H. Thomas 1924 and 1929–36; to Malcolm Macdonald 1936–7. Trustee of the Tate Gallery 1937–44. Created CMG 1908; CB 1918; CVO 1922; KCVO 1937. WSC's lifelong companion. Patron of the arts and literature. Died unmarried.

MILNER Alfred (1854–1925); High Commissioner for South Africa 1897–1905; Governor of Transvaal and Orange River Colony 1901–5; Member of the War Cabinet 1916–18; Secretary of State for War 1918–19; Secretary of State for Colonies 1919–21. Created Baron 1901; Viscount 1902. KG 1921. One of his earliest political appointments was as Private Secretary to Lord Goschen, who had succeeded Lord Randolph as Chancellor of the Exchequer in 1887. He married 1921 Violet Georgina, daughter of Admiral Frederick Maxse and widow of Lord Edward Gascoyne-Cecil.

MORLEY John (1838–1923); Liberal MP 1883–1908; Secretary of State for India 1905–10; Lord President of the Council 1910–14 when he resigned over the British intervention in the European war. His official biography of Gladstone published 1903. Created Viscount 1908.

NORTHCLIFFE Alfred Charles William Harmsworth (1865–1922); largely self-educated; founded halfpenny *Daily Mail* 1896 which pioneered popular journalism; founded *Daily Mirror* 1903; chief proprietor of *The Times* on formation of company 1908. Amassed huge fortune. Created Baronet 1904, Baron 1905, Viscount 1918.

REDMOND John Edward (1851–1918); Irish Nationalist MP for New Ross 1881–5; Wexford North 1885–91, Waterford 1891–1918; a barrister; succeeded Parnell as leader of the Irish Nationalist Party at Westminster.

ROBINSON Joseph Benjamin (1840–1929); South African mining magnate who secured valuable diamond claims at Kimberley and sank first shaft on Rand. Sympathetic to Boer cause, he quarrelled with other mine owners. After 1904 sought to show that supply of African mine labour was sufficient to dispense with Chinese coolies, thus finding favour with WSC who was responsible for carrying out Liberal pledge to end Chinese experiment. Created Baronet 1908. In 1922 Robinson was recommended for a peerage. Vehement protests caused him to decline the honour.

ROSEBERY Archibald Philip Primrose, 5th Earl of (1847–1929); Secretary of State for Foreign Affairs 1886 and 1892–4; Prime Minister 1894–5; a friend of both Lord Randolph and WSC. Always a reluctant politician, after 1901 he ploughed a lonely furrow away from his Liberal Imperialist supporters.

RUNCIMAN Walter (1870–1949); Liberal MP. Defeated WSC at Oldham 1899, but lost seat to him in 1900. Returned to Parliament 1902–18, 1924–31; as Liberal National 1931–7. Parliamentary Secretary to Local Government Board 1905–7; Financial Secretary to Treasury 1907–8; President Board of Education 1908–11; of Agriculture 1911–14; of Trade 1914–16 and 1931–7. Sent to Czechoslovakia in 1938 by Lord Halifax as 'independent mediator' between the Czechoslovak Government and Sudeten German Party. Lord President of the Council 1938–9. Shipowner: Walter Runciman & Co, Moor Line, Anchor Line. Created Baronet 1906; PC 1908; succeeded father as 2nd Baron 1933. Created Viscount Runciman of Doxford 1937.

SALISBURY Robert Arthur Talbot Gascoyne-Cecil, 3rd Marquess of (1830–1903); Conservative MP 1853–68; Prime Minister 1885–6 (unsuccessfully challenged for leadership by Lord Randolph 1886), 1886–92, 1895

to July 1902 when he resigned position to his nephew Balfour. Married
Georgiana Caroline, daughter of Sir Edward Hall Alderson 1857.

SEELY John Edward Bernard (1868–1947); fourth son of Sir Charles Seely,
1st Baronet. While on service in South Africa (DSO) where he first
met WSC, he was elected Conservative MP for Isle of Wight 1900.
Joined WSC in attacks on Mr Brodrick's Army; crossed the floor in
March 1904 on the issues of Chinese labour and free trade and was
re-elected unopposed as Liberal MP for Isle of Wight. Under-Secretary
for the Colonies 1908–10; briefly Under-Secretary, then Secretary of
State for War 1911–14, having to resign as result of his actions in Curragh
mutiny. Served in France 1914–18, commanding Canadian Cavalry
brigade; Parliamentary Under-Secretary Ministry of Munitions and
Deputy Minister of Munitions under WSC 1918; Under-Secretary of
State for Air under WSC and President of Air Council 1919; PC 1909;
Major General 1918. Created 1st Baron Mottistone 1933.

SMITH Frederick Edwin (1872–1930); Fellow of Merton College, Oxford
1896; called to the Bar 1899; Unionist MP for Walton 1906–19; KC
1908; Solicitor-General 1915; Attorney-General 1915–19; Lord Chancellor 1919–22; Secretary of State for India 1924–8. Married Margaret
Furneaux 1901. PC 1911. Knighted 1915. Created Baron 1919; Earl of
Birkenhead 1922; GCSI 1928. A brilliant lawyer and debater, he
formed a lasting friendship with WSC shortly after entering Parliament.
Smith was godfather to WSC's son and WSC was godfather to Smith's
son. WSC wrote of him in *Great Contemporaries*: '. . . our friendship was
perfect. It was one of my most precious possessions. . . . It was never
marred by the slightest personal difference or misunderstanding. . . .
The pleasure and instruction of his companionship were of the highest
order.'

SMUTS Jan Christian (1870–1950); led commando in closing stages of Boer
War. After Liberals took office December 1905, Boer party Het Volk
sent him to London to plead for responsible government for Transvaal;
met WSC while in England. Played important part in formation of
Union of South Africa 1909–10; with Botha invaded German South-
West Africa in 1914–18 war. Prime Minister of South Africa 1919–24,
1939–48. PC 1917; Order of Merit 1947.

SPENDER John Alfred (1862–1942); a contemporary at Balliol (under
Jowett) of Curzon, Cosmo Lang and Edward Grey. Edited *Westminster*

Gazette 1896–1921, which under him became an influential Liberal evening paper. Intimate friend of many members of Campbell-Bannerman's cabinet, and later his official biographer.

STANLEY (Beatrice) Venetia (1887–1948); fifth daughter of 4th Baron Stanley of Alderley. Friend of the Asquith family. Married the Hon Edwin Samuel Montagu, second son of 1st Baron Swaythling, in 1915. Cousin of CSC.

WIMBORNE Cornelia Henrietta Maria, Lady (1847–1927); eldest daughter of 7th Duke of Marlborough, aunt of WSC. Married 1868 Ivor Bertie Guest (1835–1914), 2nd Bart, who was created 1880 1st Baron Wimborne. When young, WSC frequently stayed with the Wimbornes at their house near Bournemouth. Mother of Frederick and Ivor Guest.

THE first three letters in this volume properly belong to the period covered by Companion Volume One. However, they have only recently come to light and are therefore included here.

WSC to Ivor Guest[1]
(Satinoff Papers)

25 October [18]98   35a Gt Cumberland Place

My dear Ivor,

I have postponed my departure for India until next Friday. I shall hope to come to Paris a day earlier so as to have a talk with you. I hope you read the *Morning Posts* of 25th & 27th instant. The speeches were successful but I hope to make considerable progress with practice. I speak at Portsmouth on Monday night – I think; after that no more till next year.

I will write to you and let you know my plans, as to Paris. You must have witnessed some strange scenes in the last few days. A democracy gone wrong is a terrible spectacle.

After all the only difference between us the other night was one which has long agitated the world. You follow Epicurus – I incline to Zeus. There is nobility in both. But I think more vitality in the second.

Ever yours sincerely
WINSTON S. CHURCHILL

WSC to Ivor Guest
(Satinoff Papers)

19 January [1899]   4th Hussars
India

My dear Ivor,

I was vy glad to get your letter even though its coming reproached me for not having written. But I have been busy with my book[2] and live in a strange world bounded on the north by the Preface and on the south by the Appendix & whose natural features consist of Chapters & paragraphs. I have done rather more than half of the whole work; but I am now delayed by the non-arrival of some information from Egypt. I do not think the book will bring me many friends. But friends of the cheap & worthless every-day variety are

[1] Ivor GUEST. For all names in capitals in the footnotes, see the Biographical sketches on pp. xiii–xxiii.
[2] Published in two volumes in November 1899, entitled *The River War*.

not of vy great importance. And after all in writing the great thing is to be honest.

Your letter was vy welcome and I seize the first opportunity of replying to it. I don't think you will be wise to identify yourself with the Anti-Ritual Movement very closely. The lines of division in belief run quite distinct & separate to those of party & even nation and you cannot deal with such a subject without making unexpected enemies who may do great harm. An unknown foe is twice a foe. Besides this I think that the whole question is one of great delicacy and of extraordinary complication. It is the glory of the Church of England that 'she is continually possessed by the aim of including not of excluding all shades of religious thought and opinion, all sorts and conditions of men'. You may remember my father's speech from which this is taken. 'Standing out like a lighthouse over a stormy ocean it marks the entrance to a port wherein the millions & the masses of those who at times are wearied with the cares of the world and tired of the trials of existence may reach for and may find that "peace which passeth all understanding". '

Of course if you make your harbour so large as to include *all* the navies of the world – it affords them no shelter as its wide surface is as open to tempests as the ocean itself. The whole question is one of degree. Where shall the line be drawn? And at this point whole libraries of theological treatises & every sort of religious technique is thrown into the discussion. We reach the field in which Sir W. Harcourt[1] disports himself in those lengthy letters to *The Times*. But besides this comes the even larger element of ultra-rational opinion. 'I believe this' and 'I believe that' – a volume of argument which disdains the logic it does not need to prove its own cases: which only uses reason to support faith – not faith to confirm the results of reason. The question is one of degree. The technicalities are bewildering. The disputants utterly irreconcilable – often living in different worlds of thought. Your mother – you must remember women are often intolerant and that some of the savagest persecutions in history have been inspired by kind noble women – thinks certain ceremonies odious.[2] I agree that they are distinctly Romish: and as a rationalist I deprecate all Romish practices and prefer those of Protestantism, because I believe that the Reformed Church is less deeply sunk in the mire of dogma than the Original Establishment. We are at any rate a step nearer Reason.

But at the same time I can see a poor parish – working men living their lives in ugly white-washed factories, toiling day after day amid scenes &

[1] William George Granville Vernon Harcourt (1827–1904), Liberal MP 1880–1904; Chancellor of the Exchequer 1886 and 1892–5; Liberal Leader 1896–8; knighted 1873; declined peerage 1902; father of Lewis (Loulou) 1st Viscount HARCOURT.

[2] Guest's mother was the founder of Lady Wimborne's Protestant League.

surroundings destitute of the element of beauty. I can sympathise with their aching longing for something not infected by the general squalor & something to gratify their love of the mystic, something a little nearer to the 'all-beautiful' – and I find it hard to rob their lives of this one ennobling aspiration – even though it finds expression in the burning of incense, the wearing of certain robes and other superstitious practices.

I do not for a moment say that I would not be prepared to do so. For I know that these indulgences are enervating: that peoples that think much of the next world rarely prosper in this: that men must use their minds and not kill their doubts by sensuous pleasures: that superstitious faith in nations rarely promotes their industry: that, in a phrase, Catholicism – all religions if you like, but particularly Catholicism – is a delicious narcotic. It may soothe our pains and chase our worries, but it checks our growth and saps our strength. And since the improvement of the British breed is my political aim in life, I would not permit too great indulgence if I could prevent it without assailing another great principle – Liberty. See how wide and complicated the discussion becomes, the line of thought bifurcates at every second. Who should draw the line where the maximum of human pain and doubt may be allayed and the minimum of ultra-rationalism be incurred? And having drawn that line redraw it in accordance with all other moral, political, personal & social considerations. The Sphinx is silent. Man will not know.

Well then, I don't believe that you are going to do any good by entering such a field in a spirit of controversy and agitation. I agree with you that the situation is vexatious and that certain evil people in the Church of England are subverting its monies and buildings to the furtherance of doctrines and ceremonies it detests and fears. I should like to see a strong Church Discipline Bill. But even then the application of such an act would lie with the Bishops, and – let me draw from my slender store of Latin – *'Custodes quis custodiet'*. I don't see what good will come from your agitation. I see one result daily approaching – Disestablishment. But I presume that is scarcely what your mother would like.

There is another point of view from which I would deprecate your joining ardently in the controversy. You cannot be sincere. You do not believe in the accepted forms of religion. You scoff at them. At the best, or shall I say at the worst, it is only a matter of preference to you whether people beseech what never listens for benefits which can never be granted kneeling, sitting or standing on their heads. You will therefore be an humbug – if you show zeal. And if you don't show zeal you will do no good in your agitation.

I think that legislation will have to grapple with this subject – and in a few years – but we must pray that it will be directed by moderate men – not lunatics – not by those who see only one side – not by those who have been compromised by their agitation.

Now as to Sunny. I hope that he will not take the chair at an Albert Hall meeting on this subject. I feel sure he will make many enemies and win hardly any friends – and the role of extreme orthodoxy will be very wearying – throughout a long life.[1] If he wants something to govern, the world of secular politics is wide enough. I say the same to you. 'Render unto Caesar the things that are Caesar's' & for God's sake leave God to look after his own affairs.

Let me make myself clear by one more reservation. Intervene if you like – I shall when I come home – but let your intervention be judicial, discriminating, cold, impartial – Do not fan the flames.

I shall be home early in April. Write by return to me c/o King, King & Co, Bankers, Bombay. They will forward and my movements are uncertain.

Yours ever
WINSTON S C

PS I forgot old boy to thank you for your suggestions *in re* novel.[2] They are excellent. The book has been bought by Macmillan's Magazine for publication in serial form for £100. After that it reverts to me and I will then make considerable recastings.

WSC

WSC to James B. Pond
(Hastings Papers)

31 July 1900   35a Great Cumberland Place

Dear Mr Pond,

I have received your various letters and I have this morning had a conversation with Miss Insley upon the subject of my proposed lecturing tour in the United States. Yesterday I cabled to you to this effect: 'Considering General Election here probably and Presidential States certain in October, propose coming to America Dec. Jan. & February, and use November in England'.

My plans are so unsettled because of the uncertainty of the Election here for in that event I must come forward as a candidate nor would considerations of money move me in the least.

It seems probable that the Election will be in October and between this and that date I am occupied in working up my constituency where I have a

---

[1] It is interesting to note that after his second marriage, Charles, 9th Duke of Marlborough, was received into the Church of Rome.

[2] *Savrola*, published in book form by Longmans, Green in February 1900.

majority of 1,500 against me so my time is very fully taken up. Besides your Presidential Election will take place in October and your country will be convulsed with political excitement to such an extent that I am advised by many I have talked to that lecturing would suffer – however, you are a better judge on that point than I. Reflecting on the whole situation I think it would be better for me to come to America the beginning of December and I will put myself in your hands for three months from that date.

I have had in England a good many offers of large sums to lecture at our leading towns and I propose to devote November to that purpose.

I don't think you need be afraid of unfriendly criticisms being telegraphed over. I have had some success in dealing with audiences without the aid of magic lanterns and I have dealt with facts of dry politics. Altogether my offers aggregate to over £2,000 for this single month's work, and, unless you can show me something very much better than that, I propose to carry out that arrangement. I am very much obliged to you for all your letters and for your civility and I have no doubt that when I come to America we shall be able to do business together on very satisfactory conditions. I shall leave the whole arrangements of the Tour to you, but at the same time, you must not drag me about too much and I don't want to wear myself out by talking to two-penny-half-penny meetings in out of the way places.

In all my social arrangements I shall exercise my entire discretion. When I come to Canada I shall stay with the Governor General [Lord Minto] whom I have known for some years and I have a certain number of friends in America of whose hospitality I shall avail myself.

I don't want to be dragged about to any social functions of any kind nor shall I think of talking about my experiences to anybody except when I am paid for so doing.

I shall be very glad if you will write to me quite freely, stating all your views on all points and you rely on my replying with equal candour.

Yours sincerely
WINSTON S. CHURCHILL

1

Maiden Speech

(See Main Volume Chapter I, pp. 1–13)

W SC was in Winnipeg on his lecture tour when he heard
the news of Queen Victoria's death on 22 January 1901.
On the day of the Queen's funeral in London on February 2, he
sailed from New York in the *Etruria* and arrived at Liverpool
on February 10.

On February 14 King Edward VII opened the first Parliament of the new reign and of the new century. Within an hour
of the King's Speech WSC had subscribed to the oath and taken
his seat; an hour after that he was voting in his first division
(against the leaders of his own party); and on Monday, February 18, he rose to make his maiden speech during the debate
on the Address in answer to the King's Speech.

Hansard

18 February 1901

Mr Winston Churchill (Oldham): I understood that the hon Member
[D. Lloyd George,[1] MP for Carnarvon Boroughs] to whose speech the House
has just listened, had intended to move an Amendment to the Address. The
text of the Amendment, which had appeared in the papers, was singularly
mild and moderate in tone; but mild and moderate as it was, neither the
hon Member nor his political friends had cared to expose it to criticism or
to challenge a division upon it, and, indeed, when we compare the moderation of the Amendment with the very bitter speech which the hon Member
has just delivered, it is difficult to avoid the conclusion that the moderation

[1] David Lloyd George.

of the Amendment was the moderation of the hon Member's political
friends and leaders, and that the bitterness of his speech is all his own. It has
been suggested to me[1] that it might perhaps have been better, upon the
whole, if the hon Member, instead of making his speech without moving
his Amendment, had moved his Amendment without making his speech. I
would not complain of any remarks of the hon Member were I called upon
to do so. In my opinion, based upon the experience of the most famous
men whose names have adorned the records of the House, no national
emergency short, let us say, of the actual invasion of this country itself ought
in any way to restrict or prevent the entire freedom of Parliamentary
discussion. Moreover, I do not believe that the Boers would attach particular
importance to the utterances of the hon Member. No people in the world
received so much verbal sympathy and so little practical support as the
Boers. If I were a Boer fighting in the field – and if I were a Boer I hope I
should be fighting in the field – I would not allow myself to be taken in by
any message of sympathy, not even if it were signed by a hundred hon
Members. The hon Member dwelt at great length upon the question of
farm burning. I do not propose to discuss the ethics of farm burning now;
but hon Members should, I think, cast their eyes back to the fact that no
considerations of humanity prevented the German army from throwing its
shells into dwelling houses in Paris, and starving the inhabitants of that great
city to the extent that they had to live upon rats and like atrocious foods in
order to compel the garrison to surrender. I venture to think His Majesty's
Government would not have been justified in restricting their commanders
in the field from any methods of warfare which are justified by precedents
set by European and American generals during the last fifty or sixty years.
I do not agree very fully with the charges of treachery on the one side and
barbarity on the other. From what I saw of the war – and I sometimes saw
something of it – I believe that as compared with other wars, especially
those in which a civil population took part, this war in South Africa has
been on the whole carried on with unusual humanity and generosity. The
hon Member for Carnarvon Boroughs has drawn attention to the case of
one general officer, and although I deprecate debates upon the characters of
individual general officers who are serving the country at this moment,
because I know personally General Bruce Hamilton,[2] whom the hon
Member with admirable feeling described as General Brute Hamilton, I feel
unable to address the House without offering my humble testimony to the

[1] By Thomas Gibson Bowles (1844–1922), Conservative MP King's Lynn 1892–1906;
Liberal MP Leicester South 1916; one-time proprietor of *Vanity Fair*.
[2] Bruce Meade Hamilton (1857–1936), Major-General commanding groups of mounted
columns in South African War; General 1913; GOC-in-C Scottish Command 1909–13;
Army Command Home Defence 1914–18; knighted 1902.

fact that in all His Majesty's Army there are few men with better feeling, more kindness of heart, or with higher courage than General Bruce Hamilton.

There is a point of difference which has been raised by the right hon Gentleman the Leader of the Opposition [Sir Henry Campbell-Bannerman,[1] MP for Stirling Burghs] upon the question of the policy to be pursued in South Africa after this war has been brought to a conclusion. So far as I have been able to make out the difference between the Government and the Opposition on this question is that whereas His Majesty's Government propose that when hostilities are brought to a conclusion there shall be an interval of civil government before full representative rights are extended to the peoples of these countries, on the other hand the right hon Gentleman the Leader of the Opposition believes that these representative institutions will be more quickly obtained if the military government be prolonged as a temporary measure and no interval of civil government be interposed. I hope I am not misinterpreting the right hon Gentleman in any way. If I am, I trust he will not hesitate to correct me, because I should be very sorry in any way to misstate his views. If that is the situation, I will respectfully ask the House to allow me to examine these alternative propositions. I do not wish myself to lay down the law, or thrust my views upon hon Members. I have travelled a good deal about South Africa during the last ten months under varying circumstances, and I should like to lay before the House some of the considerations which have been very forcibly borne in upon me during that period.

In the first place I would like to look back to the original cause for which we went to war. We went to war — I mean of course we were gone to war with — in connection with the extension of the franchise. We began nego-tiations with the Boers in order to extend the franchise to the people of the Transvaal. When I say the people of the Transvaal, I mean the whole people of the Transvaal, and not necessarily those who arrived there first. At that time there were nearly two-and-a-half times as many British and non-Dutch as there were Boers, but during the few weeks before the outbreak of the war every train was crowded with British subjects who were endeavouring to escape from the approaching conflict, and so it was that the Uitlanders were scattered all over the world. It seems to me that when the war is over we ought not to forget the original object with which we undertook the nego-tiations which led to the war. If I may lay down anything I would ask the House to establish the principle that they ought not to extend any repre-sentative institutions to the people of the Transvaal until such time as the population has regained its ordinary level. What could be more dangerous, ridiculous or futile, than to throw the responsible government of a ruined

[1] Sir Henry CAMPBELL-BANNERMAN.

country on that remnant of the population, that particular section of the population, which is actively hostile to the fundamental institutions of the State? I think there ought to be no doubt and no difference of opinion on the point that between the firing of the last shot and the casting of the first vote there must be an appreciable interval that must be filled by a government of some kind or another.

I invite the House to consider which form of government – civil government or military government – is most likely to be conducive to the restoration of the banished prosperity of the country and most likely to encourage the return of the population now scattered far and wide. I understand that there are hon Members who are in hopes that representative institutions may directly follow military government, but I think they cannot realise thoroughly how very irksome such military government is. I have the greatest respect for British officers, and when I hear them attacked, as some hon Members have done in their speeches, it makes me very sorry, and very angry too. Although I regard British officers in the field of war, and in dealing with native races, as the best officers in the world, I do not believe that either their training or their habits of thought qualify them to exercise arbitrary authority over civil populations of European race. I have often myself been very much ashamed to see respectable old Boer farmers – the Boer is a curious combination of the squire and the peasant, and under the rough coat of the farmer there are very often to be found the instincts of the squire – I have been ashamed to see such men ordered about peremptorily by young subaltern officers, as if they were private soldiers. I do not hesitate to say that as long as you have anything like direct military government there will be no revival of trade, no return of the Uitlander population, no influx of immigrants from other parts of the world – nothing but despair and discontent on the part of the Boer population, and growing resentment on the part of our own British settlers. If there was a system of civil government on the other hand, which I think we have an absolute moral right to establish if only from the fact that this country through the Imperial Exchequer will have to provide the money – if you had a civil government under such an administrator as Sir Alfred Milner[1] – (*Cries of 'Hear, hear,' and 'Oh'*) – it is not for me to eulogise that distinguished administrator, I am sure he enjoys the confidence of the whole of the Conservative party, and there are a great many Members on the other side of the House who do not find it convenient in their own minds to disregard Sir Alfred Milner's deliberate opinion on South African affairs. As soon as it is known that there is in the Transvaal a government under which property and liberty are secure, so soon as it is known that in these countries one can live freely and safely,

[1] Sir Alfred (later Lord) MILNER.

there would be a rush of immigrants from all parts of the world to develop the country and to profit by the great revival of trade which usually follows war of all kinds. If I may judge by my own experience there are many Members of this House who have received letters from their constituents asking whether it was advisable to go out to South Africa. When this policy of immigration is well advanced we shall again have the great majority of the people of the Transvaal firmly attached and devoted to the Imperial connection, and when you can extend representative institutions to them you will find them reposing securely upon the broad basis of the consent of the governed, while the rights of the minority will be effectively protected and preserved by the tactful and judicious intervention of the Imperial authority. May I say that it was this prospect of a loyal and Anglicised Transvaal turning the scale in our favour in South Africa, which must have been the original 'good hope' from which the Cape has taken its name.

It is not for me to criticise the proposals which come from such a distinguished authority as the Leader of the Opposition, but I find it impossible not to say that in comparing these two alternative plans one with the other I must proclaim my strong preference for the course His Majesty's Government propose to adopt. I pass now from the question of the ultimate settlement of the two late Republics to the immediate necessities of the situation. What ought to be the present policy of the Government? I take it that there is a pretty general consensus of opinion in this House that it ought to be to make it easy and honourable for the Boers to surrender, and painful and perilous for them to continue in the field. Let the Government proceed on both those lines concurrently and at full speed. I sympathise very heartily with my hon friend the senior Member for Oldham [Alfred Emmott],[1] who, in a speech delivered last year, showed great anxiety that everything should be done to make the Boers understand exactly what terms were offered to them, and I earnestly hope that the right hon Gentleman the Colonial Secretary [Joseph Chamberlain][2] will leave nothing undone to bring home to those brave and unhappy men who are fighting in the field that whenever they are prepared to recognise that their small independence must be merged in the larger liberties of the British Empire, there will be a full guarantee for the security of their property and religion, an assurance of equal rights, a promise of representative institutions, and last of all, but not least of all, what the British Army would most readily accord to a brave and enduring foe – all the honours of war. I hope the right hon Gentleman will

[1] Alfred Emmott (1858–1926), cotton manufacturer and Liberal MP for Oldham 1899–1911; Chairman of Ways and Means 1906–11; Under-Secretary of State for Colonies 1911–1914; First Commissioner of Works 1914–15; Director of War Trade Department 1915–19; Baron 1911; PC 1914. Defeated WSC at Oldham by-election 1899.

[2] Joseph CHAMBERLAIN.

not allow himself to be discouraged by any rebuffs which his envoys may meet with, but will persevere in endeavouring to bring before these people the conditions on which at any moment they may obtain peace and the friendship of Great Britain. Of course, we can only promise, and it rests with the Boers whether they will accept our conditions. They may refuse the generous terms offered them, and stand or fall by their old cry, 'Death or independence!' (*Nationalist cheers*.) I do not see anything to rejoice at in that prospect, because if it be so, the war will enter upon a very sad and gloomy phase. If the Boers remain deaf to the voice of reason, and blind to the hand of friendship, if they refuse all overtures and disdain all terms, then, while we cannot help admiring their determination and endurance, we can only hope that our own race, in the pursuit of what they feel to be a righteous cause, will show determination as strong and endurance as lasting. It is wonderful that hon Members who form the Irish party should find it in their hearts to speak and act as they do in regard to a war in which so much has been accomplished by the courage, the sacrifices, and, above all, by the military capacity of Irishmen. A practical reason, which I trust hon Members will not think it presumptuous in me to bring to their notice, is that they would be well advised cordially to co-operate with His Majesty's Government in bringing the war to a speedy conclusion, because they must know that no Irish question or agitation can possibly take any hold on the imagination of the people of Great Britain so long as all our thoughts are with the soldiers who are fighting in South Africa.

What are the military measures we ought to take? I have no doubt that other opportunities will be presented to the House to discuss them, but so far as I have been able to understand the whispers I have heard in the air there are, on the whole, considerable signs of possible improvement in the South African situation. There are appearances that the Boers are weakening, and that the desperate and feverish efforts they have made so long cannot be indefinitely sustained. If that be so, now is the time for the Government and the Army to redouble their efforts. It is incumbent on Members like myself, who represent large working class constituencies, to bring home to the Government the fact that the country does not want to count the cost of the war until it is won. I think we all rejoiced to see the announcement in the papers that 30,000 more mounted men were being despatched to South Africa. I cannot help noticing with intense satisfaction that, not content with sending large numbers of men, the Secretary of State for War [W. St. John Brodrick][1] has found some excellent Indian officers, prominent among whom is Sir Bindon Blood,[2] who will go out to South Africa and bring their know-

[1] W. St. John BRODRICK.
[2] Bindon Blood (1842–1940), Lieutenant-General commanding troops in eastern Trans-

ledge of guerilla warfare on the Indian frontier to bear on the peculiar kind of warfare – I will not call it guerilla warfare – now going on in South Africa. I shall always indulge the hope that, great as these preparations are, they will not be all, and that some fine afternoon the Secretary of State for War will come down to the House with a brand-new scheme, not only for sending all the reinforcements necessary for keeping the Army up to a fixed standard of 250,000 men, in spite of the losses by battle and disease, but also for increasing it by a regular monthly quota of 2,000 or 3,000 men, so that the Boers will be compelled, with ever-diminishing resources, to make head against ever-increasing difficulties, and will not only be exposed to the beating of the waves, but to the force of the rising tide.

Some hon Members have seen fit, either in this place or elsewhere, to stigmatise this war as a war of greed. I regret that I feel bound to repudiate that pleasant suggestion. If there were persons who rejoiced in this war, and went out with hopes of excitement or the lust of conflict, they have had enough and more than enough to-day. If, as the hon Member for Northampton [Henry Labouchere][1] has several times suggested, certain capitalists spent money in bringing on this war in the hope that it would increase the value of their mining properties, they know now that they made an uncommonly bad bargain. With the mass of the nation, with the whole people of the country, this war from beginning to end has only been a war of duty. They believe, and they have shown in the most remarkable manner that they believe, that His Majesty's Government and the Colonial Secretary have throughout been actuated by the same high and patriotic motives. They know that no other inspiration could sustain and animate the Regulars and Volunteers, who through all these hard months have had to bear the brunt of the public contention. They may indeed have to regret, as I myself have, the loss of a great many good friends in the war. We cannot help feeling sorry for many of the incidents of the war, but for all that I do not find it possible on reflection to accuse the general policy which led to the war; we have no cause to be ashamed of anything that has passed during the war, nor have we any right to be doleful or lugubrious. I think if any hon Members are feeling unhappy about the state of affairs in South Africa I would recommend them a receipt from which I myself derived much exhilaration. Let them look to the other great dependencies and colonies of the British Empire and see what the effect of the war has been there. Whatever we may have lost in doubtful friends in Cape Colony we have gained

vaal 1901; Major-General commanding Malakand Field Force 1897; retired as General 1907. KCB 1896; GCB 1909; GCVO 1932.

[1] Henry Dupré Labouchere (1831–1912), controversial journalist and Liberal MP for Northampton 1880–1906; diplomatic service 1854–64; Liberal MP for Windsor 1866, Middlesex 1867; PC 1905.

ten times, or perhaps twenty times, over in Canada and Australia, where the people – down to the humblest farmer in the most distant provinces – have by their effective participation in the conflict been able to realise, as they never could realise before, that they belong to the Empire, and that the Empire belongs to them. I cannot sit down without saying how very grateful I am for the kindness and patience with which the House has heard me, and which have been extended to me, I well know, not on my own account, but because of a certain splendid memory which many hon Members still preserve.

Hansard

18 February 1901

SIR ROBERT REID[1] (Dumfries Burghs): I am sure the House is glad to recognise that the hon Member who has just sat down possesses the same courage which so distinguished Lord Randolph Churchill during his short and brilliant career in this House. I have listened with very great pleasure to the hon Gentleman . . .

THE SECRETARY OF STATE FOR THE COLONIES, MR JOSEPH CHAMBERLAIN (Birmingham W.): . . . [a] very admirable speech, a speech which I am sure that those who were friends and intimates of his father will have welcomed with the utmost satisfaction in the hope that we may see the father repeated in the son.

19 February 1901

MR ASQUITH[2] (Fifeshire E.): . . . my honourable friend the junior Member for Oldham – whose interesting and eloquent speech last night we must all hope and believe, and especially those of us who, like myself, enjoyed the privilege of friendship with his illustrious father, was the first step in a Parliamentary career of the highest distinction . . .

[1] Robert Threshie Reid (1846–1923), first entered Parliament as a Liberal in 1880; Solicitor-General 1894–5; became Baron Loreburn & Lord Chancellor 1905; established Court of Criminal Appeal 1907; sat on Woolsack during discussion of Parliament Bill in House of Lords 1911; created Earl 1911; resigned 1912.
[2] H. H. ASQUITH.

Daily Telegraph

Unionist – One penny – Sir Edward Levy-Lawson, proprietor.

19 February 1901

Under the Clock

Mr Winston Churchill summarised the rhetorical outburst [of Mr Lloyd George] in a cluster of happy phrases . . .

It was the maiden speech of a young member who bears a name that will ever be honoured in the House of Commons. He had a great opportunity, and he satisfied the highest expectations. He held a modest page of notes in his hand, but rarely referred to it. Perfectly at home, with lively gestures that pointed his sparkling sentences he instantly caught the tone and the ear of a House crowded in every part. Among his audience were old friends, and otherwise, of his father – Mr Arthur Balfour,[1] Mr Chamberlain, Sir William Harcourt, and Sir Henry Campbell-Bannerman. Not the least fascinated section of the audience were the Irish members. They loudly cheered his remark 'If I were a Boer I should be fighting in the field.' The ringing cheers came from the other side when he added, 'But I wouldn't be taken in by a message of sympathy, even if it were signed by a hundred members,' a reference to the famous telegram to the King of Greece, when his country was at grips with Turkey, quickly seized by the House.

Not the least charming passage in a speech that instantly assured a position in the most critical assembly in the world, was the final sentence in which young Churchill thanked the House for the attention bestowed upon him, a compliment in which he recognised, not anything due to his own merit, but a tribute to 'a certain splendid memory' that still dwells in the House of Commons.

Morning Post

Unionist – One penny – Lord Glenesk, proprietor.

19 February 1901

Parliamentary Notes

The junior member for Oldham had an audience to listen to his maiden speech which very few new members have commanded; and the general opinion was that he had fully justified the expectations which had been formed – based as they were on the recollection of his father's great achievements and on his own career as writer and speaker. Every part of the House

---

[1] A. J. BALFOUR.

was crowded. The occupants of the Ladies' Gallery included his mother, Mrs George Cornwallis-West,[1] Lady Harcourt,[2] Lady Frances Balfour,[3] and Mrs Chamberlain,[4] while to the right of the clock were half-a-dozen Peers, among them his relative, Lord Tweedmouth.[5]

... We note with great pleasure that the view that the Army should be steadily reinforced was advocated last night in the House of Commons by Mr WINSTON CHURCHILL in a maiden speech, which, both in form and substance, was worthy of the traditions of the House and of those personal traditions to which Mr Churchill, in concluding, made touching reference ...

Standard
Conservative – One penny

19 February 1901

Imperial Parliament

... Mr Lloyd George made a vehement and declamatory attack upon the Government, and was succeeded by Mr Winston Churchill, who delivered his maiden speech. The Ladies' Gallery was filled by the friends of the hon member, among them being his mother (Mrs Cornwallis-West), the Duchess of Marlborough, Lady Cranborne,[6] Lady Tweedmouth, Mrs Gully,[7] Lady Hilda Brodrick,[8] Lady Harcourt, Mrs Chamberlain, Lady F. Balfour

[1] Mrs George CORNWALLIS-WEST.

[2] Elizabeth Cabot (1841–1928), second wife of Sir William Harcourt; daughter of J. L. Motley, historian and former American Minister in London.

[3] Lady Frances Balfour (1858–1931), sister-in-law of A. J. Balfour and 5th daughter of the 8th Duke of Argyll.

[4] Mary Chamberlain (1864–1957), 3rd wife of Joseph Chamberlain. She was the daughter of William Crowninshield Endicott, an American judge and statesman.

[5] Edward Marjoribanks, 2nd Baron Tweedmouth (1849–1909). Liberal MP for Berwick 1880–94; Government Chief Whip 1892–4; Lord Privy Seal and Chancellor of Duchy of Lancaster 1894–5; First Lord of the Admiralty 1905–08; Lord President of the Council 1908; married 1873 Fanny Octavia Louisa Spencer-Churchill (1853–1904), WSC's aunt.

[6] Cicely Alice Gore (1867–1955), wife of James Edward, Viscount Cranborne, elder son of 3rd Marquess of Salisbury whom he succeeded in 1903. She was the 2nd daughter of 5th Earl of Arran.

[7] Elizabeth Anne Walford (1839–1906), wife of William Court Gully, Speaker of the House of Commons 1895–1905 and daughter of Thomas Selby. Mr Gully took the title of Viscount Selby on his retirement as speaker.

[8] Lady Hilda Brodrick (1854–1901), first wife of W. St. John Brodrick, Secretary of State for War. Her eldest daughter Muriel married 30 November 1901 Dudley Marjoribanks, WSC's cousin. She was the 3rd daughter of 10th Earl of Wemyss.

and Lady Alice Boyle.[1] His speech was listened to with profound interest by a crowded House, on which the hon member made a very favourable impression. He spoke with great self-possession, modesty, and restraint of manner, and with no trace of a desire to be rhetorical. His speech was in strong support of the Government, and it drew many kindly cheers even from the Irish members. An expression that if he were a Boer he hoped he would be fighting in the field drew from the Nationalists wild cheers of approval, and his closing remark, thanking the House for listening to him with so much patience, not on his account own, but on account of a certain splendid memory, was rapturously responded to by Unionists and Opposition alike . . .

Daily Mail
Conservative – One halfpenny – Alfred Harmsworth, proprietor

19 February 1901

[Parliamentary Report]

. . . Then Mr Winston Churchill addressed the House for the first time. He did not think that the Boers paid much attention to Mr Lloyd George's verbal expressions of sympathy, and he believed no war had been carried on with more humanity and generosity. The House listened very attentively, and was evidently much pleased with Mr Churchill's contribution.

Daily News
Liberal – One penny – George Cadbury, proprietor

19 February 1901

Pictures in Parliament
[by H. W. Massingham[2]]

The tragedy of the war was destined to furnish the final interest of the evening. That interest first took the shape of a kind of duel between two young members in whose careers the House takes an interest – Mr Lloyd

---

[1] Alice Mary Boyle (1877–1958), 2nd daughter of 5th Earl of Glasgow.

[2] Henry William Massingham (1860–1924), special Parliamentary representative of the *Daily News*; Editor of the *Daily Chronicle* 1895–9; Editor of the *Nation* 1907–23, leading Liberal publicist. Massingham contributed an introduction to WSC's *Liberalism and the Social Problem* published by Hodder and Stoughton in 1909.

George and Mr Winston Churchill. Mr George never speaks now without drawing a house – a sure sign of mastery of his audience and his subject. For this task Mr George has many qualifications – a pleasing face, animated and expressive, with the natural refinement of the Celt, a voice of that rare quality which unites passion and the fine silver tone one associates with a true tenor voice, feeling and fire, the power of continuous narrative and sustained argument, and above all, the true Parliamentary style, simple, easy, and clear. All these powers Mr George displayed in his speech last night . . .

Mr Winston Churchill's reply was in very striking contrast to the speech to which it was indeed only nominally an answer. The personal contrast was as striking as that of treatment and method. Mr George has many natural advantages; Mr Churchill has many disadvantages. In his closing sentences he spoke gracefully of the splendid memory of his father. Mr Churchill does not inherit his father's voice – save for the slight lisp – or his father's manner. Address, accent, appearance do not help him.

But he has one quality – intellect. He has an eye – and he can judge and think for himself. Parts of the speech were faulty enough – there was claptrap with the wisdom and insight. But such remarks as the impossibility of the country returning to prosperity under military government, and the picture of the old Boers – more squires than peasants – ordered about by boy subalterns, the appeal for easy and honourable terms of surrender,. showed that this young man has kept his critical faculty through the glamour of association with our arms. The tone was on the whole quiet and restrained, and through the speech ran, as I have said, the subdued but obvious plea for moderation and sympathy towards the foe.

Sir Robert Reid followed with a short sympathetic speech on the side of conciliation, and then Mr Chamberlain rose. His speech was an able piece of debating – clear, rasping, coarse in tone, full of points aimed – and successfully aimed – at the average party spirit of his following . . .

But the speech was utterly without elevation – and in insight and breadth of treatment it was far inferior to Mr Churchill's.

Daily Chronicle
Liberal – One penny – Frank Lloyd, proprietor

19 February 1901

House and Lobby

The rumour had spread through the Lobbies that Mr Winston Churchill intended to speak, and, as the clock travelled towards that hour every part of the floor became crowded. The reputation of the father made everyone anxious to see whether the son was his equal, and the achievements of Mr Churchill himself increased the reputation. Mr Churchill is a medium-sized, undistinguished looking young man, with an unfortunate lisp in his voice. His style, too, is not very literary, and he lacks force. All the qualities which made his father the most daring and dauntless of recent Parliamentarians have been missed out in his son, or else they have exhibited themselves in the restless spirit of the soldier and adventurer. But he has some inherited qualities, candour and independence. The Government must have inwardly rebelled against some of the things he said last night. The speech was in many ways a good one, although it fell short of the father's wonderful skill. The last sentence was in singularly good taste. 'I thank the House for the kindly hearing it has extended to me, largely, I know, for the sake of a splendid memory.' It was modest, yet it challenged comparison with an unforgettable career, but in reality it was a filial tribute.

Daily Express
Independent – One halfpenny – C. Arthur Pearson, proprietor

19 February 1901 (front page)

Mr Churchill's Spellbinding

. . . Mr Winston Churchill then made his debut. And a very successful first appearance it was. For more than half an hour he held a crowded House spell-bound. It was not only the facility of his phrases, and the clearness of his views, but a certain youthful breeziness, a rare unaffectedness that fascinated his hearers. There was no mistaking too, the real note of genius that rang through his speech. His description of the Transvaal, his idea of the terms that should end the war, showed a statesmanlike grip that seemed strange in the almost boyish figure, with its smooth face, bright eyes, and curly hair . .

Daily Graphic
Illustrated – One penny – Carmichael Thomas, proprietor

19 February 1901

In the House

. . . During the speech [by Mr Lloyd George] the House filled up rapidly, partly to listen to Mr Lloyd George's very excellent rhetoric, and partly in

expectation of a speech from Mr Winston Churchill. The latter, who had
been sitting in the seat so often occupied by his father, was received with
loud cheers on rising to make his maiden speech. The frankness of his
manner and of his opinions appealed to both sides of the House, and certainly not least to the Liberals . . . He concluded an extremely effective and
successful Speech by thanking the House for the kindness with which they
had received him – 'a kindness which I know is not due to me personally,
but to a certain splendid memory within these walls'. After that, Sir Robert
Reid and emptiness.

Manchester Guardian
Liberal – One penny – J. E. Taylor, proprietor

19 February 1901

Sketches from Westminster (J.B.A.)[1]

Next came Mr Churchill, speaking from the corner seat of the second
bench above the gangway – the place his father used to hold. It is not often
a new member gets a cheer as well as the bestowal of curiosity and attention.
But Mr Churchill got all these things. His was a carefully turned speech,
filled with antitheses of a literary flavour. His father, with all his power,
had little literary sense, and this possession is all in favour of the young
member who started so well tonight. He was wise to stick as he obviously
did to his prepared speech, and not to be drawn away by tempting interruptions.

The Scotsman
Liberal-Unionist – One penny – James Law, principal proprietor

19 February 1901

From Private Correspondence

After dinner the debate drifted back to South Africa. It became known
that Mr Winston Churchill intended to speak, and in anticipation of his
rising the House filled. Mr Lloyd George thus had the benefit of an audience
which was far beyond his deserts . . . Mr Winston Churchill followed him at
half past ten. He was listened to by a crowded Chamber. In him a good
deal of his father survives. His voice recalls that of Lord Randolph Churchill

[1] John Black Atkins (1871–1954), London Editor of the *Manchester Guardian* 1901–05.
He had been an outstanding war correspondent and a friend of WSC in South Africa in 1899.
He described his experiences in *The Relief of Ladysmith*. Assistant Editor of the *Spectator*
1907–26.

– it has the same somewhat thin but very clear quality, and it has the same slight lisp. The manner, too, is the familiar one – ready and self-assured, and admirably adapted to Parliamentary debate. There was another point in the comparison that must have struck those familiar with the House for some years. Mr Churchill spoke from the corner behind the Treasury bench which was his father's place after he quitted the first Unionist Government. A few sentences assured the House that the young member would not belie his reputation. He handled the situation with true Parliamentary instinct when he contrasted the speech of Mr Lloyd George with the amendment that had been placed on the paper. He showed, when he got to the kernel of the question, that he had breadth of grasp as well as something of the independent and critical spirit associated with his name. As he proceeded he exhibited alertness and pungency of repartee, and when he finished the loud applause and the personal congratulations of Mr Balfour and the Ministers and members gave him gratifying assurance of the success which he had achieved.

Glasgow Herald
Independent – One penny – George Outram, proprietor

19 February 1901

Our London Correspondent

. . . This brought a maiden speech from Mr Winston Churchill, and the House filled up in every part to hear it. Mr Churchill began nervously, but managed creditably enough, and while urging the vigorous prosecution of the war to its end he drew cheers from the Opposition by advocating an ultimate settlement which should be as favourable as circumstances would permit to the defeated Boers. Occasionally there were tones and inflections of voice which forcibly recalled his father, Lord Randolph Churchill, but the hon gentleman did not show much trace of his parent's brilliancy in debate, though it would, of course, be unfair to attempt to form any final judgement on a nervous maiden effort. Readiness he had in abundance and he may develop well, but to those who remember the electrical effect of the father's maiden speech, the son's first plunge into debate was nowhere near so high a flight.

Yorkshire Post
Conservative – One penny – Lord Faber, proprietor

19 February 1901

Parliamentary Sketch

After this the resumed debate on the Address fell stale and flat. Indeed, for an hour or two dullness held sway. But about ten o'clock, when men had come back from dinner, the whisper was passed round that Mr Winston Churchill intended to speak. No young man has for a long time aroused so much interest at Westminster. When sitting in the House or moving about the Lobby he has been eyed as a new actor is eyed on the stage during rehearsals, and of whom a great deal is expected. Whether it was accident or intention, young Churchill found himself tonight in the very seat favoured by his father before he held office.

And when he rose to speak what a magnificent audience he had – the Chamber overflowing, a crowd of men about the bar, Lords and Bishops up in the Peers' Gallery, and many women's faces pressed against the grille of the Ladies' Gallery. And in that packed assembly, everybody a critic, watching to see what sort of a start he would make in politics, Winston Churchill made his debut. Those who have not seen him face to face can hardly appreciate what a boy he looks. He is twenty-six, but he is so fair, with not a hair on his lip, that you might easily take him for a lad of eighteen. He is not an orator any more than his father was. Allowing for the natural nervousness incident to this his maiden Parliamentary speech, there was a breezy frankness and yet an incisiveness, and now and then a flash of humour, followed, maybe, in a moment by a deep serious thought that lifted him away above the usual oration of a young man.

He has many of the gestures of his father, such as the sudden jerking forward of the head and clenching the fists and beating the air as though hammering home an argument. He defended the war vigorously, and at the same time praised the Boers, and hoped the Government would make it honourable and easy for them to surrender and yet painfully perilous for them to continue the struggle. And looking round the House after speaking nearly an hour he thanked it for the kindness extended to him – not, he knew, on his own account, but because of a certain splendid memory – a touching allusion to his dead father who had built up so brilliant a political reputation from that very spot where the son now stood.

Daily Dispatch (*Manchester*)
Independent – One halfpenny – Edward Hulton, proprietor

19 February 1901

Parliamentary Sketch

But the event of the evening was the maiden speech of Mr Winston Churchill. It was close on half past ten o'clock when the hon gentleman rose from the gangway seat on the second bench immediately behind the Treasury seat, the very seat which his father, Lord Randolph Churchill, occupied after he left the Unionist Government in the autumn of 1886. The House was almost crowded at the time, but the news having gone forth that the young member for Oldham was up, there was a continual inrush of members for five minutes until the Chamber was literally packed. The speech, which was brief, was well received on all sides and created an excellent impression.

Oldham Daily Standard
Conservative – One halfpenny – A. F. Stephenson, proprietor

19 February 1901

[Leading article]

The Junior Member's Speech

Mr Winston S. Churchill MP has not wasted much time after his return from America before entering upon the discharge of the duty which Oldham entrusted to him recently. With characteristic energy he did not allow the first Parliament of Edward VII to become more than a few days old before venturing to address it on a matter of the utmost importance. The House has watched the movements of Oldham's junior member with considerable interest, for it had heard much of his fight in this constituency, and was anxious to see how he fared in the more sedate atmosphere of Westminster. When, therefore, it was whispered that he would address the House the benches were rapidly filled, and by a critical assembly anxious to see if the young member realised their expectation, and doubtless compare him with the bearer of a name much honoured amongst us. By a singular coincidence he occupied the very seat favoured by his father before he held office, and the House, conscious of the significance of the incident, listened as if under a spell. The speech was closely reasoned, with logical argument, and delivered in clear and distinct style. The speaker followed each point exhaustively, and showed a balance of common sense, judgment and discretion which would have done credit to an old Parliamentary hand. Mr Churchill was given a most attentive hearing, and the cheers which punctuated his speech told how successfully he had driven home his points . . .

Evening News
Conservative – One halfpenny – Alfred Harmsworth, proprietor

19 February 1901

Mr Winston Churchill's Success

About ten o'clock the whisper went round that Mr Churchill was to interpose in the debate upon the Address, and when he rose to speak, following Mr Lloyd George, the Chamber was full – a crowd of men at the bar, Lords and Bishops in the Peers' Gallery and many ladies behind the grille in the Ladies' Gallery.

The junior member for Oldham spoke, appropriately enough, from the place which was always occupied by his father after he retired from office.

After a speech of forty minutes, a speech of breezy frankness and yet incisiveness, with now and then a flash of humour, Mr Churchill thanked the House for the kindness of its reception . . .

Pall Mall Gazette
Conservative – One penny – 1st Viscount Astor, proprietor

19 February 1901

Occasional Notes

Last night's South African debate contained practically nothing that was new about South Africa; how could it? But from the personal point of view it was full of interest. For one thing there was Mr Winston Churchill's studiously moderate and most effective speech, which evidently pleased the House. Mr Churchill sat down, not announcing that a time would come when they would hear him,[1] but thanking them for having done so, for his father's sake, as he put it . . .

[1] When Disraeli made his maiden speech on 7 December 1837 he met with a stormy reception. His biographer, W. F. Monypenny, records the conclusion of the speech: 'And then, in a voice which, by the testimony of every witness, rose high above the clamour, and which one even describes as "almost terrific": "I sit down now, but the time will come when you will hear me." '

The Globe
Conservative – One penny – W. T. Madge, proprietor

19 February 1901

Last Night's Parliament

. . . Mr Winston Churchill rose at 10.30, and spoke for half an hour in
the presence of a full and eager house, reviewing the general situation in
South Africa. He spoke fluently from the first seat behind the Treasury
bench, and, while modest in manner and attitude, his voice was that of his
father . . .

Westminster Gazette
Liberal – One penny – Sir George Newnes, proprietor

19 February 1901

Notes and Sketches in Parliament

. . . Mr Lloyd George denounced the war *ab initio* on uncompromising
lines of disapproval of the war itself in all its operations and its Generals.
Mr Winston Churchill replied in an able maiden speech, which was naturally
listened to with much interest. Although Mr Churchill has little facial re-
semblance to his father, members last night thought they could detect some
suggestion of Lord Randolph Churchill in the young member's pose while
speaking . . .

Vanity Fair
Independent – sixpence

21 February 1901

The Westminster Week by 'Jawkins MP'

. . . Later on we arrive at the second edition of the late Member for
Paddington and Chancellor of the Exchequer – much the same as Randolph
in the eighties – attitude, expression, long frock coat, delivery leaving
something to be desired, subject matter and speech first-rate.

Punch
Independent – Threepence

27 February 1901

Friday. – Still talk of WINSTON CHURCHILL's speech. Much interest pertained to occasion; high expectation; both justified. Fortunate in circumstances attending his *début.* LLOYD GEORGE obligingly bridged latter portion of dinner hour with blatant denunciation of all things British, exaltation of all things Boer. Frantic cheers of Irish sympathisers with England's enemies drew in loungers from the lobby, students from the library, philosophers from the smoking-room. Constant stream of diners-out flowed in. When young CHURCHILL rose from corner seat of bench behind Ministers, obligingly lent by CAP'EN TOMMY BOWLES, he faced, and was surrounded by, an audience that filled the Chamber. No friendly cheer greeted his rising. To three-quarters of the audience he was personally unknown. Before he concluded his third sentence he fixed attention, growing keener and kinder when, in reply to whispered questions, answer went round that this was RANDOLPH CHURCHILL's son.

Nothing either in voice or manner recalls what WINSTON in delicate touch alluded to as 'a certain splendid memory.' He has, however, the same command of pointed phrase; the same self-possession verging, perhaps, on self-assurance; the same gift of viewing familiar objects from a new standpoint; the same shrewd, confident judgment. Instantly commanding attention of the House, he maintained it to the end of a discourse wisely brief. Pretty to see SQUIRE OF MALWOOD [Walter Long][1] watching him with pleased, fatherly smile; PRINCE ARTHUR [Balfour], with glowing countenance, keenly listening from the opposite bench, doubtless thinking of days that are no more, feeling again the touch of a vanished hand, faintly hearing the sound of a voice that is still.

The Member for SARK[2] remembers over the waste of nearly a quarter of a century GRANDOLPH's maiden speech. He rose from the bench behind that from which WINSTON spoke. In those days he did not assume the prominence of a corner seat, content to find a place somewhere about the middle of the Bench. He had plenty of room to choose, for the House was not half full. The occasion was one of CHARLES DILKE's[3] crusades against small boroughs.

[1] Walter Hume Long (1854–1924), President of Local Government Board 1900–5, 1915–1916; Chief Secretary for Ireland 1905–6; Secretary of State for the Colonies 1916–18; First Lord of the Admiralty 1919–21; Conservative MP North Wilts 1880–5, Devizes 1885–92, West Derby, 1892–1900, South Bristol 1900–6, South Dublin 1906–10; Strand Division 1910, St George's, Westminster 1919–21; created Viscount Long of Wraxall 1921.

[2] A mythical MP created by Henry Lucy.

[3] Charles Wentworth Dilke (1843–1911), Liberal MP 1868–86, 1892–1911; Under Secretary of State Foreign Affairs 1880–2; President Local Government Board 1882–5; his political career ruined by involvement in celebrated Crawford divorce case 1886.

In course of his speech he had alluded disrespectfully to Woodstock, the family borough for which GRANDOLPH, not then scorning the ways of ducal cadets, was content to sit. The speech created little attention, save among two or three close observers who recognised the flash of genius in the unconventional utterance. Not the most friendly and sanguine listener dreamt of the future career of the young man who, having made an end of speaking abruptly left the House and was not heard again till after long interval.

Very different fortune attends his son when, twenty-six years later, he makes his maiden speech. WINSTON must see to it that the reversion of circumstance is not followed all along the line. The father began on a low level, and stormed the topmost towers of Ilium. The son springs into notice from a lofty plane, and will be expected to preserve his altitude.

To which end SARK, nothing if not practical, warns him to be chary of contribution to debate, at least, through his first session. Better to have the House of Commons wondering why you don't speak, than marvelling why you do.

Business done. – Still talking round Address. Accent chiefly Irish.

Sir H. Campbell-Bannerman to WSC

18 February 1901   House of Commons

Dear Mr Churchill,

I hope you will allow me to say with how much pleasure I listened to your speech.

With sincere congratulations,

Yours vry truly
H. CAMPBELL-BANNERMAN

J. Cumming Macdona[1] to WSC

18 February 1901   Palace Chambers
                                                    Westminster

Dear Winston Churchill,

I was proud to be near you last night when you made so brilliant a speech. I was touched more than I can express in words at the finish – at your exquisite allusions to his Spirit which to me seemed to hover over you, for I sat behind him when he made his last speech in the House & noticed the

[1] John Cumming Macdona (1836–1907), Conservative MP for Southwark, Rotherhithe 1892–1906. Barrister; President of the Kennel Club.

nervous twisting of his hands clasped behind him. I was also close to your mother when her emotion overcame her at the unveiling of his bust in the entrance to the Members lobby. From both sides you have inherited marvellous ability and aptitude. May God give you lengthy days and health for both influences to bear full fruit.

I am yours truly
CUMMING MACDONA

WSC to W. Murray Guthrie[1]
(*David James Papers*)

18 February 1901   105 Mount Street

My dear Murray,

Many thanks for your very kind congratulations which I know are those of a friend. It was a terrible, thrilling yet delicious experience.

Yours sincerely
WINSTON S. CHURCHILL

G. E. Buckle[2] *to WSC*

20 February 1901   *The Times*
Printing House Square

Dear Mr Churchill,

I am glad you liked the report, which I was anxious should be a good one for the sake of your father whom I knew for many years and, in spite of some acute differences, admired very sincerely.[3]

The blunder you point out I regret. But you need not blame your articulation. It is clear to me that the reporter, in his shorthand note, only took down the letters 'prls',[4] and then, in writing out, inserted the wrong vowels. It is hardly worth while to make a correction, as the general meaning of the sentence is quite clear.

With good wishes, Believe me, yours sincerely
G. E. BUCKLE

[1] Walter Murray Guthrie (1869–1911), Conservative MP for Bow and Bromley Division of Tower Hamlets 1899–1906. Married Olive Louisa Blanche, daughter of Sir John Leslie 1st Baronet and sister-in-law of Leonie Leslie, WSC's aunt.

[2] George Earle Buckle (1854–1935), editor of *The Times* 1884–1912. Co-author with W. F. Monypenny of the six-volume *Life of Disraeli*; edited *Letters of Queen Victoria* in six volumes.

[3] The report was more than one column in length. In its parliamentary summary *The Times* described the speech as 'highly successful'.

[4] 'The Government', WSC had said, '. . . ought to make it easy and honourable for the Boers to surrender, and painful and perilous for them to continue in the field.' *The Times* report read '. . . painful and *powerless* . . .'.

Lord Cromer[1] *to WSC*

27 February 1901   Cairo

Private

My dear Churchill,

I must write a line to congratulate you on your excellent maiden speech. Go on & prosper. My best wishes to you.

I should think that your views about the eventual necessity of civilian govt were quite sound. My own experience on this leads me to the conclusion that it does not so very much matter whether the subordinate agents are soldiers or civilians provided the general guidance at the top is more or less civilian. I could write a small essay on this subject but will not do so.

People use the word 'Military Government' rather loosely without defining what it means, and it may mean a lot of different things – from Genl Weyler[2] to a staff corps colonel in Burmah with a judicial training who administers a hard and fast code with the impartiality of a Lord Chancellor.

Sincerely yours
CROMER

WSC to the Editor, the Westminster Gazette

18 March 1901

'IF I WERE A BOER, I HOPE I SHOULD BE FIGHTING IN THE FIELD.'

Sir,

Your correspondents vary in their opinions, but pay me an equal honour by noticing my observations. My justification of the phrase and idea in question is briefly this. Every man owes a duty to his country, and is under a high moral obligation to bear his part in sustaining its fortunes. Again, in all great controversies the number of just and fair arguments on either side is large enough to enable most honest men to find complete conviction. Neither side has a monopoly of right or reason. Therefore, although there may be a balance of moral right on one side of the quarrel, that balance is rarely sufficient to outweigh the great patriotic considerations first mentioned.

[1] Evelyn Baring (1841–1917), Agent and Consul General in Egypt 1888–1907; created Baron Cromer 1892; Earl, August 1901.
[2] General Valeriano Weyler (1838–1930), Marquis of Teneriffe, Commander in Chief of Madrid and other parts of Spain and her possessions; Minister of War 1901–2 and 1905–6. See Main Volume I, page 277.

From this I argue that while the Boer cause is certainly wrong, the Boer who fights for it is certainly right. Much more so, then, is the Boer who fights bravely for it. If I were so unfortunate as to be a Boer, I should certainly prefer to be the best kind of Boer. Hence the original proposition.

Your correspondent who thinks that such an argument would also justify the conduct of certain Chinese in their course of massacre, treachery, and torture displays an astonishing ignorance alike of South Africa, of China, and, let me add, of reasoning, for it is evident that no patriotic obligation could justify such acts.

I am, Sir your obedient servant
WINSTON S. CHURCHILL

2

The Young Member – 1901

(See Main Volume Chapter I, pp. 13–32)

W S C continued to lecture in England during the Spring of 1901 as the following statement of receipts shows:

Lecture tour receipts

1901

			£	s.	d.
March	5	Nottingham	40	19	7
March	8	Exeter	47	17	3
March	8	Plymouth	42	1	9
March	9	Torquay	69	13	3
March	13	Hastings at 3 and 8	107	14	1
March	20	Bournemouth	91	0	1
March	20	Southampton	12	0	8
March	21	Portsmouth	39	9	2
March	27	Folkestone	61	3	10
March	27	Dover	35	5	6
March	29	Chester	38	18	7
April	17	Bedford	36	7	0
April	24	Hull	37	6	3
May	8	Malvern	30	8	2
May	8	Gloucester (cancelled)			
			£690	5	2

WSC to Lord Rosebery[1]
(Rosebery Papers)

12 February 1901   105 Mount Street

My dear Lord Rosebery,

It has been suggested to me to give another Lecture in the St James' or Queen's Hall for the benefit of the 'Princess of Wales'[2] Fund for the wives of soldiers serving in South Africa. The last time I lectured in London the *net* profits amounted to £300, and there is no reason why an equal sum should not be raised this time for such a charitable purpose.

I should like very much to help the Fund in some way and this course seems to offer better prospects than any other. To ensure success a well known chairman is necessary, and bearing in mind that you would have presided at my Edinburgh lecture merely out of personal kindness to me, I venture to ask you whether you will preside in this case should it be possible to arrange a convenient date.

At present the 4th, 5th & 7th of March are available; but I do not doubt other dates could be arranged to give you a wider choice.

I am looking forward with keen pleasure – tempered with awe – to taking my seat tomorrow in the House of Commons.

Yours vy sincerely
WINSTON S. CHURCHILL

Lord Rosebery to WSC

20 February 1901   38 Berkeley Square

My dear Winston,

Nothing will induce me to fix any engagement which may keep me in this infernal climate, so that I am afraid I cannot fill your chair. Luckily you will not in the least need me.

Let me wish you heartily joy of your maiden speech. It is a great thing to have got it over, for it is a disagreeable though necessary operation, like vaccination, circumcision and the like. But it is much more to have achieved a triumph, as you have.

Yours
AR

---

[1] Lord ROSEBERY.
[2] WSC's proposed lecture for the Princess of Wales Fund on behalf of the Soldiers' and Sailors' Families' Association seems not to have taken place.

WSC to Lady Randolph

14 February 1901   105 Mount Street

My dearest Mamma,

I enclose a cheque for £300. In a certain sense it belongs to you; for I could never have earned it had you not transmitted to me the wit and energy which are necessary.

Will you write to the Duke of Portland[1] *now:* the time is very short as the date is Nottingham Mar 6.

I feel vy guilty of indiscretion.

Your loving son
WINSTON

WSC to Lady Randolph

20 February 1901   105 Mount Street

Dearest Mamma,

I am very busy all day except just before dinner. I will ring you up then if there is an opportunity.

I have seen Gen Ian Hamilton[2] who will make it his business to see that the *Maine*[3] and its mainstay receive a complimentary allusion in Lord Roberts'[4] concluding despatch. You may regard this, I think, as settled.

Your loving son
WINSTON

[1] William John Arthur Charles James 6,th Duke of Portland (1857–1943), Lord Lieutenant of Nottingham 1898–1939; Master of the Horse 1886–92 and 1895–1905. He won the Derby two years in succession, each time with an odds-on favourite, Ayrshire (5–6) in 1888 and Donovan (8–11) in 1889. He did not preside at the meeting, but his half-brother Lord Henry Bentinck (1863–1931), Conservative MP for South Nottingham, did.

[2] Ian Standish Monteith HAMILTON.

[3] The *Maine* was offered to the British Government by the American Transport Company and converted into a hospital ship by subscriptions received by a committee of American ladies whose president was Lady Randolph. After two trips to South Africa the ship was transferred to China.

[4] Frederick Sleigh, 1st Earl Roberts (1832–1914), supreme commander of British troops in South Africa; C-in-C India 1885–93; Field-Marshal and C-in-C Ireland 1885–99; Baron 1892; PC 1895; KG and Earl 1901.

Lord Charles Beresford[1] to WSC

7 March 1901   HMS *Ramilles*
                                                 Syracuse

My dear Winston Churchill,

If I had been at home on half pay, I should have been delighted to have presided at the lecture you intend to deliver at Portsmouth during this month. I do not think that the country really appreciates how much it owes to the energy and ability of your father. He really created the Conservative working man, but his views on Imperial questions were certainly more of a National than a party character. A few more of his calibre are badly wanted now to rouse the country out of its apathetic indifference on all matters concerning its welfare, and safety.

We are becoming a nation of talkers, instead of a nation composed of men of action. We are always theorising & thinking of what might, could, or should be instead of what is. We ought to take up hard-featured practical facts and deal with them in a practical businesslike manner. May every luck attend you. You have the supreme advantage of youth combined with considerable experience. You can be of infinite use to your country.

                                          Yours very sincerely
                                          CHARLES BERESFORD

WSC to Oliver Borthwick[2]
(Bathurst Papers)

27 February 1901   105 Mount Street

My dear Oliver,

Many thanks for your kind letter: the *Morning Post* has always helped me and it is mainly through my association with it that I have become widely known.

I have forwarded your letter to my lecture agent Mr Gerald Christy [*sic*][3] who must arrange any lecturing engagements which I make – for if I were to interfere there would be great confusion.

                                          Yours vy sincerely
                                          WINSTON S. CHURCHILL

[1] Lord Charles BERESFORD.
[2] Oliver Borthwick (1873–1905), editor of the *Morning Post*; son of 1st Baron Glenesk.
[3] Gerald Christie (d. 1944). See Main Volume I, page 541.

WSC's Appointments Diary for 1901 gives some idea of his varied activities during his first year in Parliament.

APPOINTMENTS DIARY

1901

FEBRUARY

16	Dine	Marlborough	Willis' Rooms	
20	Conference	Cotton Trade	Hotel Metropole London	12 noon
	Dinner	Mr Brodrick	34 Portland Place, W.	8.15
21		Crisp[1]		10 o'c
	Lunch		35a [Gt Cumberland Place]	1.15/12.30
22		Sir Henry Wolff[2]	28 Cadogan Place	12 o'c
	Dinner	Sir James Willcocks[3]	Naval Military	8
23	Speech	Manchester bye election		
24		Taplow Court[4]	Maidenhead	
25	Dinner	Lee[5]	H of C	8 o'c
26	Dinner	Haldane[6]	H of Commons	
27	Dine	Wenlocks[7]	26 Portland Place	8.15
28		Lord Salisbury[8]	F.O.	12 o'c
	Dinner	Mrs Lyttelton[9]	16 Gt College St Westminster	8.30

[1] Charles Birch Crisp (1867–1958), stockbroker; WSC's Conservative running mate at Oldham in 1900.

[2] Henry Drummond Wolff (1830–1908), an intimate friend of Lord Randolph and his colleague in the Fourth Party; MP Christchurch 1874–80, Portsmouth 1880–5; Ambassador to Spain 1892–1900. GCMG 1878; GCB 1889.

[3] Colonel Sir James Willcocks (1857–1926), had received the KCMG, the freedom of the City of London, a sword of honour, and a mention in the King's Speech for his part in the relief of Kumasi, in the Gold Coast, in July 1900. He became a General in 1916, and was Governor of Bermuda 1917–22.

[4] Taplow Court, Buckinghamshire, the home of W. H. Grenfell, later Lord Desborough.

[5] Arthur Hamilton Lee (1868–1947), Conservative MP for Fareham 1900–18; served as British Military Attaché with the U.S. Army during the Spanish American War, 1898, when he became an intimate friend of Theodore Roosevelt; Baron 1918; Viscount 1922; Minister of Agriculture 1919–21; First Lord of the Admiralty 1921–2. Gave Chequers to the Nation 1921.

[6] Richard Burdon HALDANE.

[7] Beilby, 3rd Baron Wenlock (1849–1912), lord of the bedchamber to the Prince of Wales 1901–10 and a former Governor of Madras; and his wife Constance Mary (1852–1932), eldest daughter of 4th Earl of Harewood.

[8] Robert Arthur Talbot, 3rd Marquess of SALISBURY.

[9] Edith Sophy (1865–1948), 2nd wife of Alfred Lyttelton and mother of Oliver, 1st Viscount Chandos.

MARCH

1	Speech	L.C.C.	for S. Low[1]	
			Finsbury	
2			Newmarket	
3			Newmarket	
5	Lunch	Lady Granby[2]		1.45
	Dine		Londonderry Hse	8.15
6	Lecture		Nottingham	
7			H of C	
8	Lectures		Exeter	
			Plymouth	
9	Lecture		Torquay	
13	Lectures		Hastings	
14	Presentation	Crisp	H of C	
15	Lunch	Mrs Cholmondeley[3]	162 Albert Gate	1.30
	Dine	Lady Ribblesdale[4]	32 Green St	
16			Melton	
17			Melton	
18			Melton	
19			Melton	
20	Lectures	Stay with:		
		Tankerville	Southampton	
		Chamberlain[5] [sic]	Bournemouth	
21			Portsmouth	
22	Luncheon	Marlborough[6]/		
		Whittaker[7] & Crisp		
		Lord James[8]		4
		Lord Halsbury[9]		4.30

[1] Sidney James Low (1857–1932), journalist and historian, editor of *St James's Gazette* 1888–97; alderman in the London County Council 1901–5; knighted 1918.

[2] Violet (1856–1937), the wife of Henry John Brinsley, Marquess of Granby, who succeeded in 1906 as the 8th Duke of Rutland.

[3] Katherine Lucy (d. 1921), widow of Colonel Hon Thomas Grenville Cholmondeley, 2nd son of 1st Baron Delamere, and daughter of Sir Tatton Sykes, 4th Bart.

[4] Charlotte Monckton (1858–1911), wife of Thomas, 4th Baron Ribblesdale. She was a daughter of Sir Charles Tennant, 1st Bart, and a sister of Mrs H. H. Asquith.

[5] Tankerville Chamberlayne (1843–1924), MP for Southampton 1892–6, 1900–6; had seats at Cranbury Park, near Winchester, and Baddesley Manor, Romsey.

[6] Duke of MARLBOROUGH.

[7] Robert Whittaker (1837–1923), chairman of WSC's local Conservative Association and former Mayor of Oldham.

[8] Lord JAMES OF HEREFORD.

[9] Hardinge Stanley Giffard, 1st Earl of Halsbury (1823–1921), Lord Chancellor 1885–6, 1886–92, 1895–1905; Conservative MP Launceston 1877–85; Solicitor-General 1875–80;

MARCH

24		Ernest Beckett[1]	Virginia Water	
25	Lunch		Londonderry House	
26	Lunch	Lady Granby		
27			Folkestone	
			Dover	
28		Pearce.[2] S. Africa	House of Commons	12
29	Lecture		Chester	
31			Paris	

APRIL

1			Paris	
2			Madrid	
3			Madrid	
4-8			Seville	
9			Grenada	
10			Gibraltar	
11			Seville	
12			Cordova	
13-14			Madrid	
15			Paris	
16			London	
17	Lecture	United Service Institute	Bedford	3 pm
18			H of C	
19			Oldham	
20		Lever P.L. Annual meeting	Oldham	
23		Liverpool Conservative Club	afterwards to Town Hall Reception	
24	Lecture		Hull	
25			H of C	
27		Strafford Club	Oxford University	
28			Blenheim	

Baron 1885; Earl of Halsbury and Viscount Tiverton 1898; Senior Grand Warden of English Freemasons; 'die-hard' defender of the power of the House of Lords.

[1] Ernest William Beckett (1856-1917), Conservative MP for Whitby 1885-1905; one of Lord Randolph's literary executors; succeeded his uncle as 2nd Baron Grimthorpe 1905.

[2] Possibly Henry Pearce (1869-1925), traveller and political journalist who served as an intelligence officer during the Boer War and was commercial adviser to the Military Governor of the Orange River Colony.

APRIL

30	Dine	Conan Doyle[1]	Birmingham Athenaeum	8

MAY

1			Malvern? Worcester	
2	Polo			3.30
3		Whitefriars Club		
4	Polo			3.30
	Dine	George Wyndham[2]	35 Park Lane	8.15
5	Lunch	Lady Granby		
6	Dine	Howard Melliss[3]	Naval & Military	8.15
7		Wednesbury Institute		
8		Malvern		
9	Lunch	Bron Herbert[4]	4 St James' Square	
	Polo			
	Dine		House of Commons	
11	Polo			
12			Blenheim	
14	Lunch	Lucy[5]	42 Ashley Gdns Victoria St SW	1.30
15	Dinner		Lansdowne House	8.15
16	Lunch		17 Grosvenor Place	

[1] Arthur Conan Doyle (1859-1930), the author of the Sherlock Holmes stories, had unsuccessfully stood as Liberal Unionist candidate for Central Edinburgh in 1900. He had served in South Africa as senior physician at a field hospital; wrote a history of the early stages of the war; and in 1902 published a widely-read pamphlet justifying the cause and conduct of the war; knighted 1902.

[2] George Wyndham (1863-1913), Chief Secretary for Ireland 1900-5; Conservative MP for Dover 1889-1913; Under-Secretary of State for War 1898-1900; raised to Cabinet rank 1902; PC 1900. He married, 1899, Sibell Mary Lumley, 4th daughter of 9th Earl of Scarbrough and widow of Earl Grosvenor, eldest son of 1st Duke of Westminster.

[3] Howard Melliss (1847-1921), had befriended WSC when Inspector-General, Imperial Service Troops, India; KCSI 1897.

[4] Auberon Thomas Herbert (1876-1916), only surviving son of Auberon Herbert, 3rd son of 3rd Earl of Caernarvon, and his wife Florence Annabel Cowpe, daughter of 6th Earl of Cowpe, through whom in 1905 he succeeded as 8th Baron Lucas and 11th Baron Dingwall. Educated at Bedford Grammar School and Balliol, he rowed twice against Cambridge in the Boat Race. In the South African War he served as War Correspondent for *The Times*, and as a result of a wound in the foot a leg had to be amputated below the knee. He became Under-Secretary of State for War 1908-11, for the Colonies 1911, Parliamentary Secretary (1911-14), and President (1914-15) of the Board of Agriculture. He left office on the formation of the Coalition Government, joined the Royal Flying Corps, and failed to return from a flight over German lines in November, 1916.

[5] Henry Lucy (1845-1924), Parliamentary sketch-writer, best known as Toby MP of *Punch*, 1887-1916; knighted 1909.

MAY

16	Dine	Conan Doyle	House of Commons	
17			Oldham	
18		Lancashire & Cheshire Federations	Oldham	
21	Lunch		Brook House	2
22	Speak	Colonial Nursing Association	Londonderry House	3.30
	Dine	Clinton Dawkins[1]	38 Queen Annes' Gate	
23	Lunch		Londonderry House	
	Polo			
24	Polo			
	Initiation	Freemason	33 Golden Square	
	Dine	Lord Northbrook[2]	3 Hamilton Place	
26			Blenheim	
27			Blenheim	
30	Polo		Crystal Palace	

JUNE

1	Speech at Dinner	Cambridge University	Carlton	
2			Warwick	
4	Dine		Londonderry House	8.15
5		A. Haldane[3]		morning
	Dine	Mrs Adair[4]	30 Curzon St	
6	Preside	Midland Conservative Club	Birmingham	
7	Dine		Cumberland Place	8.15
8			Woodlands	
9			Woodlands	
10	Dinner		House of Commons	

[1] Clinton Edward Dawkins (1859–1905), Chairman of the Committee on War Office Reorganization; KCB 1902.

[2] Thomas Baring (1826–1904), MP for Penrhyn and Falmouth 1856–66; First Lord of the Admiralty 1880–5; Viceroy and Governor-General of India 1872–6; created Earl of Northbrook 1876.

[3] James Aylmer Lowthorpe Haldane (1862–1950), served in India and South Africa with WSC. He was in command of the Chieveley armoured train when he and WSC were captured and imprisoned in Pretoria. KCB 1918; retired as General 1925. He was a cousin of R. B. Haldane.

[4] Cornelia Adair, daughter of an American general and widow of the Lord of Glenveagh Castle, in Donegal, she entertained many important figures. (See Vol. I, page 286.)

JUNE

11	Dine	Mrs Cavendish-Bentinck[1]	4 Richmond Terrace, Whitehall	
12	Dine	Mrs Maguire[2]		
13			House of Commons	
14			Oldham	
15		Unionist Demonstration for J. Bagot Esq, MP[3]	Levens	
16			Taplow	
17	Dine	Harrow Fifty Club Dr Welldon[4] present toasts	Assembly Rooms Harrow	
18		Motor car	Ascot	
19	Polo			
	Dine		Wimborne Hse	8.15
20	Polo		Windsor	
21	Dine	Lady Sassoon[5]	25 Park Lane	8.30
23		Anningsley Park (Woking)	Chertsey	
24			Taplow meeting	3.30
	Dine	Lord Revelstoke[6]	26 Hill St	
25	Lunch	Loulou Harcourt[7]	14 Berkeley Square	1.45
	Dine	Mr Astor[8]	18 Carlton House Terrace	
26	Dine	Lord Derby[9]	Derby House	

[1] Ruth Mary St Mair (d. 1953), wife of William George Frederick Cavendish-Bentinck, a first cousin of Jack Leslie and great-grandson of the 3rd Duke of Portland.

[2] Julia Beatrice (d. 1949), wife of James Rochfort Maguire, a former Nationalist Irish MP, and daughter of Arthur, 1st Viscount Peel, formerly Speaker of the House of Commons.

[3] Josceline FitzRoy Bagot (1854–1913), Conservative MP for South Westmorland 1892–1906 and later for Kendal, 1910–13; married 1885 Theodosia, daughter of Sir John Leslie, 1st Bart; baronet 1913.

[4] James Edward Cowell Welldon (1854–1937), Bishop of Calcutta and Metropolitan of India 1898–1902; Headmaster of Harrow 1885–98; Canon of Westminster 1902–6; Dean of Manchester 1906–18; Dean of Durham 1918–33.

[5] Aline Caroline (d. 1909), wife of Sir Edward Albert Sassoon, 2nd Baronet, MP for Hythe 1899–1912, and daughter of Baron Gustave de Rothschild.

[6] John Baring, 2nd Baron Revelstoke (1863–1929), a partner in the banking firm of Baring Brothers and a director of the Bank of England.

[7] Lewis HARCOURT.

[8] William Waldorf Astor (1848–1919), born in New York, naturalized British subject 1899; Baron 1916, Viscount 1917.

[9] Frederick Arthur Stanley, 16th Earl of Derby (1841–1908), Conservative politician and

JUNE
27		Milner	House of Commons	
28	Lunch		Stafford House	
	Dentist			3.15
	Polo			
29			Blenheim	
30			Blenheim	

JULY
1	Dine	Lord Salisbury	20 Arlington Street	
2	Lunch	Lord Dundonald[1]	34 Portman Sq	
	Dine	Duchess of Marlborough		
3		Sir E. Cassel[2]	Newmarket	
4			Newmarket	
5			Newmarket	
6	Lunch	Ranelagh		1.45
	Polo	H of C versus Guards		
7			Hatfield	
8	Dinner	J. Morley[3] A.J.B. Mrs Grenfell[4]	H of C	
9	Dine	G. Wyndham	H of C	
10	Dine	Mrs R. Beckett[5]	26 Curzon St	
11		Charlie Stirling[6]		12
12	Dentist			10
13			Esher	

landowner; MP for Preston 1865–8; North Lancashire 1868–85; Blackpool 1885–6; Secretary of State for War, 1878–80; for Colonies 1885–6; President of the Board of Trade 1886–8; Governor-General of Canada 1888–93; succeeded his father in 1893; KG 1897; GCVO 1905.

[1] Douglas Mackinnon Baillie Hamilton Cochrane, 12th Earl of Dundonald (1852–1935), commanded the 3rd Mounted Brigade during the Boer War, entering Ladysmith with WSC on 28 February 1900; Major-General 1900; commanded Canadian Militia 1902–4; Lieutenant-General 1907.

[2] Sir Ernest Joseph CASSEL.

[3] John MORLEY.

[4] Ethel Anne Priscilla Grenfell (1867–1952), later Lady Desborough.

[5] Muriel Helen Florence (1878–1941), wife of Rupert Evelyn Beckett (1870–1955), younger brother of Ernest William Beckett (later 2nd Baron Grimthorpe).

[6] Probably Charles Richard Stirling (b. 1882) whose older brothers were at Harrow with WSC, and whose mother was Hon Mrs Gilbert Stirling, Lady Randolph's friend. Charles Stirling went on the stage and assumed the theatrical name of Eric Stirling.

JULY

14		Lady Helen Vincent[1] Esher	
15	Dinner	Mrs Rupert Beckett H of C	
16	Dine	Mrs Paget[2]	35 Belgrave Sq. 8.30
17	Dine		17 Grosvenor Place 8.30
18	Lunch		100 Park Street 1.30
	Dine	Welldon	H of C
19		2nd Degree Freemasons	33 Golden Square 6.30 sharp
	Dine	Ridleys[3]	34 Portland Place 8.30
21			Gopsall
22	Dine	Sydney Buxton[4]	H of C 8.15
25	Dentist		12
		Board of Education	3 pm
26	Lunch	De Moleyns[5]	
27	Speech	Middleton[6]	
28			Taplow
31	Dine	Lady Cranborne	24 Grafton Street

AUGUST

3–4		Lord Rosebery	The Durdans
5–7		Auberon Herbert	Wrest
	Polo		Windsor
8		Lady Helen Vincent	12
10		Demonstration	Blenheim
11			Blenheim
14		Lord Rosebery	Mentmore
17			Blenheim
19			Warwick

---

[1] Helen Venetia (1866–1954), wife of Sir Edgar Vincent (1857–1941), Conservative MP for Exeter 1899–1906, Ambassador in Berlin 1920–26, Viscount D'Abernon 1926. She was a daughter of 1st Earl of Feversham.

[2] Probably Mary ('Mimi') (d. 1919), wife of Major-General Arthur Paget and an American friend of Lady Randolph.

[3] Matthew White Ridley (1874–1916), MP for Stalybridge 1900–4, son of 1st Viscount Ridley (Home Secretary 1895–1900) and May Georgiana, sister of 2nd Baron Tweedmouth; and his wife Rosamond (1877–1947), younger daughter of 1st Baron Wimborne.

[4] Sidney Charles BUXTON.

[5] Lieutenant-Colonel Frederick Rossmore Wauchope Eveleigh De Moleyns (1861–1923), who had been Adjutant of the 4th Hussars when WSC first joined; succeeded his father as 5th Baron Ventry 1914.

[6] Richard William Evelyn Middleton (1846–1905), Chief Agent of the Conservative Party 1885–1903.

AUGUST

21	Bazaar	Lady Londesborough's[1]	Scarborough
22		Lord Ribblesdale[2]	Gisburne
25–29		Duke of Sutherland[3]	Dunrobin
30	Lecture		Goltsby

SEPTEMBER

2–5		Lord Londonderry	Wynyard
12		Lord Tweedmouth	Guisachan
16			Aberdeen
17		Asquith	St Andrews
18		Kinnoull[4]	Perth
19		Alexander Farquharson[5]	Invercauld
20			Rannoch
24			Scotland
25–26		Lady Sassoon	
29–30			Dalmeny

OCTOBER

1	Lecture		Doncaster	
2			Waterhead	
			Moorside & Clarksfield	
3			Blackpool, Westwood	
			Coldhurst, Werneth	
4			Saddleworth	
5		St James' Ward Conservative Club		
		Lytton[6]	Hollinwood Club	7.30
6		Lytton	Gisburne	
7		St Peter's & St Paul's Club		
8	Lecture	St Helens		

---

[1] Grace Adelaide Fane (1860–1933), wife of 2nd Earl of Londesborough, and elder daughter of 12th Earl of Westmorland.

[2] Thomas Lister (1854–1925), succeeded father as 4th Baron Ribblesdale 1876; Lord-in-Waiting 1880–5; Master of Buckhounds 1892–5.

[3] Cromartie Sutherland-Leverson-Gower (1851–1913), succeeded his father as 4th Duke of Sutherland 1892; Liberal MP for Sutherland 1874–86; opposed Gladstone's Home Rule Bill and became a Unionist; owned more land than any other British subject.

[4] Archibald Fitzroy George, 13th Earl of Kinnoull (1855–1916), whose seat was at Balhousie Castle, Perth.

[5] Alexander Haldane Farquharson (1867–1936), 14th of Invercauld.

[6] Victor Alexander George Robert, 2nd Earl of Lytton (1876–1947), who married Miss Pamela Plowden in 1902.

OCTOBER

8	Dine	Mayor, John Forster[1] Town Hall Esq Stay Col Pilkington[2] Rainsford Hall, St Helens	6.30
9	Distribute prizes	Co-operative Hall Oldham Show	
10		Sir M. Hicks Beach[3] Empire Theatre Marlborough	
13		Blenheim	
14	Dine	Abe Bailey[4] Carlton Hotel	
15–16		Blenheim	
17–20		Paris	
21		Ealing	
22		Hampstead	
23		stay at Glen Parva Leicester Grange	
24		Croydon	
29	Lunch	Hugh Cecil[5] Carlton Club	
30		Lytton	1.30
	Dine	G. Marsham[6] Hayle Cottage Maidstone	
31		Stoke Newington	

NOVEMBER

4	Hunt		
5		Nottingham	
6		Walsall	
7	Hunt		
8		Halley Stewart Esq[7] Wardown, Luton	

---

[1] John Forster (1853–1927), Mayor of St Helens 1900; bottle manufacturer and Liberal politician; member of St Helens Council 1884–1927; awarded OBE for munitions work and Chairmanship of the St Helens Tribunal during the First World War.

[2] Richard Pilkington (1841–1908), MP for Newton division of South-West Lancashire 1899–1906. He was a member of the great glass manufacturing family.

[3] Sir Michael HICKS BEACH.

[4] Abe Bailey (1864–1940), South African financier and mine-owner; friend of Lord Randolph; baronet 1919. John Bailey, his eldest son, married WSC's eldest daughter Diana in 1932, the marriage being dissolved in 1935.

[5] Lord Hugh CECIL.

[6] George Marsham (1849–1927), Chairman of Kent County Council, 1900–10.

[7] Halley Stewart (1838–1937), called himself (*Who's Who*) 'Advanced Liberal; advocates adult suffrage for both sexes, the land for the people, religious equality, and abolition of

NOVEMBER

9	Dine	Oldham Mayor's Banquet	
11	Shoot		
12	Dinner		Constitutional Club
13	Hunt		
		Annual dinner Cons	Banbury
		Club. Albert Brassey[1]	
14			Streatham
15	Hunt		
16	Hunt		
18	Hunt		
19	Hunt		
20	Hunt		
21	Dinner	Liverpool Debating Society	
22	Lecture		Annesley
24			Blenheim
26	Shoot		
27	Open Bazaar	for Duchess of Sutherland[2]	
29			Hanley
30	Hunt		

DECEMBER

2	Hunt		
3	Hunt		
4			Birmingham
5	Dinner	Conservative Club	Birmingham
7	Dinner	Savage Club	Hotel Cecil
9		Hooligans	
10	Hunt		
11	Present prizes	St Margaret's School	Manchester Free Trade Hall
12	Open Bazaar	Congregational Church	Oldham

---

hereditary legislations . . .' MP for Spalding, Lincs., 1887–95, Greenock 1906–10; Vice-Chairman of London Brick Co; knighted 1932.

[1] Albert Brassey (1844–1918), of Heythrop, MP for Banbury, Oxfordshire, 1895–1906; Master of the Heythrop hounds, 1873–1918.

[2] Millicent Fanny (1867–1957), daughter of 4th Earl of Rosslyn, who had married the 4th Duke of Sutherland on her seventeenth birthday.

DECEMBER

13	Canford
14 Hunt	
15	Tring
16 Hunt	
25	Gopsall

*   *   *   *   *

South African affairs continued to hold WSC's attention. On March 12 he opposed an amendment calling for an inquiry into the case of Major-General Sir Henry Colvile.[1] General Colvile had been dismissed from his command at Gibraltar because of incompetence on two occasions during the Boer War.

Sir Alfred Milner to WSC

6 February 1901   Government House
Private   Cape Town

My dear Mr Churchill,

I have your interesting letter of Dec 31. What occurs to me in reading is what occurs to me every day of my life, as I grow older, with increasing frequency, & that is that *le mieux est l'ennemi du bien.*

May we not be left alone for a little? Of course, no one expects to be spared the suggestions of busybodies having no weight. But it is a serious matter to have suggestions of pacification coming from you, with your ability, popularity & special S. African experience.

After months of intolerable grumbling, conflicting policies & contradictory Proclamations, we did settle down, something like 5 or 6 weeks ago, to a *clear line.* Mr Chamberlain's speech,[2] which I thought was surely moderate & conciliatory enough, was followed by declarations on the part of Lord Kitchener, consistent with it, which have been circulated

[1] Henry Edward Colvile (1852–1907), commander of 9th Division in South Africa, 1900; served in South Africa, Sudan, Uganda, Burma, Gibraltar; official historian of the Sudan Campaign of 1886; KCMG 1895; Major-General 1898.

[2] Chamberlain had in December 1900 explained to the Commons the Government's proposed pacification of South Africa, and attempted to justify the drastic measures such as farm-burning believed essential to crush the Boer guerillas; the bulk of the Opposition accepted his statement.

far & wide in S. Africa, though not yet everywhere, & on wh a certain number of our former enemies are now working vigorously to get their former comrades in arms to come in.

That speech & these declarations were made without any reference to me. I have no paternal interest in this. If I had been left to formulate a policy, it would not have assumed quite that form.

But the offer, though not mine, is a reasonable & practical offer, & will, I believe, be effective if we give it time to work.

Now, supposing that before we have given it a chance, before it is even generally known (even in the disintegrated state of the enemy it takes a long time for any news to circulate) we better the offer, what will be the effect? Remember that, in the interval, the enemy have been increasingly aggressive, *successful* & (apart from the question of the shooting of the peace envoy, to wh there may be two sides) *defiant*. The only effect of a precipitate bettering of our offer under these terms will be firstly, to make fools of the men who have accepted it & are working to get others to accept it, & secondly to confirm the impression, the *fatal prevalence of which is the root of all our S. African troubles,* that the only way to get anything out of the English is to hammer them, that their 'last word' never is their last word, but mere bluff wh they have only got to be sufficiently worried to abandon. Is that the way to induce people to stop fighting you? Surely, it is the strongest argument wh could be used by those who don't want any terms short of a restoration of independence, to induce their fellows to fight on.

I object most strongly at the present to any tacking at all. There are a dozen different ways in which this war might have been brought to a close since the capture of Pretoria, if we had consistently adhered to any one of them for six months. What was impracticable was to end it, when we were perpetually jerking from one to the other, till everybody was hopelessly bewildered.

But, apart from that, your terms are, as you say, not wholly what I would approve. In many of them – the honourable surrender, the immediate return of those still in the field to their homes, and assistance to restart them in farming – I quite agree. Others, like the general amnesty of rebels, I must emphatically dissent from. Please think of the effect on the loyal S. African, of whom you have upwards of 20,000 now fighting for you & probably the most useful men in the field. It is one thing to treat rebels leniently (I agree to clemency) another to *surrender the right* to treat them according to their deserts. I have no objection to 'cowing' rebels.

But perhaps what I most object to is the termination of the war by *any sort of bargain.* This is of fundamental importance for the future. State your terms – liberal ones – (we have done so), make it easy for people to accept them. But let it be submission – honourable, not 'humiliating' submission and not a treaty. You, unintentionally no doubt, quite mistake my attitude when you say that I wish to make the Boers 'cowed recipients of our favours'. I should like to strip our victory of all painful or humiliating incidents, but the fact that it is a victory must be clear, & we must keep a free hand afterwards. Otherwise I pity the man – not your humble servant – who has to superintend the subsequent work.

This letter is excessively long. You know the old saying 'Excuse this long letter, I have no time to write a short one.' But I must say one word in 'conclusion' on your second point – the financial one.

The great thing is not to burden the new countries at starting. Leave them all their resources including a reasonable amount borrowed at once to restart life as quickly as possible, & to recover their material prosperity.

But I see no reason why arrangements should not be made, that after the first year or two, the mines should contribute something substantial to the cost of the war.

If this had to be done by *general taxation of the people*, I should agree with your view. But a portion of the profits of the mines might well, in my opinion, by a carefully contrived scheme, be diverted from the pockets of non-resident share-holders to the relief of the British taxpayer. We should simply be intercepting some of the increased wealth, increased by our sacrifices, which would otherwise flow into the pockets of individual Britons, French & Germans & putting it into the Exchequer.

Yours vy truly

A. MILNER

Hansard

12 March 1901

MR WINSTON CHURCHILL (Oldham): Those who have not themselves had any actual experience of war may have some difficulty in understanding in what way the occurrence of a disaster may affect the character of a general responsible for it. I would like, so far as I may be permitted to do so, to clear that difficulty out of the way. Hon Members asked, very naturally, why, if a certain general was removed for *this* disaster, a certain other general should not be removed for *that* disaster, and indeed why all generals should not be removed for all disasters? War is a game with a good deal of chance in it, and, from the little I have seen of it, I should say that nothing in war ever goes right except occasionally by accident. The fact of a successful or an unsuccessful action being fought does not appear to be any accurate measure of the capacity or military character of the general officer who was in command. It is quite possible that in an unsuccessful action a general may show qualities of courage and resource for which there would otherwise have been no scope. General Broadwood,[1] for instance, was responsible for the command of the convoy at Sanna's Post. Such, however, was his bearing and conduct, and the high reputation which he had held and which he still holds in the Army, that after the disaster at Sanna's Post, General Broadwood's position was even more secure than before – he was even more trusted by his superiors and his men. On the other hand, there are general officers who have been responsible for no particular disaster, but who even in their success, or I should perhaps rather say their immunity from failure, have gained a most unenviable reputation. General officers or officers in high command in the Army ought not to be broken merely because they are responsible for disasters, but only if those disasters throw a light on their incompetency or inefficiency. When it is known by a competent superior officer that an officer is not a good officer, though he was not responsible for any disaster, there may be good grounds for removing him from his command, or appointing him to another command.

We have listened to two very effective speeches – one from the hon and learned Member for South Leeds [John L. Walton][2] who put the legal aspect of the question as powerfully as it could be put, and the other from the hon and gallant Member for North-West Wilts [Sir John Poynder Dickson-Poynder][3] who made a contribution to the debate which was most striking, from the fact that it came from one who had personal experience of these events. The hon and learned Member for South Leeds has put the legal aspect of the question; but soldiers are not lawyers, and their methods will not always bear the strict scrutiny of those who have given their life to the study of the law and the study of words. So long as the House is satisfied of the motives by which military officers have been actuated, it ought not to lay too great stress on technical or legal detail which may appear to have been neglected. The substance of the charge against General Colvile is the case of Sanna's Post. There may have been occasions before Sanna's Post – I do not say there were – when the conduct of that gallant officer did not give entire satisfaction. But it is upon Sanna's Post almost entirely that

---

[1] Robert George Broadwood (1862–1917), served in South Africa from 1899; Brigadier-General commanding troops in Natal 1902–4; Orange River Colony district 1904–6; Major-General commanding troops in South China 1906–10.

[2] John Lawson Walton (1852–1908), Liberal MP for South Leeds 1892–1908; Attorney-General 1905–8.

[3] Sir John Poynder Dickson-Poynder (1866–1936), succeeded his uncle as 6th Baronet, 1884. Conservative MP for Chippenham 1892–1910; Chairman, Royal Commission Indian Public Services 1912–14; Under-Secretary of State for the Colonies 1914–15; Parliamentary Under-Secretary for India 1915–18; Baron Islington 1910; PC 1911. Married Anne Beauclerk, daughter of Robert Henry Duncan Dundas of Dundas, in 1895.

the rights and the wrongs of this question stand. I venture to say that a more damning case than the one laid by the Secretary for War before the House last night, on the subject of Sanna's Post – if the representations and statements were correct – was hardly ever preferred against a general officer in this House. The hon and learned Member for South Leeds has disputed the facts. If it came to a question of balancing the evidence, I am much inclined to pin my faith to the decision come to by Lord Roberts. As to the Lindley affair, I wrote a long time ago to the War Office giving my humble opinion, having personally collected information on the spot. If the Lindley affair had been the only case against General Colvile, that would not have been worth pressing, but it must be considered together with the affair of Sanna's Post. These affairs had a cumulative aspect which rendered them much more significant. They were complicated, difficult, and technical matters, and we must trust to the men on the spot. In this case the military expert on the spot was Lord Roberts, who has been trusted, not in vain, in the greatest crisis of our history, with the largest army we have ever sent beyond the seas.

The hon and learned Member for South Leeds made a point against the Government, which I feel is a very legitimate and valid point. He said, if it be true that General Colvile made a fault, why was it that the official despatch, published since, did not make any reference to that fault or point out the blame he incurred? Perhaps it will not be entirely agreeable to many of my friends on this side of the House if I say that I have noticed in the last three wars in which we have been engaged a tendency among military officers – arising partly from good nature towards their comrades, partly from the dislike of public scrutiny – to hush everything up, to make everything look as fair as possible, to tell what is called the official truth, to present a version of the truth which contains about seventy-five per cent of the actual article. So long as a force gets a victory somehow, all the ugly facts are smoothed and varnished over, rotten reputations are propped up, and officers known as incapable are allowed to hang on and linger in their commands in the hope that at the end of the war they may be shunted into private life without a scandal. On whom does the responsibility for the continuance of the system rest? When Lord Roberts went out to South Africa he struck out a new and true line. The truth, the whole truth, was to be told to the country frankly and fairly. The House will remember the publication of the Spion Kop despatches and the reception that that publication met with from hon and right hon Gentlemen opposite. That settled the policy of candour in military matters, for some months to come at any rate. That is why the despatches contained no incriminating matter in regard to General Colvile. General Colvile was retained in his command, but it was reduced; he was put in the second line, placed practically, if not actually, in an inferior position to a general a very long way his junior in rank – General Ian Hamilton. It was no doubt thought he would be able to get out of the matter without any scandal or disturbance arising. But at length it became impossible to keep up appearances any longer. At length the crash came. Lindley was piled on Sanna's Post, there was a stormy interview, the Ninth Division was broken up, and its commander returned to England, complimented certainly, cleared in the despatches, but ruined for ever in the field. It seems to me it does not lie in the mouths of those who attacked the Government so vehemently in respect to the publication of the Spion Kop despatches to complain that now, and since that occasion, a very judicious discretion and diplomatic reticence has been practised by the War Office and the military authorities. There is some apparent misconception as to the method of removing officers from the Army, and that is because there are two ways of doing the thing. In the first place, there is the process of a court of inquiry and court-martial, and in the second place, there is the process of selection. Suppose an officer has committed no specific fault, but it is a matter of common knowledge that he is an incapable officer, would it be right that that officer should be given the command of a large body of troops? Surely it would be wrong to employ such an officer in time of peace if he was not thought good enough to employ in time of war. I have always been an enthusiastic advocate of selection, for I hold most strongly that the more nearly we can make our methods of promotion in the Army approximate to the methods employed by business firms, the more efficient the Army will be and the less soldiers we would have killed and captured in time of war.

Lord Roberts and the right hon Gentleman did not care to take the responsibility of appointing an officer to a peace command when he had just been found unfit for an important command in the field of war. I understand that hon Members opposite, including the hon and learned Member for South Leeds, differ from that view, and think it is an improper and vicious mode of procedure. Their argument is that once General Colvile was appointed to the command in Gibraltar anything that had happened in South Africa was condoned. But what about the brigade? Were 3,000 British soldiers forming the efficient part of the garrison of our greatest Mediterranean fortress not to be considered? Had they not a right to expect to be commanded by as good an officer as those best qualified to judge could get? Of course some reasonable assurance of fixity of tenure must be given to subordinates; but the paramount principle which must be held before our eyes is that the Service exists not for the benefit of individuals, but only for the advantage and security of the State. Under the process of selection mistakes are made and, unwittingly, injustice done; but the process is at work not only in the Army, but in every branch of commerce, in every walk of life, and it is nowhere more essential and more vital to efficiency than in the military service. We have to look no further than the House of Commons to see the principle of selection working in all its glory. We know that sitting around there are Members just as able, just as conscientious, quite as intelligent, as any who now adorn the Treasury Bench, but no one would think it worth while to urge the claims of anyone who has not been preferred. Selection is the only hope for increased efficiency in the Army, it is the only way in which we can prevent the upper ranks being clogged with incapable men. The principle of selection is challenged, and would be destroyed if a Commission were appointed in this case. I have been told by a distinguished general officer that, in consequence of the outcry which has occurred, already several persons against whom it had been proposed to take steps have been screwed back into their places. In regard to the selection of officers, the House ought not to interfere in any particular instance except for grievous reason. Personally, I have no hesitation in expressing my firm support of the attitude of the Secretary of State for War, and I exhort the right hon Gentleman, not only for the sake of the Army, but also in the interest of the House, not to budge an inch from the position he has taken up.

WSC to Lady Randolph

13 March 1901   105 Mount Street

Dearest Mamma,

As usual I am hunted to death. I have more than 100 letters unanswered. 30 or 40 I have not even had time to read. I am lecturing twice today at Hastings, and I shall be back here early tomorrow. It is quite evident to me that I cannot go on without a Secretary, and if you would try to get me one as a temporary measure, it would be an enormous help to me.

Speech last night was very successful. I enclose you a little note I received from Mr Brodrick after I sat down.[1] I wonder whether you waited to hear it. There is no doubt that the speech turned votes and shifted opinion at the time when the current was running very strongly against the Government. George Wyndham and all my friends think that as a Parliamentary coup it is far bigger than I have ever done. I know of several cases where people who

[1] 'That is so! May I say you will never make a better speech than you made tonight. Of course you will speak on better subjects — but you filled the House & held it — & got the debate back on to big lines. It was a great success and universally so recognised.
                                                                                            Sт. J. B.'

were going to vote against the Government decided to vote the other way, and if you read the *Daily News* or *Daily Chronicle* you will see that my intervention was by no means ineffective. I wish I had a little time to live and it is quite clear to me that unless I get a Secretary, I shall be pressed into my grave with all sorts of ridiculous things – which I have no need whatever to do. After all if I were to spend the time I take answering invitations, letters from constituents, and doing all that little business myself in writing articles I could pay the salary of a Secretary twice over. What I want is a gentleman immediately, who will come for a month or six weeks while I can look around and make some definite arrangements.

Also please try to find me a box to put letters in, a large compendious cabinet, with all kinds of drawers and holes of every kind that I can put papers in. There is a pile on my table now which quite stifles me. Lastly, I have lost the list of names of people who are to have the watches. Have you got their names? I cannot write out the inscriptions until I get them.[1]

Lord Curzon[2] to WSC

13 May 1901   Viceregal Lodge
                                                                Simla

My dear Churchill,

Just a line to congratulate you upon the successful inauguration of your Parliamentary career. I did not write to congratulate you upon your maiden speech because I have never known a case in which a young member who was expected to make a good maiden speech, has not been described as having done so. I remember in my own case making a maiden speech (I think that I ran a tilt at your father in it) which *The Times* next morning described as brilliant and which was plastered with amiable but uncritical praise.[3] All the while I knew well enough that it was execrable. I therefore never compliment maiden speeches, because with three exceptions (Disraeli's, Drage[4] and my own) I have never heard a really bad one.

[1] On 9 January 1901 WSC wrote to Lady Randolph expressing his intention of presenting inscribed watches to those who had assisted him in his escape from the Boers and enclosed a list of their names. See Companion Vol I, p. 1227, WSC to Lady Randolph.

[2] Lord CURZON.

[3] In his maiden speech, on 31 January 1887, Curzon criticised Lord Randolph's explanation of his resignation the previous month. 'The speech,' wrote Curzon's biographer, Lord Ronaldshay, 'was undoubtedly a good one . . . And yet, paradoxical though it may sound, it is difficult to resist the conclusion that it would have been an even better speech if it had not been *too* immaculately perfect.'

[4] Geoffrey Drage (1860–1955), Conservative MP for Derby 1895–1900, an expert on labour and manpower questions.

I have however been very pleased to see the manner in which you have not merely won but retained the ear of the House.

There is no more difficult position than being on the benches behind a Government. It is so hard to strike the mean between independence & loyalty.

The great thing is to impress the House with earnestness. They will forgive anything but flippancy.

Yours sincerely
CURZON

WSC to Lady Randolph

23 March 1901   105 Mount Street

My dear Mamma,

Many thanks for the picture which I value very highly, and which looks very appropriate and effective on my wall. I am very well, indeed, I think the last week my health is much improved. I polished off three more lectures at Bournemouth, Southampton and Portsmouth, and cleared about £220 out of the three.[1] I have decided definitely to play polo this year in a team which is being formed by some of my young military friends, and I think if I get two days a week at Hurlingham or Ranelagh, it will provide me with the physical exercise and mental countercurrent which these late hours and continual sittings of the house absolutely require. I search everywhere in vain for the list of names of the people who are to have the watches. Unless you can give me the list of names I cannot write out the inscriptions. Have you got them? or are they at the watchmaker's shop? and if so which watchmaker's, because I have lost your letter on the subject. I hope you are happy at Cannes and that George is making good progress. I start for Spain on the 30th or 31st, shall spend two nights in Paris and then travel direct through to Seville. I shall be back in England on the 15th of April, for I have to lecture at the United Service Institution on the 17th, not an ordinary lecture, but a special one which I have been asked to deliver, which will I think, lead to a lot of discussion among all the military sportsmen who will be present. I have been looking through the speeches with a view to boiling them down, but I do not think I shall be able to do anything in this line until the Autumn. Practically, one would miss the Spring Publishing Season now, and while Parliament is sitting I have not much time or vital energy to tackle bookmaking.

There is a good deal of dissatisfaction in the Party, and a shocking lack

[1] He was over-optimistic. See p. 25.

of cohesion. The Government is not very strong. That ridiculous Lansdowne again put us in a hole by going down to the House of Lords the day before yesterday, and reading out on the spur of the moment the result of the Tientsin negotiations without communicating the information to the House of Commons, who remained in ignorance of the whole matter until they read it in the newspapers.[1] I really think that man is a great burden for any party to carry. Meanwhile the Bartletts[2] and the Bowlses [sic] and all the other people who are disappointed, and perhaps are cruelly disappointed in the rewards their services have not received, are renewing and redoubling their attacks upon the Government, and the whole Treasury Bench appear to me to be sleepy and exhausted and played out. As for Joe [Chamberlain] he devotes his attention exclusively to the Boer business, and I am not sure that things in this direction are not looking a little brighter.

Your loving son
WINSTON S. CHURCHILL

WSC to Lady Randolph

26 March 1901   105 Mount Street

My dear Mamma,

Please *telegraph* me whether you would care to help me receive the guests at the Whitefriars Club annual banquet – at which I am to preside on the 3rd of May.

I think you will meet many interesting Bohemians and literary people.

Your loving son
WINSTON

Pamela [Lytton] is returned more lovely than ever.

*   *   *   *   *

On April 23 *The Times* reported that WSC, supported by Sir John Colomb,[3] had given notice of the following amendment to Brodrick's motion on army organization: 'That this House, while fully recognising the necessity

[1] Henry Charles Keith, 5th Marquess of Lansdowne (1845–1927), Foreign Secretary 1900–5; Governor-General of Canada 1883–8, India 1888–93; Secretary of State for War 1895–1900. A dispute had arisen between Britain and Russia over the ownership of a small strip of land at Tientsin. The dispute was referred to arbitration.

[2] Ellis Ashmead-Bartlett (1849–1902), Conservative MP for Ecclesall (Sheffield) 1885–1902; MP for Eye (Suffolk) 1880–5; Civil Lord of Admiralty 1885–92; served in Boer War; knighted 1892. Ashmead-Bartlett was an untiring advocate of British imperialism in great demand as a platform speaker.

[3] John Charles Ready Colomb (1838–1909), Conservative MP for Bow and Bromley 1886–92; Great Yarmouth 1895–1906; an influential writer on Imperial Defence; KCMG.

of providing adequately for Imperial defence nevertheless cannot view without grave apprehension the continued growth of purely military expenditure
which diverts the energies of the country from their natural commercial and
military development; and, having regard to the extraordinary pressure
under which all connected with the War Office are now working, desires
to postpone final decision on future military policy until calmer times.'

On April 27 *The Times* noted that the words 'and the plain need for
extensive reforms in the organisation of the army' had been inserted after
'Imperial defence'.

A week later the Opposition front bench prepared a different amendment
which according to Parliamentary etiquette took precedence over all other
amendments. WSC's speech was delivered during the debate on Campbell-
Bannerman's amendment.

WSC to Oliver Borthwick
(*Bathurst Papers*)

23 April 1901   105 Mount Street

My dear Oliver,

I send you herewith MS of my speech against the Army Scheme which
I hope to make in the House shortly.

It will be kind of you to give me a good report, and I should like three
or four proofs as soon as possible if you feel able to do this. I wish you could
support the view I hold. We are making a fearful mistake, which will only
fail to injure the nation because it will destroy the Conservative Party before
it can be carried out. Drop me a line to let me know your views.

Yours sincerely
WINSTON S. C.

Sir William Harcourt to WSC

24 April 1901   20 Queen Anne's Gate

Dear Winston Churchill,

I like much the flavour of your Amendment & will see what I can do.

Yrs trly
W. HARCOURT

WSC to the Editor, The Times[1]

30 April 1901   London

Sir,

The vice-president and the secretary of the Army League say that they will be interested to learn how I reconcile the amendment to Mr Brodrick's Army resolution which stands in my name with my speech at Plymouth on August 17, 1900, in which I most strongly urged the necessity of providing the forces with modern weapons.[2] I do it this way. If you have a soldier, it is evident that he must have a weapon. As he may have to fight for his life, it is desirable that this weapon should be the best that can be obtained. Now good weapons cost a great deal of money. Yet, if the expenditure is necessary, the nation though in straitened circumstances, must not grudge the money. But, if we have to provide this money for improved weapons, that is surely a reason for trying to economize in other directions; certainly it is not a reason for unnecessarily increasing the number of soldiers who are to be provided with these expensive weapons. No one who has pledged himself to Army reform need accept any scheme which may be suggested without discussing the details or counting the cost. Still less is he under an obligation to support schemes of Army increase.

A better Army does not necessarily mean a bigger Army. There ought to be ways of reforming a business, other than by merely putting more money into it. There are more ways of killing a cat, &c.

I wonder this has not occurred either to the vice-president or to the secretary of the Army League.

I am, Sir, yours faithfully
WINSTON S. CHURCHILL

WSC to the Editor, The Times[3]

2 May 1901   London

Sir,

I hesitate to occupy your space with personal matters, but I cannot admit the inconsistency in my attitude towards military policy which the vice-president and secretary of the Army League appear to consider it important to prove. Immediately after the relief of Ladysmith, when there was a good

[1] Published on May 1.
[2] In *The Times* on April 30.
[3] Published on May 3.

hope of the speedy termination of the war, I telegraphed to the *Morning Post* newspaper as follows –

'At the end of the war the nation must not be lured from the fertile fields of commerce into the stony wastes of militarism. The task before the War Office will be to fold up and pack away conveniently this splendid war machine so that it may rust as little as possible and be ready for use at short notice when next required, which, let us pray, will not be for many years. Then, having gloriously performed a necessary duty in South Africa, the Empire must turn with renewed energy to productive pursuits, and the people of England must devote themselves to stimulating and sustaining the spirit of the people by measures of social improvement and reform.'

What difference is there between this opinion and that I venture to express to-day? I confess I do not like to be judged upon such a narrow issue as a ten-line amendment; but, even so, where is the inconsistency? It is quite true that in the meanwhile – notably at Plymouth – I have urged the need of Army reform and of various kinds of reforms. But is that contradictory? Surely the desire for efficiency belongs to the same logical scheme of thought as the desire for economy. May not a man wish, and have always wished, to have a small, though perhaps elastic, Army in England, but to have the small Army very good? That, at any rate, is my position. I shall hope soon to have an opportunity of defining it and of trying to justify it. Meanwhile, if for holding these views I have deserved the epithets 'mis-chievous,' 'wrong-headed,' 'unintelligent,' which you, Sir, employ in your leading article of this morning, I am chiefly concerned to explain that I have deserved them consistently, and that no improvement can be expected in the future.

I am, Sir, yours faithfully
WINSTON S. CHURCHILL

The Argus

10 May 1901   Melbourne

THE FUTURE OF WINSTON CHURCHILL

Winston through Boer Spectacles

ENGLISHMAN, TWENTY-FIVE YEARS OLD, ABOUT 5ft 8 in HIGH; INDIFFERENT BUILD; WALKS A LITTLE WITH A BEND FORWARD; PALE APPEARANCE; RED BROWNISH HAIR; SMALL MOUSTACHE, HARDLY PERCEPTIBLE; TALKS THROUGH THE NOSE; CANNOT PRONOUNCE THE LETTER S PROPERLY; AND DOES NOT KNOW ONE WORD OF DUTCH.

Such is the official description of Mr Winston Churchill in the 'Hue-and-Cry' of the Boer authorities issued at the moment when he had managed to escape from the prison at Pretoria. It is not altogether correct; for, except to Boer eyes, the build of Mr Churchill is not indifferent; on the contrary, though slight, it is graceful and alert. In some respects, however, the description is strikingly correct, and shows both how quick is the observation of the Boer and how marked are the characteristics of the young man. Especially is the statement correct that Mr Churchill walks 'a little with a bend forward'. That, indeed, is the most characteristic thing in his whole make-up.

You see this bend forward not merely when he walks, but when he is seated; and as he is just behind the Treasury Bench, and seems to be listening eagerly – and with hot assent or ardent dissent – to everything that is going on, it gives him the appearance of a young panther ready at any moment to make a desperate spring. It is indicative of a nature full of impatience, ardour, and ambition; as I said when describing him first, it betrays the young man already in a hurry. At the same time, one must acknowledge the fine self-restraint which enables Mr Churchill to conquer his evidently fierce desire to be in the rage of battle, and to bide his time.

How far will he go?

There is no young member of the House of Commons at this moment whose future is the subject of more frequent debate and of wider interest. That he has a future nobody doubts; he is predestined to early official employment; and, after that, it all depends on himself how far he will go. He brings to political life many personal as well as hereditary advantages. Above all things, he is absorbed in his work. Never did a man enter the House of Commons more completely absorbed in his ambition, in his career, in himself. All that he has gone through hitherto has been but a preparation and an education for a political and Parliamentary career.

That eager bend forward of the head, that intense interest in all that is going on, are all proofs of this absolute and thorough absorption in the House of Commons. It is one of the curious proofs of the ascendancy he has already exercised – and personal ascendancy is one of the greatest forces in making a political career – that already he gets other men of the same age to accept his superior claims. As an example – There were other young members who wanted to speak in the Colvile debate – and who had some right to do so because of their personal experiences in the army. Mr Churchill asked one if he would oblige him by trying to catch the Speaker's eye before dinner, as he did not want to speak till late in the evening. The debate went on, and took unexpected turns, and then Mr Churchill asked his friend not to rise after dinner, as he might be cut out. In both cases the friend complied. Few are the men who would have the courage to make the request; fewer still would have the ascendancy to get the request granted.

Head – and Heart?

Has the young man heart as well as ambition? There you find different answers. Strangers think him too self-absorbed to care for any other human being. But intimates tell of many instances of real good feelings – as, for example, when he went and laid some flowers on the grave of an old nurse to whom he had been much attached, and who had been good to him in his childhood.

As to his appearances in the House up to the present, I rank them as distinctly better than those of his father. Lord Randolph Churchill was a distinctly poor speaker when he started in 1880 – which was the time he really began to speak – and it was not till he had trained himself by speaking every night for five years that he came to be really effective. And even then he never struck me as a great speaker – his speeches read better than they sounded. The one speech of his that I thought wonderfully effective was that on the Parnell Commission after the exposure of the Piggott forgery; and even that speech was marred by one coarse expression. It was force of character and a certain intuition, rather than great intellectual powers, that gave Lord Randolph Churchill his great place in Parliamentary history. Indeed, it is almost as hard to explain to anybody who did not know him the ascendancy of Lord Randolph as to explain that of Mr Parnell. In both cases it was the curious, indefinable, and indescribable thing which Americans call by the name of magnetism.

Lord Randolph's Ignorance

Young Winston Churchill, on the other hand, seems to me to speak always well – with a certain hesitation that reminds one of the father; with a certain lisp which is not altogether unpleasant; but with a facility and correctness of diction, and even with a fluency, which were not in the speeches of the father, in his earlier days, at all events. The son has this enormously great advantage, too, over the father – that his training for political life has been much better, much more thorough. Lord Randolph was incredibly ignorant when he began his Parliamentary life. I don't know whether the story is true or not; but it is said that he thanked Sir Henry Irving very much when he saw him play Hamlet; it was the first time he had ever known the plot of the play; he had never read it.

As to Mr Winston's knowledge of books I know nothing; but he has had the severe training of life and men, which, to my mind, is much better. And it is quite plain, from even a brief conversation with him, that he has the observation and intelligence to take full advantage of the tremendous opportunities he has had in this direction. I never got a more real conception of what the feelings of men in a battle are like than I got from just five minutes' talk with Mr Churchill. And nobody who read his letters from South Africa can deny him fine and very remarkable powers as a writer. I don't think his father, with all his gifts, could have written as well.

Defects and Qualities

The faults in Mr Churchill's character, that are suggested, will either pass with time or help him when he is in a position to command. It may or may not be true that on one occasion he requested that Lord Kitchener should be brought over to be introduced to him; and that at a time when the one was already a famous general and the other was still a subaltern. But, even if it were true, it shows that tremendous self-confidence and self assertion which must be in the blood of a son of Lord Randolph; and believe me that of all political talents self-confidence is the most valuable and the most triumphant.

Sir Felix Semon[1] to WSC

11 May 1901　　　　　　　　　　　　　　39 Wimpole Street
　　　　　　　　　　　　　　　　　　　　Cavendish Square
Dear Mr Churchill,

Many years ago you consulted me on account of the difficulty you experienced in pronouncing the 'S'. I told you that I thought the matter amenable to methodical teaching, but that I did not know of anybody in this country whom I could recommend to you. At last I have found a man, whom I can confidently recommend to you for this purpose. It is Mr Harry W. White, (late Vice-principal of the Training College for Teachers of the Deaf) of 13, Sinclair Gardens, Kensington, W. A few weeks ago, I saw a case absolutely analogous to your own, the patient being a little girl aged about 8. I sent her to Mr White, who just before had effected another very remarkable cure in the case of another patient of mine suffering from an uncommon form of stammering. To-day he brought the child back to me

---

[1] Felix Semon (1849–1921), throat specialist, physician extraordinary to King Edward VII; knighted 1897; KCVO 1905.

completely cured after a three weeks course, and able to pronounce the 'S' absolutely normally.

Having always taken a great interest in your remarkable career, I remembered you saying how keenly you felt the deficiency, and how seriously you were handicapped in your speaking in public by your constantly having to think of avoiding as much as possible words with 'S'. Hence this letter. I hope Mr White may be able to do you as much good as he has done for my other patients.

Believe me, Yours sincerely
FELIX SEMON

Hansard

13 May 1901

MR WINSTON CHURCHILL: I find myself differing on this occasion from the right hon Baronet the Member for the Forest of Dean, [Sir Charles Dilke] and although we are on different sides of the House, I regret that I do not differ from him in the right way at all. He is very anxious to increase the cost of the Army.

*SIR CHARLES DILKE: No.

MR WINSTON CHURCHILL: I have put the words down. I understand he is anxious to increase the cost of the Army in some respects, and he has delivered a speech which is of very great weight, coming as it does from one who is justly entitled to be considered a military expert. I think that the right hon Baronet is also a remarkable instance of a very peculiar phenomenon. I have always noticed that whenever a Radical takes to Imperialism he catches it in a very acute form. That, perhaps, explains the vigorous manner in which the right hon Baronet has defended further military expenditure at this juncture. I have no doubt the House has been powerfully impressed by the speech delivered on this side by my right hon friend the Chief Secretary for Ireland. I think we may congratulate ourselves on the return of the Chief Secretary to the theatre of war, in which he had previously earned such a distinguished reputation. We have heard from him a very illuminating and comprehensive speech on the Army question, and I for one have always regarded it as rather unfair that my right hon friend, who more than any other Minister was responsible for encouraging the nation to embark on this course of military expenditure, should escape into the secluded tranquillity of the Irish Office and leave to the Secretary for War the duty of facing the storm that this expenditure has excited and is arousing. But I cannot follow my right hon friend on this occasion as I have followed him in the past, and as I hope to follow him in the future. I wish to complain very respectfully, but most urgently, that the Army Estimates involved by the scheme lately explained by the Secretary of State for War are much too high and ought to be reduced, if not this year, certainly at the conclusion of the South African campaign. I regard it as a grave mistake in Imperial policy to spend thirty millions a year on the Army. I hold that the continued increase in Army expenditure cannot be viewed by supporters of the Government without the greatest alarm and apprehension, and by Members who represent working class constituencies without extreme dislike.

I desire to urge considerations of economy on His Majesty's Government, and as a practical step that the number of soldiers which they propose to keep ready for expeditionary purposes should be substantially reduced. First of all I exclude altogether from this discussion the cost of the South African War. Once you are so unfortunate as to be drawn into a war, no price is too great to pay for an early and victorious peace. All economy of soldiers or supplies is the worst extravagance in war. I am concerned only with the Estimates for the ordinary service of the year, which are increasing at such a rate that it is impossible to view them without alarm. Does the House realise what British expenditure on armaments amounts to? See how our Army Estimates have grown—seventeen millions in 1894, eighteen in 1897, nineteen in 1899, twenty-four in 1900, and finally in the present year no less than twenty-nine millions eight hundred thousand. Indeed we are moving rapidly, but in what direction? Sir, I see in this accelerating increase the momentum of a falling body and a downward course. I do not wish to reproach the Secretary of State for War for the enormous Estimates now presented. He is not to blame. The Secretary of State for War does not usually direct, or even powerfully influence, the policy of a Government. He is concerned with his own Department, and it is his business to get all he can for that Department. I must say the right hon Gentleman appears to have done his work remarkably well. Indeed, if the capacity of a War Minister may be measured in any way by the amount of money he can obtain from his colleagues for military purposes, the right hon Gentleman will most certainly go down to history as the greatest War Minister this country has ever had. I think this House ought to take a wider view of our Imperial responsibilities than is perhaps possible from the windows of the War Office.

If I might be allowed to revive a half-forgotten episode – it is half-forgotten because it has passed into that period of twilight which intervenes between the bright glare of newspaper controversy and the calm rays of the lamp of history – I would recall that once on a time a Conservative and Unionist Administration came into power supported by a large majority, nearly as powerful, and much more cohesive, than that which now supports His Majesty's Government, and when the time came round to consider the

Estimates the usual struggle took place between the great spending Departments and the Treasury. I say 'usual'; at least it used to be so, I do not know whether it is so now. The Government of the day threw their weight on the side of the great spending Departments, and the Chancellor of the Exchequer resigned. The controversy was bitter, the struggle uncertain, but in the end the Government triumphed, and the Chancellor of the Exchequer went down for ever, and with him, as it now seems, there fell also the cause of retrenchment and economy, so that the very memory thereof seems to have perished, and the words themselves have a curiously old-fashioned ring about them. I suppose that was a lesson which Chancellors of the Exchequer were not likely to forget in a hurry. I should like, if I might be permitted, to read the passage, which appears extremely relevant to the question now before the House. Writing from the Carlton Club on the 22nd of December, 1886, the Chancellor of the Exchequer, in resigning his office, wrote to Lord Salisbury, who had pointed out the desperate state of Europe and the possibilities of immediate war, very much in the same way as he has done recently. The Chancellor of the Exchequer replied as follows –

'The great question of public expenditure is not so technical or departmental as might be supposed by a superficial critic. Foreign policy and free expenditure upon armaments act and react upon one another.'

That has been said before in this debate, and it is what the Chief Secretary for Ireland called a hackneyed tag. I think, with as much reason, you might also call the Ten Commandments a hackneyed tag.

'A wise foreign policy will extricate England from Continental struggles and keep her outside of German, Russian, French, or Austrian disputes. I have for some time observed a tendency in the Government attitude to pursue a different line of action, which I have not been able to modify or check. This tendency is certain to be accentuated if large Estimates are presented to and voted by Parliament. The possession of a very sharp sword offers a temptation which becomes irresistible to demonstrate the efficiency of the weapon in a practical manner. I remember the vulnerable and scattered character of the Empire, the universality of our commerce, the peaceful tendencies of our democratic electorate, the hard times, the pressure of competition, and the high taxation now imposed: and with these facts vividly before me I decline to be a party to encouraging the military and militant circle of the War Office and Admiralty, to join in the high and desperate stakes which other nations seem to be forced to risk.'

Wise words, Sir, stand the test of time, and I am very glad the House has allowed me, after an interval of fifteen years, to lift again the tattered flag of retrenchment and economy. But what was the amount of the annual Estimates on which this desperate battle was fought? It may be difficult for the

House to realise it, though it is within the memory of so many hon Members. 'The Estimates for the year,' said the Chancellor of the Exchequer, in resigning, 'for the two services amounted to no less than £31,000,000, and I cannot consent to that.' What are the Estimates we are asked to vote now? We are now asked to vote, quite irrespective of the drain of a costly war still in progress, something more than fifty-nine millions for the ordinary service of the year.

This incident which I have been bringing to the mind of the House did not happen a century ago. It is quite recent history. The Leader of the House was already a famous Minister, the present Chancellor had already been Leader of the House, Lord Salisbury was already Prime Minister, when thirty-one millions was considered by the Treasury a demand which ought to be resisted tooth and nail. What has happened in the meanwhile to explain this astonishing increase? Has the wealth of the country doubled? Has the population of the Empire doubled? Have the armies of Europe doubled? Is the commercial competition of foreign nations so much reduced? Are we become the undisputed master in the markets of the world? Is there no poverty at home? Has the English Channel dried up, and are we no longer an island? Is the revenue so easily raised that we do not know how to spend it? Are the Treasury buildings pulled down, and all our financiers fled? What has happened to explain this extraordinary change? During the few weeks I have been a Member of this House I have heard hon Members advocate many causes, but no voice is raised in the cause of economy. The Financial Secretary to the War Office, who above all should keep some eye on the purse strings, speaking the other night at some dinner, boasted that he was not animated by any niggardly spirit of economy. Not one voice is raised for reduced expenditure and lightening the public burden, if I may except, in order to be quite correct, the protests raised and the cries for economy from the Irish benches – economy of money, not economy of time – and even through the Irish protests for economy, I am sorry to say, there ran the melancholy dirge, 'and how much is Ireland going to get out of it?' How can this tendency to extravagant expenditure be checked? The Opposition can do nothing. Of course, we shall outvote them. The House has no control whatever over Supply. The Treasury can do nothing against the great spending Departments, and in view of the fate that befell the last Chancellor of the Exchequer who was obdurate, can we wonder that the present distinguished occupant of that office has been compelled to bow before the storm? The Chancellor of the Exchequer gave an extraordinary reason for not objecting to, but supporting, this military expenditure. He said it had been demanded, that it was popular. Expenditure always is popular; the only unpopular part about it is the raising of the money to pay the expenditure. But if that is an extraordinary reason, it is nothing to that put forward by my right hon friend to-night, who asked pathetically, 'What are we to do with our generals?' When they come home from South Africa with no more worlds to conquer they must keep their hands in, and they must be provided with an army, even if it does cost thirty millions a year, to enable them to keep their hands in, and to save them from getting out of practice. I am, I know, a very young man, but I confess I never heard anything like that before. I had always been led to believe that the generals existed for the Army, and not the Army for the generals. The phrase 'happy-go-lucky self-indulgence,' which was used by my hon friend, seems to me to come in very appropriately somewhere about here. My right hon friend is content to arm me with a blunderbuss. Well, a blunderbuss is a traditional weapon with which the British householder defends himself from those who seek to plunder him. Though it is a very antiquated and obsolete weapon, yet at close quarters, at about the range at which my hon friend is sitting now, it has been found very effective. I stand here to plead the cause of economy. I think it is about time that a voice was heard from this side of the House pleading that unpopular cause; that someone not on the bench opposite, but a Conservative by tradition, whose fortunes are linked indissolubly to the Tory party, who knows something of the majesty and power of Britain beyond the seas, upon whom rests no taint of cosmopolitanism, should stand forward and say what he can to protest against the policy of daily increasing the public burden. If such a one is to stand forward in such a cause, then, I say it humbly, but with I hope becoming pride, no one has a better right than I have, for this is a cause I have inherited, and a cause for which the late Lord Randolph Churchill made the greatest sacrifice of any Minister of modern times. Now, bearing all that in mind, I come to the scheme of the Secretary of State. I do not propose to consider that scheme in detail, that would be an interminable labour. When the right hon Gentleman introduced the scheme – in a speech of surpassing clearness – it looked genuine, but in the weeks that have passed since he disclosed it to the House it has been sadly knocked about, crushed in the press, and exploded in the magazines, and has excited nothing but doubt in the country. The number of Amendments on the Paper shows the feeling of the House, and I know what some of the soldiers say about it. I do not feel equal to repeating their expressions here – but I shall be delighted to inform any hon Member desiring information privately. It is no good mincing matters. This is not the best scheme that could be devised. I do not say that it does not contain any wise and ingenious provisions, nor that it will not give strength to the Army. Material strength is expected even in this country to follow great expenditure of money. But if the truth must be told, although this scheme involves an expenditure of nearly £30,000,000 a year, with further increases in prospect, it nevertheless leaves most of the great questions connected with Army reform almost entirely untouched. But what could be expected? The ordinary duties of a Minister are, I have always understood, sufficiently arduous. The War office is a particularly hard job even in peace time. But we are at war. Not only has the Secretary of State to defend in this House every act of military policy big or little, but he has also to see – I hope it will not escape his attention – that an Army of more than two hundred thousand men actively engaged with enemy lacks nothing that wealth or science can produce. Now that ought to be enough for the energy even of the right hon Gentleman. Why, Sir, the labours of Hercules are nothing to it. But all this is not enough for the insatiable industry of the right hon Gentleman. He must, forsooth, rearrange the internal mechanism of the War Office. He must take his engines to pieces while the ship is beating up under full steam against the gale. That is not all. No; in the few moments of leisure that fall to a public man in this country he must thoroughly reorganise and reform the whole system of the Army. Who can wonder that he has increased the quantity of his output only to the detriment of the quality, as happens to literary men? I had put down an Amendment, which it will not be in order now to move, which to my mind possesses advantages over that we are now discussing. In the first place, it removed the question from the party sphere in which it now lies, and in which it must now be decided. In the second place, it provided the Government with a means of retreat from the very uncomfortable position in which they have managed to get themselves. I do not expect hon members on this side will agree with me, and I recognise that I am putting considerable strain upon their forbearance by the view I take of this matter, but I ask them for their indulgence while I state my view. My view is that we should have gone on with ordinary reforms which do not involve a large increase of expenditure, either of money or men, the better selection and promotion of officers, a question which the Secretary of State has shown himself willing to carry out with unflinching courage, the provision of better arms and the gradual adoption of new military material and weapons. What is called in *The Times* this morning the 'grandiose' – that is the word for which I have been looking – the grandiose portion of the scheme should be postponed until such time as the South African war has assumed its true proportions in our eyes, and the men now in South Africa best qualified to do so have come home to give their attention to the reorganisation of the Army, and until those managing the War Office are relieved from the high pressure at which they are now working. That is a tale that has not been unfolded, and this question is now before the House on party lines. I confess I am unable to support the resolution of the Government; but the Amendment of the Leader of the Opposition does not attract me any more. His differences are differences of detail, not of principle. My objections are objections of principle. I hold it is unwise to have no regard to the fact that in this reform we are diverting national resources from their proper channels of development. It may be argued that if other nations increase their armed force so must we. If you look into the tangled mass of figures on this subject you will find that while other nations during the last fifteen years have been increasing their navies we have been increasing our expenditure on our Army, which is not after all our most important weapon. I am pleading the cause of economy first of all. But I have got two strings to my bow, or perhaps I should say two barrels to my blunderbuss. Failing economy, let us have wise expenditure. My contention is that we are spending too much money on armaments, and so may impair our industries; but that if the money has to be spent, then it would be better to spend it on the Fleet than on the Army. Of course we must have an Army, not only as a training school for our garrisons abroad, but because it would be unhealthy, and even immoral, for the people of Great Britain to live sleek, timid, and secure, protected by a circle of ironclad ships. It would have been a pleasant task to examine some of the wise and ingenious provisions which the scheme of the Secretary of State for War contains. But I have assumed a more melancholy duty to-night, one, perhaps, which would be more fittingly discharged by some hon Member on the other side of the House. I contend that to spend thirty millions a year on the British Army is an unwise policy, against which the House must protest. Sir, at the late election I placarded 'Army Reform' as large as any-one. I am pledged to the hilt to Army reform. But what is Army reform? I take it to be one of two things. Either it means the same efficiency at a re-duced cost, or increased efficiency for the same cost. Perhaps it might mean greatly increased efficiency for a slightly increased cost. But the one thing it certainly does not mean is a larger number of Regular soldiers. That is not Army reform, but Army increase. In the last four years the present Ministers have added no fewer than fifty-seven thousand men to the Regular standing Army. A further increase – disguised in various ways – is contemplated in the present scheme. Sir, it is against this Army increase that I protest, first in the interests of economy, secondly in the interests of the Fleet. I complain of the increase in Regular soldiers, and particularly of the provision of the three army corps which are to be kept ready for expeditionary purposes. I con-tend that they ought to be reduced by two army corps, on the ground that one is quite enough to fight savages, and three are not enough even to begin to fight Europeans. I hope the House will let me elaborate this. The enor-mous and varied frontiers of the Empire, and our many points of contact with barbarous peoples, will surely in the future, as in the past, draw us into frequent little wars. Our military system must therefore be adapted for dealing with these minor emergencies smoothly and conveniently. But we must not expect to meet the great civilised Powers in this easy fashion. We must not regard war with a modern Power as a kind of game in which we may take a hand, and with good luck and good management may play adroitly for an evening and come safe home with our winnings. It is not that, and I rejoice that it cannot be that. A European war cannot be anything but a cruel, heartrending struggle, which, if we are ever to enjoy the bitter fruits of victory, must demand, perhaps for several years, the whole manhood of the nation, the entire suspension of peaceful industries, and the concentrating to one end of every vital energy in the community. I have frequently been astonished since I have been in this House to hear with what composure and how glibly Members, and even Ministers, talk of a European war. I will not expatiate on the horrors of war, but there has been a great change which the House should not omit to notice. In former days, when wars arose from individual causes, from the policy of a Minister or the passion of a King, when they were fought by small regular armies of professional soldiers, and when their course was retarded by the difficulties of communication and supply, and often suspended by the winter season, it was possible to limit the liabilities of the combatants. But now, when mighty populations are impelled on each other, each individual severally embittered and inflamed – when the resources of science and civilisation sweep away everything that might mitigate their fury, a European war can only end in the ruin of the vanquished and the scarcely less fatal commercial dislocation and exhaustion of the conquerors. Democracy is more vindictive than Cabinets. The wars of peoples will be more terrible than those of kings. 'Why, then,' it may be said, 'surely we must neglect nothing to make ourselves secure. Let us vote this thirty millions without more ado.' If this vast expenditure on the Army were going to make us absolutely secure – much though I hate unproductive expenditure – I would not complain. But it will do no such thing. The Secretary for War knows – none better than he – that it will not make us secure, and that if we went to war with any great Power his three army corps would scarcely serve as a vanguard. If we are hated, they will not make us loved. They are a broken reed to trust to. If we are in danger, they will not make us safe. They are enough to irritate; they are not enough to overawe. They cannot make us invulnerable, but they may very likely make us venturesome. A prudent man insures his house against fire. We are often told this military expenditure is an insurance premium. Well, there is no doubt about the premium; we are paying that all right. But I would respectfully remind the House that the premium has been put up during the last five years, and is in fact so high now that, so far as I can calculate, in order to make our insurance policy a good bargain we should have to have a war equal to the

Boer war every fifteen years. But do we get the insurance? In putting our trust in an army are we not investing in a shaky concern – in a firm that could not meet its obligations when called on? It may be said that it is not a mere question of pounds, shillings, and pence, but that it is a question of the honour and security of the Empire. I do not agree. The honour and security of the British Empire do not depend, and can never depend, on the British Army. The Admiralty is the only Office strong enough to insure the British Empire; and it can only be strong enough to do so because it has hitherto enjoyed the preferential monopoly of the sea. Moreover, the provision of these three army corps, ready to embark and attack anybody anywhere, is undoubtedly most provocative to the other Powers. No other nation makes, or has ever made, such a provision. And what of its effect on us? It is quite true that foreign nations possess gigantic armies and have lived at peace for thirty years. Foreign nations know what war is. There is scarcely a capital in Europe which has not been taken in the last one hundred years, and it is the lively realisation of the awful consequences of war which maintains the peace of Europe. We do not know what war is. We have had a glimpse of it in South Africa. Even in miniature it is hideous and appalling; but, for all our experience, war to us does not mean what it means to the Frenchman, or the German, or the Austrian. Are we not arming ourselves with their weapons without being under their restraints? What I fear is that these three costly and beautiful army corps which are to be kept ready – almost at a moment's notice – for foreign war will develop in the country, if they need developing, feelings of pride and power, which will not only be founded in actual military superiority, but only on the appearance of it. And in these days, when popular newspapers, appealing with authority to countless readers, are prepared almost every morning to urge us into war against one or other – and sometimes several – of the Great Powers of the earth, surely we ought not to make it seem so easy, and even attractive, to embark on such terrible enterprises, or to think that with the land forces at our disposal we may safely intermeddle in the European game? What is our weapon, then? The only weapon with which we can expect to cope with great nations is the Navy. This is what the Chief Secretary to the Lord Lieutenant calls 'trust to luck and the Navy' policy. I confess I do trust the Navy. This new distrust of the Navy, a kind of shrinking from our natural element, the blue water on which we have ruled so long, is the most painful symptom of the military hydrophobia with which we are afflicted. Without a supreme Navy, whatever military arrangements we may make, whether for foreign expeditions or home defence, must be utterly vain and futile. With such a Navy we may hold any antagonist at arm's length and feed ourselves in the mean time, until, if we find it necessary, we can turn every city in the country into

an arsenal, and the whole male population into an army. Sir, the superiority
of the Navy is vital to our national existence. That has been said before. No
one will deny that or thank me for repeating the obvious. Yet this tremendous
Army expenditure directly challenges the principle, and those who advocate
it are false to the principle they so loudly proclaim. For the main reason that
enables us to maintain the finest Navy in the world is that whereas every
European Power has to support a vast Army first of all, we in this fortunate,
happy island, relieved by our insular position of a double burden, may turn
our undivided efforts and attention to the Fleet. Why should we sacrifice a
game in which we are sure to win to play a game in which we are bound to
lose? For the same rule most certainly has a converse application, and just as
foreign Powers by reason of their pressing land responsibilities must be inferior to us at sea; so we, whatever our effort, whatever our expenditure, by
reason of our paramount sea responsibilities must be inferior to them on land.
And surely to adopt the double policy of equal effort both on Army and
Navy, spending thirty millions on each, is to combine the disadvantages and
dangers of all courses without the advantages or security of any, and to run
the risk of crashing to the ground between two stools, with a Navy uselessly
weak and an Army uselessly strong. We are told we have 'commitments' –
not a very cheerful expression – in three continents, and that it is in consequence of these 'commitments' that we must keep three army corps ready
for immediate expeditionary purposes. On what principle are there to be
three rather than two or eight? I had hoped that the formulation of some
definite principle governing our military needs would be a prominent feature
of any scheme of Army reform submitted to the nation. I suppose the principle
on which the army corps have been selected is, one continent one army corps.
Well, Sir, I should like to look into that. In the first place there is Asia. What
is our danger there? Of course, it is an Anglo-Russian war on the frontier of
India. But if anyone takes Lord Salisbury's advice – and sometimes he gives
very good advice – to use large scale maps of Central Asia, they will see that
any Russian enterprise against India would either have to be made with a
small force, in which case our Indian Army would be sufficient to resist it,
or else railways would have to be built, just as Lord Kitchener had to build
a railway to Khartoum, to feed the great invading forces in the barren lands
through which they must march, in which case we should have plenty of
time to levy and train as many British troops as we might think fit. Then we
have a 'commitment' in North America – a 'commitment' which is growing
more able to take care of itself every day – not a 'commitment' about which
we need feel much anxiety. Sir, we must not, however, shrink from the
responsibility. Of course, the danger which might assail us in this quarter of
the globe would only be a war with the great friendly commercial nation to

the southward. Evil would be the counsellors, dark would be the day when we embarked on that most foolish, futile, and fatal of all wars – a war with the United States. But if such a fit of madness should attack the Anglo-Saxon family, then I say both nations, having long enjoyed a glorious immunity from the curse of militarism, would be similarly placed, and no decisive events could be looked for until the war had been in progress for a year or two and enormous armies had been raised by both sides, and in this war, as in any other war of this kind, your three army corps would be merely the first few drops of the thunder shower. We shall be told 'the lesson of the South African War must not be forgotten.' 'We must profit by our experience in South Africa, and be prepared next time for all eventualities.' The present scheme of Army increase is justified mainly on the ground of our experience in South Africa. 'We must be ready next time,' says 'the man in the street.' Not for worlds would I speak disrespectfully of 'the man in the street'; but, Sir, in the first place, I cannot help hoping 'next time' may be a long way off. I trust the Government do not contemplate fighting these wars in South Africa septennially. I trust they will finish this one in such a style that future recurrence will be utterly impossible, and that an end will be made once and for all of dangers from within that continent. Dangers from without can never exist in that quarter so long as we preserve our naval supremacy. Once that is lost, such dangers would be dwarfed by greater catastrophes at home. But I will not look only to the future. I have no hesitation in asserting that even if this scheme had been carried into effect five years ago, and we had had our three expeditionary army corps ready for foreign service in October, 1899, even then the course of the South African War would not have been materially different. You would have had your three army corps ready, but would the posession of those three army corps have told the Intelligence officers and the general staff, and the Committee of National Defence that more than one army corps was needed? And even if they had advised that three army corps should be sent forthwith, that would not have been enough, for, as we know to our cost, not three army corps were needed, but six. See what inadequate security this scheme provides – if we are to embark on land enterprises against civilised peoples. The Boers were the smallest of all civilised nations. Yet this precious Army scheme, in spite of the thirty millions a year it is to cost, does not provide half the troops needed to conquer them; and if the scheme were carried into effect – as many people think it cannot be carried into effect – and the South African War, were to begin over again, you would again have to call on Volunteers, Yeomanry, and Militia to alter their original contract with the State and serve beyond the seas. Yes, against this, the smallest of all civilised nations, we should have to fall back in these emergencies on the power of unrestricted sea communication, the wealth of a commercial country, and the patriotic and warlike impulses of a people not wearied of the military yoke.

The armies of Europe are bigger than those of the Boers, and cheaper than our own. France, in this present year, for an expenditure of twenty-eight millions, can mobilise twenty army corps. Germany, for twenty-six millions, gets twenty-two army corps. Russia, for thirty-two millions, can set on foot, including twenty-three regular army corps, a total force estimated at over three millions of men. And what can Great Britain do? Taught by the experience of the South African War, rich in her commerce and the generosity of her people, guided by the unfailing instinct of the War Office, Great Britain would be defended, after this scheme has been carried into effect, by no fewer than three trained army corps and three partly trained army corps; and for this she must pay two millions a year more than France, four millions a year more than Germany, and within two millions of the total cost of the whole great Russian army. But in spite of every explanatory circumstance, after every allowance has been made, one great truth glows and glares in our faces, veil it how we may: standing armies, which abound on the European continent, are not indigenous to the British soil; they do not flourish in our climate, they are not suited to our national character, and though with artificial care and at a huge and disproportionate cost we may cultivate and preserve them, they will after all only be poor, stunted, sickly plants of foreign origin. The Empire which has grown up around these islands is essentially commercial and marine. The whole course of our history, the geography of the country, all the evidences of the present situation, proclaim beyond a doubt that our power and prosperity alike and together depend on the economic command of markets and the naval command of the sea; and from the highest sentimental reasons, not less than from the most ordinary practical considerations, we must avoid a servile imitation of the clanking military empires of the European continent, by which we cannot obtain the military predominance and security which is desired, but only impair and vitiate the natural sources of our strength and vigour. There is a higher reason still. There is a moral force – the Divine foundation of earthly power – which, as the human race advances, will more and more strengthen and protect those who enjoy it; which would have protected the Boers better than all their cannon and brave commandos if instead of being ignorant, aggressive, and corrupt, they had enjoyed that high moral reputation which protected us in the dark days of the war from European interference – for, in spite of every calumny and lie uttered or printed, the truth comes to the top, and it is known alike by peoples and by rulers that on the whole British influence is healthy and kindly, and makes for the general happiness and welfare of mankind. And we shall make a fatal bargain if we allow the moral force which this country has so long exerted to become diminished, or perhaps even destroyed for the sake of the costly, trumpery, dangerous military playthings on which the Secretary of State for War has set his heart.

The Balfourian Parliament 1900–1905
by Henry W. Lucy: Hodder and Stoughton, 1906

EXTRACT

14 May 1901

WINSTON CHURCHILL'S MAIDEN SPEECH

In debate on St John Brodrick's scheme of Army Organization, Winston Churchill, lately returned for Oldham, made his maiden speech. In modest fashion wherein a note of heredity is struck, the new member had proposed to himself to open and lead off the debate with an amendment condemning the scheme. The leader of the Opposition interposing, he necessarily gave way. Having prepared his speech, he delivered it, and has the satisfaction of reflecting that it totally eclipsed Sir Henry Campbell-Bannerman's effort.

It was, indeed, excellent alike in matter and in form, and has established the position of the young member for Oldham as a debater who will have to be reckoned with whatever Government is in office. Probably a Ministry composed of his own political friends have most to apprehend. No case is known in modern history or, indeed, in earlier Parliamentary records, where a striking personality is revived in the person of his offspring. We have to go back to the time of Pitt to find an instance where a great political personage was eclipsed by his son. Winston Churchill is not likely to eclipse the fame of Randolph, who was a statesman as well as a consummate debater. Certainly, as far as he has gone, he recalls with singular fidelity the manner and method of his distinguished father.

One priceless equipment for a Parliamentary career possessed by him is a phenomenal memory. In delivering his speech tonight he was evidently fully supplied with notes, but he did not use his manuscript for the purpose of reading a single sentence. I happened to sit next to him at dinner after his triumph in the House, and mentioned an incident observed in delivery of a speech of nearly an hour's duration. Quoting from the letter his father wrote to Lord Salisbury on the eve of Christmas, 1886, resigning the Chancellorship of the Exchequer, I noticed that when only half-way through the reading he closed the book and recited the closing passages. 'Yes,' he said 'I felt it would be easier to recite the letter than to read it from a book held in my hand, so I learned it off.'

He added that his speech, which, fully reported, filled three columns of close print, had all been written out. He then learnt it off by heart, and delivered it as if it were an extemporaneous effort, a delusion artfully assisted by occasional interpolation of sparkling sentences referring to points made by speakers preceding him through the evening. 'If,' he said 'I read a column of print four times over I commit it so perfectly to memory that I could forthwith recite it without an omission or error.'

Sir William Harcourt to WSC

14 May 1901   20 Queen Anne's Gate

My dear Winston,

I cannot resist the pleasure of joining my congratulations to the host which you must have received on the brilliant success of your speech which has established your future in the H of C on a foundation which cannot be shaken.

It is a subject of great regret to me that I was unable to be present to applaud sentiments in which I so greatly concur adorned with all the force of eloquence and reason.

                                                            Yrs sinly
                                                      W. V. Harcourt

W. T. Stead[1] to WSC

14 May 1901   *Review of Reviews*
                                                         Norfolk Street
Dear Sir,

Just a line to thank you with all my heart for your speech last night.

It confirms the hopes raised by your admirable letters from South Africa.

                                               I am, yours faithfully
                                                    William T. Stead

John Burns[2] to Lady Randolph

14 May 1901   House of Commons

Dear Madam,

Years before your son secured the position he now occupies I expressed to you a kindly hope for his future.

[1] William Thomas Stead (1849–1912), editor of *Pall Mall Gazette* 1883–9; imprisoned after sensational exposure of vice in London under heading *The Maiden Tribute of Modern Babylon*. Started *Review of Reviews* 1890; strongly opposed Boer War. Drowned on *Titanic*.

[2] John Burns (1858–1943), MP Battersea 1898–1918; President of Local Government Board 1905–14; President of Board of Trade 1914; resigned on outbreak of war.

His excellent speech of last night is by far his best effort and I write you to congratulate him, through you, on his success and to share with his mother the hope that he will go further in the career he has chosen and on the excellent lines of his courageous speech of last evening.

Yours sincerely
JOHN BURNS

Lord James of Hereford to WSC

15 May 1901   · 41 Cadogan Square

My dear Winston Churchill,

Although I cannot agree with the views expressed in your speech I must sincerely congratulate you upon its merits. It has given you a great Parliamentary position – and with the restraining influences of moderation and discretion I feel sure that you have a very broad path leading to great success before you.

When I last saw you touching Oldham magistrates I gave you two or three names of prominent citizens of Oldham occupying a non-political position. Mr Dimcust was one of them.

You promised to make enquiries about them. Can you give me any information?

Yours
JAMES OF HEREFORD

Daily Mail

17 June 1901

Two immense and amazing propositions have lately been put forward by those in high places and have, although they have remained unproved by their authors, passed almost unchallenged in Parliament and the country.

'It is by accident,' said the Secretary of State for War, in introducing his Army scheme, 'that we are a military nation; we must endeavour to make that accident permanent.'

Why? The course of our history, the geography of these islands, the character of their people, show that the Empire which it is our duty to maintain is essentially commercial and marine. No empire in human records has owed less to military strength. The greatest battles we have ever won were in point of numbers fought mainly by foreigners. The finest commanders we have produced led aliens to victory in greater measure than their own countrymen. India was conquered by a Company who employed five sepoys to one white soldier. Australia never heard the trump of war. The Cape was picked up by a navy and for a navy. Only in America were considerable military forces employed; and of what avail were they when a foreign combination had established even naval equilibrium? No people have gained more by freedom from the danger and burden of standing armies than the British.

In the opening chapters of his most famous work, Macaulay describes with beautiful precision the process by which the professional soldier was gradually evolved and specialised by the increasing complications of the art of war from the armed populations of early times; how the trained armies which replaced the ancient national levies were used by European kings at first to curb and finally to crush the Parliamentary institutions; how because we were an island the change was retarded; how this delay enabled Parliament to come through the critical period so that when the Stuarts reached out for a standing army, the constitutional forces were strong enough – just strong enough, after prolonged and horrid struggles – to control the new and dangerous engine which the advance of civilisation had produced and now required.

Many and varied are the events of English history; but there is one story running through it all. Free institutions developing manhood and commerce; commerce impatient of island limits going down to the sea in ships and breeding fleets; sea-power preserving us from Continental tumult, stimulating manufacture anew, and enabling vast but distant possessions to be conquered and kept by comparatively little armies.

'It is by accident that we are now a military nation.' An accident? We need not quarrel with the word.

The second proposition coloured the whole of the Government defence of the new Army proposals. It is wrong and unpatriotic to refuse, or even grudge, what military and naval experts consider necessary for the security of the State.

Well, let us look into that.

More people live in this island than it can feed. We have to persuade the foreigner to exchange us the food and the raw materials which he grows, for the manufactured goods which are the produce of our skill and industry. We have to make it worth his while to do this. Successful competition in trade is vital to our national and imperial existence. If we are seriously beaten in the markets of the world, the commercial strength of Britain, the very heart pulsation of the Empire, will be paralysed. We have survived defeat before. We have even risen stronger from the loss of our greatest possession. But the collapse of trade would be fatal.

It is true that this delicious island, which none can appreciate who has not travelled far, endowed by Nature with every gift of soil and climate to make it the home of a free and happy race, will always support a considerable population. But its power, and perhaps its wealth, would be gone. The majestic fabric of Empire, built up by the blood and exertion of a thousand years, would lie in ruins, and by our fault; not because we grudged our efforts to preserve it, but because we misdirected them.

Trade is vital. All taxation is a drag on trade. Long before the comfort of the people would be touched their competing power would be diminished. Therefore, the amount of money we can safely raise annually by taxation is limited. It may be a vast sum, we may not yet have reached the end, but there are limits to it. We are not drawing upon an unlimited account. We cannot gratify every desire, or indulge every appetite. The question which Parliament has to decide every year is not how to find the money to provide what the military and naval experts consider necessary, but rather how to distribute a limited income to the best possible advantage between the different public departments.

Now, if this be true, it is quite evident that it may be just as public-spirited to husband as to expend the national resources, and certainly upon the question how much should be given to each particular department there is obviously room for the widest divergence of views among people who nevertheless wish to see Great Britain powerful and respected.

We have to consider what proportion of the revenue the relative importance of the various services demands. But is there any attempt to make such an allocation? Take a single instance. No one will deny that the Navy is immensely more important to us than the Army. Yet we are spending the same share of our wealth on each, and next year the Army will actually take the larger share. Therefore, the Army is getting an undue proportion. Therefore—and this is the conclusion—we must view military expenditure with a jealous and critical eye.

Now, quite independent of these considerations, and to a certain point, as I hold, without prejudice to them, runs another line of argument. There is an irreducible minimum of military strength. There are certain military requirements which are indisputably indispensable to the security of the State, and which must be obtained even at a bad bargain. Coal may be monstrous dear, but the dinner must be cooked. Between these two arguments there is a clash, and in the compromise from their contention the truth should be found. What is the irreducible minimum of our military strength?

We are spending more than we ought upon the Army, a greater proportion
of our income than we can really afford; what is the very least we can do,
having regard to our own safety?

I will try to answer the question very briefly.

We require, first of all, by far the finest Navy in the world. In order that
the Navy can move freely about the seas we must have frequent coaling
stations. If there are coaling stations, they must have fortifications and guns.
If they have any, obviously they must have the best that money can buy.
Then comes the Army.

We want a regular Army, first, to supply our great garrisons and coaling
stations abroad; secondly, as a training school at home; thirdly, for little
native wars; fourthly, as the backbone of the civil power; and last, to hold
the land defences of certain harbours in England. We want it for nothing
else.

We do *not* want a regular Army for the defence of this island, or for foreign
war with European Powers, and we ought not to raise troops for either
purpose. In the former case they would not be needed. In the latter they
would not be enough. For native wars we must have a compact, highly
trained, central force, with regular and voluntary reserves. For the defence
of Britain we must depend upon Yeomanry, Militia, and Volunteers, made
more efficient by money saved by the reduction of the home regular establishment, and upon the highly-trained nucleus mentioned above. For European
wars, whether of defence or offence, we must trust first to the strength of the
Navy, but in the end to the wealth and patriotism of the Nation. It is the
only way.

All the legitimate military requirements could be met by a much smaller
number of regular soldiers than it is now proposed to keep at home, and
consequently at a reduced cost. If the 'linked battalion' system prevents this,
the 'linked battalion' system will have to go to the wall – it will be no great
loss – and a new system devised. It would be easy, as it would be futile, for
private persons to suggest alternatives; but that is the proper business of the
War Office, and until they have solved the riddle Army Reform will only be
a meaningless expression, and the true principles of Imperial Defence will
remain undiscovered and unknown.

WINSTON S. CHURCHILL

WSC to the Editor of The Times[1]

25 June 1901   London

Sir,

In his rejoinder to Lord Hugh Cecil, Lord Crewe[2] deals chiefly with two questions. First, if the war in South Africa is being prosecuted by 'methods of barbarism,' as Sir Henry Campbell-Bannerman contends, are the generals responsible or only the Government? Now, a military commander has nothing to say to the policy which leads to a war, nor to the conditions which it may be thought desirable to exact before peace is restored. But for the methods by which that war is waged he is certainly responsible equally with the Government at home. If the methods are of the general's own choosing, the balance of responsibility, if any exist, rests with him. No one can relieve him of it; for no authority can justify an inhuman act. And the contention that the soldier is absolved of any portion of his responsibility for the methods by which warfare is conducted would be extremely mischievous were it not altogether absurd. The ethics of slaughter are naturally obscure; but one clear principle cannot be overlooked; and the civilized combatant is obliged, at peril of being classed a savage, to avoid unnecessary cruelty to his enemy. Unless there has been unnecessary cruelty, whatever the suffering, there can be no barbarity. If there has been unnecessary cruelty, all who are in any way responsible for it are infected with the taint of inhumanity. When, therefore, Sir Henry Campbell-Bannerman speaks of 'methods of barbarism', his charge applies to generals abroad not less than to Ministers at home. When he declines to press his charge against the generals, it is evident that either his logic or his courage is at fault; and when Lord Crewe, hastening to succour his leader, informs us that 'public opinion will not burden Lord Kitchener, but will lay heavy responsibility upon the Government,' he merely affords a rare and pleasing example of party loyalty in the Liberal ranks.

The second question wich Lord Crewe raises, but which he does not answer, is of much more importance. Is the policy of concentrating the civil inhabitants barbarous? As Lord Hugh Cecil pointed out, the privations of the women and children in the refuge camps are nothing in comparison to those endured by the civil inhabitants of a fortified town during a siege. Nevertheless, as the death-rate shows, they have undoubtedly been severe.

---

[1] Published on 28 June 1901.

[2] Robert Offley Ashburton Crewe-Milnes, 1st Earl of Crewe (1858–1945), Secretary of State for the Colonies 1908–10; Lord President of the Council 1905–8, 1915–16; Lord Privy Seal 1908–11, 1912–15; Secretary of State for India 1910–15; President of the Board of Education 1916; Ambassador to France 1922–8. Married, first, Jane Hermione St Maur, daughter of 12th Duke of Somerset; and, secondly, Margaret Primrose, daughter of 5th Earl of Rosebery. PC 1892; knighted 1908; Marquess 1911. With his death his titles became extinct.

'The essential fact,' says Lord Crewe, 'is not in a distinction between fortifications and no fortifications, but between the results involved by active
resistance on the one hand, and passive submission on the other.' As a matter
of fact, the resistance of a hardy population scattered over a vast region and
continually supplying the enemy's army with food and information is plainly
more formidable than the resistance – if it can be called resistance – of the
unhappy inhabitants of an invested town. In the former case the non-com-
batants undoubtedly prolong the operations; in the other, by eating up the
food of the garrison, they terminate them. It is difficult to understand why
Lord Crewe calls the former condition 'passive submission' and the latter
'active resistance.' His expressions would be better chosen if their application
were reversed. But, putting all this aside, I would venture to observe that
'the essential fact' lies neither in the question of fortifications nor in that
of resistance, but in the actual suffering inflicted on helpless human beings.
If women and children are dying of disease and want, whether they have
offered technical resistance or not is a minor consideration The supreme
question is – Was there any alternative action by which this suffering might
have been diminished without impeding the military operations? Lord
Crewe is silent. He does not tell us – others, less careful of their words than
he, do not tell us – whether they would have faced the alternative to the
concentration camps. Would they have refused to accept any responsibility
for the Boer women and children left in the devastated districts? Would
they have said that their case was primarily a matter for the Boer generals to
consider? Would they, having trampled the crops – the enemy's commissariat
– or destroyed the houses – often his magazines – have left the women sitting
hungry amid the ruins? The mind revolts from such ideas; and so we come
to concentration camps, honestly believing that upon the whole they involve
the *minimum* of suffering to the unfortunate people for whom we have made
ourselves responsible.

I am, Sir, Yours faithfully
WINSTON S. CHURCHILL

Lady Curzon to Lord Curzon
(*Ronaldshay: Life of Lord Curzon*)

EXTRACT

21 July 1901

. . . Some of those foolish hooligans[1] (who exist to entertain lions at dinner)
invited Sir W. Harcourt to dinner last Thursday, and as Winston did not

[1] The Hooligans, or Hughligans, consisted of five of the younger and more independent
Conservatives in the Commons: WSC, Lord Hugh Cecil, Lord Percy, Arthur Stanley and

know he had been asked, *he* invited Lord Rosebery![1] Both accepted, and for the first time the Hooligan Party was confronted with a crisis ... They didn't know what to do. Lord Rosebery was put off and asked to come another night, unless he desired the pleasure of meeting Sir William. Awkward, to say the least! *Later*. Have just heard that night of dinner arrived. Lord Rosebery had been put off and Harcourt forgot to come! ...

WSC to Lord Rosebery
(*Rosebery Papers*)

24 July 1901   105 Mount Street

My dear Lord Rosebery,

I hope I may be allowed to offer my congratulations on your speech at the City Liberal Club. A good many people misunderstood your letter, and the idea that you intended to retire from public life altogether was naturally unpopular; but your speech set all that straight.[2]

We were vy disappointed that you could not dine with the 'Hooligans', but I trust you will consider yourself pledged to come next session on some Thursday.

I am afraid I disturbed your horses with my motor-car yesterday. I am learning to drive at present, so this is rather a dangerous period.

Yours vy truly
WINSTON S. CHURCHILL

Lord Rosebery to WSC

24 July 1901   38 Berkeley Square

My dear Winston,

Many thanks for your kind note.

I have an idea. If I cannot go to the Hooligans why should they not come to me on Saturday Aug 3 to spend Sunday?

Vy sincrly
AR

Ian Malcolm. They entertained distinguished politicians and for a time concerted action in the House of Commons, recalling Lord Randolph's Fourth Party.

Henry Algernon George, Earl Percy (1871–1909), eldest son of 7th Duke of Northumberland, was MP for South Kensington 1895–1909; Under Secretary of State for India 1902–3; Under Secretary of State for Foreign Affairs 1903–5. Died unmarried.

Arthur Stanley (1869–1947), 3rd son of 16th Earl of Derby, was MP for Ormskirk 1898–1918.

[1] Harcourt strongly opposed Rosebery's Liberal Imperialist outlook.

[2] In a letter to *The Times* on July 17, Rosebery had stated that he would not return to party politics. Two days later he announced that 'for the present ... I must plough my furrow alone'.

WSC to Lord Rosebery
(*Rosebery Papers*)

2 August 1901　　　　　　　　　　　　　　　105 Mount Street

My dear Lord Rosebery,

I will come down on my motor car in time for dinner tonight. The others feel they ought not to miss the Colonial Office vote; and they will telegraph to you the train they will come by tomorrow.

It is vy good of you to have us down and we are all looking forward to our visit exceedingly.

Yours vy sincerely
WINSTON S. CHURCHILL

The Hooligans to Lord Rosebery
(*Rosebery Papers*)

6 August [1901]

Dear Lord Rosebery,

We who do not agree always, are united in thinking that the Sunday we spent in your company was among the pleasantest we can remember; and we wish most sincerely to thank you for your kindness and hospitality.

Yours vy truly
HUGH CECIL: WINSTON S. CHURCHILL: PERCY: IAN MALCOLM:
ARTHUR STANLEY

PS This has taken us a great deal of trouble to make up.

My colleagues behave very badly I am sorry to say. H.C. [phrase scratched out] (stopped by the censor)

Lord Rosebery to WSC

6 August 1901　　　　　　　　　　　　　　　　　Mentmore

My dear Winston,

I cannot tell you how much I enjoyed the Hooligans' visit. It rejuvenated me. If they or any of them wish for moral repose while Parliament sits they will find it here.

Yours
AR

Lord Rosebery to WSC

9 August 1901   Mentmore

My dear Winston,
    The Hooligans will be very welcome on Wednesday. The Hoplites[1] I used to read in ancient history were accompanied by shoals of light infantry. If you wish to bring any light infantry let me know. There is lots of room.

Yours
AR

Sir Edward Grey[2] to WSC

16 August 1901   House of Commons

Dear Churchill,
    Will you dine at Brooks's with me at 8 tonight? I have been trying to get all that is left of the hooligans, but have only so far succeeded in getting one. Asquith is coming and we could join you both.

Yours sincerely
E. GREY

*   *   *   *   *

WSC to Lord Rosebery
(Rosebery Papers)

4 September 1901   Wynyard Park[3]
                                          Stockton on Tees

My dear Lord Rosebery,
    I carried away quite a queer sensation from the Napoleon picture yesterday. It seems pervaded with his personality; and I felt as if I had looked furtively into the vy room where he was working, and only just got out of the way in time to avoid being seen. I have never looked at such an impressive picture.
    There were two books of which you spoke, the names of which I do not properly remember; a book about the first 30 years after the Waterloo peace & a book about Ireland. If you find a spare moment, will you send me their exact titles; for I want to read them.
    The chief object of this note is to thank you for your kindness. It is a vy great pleasure to me to talk freely to you, and a privilege which I thoroughly

---

[1] Ancient Greek heavy infantry.
[2] Sir Edward GREY.
[3] Lord Londonderry's seat in Co Durham.

appreciate. Sir Michael [Hicks Beach] is here, apparently in good health and spirits. He has promised me to make a strong speech on economy at Oldham, on the 10th October. The rest of the party is Lady Gerard,[1] Sir F. Mowatt,[2] General Oliphant,[3] and relations of various kinds. It is warm and pleasant.

Yours vy sincerely
WINSTON S. CHURCHILL

Lord Rosebery to WSC

5 September 1901   Dalmeny Park
Edinburgh

My dear Winston,

    Martineau's *History of the Thirty Years Peace*, and Molesworth's *History of the Reform Bill* were the books I mentioned to you. Irving's *Annals of our Time* (a sort of journal) is very useful, and *I* think, interesting to read. I am very glad you enjoyed yourself with us. It is a great pleasure to me, both for your father's sake and your own, to see you whenever you like. Give my kind regards to your host and hostess.

Sincly
AR

I am pleased that you appreciated the *Napoleon* by David. I find it sometimes coming out of the canvas.

WSC to the Editor, The Times[4]

6 September 1901   Wynyard

Sir,

    As one of your many readers who have followed with attention the correspondence which has appeared in your columns upon this subject, I desire to offer some comment upon the two letters which have been signed 'J.C.B.'

---

[1] Mary Emmeline Laura (1854–1918), wife of 2nd Baron Gerard, whose only daughter Ethel in 1904 married Arnold, Count de Bendern (formerly Baron de Forest).

[2] Francis Mowatt (1837–1919), Permanent Secretary to the Treasury 1894–1903. Knighted 1893.

[3] Laurence James Oliphant (1846–1914), commanded Infantry Brigade Aldershot 1900–1; served South Africa 1901–2; commanded Home District 1903–6; C.-in-C. Northern Command 1907–11; General 1898; knighted 1907; married Monica, daughter of 1st Baron Gerard.

[4] Published on September 9.

The first letter was an attack upon the conditions under which Scottish homespuns are produced, and was avowedly designed to prejudice the public against them. The second letter was a rejoinder to the Duchess of Sutherland, who had contended that nothing in the manufacture of these homespuns justified their being singled out for criticism on the score of unhealthiness; and it was also a renewed attack upon the industry. Now we do not know what the initials 'J.C.B.' represent, nor who is the person who employs them as his *nom de plume*. Usually when a gentleman becomes engaged in a controversy with a lady he puts some chivalrous or at any rate polite restraint upon his tone. And I submit that when he all the time remains himself anonymous, the restraint, which under ordinary circumstances is merely a matter of taste, grows into something like an honourable obligation. But with that I pass from his sneers about 'versatile duchesses' and his insinuations against 'the owners of great estates who leave their crofters in a pitiable plight' to the important aspects of his letters.

The person who signs himself 'J.C.B.' has attacked, with intent to injure, an industry by which a large number of very poor people add to their slender resources; and he has attacked it anonymously. He says that 'the conditions under which Harris tweeds are manufactured are abominable'; and that 'health-respecting and scrupulously cleanly persons will hesitate to wear such garments.' He compares the weavers to 'the farmer who sends adulterated milk to market.' He infers, if he does not positively affirm, that the homespuns are produced in places where consumption, zymotic disease, and bovine tuberculosis are rife; and he asserts, with a mass of scientific phraseology which is doubtless intended to impress simple people, who do not know how easily such patter can be acquired, that the tweeds are probably 'a soil,' I quote *verbatim*, 'suitable for the retention of those tubercle bacilli or their spores – if they have spores – which can withstand desiccation, and which are not true parasites, but can live and thrive, independently of a living host, for as long as two years, retaining their virulence and capability of reproducing tuberculosis upon inoculation.' And in support of his theory he adduces two authorities as anonymous as himself.

Now, Sir, these are very serious statements; and I think we are entitled to inquire on what grounds they are made, with what motives they are made, and by whom they are made. Of course it may be possible that your correspondent is only one of those pseudo-scientific persons who have a mania for discovering bacilli in everything; and who, when they are neither anonymous nor insignificant, from time to time, and particularly in the holiday time, endeavour to alarm the British public through the columns of the newspapers. Or upon the other hand – and the importance which you appear to attach to his communications seems to favour the supposition – he may be some very high pathological authority who feels himsef compelled by the over-whelming evidence of grievous diseases repeatedly contracted through the wearing of these garments, to utter a solemn warning. If so we should be told what that evidence has been and who the authority is. Or, again – and this is a perfectly legitimate assumption – his letter may be the expression of the natural though hardly very respectable jealousy which so often exists be-tween wholesale manufacturers and independent producers.

But until we do know something definite about this correspondent and the facts which have impelled him, I venture to think the public would be well-advised to receive his injurious suspicions with reserve, and his anonymous impertinences with disapprobation.

I am, Sir, yours faithfully
WINSTON S. CHURCHILL

WSC to the Editor, The Times[1]

14 September 1901   Guisachan

Sir,

In his letter, contained in your issue of the 13th inst, 'J.C.B.' says some very rude things about me at very great length. These may be true or untrue, merited or undeserved; but they are in no way connected with the controversy, nor do they offer any reply to the complaints I urge against him.

My contentions were and are, that when a person makes attacks in news-papers which are calculated to injure an industry, and particular a poor man's industry, he should sign them with his own name, so that the public may be assured that his authority is competent and that his hands are clean; and secondly, when he neglects, and, even though challenged, declines to do this, his statements should be received with all caution and reserve.

For my own part, I have not the slightest intention of being drawn further into a wrangle with a correspondent of whose identity I know nothing, and of whose personality few persons, judging from his controversial methods, would be encouraged to learn more.

I am, Sir, yours faithfully
WINSTON S. CHURCHILL

[1] Published on September 17.

WSC to Lord Rosebery
(*Rosebery Papers*)

20 September 1901   Invercauld

My dear Lord Rosebery,
I am to lecture in Doncaster on the 1st Octr and if you would care to let me come to Dalmeny on the evening of the 28th Septr and stay with you till I go south on the morning of the 1st, I should like vy much indeed to do so.

I have seen a lot of the Liberal Imperialists lately, Haldane and Edward Grey were at Guisachan, where I passed a pleasant week; and Asquith vy kindly took the chair for me at St Andrews. I learn from them and from the newspapers that they mean to make a regular campaign this autumn, Asquith going among other places to Oldham. If I were of their forces, my inclination would be all for vigorous action; my instinct rather towards delay. However their exertions, like Kitchener's proclamation,[1] if they do no good, at any rate do no harm and cost vy little.

I wonder whether you will have followed the 'Peat Reek' controversy. J.C.B., I learn privately, is Sir James Crichton-Browne.[2] What an exhibition he has made of himself!

I suggest the following telegram to Harmsworth for the Lanarkshire election. 'Every vote given to Smillie is a vote gained to the Government.'[3]

I read your 'flower' speech with much amusement.

Yours vy sincerely
WINSTON S. CHURCHILL

[1] Horatio Herbert Kitchener (1850–1916), C-in-C in South Africa 1900–2; Sirdar of the Egyptian Army 1892–9; Chief of Staff to Lord Roberts in South Africa 1899–1900; C-in-C in India 1902–9; British Agent and Consul-General in Egypt 1911–14; Secretary of State for War 1914. Baron 1898; Viscount and OM 1902; Earl 1914; KG 1915.
Kitchener's proclamation of 7 August 1901 sought to intimidate the Boers into submission. Described by L. S. Amery as 'replete with unconscious humour', it failed to induce the Boers to surrender by the stipulated date, 15 September 1901.
[2] James Crichton-Browne (1840–1938), Lord Chancellor's visitor in Lunacy 1875–1922. Fellow, Royal Society of Medicine; published several volumes of reminiscences as a physician; knighted 1886.
[3] The candidates in the North-East Lanarkshire by-election on September 26 in a three-cornered fight were Robert Smillie, Labour, Cecil Harmsworth, Liberal, and Sir William Rattigan, Liberal Unionist. The result was: Rattigan 5,673; Harmsworth 4,769; Smillie 2,900. William Henry Rattigan (1842–1904), a former advocate at the High Court, N. W. Provinces, spent his life in India and was the author of a number of legal works. Cecil Bishopp Harmsworth (1869–1948), was a brother of Alfred, 1st Viscount Northcliffe and Harold, 1st Viscount Rothermere, and became Chairman of Associated Newspapers and a director of the Amalgamated Press. He was Liberal MP for Droitwich 1906–10, and for Luton 1911–22, and became an under-secretary of State for Foreign Affairs 1919–22. Created Baron 1939. Robert Smillie (1857–1940) was President of the Scottish Miners Federation 1894–1918, and 1921–40 and Labour MP for Morpeth 1923–29.

On October 4, WSC spoke at Saddleworth, Yorkshire. An unidentified press cutting contains the following report.

Speech at Saddleworth, Yorkshire

MR WINSTON CHURCHILL, who was very cordially received, said: I will not follow the Duke of Marlborough into the matters he has discussed in his very interesting speech. It has been most pleasant to listen to, and that is a good thing, because what I am going to say will not be altogether pleasant to listen to; but, on the contrary, I expect you will not like it at all. I have come here to-day to speak about the war in South Africa, and the conduct of that war by the present Government. This time two years ago, when I went to speak in Oldham, the war had not begun; this time last year, when I came to Saddleworth, it was over – officially over; and what is the situation to-day? It is extremely serious and disquieting. It is not less momentous than when the Boer armies paused on the frontiers of Natal before throwing themselves on the slender forces of Sir George White. It is – I believe it no exaggeration to say it – very little better, and in some respects even worse, than it was a year ago. In all that vast region which comprises the Cape Colony, the late Republics, and the Northern part of Natal, excluding only the seaports, it is not safe for a loyal British subject to walk five miles beyond the picket lines. Wherever the British columns march the British authority extends, but as they march by behind them war and rebellion raise their heads again.

The Cape Colony, our own territory, is become itself the mainstay of the enemy's cause. Trade and industry throughout South Africa are paralysed. Weariness and discontent grow apace in the hearts of the loyalists. And meantime the enemy, small in numbers, yet bold and confident, harass and disturb at every point, and frequently commit the most shameful barbarities and breaches of the laws of war. Some measure and indication of the true state of affairs must have been conveyed to you by the sharp fighting of the last fortnight. These various severe skirmishes and actions are not in themselves important. They are provoking; and to those who have lost dear friends they had already almost counted as safe, they are sad and shocking. But no one imagines they, or indeed any separate incident, are going to alter the result of the war, or change the policy of this country; and there is no need for anyone to lose his head about them, still less is there any reason for the unholy, unnatural, and ferocious exultation with which these misfortunes have been hailed by certain of the Opposition newspapers. (Hear, hear.) But as a sign of the times, as a measure of the military situation, and as showing the extent of the Government knowledge of that situation, they are of the gravest and most serious importance. In the first place, let us look to the Government. What do we learn about them? Six weeks ago they issued a proclamation. Everyone knows about that proclamation. I do not, and I did not think it a very wise or brilliant move, and not one likely materially to improve the chances of victory and peace in South Africa. A date was fixed for the Boers and the leaders of the Boers to surrender, and they were threatened with certain not very terrible penalties if they did not do so.

Now, as a Conservative member, Captain Seely,[1] has caustically observed, 'It is of much greater importance to catch the Boers who are fighting than it is to threaten what you will do to them when you have caught them.' (Hear, hear.) Moreover, by fixing a particular date – September 15 – by which the Boers were to surrender, you offered as many of them as were not disposed to surrender an incentive and opportunity of celebrating September 15 in their own fashion; and this they have naturally done in these various and unfortunate small actions, in all of which we have been ourselves on the defensive: and, furthermore, this country has been, by the failure of the proclamation, exposed to renewed ridicule and abuse in the European newspapers, and is generally regarded as having made itself look foolish. Well, that is why I have felt no enthusiasm for the proclamation. But that is not what is serious in the matter. After all, the proclamation cost nothing more, if it were worth nothing more, than the paper it was written on, and if it did no good at any rate it did very little harm, for I do not suppose that anyone here thinks its failure will affect the result of the war; and I hope no one here pays any attention to the Continental Press. They are welcome to yelp, if it pleases them.

But what disquiets me, for it is of serious and alarming import, is that the Government in August should have known so little of the real situation in South Africa, of the condition of the enemy and of their disposition, as to cherish with credulity the idea that the Boer resistance would collapse or even weaken as a result of their proclamation. There is the dangerous feature. The Government did not know the truth. (Hear, hear.) More than that, Lord Kitchener did not know the truth, for if he had known with any accuracy what the Boer feelings and resources were he would have informed the Government, and the Government would, of course, have avoided the error of issuing the proclamation or of authorising him to do so. That is the first thing that troubles me, and I can assure you that it makes me feel very uncomfortable sometimes. Now, this is by no means the first time in the war that the Government has misconceived and miscalculated the military situation. I do not think there is any reason to use harsh or bitter language

[1] John Edward Bernard SEELY.

in regard to the mistakes that have been made. All war is a prolonged muddle, and when a Government embarks on war it has to put itself in a great degree into the hands of its military advisers. And these military advisers sometimes give very peculiar and contradictory advice. I daresay the account of all the recommendations and assertions of the generals, either at the front or in the War Office, and their estimate at different times of the enemy's strength and the force necessary to overcome it, would make one of the strangest chapters in the history of the war.

If you examine in a general manner the course of the war, as those who are not military experts may examine it, you will see that it is divided into two perfectly different and distinct phases, each requiring different treatment, and the Government has therefore had to solve two separate problems. First, it had to beat the Boer armies out of our territory, and take the Boer capital towns. That was a great business. But the settling of it was plain and easy. It was only a question of putting enough soldiers in the field, and the Government had the whole Empire to draw on for men and munitions. It was like filling up a barrel from a well. If one bucket of water is not enough you bring another. 'Quantity' was the answer to the first problem. The second was wholly different. After the capture of Bloemfontein and Pretoria the second stage in the war was reached. The Boer armies had been defeated, but it was one thing to defeat the Boer armies and quite another to conquer the Boer people. The guerrilla war began within a week of the capture of Pretoria, and continues unto this day. Enormous regions are infested by small bodies of determined and often desperate men, from forty to two hundred strong, sheltered and encouraged by the inhabitants, guided and often fed by the natives, going about seeking what they may devour, and destroying what they cannot use. Now, that is not a state of things to be terminated merely by pouring in masses of troops.

Numbers cannot help you any more. It is not a case of quantity. The answer to this second problem is 'quality.' Quality, rather than quantity; leaders rather than generals; men, not masses. (Cheers.) Of course, as before, the lines of communication must be held, and towns must be garrisoned; but beyond the troops needed for this work, who are more than sufficient, a force of between fifteen to twenty thousand men must be put in the field, equal in initiative, determination, and resource, in marksmanship, mobility, and endurance to the Boer commandos: equal in all that, and superior to them in numbers, equipment, and the quality of their horses. That is a tremendous demand, a greater demand than for two hundred thousand regular soldiers on the European model; surely it is a demand which this powerful country can supply, and in the whole range of the Empire, if not indeed in the army already in South Africa, there are surely the materials out of which such a force could be organised. (Cheers.) When I speak of improving the quality of the forces in the field, naturally I do not intend to imply any reproach on the soldiers who are now fighting.

Never did a nation find more brave and devoted servants, and when I read in the papers of incidents like the fight at Tarkastad, where one poor squadron of the 17th Lancers resisted till almost every man was killed or wounded, and never one surrendered; or of that young lieutenant of the Guards who in some obscure and nameless farm, at the fag end of the war, when all the pomp and glory and excitement has faded out, who, though practically alone, and faced with the alternative of death, or only a few days' detention in the enemy's camp – for they cannot hold their prisoners – unhesitatingly preferred to die rather than dishonour his uniform, and so was shot – when we read of splendid deeds like these, worthy of the ancient Greeks and Romans, one cannot help wishing that these important military and political personages who fill great offices and enjoy superabundant honours and emoluments in safe and comfortable England would rise to the same high conception of duty that is shown by the humble soldier or subaltern in the field. (Cheers.) What is meant by improving the quality of the troops is to increase their mobility by giving them better horses; to stimulate individual initiative; to weed out of the ranks all the weaklings and the inferior men; and lastly, to prepare at home reinforcements of suitable men – I say suitable men advisedly – to refresh the fighting units.

Now, the Government which held very steadfastly to the solution of the first military problem, and continued to send out great masses of troops until the Boer armies were overwhelmed and broken up, has not, I regret to say, shown the same persistency and energy in regard to this second problem, and the efforts they have made have not been equal to the task before them. Perhaps the military authorities have raised false hopes; no doubt the wish was father to the thought, and the Government listened with eagerness to every encouraging whisper. Week after week they have expected the end of the war. Month after month they have waited bootlessly for something to turn up. And week has been added to week and month to month, till now we verge already on the third year of waste and sorrow, and the Ministers, who ought to be ceaselessly planning for the future, seem instead to drift helplessly as in a dream, hoping every moment that the hideous South African nightmare may break at last, and that they will wake to find peace returning with the morning sun. I will not now discuss with you the adjurations which are addressed to the Government to employ what is called 'the iron hand,' and to declare the Boers outlaws; except to say that I think the people who make such appeals are very short-sighted; for why should it be easier to catch an outlaw than an ordinary person; and what can keep the Boer forces obedient to their commanders better than the assurance of perpetual banishment, or even of death, if they fall into our hands.

I think we are most of us by this time agreed that it is not by threats, not by proclamations, but by the vigorous application of military force that this matter can alone be settled as it should be settled. (Cheers.) Nor will I animadvert at this moment on the over-centralisation of power and initiative in the Pretoria Headquarter Staff; an over-centralisation so extraordinary that even the appointment of a single subaltern officer to an irregular corps is a matter which must be dealt with by Lord Kitchener himself. Nor will I criticise in detail the apparently methodless manner in which columns have been moved, now here, now there, like the wind which bloweth whither it listeth, during the last nine months. These are matters for the future. But I will specify two points in particular in the later conduct of the war in which there has been a lack of vigour and of organising power, and I will do what people who criticise Governments very rarely do – I will suggest a remedy for each. I have some right to be heard on the subject, because, as you know, I was for a considerable period in the field with the Army, and, moreover, I have a very great number of acquaintances serving in many different ranks and capacities, who write to me frequently and freely. Complaint, bitter complaint, in the first place is made of the number and class of the horses supplied to the troops. If there be one department of the Army which ought by this time to be in perfect working order, so far as South Africa is concerned, it is the Remount Department, and there is none more vital to the successful prosecution of the war.

And yet regimental and squadron officers write home and complain that they cannot get enough horses; that to get horses out of the Remount Department is as hard as, to quote an actual expression, 'getting blood out of a stone,' that when they do succeed in getting remounts, they find that, first of all, these animals are very often of inferior quality; and, secondly, that they are in the poorest condition, so badly have they been taken care of; and lastly, they complain – and surely you will hear their complaint – that though the Boer commandos, who have only a ravaged country behind them, have nearly all of them two horses to every man, our columns, with the whole of the world and the wealth of the Empire to draw on, have only one horse a man, and sometimes not even that. Well, that is a very serious, and I think I may say scandalous, state of things. (Hear, hear.) Then there is the Intelligence Department. You do not need any military education to appreciate the importance of that branch. I wonder if it has occurred to you how very often the Boers seem to find out what our plans are and what troops are moving; and on the other hand how very seldom we seem to be in possession of equal information about them, or, indeed, of any accurate information at all. Take the latest examples. Two guns, with an insufficient escort, are sent out from Bloemfontein on some errand or other. What happens? Before they have marched a single day they are pounced on and captured.

Now look at the other side. The Commandant-General Botha[1] concentrates fifteen hundred men, and when that very gallant and capable young officer, Major Gough,[2] is sent out to patrol as usual, instead of his finding, as his superior officers expected, twenty or thirty Boers in the neighbourhood, the whole of Botha's force attack and overwhelm him. Look at the contrast. We cannot move a most insignificant force, compared to our Army, without the Boers knowing all about it, and the Boers can move what is a very great force compared to their Army and we know nothing about it. Now there you have the result. What is the explanation? Letters from South Africa say the Intelligence Department is mainly in the hands of soldiers who know little of the country, and nothing of its people, compared to the colonists, who have been living there all their lives; that Colonial help is not made enough use of, and Colonial opinion too rarely invited or taken, and that the whole Intelligence service is starved for want both of money and brains. Surely it is obvious that Government should undertake the reorganisation of the Remount and the Intelligence Departments; I would place at the head of each of these a man, soldier or civilian, of profound mind and proved business capacity; someone of the mental calibre of such men as Mr Clinton Dawkins, or Sir William Garstin,[3] and I would give him a perfectly free hand to spend public money and make any arrangements he thought fit to secure to the Army the greatest number of horses and the best horses; the greatest amount of information in regard to the enemy, and the best information.

I have talked a good deal about the Government and about their difficulties and shortcomings, but above all things let us be quite precise. What is the Government? In the first place, it is a body of gentlemen chosen from the great political party to which we all of us belong, and it is therefore entitled to a considerable measure of our sympathy. In the second place, it is the only Government which in the present circumstances is possible, and therefore we are bound from a national as well as from a party point of view to give it effective support. But that does not mean, certainly I do not intend

[1] Louis BOTHA.

[2] Hubert de la Poer Gough (1870–1963), with 16th Lancers in South Africa; commanded 3rd Cavalry Brigade during the First World War in which he rose to the rank of Lieutenant-General; KCB 1916; KCVO 1917. The story of Gough's capture and prompt escape is told in his autobiography *Soldiering On*, London, 1954, pp. 83–9.

[3] William Edmund Garstin (1849–1925), Under-Secretary of State for Public Works in Egypt from 1892; British Government Director of the Suez Canal Co 1907; KGMC 1897; GCMG 1902.

it to mean, that it is therefore treason to the party and even to the nation to criticise or to censure the conduct of public affairs when their conduct of them is deserving of criticism or of censure. (Hear, hear.) Who then is responsible? Is it the Chancellor of the Exchequer? I have noticed a tendency in some of the newspapers to lay the blame on the Treasury. The Treasury, it is said, grudges every penny, and will not give the money needed for the war. But I am sure you will see that when the expenditure on the war continues at the rate of a million and a quarter a week, people can hardly accuse the Treasury of being stingy. (Hear, hear.) And I myself would think it a monstrous thing if persons who were spending such vast sums of money – not in the best way – were to excuse their own blunders and mistakes by trying to lay the blame on the Treasury and on the Chancellor of the Exchequer, whose special function it is, while providing necessary moneys for the war, to guard against waste. (Cheers.)

Where shall we look? The War Office? Well, of course, in a certain sense Mr Brodrick is responsible for every matter connected with the war. He would be the last man to shrink from, indeed I think he would be the first to court that or any other responsibility. But I say it with the utmost deliberation, the country will be most unwise to allow such an assumption to be made. Nothing can be more dangerous to the public and Imperial welfare than that prosecution of the war in South Africa should come to be regarded as a departmental affair under the sole and peculiar care of a single overburdened Secretary of State. (Hear, hear.) The country looks to Mr Balfour and Mr Chamberlain, the one the Leader of the House of Commons and the apparent successor of Lord Salisbury; the other the *fons et origo* of the policy we are fighting for, and, as everyone knows, the most prominent member of the Government; and – if my voice can carry so far – I warn those two distinguished men, the mainguard of the Unionist Party, they cannot devolve the weight and burden of this tremendous enterprise – the greatest we have set our hands to since the times of Napoleon – on any subordinate Minister, or any particular department, but that it rests on their shoulders, and that with its successful conclusion is bound up their political fame and their personal honour. (Cheers.) I believe it to be the duty of everyone who is invited in these days to address public audiences to bring home to them, and through them to the Government, the overwhelming and preponderating importance of the South African situation.

It is no exaggeration to state that the embarrassments of the Empire never pressed on us in a more insidious and dangerous form, not even after that terrible week in December, 1899, or on the morrow of Spion Kop. Then, at any rate, the path of duty lay plain and clear before the country, and the difficulties were such as wealth and numbers, however ill applied, might overcome. (Hear, hear.) But now there is a most perilous apathy. We seem to regard the war as chronic. Public attention is often diverted from it. The visit of an Emperor to a neighbouring State, the murder of a President on the other side of the Atlantic; yes, even such things as the racing of pleasure yachts, turns the minds of thousands from the great public undertaking which we are pledged to carry through. Gentlemen, I appeal to you never to let the war pass out of your minds for a day. (Applause.) Think what it means to us all. Friends, brothers, or sons, fighting and toiling, ragged and hungry, while the weeks pass by, while summer grows out of spring, and autumn withers into winter. How many are there here to-night who may look in the newspaper tomorrow morning to find, as I found last week, some familiar name, and learn that some bright eye known and trusted is closed for ever. Then there is the money, the wealth of the nation, draining away, drip, drip, drip – enough to buy every month four of the largest battleships in the world. There is India. Nearly thirty thousand men detained beyond their contract with the State impatiently await relief in India. Every day increases the strain on your military organisation, and the embarrassment of your finances. The loyal districts of South Africa sicken in the grip of martial law; the gulf of hatred between Boer and Briton grows wider; and every day devastation and ruin rule over larger areas.

Surely if ever a supreme effort were needed to terminate or curtail this time of trouble, it is needed now. (Cheers.) I have had some doubt and anxiety about saying these things, which I know will cause anger to many of my political friends, and possibly draw a good deal of abuse on me; but it is not for that reason that I have been in doubt. So long as I am a member of Parliament I shall certainly say what I think it my duty to say. (Hear, hear.) My difficulty has been this: The only way to stimulate the indignation of the public, and consequently the energy of the Government, is by showing how very dangerous the prolongation of the war is to us, and what a strain on our resources, and of course words spoken with that object might have the effect – if they were spoken by someone more important – of encouraging the Boers, and also of strengthening the hands of their allies in England, who would have us find a refuge from our difficulties in a fatal and dishonourable peace. (Cheers.) But I feel with conviction – and I trust you will agree with me, for it is my excuse for so long presuming on your patience – that if the Government and the mass of the nation will concentrate their whole thought and attention on South Africa, they will infuse into the prosecution of the war a vigour and vitality which will make amends for all, which will over-come the extraordinary difficulties and dangers with which we are con-fronted, and finally lead us victoriously to a conclusion which shall combine the peace of Africa with the honour of Britain. (Loud cheers.)

WSC to Lord Rosebery
(*Rosebery Papers*)

8 October 1901   [Oldham]

My dear Lord Rosebery,
I wonder whether you will have seen my speech. It was not vy well reported, because it happened to clash with speeches by Haldane & Sir Robert Reid: but at any rate I spoke perfectly plainly and did not mince matters. Oldham agrees. I have addressed some twenty meetings here and I find everywhere the same feeling: absolute determination to force the war through: perplexity and disappointment at its prolongation (not perhaps quite so keen as one would have expected, because people are afraid that to doubt may be unpatriotic): and I must add a good deal of calm patience, more likely to flash into anger than to fade into apathy, but not yet to the point of either. I enclose you a letter from a substantial constituent; I do not know him personally but he is a typical well-to-do Lancashire Conservative of the lower middle class.
I have had a good many letters of this character; but I send this because it is the most complimentary. Please destroy it.

Yours most sincerely
WINSTON S. CHURCHILL

Lord Rosebery to WSC

18 October 1901   The Durdans
                                                            Epsom

My dear Winston,
I have not had a moment to acknowledge your letter.
I got your speech out of the *Morning Post* and liked it very much. It came at a most opportune time – but as usual things have settled down again into a relative calm. Where are the 100,000 men in this island who are being trained according to Brodrick to fill up drafts and supply South Africa? I can find no trace of them in spite of the utmost research.
You seem to have prompted Beach into a meeting which pleased him very much.

Sincly
AR

WSC to Joseph Chamberlain
(*J. Chamberlain Papers*)

14 October 1901   105 Mount Street

Private

My dear Mr Chamberlain,

I am afraid you will not approve of the series of speeches I am making in the country, if you should happen to see them in the papers; but I should like you to know what my line is.

It is not enough for the Govt to say, 'we have handed the war over to the military: they must settle it: all we can do is to supply them as they require.' I protest against that view. Nothing can relieve the Govt of their responsibility. If Kitchener cannot settle the question, you will have to interfere.

The situation is not getting better at all, according to every letter I get from S.A. I enclose only one from Burnham, the scout, a man of much local knowledge and keen intelligence.

K [Kitchener] is overworked, exhausts himself on many unimportant details, and is now showing signs of the prolonged strain. There is no plan worth speaking of in the operations except hammer, hammer, at random. The troops, which are numerous everywhere, are overwhelming nowhere. The thousands of superior men are intermingled with and consequently reduced to the level of the inferior soldiers. The mobility of the army is that of the slowest mounted man.

Moreover they are being bucketed to pieces with almost ceaseless trekking. Remount & Intelligence Departments are both vy badly managed: there is neither bold design nor clear business calculation; but only indiscriminate, methodless and haphazard energy.

How much longer is it going to last?

What I want is that the Govt should localise, delimit and assign the functions of the C in C in Africa. Should reorganise the Remount & Intelligence Depts. Should lay the army by for a short period of rest & refreshment. Should organise a picked force. Should make some sort of plan: and make sure that we end the matter with the next bitter weather whatever happens.

Believe me, yours vy sincerely
WINSTON S. CHURCHILL

F. R. Burnham[1] to WSC
(*J. Chamberlain Papers*)

7 October [1901]   6 Conduit Street
[Copy]

Dear Churchill,

This is just a line to tell you how glad I am that you have the courage to tell the *Great* leaders what the real condition of things is in South Africa. 'There is great danger of losing the loyalty of English Colonials' is the burden of my private letters from the country – also that the Kaffirs begin to doubt our power to ever whip the Boer.

This all seems so absurd when in reality Old England has not put forth one *tenth* of her strength yet.

Yours very truly
F. R. BURNHAM

Joseph Chamberlain to WSC

15 October 1901   Highbury
                                                            Birmingham
Private

My dear Churchill,

As you invite my opinion, which I certainly should not otherwise have intruded, I am bound to say that while I value your suggestions, and have in the past endeavoured to profit by them, I do not think the public discussion of them in the form of a criticism upon the government & the military authorities is profitable; and I think you must see yourself that its first result is to encourage the enemy to blaspheme, both at home & abroad.

I cannot discuss in detail the proposals of your letter, and after all in any Government which may ever be formed there must be a certain practical division of responsibility; civilians cannot do the work of soldiers, and the head of one department cannot undertake to supervise & control the details of the work of another. But, speaking generally, I agree with much that you say, and as far as my influence goes, I am working in the same direction.

I am not certain that if we had a Marlborough or a Wellington he would

---

[1] Frederick Russell Burnham (1861–1944), American scout. Entered British South African Co 1893; killed M'limo, the high priest and instigator of the revolt, in the 2nd Matabele rebellion; fought in Boer War, captured at Sanna's Post, but escaped; destroyed Pretoria-Johannesburg railway; was chief of Scouts of British Army.

be able to do much better than our present men in such a war as that which we are conducting; but it is clear that we are not fortunate enough to possess at the present time many soldiers capable of bearing comparison with the men I have quoted. Every effort has been made to secure mobile columns in every way as good as the Boers to follow up and to hang on to the small detachments of the enemy, and the recent capture of Lotter was the work of one of these columns.[1] But when small bodies of the enemy split up into absolute units, as they do, it seems to be impracticable to hunt them out of such a country as they are operating in.

The concentration by Botha of a much larger force requires different treatment, and I think there is no lack of plans, although previous experience does not justify overwhelming confidence in their success.

It is possible that, if the country were prepared to revert to the Roman system of appointing a Dictator, we should be more successful, but he would have to be given a free hand for a couple of years at the end of which he might be hanged or crowned, according to the results. For a Government to take the matter entirely into its own hands, and without considering the personal feelings of those engaged, and without their assent, to make all the changes you suggest, would be to bring about wholesale resignations and a state of anarchy which would be worse than anything which we have yet known. I do not doubt the possibility of changes which would be an improvement. I do not defend all that has been done, but neither in war nor in politics is it possible to do everything at once, and over-hurry is as bad as over-caution.

I recognise the discontent of those who describe themselves as Loyalists. I have never in my experience known them to be satisfied. They readily believe all the tales that are told them, and unless everything goes as they desire they are prepared – in words at any rate – to throw off the connection. There is another side to this, and before I should allow them to be arbiters in the matter they must be willing to make the sacrifices in purse as well as in person which have been cheerfully made by the mother country.

Possibly, if it were not for the difficulties caused by the presence of a majority of Dutchmen in South Africa, the British there would be more worthy of their name; but, as it is, if we came to balance complaints, I am by no means certain that it would be in their favour.

Believe me, yours very truly

J. Chamberlain

---

[1] Commandant Lotter was sentenced to death for treason and murder by Court Martial at Middelburg, Cape Colony. The sentence was carried out on October 11.

WSC to Lord Rosebery
(*Rosebery Papers*)

23 October 1901   105 Mount Street

Private

My dear Lord Rosebery,

I am in a state of jumps this morning, because I am off to Leicester to make another speech on much the same lines as the last; but I cannot resist writing to tell you with what enthusiastic joy I read your remarks about 'Peat-Reek and Harris Tweeds'. Certainly you have smiled J.C.B.'s bacilli away. I had thought of writing to point out what pain and annoyance must have been caused to Sir James Crichton-Browne, by the unscrupulous use which had been made of his initials. But I have preferred to put it all in the credit account. A day will come!

I pass to another person 'distinctly the reverse of anonymous' – Buller! Poor old man – I cannot help being sorry for him, but it was evident after his exposure that he would have to go. The Government would have sent him away long before had they dared; but they were tactless and cowardly in the matter, and the result is to bring all sorts of humiliation upon the general which might have been spared him if he had been given a peerage instead of an army corps.[1]

I wonder what Mr Chamberlain will say at Edinburgh! I had a vy civil and kind letter from him the other day. I am sure he is profoundly dissatisfied with the situation, and would like to [take] it more into his own hands.

I continue to receive uniformly bad news from S. Africa: I put no faith whatever in the crumbs of comfort we get from time to time in the newspapers: the last thing I hear – on excellent authority – is the strain is telling markedly upon K. [Kitchener].

I hope you will not think it necessary to answer this letter – at any rate not with your own hand.

Yours vy sincerely
WINSTON S. CHURCHILL

[1] Despite the reverse he suffered at Spion Kop and his half-hearted effort to relieve Ladysmith, Sir Redvers Buller (1839–1908) was in September 1901 appointed to command the First Army Corps at Aldershot. The appointment was strongly criticised in the Press. At a luncheon in Westminster on October 10 Sir Redvers sought to defend his record. His speech was thought to be so lacking in judgment and self-restraint that on October 23 the War Office relieved him of his command and placed him on half pay.

Lord Rosebery to WSC

10 November 1901   38 Berkeley Square

My dear Winston,

I had your speech of Oct 23[1] cut out to read, but mislaid it, and only found it and read it tonight. It seems to me to express what has become the patent truth in a striking way, while it chaffs the heads of your own and Percy's families in most effective fashion. Thanks too for your letter. I am passing through London on my way North tonight. When do you return hitherwards?

Sincly

AR

Duke of Marlborough to WSC

EXTRACT

12 November 1901   Warwick House
                                                     St James's

My dear Winston,

I am distressed that your letters to me have not been attended to before. The meeting at Leicester went off all right. Your speech was appreciated by those who were present and I think every one was satisfied. The reports in the Press were poor but of that I do not mind.

I stay here till Monday when I go to Blenheim. Your telegram has just come. I shall be out hunting on Saturday and I shall hope to see you out. Lilian is full up here, as the House is only a tiny one. Where will you stay? I beg you will arrange with Wright concerning your Horses, I cannot interpret your wishes nor do I know when you will hunt. Pray write to him and tell him what your plans are and when you will be home. It occurs to me that you attempt too many things at the same moment. No doubt you are of the same opinion. I am sorry your Horses will be unused for so long. Hunting is expensive and is economical in proportion to the number of days that one hunts. You propose to hunt for 8 weeks i.e. 50 days. That is let us say, 20 days hunting. Four horses cost you nearly £400 per annum. The Hunting that you will do will therefore cost you £20 a day. I consider your arrangements therefore needlessly extravagant. Wright has just come in and had a conversation re your horses. If you do not mean to hunt till Feb he urges you selling now at Leicester, and hiring when you come home.

---

[1] In a speech at Leicester WSC had assailed the Dukes of Northumberland and Marlborough for their 'vain and discredited optimism' about the Government's conduct of the South African War.

Where do you mean to hunt next year i.e. Feb and March. From Blenheim? If so Hawes could supply you with good enough animals for the Bicester Hunt? But all this you must think out and settle for yourself. I shall hope to talk [to] you about it on Saturday.

We have had good fun here and we have had 1st Class Sport. Lumley[1] has sent me a document about your Life Policy! What do you wish to have done in this matter. I gathered that you wished to surrender it or do you wish to keep it up. Let me know what you propose when we meet, as I do not quite understand his communication to me. . . .

Where is Jack?[2] I have heard nothing of him.

I shall look forward to seeing you Saturday.

Your aff
SUNNY

W. St John Brodrick to WSC

16 November 1901   War Office

Private

My dear Churchill,

A line of thanks none the less for your nice letter.

I hope the outlook is not a 10 yrs one. My comfort is that every prediction about South Africa is wrong!

The Oxfordshire Hussars pleases me doubly – you are evidently insuring agst compulsion of some sort – and surely under the Army Act your utterances must now be cut to the liking of the C in C!

Yours ever
ST JOHN BRODRICK

H. G. Wells[3] to WSC

19 November 1901   Spade House
Sandgate

Dear Sir,

I am greatly flattered & interested by your letter and glad indeed that my publishers have done me the kindness to send you a copy.[4] But you bring home to me very clearly that – very probably because of my desire to win

---

[1] Theodore Lumley (d. 1922), member of firm of Lumley & Lumley, WSC's solicitors for many years. Sometime Solicitor to Portuguese Government.

[2] Jack CHURCHILL.

[3] Herbert George Wells (1866–1946), prolific author of novels (*Kipps, Love and Mr Lewisham*) and scientific fantasies (*The Time Machine*); early Fabian and socialist writer. One of the prized possessions in WSC's library was an almost complete set of H. G. Wells' books, each individually inscribed by the author.

[4] *Anticipations.*

some scientific & medical people to my views – I have failed to give the proper value to one very important point. My predominating people to come are to be 'educated not trained' (see pages 86 & 140) and in your litany when it came to 'from the dream of all specialists' I too will most heartily join in the 'God shall deliver us', with you. Indeed, in another book, *The First Men in the Moon*, which Newnes is publishing, I have been guying the specializer soul to the very best of my ability.

That you should find my estimate of the rapidity of development excessive is simply due to the difference in our social circumstances. You belong to a class that has scarcely altered internally in a hundred years. If you could be transported by some magic into the Household of your ancestors of 1800, a week would make you at home with them. In that time the tailor, hairdresser & the atmosphere of different manners only have done all that was needed. But of the four grandparents who represented me in 1800 it's highly probable two could not read & that any of them would find me and that I should find them as alien as contemporary Chinese. I really do not think that your people who gather in great country houses realize the pace of things.

I must repeat my gratification to find you have read my book. I have had an immediate aim in writing it. I do sincerely believe that Liberalism (as Gladstone knew it) is as dead as Adam and that there is an urgent need for an ordered body of doctrine that will serve for the good intentions that are the soul of Liberalism to come together upon. I have proposed (preferred?) an ordered body of doctrine. Take it or leave it, it is a more coherent & consistent thing than any political leader can produce today.

Yours v sincerely
H. G. WELLS

H. G. Wells to WSC

21 November 1901   Spade House

My dear Sir,

I should certainly like the discussion you suggest and I hope you will remember your suggestion when Parliament is sitting. It will interest me tremendously to make your acquaintance. To me you are a particularly interesting & rather amiable figure. Believing as I do that big sliders & new fissures are bound to come in the next few years, I fancy at times that you are a little too inclined towards the *Old Game*. More than anything else I speculate whether you anticipate that when you are sixty you will be in or

upon a Conservative Party with a Liberal opposition & an Irish Corner in a
British or Imperial Parliament & if not – where you expect to be.

Yours very faithfully
H. G. WELLS

Sir Ian Hamilton to WSC

EXTRACT

24 November 1901   Union Castle Line
RMS *Briton*

My dear Winston,

 ... [I] beg you like a dear boy not to lose sight of that question of the Boer
prisoners. I don't think you ever quite troubled to consider the matter carefully, but the more I ponder over it the more vital does it seem to me to be.
Of course if I were Napoleon I would clear out Essex of its present muddle-
headed peasantry (with due compensation) and settle them down there with
their wives & children in small farms. Thus we should secure some population which was immune from the disease of loving the town better than
the country and would revivify our blood from a splendid, semi-civilized,
robust stock possessing endless potentialities. I am not Napoleon & this of
course is a dream. *But*, something can be done, I am perfectly certain, to
bring these people into line with us . . .

WSC to the Editor, The English Churchman

25 November 1901   105 Mount Street

Sir,

Your worthy correspondent 'A Protestant Churchman and Conservative,'
is pained unnecessarily.

I am not a Ritualist – whatever that may mean – but, on the contrary, I
adhere to a plain service, and dislike ceremonial forms. That is my personal
and private feeling on the subject. As the representative of a Parliamentary
borough, I am frequently invited to become a patron of bazaars. These
invitations, provided the object of the bazaar is a lawful one, I am usually
willing to accept. I have not heard of any illegalities being committed in St
John's Church, Werneth, Oldham. Therefore, I have no objection to allowing
my name and influence to be used in support of the charitable purpose of
the Vicar's bazaar. I should be equally willing to associate myself with a

Methodist or a Roman Catholic charity, but in no case would my association imply that I shared the religious views of the body in question; still less would it prove, as your correspondent rather unjustifiably suggests, the existence of some dark and secret compact wrought during the late election.

I may add that this morning I have agreed to become a patron of the Oldham Association for the Deaf and Dumb, but that agreement in no way pledges me to become a deaf mute myself.

WINSTON S. CHURCHILL

*   *   *   *   *

Speaking at Hanley on November 28 WSC said that when he had suggested that Lord Kitchener should be relieved of what he called the superfluous duties with which he had been encumbered, 'Mr Walter Long for whom I have the greatest respect, who was speaking at Liverpool, said that my suggestion was a very ridiculous one. But what happened? Within ten days of Mr Long's speech the Government sent out to South Africa General Ian Hamilton, a most capable officer, to be the chief of the staff of Lord Kitchener and to help him in discharging the difficult and multifarious duties which had been imposed upon him . . . I rejoice that the Government have sent this General out to South Africa . . . When my friend Mr Walter Long talks about it as being ridiculous really I think he ought to be more careful of the language he uses towards his colleagues of the Cabinet.'

Walter Long to WSC

3 December 1901   Local Government Board

Private

My dear Winston Churchill,

I trouble you with these few lines in reference to your late speech on purely personal grounds. I can assure you I never 'ridiculed' any suggestion of yours. So far as I know my only reference to you was made in a speech I delivered at Liverpool, & if you will be good enough to read the marked passages in enclosed report I think you will agree that there is no word to which you could take exception.

The only other allusion I made was to your suggestion that this Government should not 'assist' Kitchener, but 'localise, limit & assign' his duties. I said I thought this would involve an interference with the discretion of the C in C in Africa which would not commend itself to the Government or this country.

I am sorry to bore you with all this and my words are of little interest to anybody but I am anxious there should be no misunderstanding. Nobody has watched your political career with greater pleasure than I have, not only on your account and that of our party, but also because you are the son of one whom it was my pleasure and pride to follow, and whose personal friendship I had the good fortune to enjoy.

Sincerely Yours

WALTER H. LONG

Walter Long to WSC

5 December 1901   11 Ennismore Gardens

My dear Winston Churchill,

Thanks many for yours. I entirely share your view as to public criticism – but 'ridicule' I felt could not be thrown by me on practical suggestions & I only wanted to put that right.

Yours sincerely

WALTER H. LONG

John Morley to WSC

Post card

12 December 1901   57 Elm Park Gardens

I find my copy of the book I commended to you has been lent. 'Tis sure to be on the table at the Carlton. *'Poverty: A Study of Town Life.'* It is not nearly so big as it looks.

Yrs

J. MORLEY

WSC to Lady Randolph

13 December 1901   105 Mount Street

My dear Mamma,

I fancy your box is as near perfection as we are likely to attain. Of course I cannot be quite sure till I use it; but so far as I can judge by looking at it, I should say that no improvement could be made. Thank you vy much indeed for it and for the thought involved.

I had a wretched day yesterday. I started by the 10.15 train to open a bazaar at Oldham. I shd have arrived at 2.30. The bazaar was at 3. But when I got to Stafford all the telegraph wires were broken by the gale and the poles in many cases lay across the railroad; so that it was 4 o'clock before I even reached Crewe. Then I came back to London, it being useless to proceed further, and reached Euston at 10 o'clock after a most unprofitable day. Today we have shot 500 rabbits in the park, wh was good fun as we were but three guns. Tomorrow I hunt: Sunday – Tring: and then if only the weather keeps open I shall get 6 days hunting next week, for I have my own 4 horses and some of Sunny's.

Two years ago I was in solitude with the vulture sixty miles from Pretoria & 250 from the frontier. It is strange to look back on these anniversaries from amid such peaceful surroundings.

I dined with John Morley on Wedy night: most pleasant: Buckle, Mowatt, Saunderson,[1] Spender[2] (of the *W.G.* [*Westminster Gazette*]) & Goschen.[3] Everybody most kind and caressing, particularly the host, who like so many of these Liberals commands my affection at once.

No my dear, I do not forget you. But we are both of us busy people, absorbed in our own affairs, and at present independent. Naturally we see little of each other. Naturally that makes no difference to our feelings.

I remain always, Your loving son
WINSTON S.C.

WSC to Lumley and Lumley

[Copy]

17 December 1901

While my mother's position continues unchanged, I recognise that it is difficult for her to make me or my brother any allowance, and I feel it my duty on the other hand to assist her in any manner possible without seriously prejudicing my reversionary interests. I therefore forego the allowance of £500 a year she and my father had always intended to give me. I also defray the expenses of the loan of £3500 I contracted at her suggestion

[1] Edward James Saunderson (1837–1906), Whig MP for Co Cavan 1865–75; Conservative MP for North Armagh 1885–1906. Married Helena Emily de Moleyns, daughter of 3rd Baron Ventry.

[2] John Alfred Spender (1862–1942), Editor of the *Westminster Gazette* 1896–1922; biographer of Campbell-Bannerman and Asquith; CH 1937.

[3] George Joachim, 1st Viscount Goschen (1831–1907), who in 1886 succeeded Lord Randolph as Chancellor of the Exchequer, shortly after he and the Marquess of Hartington had formed the Liberal Unionist Party; Viscount 1900.

for my brother's allowance and my own from 1897–1900, amounting to
£305 per annum.

I view the question of the £1100 in the same light, and will raise no objection
to its dissipation as proposed.

What I desire in my brother's interest as in my own is that there should
be a clear understanding necessarily not of a legal nature, that in the event
of Mr George Cornwallis-West being at some future time in a superior
financial position my mother will make suitable provision for her children
out of her own income; in other words that she will reciprocate the attitude
I am now adopting.

*   *   *   *   *

On December 18 there was a riot at Birmingham, and the 'pro-Boer'
Lloyd George had to escape from the Town Hall disguised as a policeman.
One man was killed; many, including policemen, were injured.

WSC to J. Moore Bayley[1]

19 December 1901   105 Mount Street

[Copy]

Private

My dear Moore Bayley,

I am disgusted to read today's papers upon the riots in Bham. I hope the
Conservative Party have kept their hands clean.

It is a curious thing what a long time bad habits take to eradicate. 'Forged
tickets'! I thought almost I was reading a much older story.[2]

Yours vy truly
WINSTON S. CHURCHILL

PS What do you think of Lord R's [Rosebery] speech?[3]

[1] J. Moore Bayley (1858–1911), solicitor and Conservative politician; Birmingham City
Councillor 1893–7; founder member of Midland Conservative Club and, at different periods,
member of Executive Committee of Birmingham Conservative Association and president of
Birmingham Central Division Association; an ardent admirer of Lord Randolph whose
candidature for Central Birmingham he promoted in 1884 and 1889.

[2] A reference to the Aston Riots in 1884, when a Conservative meeting addressed by Lord
Randolph and Sir Stafford Northcote was broken up by the supporters of Joseph Chamberlain's – then Liberal – Birmingham caucus many of whom, it was alleged, had gained admission to the meeting in Aston Park by means of forged tickets. Moore Bayley was one of the
principal organisers of the meeting.

[3] In his famous speech at Chesterfield on December 16, Lord Rosebery urged the divided
Liberal Party to 'clean the slate.' He also advocated discussion of peace terms with the Boers.
Although the speech failed to repair the breach within the Liberal Party, it did create an
atmosphere in which negotiations with the pro-Boers became possible. Several prominent
Liberals rallied round Rosebery.

WSC to J. Moore Bayley

23 December 1901   105 Mount Street

[Copy]

My dear Moore Bayley,

Many thanks for your long letter. I do not agree in the least with your view of the Birmingham riots, and I think such methods equally disgraceful whether they are employed for or against the Conservative Party. You will find that the public opinion of the country will regard the whole episode as a blot upon the civilisation of Birmingham. If people say things which are treasonable and within the scope of the law they should be prosecuted and dealt with accordingly, but within the law every man has a perfect right to express his own opinions, and that they should be shouted down because they are odious to the majority in the district is a very dangerous, fatal doctrine for the Conservative Party, who may not always have the weight of numbers on their side to encourage. I shudder to think of the harm that would have been done to the Imperial cause in South Africa if Mr Lloyd George had been mauled or massacred by the mob. If your head clerk had made his presence known, he would have run a very great chance of being made answerable for the consequences. Personally, I think Lloyd George a vulgar, chattering little cad, but he will have gained a hundred thousand sympathisers in England by the late proceedings. We have all been very pleased to see in London, the Conservative Paper, the *Daily Gazette*, has clearly repudiated any sympathy with the outrage.

Will you please send me a copy of your Speech on the Housing Question and the Outline of your practical suggestion as to the purchase of property. I have lately been reading a book by Mr Rowntree called *Poverty*,[1] which has impressed me very much, and which I strongly recommend you to read.[2] It is quite evident from the figures which he adduces that the American labourer is a stronger, larger, healthier, better fed, and consequently more efficient animal than a large proportion of our population, and that is surely a fact which our unbridled Imperialists, who have no thought but to pile up armaments, taxation and territory, should not lose sight of. For my own part, I see little glory in an Empire which can rule the waves and is unable to flush its sewers. The difficulty has been so far that the people who have

---

[1] Benjamin Seebohm Rowntree (1871–1954), Chairman of the family chocolate business in York 1925–41; was the author of several works of social research. His *Poverty: a Study of Town Life*, published in 1901, is acknowledged as an important milestone on the road to the Welfare State. CH 1931.

[2] WSC had been introduced to Rowntree's book at a dinner given by John Morley at the Athenaeum on December 11.

looked abroad have paid no attention to domestic matters, and those who are centred on domestic matters regard the Empire merely as an encumbrance. What is wanted is a well-balanced policy midway between the Hotel Cecil and Exeter Hall,[1] something that will co-ordinate development and expansion with the progress of social comfort and health. But I suppose the Party machinery will carry everything before it, and, as heretofore, the Extremists on both sides, whether progressive or reactionary, will set the tune and collar the organisation, and all we wretched, unorganised middle thinkers will either be destroyed between the contending forces, or compelled to serve in support of one disproportionate cause or the other. But I shall watch the Chesterfield experiment with interest.

Yours vy sincerely
WINSTON S. CHURCHILL

[?*Unpublished*] *Review by WSC of Seebohm Rowntree's*
Poverty: A Study of Town Life

The ancient and prosperous city of York is encircled by strong walls of stone which were raised along the lines of the Roman ramparts by the labours and the necessity of the thirteenth century and which today attract the attention of the traveller as the train moves out of the North Eastern Railway station. In the olden times these fortifications divided the comparative security of the citizens from the perilous disorders of the open country. The days of internal violence have long departed; the walls crumble in the steady grip of time and at frequent intervals are pierced by broad unbarred roads leading in all directions to extensive suburbs. Yet although peace and order reign throughout the land, though public strife & private feud have almost vanished in the vistas of the past, though a man may walk freely from village to village and encounter nothing more alarming than a motor car the townsfolk are huddled together within their walls not less closely packed than on the morrow of the Towton (Wakefield?)[2]; and while the land is interlaced with railways and the seas are scarred with steamships bearing and distributing all manner of food in plentiful abundance, a large proportion of the Yorkists endure all the privations which are usually associated with a state of siege.

[1] An allusion to Salisbury's Administration on the one hand, and the negrophilistic missionary movement on the other. Exeter Hall was in the Strand and was used for religious and philanthropic assemblies until 1907.
[2] The Yorkists defeated the Lancastrians at the Battle of Towton, 11 miles SW of York, in 1461. In 1460, Richard, Duke of York, was defeated and killed by the Lancastrians at the Battle of Wakefield.

Such a remarkable phenomenon has lately been the subject of a most minute and persevering examination the results of which are made known to the public in the pages of Mr Rowntree's latest book. This gentleman happened to possess a temperament equally inquisitive and pertinacious, and could also command a considerable and varied experience of urban and social problems; and in the autumn of 1899 he set to work upon a house-to-house enquiry to obtain 'exact information regarding the housing, occupation & earnings of every wage-earning family in York, together with the number and age of the children in each family.' Not content with this he counted the number of people of each denomination who attended divine service on Sunday, noted their costume and appearance, and whether they attended in the morning & the evening: he catalogued the customers of the various public houses, & the members of the different clubs, recorded carefully at what hours of the day they entered, how long they remained, in what condition they departed, and how their numbers were affected by the state of the weather outside or the attractions offered within; he mastered the municipal statistics of health, vitality and education and accurately weighed, measured and physically tested 1919 boys & girls; he probed the influence exerted upon the working class in the city by Friendly Societies, Insurance companies & Trade Unions. No task was too large for him, no detail too small; and in an investigation which extended over the greater part of two years he acquired particulars of a more or less intimate nature concerning '11,560 families living in 388 streets and comprising a population of 46,754.' As the course of his inquiry was not interrupted by popular irritations, it is only fair to conclude that his industry was equalled by his tact. The result was a formidable accumulation of facts and figures, less misleading and more manageable because confined to one locality than the extensive & improving statistics of the Board of Trade. In other words he discharged for York on a smaller scale and with consequently more precision and minuteness much the same service as Mr Charles Booth[1] has rendered to London.

Trusting in this broad foundation Mr Rowntree enters upon his argument. He wastes no time (as we shall presently see) in moralising upon the conclusions at which he arrives and he finds no room in his pages for sentiment or indignation. The subject is handled in the style of a mathematical treatise. The figures are assembled; the averages are struck & the results proclaimed in an unpretentious fashion and with grim and passionless deliberation. The general scheme of his argument is extremely simple. It is shown in the first place that York is a typical provincial town; neither a sea port nor a

[1] Charles Booth (1840–1916), shipowner and social investigator; author of *Life and Labour of the People in London* (9 vols, 1889–97).

purely industrial district; neither peculiarly poor nor very rich; neither unusually overcrowded nor abnormally salubrious; but upon the whole fairly representative of the conditions which prevail in other English cities. Therefore it is intended that what is said about York would in all probability apply equally to the urban population in general; and this view obtains some confirmation from the fact that many of Mr Rowntree's statements tally very closely with those which Mr Charles Booth, working by somewhat different methods, has set forth in regard to London. Therefore the proportion of those in poverty in York is a rough measure of those in poverty throughout the cities of the land.

We are next invited to consider a definition of poverty. Gibbon has observed that human imagination has been much more successful in depicting hell than heaven, and no doubt that is especially true of the theological mind: but when we return to earthly things it is evident that an inverse principle prevails. We indulge day dreams of fairy castles and bright hopes which can never be realised. We rejoice in the idea of Aladdin and his wonderful lamp. Desire lends force to fancy. Who has not considered how he would spend vast wealth? But from the ugly things of life, from its darker facts and hideous possibilities imagination recoils or is deliberately recalled. It is pleasureable to dwell upon the extremes of wealth. We do not wish to contemplate the extreme of poverty. The splendour of the palace, the glitter of the cavalcade, all the pomp & pageantry of life are familiar to enormous numbers of homely comfortable people: the slum, the garret & the gutter are strictly relegated by social arrangement & mental habit to their own peculiar limits. And so we think that the author is quite right in setting his definition of poverty at the outset.

Certainly it is not one which stirs the imagination. It is more like a clinical formula; purely material in character. Families whose total earnings, however judiciously expended, are not enough to supply them with the food necessary to sustain the human animal in ordinary physical efficiency are described as being in a state of 'primary' poverty. Families whose total earnings, though otherwise sufficient, are by reason of folly or misfortune, not enough for the above purpose are said to be in 'secondary' poverty. Surely no person however optimistic and contented with the present state of affairs would quarrel with such a definition. How are we to tell what amount of food constitutes 'enough'? Science both European & American – particularly the latter – provides ingenious and delicate calculations. The waste of tissue & strength in a human body varies with the exertions which are demanded of it; and if physical efficiency is to be maintained that waste must be made good in protein and fuel, fats & carbohydrates the former of which food-constituents makes muscle, & the latter warmth and energy.

The amounts have been accurately estimated, and a man should eat each day food which yields from 112 to 150 grains of protein & from 3000 to 4500 calories of fuel value, according to the degree of the work he performs. These estimates have also been checked by actual experiment upon unfortunate convicts and paupers whom it was possible to keep under close and continual observation.

The next step was to select a standard diet which would yield at the cheapest possible price the nutritive values required. We look to the workhouse for information. As the result of an inquiry concluded in 1897, the Local Government Board on the 25th of March 1901 issued a new general order regulating within certain clearly defined limits all workhouse diets in England and Wales. The estimate is therefore of the most modern character. It almost coincides in food value with the proportions considered necessary by the United States Board of Agriculture for the maintenance of physical efficiency. It is satisfactory to reflect that while the workhouse is scarcely a glutton's paradise, our paupers even from the chemical point of view have enough to eat. Moreover the regulations prescribe that not fewer than two boiled or roast meat dinners must be given weekly, and that the dietary shall be of a varied character. Nothing so luxurious would be of use to Mr Rowntree. He seeks to find the irreducible minimum; and by judicious selection of the *cheapest* foods specified by the Local Government Board for use in workhouses he frames a dietary which though more unappetising & less generous than that given to paupers satisfies the nutritive standard. He estimates that such a dietary would cost 3/– a week for adults and 2/3 a week for children, exclusive of the expense of cooking. Therefore families who cannot provide this necessary sum, or who, providing it do not select their food with like discrimination are *underfed* and come below the 'poverty' line.

And then Mr Rowntree comes to his figures. We will not attempt to follow him into the elaborate allowances and complicated calculations he has made in a conscientious effort to approximate to exact truth. They may be followed with profit and not without interest in his pages. It will be sufficient to state their features. The population of York was during the period covered by the inquiry 75,812. Of these 1957 persons belonged to families whose total income was under 18s. per week: 4,492 between 18/– & 21/–: 15,710 between 21/– & 30/–; & 24,595 over 30/–. The next remaining 29,058 are in calm water as domestic servants, in public institutions or belong to the 'servant keeping class'. Applying figures to the minimum food standard Mr Rowntree estimates that 7,230 persons in the city of York are in 'primary' poverty, & 13,072 in secondary poverty; that is to say that 20,302 persons equal to 43 per cent of the wage earning class and to 28 per cent of the total population were living in poverty, in that their food was of less than the nourishing value necessary to the maintenance of physical efficiency, and below the standard of that supplied to paupers.

That is a state of circumstances not upon the face of it very satisfactory: and this impression is not removed but rather deepened by a closer examination. The causes of 'secondary poverty' are too complicated, too subtle to be catalogued even by so patient an investigator: but 'Primary Poverty' is more tangible. There were found to be 7230 persons men, women & children in York living in the latter condition; and the immediate causes of their destitution can be grouped under six heads as follows:—

167 through the chief wage earner being out of work;
205 through irregularity of work;
370 through illness or old age of the chief wage earner;
1130 through his death; 1602 through the largeness of the family; and 3756 through the low wage earned by unskilled labour even when regularly employed.

But many of these causes are transient and accidental; and the 7230 persons shown by Mr Rowntree's inquiry to be in a state of primary poverty must not be supposed to live all their lives in that state, nor to represent the only persons in the population who pass through that state; but 'merely the section who happened to be in that state at the time the inquiry was made.' Therefore – and it is a big 'therefore' – any evils or privations which may accompany this condition really react upon a much larger class than are passing through it in any one period and are spread over a wider area.

'The life of the labourer' says our author 'is marked by five alternating periods of want and comparative plenty'; and thereupon he draws a neat and significant little diagram after the fashion of a meteorological chart – which shows the fluctuations of the labourer at different periods of his life above and below the 'poverty line'; shows that, and shows moreover that even in this, the lowest stratum of society, and between the narrow limits of being more or less underfed, there is yet room for all the agitating emotions, variations and vicissitudes which are experienced in a larger & more generous condition of life, and the obscure struggler is still hammered on the anvil tantalised with hopes hardly ever realised, haunted by apprehensions too often verified by time. He is born in poverty and in poverty he remains till he reaches 14 or 15 years of age and begins by his own earning to supplement the family income. There follows a period of comparative prosperity & perhaps of thrift culminating in marriage at, let us say, 23. This may endure till he has two or three children when the family sink again gradually below the poverty line, and these continue till at about 40 his children – hitherto dead weight – begin to earn and the family floats again to the surface. There they remain, again under the sky until the children marry and leave home (to repeat the evolution for themselves) while the old couple, if still united, both past work are again gradually and this time finally submerged and after a more or less protracted choking find oblivion – if nothing better – in the grave.

Leaving the question of food we come to housing. Our author provides carefully detailed information with diagrams and plans describing and illustrating all the various classes of dwellings occupied by the working people in York. Into all this space will not allow us to plunge. But the fact which emerges most plainly – and it is a very curious and startling fact – is that a certain proportion of the poor of every city require for their home, the most filthy, the most insanitary, most dilapidated and cheerless kennel which they can by great perseverance and constant search discover. Indeed they sometimes spend whole nights prowling about the city in the hopes of finding by great good fortune some den close to a slaughter house, where there is a hateful smell of offal or chemicals, where the roof is tumbling in, or where high factory buildings opposite shut out all sunlight and the air. These conditions, fatal to health and dangerous to life, are in themselves attractions. They are to the very poor what bracing climate, salubrious soil, convenient communication with the metropolis, conservatories and pleasant gardens are to the rich or well-to-do. Whatever persons with any power of choosing shrink from in a house, the poorest of the poor regard as high qualifications. Why? Not because they do not suffer. Even the jelly fish can feel pain; but because there will be less rent to pay; and less rent means more money to be spent on food, means more strength to work, perhaps the capacity to earn more wages; in fact, brings the star of hope once more above the horizon. Therefore whatever the healthy prosperous animal shuns, these poorest seek and welcome, and a house abandoned by all is treasure-trove to them.

And this raises the question of rent. The average rent among the working classes in York is one and sevenpence a week for the first room and about a shilling more for every other room, and as most of the houses contain three or four rooms, and nearly every family occupies one house, the rent paid by each household varies from between 2s 11d in the case of those whose weekly earnings average 10s. to seven shillings when the earnings average over seventy shillings. Now to pay seven shillings in rent out of seventy shillings income is a very different matter than to pay 2s. 11d. out of ten shillings income: and we see that whereas rent absorbs only about 10 per cent of the incomes of the prosperous working class, it absorbs 29 per cent of the total income of the very poor. There is a minimum standard of rent – about three shillings: there is no minimum standard of earnings: and hence the night prowling after a bargain; some miserable shelter with less to pay, a little more to eat, & a little larger chance of life bought not so much at the cost of the wretched inhabitant, for 'all living things tend to adapt themselves to their environment' – but at the common peril. Now the public health acts are quite sufficient if they be rigidly enforced, as they should be, to clear these insanitary dwellings; but where are their denizens to go?

Consider the peculiar case of these poor, and the consequences. Although the British Empire is so large, they cannot find room to live in it; although it is so magnificent, they would have had a better chance of happiness if they had been born cannibal islanders of the Southern seas; although its science is so profound, they would have been more healthy if they had been subjects of Hardicanute. But it would be absurd to trust to such arguments, impudent to urge them upon a Parliament busy with matters so many thousand miles from home. There is a more important consideration. Not the duty of a man to man, nor the doctrines that honest effort in a wealthy community should involve certain minimum rights, nor that this festering life at home makes world wide power a mockery, and defaces the image of God upon earth. It is a serious hindrance to recruiting.

Let it be granted that nations exist and peoples labour to produce armies with which they conquer other nations, and the nation best qualified to do this is of course the most highly civilised and the most deserving of honour. But supposing the common people shall be so stunted and deformed in body as to be unfit to fill the ranks the army corps may lack. And thus – strange as it may seem, eccentric, almost incredible to write – our Imperial reputation is actually involved in their condition.

It is because I desire to contribute something to the recruiting problem that I would ask for a patient consideration for what is written. Of course it is a vy great nuisance that statesmen should have their minds diverted from the issues of war, diplomacy or colonization, to have to attend to such parochial matters, and I do not wonder that clever people write to the *Times* to show how much better it would be if the same sort of British legislative assembly were instituted to deal with local affairs and to provide the money while the Imperial senate concerned itself only with the high & important question of how to spend it. But in the present circumstances of the British Constitution – for which no loyal conservative can have any respect – we are unfortunately compelled to burden these great men with all sorts of business which affects these small islands; and therefore for the present and until we can make some arrangement, more suited to the spirit of the age, they must in some degree be held responsible if the manhood of the British nation deteriorates so much that she can no longer provide a status of recruits fit to fall in line with our colonial brothers.

3

The Young Member–1902

(*See Main Volume Chapter I, pp. 33–47*)

Lord Hugh Cecil to WSC

28 December 1901   Hatfield

My dear Winston,

If you think moving about Lynch[1] wd interfere with your chance of getting called on the address, what do you think of seconding? That wd not seem 'putting yourself forward' & might be very briefly done; but it would amply redeem yr speech in the country. Percy might move – I want to wait to reply – & you might second. If you think this wd do I will write to P accordingly – I enclose on a separate paper my view of the right procedure.

As to the Imperialist & his Middle Party, I will send you in a week or so a full statement of my views about negotiations: shortly they amount to this – unconditional surrender is best but may be too costly to attain. But as to joining a Middle Party, that may be a very proper course when there is a Middle Party to join. Now there is none. And the (Imperialist's) best friends cannot deny that his aspirations are not always realised. So that whatever it might be wise to do if for instance you were offered office in a Rosebery administration, now it would be madness not to remain unequivocally Unionist.

That of course does not in the least preclude honest criticism of the Govt.

---

[1] Arthur Lynch (1861–1934), physician; elected as Irish Nationalist MP for Galway 1901 while serving with the Boers in S. Africa as Colonel of an Irish Brigade. In answer to a question from Earl Percy on 17 January 1902, Arthur Balfour announced that Lynch would be arrested as soon as he landed in Great Britain. Lynch was arrested on 11 June 1902, tried and convicted of high treason in January 1903. On 2 March 1903 Churchill, Ian Malcolm, and Lord Hugh Cecil voted with a minority of MP's to disfranchise Galway until the end of the session. Lynch was released after spending less than one year in gaol. WSC wrote to him on 9 February 1904: 'It was repellent to me that after the conclusion of the war you should be imprisoned as a felon for acts which however reprehensible involve in my opinion at any rate no moral turpitude: and I therefore am glad to be able to congratulate you upon regaining your liberty.'

But it means that it should be clear to the audience that you are criticizing not for the sake of finding fault (in the manner of Tommy Bowles) but because you believe the criticism to be a just one. It also means that the criticisms should be moderately & courteously expressed & that fair opportunities should be taken for criticizing the opposition including the Lib Imp tho' there too urbanity would be wise in view of possibilities of future co-operation.

In short as we agreed at Blenheim it is wise to play a waiting game & not to respond to the (Imperialist's) invitations until he has built himself a house to entertain you in. Now he has only a share in a dilapidated umbrella!

Of course all these tactical considerations ought to be subordinated to the duty of honestly pressing views you believe to be sound. As long as one is conscious of acting for a principle or cause I shouldn't bother myself about parties, Unionist or Middle, – they are only instruments after all. But in so far as tactics may rightly be considered I am sure the part of wisdom is to keep both feet securely planted on Unionist terra firma until there is equally firm land, Middle or other, to step on to.

Forgive this long & hortatory letter.

Yours ever

Hugh Cecil

Send back the Lynch paper for transmission to Percy if you decide to move.

Lord Hugh Cecil to WSC

30 December 1901   Hatfield

My dear Winston,

Many thanks for your note & Vincent's letter. I think there is force in what he says. But I don't much like an amendt to the address. The 'vote of censure' convention comes in: & the division becomes an absurdity.

I hope you have got my letter by this time:—it was sent to Blenheim & posted on Saturday 'to be forwarded'. I don't think our Lynch plan will be out of order on the ground you suggest. The procedure I have indicated closely resembles – nay is the same as – that followed – not at the outset of the Bradlaugh row[1] – but after he had been re-elected in 1881, when Sir S. Northcote[2] made a motion just like what I have sent you.

[1] Charles Bradlaugh (1834–91), atheist, founder of the National Secular Society, was five times elected MP for Northampton before being permitted to take the oath of allegiance and take his seat in the House of Commons.

[2] Henry Stafford Northcote (1818–87), Conservative leader in the House of Commons whom Lord Randolph described as fit only to lead 'the old men crooning over the fires at the Carlton'; Secretary of State for India 1866–8; Chancellor of the Exchequer 1874–80; suc-

What I am afraid of is a ruling of Speaker Peel's at the opening of the 1886 Parlt that a member was only fulfilling a legal duty in taking the oath, & he could not allow it to be questioned. This ended the Bradlaugh controversy. Then in a moment of imbecile sentiment (so like the H of C!) when Bradlaugh lay dying the motion (Wolff's) of 1880 was expunged from the Journals. These are obstacles. But I rely on the clear precedent of 1881. We can but try.

Yours ever
HUGH CECIL

WSC to Lord Rosebery
(*Rosebery Papers*)

17 January 1902   105 Mount Street

My dear Lord Rosebery,

I laughed inordinately at your speech today[1] and was reproved – with a good many other members of the H of Commons (who form a better audience, I think, than 'the noble lords') for doing so by the usher: but what pleased me enormously was your praise of Victor Lytton.[2] His success impresses me anew with what I often notice about myself – that I am never wrong. I was certain after talking with him for an hour that he had the necessary qualifications; and perhaps you remember my speaking to you on the subject at Mentmore. I don't think he will be a good *party* politician.

Sarum [Lord Salisbury] was vy pathetic and really ought not to be allowed.

From a consultation with the Speaker I gather good hopes of getting in on Monday at about 10 p.m.: or better still of getting leave to move the adjournment wh would give me the right to re-open the debate on the Tuesday. I shall be so unpopular thereafter that I propose to avail myself of the open weather – now returned thank Heaven! – to hunt for at least a week.

The Tory Party are in a vy brutal and bloody frame of mind.

Yours most sincerely
WINSTON S. CHURCHILL

---

ceeded Disraeli as leader of the House of Commons in 1876; First Lord of the Treasury 1885–6; Foreign Secretary 1886. 1st Earl of Iddesleigh 1885.

[1] In the debate on the King's Speech.

[2] Lord Lytton had seconded the Address in answer to the King's speech.

WSC to Lord Rosebery
(*Rosebery Papers*)

22 January 1902   105 Mount Street

My dear Lord Rosebery,

I will knock at your door at 11.15 on my way to the House (where Percy[1] is to speak on Persia), in the hopes of finding you disengaged for ten minutes. If you are busy, will you tell the servant to let me know?

Yours vy sincerely
WINSTON S. CHURCHILL

WSC to Lord Rosebery
(*Rosebery Papers*)

21 February 1902   105 Mount Street

My dear Lord Rosebery,

The enclosed letter[2] was written to me under the seal of friendship; but I feel that it might interest you and perhaps be of use in confirming your opinion, and I do not think I am prohibited from showing it in confidence *pro bono publico*.

But I gathered from Brodrick over whom I threw a fly that he had been shown the letter by Lord Roberts so that any phrase might be recognised and perhaps get my friend into trouble. Will you let me have it back when you have done with it.

The general has rather a sentimental & imaginative nature; but I am not certain that that is any hindrance to forming a true view of the S. African question.

So the breach is at last open![3]

Yours vy sincerely
WINSTON S. CHURCHILL

[1] Percy seconded an amendment to the address moved by a Liberal, John Walton, asking that adequate measures be taken to safeguard British interests in Persia. Both had travelled in that country and were concerned at the extension of Russian influence in northern Persia.

[2] See letter from Ian Hamilton immediately below.

[3] On February 21 *The Times* published a letter from Rosebery in which he wrote of 'this moment of definite separation' between himself and Campbell-Bannerman on Liberal policy, the war, and Home Rule.

Sir Ian Hamilton to WSC

EXTRACT

20 January 1902   Pretoria

Private

... It was kind of you to write me such a nice long letter, dated 23rd December, and to say that you will take in consideration my ideas with regard to Boer prisoners of war, with a view to putting them forward on some suitable opportunity. They are now volunteering in crowds to join the National Scouts out here, and of course if they are trusted to do that, by so much the more might they have been trusted to do garrison work for the Empire in outside countries, where they would have no temptation to go wrong. ...

I cannot tell you how strongly I feel that if we could incorporate these Boers into the Empire, we should be doing a vast deal more for the future of our race and language, than by assimilating a million Johannesburg Jews. They have first class natural ability, and their brains, having lain fallow for about 200 years, will like all virgin soil produce magnificent crops, as soon as cultivation is commenced.

At present we are trying to make the Boers come in and lick the boots of the Johannesburghers whom they thoroughly despise. If the Johannesburghers were good honest Englishmen who looked at things as we do, it would not so much matter, but then in that case the Johannesburghers would not ask for it. ...

Yours always

IAN HAMILTON

PS One point I do not like in Lord Rosebery's speech. It is the idea of approaching Kruger,[1] Leyds,[2] & Co. I should imagine it would give foreign diplomatists chances of interference but this you would know better than I can do. But what I know better than you can do is that neither Botha or De Wet[3] would accept such terms unless they were terms that they themselves would have accepted at first hand. ...

[1] Stephanus Johannes Paulus Kruger (1825–1904), ex-President of the Transvaal Republic exiled in Holland; Commandant-General of the South African Republic 1863; President of the Transvaal Republic 1882–1900.

[2] Willem Johannes Leyds (1859–1940), Envoy Extraordinary and Minister Plenipotentiary of the Transvaal Republic in Europe; appointed State Attorney of the Transvaal Republic in 1884 at the age of 25; State Secretary (principal adviser to Kruger) 1888–98.

[3] Christiaan Rudolf de Wet (1854–1922), farmer, politician and soldier, Chief Commandant of the Orange Free State 1900–2; Minister of Agriculture and Member of the Legislative Assembly for Vredefort 1907–10; participated in the rebellion of 1914, was sentenced to six years' imprisonment, but was released in December 1915.

WSC to Lord Rosebery
(*Rosebery Papers*)

2 March 1902   In the train

My dear Lord Rosebery,
We are all vy glad you will come on the 17th. It is thought that no one else should be invited and that we should keep you to our-selves, wh is selfish & greedy but probably more pleasant. I think however I must ask Westminster[1] who is young and enthusiastic, may have brains, and certainly would enjoy coming.

Yours vy sincerely
WINSTON S. C.

WSC to Lord Rosebery
(*Roseberv Papers*)

7 March 1902   105 Mount Street

My dear Lord Rosebery,
Two requests. First Hugh Cecil wants you to let the leaders of the Hooligans – (the Whip being still in Burmah, and 'the party' down with influenza), therefore three in all – come to lunch with you some day; and it will be vy kind of you to say 'Yes'.
Secondly: the Duchess of Marlborough has asked me to put this matter before you. Her father Mr Vanderbilt[2] has a horse running in the Derby,[3] and, as I understand it, this is a vy nervous horse; and it would be a real advantage, as well as a courtesy greatly appreciated, if you would allow it to stand in your stables at Epsom for the night before & the night after the race, so that it could walk straight on to the course and minimise crowds and confusion.
I don't know what you will think of this, but I am sure you will not mind being asked.
I had an encounter with 'CB' [Campbell-Bannerman] last night on the word 'efficiency', *vide The Times*; but it was vy good-humoured. He is always

[1] Hugh Richard Arthur Grosvenor, 2nd Duke of Westminster (1879–1953), who had served with WSC in the Boer War and who in February 1901 had married Constance Edwina, sister of George Cornwallis-West. He became a life-long friend of WSC.
[2] William Kissam Vanderbilt (1849–1920), grandson of Cornelius Vanderbilt.
[3] Ellsmere, a brown colt by Hanover out of Ella Pinkerton. He had won a handicap race at Maisons Laffite in October 1901 but was a non-runner in the Derby and in fact did not race again. The Derby was run on June 4 and won by Mr J. Gubbin's Ard Patrick.

in his place and works harder than any one on the front opposition bench; but what a vicious speech at the dinner![1]

Yours vy sincerely
WINSTON S. C.

Lord Rosebery to WSC

7 March 1902   38 Berkeley Square

My dear Winston,

Friday is the first day on which I expect to lunch again in London. But then I have to lunch at the City Liberal. Any day after that you like – when we can talk over Vanderbilt's wishes, as to wh I am full of good will.

You did well last night.

Yrs
AR

WSC to Lord Rosebery
(*Rosebery Papers*)

10 March 1902   Blenheim

My dear Lord Rosebery,

If you find Friday 21st a suitable day we should like to come and lunch then. You will be able to say whether or no when you dine with us – (please let this remind you) on Monday 17th at 8 oclock.

I think Glasgow is better than Liverpool and the end of it better than Chesterfield. 'Seven years lost to all social and human causes'.[2]

Neil [Primrose][3] is coming over here to shoot tomorrow. Alas Poor Methuen![4]

Yours vy sincerely
WINSTON S. C.

[1] In a speech at the National Liberal Club on March 5 Campbell-Bannerman had warned the Liberal Imperialists against 'associating themselves in hostility to the central organisation of the party'. The speech was described by *The Times* as 'a declaration of war against Lord Rosebery'.

[2] At Glasgow on March 7 Rosebery elaborated on the differences between the Liberal League and the official Liberal Opposition.

[3] Neil James Archibald Primrose (1882–1917), 2nd son of 5th Earl of Rosebery, Liberal MP for Wisbech, 1910–17; Parliamentary Under-Secretary to Foreign Office 1915; Parliamentary Military Secretary to Ministry of Munitions 1916; Parliamentary Secretary to Treasury 1916–17; PC 1917; married Victoria Alice Louise Stanley, only daughter of 17th Earl of Derby, in 1915; killed in action Western Front, November 1917.

[4] Paul Sanford Methuen (1845–1932), Commander, 1st Division 1st Army Corps, South Africa 1899–1902; Major-General 1890; C-in-C Eastern Command 1903–8; GOC-in-C South Africa 1907–9; Governor of Natal 1909, Malta 1915–19; Field-Marshal 1911; GCB 1902; GCMG 1919; GCVO 1910. On March 7 1902 the Boers defeated a column under his command. He was wounded and taken prisoner.

Sir Ian Hamilton to WSC

23 March 1902   Pretoria
Private & Personal

My dear Winston,

I have sent you my views at length, shorthand, I do not do myself much
justice by that method but work is heavy & I could not otherwise write you
at all. I am entirely satisfied with your action regarding my last letter &
you may either treat this one likewise, or keep it to yourself, just as you
think proper – I can't write to Cabinet Ministers for the only one I know
well is Brodrick and although I like him very much as a private individual,
I am entirely out of sympathy with him as a S of S. He would not understand me & I could only do myself harm without doing the Cause I have at
heart any good.

As regards yourself: Lord K is rather super-human in some respects. He
disliked you as a soldier; as an MP or Pressman he would look on you
without any sort of prejudice. You may, I know, rely absolutely on receiving
no petty annoyance at his hands.

On the other hand I would advise you *not* to come out now. The Press
censorship is severe & would be intolerable to you.

Facilities for going about are also much restricted. If you *do* come get letters
from Chamberlain to K & Milner just as if you had never been with them
before & you will be then as well off as anyone but that is not saying much
& I advise you put off until the War is over.

Yours ever
IAN HAMILTON

PS Lord R [Rosebery] did *not* show my last to Mr Brodrick, as you fancied
he must have done.

IAN H

Sir Ian Hamilton to WSC

EXTRACT

30 March 1902   Pretoria
Private

My dear Winston,

I wish rather I had not written you my last letter for it forces me to write
you another, as I do not wish to give a false impression if I can help it.

Even writing you now I must be cautious, for what Reitz[1] thinks at the present date may be much modified after his talk with His Honour Mr Steyn.[2] I will only remark then that these civilians do not seem to hold identical views with Botha. Thus they do not attach as much importance as I thought they did to an amnesty to rebels, as they profess certitude that the King would exercise his prerogative of mercy at the Coronation and say that even if he did not do so, no political party ever formed in England could keep large numbers of men indefinitely imprisoned or banished for mere political crimes. This has always been my own theory as you very well know! Then again they seem fairly confident that there will be no *impasse* over the rebuilding of farms questions [*sic*]. They expect to get a joint commission to assess damages.

Per Contra they do seem bent upon extracting some definite promise of representative Government within some definite period, subject of course to complete quiescence of country during the interregnum. They recognise that there must be an interregnum – I think the thing might be worked on a 3 years basis. But they mean to try and insist on something definite. They dislike Lord Milner & would prefer the conference without him, like Hamlet & the Play, but being clever men they recognise the impracticability of their desire. I believe in Peace this time if a sharp eye is kept on the conference.

The loyalists would be enchanted if it fell through, for one more year of this would eliminate the Boer factor altogether. But England, whose army is entangled and who pays the piper, should keep a keen look out & see fair play at the Pow Wow. . . .

. . . Please, dear Winston, justify my high opinion of your discretion regarding this letter. Let such facts as I give you serve as a guide to your steps, &, if you like to those of one or two intimate – & reliable friends who do not talk of *how* they hear things – Nothing more.

Yours ever

IAN HAMILTON

[1] Francis William Reitz (1844–1934), barrister and judge; State Secretary, Transvaal Republic 1898–1902; President of the Orange Free State 1889–95; President of the Senate, Union of South Africa, 1910–29.

[2] Marthinus Theunis Steyn (1857–1916), lawyer and farmer; President of the Orange Free State 1896–1902; Judge of the High Court, Orange Free State 1889–96; Vice-President of the South African National Convention 1908–9.

Sir Ian Hamilton to WSC

EXTRACT

5 April 1902   Pretoria

... I enclose you, very privately, a letter I have just received from a friend,
who shall be nameless. You will observe that it more than substantiates my
suspicions, as to the views held by Lord Milner. It is clear to me that the
High Commissioner wishes to bite off more than he can chew, in planning
to exercise despotic control over a vast continent, which two late republics,
plus the Cape Colony, certainly is.

If the Conference gets into difficulties about the time you receive this
letter, you will have a very shrewd idea of one of the reasons. . . .[1]

[PS] After thinking it over more carefully I think I have no right to send
you a copy of this letter. Some day I may show it to you. Meanwhile treat
my view of Milner's attitude as merely an opinion unsupported. . . .

Sir Michael Hicks-Beach to WSC

16 April 1902   11 Downing Street

My dear Churchill,

We may have got to evening Wednesday sittings by May 14th – and if so,
I can't be certain of being able to get away from H of C. But, barring that,
I shall be very happy to dine with you at the Marlborough on that evening –
I suppose about 8.15, as usual.

Yours sincerely
M. HICKS-BEACH

Sir Edward Hamilton[2] to WSC

20 April 1902   Holdenby House
                                                  Northampton

My dear Winston,

I have never had a moment this week to write to you, as I have intended
doing. Please accept the excuse.

I want to congratulate you on your speech last Monday. It was excellent,

---

[1] Hamilton wrote across these paragraphs: 'Strictly private. Only for Winston Churchill.
Ian H.' The Boers were about to begin negotiating a peace settlement.

[2] Edward Walter Hamilton (1847–1908), Joint Permanent Financial Secretary and joint
Permanent Secretary to the Treasury 1902–07; Assistant Financial Secretary 1892; Assistant
Secretary 1894; Permanent Financial Secretary 1902. A former private secretary and intimate
confidante of Mr Gladstone; eldest son of Walter Kerr Hamilton, Bishop of Salisbury. KCB
1894; KCVO 1901; GCB 1906; PC 1908.

& did you great credit.[1] It was the best success you have had & I hope it will be an encouragement to you to pursue the subject of finance. Nothing is more important. & there are very few who have got the power to grapple with it.

Please remember that the doors of the Treasury are always open to you. I shall be delighted at all times to render you any assistance, for your father's sake as well as your own.

Yours sincerely
E. HAMILTON

WSC to James Dyson

26 April 1902   105 Mount Street

[Copy]

Dear Sir,

In reply to the Resolution you have forwarded from 21 Radical Clubs at Oldham respecting the Corn Tax and the Education Bill, I beg to inform you that I shall support the Government policy in both matters. In the former because it is the most convenient method of raising the money for purposes of which the electorate have approved, and because unless the whole community bear a share in the burden of taxation, what check is there upon expenditure? In the latter because I believe that the present Education Bill will without wasting or destroying the existing machinery go a long way towards simplification and efficiency.[2]

Yours faithfully
WINSTON S. CHURCHILL

*   *   *   *   *

The following correspondence was published in the *Oldham Evening Chronicle* on May 13.

John Harrison to the Editor, the Oldham Evening Chronicle

12 May 1902   51 London Road
                                                          Oldham

Sir,

Will you please publish the following correspondence with our junior MP relative to vaccination and smallpox, and inoculation for enteric fever.

Yours &c
JOHN HARRISON

[1] On April 14, during the Budget debate, WSC had protested against the 'shocking lack of Cabinet control' over expenditure.

[2] In his Budget speech on April 14 Hicks-Beach announced a registration duty on corn and flour – a duty abolished in 1869. The 'Corn Tax' was inevitably denounced as a tax on the food of the people. Radicals – and non-conformists – opposed the Education Bill largely because it placed the cost of sectarian schools on the rates.

John Harrison to WSC

21 April 1902   Oldham

Sir,

In your address at Royton a short time ago you stated that it was your intention to be re-vaccinated in order to be protected against the epidemic of smallpox then raging. I beg to ask if you have submitted to the operation since you made reference of your intention to secure the supposed advantages of the vaccine rite. All epidemics and endemics are due to insanitary conditions. There can be no mistake about it. Their first causes, if properly traced, would show that they were owing either to personal uncleanliness, to a vitiated atmosphere, to impurities in the water supply, to the cesspool nuisance, defective drainage, or to some of their lineage, or to overcrowding where you find the breeding ground for original specimens. Cleanse the house, ventilate it, and stop overcrowding and you will have no smallpox. We maintain that there is no scientific support for vaccination – that it affords no protection against smallpox. It has no power apparently over epidemics. What a lesson is presented by London and Glasgow of its uselessness! Further it would be interesting to know why you objected to inoculation with anti-toxin serum against enteric fever before leaving this country for South Africa? What a commentary upon the wretched business is the shocking mortality from enteric fever now raging among our brave soldiers in South Africa, all of whom were 'protected' before leaving this country! How many of our soldiers have had their health and constitutions ruined by this superstitious blood-poisoning we shall probably never know. This inoculation business is a very serious matter. It is not only that the blood of our children is being poisoned as the result of this fashionable craze, but in order to keep up a supply of these multitudinous serums thousands of animals are being lingeringly tortured.

Yours sincerely

JOHN HARRISON

WSC to John Harrison

25 April 1902   105 Mount Street

Dear sir,

In answer to your interesting letter of the 21st, and the questions it contains. I beg to inform you that I have most certainly been re-vaccinated without any evil consequences attending the operation, and with very satisfactory and comfortable results to my peace of mind both as regards myself and the community in general, during a time when the terrible scourge of smallpox is abroad in the land.

Yours very truly

WINSTON S. CHURCHILL

John Harrison to WSC

29 April 1902   Oldham

Sir,

Thanks for your answer to my first question, but I beg to remind you that you have not answered my second question. As you are well known to be a man of independent mind, of straightforwardness, and of having the courage to avow your convictions, I hope you will oblige me in this matter. It seems to me that you ought to have the same satisfaction, the same comfortable results to your peace of mind, that you did not submit to be inoculated to prevent enteric fever, which has proved such a terrible scourge in South Africa.

Yours, &c
JOHN HARRISON

H. W. Carr-Gomm[1] to John Harrison

5 May 1902   105 Mount Street

Sir,

In reply to your letter, I am desired by Mr Winston Churchill to say that in comparing inoculations to prevent enteric fever with vaccination as a safeguard from smallpox, it is his opinion that the medical evidence is much less weighty; the experience much more scanty; the risks of infection far less in the former inoculation than in the latter.

I am, Sir, yours faithfully
H. W. CARR-GOMM

Sir H. Campbell-Bannerman to WSC

15 May 1902   6 Grosvenor Place

Dear Mr Churchill,

It will give me great pleasure to dine with you & your friends on Thursday the 29th.

Yours vy truly
H. CAMPBELL-BANNERMAN

---

[1] Hubert William Culling Carr-Gomm (1877–1939), Liberal MP, Rotherhithe Division of Southwark 1906–18; Assistant Private Secretary to Sir Henry Campbell-Bannerman, 1906–8.

John Morley to WSC

25 May 1902   Hawarden
                                                         Chester

Your telegram finds me at the Mecca of the economist. I wish I could have come, but I don't leave here until later in the week. It is most kind of you to ask me.

Ever yours sincerely
JOHN MORLEY

Mrs Humphry Ward[1] to WSC

26 May 1902   Stocks
                                                         Tring

Dear Mr Winston Churchill,
    Perhaps you will remember that we met at luncheon at Mentmore last August, and that you said you would come & see me in town? I have been in the country or abroad ever since, but now I am to be a few weeks in London, & it would be very pleasant to see you. Are you by happy chance disengaged for dinner on Friday June 5th at 8.15? And if so would you dine with us then – at 25 Grosvenor Place? I hope President Roosevelt's sister, Mrs Douglas Robinson may be with us; and my son who has followed on your traces in the Sudan & in India would be particularly glad to make your acquaintance. I hope we may find you free. Could you send a line to Grosvenor Place, by tonight's post?

Yours very truly
MARY A. WARD

John Morley to WSC

29 May 1902   57 Elm Park Gardens

I will dine with you on Monday next, June 2, with all the pleasure in life.

Yours
JOHN MORLEY

---

[1] Mary Augusta Ward (1851–1920), novelist best known for her novel *Robert Elsmere*, 1888, an attack on evangelical Christianity. She was a niece of Matthew Arnold, and a grand-daughter of Thomas Arnold of Rugby.

James M. Tusby to WSC

29 May 1902   23 Warwick Gardens

Dear Sir,

You will probably remember my asking you in the Lobby at the House the other night if you would undertake to write a description of the Coronation for the *World*. I have since been in communication with the Editor and I find that you were right in supposing that the sum you mentioned would be too high for the *World*. The Editor, in fact, cables that he thinks One Hundred Pounds would be a fair honorarium for the work, relying apparently on the fact that this is a larger amount than he paid one of the most prominent literary men in England to describe the Jubilee Procession.

I am however very unwilling to abandon the hope that the *World* may have the advantage of your work and name, and if you were disposed to come, to any extent, to meet the *World* I should be glad to make a further proposal. I may say that my own impression is that £200, is the limit to which they might be induced to go, and if I could make them a final offer of that amount I should get an answer immediately one way or the other.

As we, in common with the other leading New York papers will have representatives of our own in the Abbey, it is not a question of getting facilities that is in point.

Awaiting the favour of a reply and thanking you for your courtesy. I am,

Yours Very Truly

JAMES M. TUSBY

*   *   *   *   *

In July 1902 a Select Committee on Expenditure was appointed. In the House of Commons on 24 April 1902 WSC had asked A. J. Balfour whether the Government would consent to the appointment of a Select Committee 'to consider and report whether National Expenditure cannot be diminished without injury to the public service, and whether the money voted cannot be apportioned to better advantage than at present'. Balfour replied that the terms were too general to make an enquiry possible or fruitful. In answer to a second attempt to raise the matter Balfour replied on May 5 that he could see no advantage in the appointment of such a Committee. In the debate on the Finance Bill seven days later WSC charged the Government with allowing the National Expenditure to 'get beyond the points of prudence and reason'. After the following letters between WSC and Balfour had been published in *The Times*, a decision was taken, against Treasury advice, to set up a committee of inquiry.

WSC to A. J. Balfour

8 May 1902   105 Mount Street

Dear Mr Balfour,

I shall not conceal my disappointment at your answer as to an inquiry into the distribution of public expenditure.

I heard with surprise that the Cabinet have the leisure to make any detailed survey of the Estimates and to weigh and examine departmental projects which are not of first magnitude. It did not indeed seem possible that in the comparatively short time available for their deliberations supervision other than of a rough and ready character could have been exercised over the administrative sphere; and in regard to policy, while there are main objects upon which the opinion of the party is in full agreement with the Government, yet it would seem that there must also be items which involve considerable sums of money which belong partly to the province of policy and partly to that of administration, concerning which it is perfectly legitimate for their supporters in the House of Commons to adopt an independent position.

It may be quite true that the Cabinet is the only body which can control and apportion; but the Cabinet however efficient, must be governed strongly in its action by the varying personal influence of individual Ministers and by the fortuitous course of events. It would therefore seem desirable that from time to time the outlay sanctioned by Cabinets should be retrospectively examined in order that disproportionate investments may be detected and readjustment made if necessary. If this be true of ordinary periods, with how much greater force does it apply now; for the sudden immense increase in expenditure may not only have increased the unavoidable percentage of waste, but has certainly made that percentage operative over a much larger area. Apart from these considerations it would seem that an augmentation of nearly 40 per cent in national expenditure within the course of a few years is a fact which in itself calls for scrutiny and reflection. This revision – at once healthy and prudent – would under ordinary circumstances have been made by another political party. That the Government is now enjoying a second term of office devolves the responsibility with added weight upon them.

The character and composition of the committee and even its terms of reference are not of first consequence; but it appears to be of great and vital importance, in these days when so much pressure of all kinds and from all quarters is put upon the Government to incur fresh liabilities, that there should be some counter influence such as a Parliamentary inquiry would afford.

Trusting that you will not hold me presumptuous to address you upon this grave matter, fraught as I believe it with supreme consequences to the Conservative party.

Believe me yours sincerely
WINSTON S. CHURCHILL

A. J. Balfour to WSC

15 May 1902   10 Downing Street

Dear Winston Churchill,

I cannot agree with you that the 'character and composition, and even the terms of reference' of any Committee appointed to enquire into expenditure are 'not of the first importance'. On the contrary, the difference between us would, as it seems to me, be narrowed down to much more definite issues if I understood precisely what it was that your proposed Committee is intended to effect, and how it is intended to effect it.

The main elements in the growth of expenditure during the last seven years have been in the Army and the Navy. Is your proposed Committee to discuss whether we have too large an Army or too large a Navy? If so, the problem before them would touch every aspect of our relations with Foreign Countries and with our Colonies, would involve an examination into the military position of India and into the military and maritime strategy which we should have to follow should war break out with any Power or combination of Powers. This is not a task which could, in my opinion, properly be thrown upon any Committee outside the Government itself.

An even stronger case can be made out against entrusting to a Committee the task of forming an estimate of the comparative importance of different branches of expenditure. Next in magnitude to the increase in Army and Navy Estimates is the increase in the Estimates for Education. Now it may be that the money spent on Education is not spent to the best advantage. But a Committee which could give any valuable opinion on such a point, would have to be very differently composed from a Committee fitted to deal with Imperial Defence or Army and Navy Expenditure, and neither one Committee nor the other would be qualified to determine whether, if economies are necessary, they had best be effected by diminishing expenditure on armaments for the sake of Education, or expenditure on Education for the sake of armaments.

It may be, however, that the Committee you desire is not to discuss policy but to check waste, if waste there be. To this I have no objection in principle. On the contrary, when introducing the new rules, I expressed on behalf of the Government a desire for some reform of our parliamentary machinery for the purpose of effecting this object: and I have placed on the paper a motion for a Select Committee to advise as to the best way of carrying it out. But I cannot persuade myself that it is likely to result in large or important economies: and for this reason – the chief danger to economical administration under our modern system (next to House of Commons pressure) arises not so much from the addition to the estimates of new items which are unnecessary, as from the retention of old ones whose necessity has disappeared. Treasury control is from the nature of the case more effective in preventing the first evil than the second. But on the other hand the second is much more likely to beset us in a period of 'surpluses', diminishing taxation and diminishing departmental work, than at a moment like the present when the labours thrown upon every department by legislation or by the growth of population and Empire are increasing, and when, unhappily, taxation and expenditure are increasing with them. The path of a Minister making financial demands upon the Chancellor of the Exchequer and the Cabinet at such a time is not a smooth one. It is his interest, and the interest of his Department, to make economies wherever they are possible, as some counterpoise to the new charges proposed to be thrown upon the Exchequer, and he has the strongest inducement to economical administration. I suspect that whatever other discoveries might be made by a Committee enquiring into the expenditure of such Offices as (for example) the Foreign Office or the Local Government Board, it would probably find that these were understaffed rather than the reverse, and that official administration was more thriftily conducted at the present time than it was twenty or thirty years ago: in other words, that the cost of the Departments has not grown in proportion to their work.

I gather, however, that your scheme is more ambitious in its character. You appear to suppose that 'a parliamentary enquiry would provide a counter influence to the pressure of all kinds and from all quarters which is put upon the Government to incur fresh liabilities'. I fear this is an illusion. The quarters from which this pressure now comes are parliamentary quarters, and there is no reason to believe, either from experience or theory, that a Committee of the House ranging over the whole field of imperial and domestic policy would behave differently from the House itself. A Government has stronger motives for desiring economy than any Committee. It has a corporate responsibility to which no Committee, drawn from different political parties, and existing as a unity only during its occasional hours of meeting, can make pretence. A Committee would gain no popularity from the diminution of our financial burden – and suffer no inconvenience from its increase. If in accordance with their advice national armaments were cut down below the point of safety, it is not they who would be attacked in case of disaster, but the Government. If on the other hand, (as is at least as probable) they advised an inflation of military or other expenditure, it is not they who would have to devise new taxation: nor would they have to defend it. Cabinet control is doubtless imperfect: ministerial responsibility is not everything in practice which it is sometimes represented to be in theory. But on the whole it will be found that the control would not be more effective if shared with a Committee, and that the responsibility must be weakened if you endeavour to divide it. Legitimate therefore as is the misgiving with which we may contemplate the rapid growth in our annual estimates, I cannot believe that the work of the nation would be better done if your plan were adopted. I do not even believe that it would be done more cheaply.

Yrs sinly
ARTHUR JAMES BALFOUR

Memorandum by WSC

1902

1. The task assigned to the Select Committee was not to pronounce upon past expenditure but to invent, if it were necessary, new machinery whereby not so much the control of the Treasury nor the control of the Cabinet but rather the control of the House of Commons itself could be made better and stronger as regards the expenditure of the future.

2. Financial control by Parliament must be enforced in two ways: – a. Audit of accounts; b. examination of estimates. –

Audit of Accounts. – The existing machinery for this is very good and powerful. First there is the Comptroller or Auditor-General, a Parliamentary officer almost as independent of the Executive as a judge, absolutely independent of the departments whose accounts he audits, with a permanent office and an extensive highly-trained staff who not only scrutinise the accounts but have regular access to the departments while they are in preparation. Thus enabled evenly and thoroughly to survey as an auditor the whole field of expenditure, the Comptroller & Auditor-General is in a position to give to the Public Accounts Committee accurate information on any point in the Accounts, and to direct their attention to any irregularity. The matter now passes into the hands of the Committee. They are usually a strong Committee; there is considerable desire among members to serve: a member of the Opposition is by practice appointed Chairman. Their proceedings are businesslike and devoid of party feeling. Accurate knowledge collected by a trained official is at their disposal, and may, if so desired, be checked or extended by the examination of witnesses or the production of documents. With all these advantages, the Public Accounts Committee make authoritative reports which the House of Commons may act upon or ignore as is decided. Indeed the only broken link would appear to be the lack of any definite day or days allocated in Supply to the consideration of their reports.

3.   Contrast all this with the *Examination of Estimates* by the House of Commons. –

The colour of the discussions is nearly always partisan, their nature frequently factious or obstructive; and the time available altogether insufficient. Few questions are discussed with accurate knowledge; hardly one is settled on its merits. 670 members, circumstanced as they are, influenced above all by party ties, occupied with all manner of other work and interests, cannot pretend that by strolling in and out of the chamber during the 22 supply days they achieve any real examination of the immense and complex estimates now annually presented; and even so could not challenge a single sixpence in the bill without at the same time voting for Home Rule or other ideas from which they might equally recoil. The fact is well known that in practice the Estimates are used by the House not for the purpose of financial scrutiny but simply to provide a series of convenient and useful opportunities for the discussion of all kinds of questions of policy and for obtaining Parliamentary decisions upon them.

4.   What is wanted therefore is to make the examination of Estimates so far as possible as real and thorough as the audit of accounts, and I suggest that this will be achieved if and in so far as the machinery for auditing accounts can be applied to the examination of Estimates. But considerable limitations are evidently necessary. Accounts are matters of arithmetic and may be settled by rule; Estimates are matters of opinion, often mixed up with policy. Party feelings banished in the one case might return with renewed vigour in the other. No Cabinet is likely to create a committee for the purpose of discussing at large whatever questions of high policy might take their fancy; and Parliament would certainly not endow them with the power of deciding upon them. If estimates had to pass a committee before being presented to Parliament, the responsibility of the Minister framing them would be greatly diminished if not destroyed and the work of the

Treasury hampered. Time would not allow a committee to examine them properly between the date of their completion and the date of their presentation to Parliament or between the date of their presentation and the time when they might be considered by the House of Commons; and it is by no means certain that the tendency of such arrangements, even if practicable, would be towards economy.

5. Let me now indicate the limitations which the foregoing difficulties impose. –

Public expenditure may be considered in three aspects: policy, merit, and audit. To take a hypothetical instance: whether the standard of professional skill in the Royal Army Medical Corps should be improved or not is *Policy;* whether this result should be sought by building a special hospital for army surgeons, or whether arrangements should be made with existing civil hospitals to afford them opportunities of practice and study; whether in the one case the contracts for the hospital are the best that can be made, or in the other the arrangements are economical and efficient – all this may be called *Merit;* and whether in fact the money provided is expended faithfully and with proper authority is *Audit.* In other words – What should be done is a question of *policy:* in what way it should be done is a question of *merit:* and whether it is honestly done is a question of *audit.*[1]

Now Policy is the province of the Cabinet and of the House of Commons itself, and no interference by a committee is possible or necessary. Audit has, as I have said, been delegated by the House of Commons with satisfactory results to the Public Accounts Committee and the Comptroller & Auditor-General. But over the merit of expenditure no real Parliamentary control at present exists; and an immense number of items involving in the aggregate vast sums of money, because they are too small for the Cabinet, too complicated for the House of Commons and too large for the Public Accounts Committee are settled entirely by officials without any external check. Here then is the lacuna bounded on the one hand by questions of policy decided by the cabinet and ratified by Parliament, and on the other by questions reserved for auditors and accountants across which the new network needs to be spread. And it is worth noting – as an instance of the adaptable and elastic nature of Parliamentary institutions – that the Public Accounts Committee and the Comptroller & Auditor-General have latterly been more and more inclined to stretch out almost instinctively beyond the region of simple audit and to discuss questions on their merits.

6. The first limitation is therefore the restriction of a committee on estimates to the 'merit' or 'value for money' aspect of expenditure and their

[1] The argument and phraseology of this paragraph were repeated by WSC in a speech in the House of Commons on 26 July 1905.

exclusion from matters which have been decided by the Cabinet. Next as to time: how long would a committee have to sit to consider the merit of estimates. I say frankly it would be a task quite beyond any committee; but it is not a task beyond the scope of machinery which exists or could be devised within the Audit Department, and if the estimates were examined in the Comptroller & Auditor-General's office by officials trained for that very purpose the Parliamentary Committee could have their attention directed to the tender points and would not have to toil through the whole mass. Then comes the question of ministerial responsibility which seems to require that once the Estimates have been thrashed out among the ministers themselves nothing should stand between them and the decision of Parliament. Therefore a committee on estimates must deal with the Estimates after they have been presented to and perhaps voted by Parliament. Would that be any use? Certainly, because first nearly all expenditure is recurring expenditure and information as to the estimates of the previous year would nearly always be applicable to the current year; and secondly because a realisation of the extreme probability that departmental extravagance would be exposed and would form the subject of well informed Parliamentary discussion would operate as a powerful incentive to economy.

7.   Bearing all this in mind, I suggest the following scheme for applying to the Examination of Estimates similar machinery to that employed in the Audit of Accounts. –

a.   The Public Accounts Committee shall be enlarged to 25 members, called the Public Finance Committee, and sub-divided into two sub-committees called respectively 'The Accounts Committee' and 'The Estimates Committee.' The Comptroller & Auditor-General's Department shall be divided into two Branches: the Estimates Branch under an officer called the Comptroller; and the Accounts Branch under an officer called the Auditor.

b.   'The Accounts Committee' shall consist of 15 members, 5 of whom shall also belong to the Estimates Committee; and seven shall constitute a quorum. Its duty shall be that of the present Public Accounts Committee but strictly limited to questions of audit. It shall be guided and served by the officer called the Auditor, and shall report to Parliament upon the accounts of the current year at convenient intervals.

c.   'The Estimates Committee' shall be similarly constituted. Its duty shall be to hold a kind of post-mortem examination upon the Merit of the Estimates after they have been presented to and (perhaps) voted by the House of Commons, and to report thereupon; and for this purpose it shall be guided and served by the officer called the Comptroller, supplied by him with all requisite information, and shall have power to examine witnesses and to call for papers always providing that the Comptroller & Auditor-General shall take care that no military or naval information or papers be divulged contrary to the public interest or in regard to specific matters of policy which have been or may be at the time under the consideration of the Cabinet.

The Estimates Committee shall report to Parliament as early as possible in each session upon the Estimates voted *in the previous year*, drawing attention to any waste or wasteful practice they may have discovered, and not less than two days in supply shall be allocated to the consideration of their reports.

8.   Such a system – and no doubt it is capable of improvements – would not lessen the control of the House of Commons but would increase it by supplying accurate knowledge of the Estimates derived from independent and experienced sources. So far from diminishing ministerial responsibility it would rather accentuate it by the anticipation of a more severe ordeal. It avoids all temporal difficulties. It does not clash with Treasury control. It would safeguard military and naval secrets and exclude matters of policy, for the Comptroller & Auditor-General while charged to aid to his utmost the Audit and Estimates Committees in their investigations would equally be charged by Parliament not to reveal matters outside the assigned limits of these investigations: and in regard to this he would, though essentially a Parliamentary officer, be easily accessible to ministers who would specify what were official secrets and matters of cabinet policy: and if, on the other hand, the committee were dissatisfied with a refusal to supply information on any point they would report the matter to the House of Commons accordingly and a Parliamentary decision would follow.

The labour imposed upon the Committees would neither be too severe nor disproportioned to the time at their disposal, for they would only weigh and pronounce upon the information collected for them by the Comptroller and the Auditor. Lastly, the creation of the Finance Committee, embracing as it would twenty-five selected members who from their positions on either the Accounts or Estimates Committees or on both would have a close and accurate knowledge of questions relating to estimates, and also from the fact of their selection would probably be interested and versed in finance, could not fail – quite apart from the reports of the Committees – to strengthen in the House of Commons those influences which make for thrifty and efficient administration.

WSC to Lord Rosebery
(*Rosebery Papers*)

18 May 1902   Blenheim

My dear Lord Rosebery,

Please consider June 11th definitely fixed for our dinner. I send you enclosed Ian Hamilton's letter, wh I will ask you for at the Durdans on Sunday.

Josephus made a fine speech at Birmingham; but was unnecessarily aggressive[1]; and I hope he will not think it desirable to 'run up another bill, just as big as that of the Boer War' just to impress the foreigners – at present at any rate.

Yours most sincerely
WINSTON S. CHURCHILL

Lord Rosebery to WSC

1 June 1902   The Durdans

My dear Winston,

Alas! Alas! I am bidden to the American Ambassador to dinner on June 11 'to meet the King and Queen', and I fear that that must be considered as a command. I cannot therefore dine with you, and though I rend my garments I have no option.

Yrs
AR

WSC to the Editor, The Times[2]

1 June 1902   105 Mount Street

Sir,

Although it is still a good two months before the silly season, 'J. C. B.' and his bacilli are again in the field. Now from the point of view of Harris tweeds this is a most opportune occurrence; for, as it happens, there is to be a sale of those homespuns at Stafford-house upon the 9th of the month, and, no doubt, they will profit from his abuse not less upon this occasion than during the past year. But, putting aside for a moment the material advantage and advertisement to the tweeds, of which 'J. C. B.' is the unwilling and the

---

[1] In a vigorous vindication of the Government on 16 May, Joseph Chamberlain repudiated Rosebery's charge that the Unionists' legislative record was a sterile one.
[2] Published on June 2.

unworthy cause, I feel bound to repeat my former protest against his practice of making malicious attacks upon an industry, and lavishing personalities upon individuals, while himself remaining all the time anonymous. Such conduct, Sir, would merit severe censure under ordinary circumstances; but in this case it is infected with a peculiar degree of evil. It may, perhaps, have occurred to many of your readers that the letters 'J. C. B.' are the initials of Sir James Crichton Browne. To strike living persons from under the cover of anonymity is already sufficiently questionable; but what shall we say when the correspondent, not content with sheltering in obscurity, deliberately – for it cannot be a coincidence – assumes the initials of a distinguished man, well known alike in science and in literature? I have not the pleasure of the acquaintance of Sir James Crichton Browne, but I can well imagine how keen must be his own annoyance and the embarrassment of his friends when the name he has elevated and adorned is, as it were, dragged in the mire through the quackery and pretensions of some imposter.

It is easy to understand – indeed, it is impossible not to sympathize with – the feelings of modesty and reserve which cause scientific genius to shrink from publicity of all kinds. But this matter has now gone too far. It has even been openly stated in an evening newspaper – not infrequently well informed – that 'J. C. B.' is, in fact, Sir James Crichton Browne; and I therefore venture to appeal with all respect to that learned and vivacious person, in the interests of the reputation he has achieved, in the name of his many admirers, and for the sake of the truth, forthwith and without compunction to repudiate the busybody who is masquerading in his livery.

I have the honour to be, Sir, your obedient humble servant
WINSTON S. CHURCHILL

J. C. B. to the Editor, The Times

3 June 1902   London

Sir,

In a letter which appeared in *The Times* of September 17 last Mr Winston Churchill expressed his determination to withdraw from the 'wrangle' as to Harris tweed upon which, as I pointed out at the time, he had entered uninvited and without any special qualifications to warrant his intrusion. I regarded him, therefore, as again a fugitive correspondent. But during these nine months he has recovered his stomach for fighting, and now re-enters the field with his usual arrogance. He knows really nothing about Harris tweed or its manufacture, and could not, I am sure, distinguish bacteria from shorthand; but he must be in evidence, and so professes to

be much exercised over my anonymity, and waxes witty, as he fancies, in his
attempts to draw me. But I am not to be unearthed by mere yelping. My
anonymity is no business of his, and has no bearing on the points at issue,
for the original indictment against Harris tweed was launched not on my
authority, but on that of Mr Newlands, Inspector of Factories for the North
of Scotland, and until Mr Winston Churchill can 'rail from off' page 339
of the report of the Chief Inspector of Factories and Workshops published
last year the passage describing the conditions under which the Harris tweed
industry is carried on, he, like Gratiano, 'but offends his lungs to speak so
loud.'

It appears that an evening newspaper has surmised that Sir James
Crichton Browne is the author of these letters of mine, and Mr Winston
Churchill is concerned for the reputation of that gentleman, whom he has
taken under his protection. But it should be scarcely necessary to remind
Mr Winston Churchill that such guesses are always risky and often wrong,
and that it is well to take no notice of them. A recent correspondence in
your columns as to the ownership of the initials 'A. A.' ought to have taught
him this; and curiously enough I can recall an instance in which the much
commoner combination of initials I have used – viz., 'J. C. B.' – led to
flagrant error. A number of years ago a series of letters on Homœopathy
to which the initials 'J. C. B.' were attached appeared in *The Times*. These
letters were immediately fathered, I suppose by some evening newspaper,
on the late Sir John Charles Bucknill, who calmly bore the brunt of the fierce
personal attacks of rash controversialists like Mr Winston Churchill, and
when the correspondence was over announced that he had had nothing
whatever to do with the letters in question. Perhaps Sir James Crichton
Browne is adopting similar tactics, and may desire to defer his declaration,
one way or the other; but, at any rate, he must be amply compensated in
the meantime for any annoyance the ascription of these letters to him may
have caused by the handsome and complimentary way in which Mr Winston
Churchill has referred to him. To be described by so uncompromising a
critic as 'learned and vivacious,' 'distinguished in science and literature,'
'bearing a name elevated and admired,' must be a gratifying experience.
It is clear that, were Sir James Crichton Browne the author of these letters,
he dare not now avow the fact, for that would be to deal a fatal blow at the
reputation for discernment of his patron and protector Mr Winston
Churchill, who would in that case stand convicted of having attributed to a
'pretentious imposter' the weighty lucubrations of a 'learned and distinguished' man. To a precocious politician discernment is everything; so it is
Mr Winston Churchill who now requires shelter behind the veil of anonymity.

It is not I who have reopened the discussion on Harris tweed, but the local authorities in the North, who, instead of setting their house in order, have attempted to whitewash it, and issued statements which, in the interests of public health, required correction.

About homespun generally I have had nothing that is not approbatory to say, and as regards Harris tweed, as I have repeatedly pointed out, a few simple precautions will make it not only an unobjectionable, but an admirable fabric.

I hope much good will result from the exhibition at Stafford-house, and I sincerely wish success to those excellently-planned technical schools which, by the liberality of the Duke and Duchess of Sutherland and Mr Carnegie, are being established in the northern counties of Scotland.

Their teaching and influence will soon put the Harris tweed and all other homespun industries on a sound and sanitary basis.

I am anxiously awaiting Mr Winston Churchill's views on the Colorado beetle.

Your obedient servant
J. C. B.

WSC to Lord Rosebery
(Rosebery Papers)

4 June 1902   105 Mount Street

My dear Lord Rosebery,

I am so vy sorry that you cannot come on the 11th. In the matter of dinners etc the King exerts an authority more tyrannical and oppressive than that of the Czar; and as for the American Ambassador – I confess I feel that Anglo-Saxon brotherhood has declined several points.

I wonder whether the enclosed met your eye. Please put it in the waste paper basket when you have done with it. I am awaiting the retort, with a weapon which will cut both ways.[1]

One piece of gossip wh will interest you – but is at present a party secret – Ian Malcolm is to marry Mrs Langtry.[2] The union is one upon which I shall not permit myself to comment.

Most sincerely yours
WINSTON S. C.

[1] See WSC's letter to *The Times* 1 June 1902.
[2] They were married on June 30 1902.

Lord Rosebery to WSC

4 June 1902   38 Berkeley Square

My dear W.

Never did I read such a letter as yours in *The Times* on Monday. It is of the true Corinthian brass. Contrast it with the chaste and dignified epistle on the Eton memorial in the same paper.[1] How about Ian Malcolm? Does he leave the Hooligans?

Yrs
AR

WSC to the Editor, The Times[2]

6 June 1902   105 Mount Street

Sir,

During the autumn of last year an anonymous writer, styling himself 'J. C. B.,' published a series of letters in *The Times* the evident object of which was to discourage the public from purchasing Harris tweed upon the grounds that it was dangerously insanitary and no sufficient protection against the weather. At a very early stage in this correspondence his letters became garnished with all kinds of personalities about those gentlemen – some of them my friends – who ventured to dissent from his opinions, and they included an insinuation against the management of some Scottish estates so gratuitous and so gross that you, Sir, thought it proper to rebuke him in a leading article.

Under these circumstances I was emboldened to enter the controversy. It is true that I did not wait for an invitation from 'J. C. B.'; for I did not know that one was necessary. It is also true that I had no 'special qualifications' to discuss Harris tweeds, or peat reek, or *bacilli* of any kind; and for that reason I refrained from discussing any of them. My point was simple. I stated it then as clearly as possible. I repeat it now: that those who assail industries, particularly industries of the poor, ought to do so above their own names; and, moreover, that honourable men do not usually make personal attacks upon private people from the cover of anonymity.

Such was the issue – of which others may judge – and for my part I was

---

[1] On May 31 Lord Rosebery wrote to *The Times* urging Old Etonians to subscribe to a Memorial Hall 'where the whole school can be collected together'. He suggested that the Hall should be erected as a memorial to Queen Victoria, rather than in memory of the Old Etonians who had died in the South African War. His letter was published on Monday, June 2.

[2] Published on June 7.

content to leave it there. But it has subsequently been remarked that the initials which this correspondent assumed or employed might be mistaken for those of a well-known scientist, and that consequently his opinions might seem invested with an authority to which they may have no right. It therefore appeared desirable to elicit from Sir James Crichton Browne some explicit disclaimer; and it is greatly to be regretted that such has not so far been forthcoming. But whatever the previous offences of 'J. C. B.' may have been, they are almost eclipsed by the amazing letter published in your issue to-day, in which he sedulously endeavours to convey the impression to your readers that he is actually the eminent person in question, and in which by no single word or expression does he in any way contradict the suggestion which has now been so openly made.

I will confess, Sir, that after I had written to you last week I was seized with a violent feeling of apprehension – almost of panic. What if Sir James Crichton Browne were really the author of such letters! The idea was preposterous; its monstrous improbability was comforting; and yet I trembled. But not for myself. My reputation or my 'discernment' were not at stake, as 'J. C. B.' seems to think. It is quite possible that a man may possess great scientific attainments and have rendered notable services, and yet may cut no better figure in the columns of a newspaper than a gallant officer when he makes an after-dinner speech. And, indeed, with all my respect for Sir James Crichton Browne, it would seem that a life so largely devoted to the study of lunacy might not perhaps be the training which would best fit him for public controversy. One may easily imagine that the provocations and vicissitudes of such a career might engender in the student a distorted sense of his own superiority, an irritability of temperament, a desire to override the opinions of others, which, although of small consequence compared to the benefits derived by society from his labours, would nevertheless constitute a serious personal disadvantage. Indeed I find in this very reflection my chief reason for admiring such men, who with their eyes open to all the dangers do not hesitate to face an atmosphere of mental contagion, and, like Father Damien, while saving others, sacrifice themselves.

My dread, Sir, certainly not selfish in its nature, was of the pain which we should feel to see an honoured name covered with reproach, and a reputation stained. I am, however, persuaded, from what I learn of Sir James Crichton Browne, that, were he the writer of the letters, no undue regard for my feelings would, as 'J. C. B.' suggests, deter him from openly avowing their authenticity. For this reason 'J. C. B.' in his letter of to-day exposes his ignorance of the character of the man behind whom he has endeavoured to shelter; and in spite of his attempt to foster the supposition that he is actually Sir James Crichton Browne – a trick similar to that which, as he cynically informs us has already upon an earlier occasion met with ill-deserved success at the expense of the late Sir John Charles Bucknill – the public will be well advised to continue to regard him as a person to whose opinions no especial weight or credence need be attached.

From new or further controversy with such a correspondent I have no reason to shrink. But let us deal with one mysterious plague at a time. It will be soon enough to discuss the Colorado beetle after we have settled with 'J. C. B.'

I have the honour to be, Sir, your obedient, humble servant

WINSTON S. CHURCHILL

WSC to the Editor, The Times[1]

12 June 1902   105 Mount Street

Sir,

I feel compelled to make public a painful discovery. To the last I refused to be convinced, and even when hope had disappeared I clung to doubt; but, as I need scarcely say, through the agency of no person connected with *The Times,* I have been confronted with conclusive evidence of a fact, which it would no longer be honest to your readers to conceal. 'J.C.B.' is Sir James Crichton Browne.

Comment is difficult. We have before us a highly diverting revelation of the dual nature of the human mind. And this eminent scientist, 'created half to rise and half to fall,' leading, as it were, a double life; upon the one hand, devoting his talents to the service of society and, building up an honourable reputation; and all the time relieving his baser nature by anonymous exercises of the kind which have lately soiled your columns, is a spectacle so strange and striking that at an earlier period it might well have furnished the late Mr Stevenson with the original inspiration for *Dr Jekyll and Mr Hyde.*

I had no wish to offend Sir James Crichton Browne. Indeed, speaking for others besides myself, had we known in the beginning that he was the author of the attacks, much though we might have regretted his action, widely as we should have been found to differ from his conclusions, we should not in any case have treated him with disrespect; and now, Sir, in the face of this exposure, I will say nothing to add to his evident annoyance. No one will deny his right to embark upon such a controversy; and so long as he is sincerely convinced that Harris tweed constitutes a real and serious danger to the public, he is, of course, quite justified in allowing no

[1] Published on June 14 1902.

consideration of the welfare of those engaged in the industry to weigh with him. But let me ask him a single question. How is it that, while he believes that the danger from these homespuns is so great, he could permit himself to visit the centre of infection at Stafford-house during the sale last Monday, and run the risk not only of being stricken himself, but of disseminating the germs of sickness among his fellows?

Only one further observation, and that of a more intimate nature. Surely the statement of 'J.C.B.,' 'I never made an insinuation against the management of any one Highland estate' requires to be carefully reconsidered by Sir James Crichton Browne!

I have the honour to be, Sir, your obedient servant
WINSTON S. CHURCHILL

*   *   *   *   *

WSC to the Honorary Secretary, the Newcastle Anti-Bread Tax Committee[1]

5 June 1902   London

Dear Sir,

I desire not less strongly than your committee that the reduction of our national expenditure may render the withdrawal of the corn tax possible. But I am of opinion that before it is withdrawn the sinking fund should be resumed, and that when this condition is established the reductions of taxation should be effected without altering in any serious degree the existing balance between direct and indirect taxation. Meanwhile it is idle to talk of an agitation against the corn tax being of a non-party character. As a fiscal measure the corn tax is the best practical method of raising the money needed under the present Budget, and all who have confidence in the present Government are bound in ordinary common-sense to support it.

WSC to W. St John Brodrick

7 June 1902   105 Mount Street

[Copy]

I have heard some rumours that in consequence of the Report of the Committee upon the education of officers, it is proposed, inter alia, to prohibit inter-regimental polo tournaments, and I venture to put my view

[1] Published in the *Western Mercury* on June 9.

upon the subject before you in the hopes that you may consider it when making up your mind upon the subject.

You will certainly not be blind to the great advantages of polo as a recreation, and even as an education for officers, particularly of mounted forces. It is, to my mind, a game which develops very strongly qualities of nerve and of judgment quite apart from horsemanship, and I imagine that on this point there is a general concensus of opinion even among senior officers. I have not the means of making the calculation, but I think it would be very instructive to find out how officers of cavalry regiments who have played for their regiment in polo tournaments, and often in the winning teams, in polo tournaments, have behaved in South Africa. My own impression is that in almost every case when a cavalry officer or a mounted infantry officer has made a reputation for himself, has been mentioned in dispatches repeatedly, has been several times wounded or awarded some military decoration, he has been a good polo player, and certainly in all the cavalry regiments I have known the men who formed the polo team have been the strongest and the leading personalities in the regiment, and this because of their character, and not because of their proficiency at the game.

Now I should be the last to overlook the urgent need of making the cost of living less in cavalry regiments, but I do not think it has ever been proposed to abolish polo altogether, for that would undoubtedly be a great injury to the Service, and I think a very tyrannical exercise of authority over the private amusements of officers when not on duty. What is wanted is some reform which, while not discouraging the playing of polo in the Army, will make it possible for it to be played at something less than its present expense. To do this you must endeavour to dissociate army polo from civilian polo, for it is the wealthy civilians who in the last 8 or 10 years have been playing polo all over England in increasing numbers, who have so greatly increased the price of polo ponies. Now, if you abolish the inter-regimental tournament you will, I believe, place a serious obstacle in the way of this separation which would be so beneficial, and I think that if it were properly handled the inter-regimental tournament ought to be the weapon with which the cost of polo ponies in use throughout the Army should be substantially reduced.

The soldiers ought to take its regulation into their own hands. There should be in England as in India an Army Polo Association. The regulations of the inter-regimental tournament should be framed so as to discourage the use of very high priced polo ponies, and so as to prevent altogether the sort of practice lately indulged in by some regiments of buying a great number of expensive ponies shortly before a match. These could very easily be done if such conditions as these were insisted upon: that not more than a certain number of ponies should be played by any team: that all of these ponies should have been the property of officers in the regiment for at least 6 months: and that not less than half of the ponies should have been actually trained to polo in the regiment and not bought as made ponies. The value of this last condition is evident, for an unmade polo pony is very cheap, and the task of training him requires and develops all those higher qualities of horsemanship which are of such value. Its possibility and practicability is abundantly proved by the history of the Durham Light Infantry who possessed themselves of the finest team of polo ponies in the whole of India without indulging in the slightest extravagance and with results most profitable to themselves. If the conditions of the inter-regimental polo tournament and of Army Polo generally were framed and regulated by an Army Polo Association on the lines I have indicated I believe that more polo would be played in the Army, that it would cost much less than at present, that the Army would, as it were, be isolated from civilian competition, and that the winning team of the polo tournament each year would not represent merely the most wealthy or the most sporting regiment, but the regiment who were the finest masters of horsemanship and in every sense the best players of the best of games.

Sir Ian Hamilton to WSC

EXTRACT

8 June 1902   Pretoria

My dear Winston,

   This is probably the last letter I shall write you from South Africa. Thank God, all has gone well, and by going well I do not only mean that the victory is complete, but also that I think history will say Lord K has done all that he could do, even during that first flush of success which turns some people's heads, to lay the foundations for a permanent friendship and peace between the Dutch and English sections which may, D.V., end in complete amalgamation. Someday, in safe England, I will tell you perhaps something of the vicissitudes and struggles through which this has been accomplished. It is wonderful to think how smooth and easy it must all seem to some of the outside world when one has an intimate knowledge of the ups and downs of the struggle. . . .

   There is only one troublesome matter now left on my mind, and I do not think I can give a better notion of it than by the following extract from a letter which I have just written to Lord Roberts. . . .

' . . . The Pan-Germanic League have asked Botha and De la Rey[1] to go on a tour through Germany to make speeches, and have baited their hook with the promise that they will be able thereby to raise a very large sum of money for the widows and children of those who have fallen. This idea has caught on, and Botha certainly (with his secretary De Wet), and probably also De la Rey, are going. After all, they are British subjects, and, being so, cannot well be prevented from travelling where they like. . . .

. . . Their feelings towards us at present are all that any Britisher could desire. Start them, however, on a tour of speechifying in Germany, and the local anti-British atmosphere would turn their heads as they saw time after time how any reference to ill-treatment or farm burning was received with applause. It is hardly in human nature, certainly not in Boer nature, to resist going further and further on the denunciatory tack. There might be no great political harm in this on the Continent – of that I am no judge – but as regards this country the effect would be damnable.

Now, there is a perfectly easy way of preventing all this mischief and trouble, or rather there are two ways. The first I hardly venture to press. It is that Commissions, at any rate honorary, should be given to Botha and De la Rey, which would stamp them definitely as British and render any anti-British remarks uttered in their presence insulting to them, but I feel that in expressing this wish I am going a bit ahead of your views and those generally held in England.

The second method is far simpler, and, if well worked, would, I believe, be equally effective. You have simply to let Botha come home in the ship with Lord K, and appear a few times to enthusiastic meetings in London. He would then publicly give himself away to such an extent by declaring his real feelings as regards our treatment of prisoners and general conduct, that he would cease to be worth a cent to the blighters of the Pan-Germanic League. . . .'

We have just had our Thanksgiving Service. K surpassed himself. He was Archbishop, Choir and Congregation in one. I could not deny him the tribute of my warmest admiration.

Goodbye, my dear boy. More power to your elbow, and

Believe me, Yours ever

IAN HAMILTON

[1] Jacobus Herculaas De la Rey (1847–1914), farmer, politician and soldier; Assistant Commandant-General of the South African Republic 1900–2; Senator for the Transvaal 1910–14.

WSC to Lord Rosebery
(*Rosebery Papers*)
EXTRACT

10 June 1902   105 Mount Street

My Dear Lord Rosebery,

I am going to make a speech in the Debate on the Address, taking your view about the S.A. settlement; viz that it must be one in which the Boers acquiesce by some deliberate corporate act. I am also going to trounce Brodrick on the military mismanagement. They will not be vy pleased with me afterwards.

I cannot make speeches in the country with any satisfaction now. I cannot work up the least enthusiasm on the Govts behalf: and yet popular audiences seem to gape for party clap trap.

The two faithful Hooligans are in a vy satisfactory state of mind and both seem to develop that invaluable political quality – a desire for mischief. We propose to demonstrate against Mr Lynch, which will be great fun.

I go to Trentham for the Sunday.

Yours vy sincerely
WINSTON S. CHURCHILL

Lord Charles Beresford to WSC

17 June 1902   Gilmuire
                                                                                       Ascot

My dear Winston,

Try and be in the House on Friday next and support my effort to get direct responsibility for efficiency. To control the wicked waste & extravagant expenditure that now goes on in the Services. The keynote for Reform must be direct responsibility for efficiency.

Yours very truly
CHARLES BERESFORD

WSC to Sir Ian Hamilton
(*Hamilton Papers*)
EXTRACT

25 June 1902   105 Mount Street

My dear General,

Many thanks for your last three letters, all of which have been most pleasant to read and to receive.[1] How thankful you must be at the result which has been achieved, and to think that you yourself were able to exert a powerful and effective influence, not only upon the War but upon the negotiations. I am quite certain that the Boer leaders have been powerfully impressed by the courtesy and respect which is entertained for them by the English Commanders. As a Nation it seems to me they possess qualities quite different to their individual qualities, and instead of being a matter of fact, secluded, sober, plainly dressed folk, they are, when they get together, as full of military vanity and desire for glory and renown as any Nation has ever been; and they have moreover (so it has always seemed to me) a very curious and complete comprehension of the soldier's mind and the soldier's point of view. If this be true, I find myself able at once to understand how beneficent an influence men like Kitchener and yourself must have had upon the course of events.

We are all very much impressed over here by the loyalty of the Boers in carrying out the spirit of the capitulation, and I hear it on all sides said what an extraordinary people they are. For my part I see nothing in their behaviour which is not perfectly logical and consistent, marked by the same shrewdness and boldness which has characterised all their previous plans. They have fought the British Empire; they have been defeated; they recognise that they cannot beat the British Empire; and they have decided to have it on their side. I am bound to say if they play their cards with their usual skill they will most certainly succeed. They do not mean to be handed over to the tender mercies of the Loyalists of South Africa, and it is in my opinion a shrewd and a practical policy on their part (an act all the more shrewd because it will be evidently sincere) to try to stand of all South African factors nearest the Imperial throne. For my part I think that if henceforward they associate themselves with us, we are absolutely bound to give them every kind of encouragement. I have very little admiration or respect for the Loyalists of Capetown, and with a few exceptions for the Uitlanders of Johannesburg, and I am certain of this that if we can make the Boers one of the foundations of our position in South Africa, if not indeed the chief foundation, we shall be building upon the rock.

[1] See Hamilton's letters of March 30, April 5 and June 8 on pages 119, 121 and 144.

I envy you very much your dinner with De Wet and the others, and it must have been indeed to you the most interesting event in your life. How very seldom opportunities have been provided in history for distinguished commanders on both sides to fight their battles over again. I wish I had the power to make the appointments[1] you suggest, but I know that Mr Chamberlain is fully alive to the value of the help he may receive from the Boer leaders; and you may be quite sure that in politics he will always be a good friend to any one who can give him the least assistance. Of course, the Government will use the Boers if they find from them a stronger support than from elsewhere.

Turning now to your letter about court-martialling officers for failure – I quite agree with all you say, and I think the comparison between Naval and Military conditions most effective. It had often occurred to me how absurd it is to draw any analogy from the Navy. War is a gamble. Seamanship is a science. And I think the two examples you give of the Cavalry Colonel and the chalk pit, and of the Infantry Colonel and the railway tunnel very witty and conclusive. But I do not think that any one has really suggested that officers should be proceeded against in any way for failure arising from circumstances beyond their control, or from errors of judgment. What has been urged is that where some obvious military precaution has without any countervailing reason been neglected, and consequently an act has been committed of a highly unmilitary character, disciplinary action should be taken; and I am bound to say that without prejudice to your letter, there seems to be a good deal to be said for this. Let us take the case of an officer who bivouacs at the base of a hill and puts no pickets of any kind on the top of the hill, or the officer who bivouacs on the top of a hill and takes no steps to defend it from attack, or let us say an officer who is posted for several weeks in a town (like Dewetsdorp!) and never makes any preparation for putting it in a state of defence. All these gross, primary military errors arising either from stupidity or carelessness ought to be judged, if only in justice to the private soldier, by military courts. There is 'that *crassa ingnorantia* and that *crassa negligentia* on which the law animadverts in magistrates and surgeons even when actual malice or corruption are not imputed.' And I think that surely you would not take the position of saying that no officer should be court-martialled except for disobedience or disloyalty.

You will be easily able to imagine what a very painful shock we have had here about the Coronation. What an appalling waste of money and labour, and what a terrible disappointment for so many thousands of poor people who had been put to trouble and expense, and had their hopes raised. The whole event stands in a very curious, ironical light. Here was to be the greatest

[1] Note in Hamilton's hand: To give Botha a Brigade at Aldershot.

concourse of human beings ever gathered together under the sun. All these millions were to participate in a ceremony. Of all those millions one was indispensable. Yet of all those millions it is that one who has been chosen. A week ago we apprehended rain to spoil the ceremonies, but no one dreamed of anything else. Today when all is cancelled the sky is cloudless – the heavens themselves wear a bland sardonic smile. Do you remember Meredith on life – 'a supreme ironic procession – with laughter of the gods in the background'?[1]

John Morley to WSC

30 June 1902   57 Elm Park Gardens

My dear Churchill,

Your most kind note gives me the liveliest pleasure, and I thank you for writing it.[2] As you say, there is no reason to suppose that Cato would have worn a riband at a Roman evening party. But I will not be bound by his precedent. For instance, at last he fell upon his sword. That is not at all my notion of the best use for my poor weapon. The Romans were undoubtedly frugal in their rewards for public service, as you will remember from a famous computation of Swift's, comparing the cheap laurels of Cincinnatus, Fabius, and I know not whom besides, with the copious & lavish generosity of England to an immortal John Churchill whose memory must be cherished by you – unless the spirit of the Economist within you should cloud his fame.[3]

Nonsense apart, I am delighted to have your salutation.

Ever yours
JOHN MORLEY

[1] This last paragraph was in holograph, the earlier part having been typed. WSC, possibly thinking he had written a PS, did not sign the letter.
[2] Among the recipients of Coronation honours announced on June 25 was Morley, who received the newly-created Order of Merit.
[3] Swift's attack on British generosity to Marlborough is in *The Examiner* No. 16, quoted in full in *The Works of Jonathan Swift* 1824 edition, Vol. III. Thirty-five years later WSC dealt with this attack in *Marlborough His Life and Times* Vol. IV p. 362. By a slip of the pen WSC referred to No. 17 of *The Examiner*.

Sir William Nicholson[1] to WSC

4 July 1902   War Office

Private

Dear Churchill,

Very sorry that such a formal reply was sent you in reply to your request for information on certain points connected with the S. African War. I felt bound to enquire whether Mr Secretary Brodrick had any objection to the compilation of the statistics you wanted, as naturally he does not like independent MP's to be better informed than himself.

All I did was to ask the Private Secy whether Mr Brodrick would allow me to give you the data you wished for. There was no official correspondence on the subject.

Yours very Sincerely

W. G. NICHOLSON

*   *   *   *   *

WSC to the Editor, The Times[2]

7 July 1902   House of Commons

Sir,

Although it has not been found possible to discuss the Sandhurst affair in the House of Commons, the case is one which may perhaps be thought worthy of the attention of your readers.

During the course of the last term five fires – presumably the work of incendiaries – occurred in the college. The first two outbreaks were on April 23 in the quarters of C Company. The third fire was in the quarters of A Company on May 7, and the fourth occurred on June 7 in an office between B and C Company, but equally inaccessible to both. In consequence of these occurrences all the leave in the college was stopped by an order from the War Office until the guilty parties should be discovered. It was in vain that the cadets protested that they did not know who the offender was. Their asseverations were ignored, and the natural indignation at this injustice found vent in some sort of serious horseplay on the occasion of the Camberley Fair. An inquiry was held. Three cadet corporals were reduced to the ranks, some minor punishments were inflicted on a small number of cadets, and the matter then dropped.

---

[1] William Gustavus Nicholson (1845–1918), Director-General of Mobilisation and Military Intelligence, War Office 1901–4; Chief of General Staff 1908–12. KCB, 1898; GCB, 1908; Baron 1912.

[2] Published on July 8.

Upon June 24 the leave of the college was restored, and this seems to set the seal upon the condonation by the authorities of the disorder; but, whether or not, what follows stands by itself. At about 3 o'clock on the 25th another fire occurred in a room occupied by three cadets of C Company. It was easily extinguished. The three cadets were placed in arrest and brought before a Court of inquiry composed of three Regular officers. The Court sat from the 26th to the 28th, and nothing having been proved against the cadets they were released from arrest. But on the 30th the following telegram arrived from the War Office and was read out to the cadet battalion: – 'Unless within 48 hours the author, or authors, of the fires which have occurred at Sandhurst has been found, all C Company will be rusticated and all servants will be discharged unless they can successfully prove they were not in the college at the time of the fires.'

At the expiration of the specified time all the cadets of the company were brought before the commanding officer; no evidence was taken on oath; no defence of any kind was allowed; and all who were unable to prove that they were on the cricket ground or otherwise engaged outside the building were summarily sent down. Among them were the three cadets who had already been exonerated by the Court of inquiry; and – to make injustice even-handed – three wretched servants, old soldiers of the highest character, were also flung out.

Mr Brodrick informed the House of Commons that all the fires had taken place in the quarters of C Company; but this is, in fact, inaccurate, for two fires have occurred in other parts of the college; and, in any case, it is perfectly easy for cadets from all companies to move freely about the building; and there is no especial reason to suppose that the incendiary was a member of the particular company selected for vengeance. It is, therefore, more than probable that the culprit, if he be a cadet at all, is not among the 29 scapegoats; and, even if he were, the silliness – apart from its impropriety – of the course adopted by the War Office is patent, for, according to their arrangements, the incendiary will now return at the beginning of the winter term, and the college will have the benefit of his presence for an additional six months. It was not pretended at Sandhurst that these 29 cadets were proceeded against because of disorder at the Camberley Fair; and most of them had not been in any way concerned with it; yet this bad reason is thought good enough to bring forward in the House of Commons to confuse the issue and to support other reasons which are worse.

The following official notification of this action was sent to the parents: –
'From the Assistant-Commandant R.M. College, Camberley.

'3rd July 1902.
'I beg to inform you that in accordance with instructions received from

the War Office your son Gent Cadet . . . . has this day been rusticated until
the end of the term on account of his being unable to prove an *alibi* on the
afternoon of 25th ulto, when an outbreak of fire occurred in C Company's
quarters.

G. Cadet . . . . should rejoin the Junior Division on Wednesday, 17th
September next, before 8 p.m., unless another date is fixed, which will be
duly notified to you.

'Kindly acknowledge receipt.

'J. S. TALBOT, Lt-Col,

Asst Commandant RM College.'

I will not take occasion here to comment upon this travesty of justice
further than to point out three cardinal principles of equity which it violates–
that suspicion is not evidence; that accused persons should be heard in their
own defence; and that it is for the accuser to prove his charge, not for the
defendant to prove his innocence. But it is necessary to observe the effects.
Twenty-nine cadets have been rusticated, and will, in consequence, forfeit
six months' seniority, a matter of vast importance to a soldier. They will
rejoin in September and go through exactly the same educational course
again, step by step; and, moreover, they will lie all their lives under a very
serious and damaging suspicion.

Such are the consequences to them; to their parents they are not less
cruel. Sandhurst is the poor man's road into the Army, and it is by that
course that nearly all the Indian Staff Corps officers make their way. The
college fees are high – indeed, according to the recent Committee on
Military Education, they are excessive. To find £60 a term for two terms,
together with £30 for outfit, is a serious problem for most of the parents concerned. One gentleman is a 'struggling country parson,' with a nominal
income of £120 a year, and a family of eight children. His eldest son has just
returned from South Africa after 29 months of active service, having won
the Distinguished Service Order. Two other of his sons are in the Navy.
It is doubtful whether the extra money can be found for the Sandhurst cadet.
This is the kind of person who is struck; yet surely such a one deserves some
consideration from the State!

The father of another cadet, a master at Uppingham, is so badly off that
the boy was only enabled to go to Sandhurst through the liberality of a
relation, who found the necessary £150. 'The boy himself,' writes the headmaster of his public school, 'is most conscientious and has worked like a
trooper to get into Sandhurst and out again, for he is not clever. His prospects
are entirely blighted, for the money cannot be found for another term, and

the boy is broken-hearted at the failure of his hopes. Had he been on '*mufti leave*,' like so many of the others, his *alibi* would have been accepted; but he was working hard, *more suo*, for the examination which was to begin the next day.'

These cases would be pitiful even if a serious charge were fully sustained. But no charge whatever has been made against any of these cadets. No opportunity of defence has been allowed. No evidence on oath has been taken. Nothing having the remotest semblance of a judicial inquiry has been held. The sole reason which is given these unfortunate gentlemen for the treatment of their sons is contained in the monstrous confession of the official memorandum, that they were 'unable to prove an *alibi*.'

It is only necessary to state that all the cadets I have seen strenuously deny any complicity with the offence; that they do not know who the offender is; and they affirm that if they did they would have no hesitation in surrendering him. They and their parents only ask that they may be permitted to substantiate their statement upon oath, and several have already forwarded affidavits.

Mr Brodrick has stated in the House of Commons that he approves and that Lord Roberts approves of these proceedings. I therefore invite them to answer three questions: – What is the charge against these 29 cadets? What is the evidence in support of it? When and before whom has it been proved? These are short, plain questions, which not only involve the interests of innocent and deserving people, but also raise various ancient and valuable principles; and, if fair play is still honoured in the British Army, they ought to be answered.

Your obedient servant
WINSTON S. CHURCHILL

WSC to the Editor, The Times[1]

8 July 1902   105 Mount Street

Sir,

The Headmaster of Sherborne writes you a truly remarkable letter. He says that a large part of the prosperity of the British Army depends upon learning of the lessons of general punishment. 'The innocent, doubtless, suffer with the guilty; but then they always do. The world has been so arranged.' Has it indeed? No doubt he has taken care that the little world over which he presides is arranged on that admirable plan, but it is necessary

[1] Published on July 9.

to tell him that elsewhere the punishment of innocent people is regarded as a crime or as a calamity to be prevented by unstinted exertion.

So long as the delinquencies of a schoolmaster are within the ordinary law the House of Commons has no right to intervene; but when a Commander-in-Chief and a Secretary of State are encouraged to imitate him, it is time to take notice.

Does Mr Westcott[1] flog his boys in their corporate capacity?

Your obedient servant

WINSTON S. CHURCHILL

Benjamin G. Horniman[2] to the Editor, The Times

8 July 1902   Westminster

Sir,

For the sake of the discipline of the Army, the preservation of which so largely depends on the impression now made upon those who in the future will be called upon to maintain it, it is to be hoped that the authorities will ignore the agitation concerning the Sandhurst scandal which Lord Hugh Cecil and Mr Winston Churchill are endeavouring to foster.

It would appear from the statement of the facts made by Mr Churchill that the authorities have taken the only course open in a matter which called at once for the most stringent treatment; and from Mr Churchill, it must be remembered, we get only one side of the case. The affair from beginning to end, and more especially the Camberley Fair incident, points to the existence of a dangerous spirit of insubordination among the cadets; and it would have been culpable in the extreme to let the matter go further without taking action, while as for the mode of punishment and the possible inclusion of the innocent with the guilty, Lord Hugh Cecil, at least, should know that these matters cannot be dealt with on the principles which govern civil judicial procedure, and that, if they were to be, we might surrender finally all hope of keeping a proper state of discipline in the service. A natural feeling of sympathy with the spirit of Hooliganism, no matter in what walk of life it be found, must have led Lord Hugh Cecil into this curious attitude.

Some of us may be pardoned for declining to believe that incendiarism can be so persistently practised in an establishment like Sandhurst while all the inmates remain in ignorance of its authorship. But I do not wish, like Mr Churchill, to come to a judgment while not yet in full possession of the

---

[1] Frederick Brooke Westcott (1857–1918), headmaster of Sherborne 1892–1908; Archdeacon of Norwich 1910–18; Chaplain-in-Ordinary to King Edward VII and King George V 1910–18.

[2] Benjamin Guy Horniman (1873–1948), journalist and author in England and India.

facts as they are known to the authorities. The case of the servants, however, stands by itself. They were obviously unfit for their duties if they were unable to prevent the outbreaks or detect the culprits.

As for the hardships which fall upon the parents of the rusticated cadets they have no more to do with the question of the justice or the expediency of the measures taken by the Commander-in-Chief than the fact that Mr Churchill apparently numbers some of the victims among his friends. The whole of the 29 cadets might (for the sake of argument) have been tried and sentenced in a civil Court. The sad circumstances he mentions would then have been infinitely more sad, but they would have been still without application to the treatment of the individual offenders. Mr Churchill, apparently, has yet to learn that justice is governed by fact and circumstance, and not by sentiment.

There was never a time, Sir, when it was more important to support the Commander-in-Chief in his task of asserting the military profession as a serious business. If our officers at the commencement of their careers are to be encouraged in the belief that the authority of their superiors can be negatived by an appeal to the meddling officiousness of irresponsible members of Parliament it will strike at the very root of the reform which the service so urgently needs.

May I say, in conclusion, that the country is to be congratulated on the failure of Mr Winston Churchill and his friends to obtain a motion for the adjournment of the House last night? The public are heartily tired of the way in which the time of Parliament is wasted in discussions which, while so much important legislation is awaiting attention, are merely frivolous.

I am, Sir, your obedient servant
BENJAMIN G. HORNIMAN

Lord Hugh Cecil to WSC
(Rosebery Papers)

8 July [1902]   20 Arlington Street

Dear Winston,

Go round & see the Imperialist [?] & urge him to back Carrington[1] in the Lords tonight. You might give him your papers & letters.

I wish they wd have a motion & divide more.

Yrs
HC

[1] Charles Robert Wynn-Carrington, 1st and last Marquess of Lincolnshire (1843–1928), succeeded to barony of Carrington 1868; Governor, New South Wales 1885–90; President of Board of Agriculture and Fisheries 1905–11; Lord Privy Seal 1911–12; Marquess 1912.

WSC to Lord Rosebery
(*Rosebery Papers*)

8 July [1902]   105 Mount Street

My dear Lord Rosebery,
    The Sandhurst affair is I believe to come up in the House of Lords today
as the result of a question from Carrington. In case it is a matter wh excites
your indignation as a father etc, you will find me full of information on the
point.

Yours vy sincerely
WINSTON S. CHURCHILL

WSC to the Editor, The Times[1]

[?10] July 1902

Sir,
    On Tuesday last you allowed me to lay before the public a general
statement upon the Sandhurst punishments. Let me now deal with a particular instance.
    Gentleman Cadet J. S. Oldham has been at the Royal Military College for
almost a year. At the beginning of his second term he was promoted to be a
cadet corporal. These posts are very much coveted by the cadets, and the
keenest competition takes place among them in smartness, obedience, and
punctuality. Corporal Oldham's record was indeed exemplary, and contained
no entry of any kind whatever until his rustication on July 3, three weeks
before he would have received his commission.
    'All the cadets,' said Mr Brodrick in the House of Commons (*vide The
Times* report, July 8), 'mutinously broke bounds on the evening following
the Commander-in-Chief's order that leave was suspended and that bounds
must not be broken. There was a mutinous outbreak, in which the very
cadets implicated (in the fire of the 25th ult) broke bounds and created a
disturbance in the neighbouring village.' Now what is the truth about this
'mutiny'? A large number of cadets – how many was never ascertained, but
probably about 150 – irritated, no doubt, at the general stoppage of leave,
did undoubtedly break bounds on the night of the 11th, smashed three lamps

---
[1] Published on July 11.

in the town of Camberley, and pushed a roller into the lake. It is noteworthy that according to all accounts their indignation was directed, not towards any of their officers, nor to the Governor of the college, but against the War Office, whose ignorant and capricious interference they not unnaturally resented. Be this as it may, these cadets committed an undoubted offence against military discipline, and if the Commander-in-Chief had rusticated or expelled all against whom the offence was proved no complaint of their treatment could have been made upon the score of injustice.

An official inquiry was immediately held. Sir Robert Grant,[1] who was sent down on purpose by the War Office, presided. Very few arrests had been made, but about 120 cadets, most of whom were mere spectators, voluntarily confessed their fault. No attempt was made by the authorities to prove that the indiscipline shown in this affair was to be connected with the dangerous incendiary fires, of which four had already occurred. Sir Robert Grant made a full report to the Commander-in-Chief; 'and,' to quote Mr Brodrick again, 'it was as the result of this report that the Commander-in-Chief took the very lenient action he did, desiring to treat the whole matter as a schoolboy freak.' Four cadet corporals were reduced, and about 30 cadets were punished with restriction drill for various periods. Thus by punishment or condonation the matter was completely disposed of, and upon June 24 the leave of the college was restored.

To revive this charge in a new and serious form upon a subsequent occasion is a violation of the principle which generally obtains in the Army – that no man may be punished, or even tried, twice for the same offence, a principle so venerable that it reaches back to the ancient Norman formula to this day employed in our Courts of justice, *Autre fois acquit*. But that is not the position of Corporal Oldham. However the former charge may be utilized to make up a Parliamentary case, it does not affect this gentleman. He was not at Sandhurst when the Camberley disorder took place, but in London upon sick leave for special treatment to his knee; and this fact could easily have been ascertained by the War Office authorities if, in their hasty and haphazard act of vengeance, they had taken the trouble to consult the college registers.

At 3 o'clock on the afternoon of June 25 Corporal Oldham was on duty as one of the corporals supervising the defaulters' drill. When this parade was over, he returned to his quarters in order to put away his belt, and thus walked into the trap which the War Office orders had formed and came, by something less than five minutes, under their interpretation of 'being unable to prove an *alibi*.' Had he not been on duty he would have been

---

[1] Robert Grant (1837–1904), Lieutenant-General (retired); commanded Royal Engineers, Soudan Expedition 1885; Inspector-General of Fortifications 1891–8; GCB 1902.

playing cricket, and so would have escaped. On hearing the fire alarm sounding, he hurried to the scene and helped to extinguish the flames.

He has never been accused of lighting the fire, of being accessory to the act, or of concealing evidence which might lead to the detection of the offender; and Mr Brodrick would not charge him with any of these things outside the privileged precincts of the House of Commons, for there is no scrap of evidence in support of them which any jury in a libel action would consider for a moment. No charge of any kind has ever been brought against him. No opportunity was afforded him of testifying on oath. He was not confronted with evidence or witnesses. Yet he was sentenced to lose six months' seniority, and lies, moreover, at this moment under suspicion – suspicion all the more hateful since, unless Parliament insist, it can never be cleared without committing or abetting a felony.

Corporal Oldham is a King's India cadet, a fact which marks him as a poor man's son. His father, Mr W. B. Oldham, CIE, is a retired Indian Civil servant, now living in Ireland with very bad health and a small pension, the joint results of a life of service in the East. I commend this case particularly to the attention of Lord Roberts, not in order to secure for it exceptional treatment, but to bring before him clearly the consequences which have followed from the callous, careless, and utterly unjust action taken under his name and authority.

Your obedient servant
WINSTON S. CHURCHILL

The Times

11 July 1902

The 'regrettable incident' of the Sandhurst punishments, which has been under discussion in our columns for a week past, was yesterday transferred to the high and generally serene atmosphere of the House of Lords. It gave rise to an animated and important debate, which goes far to render unnecessary the discussion in the House of Commons which Mr Winston Churchill desires and for which Mr Balfour declines to grant special facilities. The debate in the Lords was such as to indicate that the gravity of the affair is recognized in the highest quarters. A discussion in which the Commander-in-Chief personally intervenes, and is supported by the Foreign Secretary, the Lord President, and the Under-Secretary for War, while the other side is represented by Lord Rosebery and Lord Carrington, together with several peers who commonly support the Government, is one of considerable moment. Matters must be serious when all this force has to be directed upon them; and serious they are, in two ways. In the first place, the War Office has met a disciplinary difficulty in a manner which, to say the least, has made a number of intelligent people very indignant; and, in the second, the whole story throws an unpleasant light upon the condition of the Royal Military College. From both points of view the incident is extremely unfortunate. We do not want a state of things which is, by any degree of ingenuity, capable of being twisted into a miniature *affaire Dreyfus* – a case which would seem to show that military justice is not of the same nature as civil justice. Nor do we want to be so quickly and so painfully reminded of the sweeping censure passed upon Sandhurst by the recent Commission upon Military Education. Whoever may be primarily at fault, the state of the College cannot be satisfactory when these things happen there. It is not pleasant to have exposed to the eyes of the whole world – including our foreign critics – visible proof that the Commission was justified in its sharp criticisms.

The discussion in the House of Lords was opened by Lord Carrington, who gave a brief *résumé* of the facts with which the letters of Lord Hugh Cecil, Mr Winston Churchill, and others have made our readers familiar. He spoke of the fires which broke out at Sandhurst in the spring; of the War Office order stopping all leave pending the discovery of the culprit; of the breaking out of bounds and of the rather riotous conduct of some 120 cadets at Camberley Fair; of the special Commission sent down to inquire; of the confession of the cadets, and of the very lenient action of Lord Roberts, who only rusticated the two ringleaders and reduced three other corporals. On June 23 leave was restored, so that the cadets should be able to come to London for the Coronation. Unfortunately, a fifth fire broke out on the afternoon of June 25; and it is out of that, and the subsequent action of the War Office, that the present disagreeable situation has grown. In the course of a clear and moderate speech, Lord Raglan[1] dwelt effectively upon what appears to be a fact, and a deplorable fact, that Sandhurst has in all this matter shown less disposition to 'police itself,' to keep order in the interests of all, than is common, in fact universal, in the public schools. As the Duke of Northumberland[2] remarked later, the absence of this kind of public spirit in a school or college implies that there is something very wrong in the authorities. Lord Roberts, who followed, was naturally listened to with

[1] George Fitz-Roy Henry Somerset, 3rd Baron Raglan (1857–1921), Under-Secretary of State for War 1900–2; soldier and writer on military and sporting subjects; Lieutenant-Governor, Isle of Man, 1902–19.

[2] Henry George Percy, 7th Duke of Northumberland (1846–1918), succeeded 6th Duke 1899; Conservative MP for North Cumberland 1868–85; Treasurer of the Household 1874–5; President of Archaeological Institute 1889–92; Lord Lieutenant of Northumberland.

respect and interest, and his speech had that character of straightforwardness, and revealed that desire to avoid all harsh measures and harsh language,
which might have been expected from him. It was soon made evident that
the Commander-in-Chief – who is *ex officio* president of the College as well
as responsible for the discipline of the Army – had given close personal
attention to this Sandhurst affair. After conferring with Sir Edwin Markham[1]
the Governor, he came to the conclusion that none of the ordinary detective
agencies could be employed to discover the author of the fires; and, some
time later, that unless the cadets volunteered to give up the culprit the latter
could not be discovered. Then followed the result we know. On the outbreak of the fifth fire, on June 25, the order went forth that unless the
name of the criminal were given up within 48 hours the whole of the
cadets of C Company who could not prove an *alibi* would be rusticated,
and the servants dismissed. The sentence was carried out in the case of 29
cadets and three servants – old soldiers, it may be remarked, who were
doing their work on what the Commission has called the inadequate wage
of 18s. a week. It should not be forgotten that these very servants were, in
the words of the Commission, 'not only underpaid, but overworked'; a fact
not without its bearing upon the question of why the author of the fires has
never been discovered. Thus the principle of general or collective punishment came to be applied; a confession of weakness, as all the Government
speakers admitted, but, in their view, the only kind of deterrent that could
be applied in the difficult circumstances of the case.

Lord Roberts supplemented a previous statement of Mr Brodrick by
announcing an important concession. The Secretary of State had promised
that the rusticated cadets, the time for whose final examination is approaching, should be examined this month in London; and that, 'if cleared,'
they should thus not forfeit any seniority. The value of this will be apparent
to all military men. Lord Roberts adds the not less important promise
that he himself 'will go carefully into each individual case.' That is the
right way to proceed, and, now that the matter has assumed such a painfully
public character, the only way. We feel sure that one of the first cases
to be examined will be that of Cadet-Corporal Oldham, which Mr Winston
Churchill describes for us this morning; and if the facts are found to be
as his effective advocate represents them, this gentleman will, we presume,
be reinstated. So, surely, will be all those who will declare on their honour
that they had no part in the fires and do not know who the criminals are.
We do not see that any answer is possible to the argument that has been

[1] Edwin Markham (1833–1918), Governor of Royal Military College, Sandhurst 1898–
1902; served in Crimea 1854–5; India 1857–8; Inspector-General of Ordnance at Headquarters 1895–8; knighted 1897; Lieutenant-General.

employed so freely in the matter: – These young men are gentlemen, about to become officers of the King's forces. Practically they are officers now; and the word of an officer must be accepted, or what becomes of the Army and of the fundamental canon of military honour? We do not say that in this way the author of the very serious offence would be discovered; but we should get rid of a very unpleasant application of the principle of general punishment to a case in which it should not have been resorted to.

* * * * * *

WSC to J. T. Travis-Clegg[1]

21 July 1902   House of Commons

Dear Mr Travis-Clegg,

   I am very glad of the opportunity provided by the annual report of writing a not too lengthy letter on the general course of public affairs, so that it may thus come into the hands of those most trusted with the work of maintaining the Conservative cause in Oldham.

   The long Parliamentary session, now approaching a brief interruption, leaves the Unionist party in a position of undiminished strength. We have lost two, at least, of the leaders under whose direction and guidance that party was formed; but although it may be difficult to fill the places of Lord Salisbury and Sir Michael Hicks Beach with men of the same supreme distinction and authority, the confidence of the House of Commons, and of the country, is freely given to Mr Balfour; for it is well known that as regards all great questions which have been before us of late years, the policy of the party remains unchanged and rests in hands long trained to execute it. The generous and disinterested support which the new Prime Minister receives from Mr Chamberlain is only another instance of the healthy and honourable condition of public life in England, and another pledge of good faith and loyalty between Conservatives and their powerful and patriotic allies.

   Outside the variations in the leadership, there has come another immense change. We have passed from war – dragging, draining, dangerous war – to victorious peace. From the bottom of my heart I rejoice in the settlement that has at length been reached by so much skill in negotiation, and so much persistence in the field. It is a settlement based not entirely upon the exhaustion and despair of a brave enemy, but rather on an honourable agreement between fighting races who have learned in the hardest of schools

---

[1] James Travis Travis-Clegg (1874–1942), Chairman of the Oldham Conservative Association until he resigned in April 1906 to become prospective candidate for Stalybridge; knighted 1933.

to respect each other's qualities. It is a settlement which secures to the British all that right and prudence demanded, and gives to the Boer all that generosity required. As such I believe it will establish, upon enduring foundations, the real achievement of the war, namely, that South Africa shall be a British Commonwealth and not a Boer Republic. Surely this must be almost the first peace in English history about which agreement was so complete that no debate of any kind was necessary!

Now that the war is out of the way, Finance steps into the first place. You know enough of my views to understand with what satisfaction I welcomed the recent appointment of a Committee of the House of Commons to inquire into the system of Parliamentary control. With Imperial expenditure leaping forward by nearly seven millions every year; with an increase in six years of more than forty millions, with the growth of debt, and the imposition of new taxes – all of them necessary, but some of them burdensome – with municipal expenditure and indebtedness keeping pace, step by step, in this dangerous progress, it is high time that every thinking man turned his attention to financial problems. When we reflect that the House of Commons cannot refuse a single sixpence of the immense bill presented to Parliament every year without at the same time voting for Home Rule, Disestablishment, and the rest of the Radical programme, it would seem on the face of it that some improvement of our machinery of control is urgently and vitally needed. Something to this end may be achieved by a committee; but public opinion, boldly expressed, must be the main instrument.

I hope to have an opportunity when I come before my constituents at the general meeting we are to have in the Colosseum Theatre on the 23rd of October (which I trust all the officials and workers of the party will endeavour to attend), of dealing with another formidable question towards which the increase of expenditure is steadily drawing us – the question of what is called Fair Trade. The time is, I think, coming near when men will have to make up their minds on this great issue to formulate their opinions, and set them forth without hesitation or doubt. But you will certainly not expect me to attempt such a matter within the narrow compass of this letter.

There is, I understand, a very general agreement throughout the party in Oldham, and even in some quarters beyond it, that the Education Bill now before Parliament will in fact effect a real and substantial improvement in the existing system, that it will increase the volume and improve the quality of education, that it gives to Voluntary schools a long-delayed, urgently needed measure of justice, and that for all these reasons it deserves consistent support. Such is the determination of the Government in this undertaking, that you need have no fears of the Bill not passing into law.

Turning, in conclusion, to our own affairs, I need scarcely repeat how glad I am that you have found it possible to place your most valuable services at the disposal of the party in Oldham. Very great improvements in the organisation have been carried out during the past year, both in regard to actual efficiency, for which our able and energetic agent, Mr Ware, is so largely responsible, and also in the direction of increasing the popular character of our machinery and strengthening the control exerted by the workers generally. Indeed, there is every reason to hope that by persevering on our present lines we may, in the course of a few years, make the Unionist organisation in Oldham a model to Conservatives in surrounding constituencies, and a deep and legitimate cause of anxiety to our Radical friends.

Yours sincerely
WINSTON S. CHURCHILL

WSC to Lord Rosebery
(*Rosebery Papers*)

24 July 1902   105 Mount Street

My dear Lord Rosebery,
   I am sending round to find out how we can get out of other engagements. But of course we should all be delighted to come.
   I will let you know definitely tomorrow. Do you realise we are five?

Yours vy sincerely
WINSTON S. CHURCHILL

WSC to Lord Rosebery
(*Rosebery Papers*)

25 July 1902   105 Mount Street

My dear Lord Rosebery,
   Percy, Ian Malcolm and I will be proud to accept your invitation – I presume to the Durdans. Hugh Cecil is trying to get out of his engagement, but suffers from the inconvenience of high moral principles in social matters. Arthur Stanley cannot come. Unless therefore I hear from you to the contrary we three will duly present ourselves; and I will let you know about Cecil tomorrow or Saturday at latest.

Yours vy sincerely
WINSTON S. CHURCHILL

Sir William Harcourt to WSC

26 July 1902   Malwood
                                                               Lyndhurst

My dear Winston Churchill,
    I was pleased to receive your letter. As one grows older one takes more
interest in the generation that is to come. I do not wonder that the general
state of politics perplexes you. In a long public life I have never [?] beheld
Man [?] in so unsatisfying a condition.

                                                          Yours sincerely
                                                      W. V. HARCOURT

George Wyndham to WSC

14 September 1902   Chief Secretary's Lodge
                                                           Phoenix Park
                                                                 Dublin

My dear Winston,
    Many thanks for a very interesting letter. You have 'got the hang' of
the matter & your four divisions cover the field of discussion.
    But you must come *here*. The Irish Office in London is but an empty
shell when the Chief Sec is in Ireland. So run over & I will see that you
are supplied with facts to support yr conclusions.
    If you cannot come I will send you material; it will help the cause &
your friend G.W. if you can say something on point 4, 'Education &
C[atholic] Hierarchy'. But I see yr difficulty from an Oldham point of
view. On 3, Remedial legislation supported by grants from British Treasury,
there is much to be said, but more to be done.

                                                              Yrs ever
                                                      GEORGE WYNDHAM

WSC to Lady Randolph

27 September 1902   Balmoral

Dearest Mamma,
    I have been vy kindly treated here by the King, who has gone out of his
way to be nice to me. It has been most pleasant & easy going & today the
stalking was excellent, tho I missed my stags.
    You will see the King on Weds when he comes to Invercauld; mind you

gush to him about my having written to you saying how much etc etc I had enjoyed myself here.

I go to Dalmeny with Lord R tomorrow morning by car. Write me a line there & send me your notes – if you have done them! I daresay other attractions have interrupted and delayed the task.

Ever your loving son
WINSTON S. C.

PS Address till 1st Dalmeny House, Edinburgh
                 2nd Crompton Hall, Shaw, Oldham
After that 105 . . .

Sir Michael Hicks Beach to WSC

5 October 1902   Coln St Aldwyns
                                                           Fairford

My dear Churchill,

I have no objection to the publication that you ask for. But as it may as well be correct, I enclose a report from the Bristol Liberal paper (*Western Daily Press*) with some necessary verbal corrections.

I wrote a long letter to you on Friday at 35a Cumberland Place on other matters – which I hope you will receive.

Your letter of 3rd only reached me to-day, when it was too late to telegraph.

Yours sincerely
M. HICKS BEACH

WSC to Lord Rosebery
(*Rosebery Papers*)

6 October 1902   105 Mount Street

My dear Lord Rosebery,

I telegraphed to you this morning the reply I have received from Beach. I now forward a corrected copy of his speech. In case you make use of it I do not think he would wish it to be publicly stated that he had revised it for the L.L. [Liberal League]. But the letter I wrote him asked about the economy & efficiency part only – so that I take it you are at liberty either to print the whole speech or leave out what refers to education.

I was very pleased with my visit to Oldham, where I was caressed by both parties with a cordiality most satisfactory & even surprising – for I have not been with them for 6 months.

I have broached the plan I spoke to you about – wh under certain contingencies it might be desirable to follow – to my two chief myrmidons. I think they would do anything I asked.

Yours ever

WINSTON S. C.

PS I see 'Beach' is in the 3rd person. Surely before it is printed it should be put into a direct form.

Lord Rosebery to WSC

7 October 1902   Rosebery

Private

My dear Winston,

Many thanks for your letter and the speech. This last I have urged the L.L. Publication Committee to produce.

I think with the heading 'Sir M.H-B on Efficiency and Economy' we might publish only two parts. I have not read the Education part, but it is of course governmental. Perhaps, however, as I am very scrupulous in such matters you might get HB's assent to my suggestion. Of course it would be made clear that the speech was not the entire speech.

What you say about your conference with your two myrmidons is most interesting. But politics & parties are at this moment in a witches' cauldron and I would not have you precipitate.

Yrs

AR

A. J. Balfour to WSC

EXTRACT

8 October 1902   Whittingehame

Private Dictated

My Dear Winston,

. . . I am interested in what you tell me about the feeling of Oldham, which quite squares with other opinions that reach me.

Your suggestion about the Public Accounts Committee and the Auditor-General is, so far as I know, novel, and most certainly deserves to be considered. I shall be very glad to talk it over with you. I suppose the Committee have it before them in some formal shape.

Yours very sincerely

ARTHUR JAMES BALFOUR

WSC to Jack Churchill

EXTRACT

9 October 1902　　　　　　　　　　　　　　　　　Canford Manor
　　　　　　　　　　　　　　　　　　　　　　　　Wimborne

My dear Jack,

I was very sorry not to see you going through London, and I earnestly hope you have not begun working too soon. I shall be back in London on the 15th for the opening of Parliament and hope to find you flourishing.

I have accepted Cassel's invitation to go to Egypt for the opening of the Dam and I start on the 20th of November and shall not be back until the 15th December. During this period you could hunt my horses two days a week, and I think, if it would do you no harm physically or financially, you should make arrangements to get that month away from the City. I think it very important that you should have fresh air, etc and should live quietly at Blenheim, or at Oxford (if they are not there) for that period, and if there is any difficulty from the City point of view, I will talk to Cassel about it. Cassel has secured me £10,000 of the Japanese Loan, on which I hope to make a small profit. You ought to go and see him, he told me he had asked you to do so, and as you know, he is laid up with Water on the Knee. Please recollect that I have told him nothing.

I have been all through the letters, which you looked over, and find your work very useful indeed. There are here, in addition, some of the most interesting Scrap Books, collected by Cornelia, that I ever saw in my life, which are of inestimable value to me in my work. Indeed, I may say I now have all the information I require.

　　　　　　　　　　　　　　　　　　　　　　　　Yours ever
　　　　　　　　　　　　　　　　　　　　　　　WINSTON S. C.

WSC to Lord Rosebery
(Rosebery Papers)

10 October 1902　　　　　　　　　　　　　　　　105 Mount Street

Most private

My dear Lord Rosebery,

Beach is departed for foreign lands; but his consent to my letter fully authorises the publication of that part of his speech wh deals with economy & efficiency; & I will be responsible that this is so, and that the educational part need not be included. But if I were printing it I should begin 'After dealing with the Education Bill wh he defended & supported, Sir M.H.B. said: –' for this is not only scrupulously fair to him, but even lends weight to what follows by vindicating the toryism of the speaker.

I enclose you a letter from the man of my committee on whom I chiefly depend. It is a striking letter. If by an 'evolutionary process' we could create a wing of the Tory party wh could either infuse vigour into the parent body or join a central coalition, *my plan* would become most important as an incident in or possibly as the herald of the movement. But the risk & peril of it would be vy great, & it would carry consequences to me wh I cannot foresee; & only the conviction that you are upholding the flag for which my father fought so long & so disastrously would nerve me to the plunge. The Government of the Middle – the party wh shall be free at once from the sordid selfishness & callousness of Toryism on the one hand & the blind appetites of the Radical masses on the other – may be an ideal wh we perhaps shall never attain, wh could in any case only be possessed for a time, but which is nevertheless worth working for: & I for my part, see no reason to despair of that 'good state'.

But I should like to bring you & Beach together. There lies the chance of a central coalition. 'Tory-Liberal' is a much better name than 'Tory Democrat' or 'Liberal Imperialist': & certainly neither paradoxical nor unprecedented. The one real difficulty I have to encounter is the suspicion that I am moved by mere restless ambition: & if some definite issue – such as Tariff – were to arise – that difficulty would disappear.

Yours always
WINSTON S. CHURCHILL

The settlement of the Education Bill must of course precede everything else.

Lord Rosebery to WSC

12 October 1902   Dalmeny

Private

My dear Winston,

Many thanks for letting me see the enclosure, which I return. It is full of sound sense. You must not compromise your career by premature action. Some day, perhaps not long hence, the psychological moment may come for a new departure, but it is not yet.

The fact is people in this country fight about names and not things. Their first object is to enfold as many people as possible behind some obsolete crumbling ramparts on which they have hoisted a pole which once held a flag. Why the people are there or why in the other they can scarcely say themselves. As for me, I am fighting the 'machine', and the 'machine' will probably win, as your friend surmises. But I can do no other.

I am off to London tonight for a few days.

Yrs always
AR

WSC to the Editor, the Oldham Chronicle

28 October 1902   House of Commons

Sir,

The main propositions of Free Trade do not touch methods of raising revenue. Money has to be found for carrying on the government of the country, and when revenue alone is the object of the tax no violation of Free Trade principles occurs. The corn-tax and the sugar-tax were both imposed for revenue purposes, and for revenue purposes alone. They were imposed during a period of war when it was absolutely vital to find the necessary money, and they were an alternative infinitely to be preferred by an economist to a larger proportion of borrowing. Therefore there is no inconsistency whatever between the vote which I gave in support of this taxation and the principles of Free Trade, of which I must confess myself a sober admirer. No one knows this better than the able writer of your article on Saturday last, and I am therefore rather surprised at the false conclusions he allows himself to draw.

The questions of shipping subsidies, of the Brussels Sugar Convention, of the desirability of taxing food stuffs or necessaries, or of making preferential distinctions in taxation raised honestly and primarily for revenue purposes, are complicated special cases, which must be considered separately on their merits as they arise; and their aspect in an economic sense, though a very important aspect, is by no means the only one which should be examined.

You allude especially to the Brussels Sugar Convention, and as you may value in others a precision and candour of statement not always evident in your own practice let me add that I have not yet been able to discover arguments sufficient to vindicate the Brussels Sugar Convention as a wise act of policy, and that, as at present advised, I do not propose to vote for its ratification.

Yours faithfully
WINSTON S. CHURCHILL

Lawrence C. Tipper[1] to WSC

3 November 1902   Ribbesford
                                                   Moseley
                                                   Birmingham

Sir,

I note by a report from the *Manchester Courier* of October 24th, you state, 'that Lord Randolph Churchill was inclined to be in favour of Fair Trade, but afterwards he might be said to have been a moderate Free Trader.'

As you practically deny the assertion of Sir Howard Vincent MP,[2] the worthy champion of the Protection of British and Colonial Industries, I wish to correct the error into which you have fallen.

The late Lord Randolph Churchill was undoubtedly a Fair Trader at heart up to the end. In the Committee Room of the Birmingham Town Hall, after one of his great Meetings, at which Meeting I intended to criticise his conduct for deserting and throwing over the Fair Trade party, his Lordship said 'Within these walls I am a Fair Trader, outside I don't know anything about Fair Trade. When the Masses shout for Fair Trade then I shall be willing to take up and champion the Cause.'

Some few years since I made this known publicly at St James's Hall, London.

I am, Sir, Your obedient servant
LAWRENCE C. TIPPER

Note by WSC:

1. Ask Mr Moore Bayley of Birmingham what he thinks of the enclosed answer to Mr Tipper & whether he would recommend its being sent.
2. Retain letter.
3. Copy answer.

---

[1] Lawrence Clarke Tipper (1855–1939), principal director of B. C. Tipper and Sons, Veterinary Medicine Manufacturers; sometime Chairman of the Birmingham branch of the Fair Trade League and an eye-witness of the Aston Riots in 1883. The Tippers specialised in: 'Vitalis', a stock medicine for general treatment of animals, Cow Relief for Hard Udders and Sore Teats, Cod Liver Oil Condiments and Veterinary Vaccines and Calf Feeders.

[2] (Charles Edward) Howard Vincent (1849–1908), Conservative MP for Central Sheffield 1885–1908; Chairman, National Union of Conservative Associations 1895; a prominent tariff reformer; brother of Sir Edgar Vincent; KCMG 1899.

WSC to Lawrence C. Tipper

4 November 1902

[Copy]

Sir,

The remarkable account which you give of your treatment of the confidences of the late Lord Randolph Churchill does not encourage me to embark upon a personal correspondence with you.

Yours faithfully
WINSTON S. CHURCHILL

Lord Dudley[1] to WSC

9 November 1902   Vice Regal Lodge
                                                    Dublin

My dear Winston,

I am glad to hear that you enjoyed your visit to Dublin and that you were interested by what you saw over here.

We were very pleased to have you staying with us and if you ever care to come again you have only to let us know when it would suit you to come.

As I told you the other day, if at any time you care to see Ireland for yourself and study Irish questions on the spot, we both hope that you will look upon this house as your headquarters for as long as you like.

I hear that you made an excellent speech the other night and that they gave you a very cordial reception.

Please don't be too extreme a Free Trader, or refuse to listen to any question of a protective tariff. I agree with you absolutely that the prosperity of this country depends on cheap food and cheap raw material and that we must do nothing to permanently interfere with our power of obtaining both these things, but at the same time I am convinced that before long we shall be forced to make bargains in trade matters both with our Colonies and other countries.

Free Trade notwithstanding, we are gradually but surely being beaten by Germany and the US in colonial and other markets and the defenceless position that our present system leaves us in, makes us powerless to arrest the downward tendency.

A commercial war is being hotly waged against us and yet because we are cowards we refuse to avail ourselves of arms to combat our enemies.

[1] William Humble Ward, 2nd Earl of Dudley (1867–1932), Lord Lieutenant of Ireland 1902–6; Governor-General of Australia 1908–11.

We are afraid of the temporary consequences of touching our free trade policy and we therefore allow our enemies to ravage our territories unchecked. Just as well might we say that because we are a Christian people and abhor the bloodshed of war, so therefore should we refuse to maintain our rights or defend our property by force of arms – At this moment our Colonies are enthusiastically Imperialistic – and would much rather trade with us, where local manufactures are not concerned, than with other countries. They are prepared to give us considerable preferences but they will not continue to do that unless we can give a *quid pro quo*.

Such however is for the moment impossible because of the extreme character of our trade arrangements.

If therefore we are to count upon Colonial markets as primarily open to our goods, we must in turn be prepared to give to the Colonies opportunities of supplying us with what we require on better terms than those open to other countries.

And this we can only do by the inauguration of a system of preferential tariffs and some modification of our present free trade policy.

And so long as prices in this country are not permanently affected I cannot see why anyone should object. If Canada, as she might do in 10 years, can supply us with bread as cheaply as Russia or the Argentine, why shouldn't she. If Australia can send beef and mutton into England at the same price as the United States why not depend upon Colonial supplies; we in return getting a preference in their markets for all those goods (and they are many) which do not compete with Colonial manufactures. I grant that the subject is a difficult one, but it is only by open-minded discussion that we can arrive at a conclusion and I am afraid that if the bigotry of the Manchester School is allowed too much scope we shall postpone considering these vital questions till too late.

Talk to Chamberlain some day if you get a chance on these matters and I shall be surprised if he doesn't express the opinion that a large body of commercial men in England are in favour of some policy of this kind.

Goodbye old man. Good luck on your trip to Egypt.

Yrs ever

D

Joseph H. Choate[1] to WSC
EXTRACT

11 November 1902   American Embassy
                                        London

Dear Mr Churchill,
  ... Your friends at Oldham have been very kind and cordial before in
inviting me to come to them, but I have never been able to do so. And
this time again I am sorry to say that it will be quite impossible for me to
accept their invitation. It seems now to be settled that I shall be absent 'on
leave' during the whole time mentioned in your letter, and probably later.
At any rate I should not be willing to make any such engagement to call me
back in case I wanted to stay away longer. I am greatly obliged to you for
your kind interest in the matter and to your good friends at Oldham for their
good will and hospitable intentions.

                                        Yours most truly
                                        JOSEPH H. CHOATE

Ernest Fletcher[2] to WSC

13 November 1902   The Hindles
                                        Atherton

Dear Sir,
  May I ask you as an ardent Free Trader to be so kind as to enlighten me
on one or two points, or to recommend me some publication or publications
that will help.
  I have started at our local Conservative Club various discussions, & we
are to have shortly some arguments in favour of protection, *as an Empire*,
that is against all except our own Colonies.
  I want to be able to argue against this, but in my own mind I am inclined
to consider it the right thing.
  In your opinion
1) Would there be any objection to this if we were self supporting, with the
assistance of our colonies?
2) Are we so? Can we get from our own selves & our colonies all that we
require, in the way of food stuffs & raw material.

[1] Joseph Hodges Choate (1832–1917), United States Ambassador to the United Kingdom
1899–1905.
[2] Solicitor, member of the firm of Watkins, Son and Fletcher.

I can understand that our system of allowing other countries' goods to come in free is good for this Country because we cannot get on without such goods, but in a case like the *following*, is not an import duty advisable.

'America or Germany overproduces for some time; & rather than not get rid of the article overproduced sends it into this country & (at a loss) sells it at of course a price with which we cannot compete, & spoils the market for the home article.'

Your views on these points would be much valued by me both for the purpose mentioned & for general use.

My excuse for writing is a profound ignorance on the subject coupled with a wish to learn, without knowing what to read to enlighten me.

Any reply to this is of course not in any way for publication.

Trusting to be favoured with a reply, & apologising for occupying your time.

Yours faithfully
ERNEST FLETCHER

PS I cannot unfortunately apply to my own member for help, as we are 'represented' by C. P. Scott.[1]

WSC to Ernest Fletcher

14 November 1902   105 Mount Street

[Copy]

Dear Sir,

I have never described myself as 'an ardent Free Trader' but as a 'sober admirer of Free Trade principles' which is not quite the same thing.

I think that the discussions which you have inaugurated at your Club must be of great value and use and I most heartily wish you success.

As to the question of 'a protected Empire', I could not pretend to put any arguments at length before you but it would seem to me a fantastic policy to endeavour to shut the British Empire up in a ringed fence. It is very large, and there are many good things which can be produced in it but the world is larger & produces some better things than can ever be found in the British Empire. Why should we deny ourselves the good and varied merchandise which the traffic of the world offers, more especially since the more we trade with others, the more they must trade with us; for it is quite clear that we give them something else back for everything they give to us. Our planet is

[1] Charles Prestwich Scott (1846–1932), the great editor of the *Manchester Guardian* 1872–1929, was Liberal MP for the Leigh Division of Lancashire 1895–1905. Opponent of Free Trade.

not a very big one compared with the other celestial bodies, and I see no particular reason why we should endeavour to make inside our planet a smaller planet called the British Empire, cut off by impossible space from everything else. The idea does not attract me as an idea, because, although it may be worth while as circumstances arise, to make commercial treaties in special cases, either with our Colonies or with Foreign countries, I for one, should scrutinize these projects very carefully.

[Winston S. Churchill]

WSC to Lady Randolph

19 December 1902   Savoy Hotel
                                                                Cairo

My dearest Mamma,

It was very kind of you to open the Bazaar & I am sure those people were vy pleased at your going. I don't know what I should have done if you had failed me. They were already put out at my absence & if no one had taken Consuelo's place would have been – not perhaps altogether unnaturally – sulky.

Well here we are back in Cairo after what I would say has been a satisfactory and pleasant expedition. I have seen all the temples and sights and have pressed forward with my writing also to no inconsiderable extent. Cassel is an excellent host – never exacting or touchy, always the same – and most anxious for everybody's comfort & contentment. Mrs Keppel[1] is vy good company & we have made other friends. Now there is a scheme – of which I have been given the arrangement – for a four days tour through the desert on camels to Fayoum, an oasis about 70 miles away from the Nile. We start on Monday so I shall not be able to catch my boat before the 29th via Brindisi or possibly even the 1st via Naples. I wonder whether we could meet in Paris. I do not want to be back in England if it is freezing until 10th or 11th. Perhaps you will send me a telegram here on receipt of this, if any arrangement is possible. In any case I shall stay two days in Paris, for I want to drink some claret at Voisins.

Beach & the Beach family were really quite an accession. I rejoiced in my talks with him. He is such a good and true friend; & we agree in almost everything political. I only wish he were going to be back in Parliament during the early part of the session for I foresee many possibilities of co-operation: & in regard to the book he has been vy diligent & ready to help

---

[1] Alice Frederica Keppel (1869–1947), wife of Lieutenant-Colonel George Keppel, 3rd son of 7th Earl of Albemarle; youngest daughter of Admiral Sir William Edmonstone, 4th Baronet. The friend of King Edward VII.

Gorst père is also here: I think he will have to advise the new 'group' on questions of procedure next session. Did you see that that silly Brodrick was compelled to withdraw his proposals about the Yeomanry owing to the opposition of Ernest Beckett, Seely & others of our little band. It has been a vy good preliminary canter and has no doubt increased the possibilities of further combined action in the future.

I have learned 'bridge' & we now play every day at least four rubbers. It amuses me. Mrs Cassel talks more than ever in broken English & is a little on my nerves; but she is a harmless and well meaning creature.

This land is overflowing with agricultural prosperity and the people sprawl continuously on full bellies under a genial sun. I fear our poor folks at home are far from this happy state now that the winter threatens to be such a hard one. You will see in the near future what vindication my views of two years ago on economy and Army policy will remain and how much support they will get.

Always your loving son
WINSTON

WSC to Lady Randolph

[December 1902]   Assouan

Dearest Mamma,

It was very pleasant to get your letter, and makes me realise that we may lose much by not writing more. But I have to use my pen so often & here I can find no shorthand writer.

I am not very well, having a touch of fever and – so the doctor asserts – of rheumatism, and today I am left alone on deck while everyone else is gone to see the dam. The Connaughts and Leonie arrive tomorrow & I still hope to attend the function. But after all that was not my only object in coming to Egypt. The trip so far has been vy comfortable & everything has moved on smoothly oiled wheels. The steamer is magnificent – the food good – too good I fear for me at present, and the company very kind & good tempered.

For the last two days we have had the Beaches – 5 in all. He has taken great interest in my work (which I persevere in every morning) & has given me plenty of information on important points. Altogether the book is making progress & I begin to see its limits in every direction. It ought to see the light in March 1904 – as I originally designed.

I have seen various temples. Carnac was a disappointment. Ruin has made too great progress and the fall of eleven more columns has much diminished the grandeur of the great hall. On the other hand there are some new excavations which are worth seeing. I have also visited Dendera & Sakkara – the latter not much to see – but very wonderful to think about.

The Trade Union matter is as you suppose tiresome & difficult. There is much reason in their case: yet they make unreasonable demands. These demands the Conservatives meet with flat refusal. I want to see them grapple with the difficulties & remove the force from the demand by conceding all that is just in it. But middle courses are proverbially unpopular. As to the next election – my mind is at present a blank. But we shall have some clearer light to work in before then. Aird[1] wants me to speak in Paddington. I have said Yes.

I often think of you and Jack: and feel vy anxious about him. Please concentrate your attention on him. He is rather untamed & forlorn.

Always your loving son
WINSTON

[1] John Aird (1833–1911), Conservative MP for North Paddington 1887–1905; baronet 1901.

4

Free Trade

(See Main Volume Chapter 2)

D URING the early part of 1903 WSC continued to attack the Government's Army scheme, and on February 24 he made a particularly successful speech in the House – 'his finest effort', said the *Morning Post*: Lady Randolph was in the Gallery; so was Lord Rosebery.

> WSC to Lord Rosebery
> *(Rosebery Papers)*

24 February 1903   105 Mount Street

My dear Lord Rosebery,

I am so glad you were there & approved. I think it is the most successful speech I have yet made – and the House of Commons purred like an amiable cat.

Our advance guard action has really been most successful. If the Irish had voted with us the Government majority would hardly have been 50 – and what a fifty! 18 Unionists voted against them: about 15 deliberately abstained.[1]

Our friends are all extremely well satisfied and more full of fight than ever. There were indications both in Brodrick's & AJB's speeches of an impending change in military policy.

My only fear is that we may succeed too soon.

If France had made peace after Worth[2] perhaps the German Empire would never have been formed!

Yours ever
WINSTON SC

[1] An amendment hostile to the Secretary of State for War was moved by Ernest Beckett and seconded by Jack Seely – both Unionists. It was rejected by 261 votes against 145, eighteen Unionists, including WSC, voting for the amendment.
[2] The first French disaster of the Franco-Prussian War, August 1870.

PS Supposing you were going to walk in the Park this morning & would like my escort would you let me know.

WSC

WSC to Sir Henry Campbell-Bannerman

26 March [1903]   105 Mount Street

Private

Dear Sir Henry Campbell-Bannerman,

Some of my friends were vy much perplexed last night at the compromise which was effected between the front benches at 11.45. We had intended to vote in support of Pirie's motion and on a clear issue, such as the refusal of the Government to accept it, a good division might have been obtained. We were therefore much embarrassed when at an hour when no explanation was possible an amendment was sprung upon the house & received your blessing. Of course we had assumed that your only desire would have been to persuade as many Unionists to vote against the Government as possible.

The difficulties & dangers which confront those who from our side of the house are attempting to arrest the Army Policy of the Ministry must be my excuse for this letter.

Yours vy truly
WINSTON S. CHURCHILL

J. T. Travis-Clegg to WSC

21 April 1903   Shaw Lodge
                                                       near Oldham

Draft

My dear Mr Churchill,

Now that you are able to resume your Parliamentary work, I have to thank you for sending me a copy of your pamphlet on *Mr Brodrick's Army*.

I trust you will not be deterred by any such correspondence from carrying on your campaign for 'economical efficiency', the plan of which is contained in your speeches, and with which all those Unionists who are not blinded by party passion or prejudice will heartily agree.

I am, Yours sincerely
JAMES T. TRAVIS-CLEGG

24 April 1903   House of Commons

[Copy]

Dear Mr Travis-Clegg,

I am very much encouraged by your kind letter and by the confidence which you express: but it may be just as well for me to make my position quite clear to our friends at Oldham.

You will remember that at the last election I pledged myself in the plainest terms to the cause of Army Reform; and it was therefore with much disgust that I saw the Government, within a month of the meeting of Parliament, commit themselves to a policy not of Army Reform but of Army Increase and try to varnish over the defects revealed by the War with a grandiose scheme and a lavish outlay of public money. Since then I have taken several opportunities of complaining both in and out of the House of Commons. But it is of course utterly impossible for any private member acting alone to influence in the slightest degree the policy of a powerful government. He may make speeches; but that is all. Hardly any question is ever decided on its merits. Divisions are taken on strict party lines and Ministers have at their disposal a monopoly of expert opinion for and against every conceivable course, a battalion of drilled supporters and the last word in all debates.

Seeing therefore on the one hand the disquieting condition of the Army and upon the other the difficulties which confront any one who would expose it, I felt it my duty last autumn to join with a number of Conservative & Liberal Unionist members, who, in company with Mr Ernest Beckett, the Conservative member for Whitby, had resolved to pay great attention to all Army questions, and to take common action in the cause of Army Reform. That association as I understand it – and of course I speak only for myself – is in its action limited to questions affecting the size and efficiency of the Army, to the finance connected therewith and the expenditure necessitated thereby. Its definite and immediate object is to secure a substantial modification of Mr Brodrick's Army Scheme of 1901 in respect of organisation, numbers and cost. It is in that intention that the debates have been conducted this session. I have every reason to believe that the same course will be pursued in the future: and if the object for which we are working should be attained, I do not at present see any reason why the association should continue.

Now of course it has been very much easier for the defenders of the War Office to traduce the motives of their critics than to justify themselves. The Government declare that every question connected with the Army is a question of confidence. Every vote given against the Army scheme is a vote against the most sacred principles of the Conservative party. The Empire, the constitution, the established Church, the Union, the rights of property and the liberties of men – all are discovered to stand on the foundation of six Army Corps. There is no middle path between 'pro-Brodrick' and 'pro-Boer'. When it is found that these thunders, which if effective would reduce every Unionist Member to a puppet contrived mechanically to vote in the same lobby with Sir Alexander Acland-Hood,[1] are heard with some amusement by the Press and the public, and leave the persons at whom they are especially directed quite undisturbed, other methods are employed.

These other methods, adopted without their approval, must have caused a great deal of embarrassment to Mr Balfour and Mr Chamberlain; but they have afforded a fine opportunity for the talents of Tadpole and Taper.[2] By gossip in the Lobbies and by anonymous letters to faithful newspapers it has been represented that the movement of opinion against the Army Policy – whole-hearted, honest, practically spontaneous as it is – is in fact only a dirty intrigue depending on an agreement with the Liberal Imperialists and having for its object the ousting of Mr Balfour from the leadership of the Unionist party and the installation of a Rosebery government by which the Army Reformers would be paid for their trouble. I am glad you have taken these allegations at their proper worth. They are false statements, made it is to be hoped by persons ignorant of the truth.

In spite of these methods an immense advantage has been gained to the Empire by the debates of the present session. Great principles connected with Imperial Defence have been established and are generally recognised, although only last year they were denied or ignored: the War Office, instead of setting the pace to the Conservative party, is now only anxious to make a retreat with as much baggage as possible. All sorts of people who laughed at economy – who looked at it indeed as if it was something positively immoral – are beginning to wag their heads over the pounds, shillings and pence; and already the Budget of 1903 casts its shadow upon the Army Estimates of 1904.

Army Expenditure does not stand alone. It is the keystone in an arch of extravagance.

The profuse example of the War Office corrupts other Departments; and the self respect of Ministers is sapped by the constant necessity of defending

[1] Alexander Fuller-Acland-Hood (1853–1917), Conservative MP for West Somerset 1892–1917; Parliamentary Secretary to the Treasury 1902–06; succeeded father as 4th Baronet 1892; PC 1904; Baron St Audries 1911; married Mildred Rose Eveleigh-de-Moleyns, 2nd daughter of 4th Baron Ventry 1888.
[2] Fictitious MPs in Disraeli's Coningsby who indulged in fruitless political speculation and gossip.

what they know to be unsound. The attempted preparation of enormous land forces distorts the sense of political, financial and strategic proportion. England is forgotten amid the splendour of her Empire. I have not any lengthy experience of politics, yet even in the five years which have passed since I formally became associated with the Conservative party, considerable changes have been effected in its policy and character. Five years ago the sagacious statecraft of Lord Salisbury was preserving us in spite of the taunts of the Imperialist section of the opposition, from one terrible war about China, and kept us clear of other perils in Eastern Europe into which we might have been drawn by the more sentimental Radicals. Five years ago the Army cost only 18 millions; taxation was light, wages were up, commodities were down and notwithstanding the growing wealth of the country a judicious economy was enforced in the public departments. Five years ago the Workmen's Compensation Act had conferred an immense benefit upon Labour; and the Conservatives and Liberal Unionists by this compact seemed almost to have attained that grand ideal of a National Party of which Lord Randolph Churchill dreamed and for which he toiled.

Yours vy truly
WINSTON S. CHURCHILL

*   *   *   *   *

On 15 May 1903 Joseph Chamberlain, in a speech in Birmingham, proposed that a system of Imperial Preference be introduced in order to promote imperial unity.

WSC to J. Moore Bayley

20 May 1903   105 Mount Street
Private

[Copy]

My dear Moore Bayley,

I was extremely glad to get your very sensible letter with which I cordially agree. I do not think this preferential tariff cock will fight long. The almost insuperable difficulties of framing any scheme which would satisfy all the Colonies, & the certainty of future bickerings and hagglings are alone enough to discourage any but old men in a hurry! The only way in which we can help the Colonies is by paying duties on raw materials and foodstuffs – the very commodities taxation of which cannot be of the slightest use or value to the manufacturer.

Is it conceivable that the manufacturer will be content to bear this burden all by himself and let both English agriculturalists and Colonial producers gain the benefit? No, he will infallibly demand a *quid pro quo;* and as surely as we embark upon the slippery path of protection, we shall finish up amid a tangle of high protective tariffs of all kinds. If that be so, exit for ever the banking, broking, warehousing predominance of Great Britain.

I do not want a selfcontained Empire. It is very much better that the great nations of the world should be interdependent one upon the other than that they should be independent of each other. That makes powerfully for peace and it is chiefly through the cause of the great traffic of one great nation with another during the last twenty five years that the peace of Europe has been preserved through so many crises.

And even if it comes to an European war, do you not think it very much better that the United States should be vitally interested in keeping the English market open, than that they should be utterly careless of what happens to their present principal customer?

I deprecate very much the raising of this controversy, it is premature, it is ill considered, it is unsound. It is far more sensible to try to get the Colonials gradually to adopt our free trade system, than that we should try their vicious policy of protection. If, as I fear may be the case, this question is raised as a vital issue, great harm will be done to Imperial sentiment by the language which will be used about the Colonies and their share in the burdens of the State; and most certainly it will split and tear the Unionist party from one end to the other. I earnestly hope you will practise the greatest caution. The Fourth party is perfectly sound.

Yours vy ty
WINSTON S. CHURCHILL

Please keep me in touch with B'ham & Midland feeling.

WSC

WSC to A. J. Balfour

EXTRACT

25 May 1903   [House of Commons]

Most private
Dear Mr Balfour,

You have shown me so much kindness in the past that I am encouraged to write to you frankly now about Mr Chamberlain's recent statements, & indeed the matter seems to me so important that it is my duty to do so.

At Birmingham he advocated Preferential Tariffs with the Colonies; in his

letter of Monday to a Mr Lovesay he revealed plain Protectionist intentions;
& in the House on Friday last he showed himself prepared to use Old Age
Pensions as a lever to attain these ends. Now I see it stated by Mr Bonar Law
that you are agreed with him in all this.

I earnestly hope this is not true & that you have not taken an irrevocable
decision. Hence this letter.

I am utterly opposed to anything which will alter the Free Trade character
of this country; & I consider such an issue superior in importance to any
other now before us. . . . I am persuaded that once this policy is begun it
must lead to the establishment of a complete Protective system, involving
commercial disaster, & the Americanisation of English politics. I do not now
attempt to argue all this. But I submit these two points to you: 1. From a
national point of view there is no case for a fiscal revolution . . . 2. From a
party point of view the government is probably less unpopular than any
which has ruled 8 years in England.

Their record – army & expenditure apart – will make a fine page in
history. They have no reason to dread an appeal to the constituencies; and
even if a general election should result in a transference of power, the conservative party would be in a strong minority to protect those causes and
institutions which they cherish. In five or six years a healthy operation of
opinion would recall them once more to power. Why is it necessary to play
such desperate stakes?

. . . I should like to tell you that an attempt on your part to preserve the
Free Trade policy & character of the Tory party would command my
absolute loyalty . . . But if on the other hand you have made up your mind
& there is no going back, I must reconsider my position in politics.

Please do not consider this letter disrespectful or anything but a statement
of fact, I should be very sorry to cause you annoyance of any kind. . . .

Yours vy sincerely
WINSTON S. CHURCHILL

A. J. Balfour to WSC

26 May 1903   10 Downing Street

Private   Dictated

My dear Winston,

I am very much obliged to you for your letter.

I have not seen Chamberlain's letter, and am mildly surprised that Bonar
Law[1] should have taken us under his aegis, as you tell me he has done.

[1] Andrew BONAR LAW.

I have never understood that Chamberlain advocated protection, though, no doubt, he is ready and, indeed, anxious – for a duty on food stuffs, which may incidentally be protective in its character, but whose main object is to provide an instrument for fiscal union with the Colonies. This is a very different thing from protection, both in theory and in practice. But undoubtedly the matter is one of difficulty, and requires the most wary walking.

Yours sincerely

A. J. BALFOUR

WSC to Lord Rosebery
(*Rosebery Papers*)

29 May 1903   105 Mount Street

Private

My dear Lord,

What a pity your lieutenants were not in their places yesterday![1] Asquith would have had an opportunity after Chamberlain sat down which may not recur. The whole burden of protest was left to us.

I am absolutely in earnest in this business & if by the aid & under the aegis of Beach we cannot save the Tory party from Protection, I shall look to you.

Yours vy sincerely

WINSTON S. CHURCHILL

WSC to Lord Hugh Cecil

(*Quickswood Papers*)

29 May 1903   105 Mount Street

My dear Linky,

I sent round to you this morning in the hopes of catching you. You will get my letter with an enclosure from Beach in due course. I send you a copy of a letter I have written to Campbell-Bannerman about the amendment to the Finance Bill. Please return it when read. I hope you will agree with the suggestion I have made. To my mind it is of vital importance that whatever the decision of the Conservative Party, it should be arrived at as soon as

[1] On the motion for the adjournment of the House over the Whitsun recess, in which Sir Charles Dilke drew attention to Chamberlain's speeches on fiscal policy. WSC, who spoke immediately after Chamberlain, warned that Chamberlain's proposals, if carried out, would lead to the Conservative Party being replaced by a party based on tariffs. During the debate Balfour stated that the Government would not alter its fiscal policy before a dissolution.

possible after the Whitsuntide holidays, for nothing can be worse than continued disagreement. That being so, all we have to look for is a clear issue. According to Ludlow,[1] whom I met this morning, Balfour must be taken to be irrevocably committed to Chamberlain. I am still in hopes this may not be true.

I have written to Beach persuading him to address a Meeting in the St James's Hall, and when I hear from you I will make a suitable announcement in the papers and put all arrangements *en train*.

I shall come up to London next week to see various people, and perhaps if I let you know, we might meet for a meal.

Write to me at Blenheim.

Yours ever

WINSTON S. CHURCHILL

Ivor Guest to WSC

29 May 1903   Canford Manor
                                               Wimborne

Dear Winston,

Your letter to hand.

Joe's move is most astute and places Unionist Free Traders in a very difficult position.

The fallacy, if fallacy there be in his new policy, is remote and concealed winding intricate arguments to expose and experience to substantiate while the advantages are palpable and immediate [*sic*].

I doubt whether a tax on foodstuffs – small in the first place – would be much felt or resented by the masses while the bribe of Pensions – to be covered in the first sessions of the new Parliament favourably introspective in character – would I think be powerful.

I don't see how the great Agricultural Industry can be expected to reject protection. Manufacturers will be seduced by the promise of the Home Market Monopoly and Retaliation.

These three interests may be sufficient to win the election. Moreover the introductions of a quite new issue would check the tendency which favours alternative parties in power. Still it is by no means certain that Joe will succeed though I am bound to say that I think the odds are just a shade on him at present.

Because, you see, if AJB gives a temporising acquiescence such as will not wholly alienate and dismay his supporters, Joe will be able to foist his

[1] Henry Ludlow Lopes (1865–1922), barrister; succeeded father as 2nd Baron Ludlow 1899.

ideas upon the party to the extent of having them included in the official programme.

No doubt they will be dexterously kept in the offing – ideals, vaguely defined, of great promise which need a 'mandate' to investigate.

Once successful in the country it will be easy to declare that the mandate – not for enquiry – but action has been obtained, and that this Party is pledged to protectionist socialistic Imperialism.

It is quite possible that by this skilful indefiniteness and by AJB's weakness and love of ease that nine tenths of the present Unionist members will remain in the double fold and go to the country in apparent agreement.

Those who revolt will in most cases lose their seats – however disagreeable they may be able to make themselves at the country elections – and should the Election go for the present Government something very like political annihilation will await all but the most distinguished of their Members. I don't anticipate that many of the present cabinet will be found among the conscientious objectors. Salary, loyalty, Balfour's personal and intellectual charm will hold them together. Even Beach is not quite clean handed with his corn tax.

Then take the party as a whole. Here is a chance – the only chance probably – of another term of power and for individuals of a seat in the House.

To fight on the record of past achievements would not be very inspiring to any constituency. Will they not think thus, the majority of them?

So far politically then as to the economic question who can dogmatise?

Altogether I keep rather an open and empty mind on the subject. I am too far away here to feel in touch with things.

I think that if this policy became officially recognised and if I totally disagreed with it that it would be better not to contest the next election. This may seem pusillanimous but I am not sure if it would not be more prudent than to court defeat.

Then there is something undignified in trying to split your own party's vote elsewhere out of mere spite.

In any case if one stood I think it should be as an independent elsewhere. I dont see how I could do it at Plymouth with Duke representing the official view in sharp antagonism to myself.

However much depends upon the events of the next two months and of how far Joe can lead AJB and the party by the nose. I should like to discuss it all with you. After my Yeomanry is over I go to Plymouth Thursday for a couple of nights. Saturday will find me at Blenheim. Do come and instruct me.

Yours ever
IVOR

WSC to Sir Henry Campbell-Bannerman

29 May 1903   105 Mount Street

[Copy]

Most Private

Dear Sir Henry Campbell-Bannerman,

I am anxious about your amendment to the Finance Bill, which seems to me to court a decision of first importance upon a false issue. After all we like the Finance Bill, and refusing to proceed with it will unite the whole Conservative party: protectionists who will be glad to triumph over you: Free Traders who are bound to support Ritchie[1] and the repeal of the corn tax. The result can only be a disastrous division and an immense victory for Chamberlain. This is Sir Michael Hicks Beach's opinion as well as that of my friends.

Is it not possible for the discussion, for which we are all anxious, to be raised in some other way? You are quite justified in asking the Government to put down a resolution, or in moving a vote of want of confidence on the ground that their public utterances conflict with their declared fiscal policy – and Mr Balfour would be bound to give full opportunity. But let us at any rate have a discussion which can be terminated by a division on a fair issue.

You will of course understand that the position of those Conservatives who are unalterably opposed to the impending fiscal change is one of great difficulty and danger; and I earnestly hope you will consider us in the course you take.

Believe me, yours sincerely
WINSTON S. CHURCHILL

Lord Hugh Cecil to WSC

[30 May 1903]   Hatfield

My dear Winston,

I am greatly put out at your writing to CB without consulting me. It is scarcely fair; & I am far from feeling sure that the tactics are not a profound mistake.

It is of course difficult to say (at the pace we are moving) what will be the situation a fortnight hence. But at this moment nothing would be more

[1] Charles Thompson Ritchie, 1st Baron Ritchie (1838–1906), Chancellor of the Exchequer 1902–3; Conservative MP for Tower Hamlets 1874–85; St George's-in-the-East 1885–92; Croydon 1895–1905; President of Local Government Board 1886–92; Board of Trade 1895–1900; Home Secretary 1900–2.

:alamitous than a division on a clear issue. We might get thirty people on our
ide to vote with us. I want to get a hundred or 150. Our game is at all
1azards to avoid a division in wh we should vote with the Opposition. An
1mmense section of the party have not yet anything like the courage or
disloyalty' to go into the lobby on a vote of censure with the leaders of the
Opposition. Yet they may be Free Traders at heart. It is much better to
begin an agitation on as large a scale as possible & tempt trembling sheep
on to our platforms. After Arthur's speech no one can call this disloyal &
many may be coaxed over to us who wd now shudder at the thought of
voting with the Opposition against the Govt. Indeed if the Opposition do try
& raise a clear issue I think it would be wise for me to try & find an ingenious
way of voting myself with the Govt so that the issue shd not be clear but
confused. But in any case it wd be a calamity.

An additional but minor objection is that we ought not to act with CB at
all. Rosebery & Grey are our friends. We must try & split their party as well
as our own.

Generally: – 1. Our first object is to get as many MPs on our side as we
can. We must be most decorous & respectable; & put Beach & Goschen (if
he will come) in the forefront of all we do. We must avoid a 'Fourth Party'
atmosphere; & ask ourselves constantly what wd (e.g.) Sir J. Fergusson[1] think
of this?

2. It's no use angling any further for Arthur. He must go his own way. He
knows clearly what we think.

3. As much as possible we must throw the discredit of splitting the party on
Joe. There must be no secession unless in answer to some act of war on his
side. Happily Arthur has given us licence to discuss & that justifies agitation
and even a Free Trade League.

4. For all the foregoing reasons I am against any divisions in the House
& in favour of meetings.

But beyond & above all I must ask you as a condition of co-operation not
to take any public or important action without consulting me or Beach whom
I am quite willing to regard as a leader & trust as such. I will in like manner
consult you or him.

I thought your interview with the *Westminster* [*Gazette*] rather unwise – I
am sure it wd offend the trembling sheep.

Yrs ever

HUGH CECIL

[1] Sir James Fergusson, 6th Baronet (1832–1907), Conservative MP North East Manchester
1885–1906; politician and colonial administrator; Governor and C-in-C South Australia
1868; New Zealand 1873–5; Governor of Bombay 1880–5; Under-Secretary of State for
India 1860–7; Home Office 1867–8; Under-Secretary of State for Foreign Affairs 1886–91;
Postmaster-General 1891–2. He was killed in an earthquake in Jamaica.

WSC to Lord Hugh Cecil
(Quickswood Papers)

30 May [1903]   Blenheim Camp

My dear Linky,

I was fortunate enough to meet Beach last night on my way down here & had a long talk. He is quite ready & determined to fight & seemed overjoyed to see me. He believes that it will be better to hold meetings *after* an Association or Free Trade League is formed, & he has written to Lord Avebury[1] to consult how this can be done in conjunction with important interests in the city. Till then he was doubtful whether we were strong enough. He evidently counted upon Goschen. I am to see him again on Wednesday. He had seen Harcourt & told him the CB amendment was rubbish. Harcourt thoroughly agreed & perhaps we shall hear no more of it.

Beach was most anxious that the fight should be fought strictly in the party, & that only when that had failed could we look elsewhere. He did not want to be led by the Opposition he said. He was hopeful but not sanguine as to the result: inveighed against Chamberlain's wanton ambition, & particularly desired to know whether under any circumstances Lord Salisbury could be induced to pronounce against him.

Meanwhile I have written to Galloway[2] about the Manchester meeting, & if he likes the business that can go forward separately. I propose to inform my constituents that I am not prepared to support proposals for the protective taxation of foodstuffs & that if I am to fight as a Conservative it must be on a F. Trade platform. I will if possible secure an overwhelming vote of confidence.

Do write letters to collect all your chickens. The following may I think be counted. I have written to a good many.

Certain	Probable	Possible
H. Cecil	Cust[3]	
E. Beckett	Malcolm	Renshaw[5]
Ed Vincent	Pemberton[4]	Flannery[6]

[1] (Sir) John Lubbock (4th Baronet), 1st Baron Avebury (1834–1913), banker, scientist and author. Liberal MP for Maidstone 1870–80; University of London 1880–5; Liberal Unionist MP for University of London 1885–1900; PC 1890; Baron Avebury 1900.

[2] William Johnson Galloway (1866–1931), Conservative MP for Manchester S.W. 1895–1906.

[3] Henry John Cockayne Cust (1861–1917), Conservative MP for Stamford 1890–5; for Bermondsey 1900–6; Editor of the *Pall Mall Gazette* 1902–6.

[4] John Stapylton Grey Pemberton (1860–1940), Conservative MP for Sunderland 1900–06.

[5] Charles Bine Renshaw (1848–1918), Conservative MP 1892–1906; Chairman, Board of Referees for Excess Profits Tax 1916–18; baronet 1902.

[6] James Fortescue-Flannery (1851–1943), Unionist MP 1895–1906, 1910–22; knighted 1899; baronet 1904.

Certain	Probable	Possible
Sir Poynder	Peel[4]	G. Parker?[10]
J. Seely	Goschen	R. Greene[11]
[?][1]	Galloway	Faber[12]
Gorst[2]	Hatch[5]	Mowbray[13]
Bowles	Agg-Gardner[6]	6
Ivor Guest	Yerburgh[7]	
Sir M. Hicks Beach	Vicary[8]	
Churchill	Kemp[9]	
Wilson[3]	11	
12		

Will you supplement this list as far as possible & let me know what names you can add. Will Evelyn Cecil[14] go?

I find Marlborough who has not been to London quite sincerely incredulous, & much amused to see, as he thinks, Chamberlain gone quite

[1] Unidentifiable.

[2] John Eldon Gorst (1835–1916), Conservative MP 1866–8, 1875–1906; contested Preston as a Liberal in the election of 1910; Solicitor General 1885–6; Financial Secretary to Treasury, 1891–2; knighted 1885.

[3] Arthur Stanley Wilson (1868–1938), Conservative MP for Holderness 1900–22.

[4] Arthur Wellesley Peel (1829–1913), 5th son of Sir Robert Peel 2nd baronet, Liberal MP 1865–1895, Speaker 1884–95; Viscount 1895.

[5] Ernest Frederic George Hatch (1859–1927), Conservative MP for Gorton 1895–1906; married Lady Constance Blanche Godolphin Osborne, youngest daughter of 9th Duke of Leeds; baronet 1908; KBE 1920.

[6] James Tynte Agg-Gardner (1846–1928), Conservative MP for Cheltenham 1874–80, 1885–92, 1900–10, 1911–28; knighted 1916; PC 1924.

[7] Ralph Armstrong Yerburgh (1853–1916), Conservative MP for Chester 1886–1906, 1910–16.

[8] Vicary Gibbs (1853–1932), Conservative MP for St Albans 1892–1904. Second surviving son of 1st Baron Aldenham; barrister, merchant and banker. Editor of the *Complete Peerage*.

[9] George Kemp (1866–1945), Liberal Unionist MP 1895–1906; Liberal MP 1910–12. Married Lady Beatrice Egerton, 3rd daughter of 3rd Earl of Ellesmere; knighted 1909; created Baron Rochdale 1913.

[10] Gilbert Parker (1862–1932), poet, playwright and novelist; Conservative MP for Gravesend 1900–18; knighted 1902, baronet 1915; PC 1916.

[11] Walter Raymond Greene (1869–1947), Conservative MP for Chesterton 1895–1906, for North Hackney 1910–23; succeeded his father as 2nd baronet 1920.

[12] Edmund Beckett Faber (1847–1920), Conservative MP for Andover 1901–5. Senior partner in Beckett's Bank, Leeds and York; Baron Faber of Butterwick 1905 *or* George Denison Faber (1851–1931), Conservative MP 1900–1918; Partner in Beckett & Company, bankers; married Hilda Georgiana, youngest daughter of Sir Frederick Graham, 3rd Baronet of Netherby, 1895; Baron Wittingham of Wallingford, 1918.

[13] Robert Gray Cornish Mowbray (1850–1916), Conservative MP 1886–95, 1900–06. Parliamentary Private Secretary to Chancellor of the Exchequer 1887–92; succeeded father as 2nd baronet 1899.

[14] Evelyn Cecil, 1st Baron Rockley (1865–1941), Conservative MP for East Hertfordshire 1898–1900, Aston Manor 1900–18, Aston 1918–29. Private secretary to his grandfather, Lord Salisbury 1891–2, 1895–1902; PC 1917.

mad. The country gentlemen in the Yeomanry seem to reflect this view. I wonder if this attitude is typical.

Yours ever

W

I met E. Grey at Oxford last night & rebuked him for his absence. He was at York. I said that was no answer.

Jack Seely to WSC

30 May 1903   Hampshire Yeomanry Camp
                                               Ringwood

My dear Winston,

Your letter was most interesting, but so, indeed, is the whole situation – the more I think of it, the more certain I am that we are right and JC wrong. But whether the majority will see it is another matter. Do write to me again when you have time – would Beach be President of a Free Trade Committee? If he would I believe we could kill the zollverein proposal in a few months – so far, no old 'safe' man of great reputation has said a word against the scheme.

I have ridden about 40 miles today in order to conduct that very silly and useless proceeding, a sham fight, and am tired out – still I am very fit and full of parliamentary zeal.

I am here till Saturday 6th on a yacht from then till Monday 8th when I will be at the House.

Yours ever

JACK

The average man I meet seems puzzled but favourable to the scheme – if we let him alone too long his opinion will crystalize in favour of it. I have useful 1st hand information about guns, recruits, Army Corps – recruiting fell off a half when they asked for characters – the Horse Gunners condemn our old gun etc. etc.

Sir Henry Campbell-Bannerman to WSC

31 May 1903   6 Grosvenor Place

Private

Dear Mr Churchill,

I am much obliged for your letter.

The debate on Thursday and the statement of policy made on the part of the Government, have of course rendered my amendment inappropriate and therefore superfluous, and it will not be moved. There is still much to learn as to their plans, but we have ascertained enough for the basis of a general discussion.

I should think this must be generally obvious, but I have taken means to make it publicly known.

Yours very truly
H CAMPBELL-BANNERMAN

WSC to Lord Hugh Cecil
(Quickswood Papers)

31 May [1903]   Blenheim
Private

Linky – No harm will have been done by my letter to CB: for Beach had already spoken to Harcourt. There is no reason why I should not keep my communications open in that quarter; not that there is any question of agreement in policy or action, but because the Leader of the Opposition has powers in regard to the time of the House which no one else has. However I will not write again without consulting you, & I would not have done so in this case had you been in London.

Lady Howe[1] is giving a dinner for me at Curzon House on the 23rd. AJB & a great many friends are coming & I am to bid you be of the number.

Yours always
WINSTON S. CHURCHILL

Lord Hugh Cecil to WSC

Whit Monday [1 June] 1903   Hatfield
Private

My dear Winston,

In my disapproval of yr letter to CB I forgot to say, though I implied, that I am strongly in favour of the St James's Hall Meeting. Don't fix on day on which we shall be discussing the Budget Bill: I suggest an afternoon (not Friday) in the week beginning the 13th, or the week after.

As to my father, he is quite ag'st JC's policy, but whether he will say so I don't know. The best way of trying for him wd be for Beach to write to him.

---

[1] Georgina Elizabeth, Countess Howe (1860–1906), wife of 4th Earl Howe; daughter of the 7th Duke of Marlborough; WSC's aunt.

His health wd not allow a speech but possibly he wd write a short letter – e.g. in answer to Beach & allow its publication. If Beach does write he shd *not* mention me.

Yrs

Hugh Cecil

WSC to Lord Hugh Cecil
(*Quickswood Papers*)

1 June 1903   Blenheim

My dear Linky,

I am sorry you have been vexed. Of course I quite understand what you say about consultation & indeed I am hardly likely to act against your advice or without it. In this case I thought the matter self-evident after Beach's letter. But I see your point about a decisive division & am glad no harm has resulted from my letter. Here is CB's answer (which I have merely acknowledged politely) & which together with the announcement in today's papers show that the Opposition propose a full dress debate on the 2nd Reading of the Finance Bill before any amendments come on, so that there will be entire liberty of discussion & no division. This is what you want. All the same I am ready to admit that I deserve rebuke. I quite accept for the future your conditions of consultation before any public or important action! Do you consider an interview in the *W.G.* [*Westminster Gazette*] 'important'?

I am sure you will see that it will be of great advantage for me to preserve a channel of communication with CB. We can shape the course of business far better through him than any other way at present open. No one else need be compromised & I will not employ it without your consent.

I generally agree with all you say in your letter: especially about splitting their party as well as ours, if ours must be split at all. I do not expect any course I can take however will win the approval of Sir James Fergusson!

I enclose also a letter from Ivor. He is gloomy. Do write him a very short line to encourage him. He will fight all night in the end. I do trust you are writing to your friends. I am to see Beach on Wednesday & after that I shall have more to report. A letter here posted Tuesday will apprise me of any points on wh you wish Beach to be consulted or directed.

For the rest I am writing vague letters to my own personal friends begging them not to commit themselves to Joe's policy.

I shall hear from my constituency in a day or two and I will then discuss with you what course to take.

Marlborough would be vy glad to see you here any day till Monday; & it vould be very convenient if you could come. Why not Thursday or Friday.

Yours always

WINSTON S. CHURCHILL

)o come here, we shall be delighted to see you any day.

'S Send these letters back. I keep everything. WSC

J. St. Loe Strachey[1] *to WSC*

Tuesday   Hotel St Romain
ι June 1903   Paris

)ear Churchill,

I was greatly delighted to get your letter & to hear that Beach was not ·nly sound but willing to lead us if need be.

The name you suggest for our League is good, – in fact necessary. We nust never allow Joe & Co to ticket us as non-Imperialists. We oppose him)ecause we are determined that the Empire shall not be smashed by the ·eversal of the policy which has made it great. You may therefore assume ·hat I shall back *up any Imperialist Free Trade League for all I am worth*. I am ·repared to fight this thing out even if it ruins the *Spectator*. It won't of course ·o that but it may cost me half my readers & I am quite prepared to see it ·o so.

Just as I got your letter I was preparing to write an article on 'The duty of ·mperialist Free Traders', & to say that in face of the declaration by Cham·erlain & Balfour they must organize themselves – unless of course the other ·ide announced that they had given up their propaganda *absolutely & nreservedly* which of course is improbable. I shall still write on these lines ·ut shall of course say no word about what you write.

I had a good letter from Goschen who is of course sound.

I saw the Asquiths last night. They are not unnaturally in a state of ·ewilderment. His is the frame of mind which will be very useful if it comes ɔ a big fight. But I hold that it is we Unionists who must stop the business. Ve must refuse to allow it to be the essential business of the Opposition & not ·urs to fight for Free Trade. The new Protection must be knocked on the ·ead within our own party & before it becomes an inter-party fight. I am sure ·e can do it if we organize & show ourselves ready to fight to the end.

Yrs tly

J. ST LOE STRACHEY

[1] John St Loe Strachey (1860–1927), editor and proprietor of the *Spectator*, 1898–1925; ·litor, *Cornhill Magazine*, 1896–7.

PS I am going back on Thursday so as to be able to see the next *Spectato*
through the Press & to write our article. I shall be at the *Spectator* office or
Thursday afternoon to pick up letters & there all *Friday morning* if you have
anything to communicate. I shall be living at Newlands Corner, Merrow
Guildford, all the summer coming up to the *Spectator* office every day excep
Saturdays & Sundays.

JS:

Lord Hugh Cecil to WSC

Whit Tuesday [2 June] 1903   Hatfield

My dear Winston,
  I suggest the following points to be submitted to Beach's judgement:
  1. The formation of a League. If yes what name? Wd Free Trade League
     do? Wd it please *Tories?* How wd Anti-Food Tax do?
  2. An organized system of meetings in all the great towns. How to
     arrange these? What dates? Whence to get funds, for this & othe
     purposes of agitation?
  3. What plan for next week's debate? When will Beach speak? Shall yor
     & I speak or not?
  4. What line are we to take about *Retaliation?* Suppose AJB adopts tha
     as *his* policy (not an unlikely thing), how far ought we to go in orde
     to meet him & enable him to get away from JC's more extrem
     counsels? Wd it be proper to say 'Retaliation defensible in theory
     difficult in practice: we will wait & see particular proposals'.
  5. Ought not Ritchie to be urged *not* to resign but frankly to criticis
     JC's proposals in his speech on Finance Bill? If AJB does no
     approve this he must take responsibility of turning Ritchie out. Bu
     this wd be to abandon the free discussion position.
  6. The question of Beach writing to my father (see observations in previou
     letter) Also to Goschen. Also to Devonshire.[1]
  I think of writing both to Ritchie & Goschen myself. Do you approve of this
  Ivor's letter shews a very clear sense of the dangers of the situation. But i
we have a strong party (say 100 MP's) with an organisation we shall b
able to secure I hope the neutrality either of the orthodox Unionists or of th
Radicals. They will hate one another more than they will hate us. Howeve
I don't think there will be an election till next year; in which case there i
time to look round.
  My father is evidently of opinion that Joe will be utterly beaten. He use

---

[1] Spencer Compton, 8th Duke of Devonshire (1833–1908), Secretary of State for Wa
1866; Chief Secretary for Ireland 1870; Secretary of State for India 1880–2; War 1882–5
President of Board of Education 1900–02; Lord President of the Council 1895–1903.

ɔ be a very good judge of currents of feeling, so I am encouraged. But of
ourse he is old now & moreover only gives a corner of his mind to a subject.
   We very much want a good statistical criticism of JC's scheme – an
rticle or speech shewing in detail the probable effect of a 5/- or 10/- duty
n corn on Colonial and on foreign trade. I suppose the Cobden Club are
oing something of this kind. Wd you go round to them & ask them to send
ɪe their publications relating to Preferential Tariffs & Retaliation?
   I cannot come to Blenheim; I must be at home for a little bit. Very many
ɪanks all the same to Marlborough. I shall be in the House on Monday.

Yrs
H.C.

WSC to Lord Hugh Cecil
(*Quickswood Papers*)

June 1903   Blenheim

ɪy dear Linky,
   I am vy glad to get your letter & will inquire about all these points today
om Beach. I have a letter from Ritchie in which he says 'It is a deplorable
tuation which will shatter our party to pieces' & nothing else of conse-
uence. I quite approve of your writing to him; & that you should advise
im to make a detailed criticism of Chamberlain's proposals on the Budget
ɪll – quite friendly in tone – pitiless in character; but on no account to
:sign his office. He will count much more in the country if he is dismissed.
he working man understands & sympathises with a person who is 'sacked'.
   I have written to H. Cox[1] of the Cobden Club for them to send you their
terature, and to suggest the detailed statement of the results of a five shilling
uty on wheat.
   There is a book by Sir T. Farrer (now Lord Farrer) *Free Trade V. Fair
'rade*, written in 1887 & finally dealing with the arguments of the Fair
'raders. I was surprised to find nothing new in what Ch has said. Every
ord is taken literally from the programme of the Fair Trade League 1885.
have written to Mr Bain to try to get another copy of this most useful work
ɪr you. It is out of print.
   Do write to Goschen too.
   Ritchie is to meet the Duke at Lismore on Friday. I believe Devonshire is
ɪund.
   E. Beckett is evidently collecting his friends of the old groups & is

---

[1] Harold Cox (1859–1936), Secretary of the Cobden Club 1899–1904; Liberal MP for
:eston 1906–09; editor *Edinburgh Review* 1912–29.

entertaining steadily at Woodlea. Galloway writes from there. This is all
right.

Moore Bayley of Birmingham who is a forceful local politician & was
one of my father's most trusted agents, has been to see me here. He is
making enquiries as to feeling etc but is himself vy anxious to fight. He is
doubtful about the Midland Conservative Club; but he thinks the organisation of the Central Division (of wh he is President) can be made use of in an
emergency.

If this comes to a fight in the country the great cities of Birmingham &
Manchester will be the two principal battlegrounds. We must carefully
guard our right of entry into B'ham. It is just as well that you are President
of the Midland C.C. for this year.

Yours always
W

Lord Hugh Cecil to WSC

3 June 1903   Hatfield

My dear Winston,

I return you the letters you have sent me. I do not think there is any
advantage in my writing to Peel or Galloway. They are not likely to commit
themselves in the wrong sense and a letter is not a convenient way of discussing a difficult question. I do not think the tactical difference between us
and Peel is very great. It will certainly be wise to try and find out what we
can in the course of the Budget debate and there is no serious objection to his
not committing himself until the close of that discussion.

I suspect Galloway is right about the impossibility of holding meetings in
the provincial towns during the summer, though of course it is a pity that
it should be so. We ought at any rate to make arrangements for such meetings
in October.

You will not have forgotten that I am going to Highbury on Saturday and
I expect to be able to judge exactly what Chamberlain does intend and
whether there is any prospect of his receding. The article in *The Times* today
has the air of being inspired by him and looks as if he was going altogether
for protection. In that case I imagine he will resign at once.

AJB has never written to me after all. I have difficulty in understanding
exactly why.

You will, of course, write to me the result of your conference with Beach
to-day. You must bear in mind that it is impossible for us to force our friends
beyond the pace they think it wise to go. It may be in the abstract quite true
for instance, that Peel is too prudent, but his inclinations are one of the

factors in our problem and we must often be content to take what we believe to be the less wise course in order to secure the co-operation of others.

Yours ever
HUGH CECIL

WSC to Lord Hugh Cecil
(*Quickswood Papers*)

3 June 1903 Blenheim

My dear Linky,

I have just seen Beach. He is determined but rather oppressed by the odds against him, & no doubt old men (except Joe) do not possess reservoirs of combative energy. He had written to Avebury & had received a vy unsatisfactory reply. Avebury is evidently a weak man & is inclined to make all kinds of damaging admissions about reciprocity & retaliation, while feebly protesting his devotion to Free Trade. Beach will write to Goschen & to Lord Derby. He holds himself prevented from writing to Devonshire as the latter is a member of the Government.

As to the formation of a League the course he proposed is this: – Nothing can be done this week. Next Monday if we can collect about 30 members who would be willing to attend a meeting in the House of Commons & if they liked the general line of Beach's speech on Tuesday, he would himself send out summons to them for a meeting on Wednesday. He did not want to court refusals. He thought less than thirty would be of little advantage. Peers might come too. He said nearly all Tories were Protectionists at heart & therefore 'Imperial Free Trade League' might not be a good name. He liked best the 'Anti-Food Tax' idea, but said someone must hit upon a good name. We must all set to work & think. I said 'Party or non party' being myself strongly in favour of 'without distinction of party' for many reasons wh I will explain when we meet. He inclined to my view. It is a matter to be carefully considered.

2. As to meetings: he said organisation must precede the meetings. When we have some sort of machinery we can easily arrange the campaign. We must consider the money question at our meeting. I hope Edgar Vincent, Ernest Beckett & Marlborough will come forward.

3. As to the course of debate. He said Speaker would certainly call on Chaplin[1] now opposition amendment was out of the way. He would write

---

[1] Henry Chaplin (1840–1923), Conservative MP Mid-Lincolnshire (afterwards Sleaford) 1868–1906, Wimbledon 1907–16. Chancellor of the Duchy of Lancaster 1885–6; President of the Board of Agriculture 1886–92; of Local Government Board 1895–1900; member of Tariff Commission and Chairman of its Agricultural Committee 1904; PC 1885; Viscount Chaplin 1916.

to ask Speaker whether he could deal with the whole question on that. If not he would speak twice. I thought this vy undesirable. I urged importance of full dress debate in which our arguments & speakers could show to advantage. (Observe: Opposition have half the speeches & all are agst Govt. If we get half the next – $\frac{3}{4}$ of the speaking is agst them. This is one of our most promising conditions.) He said 'All very true but how to obtain it' I said 'utilise CB.' He would not do this himself (CB was a fool & did not possess the power to say yes or no); but what I might do was no concern of his in that respect. He thought on the whole that the best line for the Opposition would be to ask for full facilities to discuss a substantive motion – quite apart from the Finance Bill. I suggest that you allow me to write to CB to find out what his intention is & (2) tell him what we wish him to do. Beach thought Asquith the better man. I disagree. The Leader of the Opposition is the only person who has the power.

4. Beach was against any form of Retaliation – especially now. I concur. It is a great mistake to break into general principles during a battle. The clemency of conquerors or the conditions of a compromise may make a difference afterwards.

5. He would speak to Ritchie in the sense you recommend.

6. He will write to your father & ask him whether he would consent to write a letter or receive a deputation. If necessary he would come to see him. I impressed upon him not to mention you.

Beach evidently means to do his best for us & fight as hard as he can; but he said that he was not capable of stumping the country. Two meetings would probably be all his strength would allow. I said that would be quite enough. When it comes to the point we will get three out of him. He said that if it came to real fighting we shall be forced to make an arrangement with the Liberal Imperialists respecting seats. Edgar Vincent has just wired to me about putting down an amendment to the Finance Bill raising the issue & squaring the Opposition to adopt it, as we did about the army on the address.

You must make up your mind about procedure on Finance Bill. I will accept what you decide & I think Beach will probably agree. (He thought we should both be prepared to speak.) Let me know as soon as you can what course seems most desirable.

He authorised me to write to Ernest Beckett and other friends and explain his attitude. I propose to do this & suggest to Ernest B to call the group together for luncheon on Monday. Prejudice or no prejudice – that is the only effective nucleus at present, & how else are we to get the necessary thirty. Do you agree? Beckett will be offended if he is not kept *au fait*.

I enclose a letter from the Editor of the *Daily Graphic*. The press will fight while there is a chance of victory, but they melt in the hour of defeat. Recollect that our two main cards are (1) Debating & speaking ability in the House of Commons (2) The Anti-Food Tax cry in the country. What a shocking long letter.

Yours ever
WINSTON S. C.

Lord Hugh Cecil to WSC

4 June 1903   Hatfield

My dear Winston,

Plainly it won't do for Edgar Vincent or any of 'our side' to move an amendt to the 2nd Reading of the Finance Bill. It is a Free Trade Bill & we must support it to the uttermost. Anything hostile to it would have a most factious, unreasonable appearance.

Nor do I like yr plan that CB shd ask for a day for a motion. Arthur wd certainly contrive to treat it as a vote of censure; & he wd urge with great effect that the Govt were only committed to enquiry & that it was astonishingly narrow minded & factious to censure them for enquiry. This wd sweep all the wobblers away & perhaps a dozen of us wd be left to vote with the Opposition & forfeit much influence both in & out of the House by doing so. One must bear in mind that the Opposition will play the game very badly & Arthur & Joe very well.

I am therefore against both an amendt from us and a motion from the Opposition. Far the best thing would be that the Protectionists, Harry Chaplin & Co shd raise the question on the Finance Bill. Then we shd be in the position of defending the Govt & *they* would divide a mere handful shewing the weakness of Protection & covering Joe with discredit. And I hope this may come to pass. Harry: oratorical vanity will strongly incline him to make a speech to a crowded House on *the* topic of the day. If the Speaker holds the matter out of order on his present amendt he can easily modify the wording so as to make it in order.

I enclose an artful note which he will get (if you post it) at any rate on Monday, & which is intended to draw his attention to the point of order without displaying too suspicious an anxiety for him to alter his amendt – if you think he will see through it, don't send it: it will better to trust to the unassisted working of his mind. But if you approve post it. He is not Sherlock Holmes enough to notice post-marks.

Yrs
HUGH CECIL

A little anxiety on my part to have the amendt in order will seem natural & harmless enough.

Lord Hugh Cecil to WSC

5 June 1903   Hatfield

Private

My dear Winston,

I am sorry to say my father has become very ill.[1] This complicates matters for me a good deal. I have thrown over Highbury & may not be able to come to London next week.

Don't say much about the matter as it's only a bother to have alarming reports in the papers or even current among friends. The fact is however that he as nearly as possible died from heart-failure last evening. The ultimate cause seems to be congestion of the kidney from a chill (he has been weak there for some years). Happily he is a good deal better today, but at his age such illnesses must be very serious.

The upshot is that I must withdraw my insistence on consultation. You must decide things: – I hope you will consult Beach whenever you can. Try & believe that in politics it is sometimes better to do nothing, & very seldom well to act in a violent hurry. A night's rest before important decisions is a capital thing.

I wrote about tactics yesterday & Vincent seems very sound.

Yrs
H.C.

WSC to Lord Hugh Cecil
(*Quickswood Papers*)

5 June [1903]   Blenheim

My dear Linky,

Please dine with me on Monday night at Willis at 8. I am asking a few people of sound views. Don't let his electric eel paralyse you. He is a deadly creature.

I am waiting to hear from you about tactics before replying on that point to E. Vincent, whose satisfactory letter I enclose.

Yours ever
WINSTON S. C.

[1] Lord Salisbury died on August 22, aged 73.

WSC to Lord Hugh Cecil
(*Quickswood Papers*)

6 June 1903   Blenheim

My dear Linky,

Your note to Chaplin has gone on. I thought it very deep. You have not answered about dinner Monday or dinner 23rd June.

I agree entirely about procedure; but I would suggest that CB should be told to use his influence to stop the debate coming to a close before Thursday night. We are vy strong in speaking & cannot afford to throw away any points.

My feeling is that the tide is running agst Joe; but that he will make a magnificent speech in reply to HB. I beg you not to be drawn into making admissions to Chamberlain about retaliation. The more you can discourage him, the better; even if he thinks you a fetish worshipper. But you have nothing to learn from me in tactics! Turn over in your mind whether Marlborough would not be a vy suitable person to *organise* the League – if such should be formed. He has three years experience with the P.L. [Primrose League] as Chancellor; & much knowledge of machinery. He would (I think) accept it if it were put to him.

Your ever
W

WSC to Lord Hugh Cecil
(*Quickswood Papers*)

7 June 1903   Blenheim

My dear Linky,

I am very sorry indeed to hear your news, & sympathise most deeply with you in your anxiety. I hope after all that this trouble may pass away again, & I am encouraged by your later report.

As to consultations – this is a great comfort & advantage to me & there are few things I value more. If however these political matters offend you now you must let me know as otherwise I will continue to refer to you & only act without you if circumstances are urgent. I therefore enclose a letter from Beach & a note from the Speaker. They are not vy satisfactory: & I do not want the effect of Beach's pronouncement to be marred by interruptions of order. Evidently the debate will take its own course.

Yours always
WINSTON S. C.

PS If you cannot come to London please send instructions about the

D.W.S. [Deceased Wife's Sister] on Wednesday and about your amendments either to me or Talbot.[1]

WSC

I am sending Farrer's *Free Trade versus Fair Trade*. It is very useful.

Sir Michael Hicks Beach to WSC

12 June 1903   Londonderry House
                                                              London

My dear Churchill,

I shall be happy to dine with you at the House next Tuesday. On Wednesday night I have an engagement in Gloucestershire. I shall be in town again on Thursday & Friday.

I met the Master Cutler of Sheffield, at the Merchant Taylor's last night. I enclose a note from him just received. I think he ought to be one of our 'respectables'. I should think we might get their meeting on Friday afternoon or Saturday morning. I think Gorst must attend it: so you might tell him in confidence. Perhaps also A. Cross[2] (though a crank) & Mark Stewart,[3] as typical Scotchmen. I will ask Ld Ridley[4] to come.

Your Chairman's letter is most satisfactory: and I am delighted by the hopes of Salisbury. If *that* comes off, we are right enough.

Yours sincerely
M. HICKS BEACH

Duke of Marlborough to WSC

30 June 1903   Blenheim

My dear Winston,

Enclosed you will find cheque. I am sorrowful to think that we are at the parting of the political ways, and I am also grieved to feel that you are going to take such an aggressive part in opposition to the Fiscal proposals of AJB

[1] John Gilbert Talbot (1835–1910), Conservative MP for W. Kent 1868–78, and Oxford University 1878–1910; Parliamentary Secretary to Board of Trade 1878–80; PC 1897.
[2] Alexander Cross (1847–1914), Liberal MP for Camlachie division, Glasgow, 1892–1910; baronet 1912.
[3] Mark John MacTaggart Stewart (1834–1923), Conservative MP for Wigtown Burghs 1874–80; baronet 1892.
[4] Matthew White Ridley (1842–1904), MP N. Northumberland 1868–85; Blackpool 1886–1901. Under-Secretary of State for Home Department 1878–80; Financial Secretary to Treasury 1885–6; Secretary of State Home Department 1895–1900; Viscount Ridley 1900.

and JC. It will mean your ultimate severance from the Tory party and your identification with Rosebery and his followers.

I deplore the hasty position that you have taken up; however I will not pursue a topic further over which it is impossible for us ever to agree upon.

Yrs ever

SUNNY

I come to London tomorrow.

* * * * *

WSC to J. H. Lawton

1 July 1903   105 Mount Street

Private

[Copy]

Dear Sir,

Protection, is, in the first instance, undoubtedly beneficial to the protected trade whatever it may be. It is secured from foreign competition and can enjoy a practical monopoly of the Home Market. This advantage is however obtained at the expense of the general consumer, who, being deprived of his right to buy in the cheapest market, has to pay rather more for home made goods, and, in the second place, the quality of the goods is apt to deteriorate under the unhealthy conditions of monopoly. It may be urged that there is enough competition within the country to prevent these evils, or, at any rate, to prevent anything like a monopoly being established, but I would point out to you that the natural consequence of protection is an attempt on the part of the manufacturers to form trusts, and as they are very often able to agree among themselves, the great development of the Trust system, which we have seen with such striking results in the United States, may easily follow.

Now it should be remembered that what happens in the case of one protected trade may happen in the case of all protected trades. Therefore the consumer will pay more for the articles which he uses and will perhaps not get such good articles in the end. His loss will be more or less severe in proportion to the amount of protection given and to the number of industries protected. But the consumer's loss does not stop with the consumer. It operates in two ways upon trade generally. In the first place, by making the cost of living higher, it increases the cost of production and consequently hampers our competition in the neutral, foreign and Imperial markets, and when we think that a great portion of our export trade is absorbed by native populations in India, China and Africa, it must be clear to you that cheapness of production is a matter of almost vital importance. And this is particularly true of the Cotton Trade which constitutes one fourth of all our exports, and which has to depend and will increasingly have to depend upon the demand of the less civilised and native population of the world.

Secondly the increased cost of living to the consumer reduces the general demand for commodities. He has spent more money on this or that manufactured article because it is a protected article, he has therefore less money left to spend on other things. So much for the general theory which underlies the position adopted by Free Traders in regard to Fair Trade. We do not deny that industries may be made to flourish by artificial means in the power of the State to administer, but we contend that the Government must look to the wellbeing of the country as a whole not to that of any particular class or section and we believe that if a Government honestly pursues the greatest good of the greatest number, they will have established a system of society which will be more favourable than any other to the development of special interests and which will secure the supremacy of the best.

It is often urged that by threatening to tax foreign manufactured articles we might persuade foreign nations to admit ours free, and this is what the reciprocitarians and retaliationists desire, or affect to desire. But these methods of retaliation have been tried by all the protectionist countries for generations, and the result is that so far from arriving at free trade, they have only raised their tariffs higher and higher. And today we, the one free country in the world, are, in relation to all the other nations of the world, no worse off but are better off for trading purposes than any of the protected nations, for we enjoy with nearly every country the most favoured nation treaty; and although I should be far from saying that this treaty was always observed faithfully by other countries, yet in the balance its advantages are very great.

I agree with you that the taxation of food should come last in the list of proposals and I am hopeful that we shall never get so far as to reach it. I have no leisure to discuss with you the Zollverein proposal which is quite distinct from the fair trade proposal, but since you have taken the trouble to write to me so courteously, I venture to direct your attention to Mr Chiozza's book *British Trade and the Zollverein Issue* (obtainable from The Commercial Intelligence Publishing Co Ld. 166, Fleet St E.C.)[1] which, I think, puts some direct practical considerations forward with a force difficult to ignore.

Yours faithfully

[WINSTON S. CHURCHILL]

[1] Leo (George) Chiozza Money (1870–1944), Managing editor of *Commercial Intelligence* 1898–1903. Liberal MP for North Paddington 1906–10, East Northants 1910–18; defeated as Labour candidate for South Tottenham 1918. Parliamentary Secretary to the Ministry of Pensions 1917, Ministry of Shipping 1916–18.

Colonel J. Mitford to WSC

2 July 1903   Old Town
                                                  Northumberland

Dear Sir,
   I see in the newspapers that you have announced yourself to be a 'Conservative Free Trader', and as that is what I have myself been *for over 50 years* without my principle having been realized, I would be very glad to know how you expect or propose to arrive at a system of Free Trade so long as Foreign Countries refuse to sanction it. You do not appear to support Mr Chamberlain's suggested scheme of tariffs in favour of our Colonies, and I take it therefore that you have an alternative scheme which will bring us the advantages of Free Trade in accordance with our professed principle. There are many 'Conservative Free Traders' in this District who, like myself, would be only too glad to know the means whereby our principle can be established, and who, in the absence of any intelligible scheme, will assuredly support Mr Chamberlain at the next General Election.

                                 I am, Dear Sir, Yours faithfully
                                               J. MITFORD
PS If you favour me with a reply I should like to make it known amongst *our* fraternity hereabout if you do not object.

WSC to Colonel J. Mitford

9 July 1903   105 Mount Street
[Copy]

Dear Sir,
   Of course it stands to reason that we are all in favour of the consolidation of the British Empire, of compelling foreign nations to adopt Free Trade and of increasing British commercial prosperity; and if Mr Chamberlain's fiscal proposals can be shown to produce these desirable ends, they would claim wide if not universal support. But I should like to point out to you that so far as this controversy has advanced, Mr Chamberlain, although he has enlarged upon many benefits which we should all desire, has made no definite proposal by which these benefits can be secured, and I myself as a Conservative Free Trader gravely doubt whether any fiscal change will bring them within our reach. I fear that a policy of Preferential Tariffs will lead to much friction between the Colonies and the mother country, and if it

is based upon the taxation of food, will estrange the masses of our countrymen from the Imperial idea.

Retaliation has been tried by all the protectionist nations for many years,
and so far from arriving at free trade, they have only raised their tariff
walls higher and higher; and even now Free Trade England has better terms
in respect of all other countries of the world taken together than any one of
the highly protected states.

Thirdly, I would look to improvements in scientific and technical education, to light taxation, to pacific policy and to a stable and orderly state of
Society, as the best means of stimulating the commercial prosperity of our
country. But the burden of proof is admitted to rest with Mr Chamberlain
and his supporters. They invite the richest nation in the world to change its
fiscal system. They have first of all to prove that the old system has failed;
they have in the second place, to state plainly and definitely the new system
they propose to establish, and in the third place, they have to show that
their new system will in fact achieve the ends they have in view and work a
real and substantial improvement in our condition. Until they have done
these things, Free Traders are not called upon to put forward any alternative
scheme for we are in the position of adhering to the principles which have
been long accepted in this country.

I may add, however, that I think the question of (a) spasmodic dumping
likely to cause temporary dislocation of trade and arising either from the
action deliberate or otherwise of foreign trusts and (b) leverage for negotiating commercial treaties, are questions upon which the public mind is
seriously disquieted, and questions which would form very suitable subjects
for scientific investigation by a strong Royal Commission with a strictly
limited reference. I do not think that either of these two references are
capable of being suitably dealt with in an electioneering campaign; for
under such circumstances the scientific aspect is entirely overshadowed by
the prime necessity of getting votes. Already the most loose statements have
been made, and various kinds of promises, not easily distinguishable from
bribes, have been put forward, and an attempt to snatch an ill-considered
verdict from the Electorate by widespread promises of help for local interests,
and by general schemes which cannot be checked or closely examined, would
be a political manoeuvre demanding the most strenuous resistance which a
Conservative could offer.

[WINSTON S. CHURCHILL]

Colonel J. Mitford to WSC

13 July 1903   Old Town

Dear Sir,
    I beg to thank you for your courteous reply to my letter of the 2nd instant,
and to say that I am pleased to see it in the newspapers of to-day, though I
cannot but think it would have been better understood if you had published
my letter with it. Your reply however does not touch the main point of my
inquiry upon which I, like many other people, wish for information, viz: –
'how you expect or propose to arrive at a system of Free Trade so long as
Foreign countries decline to accept it.' You and I may go on calling ourselves
'Conservative Free Traders' till all is blue, but we shall never get it unless
something is done to bring it into existence, and we shall remain barren as
long as our ruinous system of one-sided Free Trade continues. How you can
hold on, as you seem to do, to this one-sided Free Trade and call yourself a
'Conservative Free Trader' puzzles me entirely. If you will turn to the late
John Stuart Mill's Book on Political Economy you will find that he emphatically condemned one-sided Free Trade by stating that any country adopting it
must inevitably be ruined. Then again if you turn to our Board of Trade
Returns is there not a great lesson of warning against our present system!
They are, to my mind, alarming, and no 'Royal Commission' or any other
Commission is needed to prove to Englishmen the wisdom of Mr Chamberlain's initiative to 'wake up' England to her dangers.
    I fail to see in Mr Chamberlain's proposals for inquiry anything calculated
'to estrange the mass of the people from the idea of Empire,' on the contrary, are not all our Colonies, without exception, in favour of them? and,
if I know my countrymen, as I think I do, let me tell you that 'the mass of
the people' will be found to be in favour of them also.
    May I further ask for an explanation of your term 'Free Trade England'
for I am not aware that England has ever enjoyed it?
    It is pretty evident, I think, if the present system be not abandoned there
will be no trade left to dear old England a decade hence, seeing what has
taken place in the last ten years; and the bogus of 'taxing of foodstuffs' will
be left to some other nations to which Englishmen will be driven when we
shall have been fully robbed of our trades.

                                                 Yours very truly
                                                 J. Mitford

WSC to Colonel J. Mitford

14 July 1903   105 Mount Street

Private

[Copy]

Dear Sir,

I am glad to hear from you that you did not object to my publishing my answer to your letter. It enabled me to deal with much correspondence at the same time, and also to put forward a view which I was anxious to make clear.

You say that I have not answered the principal question in your letter, namely, how it is proposed to arrive at a system of Free Trade so long as foreign countries decline to accept it.

Free Trade is a theory as well as a condition. We have not yet attained the condition in the world, to our loss, to the loss of foreign nations and to the world's loss. But we believe in the theory. We do not adhere to a Free Trade system in England in the hopes of foreign nations adopting that system also, but because we believe that that is commercially and economically the best thing we can do for ourselves. If it were proved to me that a system of protection or of Fair Trade were better for this country, I should of course have no more to say. There should be no question of sacrificing England to a theory, however lofty and inspiring that theory might be. It is as a bread and butter policy that our system of free imports is to be defended; the theory of Free Trade as expounded by the leading economists, shows that with certain exceptional modifications it is profitable to the nation at large, whatever it may be to special interests, to fight hostile tariffs with free imports. A practical proof may be found in the immense and growing wealth of the world.

At the same time our manufacturers are no doubt unhappy and it may be possible that we have purchased a general advantage to the community at the disadvantage of certain classes. If that were proved as a result of scientific investigation, it would no doubt suggest modifications in our policy to afford a greater encouragement and security to manufacturers. But I say emphatically that that has not been proved nor attempted to be proved. Neither has any definite remedy been suggested nor has it been proved that any remedy would be likely to be effective. And I cannot believe that an electioneering campaign is likely to throw any light upon the question.

Yours very truly

[WINSTON S. CHURCHILL]

*   *   *   *   *

WSC to the Duke of Devonshire

13 July 1903   House of Commons

Private

[Copy]

Dear Duke,

Mr Hobhouse[1] has put down a motion, nominally to ask for papers, but in reality to serve as a vehicle for a full & free debate on the proposed changes in Fiscal policy, without an embarrassing division at the end. More than fifty Unionist members of Free Trade complexion desire that this opportunity should be given. If it is refused they will be embittered & disheartened. Mr Chamberlain has said that 'the House of Commons ought eagerly to welcome the opportunity of discussion.' Mr Balfour has said 'that it would be ridiculous to make fiscal opinions the test of party loyalty.' Under these circumstances how can the Government with candour refuse all opportunities of debate other than on votes of censure?

Perhaps you may have heard of some of the steps wh are being made by the Protectionist party to promote their views in the constituencies; and it is unfair to deny to members thus attacked all chance of making their case good in Parliament. Few private members have access to the public except when Parliament is sitting & through the publicity of debate. Money, organisation, popular repute – all are on the side of the Protectionists in our party. I want to urge upon you that fairness & impartiality in this controversy will be altogether destroyed if an unprejudiced debate is prevented in the House of Commons. Quite apart from the injustice to individuals, it cannot fail to injure the House itself, that it should be the one place where discussion of the question of the hour is forbidden; & I cannot believe that Mr Balfour would knowingly lend himself to such a manoeuvre. There is no desire on the part of any of the Conservative Free Traders to take a course hostile to the Government; but inactivity & silence would most certainly be interpreted in the country as weakness & indecision – & perhaps justly so interpreted. We want a debate and the meeting today was unanimous in thinking that a debate would greatly advance the cause of Free Trade, & that no debate would greatly prejudice it. I feel sure you will not mind my putting the case before you. Don't think it necessary to answer it.

Yours sincerely
WINSTON S. CHURCHILL

---

[1] Henry Hobhouse (1854–1937), Unionist MP for Somerset East 1885–1906. PC 1902; married Margaret Heyworth, 7th daughter of Richard Potter and sister of Beatrice Webb.

WSC to Sir J. Dickson-Poynder

14 July 1903   105 Mount Street

[Copy]

My dear Jack,

I had been meaning to write and tell you how very sorry I am to hear of your illness. I wish I had been able to come to see you the other morning so as to have a talk, but I was kept at the House on a beastly Committee now happily concluded.

I do beg of you to take most complete rest. I do not think it at all likely that there will be a General Election in the autumn, and if you are fit again by October, you will be in plenty of time to bear your share in the Battle. Meanwhile, I should seek the very best medical advice in the world and I should absolutely follow it. I have read your letter and I think our views on the question are almost exactly the same. Our manufacturers are no doubt unhappy, but whether they are legitimately unhappy or not is a question, but whether legitimately or illegitimately unhappy, they complain, and they have a right to have their case considered. But that consideration must be of an impartial, dis-interested and scientific character very different from the campaign of bribery and plunder which Chamberlain contemplates.

I am purposely taking a very moderate line now because if we can get moderate men on our side in the beginning, there is no doubt that when Chamberlain becomes violent as he cannot fail to do, they will be confirmed in their agreement with us.

We had a capital meeting yesterday[1] and its spirit was very remarkable, absolute unanimity, considerable determination and implicit confidence in Beach. Nothing could exceed the cleverness with which Beach put his case for a Debate in the House of Commons. He had grave doubts about the course he is now taking, but when he finally decided in favour of it, he neglected nothing to carry the Meeting with him and he used his doubts most ingenuously as the very strongest arguments in favour of what he proposed. Now we shall see what happens. My own opinion is that the Government will not be able to refuse a Debate.

As regards electoral prospects and the party situation, let me say in the strictest confidence, that my idea is, and has always been, of some sort of central government being formed. I do not myself see any reason why if the Balfour Cabinet breaks, the Duke of Devonshire should not be sent for by the King and although his tenure of office would be short and precarious, the machinery of Government would place us in a much better position for

---

[1] Some 60 Unionist MPs, under the chairmanship of Hicks Beach, inaugurated the Unionist Free Food League.

making our terms with the Liberals and in the constituency. Of course this
is all very vague and at present chiefly confined to my own cranium. But the
Conservative party will not like the idea of a general election under these
conditions and numerous forces will be at work to prolong the supremacy of
Conservative forces. One must not be in a hurry. I cannot believe that there
will be a general election before April and possibly not before next October.

[WINSTON S. CHURCHILL]

Mrs Sidney Webb[1] *to WSC*

[14 July 1903]   41 Grosvenor Road

Dear Mr Winston Churchill
    When I had the pleasure of meeting you at my sister, Mrs Hobhouse's, you
asked me to suggest a German Socialist Leader who wd be likely to give a
'wise' answer with regard to the working class feeling against taxes on Food
& its relation to the growth of Socialism. We think your best [? choice] would
be Herr Bernstein,[2] Berlin W.30 Hohenstaufen Str 37. He is the rising light,
and a highly educated man who has lived in London for many years & is
now a member of the Reichstag – he belongs to the new school of constitutional or Fabian Socialists among the German Democratic Socialists. If you
write to him you had better mention our name – he is an old acquaintance
of ours & translated one of our books into German. I do not know of course
whether he wd be sufficiently detached to be willing to attribute Socialist
successes to any less abstruse cause than faith in Socialist doctrine.
    Do you really require a young economist to work out statistics for you?
If you do I think we could recommend one or other of some of the young
men working at the School of Economics at Clare Market.
    Might I venture to suggest that you should look at the Appendix on 'The
Relation of the Free Trade Controversy to Parasitic Industries' in our
Industrial Democracy: I think you would find therein the [?] answer to Mr

[1] Beatrice Webb (1858–1943), writer and social reformer; married Sidney Webb, later
Lord Passfield; author of *The Co-operative Movement in Great Britain* 1891; and, with her husband, *The History of Trade Unionism* 1894; served on Royal Commission on Poor Law and
Unemployment 1905–9; member of Fabian Society of which she became President.
[2] Eduard Bernstein (1850–1932), German writer and politician; joined Social Democrats
1872; was forced to leave Germany in 1879 and published *The Social Democrat* in Zurich
1881–90. Lived in London 1888–1901 where he became acquainted with Engels; returned to
Germany 1901; member of Parliament 1902–6, 1912–18, 1920–8; his importance lies in the
fact that after quarrelling with orthodox Marxism, he ensured that Revisionism gained the
upper hand in the Social Democratic Party.

Chamberlain's contention that high prices mean high wages. Forgive me for recommending our own brand of [? powder]!

Sincerely
BEATRICE WEBB

Sidney Low to WSC

23 July 1903   Durham Place

Dear Winston Churchill,

I am assured that a draft Birmingham Tariff *has* been seen by a chosen few. If I could get hold of it, I would get it published in the *Standard*, with – I think – an useful educational effect. But I expect 'Consistent Birmingham' is sitting upon its compromising documents just now.

Thanks for your friendly hint about Sir MHB & your pleasant references to the attitude of the *Standard*. I am not, as you know, responsible for the policy of that journal; but I endeavour to keep before its conductors certain of those elementary propositions which many people forget or ignore in these days. I suppose the multiplication table will be called a 'shibboleth' soon & we shall be encouraged to cultivate an 'open mind' upon it. The confusion & ignorance which prevail upon all economic questions are of course Mr C's most powerful ally, or rather his *second* most powerful. His chief asset is the exaggerated & extravagant pseudo-Imperialist idolatry which he was allowed & assisted to set up. I always thought he would make the Unionist party 'Nay-Nay-Nay' for that orgy.

Can you give me the pleasure of lunching with me on Wednesday of next week, the 29th, at the Garrick Club at 1.30?[1] My brother Maurice Low,[2] a journalist in Washington, U.S.A., is here. He is much in the confidence of Roosevelt,[3] Hay[4] & others & knows more than most people of the way of things in America. I think you might be interested to meet him.

I am yours sincerely
SIDNEY LOW

[1] WSC wrote across this sentence: 'Yes delighted. Telegram.'

[2] A. Maurice Low (1860–1929), was Chief American Correspondent of the *Morning Post*; knighted 1922.

[3] Theodore Roosevelt (1858–1919), 26th President of the USA 1901–8, to which office he succeeded on the assassination of President McKinley and was re-elected in 1904. Was awarded the Nobel peace prize in 1906 for his intervention in the Russo-Japanese war which resulted in the treaty of Portsmouth N.H.; a distant cousin of F. D. Roosevelt.

[4] John Hay (1838–1905), American statesman and author. Private Secretary to Abraham Lincoln 1861–5; ambassador to Great Britain 1897; negotiated Hay-Pauncefote Treaty between Great Britain and United States for the construction of the Panama Canal 1901.

Andrew Hogg to WSC

30 July 1903   Edinburgh Conservative Working Men's Association
Edinburgh

Dear Sir,
  Referring to your letter of 29th May last the Committee have had under
consideration the provisional engagement which you then made to deliver
a political address under the auspices of the Association on November 11th.
They have reluctantly come to the conclusion that they must take advantage
of the option which you so generously gave them by that letter to cancel the
engagement. In view of the great public interest which is being taken in Mr
Chamberlain's fiscal proposals, they feel that your proposed address must
almost of necessity have dealt with this subject. Looking to the strong
attitude which you have adopted against these proposals, the Committee,
while some of their number favour your views, do not think it prudent for
various reasons to have the proposed address.
  I need scarcely say that it is with very great regret that the Committee
have come to this conclusion, as they fully appreciate the honesty and great
ability with which you have expressed your views, and it is a distinct disappointment to them that circumstances should have compelled them to
take this step.
  I have to thank you for your great courtesy and kindness in this matter.
                                        I am, Dear Sir, Yours very truly
                                             ANDREW H. HOGG
                                             Honorary Secretary

WSC to Andrew Hogg

1 August 1903   105 Mount Street

[Copy]

Dear Sir,
  I beg to acknowledge the receipt of your letter of the 30th July and I
thank you for its courteous tone.
  In reply I would observe that I never sought the honour of addressing a
Meeting under the auspices of your Association, but only consented at your
urgent request to do so, and I therefore in nowise regret being relieved of the
task. But I am sorry to learn that there is so much intolerance and prejudice
among Conservatives in Edinburgh upon this question of Fiscal Policy that
they cannot even contemplate its free discussion.

The Conservative party may not always enjoy the support of a great majority and may in the future have to fight hard for many causes that have been long unchallenged. And if such a spirit of intolerance were to result in driving from their ranks those who adhere to Free Trade principles – a contingency I earnestly hope may be avoided – there may be cause for regret in the years that are to come.

Yours very truly

[WINSTON S. CHURCHILL]

Lord James of Hereford to WSC

4 August 1903   41 Cadogan Square

My dear Winston Churchill,

When we were having our talk this afternoon I forgot that I had arranged with Goschen not to take an active part in the affairs of the Free Food League without communicating with him. I will come to the meeting on Thursday – but please let no publicity be given to it on Thursday – 8.15 please.

Yours

JAMES OF H

WSC to H. Mayall[1]

6 August 1903   105 Mount Street

[Copy]

Dear Sir,

I beg to acknowledge the receipt of your letters of the 5th instant forwarding me the resolutions passed by the Marlborough Conservative Club.

In respect of the first resolution which refers to my own action, I may be permitted to point out that Mr Chamberlain's proposals were put forward in a vague and general form avowedly for the purpose of raising discussion and inquiry; that Mr Balfour has himself distinctly stated that fiscal opinions are not to be made a test of party loyalty; and that in expressing a perfectly honest and sincere conviction on the proposals so far as they may at present be apprehended, I have in no way departed from the principles of the Conservative party. I think that under the circumstances the Marlborough Conservative Club might at any rate have afforded me an opportunity of justifying my position to their members before reflecting upon my conduct as their representative.

[1] Secretary of the Marlborough Conservative Club, East Oldham.

But if it is their view, as expressed in the first resolution, that no definite pronouncement should be made by Conservatives upon Mr Chamberlain's proposals 'before the said scheme has been explained in detail for the consideration of the people', and if I am to be reproached for so pronouncing, then I do not understand how it can be consistent or logical to proceed in the second resolution to express a definite and decided opinion 'that such a policy would if enforced tend to the revival of our industries and be beneficial to the country generally.'

Yours faithfully

[WINSTON S. CHURCHILL]

WSC to Lady Randolph

12 August 1903   105 Mount Street

Private

Dearest Mamma,

I send you another crop of newspaper cuttings. I daresay they will amuse you.

I have had eight small meetings in Oldham of 200 a piece, and have been extremely well received as you will see from the papers, and the Central Executive there have passed a unanimous vote of confidence in me although I have expressed myself unequivocally against the great man.

There are of course a lot of Protectionists and Fair Traders in the party there, and there is no doubt that everything will have to be handled very carefully; but they are all quite agreed in recognising that I am the only person that has got the slightest chance of winning the Election for the Tory party there, and in consequence, they are prepared to give me very wide liberty. In addition to this, there is a great deal of personal enthusiasm and I find that the working classes are very much attracted by the idea of a representative whose name they read frequently in the newspapers, and who as they think, confers distinction on the town.

All the evidence that I get here goes to show that Arthur Balfour is going to break with Chamberlain, and that Joe will leave the Government with a certain following and will drive on his own wild career as an independent person. This means his ruin. I cannot contemplate such a prospect without a melancholy feeling, because, although I disagree with him so utterly, yet he has been very kind to me.

Last night Jack Seely and I gave a dinner at the House of Commons which 'AJB', Austen Chamberlain,[1] George Wyndham, St John Brodrick, Cecil & Ivor Guest with some others attended. We had a most pleasant evening. AB was most amiable and good humoured in spite of the fact that Cecil and I had been very rude to him in the House of Commons in the afternoon, as you will see if you read the Debate.[2] He chaffed and chatted in the best of spirits. Austen, on the other hand, was most depressed, and although very friendly to me and Linky, evidently somewhat estranged both from AB & George Wyndham. I can quite understand that if AB is at length turning against Joe, there would be more bitterness felt in Chamberlainite circles towards those in the Cabinet who had encouraged him and who seemed ready to support him up to a certain point, than against those, who like Cecil and me, have been from the beginning uncompromisingly opposed to his plan. After dinner AB made us go into his room where we sat and talked a long time – (Jack (our Jack) was there too –) and when I came out of his room to go to a Division, of course I ran straight into JC who gave me an extraordinary look of reproach as much as to say 'how could you desert me' and I confess I felt very sorry for him indeed. I have far more respect for him than for those time-servers who have been waiting to see which way the cat will jump, and who, although perhaps only a week ago were ready to shout down people like Cecil for daring to question Chamberlain's policy, may easily in the near future be occupying themselves with destroying his influence.

I cannot help admiring Chamberlain's courage. I do not believe he means to give way an inch, and I think he is quite prepared to sacrifice his whole political position and Austen's as well, for the cause in which he is so wrapped up. Of course the Unionist Free Traders will support Mr Balfour with great determination if Chamberlain should leave the Government. Such a solution would not be so satisfactory as the Devonshire plan, but there could be no question of rejecting it.

I spent Sunday at Keele[3] which is a charming house.

The Session is over on Saturday but I do not think I shall wait for the end of it. I expect to go to Warwick on Friday for two or three days thence to

---

[1] Austen Chamberlain (1863–1937), eldest son of Joseph Chamberlain. Unionist MP for E. Worcestershire 1892–1914, Birmingham 1914–37; Chancellor of the Exchequer 1903–6, 1919–21; Secretary of State for India 1915–17; Secretary of State for Foreign Affairs 1924–29; KG 1925.

[2] On 11 August 1903, during the second reading of the Consolidated Fund Bill, Lord Hugh Cecil challenged Balfour to explain why Joseph Chamberlain had been allowed 'to publish on a scale of almost legendary magnitude' leaflets on the fiscal issue 'and to distribute them broadcast over the whole country'. Cecil asked Balfour whether or not this constituted a misuse of Chamberlain's prestige as a Minister of the Crown. When Balfour interrupted Cecil on a point of order he interjected: 'Oh; muzzle the House of Commons.'

[3] House of Mr Ralph Sneyd.

Blenheim for two or three days, thence on the Friday afternoon to Beach for a night, then for two days to Tranby [Croft]¹ on my way north, and on the 25th I shall be at Dunrobin. We must try to see something of each other in Scotland.

I hope your cure has been satisfactory. I find myself in very good health but I shall be glad to lead a quiet, regular, temperate life, for a month. I shall do my exercises every day.

Sunny is extremely pleased with his appointment.² He made an extremely good speech in the House of Lords on the Sugar Convention and everybody is loud in his praise. What a difference it makes to a man to get the 'claque' on his side. I see a great deal of him now and our relations are most cordial.

I think you should write me a nice long letter in answer to this.

Ever your loving son
W

Joseph Chamberlain to WSC

15 August 1903   40 Princes Gardens

Private

My dear Churchill,

I am sorry that my looks should have belied me, but I can assure you that I have not *consciously* regarded you 'with reproach' since you definitely announced your position on Fiscal Policy. I am afraid that my short sightedness is in fault, and I may have passed you in the lobby without seeing you, but you may be certain in my case that I bear no malice for political opposition.

I have felt for a long time – in fact from your first confidences to me – that you would never settle down in the position of what is called a 'loyal supporter'. I do not think there is much room in politics for a dissentient Tory, but Heaven knows that the other side stands much in need of new talent, and I expect you will drift there before very long. No one can really pretend to foresee the future, and I have myself at the present moment not the slightest idea of what will be the result of the next election; but I have no hesitation in predicting that whenever the natural change takes place from prosperous trade to commercial depression the demand for an alteration of our fiscal system will be irresistible.

---

¹ Home of Mr Arthur Wilson, a wealthy shipowner, and scene of the famous baccarat scandal of 1891, when Sir William Gordon-Cumming was accused of cheating and the Prince of Wales, who had been present, gave evidence during his unsuccessful action to clear his name.

² As Under-Secretary of State for the Colonies.

In any case, and whatever happens, if you fight your battle fairly and squarely, you may rely on my interest and good-will.

Believe me, Yours very truly

J. CHAMBERLAIN

PS Is it really necessary to be quite as personal in your speeches? You can attack a policy without imputing all sorts of crimes to its author. Mr Gladstone was a good model in this aspect & in all the Home Rule controversy he almost entirely avoided personal attack.

Sidney Low to WSC

EXTRACT

17 August 1903   2 Durham Place

. . . It strikes me that if you 'stern and unbending' Free Trade Unionists want a proper 'show' in the Press, you will have to put some of your millionaires on to starting or buying a newspaper, and running it on uncompromising anti-Protectionist lines. As far as I can see that cause will be very badly served in the Press – London and provincial – when Mr C. drops or reduces his food taxes and tries to get the party into line on Retaliation & taxing foreign manufactures. *The Times* and *Telegraph* will go all the way with him; so in a less degree the *Morning Post*, the *Pall Mall*, *Globe*, *St James's* & *Daily Express*. The *Daily Mail*, which will not stand food taxes, is crusading against 'dumping', even the *Standard* has a certain tendency that way. It is the same with the country Unionist journals. They incline to look favourably on Retaliation &c. though they denounce food taxes, and the Protectionist issue, once raised, won't be dropped after the next election. A few free Trade capitalists might do worse than run a decent Unionist paper if only to prevent the defence being left to the Radical press. They would not lose their money. A Free Trade journal, advocating 'efficiency' & progressive Conservatism if well managed, might prove a paying property . . .

Lord Rosebery to WSC

19 August 1903   Gastein

Private

My dear Winston,

Many thanks for your admirable and interesting letter. Balfour must feel the joy of a reprieved criminal now that the Session has closed, and I, too, rejoice, for the spectacle was painful and degrading. What this Government has done to deserve such an opposition I cannot conceive. To the numberless chances they (the O.) [the Opposition] have missed during the last few years they now have added another. Fate does not really forgive such disregard of fortune. You must have been glad to have fired the parting shot, and you have every reason to be satisfied with the decision.[1] I am delighted to hear that Oldham is also satisfied with your attitude.

You say that people of 70 are not easily convinced. That is true. But this is also true – that the person you speak of [the Duke of Devonshire] is a very bad resigner. He has more than once been in the position when he should I think have resigned, but he is easily persuaded to stay.

The Education Bill of last year is the real obstacle to a central party. Pray come to Dalmeny. I hoped that Hugh Cecil would have come. But I fear his father is dying.

Do you by any chance know of a young fellow who would be a good assistant and understudy to Waterfield my private secretary? There are only two indispensable requisites – he must be a gentleman and must write shorthand. But do not let it slip out, even in your sleep, that I want such a thing, or I should have my hall-door forced by a hungry crowd.

I hope to be in England before the end of next week, but you will be in Sutherland.

Yrs ever
AR

WSC to J. T. Travis-Clegg

20 August 1903   105 Mount Street

[Copy]

Private

Dear Travis-Clegg,

I am sorry that you had a stormy meeting. It will be the first of many I daresay. There is however, no necessity for any definite division until after Mr Balfour's speech at Sheffield. And then perhaps we shall be found to have the whole official authority on our side. I therefore concur in the course

[1] On the last day of the session WSC confessed that an 'unworthy doubt' about Balfour had crossed his mind: 'I have sometimes doubted whether the right hon gentleman's policy has been so disingenuous, so haphazard, so dictated by circumstances beyond his control, as I would gladly believe, whether in fact it is merely a serious and honest, but a somewhat undignified, attempt to keep the Cabinet together rather than a tactical deployment to commit a great Party to a new policy against which its instinct revolts and distrusts.'

you have adopted with respect to leaflets. For the present nothing need be done by us. But later on an organisation will have to be formed for the purpose of distribution.

Please find out for me the name of the League that has been communicating directly with the Ward Committees and the Clubs. If possible procure one of their letters. I will make a complaint to Mr Balfour, if this League is in any way connected with Mr Chamberlain. The proceeding is admittedly irregular.

I hope the Free Traders will go to work in earnest in the constituency and will not allow a loud mouthed section to frighten them. The Fair Traders will never carry the working men although they may split conservative organisations.

You may let it be known in the Inner Executive that if a Fair Trade Candidate were adopted by the Association, I should not contest the seat. If he were adopted by any outside body, or improvised organisation, I will most certainly contest it: but this last you may keep to yourself.

Don't get downhearted. The position will improve greatly in the near future.

Yours very sincerely
WINSTON S. CHURCHILL

Lord Hugh Cecil to WSC

31 August 1903   Hatfield

My dear Winston,

First about myself. I am not very unhappy but I am exhausted rather & not inclined for much exertion – moreover I certainly incline to leave politics tho' I shall come to no decision for some months.

As to Harmsworth[1] I shd not advise taking him too far into confidence. He is not a very trustworthy man; & apart from that – nothing would be more deplorable than to give the impression that the Duke of Devonshire was being run by you & me & the *Daily Mail!!!* Indeed let me repeat again the desirability of great reserve in conversation. I tremble as to what you may have said to Mrs Grenfell!

But I am inclined to fear the design is visionary. Is the Duke at 70 the man for such an enterprise?

Arthur [Balfour] has been here – very charming & lovable, all his best qualities coming out on such an occasion. I have had no political talk with him: but casual observations convince me that he is confident that his Govt is not going to break up this autumn. Joe may be going to resign: or AJB

[1] Alfred Harmsworth, later Lord NORTHCLIFFE.

may hope to smooth things over. But then AJB is the most sanguine of optimists & may very likely turn out wrong.

I arrange possibilities in this order of preference.

Best – JC to resign
2nd   – Devons. & Rosebery resigning
3rd   – Smoothed over present Govt
4th   – Spencer & CB resigning
5th   – Ritchie to resign without the Duke

Any of the three last would be very bad. This order is not one of probability but of wish.

Why does the *Daily News* run Devonshire? From our pt of view their advocacy does harm.

Argyllshire[1] is partly cheering, partly not. JC is clearly beaten. But on the other hand will not the whole Unionist party be swept away – including ourselves?

Yrs ever
HUGH CECIL

PS Joe's letter is very interesting & comic. He clearly thinks himself the standard of Tory orthodoxy from which we are 'dissentients'. There is truth in what he says about personalities – but it is humorous from him!

S. Smethurst[2] to WSC

EXTRACT

11 September 1903   Coldhurst House
                                                     Oldham

My dear Mr Churchill,

. . . I suppose at an early date now your annual address to your constituents will be due. If you are taking up the position of the Free Food League of supporting the official programme – I will not say Balfour – and opposing Chamberlain the sooner you say so the better. There is a strong Pro Chamberlain feeling in the Constituency and I am afraid it is growing and it will have to be dealt with very tactfully.

. . . It seems to me . . . that Ashton[3] knowing of the disaffection of the

---

[1] In a by-election on the death of the sitting Conservative MP, the Liberal candidate converted a 600 vote deficit to a 1500 vote majority.

[2] Samuel Smethurst (1854–1931), building contractor and Conservative leader in Oldham; sometime member of Oldham School Board, Royton Urban District Council and Lancashire County Council; Conservative candidate for Oldham 1922 and 1923.

[3] Thomas Ashton (1844–1927), prospective Labour candidate for Oldham; General Secretary of the Miner's Federation of Great Britain 1889–1919; PC 1917.

Tory working men (which seems to prevail to a wide extent) with your attitude is going to bid for their vote by appearing to make some concession to your view.

Yours truly

Sam Smethurst

Alfred Harmsworth to WSC

14 September 1903   1 Carmelite House
Private

Dear Churchill,

I will see your friend with pleasure. I am now really at a loss to know who to ask for the 26th; that is, who would be of use. I know, as you do probably, a large number of inefficients.

When I wrote to you I had great hopes of hearing that Lord R [Rosebery] was about to start on an active political campaign. If he does not do so, a Radical Government is, in my judgement, certain. And when I say Radical, I mean a Government into which Grey and Asquith would be forced.

Lord R does not realise how much his lack of activity injures him in the country, & especially in the provinces.

I almost despair of politics at the present time. Unless I can see some party to which to attach myself, I shall give up politics & go in for buying and organising more newspapers.

I warn you that ours is a very quiet circle at Sutton Place – strictly journalistic – and I am not so hopeful of anything resulting from our conference as I was when I wrote to you & before R's state of inanition at that critical time. However, discussion will do no harm.

Yours very truly

AH

WSC to Lady Randolph

18 September 1903   Invercauld

Dearest Mamma,

I am indeed sorry to miss you here: but we shall see each other often in the autumn, & I may need your assistance in Oldham, if you have time & inclination.

The situation is most interesting & I fancy a smash must come in a few days. Mr Balfour is coming to Balmoral on Saturday. Is he going to resign or reconstruct? If he resigns will the King send for Spencer or Devonshire? If for either will he succeed in forming a govt & what kind of government? If he reconstructs – will it be a Protectionist reconstruction of a cabinet wh does not contain the Free Trade Ministers, or a Free Trade reconstruction of a Cabinet from which JC has resigned? All these things are possible.[1]

I go to Dalmeny tomorrow. Write to me there. I have put my name down at Balmoral – but I fear I am still in disgrace.

Yours loving son
WINSTON SC

Lord Hugh Cecil to WSC

[Undated]   Cranborne

My dear Winston,

I shd have written before but that I have been busy with other things.

The situation is very obscure. Why did Ritchie resign? Potential Retaliation as the *Daily Graphic* happily calls it need frighten no one. But if there is more why did not the Duke resign. Or has Ritchie been virtually turned out to save Joe's face? If the last Ritchie ought to have stuck like a limpet & made the situation scandalous.

Our part seems to me at present to be triumphant over the withdrawal of Preference as a Govt policy; to fight Joe in the country as hard as we can; in regard to Retaliation to be critical but not absolutely hostile 'all very well in theory. What exactly do you propose? We see great difficulties etc.'

Generally the object of our strategy must be to damage Joe without producing the total ruin of the Unionist Party. This last point must bulk rather more largely in our plans than formerly in view of the very strong stream that is running against them. We don't want a Radical majority independent of the Irish if we can help it.

As to (Imp:) find out from him what he will do if the General Election which cannot be later than June, I think, results (a) in a Liberal majority

---

[1] On September 18 the resignations were announced of Chamberlain, and of two opponents of his fiscal schemes, Ritchie, Chancellor of the Exchequer, and Lord George Hamilton, Secretary for India. Both were unaware of Chamberlain's resignation. These were followed by the resignations two days later of Lord Balfour of Burleigh, Secretary for Scotland, and Arthur Elliot, Financial Secretary to the Treasury. The Duke of Devonshire's resignation as Lord President of the Council was made public on October 6.

with the Irish (b) in such a majority without the Irish & what he expects
Asquith & Grey to do. What prospect does he think there is of any co-
operation after the Election between the Free Traders & Lib Imp?
Generally in short find out as much as you can.

It is too early to determine next Session's tactics. I shall see you 25th –
uncertain about 24th; will write or wire.

In great haste
HC

Lord James of Hereford to WSC

22 September 1903   Kennet
                                                        Alloa

Strictly confidential

My dear Winston Churchill,

I need not tell you how distressed I am by the extraordinary action of
the Duke.[1] It is as disastrous as it is inexplicable.

I cannot tell you how troubled I am especially in regard to the future of
Unionists Free-Traders.

What are your movements? If I do not hear from the Duke in the course of
this afternoon I leave here tonight and go through to Breamore. I shall be
most pleased if you can come there to talk over future operations. I have
written to Goschen asking him to come on Saturday. I shall be there for the
rest of the autumn – but come as soon as you can.

Yours
J. OF H.

Your journey with the Duchess must have been very interesting. I went
over to Invercauld on Saturday but found you had left.

Lord James of Hereford to WSC

23 September 1903   Breamore
                                                        Salisbury

My dear Winston Churchill,

Please send me a telegram saying if you can come here on Saturday.
Goschen is coming – and I have asked Hicks Beach. I shall be at the meeting
on Friday but send me a wire as soon as you can.

Yours
JAMES OF H

---

[1] See Volume II, page 66, for a commentary on the Duke of Devonshire's 'extraordinary
action.'

Lord Hugh Cecil to WSC

6 October 1903   The Cottage
                                                       Great Brington
                                                       Northampton

My dear Winston,
    What a thunder clap.[1] I confess my sympathies are largely with AJB
but we must of course stand by the Duke. Moreover Arthur's answer making
no reply to the accusation of being a Protectionist is almost fatal.
    I shall lunch to-morrow at the Carlton at 1.30.

                                                       Yrs ever
                                                       HUGH CECIL
Let us not say anything public till we meet.

WSC to Lord Rosebery
(Rosebery Papers)

9 October 1903   105 Mount Street

Private

My dear Lord Rosebery,
    I am looking forward anxiously to your speech next Tuesday. So much
seems to depend upon it & I think the odds against us are vy heavy. No one
pays any attention to Asquith. Beach & Goschen are old & husky. *We* are
children. Joe's electric strength carries all before it. You alone can counter
him & stem the tide. I hope you will make some conjunction with the duke,
so that at Sheffield you may be able to say that you join with him in fighting
for Free Trade & would if necessary serve under him.[2]
    Our meeting of Free Traders yesterday was vy determined & in all
respects satisfactory. We have adjourned till this afternoon to allow Beach to
consult the duke.

                                                       Yours ever
                                                       W

---

[1] The resignation of the Duke of Devonshire.
[2] At Sheffield on October 13, Rosebery explained his objections to preferential tariffs in a
way which suggested he might resume an active role in politics. This illusion was dispelled
by later speeches.

Lord Rosebery to WSC

10 October 1903   Dalmeny

My dear Winston,

I am very grateful for your letters but should have liked more about Sheffield and less about AB. It is of no use my seeing him as he has gone over definitely to JC. As to your suggestion about the Duke I can hardly throw myself into his arms – at any rate till I know they are open. Moreover, the Education Act!

I doubt if I shall be in London this month, but shall be there the beginning of next.

Yrs

AR

WSC to J. T. Travis-Clegg[1]

9 October [1903]   105 Mount Street

Dear Mr Travis-Clegg,

Sheffield and Glasgow have come and gone, and it is necessary to consider where they leave us. No one can misunderstand Mr Chamberlain. His policy is perfectly plain, and now that he has left the Government he has an absolute right to urge it. He stands forward plainly and boldly as a thoroughgoing protectionist. He cares little or nothing for 'the freedom to negotiate' for which the Prime Minister pleads. He demands a tariff not as a means of doing evil that good may come, but as an institution good in itself. He cares less about lowering the tariffs of foreign countries than of building up a tariff round our own. He proposes permanent taxation, protective to the home producer, on bread, beef, mutton, butter, cheese, eggs, and fruit, as well as upon manufactured and semi-manufactured articles. With him imports are evils and free-traders fools. He admires the policy of protectionist countries and extols the wisdom of protectionist statesmen. Mr Chaplin and Sir Howard Vincent adorn his platforms; Mr Seddon[2] signals encouragement from the Antipodes, and the methods of German finance are advocated by the methods of American politics.

I do not complain. His policy may be unwise; his arithmetic may be queer; his electioneering may be crude; but we recognize a real man putting forth a real policy with faith and courage. Would all our statesmen were

---

[1] Published in *The Times* on October 12.
[2] Richard John Seddon (1845–1906), Prime Minister of New Zealand.

equally outspoken! I do not wonder that the protectionists follow him. They will never get such a chance again.

Like you, I find myself bluntly and flatly against the policy he has declared, I do not underrate the strength of the appeal that he will make, but I believe absolutely that it will be rejected, and I fear that its rejection will bring our venerable party clattering in ruins to the ground. Perhaps, indeed, when Mr Chamberlain talked to his Glasgow audience of the fall of the Campanile at Venice he had also in his mind the plan of the brand new German-American structure which he would set up in its place.

But, like all the advocates of quack remedies, he protests too much. Nobody is to suffer, everybody is to gain. Employment will be regular, wages will rise. The miller is to be protected. The labourer will return to the land. In Ireland two pigs are to grow where one pig grew before. Sugar refining will revive at Greenock. There will be a boom in Rochester cement. The cost of food will remain unaltered, but those who sell it are to get a better price. Manufacturers will make larger profits, but the consumer will pay no more. By a proposal so small as not to dislocate our trade our industries are to be sustained and our Empire consolidated and without any extra charge to the taxpayer the Exchequer will be embarrassed every year with a mighty surplus. How is it to be done? It is as easy as thimble-rigging. All is to be paid by the dirty foreigner, all except a tax on bacon. Apparently the foreigner will not pay a tax on bacon. It is the food of the poor, and perhaps for that very reason the foreigner – who will pay all the others – with callous villainy refuses to pay it. And here, again, is an argument for retaliation. It is a wonderful plan. Will the people be taken in? I think not. Labouring men must view with unalterable suspicion a scheme for reducing the cost of living by taxing every mouthful they eat. The Colonies will reject proposals to cramp their economic development, like the Chinese women tie up their children's feet. The commercial classes will shrink from the disturbance of an utterly unnecessary revolution. And trade unionists will not be such fools as to hand themselves over to capitalist combinations at the very moment when, owing to the state of the law, they have lost much of the power and freedom which Lord Beaconsfield intended them to have. I have not concealed from you my opposition. I hold that, though free trade, like every other policy, has its defects in this imperfect world, still on the whole the abundance of commodities, the simplicity of our Customs arrangements, the freedom of our ports, the adaptiveness of our industries, the purity of our public life give to our workers much more than foreign nations are able to gain by tariff juggles, usually stupid, often corrupt. And the proof I find in the published official returns which are the result of the inquiry, and which show beyond all doubt that notwithstanding four years of profligate expenditure, for which Mr Chamberlain is largely responsible, the material well-being of the people is steadily increasing, and, that in wealth and productive energy we are far the superiors of any other nation in the world. But Mr Balfour is a mystery. He asks for 'freedom to negotiate,' and who shall refuse it? It may be that there are times when fiscal threats or fiscal bribes judiciously applied might procure advantages or prevent misfortune. Let us give the Government of the King full power to make proposals to Parliament, and let Parliament be the judge. But I hope myself that they will not use this 'freedom to negotiate' to make any more treaties like the Sugar Convention, which has already succeeded in making every Englishman pay more and every Frenchman pay less for his sugar, and which, without restoring those industries which have suffered from unnatural foreign competition, hurts those greater industries which have resulted from it. If the Government make foolish treaties they will be blamed. If they make wise treaties they will be praised; but their right to make such treaties is undisputed and indisputable, and if they doubt it by all means let us reassure them. So that I am perfectly willing as a Conservative member to accept provisionally the principle of negotiation which Mr Balfour declares is the Test Act of the party.

I say 'provisionally' because it is impossible altogether to shut out suspicion. If this were all, where was the need for such a fuss? Is Mr Balfour asking only for 'freedom to negotiate,' or is he using this vague and platitudinous formula to cover Mr Chamberlain and to coax or cozen us into protection? Observe the signs of the weather. Mr Balfour and Mr Chamberlain reciprocate endearments. The Prime Minister has never a good word for free trade, and never uses a phrase to disparage protection. The free-trade Ministers are ejected from the Cabinet. Their places are filled by some of the most rabid protectionists in the House of Commons. Mr Austen Chamberlain, the echo and exponent of his father, is sent to guard the public purse. *Custodes ipsos quis custodiet!* The partisans of both distinguished men assert that there is real collusion, that no differences exist between them; that, in the words of *The Times*, 'they are playing their game with the skill of accomplished whist players.' Lastly, the Duke of Devonshire, who knows the truth from within, has resigned, and Mr Gerald Balfour tells us with much candour that, though food taxes are not the present official policy of the Government, if Mr Chamberlain's campaign proves popular they are likely to become so. A month ago the Prime Minister's friends would have rejected such suggestions with scorn; but some things have happened at present unexplained which have weakened the foundations of belief.

Now if it be true that 'freedom to negotiate' is only a trick and a pretence, I for one would unhesitatingly prefer Mr Chamberlain with his honest, downright thumping. If we are to tax our food let us do so because we think it right, not because it is found to be popular. Let us do it for the sake of Empire, and not for a party caucus. Let us look to the harvest of the future, and not to the general election. I assume, however, since it affords a last hope of reunion, that Mr Balfour is conscientiously opposed to taxes on food and to an average 10 per cent protective duty on manufactured articles, and that, whether these things be popular or unpopular, he will not himself consent to them. But while the Unionist free trader recognizes the flag of truce, he would be wise to keep his finger on the trigger. And, after all, I sometimes wonder whether, if Mr Balfour has the will, he has the power to stop. These great debates, which convulse our public life once at least in every generation, do not lend themselves to compromise. Present friendships and old associations will avail little to mitigate the fierceness of the conflict. Existing bonds and existing prejudices will fade together. Party machinery, smooth speeches, ambiguous and adroit procedure must utterly fail to avert or even long to delay the taking of a great decision. The armies are drawing up for battle, and the middle ground will soon be swept with cross-fire. The administration of the trimmers will either be extinguished or be enlisted in the forces of protection. Men must choose, and by their choice they will be bound in the years that are to come. Liberals and Tories alike may try to vex or complicate the issue, but on the day of voting the electors will see only the simple and supreme alternative – protection or free trade. Mr Chamberlain may in perfect good faith declare that he has no wish to supplant Mr Balfour. But if he wins the victory will be his, and those who have won it with him will certainly not be content with the half-hearted declarations of Sheffield.

Therefore you will justify me in accepting the policy of the party as declared by Mr Balfour under some reserve. I wish to be perfectly frank with our friends at Oldham. I look forward to many occasions of pleading to them the great cause we are trying to uphold, a cause always so intimately associated with the political history of the town. During the winter I shall ask you to invite to your platform more than one speaker of eminence and repute, and if any distinguished protectionist should desire a hearing also he will assuredly find that in Lancashire, at any rate, free trade and free speech are equally esteemed.

Yours sincerely

WINSTON S. CHURCHILL

J. T. Travis-Clegg to WSC

EXTRACT

11 October 1903   Shaw Lodge
                                                   Nr Oldham

My dear Mr Churchill,

I have not written you sooner as I expected that you would be sufficiently busy without my bothering you with correspondence.

I think your letter excellent & better still, 'all of it is true'. There is no doubt Mr Chamberlain is a most dangerous opponent & with all the wealth & influence he evidently has on his side he will be still more so . . . I think it would be a good plan, as you suggest, to have a series of meetings during the winter, but when they are over & the electors are better informed by both sides on the question it would then be wise for you to take a vote of the Executive on your attitude & to decide once for all if you are going to be the Candidate.

You would look foolish if when the election came the majority of your own side decided not to run you as their Candidate, & furthermore we cannot afford to let you be out of the next Parliament & if you are not going to have any chance in Oldham you will be better employed in fighting a Constituency where at least the majority of your *own party* are in favour of you. Again it would be a good thing if the Protectionists could say that you, almost the chief leader of the Free Trade party, had lost a seat in Lancashire. You will gain no party advantage in Oldham from being a Free Trader as both your opponents are the same. I am not saying all this to dishearten you, because I think it quite possible after the people are better informed they will see the fallacy of Protection. All that I advise is that after the meetings in Oldham have been held & after you have spoken (as you probably will) all over the Country, you should get to know how you stand with your own party in your own Constituency, & not wait till close on to the election time. If the executive decided against you I should resign my Chairmanship of the party and take no further active part in the Election. I am afraid you are only too correct when you say this unhappy question 'will ruin our venerable party', I want if possible to avoid your being even temporarily crushed in the debris. I think it absolutely essential that you should be in the next Parliament as member of somewhere, Oldham for preference.

I shall like to have a talk over matters with you next week. You will perhaps let me know later exactly when to expect you.

                                                   I am
                                          Your very sincerely
                                          J. T. TRAVIS-CLEGG

Lord James of Hereford to WSC

12 October 1903   Breamore
                                                       Salisbury
My dear Winston Churchill,

Very many congratulations on your most able and incisive letter. 'Tis most useful.

Can you come here any time during the coming month? Choose your own time – always glad to see you. I have written in same sense to Hugh Cecil. Wish you would come with him.

Yrs

JAMES OF HEREFORD

Daily Mail

12 October 1903

'A FEAST FOR PIGS'

Three of the most adroit critics of Mr Chamberlain's policy – Mr Churchill, Mr Lloyd-George, and Mr Robson[1] – have made pronouncements on the fiscal proposals.

As a phrase-maker, Mr Lloyd-George found material to his liking, especially in the consideration that is to be shown for the pig. 'A policy of dear food and cheap offal,' 'A perpetual feast for pigs,' were among his achievements.

Mr Churchill has written a very long letter (from which we give extracts) to explain his reasons for accepting the policy of Mr Balfour 'with reserve'.

Thomas Marlowe[2] to WSC

13 October 1903   *Daily Mail*
                                                   3 Carmelite House

Dear Mr Churchill,

Mr Harmsworth tells me you have suffered some annoyance in conse-quence of the heading under which your letter appeared. I regret this very

---

[1] William Snowdon Robson (?–1918), Liberal MP South Shields 1895–1910; Solicitor-General 1905–8; Attorney-General 1908–10; knighted 1905; PC 1910; Baron Robson of Jesmond 1910.

[2] Thomas Marlowe (1868–1935), Editor of the *Daily Mail* 1899–1926; Chairman, Asso-ciated Newspapers Limited 1918–26.

much and hope that we may find an early opportunity of repairing the injury. The phrase was taken from Mr Lloyd George's speech and was intended to apply to that speech alone. This must have been clear to anyone who read the column, but I can quite understand that it would convey a wrong impression to a casual reader. Of course I ought to have seen this in time to alter it and I am sorry to have overlooked it.

With renewed apologies, Believe me, Yours sincerely
THOMAS MARLOWE

Alfred Harmsworth to WSC

13 October 1903   Carmelite House

My dear Churchill,
I had nothing to do with the matter of which you complain. It was simply a piece of stupidity.

I have been extremely unwell for some days, & do not know whether I shall be fit enough to see anyone this week.

My views on the matter are exactly as I told you, & I enclose you a copy.

Sincerely yours
ALF HARMSWORTH

Alfred Harmsworth to WSC

14 October 1903   36 Berkeley Square

My dear Churchill,
I am here in Berkeley Square in bed & shall be till tomorrow afternoon. I shall be very glad to see you at any time between now & then.

I hope my note yesterday did not seem very cross. I was at the time in much pain & mentally annoyed at being knocked over on the eve of starting a new newspaper [the *Daily Mirror*]. But my doctor cheers me up & says I shall be about again tomorrow.

Sincerely yours
ALF HARMSWORTH

J. T. Travis-Clegg to WSC

13 October 1903   Shaw Lodge

My dear Mr Churchill,

The Unity Hall has been taken for 21st, the meeting to commence 7.45. I really think your best course now is to take the bull by the horns & declare your policy on which you will stand. If you do as you propose & bring men like Lord Goschen down & invite the Protectionists to bring Austen Chamberlain or Earl Percy to state their side you will do what Hilton[1] & his friends expressly desire & you will, I fear, also cause a split in the party which would be fatal to your chances. I hear that Tom Ashton is thinking of 'trimming' to the Chamberlain idea. You may also have seen that Blatchford[2] in the *Clarion*, is declaring against 'Free Trade', though from a different point of view to Mr Chamberlain. He advocates it from the Socialistic side as being of possible use for the 'Producers', i.e. the working men's benefit. This is just what I told you I feared, that protection would rouse the dormant socialism in the country. Once roused I believe it will be irresistible, because there is no curbing power here like there is in Germany.

You will see how Lord Hugh takes next week & that might be a guide for your future action.

There is the monthly meeting of the General Purposes Committee to-morrow evening, there will probably be a row & if so I shall put the question straight to them & ask them if they are prepared to sacrifice you, & if so to say so, if not then they must give you their absolute wholehearted support. I am not going to see you fooled, at any rate with your eyes shut.

Lord Goschen did speak in the Theatre in Oldham when he was Chancellor & had a magnificent reception. I have his speech now, but I dont know how he would be received at present. He would certainly carry respect if not enthusiasm. I fear, at any rate just now, that the Chamberlain mania is pervading our party.

Yours very sincerely
J. T. TRAVIS-CLEGG

PS I have had a long talk with Smethurst this morning. We are agreed.

---

[1] W. Hilton, Secretary, St Peter's Ward Conservative Club, Oldham.

[2] Robert Blatchford (1851–1943), editor of *The Clarion*; socialist and imperialist who devoted many years to trying to arouse his countrymen against the 'German menace'.

Lady Moyra Cavendish[1] to WSC

13 October 1903   Gosford
                                                Longniddry

Dear Mr Churchill,
    I can't help writing one line of congratulation to you on your letter, which
we all think *quite* excellent. You will probably think it very unnecessary my
writing but it was so exactly what Dick & I feel & so wonderfully expressed
that I could not resist congratulating you on it & of *course* you won't think of
bothering to answer otherwise I shall be sorry I wrote.

                                            Yours v. sincerely
                                            MOYRA CAVENDISH

Andrew Carnegie[2] to WSC

13 October 1903   Skibo Castle
                                                Sutherland

My dear Mr Churchill,
    The Iron & Steel Institute is very anxious to have you at its next Banquet,
May 6th. At the Banquet in May last, we had the leaders of both parties,
including the Prime Minister. This time, we are inviting the Prime Ministers
and Leaders of the future.
    The Autumn meeting of the Institute is to be held in New York. For the
first time in its history, it has a President who is an American Citizen. This
gives the coming Banquet and the Meeting somewhat of an international
flavor, which the Council feels would be strengthened by your co-operation.
    Expressing the hope, personally, that you will be able to attend, and sup-
port me, I am

                                        Always very truly yours
                                        ANDREW CARNEGIE

----

[1] Moyra de Vere Beauclerk Cavendish (1876–1942), 3rd daughter of 10th Duke of St
Albans; married, 1895, Lord Richard Frederick Cavendish (1871–1946), younger brother
of 9th Duke of Devonshire.
[2] Andrew Carnegie (1835–1919), the American steel millionaire and philanthropist, was
the President of the Iron and Steel Institute. He retired from business in 1901 after con-
solidating various American steel works in the gigantic cartel, United States Steel Corporation.

John Morley to WSC

14 October 1903　　　　　　　　　　　　　　　Flowermead
　　　　　　　　　　　　　　　　　　　　Wimbledon Park

My dear Churchill,

I was just going to write to thank you for your brilliant, powerful, decisive letter.

I should much like a talk with you, for all sorts of reasons. But I cannot dine on Friday, I'm sorry to say. When I come back from Lancashire? Many thanks to you.

　　　　　　　　　　　　　　　　　　　　　Yours sincerely
　　　　　　　　　　　　　　　　　　　　　J. MORLEY

J. T. Travis-Clegg to WSC

1.30 pm　　　　　　　　　　　　　　　　　　Shaw Lodge
14 October 1903

My dear Mr Churchill,

I have just come back from the association meeting in Oldham & I am sorry to say that my fears as to your position with them are only too well-founded. Except Smethurst & myself everyone there including Horrobin who is a supporter of yours & a strong Free Trader, & Schofield[1] of Waterhead who is a Free Trader with an 'open mind' deprecated the tone of your letter to me & protested against the holding of the meeting to be addressed by Lord Hugh & yourself next Wednesday. Hilton was desirous of moving a resolution of confidence in Balfour tonight but was restrained, but finally the following resolution was passed practically unanimously only Horrobin dissenting: 'That this meeting regrets the tone of Mr Churchill's letter to Mr Travis-Clegg, & trusts that at the coming meeting in the Unity Hall he will clearly define his position on Mr Balfour's policy.' This resolution means that unless you are prepared blindly to follow Mr Balfour's Policy your candidature at the next election in Oldham will only be backed by a small minority of your party. The protectionists are not now asking for a 'Chamberlain Candidate' but a 'Balfour Candidate', which is to my mind a distinction without a difference, but it gives them the strong argument of being in accordance with their leaders. Both Smethurst & I told the meeting straight that what they had to decide really was whether they would give you their wholehearted & united support as a Free Trade Unionist, or lose you

[1] Secretary of the Oldham Conservative Club.

altogether. Hilton at first threatened to move a hostile resolution from the platform on Wednesday, but I got him to promise after the passing of the resolution at the close of the meeting that he would not attend the meeting at all. I don't think any of the Committee except Smethurst, Brierley[1] & myself will attend.

What it comes to is this that unless you satisfy them by swearing allegiance to Balfour on Wednesday you will have to face a hostile vote of the Executive.

I told them that in the event of your giving up the Candidature at the next election I should resign the Chairmanship & Smethurst told them he would not support a Protectionist Candidate.

It was decided that as the meeting for Wednesday is placarded it would cause too much of a scandal to abandon it, but I fear the climax will take place afterwards unless you satisfy them on the lines I have mentioned.

Shall I call a meeting of the full Executive for Friday evening next week after a meeting of the General Purposes Committee at both of which you should be present?

I am, Yours very sincerely
J. T. TRAVIS-CLEGG

J. T. Travis-Clegg to WSC

15 October 1903   Shaw Lodge

My dear Mr Churchill,

I had a long conversation with Smethurst this morning & as a result we sent the telegram to you.

I think there is no doubt that unless you agree blindly to follow Mr Balfour the party in Oldham will repudiate you. I think it quite possible your meeting on Wednesday may be broken up. I certainly think the climax has arrived & Smethurst agrees with me that it will be more dignified to retire than be kicked out.

Unless I hear from you to the contrary by midday tomorrow I will have the full executive called for Monday.

Chamberlain has completely captured the party.

I am Yours very sincerely
JAMES T. TRAVIS-CLEGG

[1] Frederick Brierley (1867–1927), honorary secretary, Oldham Conservative Association until, like WSC, he broke with the Association over free trade and became a Liberal; an accountant and former Collector of Taxes, he was for many years an Oldham Borough Councillor.

Lady Wimborne to WSC

15 October 1903   Wimborne House

Dearest Winston,

You know, I am sure, how deeply interested I am in your career & dear Ivor's. I feel the present moment is such a critical one for your fortunes & his that I should so like to see you & have a chat. Do come round & see me anytime before I go away on Saturday afternoon. I thought your letter quite excellent & it reminded me of your Father's way of going straight to the point. Of one thing I think there is no doubt & that is that Balfour & Chamberlain are one, and that there is no future for Free Traders in the Conservative party. Why tarry?

Yrs affecly
CORNELIA WIMBORNE

Lord Rosebery to WSC

16 October 1903   Dalmeny

My dear Winston,

Many thanks for your amusing telegram. Everyone was talking of your letter when I arrived at Sheffield. I think it has really (and justly) produced an effect.

Yrs always
A R

Tell me about your league.[1]

J. T. Travis-Clegg to WSC

17 October 1903   Shaw Lodge

Dear Mr. Churchill,

Smethurst & I have had a long conversation about your letter this afternoon. We are afraid you totally misunderstand the position in Oldham. It is

---

[1] The Unionist Free Food League. On October 16 the Duke of Devonshire joined the League. He was elected president a week later. Other officers were Lord Goschen, Sir Michael Hicks Beach and C. T. Ritchie – vice-presidents; Lord James of Hereford – treasurer; F. H. Manners-Sutton – secretary.

entirely out of your power either to postpone a vote of no confidence till next year or to obtain a Conservative Platform in Oldham. The vote will be decisive on Tuesday night and unless you agree to support Mr Balfour absolutely you will find that you will be absolutely repudiated by the party; they will probably pass a vote saying you are no longer their representative. the organisation will be taken from you & you will receive no Conservative support. Even the strongest Free Traders are against your attitude & even I could not split the party by appearing on the platform after you were repudiated as the party member.

I fear there is nothing for it but either declaring yourself against the Government, & saying you will hold your seat till the next election, but will not contest Oldham again as a Conservative, or swallowing Balfour's Policy. The party has made up its mind & will act on Tuesday night.

You can no more stop it than you could a whirlwind. Both Smethurst & I think it essential that Wednesday's meeting must be stopped. I could not take the chair at it as Chairman of the Party if the Executive pass an adverse Resolution on Tuesday night & I should have to resign the Chairmanship right away.

Tuesday night is so near to the Wednesday's meeting there is no room to turn round. If you will be guided by our advice, postpone Lord Hugh Cecil's meeting on Wednesday. Am sending this by express post as stated in the telegram sent by Smethurst.

It is impossible to convey by letter the feeling there is in the constituency about this matter. You entirely misunderstand it.

I am
Yours very sincerely
J. T. TRAVIS-CLEGG

Wire me as soon as possible.

C. E. G. Webb to WSC

18 October 1903   High Street
                                                   Harrow

Dear Sir

With reference to my personal invitation to you on Wednesday last to come and speak at Harrow on the Fiscal Question I now write you. I presume you are still of opinion that you cannot go so far, at present, as to address an audience at *the Harrow Liberal Club*. Harrovians would give you a most cordial welcome.

If you must insist in replying in the negative may I hope that should later there be a development that I can successfully approach you for a meeting.

Your reply I will communicate to the Exchange Telegraph Co for the Press.

Yours truly
C. E. G. WEBB

WSC to C. E. G. Webb

18 October 1903   105 Mount Street

Copy

My dear Sir,

I have carefully considered the invitation you have sent me to address a meeting in the Harrow Liberal Club upon the Fiscal question, and I can only repeat the answer which I gave to you personally on Wednesday last. While I am a Conservative member it would be obviously improper for me to appear upon a Liberal platform. It is no doubt true that this controversy raises social and Imperialistic issues which transcend party considerations, and may before it is finished change the character, composition, and balance of English political organisations. But it is the plain duty of a Unionist Free Trader first of all to fight the battle steadfastly within his own party and not easily to give up the hope of so restraining the present movement as to prevent at any rate a general reversion to Protection such as Mr Chamberlain seems to desire. And now that the Duke of Devonshire has come forward to lead us, who will be bold enough to say that that battle is hopeless? I have seen enough war not to try to prophesy the result of engagements before they are fought; and until the event is actually decided, I can only thank you for the courtesy which you have shown to me.

Yours very truly
[WINSTON S. CHURCHILL]

S. Smethurst to WSC

18 October 1903   Coldhurst House
                                   Oldham

Dear Mr Churchill,

I wired you yesterday after consultation with Travis-Clegg believing that your letter indicated you had a wrong conception of how matters stood at

Oldham. The decisive vote of committee we anticipate is that they will pass a vote of confidence in Balfour which may be construed if not put definitely in that form as want of confidence in you. In regard to Wednesday's meeting I was thinking more of the reception Lord Hugh Cecil would get and whether you had led him to expect a different state of things.

It is quite possible the majority of those present at the meeting may be Radicals and so sympathetic with your views, but, except something outrageous is said, I think the meeting will listen with respect. I should be sorry to think otherwise. Of course a great deal depends upon the tact you & Lord Hugh exercise for you are dealing with very combustible materials. I take it, now, you are going to fight the matter out to the bitter end in Oldham. If so are you going to declare to your Committee & Executive unequivocably you are a Unionist and a Unionist you will remain and if you are defeated you will at least for a time go out of politics rather than acquiesce in a course you think so detrimental to the true interest of the Country? Because there is a very general opinion you are only waiting an opportune time to go over to the other side, a clear deliverance on this matter would immensely strengthen you, if you can make it.

Yours truly

SAM SMETHURST

WSC to Lord Hugh Cecil

24 October 1903   105 Mount Street

Not sent

Most private

My dear Linky,

I want to impress upon you that I am absolutely in earnest in what I said to you yesterday & I do not think that anything is likely to happen to turn me.

I understand your plan vy clearly; and it is not mine. I do not want to be enrolled in a narrow sect of latter day Peelites austerely unbending in economics, more Tory than the Tories in other things. I do not intend to be a 'loyal supporter' of the Unionist party or of this present administration, & I object to be so labelled. These old ministers who have come forward to help us on Free Trade are involved in varying degrees – but all vy deeply – in the blunders and follies of the last four years. They all feel – as I cannot feel – identity with the earlier glories of the Unionist party. It seems to me certain that the Duke will be a paralysing influence. He is according to Victor

Cavendish[1] to be 'a drag' on the Fiscal policy of the Government; & no doubt he will also be their defender in all other things. This is all vy well for a peer; but for a member dependent upon the vote of a constituency the position is quite untenable. No one will know better how to profit from it than Joe. I do not object to fighting against heavy odds. I do object to being compelled to choose bad ground to fight on. Much may be done by even a few men whose position is clear and logical. But to proceed making perfervid protestations of loyalty to the 'party' & yet to trample on the dearest aspirations of the party & thwart its most popular champions is to court utter ruin.

You like this sort of thing. You derive a melancholy satisfaction from the idea of being driven out of politics nursing your wrongs. And when I think that no one will be more mercilessly outspoken than you I think you will have your martyrdom as you wish.

But I do not share this view. I am an English Liberal. I hate the Tory party, their men, their words & their methods. I feel no sort of sympathy with them – except to my own people at Oldham. I want to take up a clear practical position which masses of people can understand. I do not want to stay splitting hairs upon retaliation and contracting all sorts of embarrassing obligations. Already I have freely against my inclination taken a backward step in subscribing to A. Balfour's policy. I have done this simply & solely because I want to cover the formation of your League & it was the only way of staving off the crisis. I feel vy uncomfortable about what I have said, & am not sure even of its honesty. To go on like this wavering between opposite courses, feigning friendship to a party where no friendship exists, & loyalty to leaders whose downfall is desired, sickens me. Moreover from a tactical point of view it is the surest road to destruction.

I entirely dissent from your doctrine that no forethought should be exercised. It is madness when dealing with such antagonists as we have to face. The Tory party would show me no mercy, & I do not expect it or desire it. But upon the other hand I want to be free to defend myself – and I mean to be. It is therefore my intention that before Parliament meets my separation from the Tory party and the Government shall be complete & irrevocable; & during the next session I propose to act consistently with the Liberal party. This will no doubt necessitate re-election which I shall not hesitate to face with all its chances.

It troubles me much to write all this; but I am convinced that the position you wish to take up is neither practical nor consistent. Free Trade is so

---

[1] Victor Christian William Cavendish (1868–1938), succeeded his uncle as 9th Duke of Devonshire in 1908; Liberal Unionist MP for West Derbyshire 1891–1908; Treasurer of HM Household 1900–3; Financial Secretary to the Treasury 1903–5; Civil Lord of the Admiralty 1915–16; Governor-General of Canada 1916–21. PC 1905; KG 1916.

essentially Liberal in its sympathies & tendencies that those who fight for it must become Liberals. The duty of those who mean to maintain it is not to remain a snarling band on the flank of a government who mean to betray it, but boldly & honestly to range themselves in the ranks of that great party without whose instrumentality it cannot be preserved.

Nothing need happen until December at any rate, unless Oldham explodes: but I cannot leave you longer in doubt as to my intentions, & you will of course have to steer accordingly. It would be far better for the country in the long run if you were to face the real facts of the case and help to preserve a reconstituted Liberal party against the twin assaults of capital & Labour. And wherever you go you can only do your best for those religious causes which you care about – and your efforts would be more effective on the Liberal side than on these Tory materialists. But you must choose, as I have done, for yourself.

Yours ever
W

I should like you to show this letter to Jack Seely and talk to him on the subject.

Lord Hugh Cecil to WSC

27 October 1903   Brooke House
                                                         Isle of Wight

My dear Winston,

Just a line about Beach's manoeuvre at Bristol. At first it rather ruffled me but on reflection I think it may turn out well.[1] The Joeites are already nervous & dissatisfied with AJB & civility from Beach to him may easily drive them into attacking him wh will bring grist to our mill. We want more people very badly. We had only 42 MPs present & ... [?] sympathy on Friday! [Sir Robert] Peel began with 119 & the Lib Uns with 93. We must get more. Now if we can coax some more into declaring against Joe they will be ours ultimately or most of them – for all purposes.

I entreat you therefore to moderation. I didn't think yr speech to the Press wise – jokes about party loyalty are a mistake just now. Remember we are engaged on a task of quite extraordinary difficulty and delicacy against the ablest political tacticians of the day! Please be careful at Birmingham & remember that the newspaper reader of tomorrow is much more important than the audience of tonight.

[1] Hicks Beach and Balfour appeared on the same platform at a banquet at Bristol on November 13.

I am staying with Jack Seely here – a very nice place if you like the sea &
storms as I do.

Yrs ever

HUGH CECIL

Lord Hugh Cecil to WSC

[Undated]   Cranborne

My dear Winston,

1. Bob[1] wants to know times and plans for B'ham. You better send him 12
platform tickets to 20 Manchester Square. 2. As to watchmaker it is curious
and pathetic. But note it is mainly Swiss competition – therefore not 'dumping'. I suspect the poor man is incompetent.

3. I don't think your tactics are the right ones. We can never do very
much in the country; and we are not doing nothing now. Consider this
month Goschen, Beach, Balfour of B, the Duke, you and I at B'ham, Gorst
at Oxford (where I take the chair) are all to speak. That is not bad for the
month. Quite enough to make a show. Supposing we were ever so definite
and clear headed we shd not do much more. Nor shd we excite much more
support. There is much more general apathy on the question than you
reckon with. People outside the Parly circle are by no means so excited
as we are. After all the actual proposals are in the dim distance – next Parlt
or next Parlt but one. And that takes the fire out of the contest. I don't
think anything we can do wd make any perceptible difference, and I am
not dissatisfied – we seem to me to be doing quite nicely.

Then as to Parlt I am sure you are quite wrong. Any secession would
weaken us there. What we want is not a band of guerillas but a number of
votes on a free food division. I am sure that division is the most important
thing to think of. I am only disturbed to think how much influence I have
myself thrown away by too much violence. After the division if the Govt
survive it will be quite time enough to rearrange our tactics. But even then
I think I shall be against a constant attack. We don't want pin-pricks, we
want a stab to the heart or not at all.

Finally I entreat you to give up 'candour' and 'clearheadedness' and
'looking facts in the face' so far as our comtees go. You did nothing but
mischief last time. Keep rigid command of your face. Never try to state the

---

[1] Lord (Edgar Algernon) Robert Cecil (1864–1958), 3rd son of the 3rd Marquess of Salisbury; Conservative MP East Marylebone 1906–10; Independent Conservative MP Hitchin
1911–23; Minister of Blockade 1916–18; Assistant Secretary of State for Foreign Affairs 1918;
Lord Privy Seal 1923–24; Chancellor of the Duchy of Lancaster 1924–7; PC 1915; CH 1956;
created Viscount Cecil of Chelwood 1923.

whole truth; and be well satisfied to keep everyone together in a muddled sort of way. If you really want more meetings go and address Trades Unionists and Cooperators on your own hook. But probably even so yr speeches will be too violent to do much good. There! After all Fisher[1] is no unfavourable type of the sort of man we want to gain. If we alienate him whom are we going to convert?

As to the London meeting, I've no doubt that difficulty will be easily got over. The Duke must make his own speech his own way: and the resolution must be ag'st protection in such terms as Fisher can accept.

I return Beach's letter – I hope he won't dream of retiring. His power in the House is great and his retirement wd be a heavy blow. As I have indicated I think both you and he are too pessimistic. Otherwise I mainly agree with him.

Yours ever
HUGH CECIL

WSC to Lord Rosebery
(Rosebery Papers)

30 October 1903   105 Mount Street
Private

My dear Lord,

Beach is all right; but our difficulties in the Free Food League are immense. The pressure of the local organisations upon the members is severe & there are eight or ten old women who paralyse the sword arm and prate of loyalty where it is not returned. The duke is excellent. I wish you could get into communication with him. He is to address a great meeting in London on the 24th.

As to Oldham – I nourish a great & dark design in which I need your help: & which I will impart to you when you come to London. I hope that will be soon.

Linky & I go to B'ham on the 11th. Such mean opposition & cowardice you never saw. But all is now moving steadily forward. I am in better spirits tonight than for the last day or two. I am quite sure that Joe is *not* carrying the electorate whatever he may have done to the editors.

I liked your letters about his inaccurate quotations. I think it would be a good thing for you to attack him. Only a gentleman can really throw mud in politics!

I am sending you the *Monthly Review* with some stuff by me.

Yours vy sincerely
WINSTON S. C.

---

[1] Possibly W. Hayes Fisher (1853–1920), Conservative MP for Fulham 1885–1906, 1910–1918, who had recently resigned as Financial Secretary to the Treasury.

J. T. Travis-Clegg to WSC

30 October 1903   Shaw Lodge

My dear Mr Churchill,

I have thought carefully over your letter. The situation is very puzzling. I think before deciding anything it will be better to wait & see what step the 'Hilton' section of the party is going to take in reference to the proposed meeting. I have written them that if they attempt to get Crisp down I shall write to Capt Wells[1] as Chairman of the party & tell him that Crisp's advent at the present time would mean a party split straight away. I have been told that Hilton has said that, 'They have the speakers & that the meeting will take place'. I think it will be well therefore for you to keep out of Oldham till you see what they are going to do & if they force a split the responsibility will rest on their shoulders. I will write you again when I have any further information. I have arranged to get information at the earliest possible moment.

Yours very sincerely
J. T. TRAVIS-CLEGG

I shall tell them that you are willing to ask Bonar Law to come if they specially want him though I should recommend a Balfourian speaker like Lord Stanley[2] or Sir R. Finlay.[3] I am told that the latest idea is to work their meeting from one of the Ward Conservative Clubs & not from the Assn at all.

WSC to Lord Salisbury[4]
(*Hatfield Papers*)

2 November 1903   105 Mount Street

My dear Cranborne,

Thank you vy much indeed. I will of course consult you about the pub-

---

[1] Lionel de Lautour Wells (1859–1929), chief agent of Conservative party 1903–5; Captain RN; Chief Officer Metropolitan Fire Brigade and originator of many fire-fighting techniques; knighted 1921.

[2] Edward George Villiers Stanley, 17th Earl of Derby (1865–1948), Postmaster-General 1903–5; Financial Secretary to the War Office 1900–3; MP West Houghton 1892–1906; Under-Secretary of State for War 1916; Secretary of State for War 1916–18, 1922–4; Ambassador to France 1918–20; succeeded father in 1908. PC 1903; KG 1914.

[3] Robert Bannatyne Finlay, 1st Viscount Finlay (1842–1929), Attorney-General 1900–6; Conservative MP Inverness Burghs 1885–92, 1895–1906, Edinburgh and St Andrew's Universities 1910–16; Solicitor-General 1895–1900; Lord Chancellor 1916–18; knighted 1895; Baron 1916; Viscount 1919.

[4] James Edward Hubert, 4th Marquess of Salisbury (1861–1947), had succeeded his father on August 22. Conservative MP Darwen Div 1885–92, Rochester 1893–1903; Lord Privy Seal 1903–5, 1924–29; President of Board of Trade 1905; Leader of the House of Lords 1925–1931.

lication of all matters referring to your father. You had better bid Linky
farewell before Birmingham. You may never see him again!

Yours vy sincerely

WINSTON S. CHURCHILL

WSC to Lord Hugh Cecil

EXTRACT

3 November 1903   105 Mount Street

Private

[Copy]

My dear Linky,

I do not care very much if there was nobody on the platform except our
own party of friends, indeed if there were a row of blank chairs the effect
would not necessarily be altogether prejudicial.

I think it would be a very good thing if the Duke would write a letter to
Moore Bayley or to yourself about the meeting. I suggested it to Moore
Bayley and he jumped at the idea. The Duke is dining with my mother to-
night and I will consult him about it.

I have carefully revised my speech so as to avoid provocative terms of
phraseology and I think I shall have no difficulty in getting the audience to
listen to it.

Yesterday I met John Morley who told me he thought it most unlikely
that Chamberlain would allow anything to be done to disturb the meeting
and he said he was perfectly sure nothing would be done unless he wished
it to be done.

I am of opinion that you should ask two or three members of Parliament
to go down with you. It would come better from you than from me because
I am so much younger.[1]

I understand that you are going to be at Liverpool on Friday to support
Goschen and we shall meet there. I shall return the same night to London.

Rosebery sent for me yesterday and we had a talk. I suggested to him that
it would be very desirable for him to get into touch with the Duke personally.
He replied that the latter was a very bad horse to go up to in the stable, and
that he would let him know if he wanted to see him soon enough. This
morning however, I met R and he tells me that a meeting is arranged
between them.

[1] WSC was approaching his 29th birthday: Lord Hugh Cecil had just turned 34.

I do feel so strongly that some steps should be taken by us, and those who think with us, which would command public interest and perhaps enthusiasm. So many people are doubting and hesitating now what to do, and a good plain lead would be worth anything. I know you will not agree with me, but I know if these two persons would appear on a common platform in the near future, it would be a *coup de théâtre* with resounding effects throughout the land. Moreover such an alliance is natural and reasonable from every point of view, would not be dishonourable or have about it the smallest suggestion of intrigue.

I dined with Tweedmouth last night and had a long talk with him, the result of which I found not satisfactory. He declares to me positively that he was sure that if the sense of the constituencies were tested, as I have indicated to you, by some of us early in the Session, we should only obtain official Liberal support if we came forward as fair and square Liberal candidates. He is very anxious to help, but their Liberal machine seems to be just as stupid and brutalized as ours, so I told him it was useless to go on discussing on that basis and that I would not go and see H. Gladstone[1] to-day as had been arranged. I was glad to see he was disappointed at this and I have left the matter where it stands at the present.

I am convinced that Lord Rosebery will refuse utterly to have anything to do with a Liberal Government on settled lines and cares more about working with us than anything else.

I do not mean to be put off by any difficulties which wire pullers may raise, and I think that whatever the result of the by-election, it is the only sensible and honest course for me.

I go to Manchester on Friday morning.

Do write to Freddy Lambton[2] and have him at our meeting on Saturday. About the Birmingham resolution, let us leave that for a little. I think it is best to be guided by what the Meeting is like. If I am to speak first I shall know before I am half way through, whether such a resolution as you have drafted, could safely be put and I could easily ask you while the Meeting was going on whether I shall move it at the end or not.

I am very sorry for Moore Bayley. I think we may very easily under-rate the enormous pressure and difficulties which a provincial man like that has to encounter, when every single friend and companion turns his hand against him. I think he is inclined to be excitable and even hysterical but I believe he will go through the business now.

I asked Beach to tackle Joe's position at Manchester and not to worry

---

[1] Herbert GLADSTONE.
[2] Frederick William Lambton, 4th Earl of Durham (1855–1929), Conservative MP for Durham South East 1900–10; Durham South 1880–5; succeeded his twin brother in 1928.

about his agreement with AB and he has replied that that is his intention.
Let me know when you come up to town.

I have had a very nice letter from your brother about your father's papers
and I am sure I should be grateful to you for your good offices in the matter.

Yours ever

WINSTON S. CHURCHILL

The Duke of Devonshire to J. Moore Bayley[1]

9 November 1903   Devonshire House

My dear Sir,

I need scarcely say that I feel a great interest in the success of the meeting
over which you are going to preside as chairman, and which is going to be
addressed by Lord Hugh Cecil and Mr Winston Churchill. The discussion on
the fiscal question which has been invited by the Government has disclosed
great differences of opinion in the Unionist party, and a policy has been
advocated which goes far in the direction of change beyond that which has
been announced as the policy of the official leader of the party. Every loyal
Unionist must desire that full expression should be given to conflicting
opinions on both sides before the party is finally committed to either of them.
The arguments on one side have been already fully stated in Birmingham,
and I am sure that the city which had the honour of being represented for so
many years by Mr John Bright would desire that a fair hearing should be
given to the exponents of the opinions of which he was one of the foremost
champions, and in support of which, either as a Liberal, or, as in his later
days, a staunch Unionist, he never varied.

I remain, yours sincerely

DEVONSHIRE

J. Moore Bayley to WSC

                                                    47 Temple Row
10 November 1903   Birmingham

Dear Churchill,

Things were getting so disgraceful here to-day, with sandwich men walking
about with bills calling upon people to attend at the Town Hall to-morrow
to oppose our meeting, that I decided to issue the Duke's letter to-night, so
that we could have the benefit of it in all the evening papers throughout the

[1] Published in *The Times* on November 11.

country to-night, and also in the daily papers to-morrow morning. If I had kept it back for the morning papers, the evening papers to-morrow would be no good to us.

The point raised against us, with which we have to contend, is that we have been using a Radical organization to convene and pack a Radical meeting, and pass a resolution as coming from Unionists. This is how they are working things against us, and it is the only point which prevents hundreds of Unionists from coming to our side. Enclosed I send you copy of resolution which I want proposed at the meeting to-morrow, and if this could only be handed in to the Press Association to-night we should completely annihilate our opponents. Any Radicals present will vote on this resolution, and Mr Chamberlain's friends cannot vote against us, and all supporters of the Government would have to vote with us. It neutralises any element we may reasonably have to contend with, and I am sure its effect would be excellent.

If you and Lord Hugh Cecil would not like to be committed by this resolution you can make your speeches first, and I would, from the chair, move the resolution myself. I have written Lord Hugh, and wired him fully to this effect this afternoon, but up to the time of despatching this, have not heard from him. If you by any chance get this in time to see him to-night you might hand it in to the Press Association. You can ring up any of the leading papers, and they will do what is necessary for you. It is very hard fighting a matter like this on the spot absolutely alone, and not altogether having a free hand. I consider the enclosed resolution is excellent, and will supplement Sir Michael's action at Bristol, and generally strengthen Mr Balfour as against the unauthorised programme.

There has been a marked tone in the local press this evening, and if I were sure of your accepting, as I think you should do, the enclosed resolution, I should score heavily in the morning by its appearance in the papers. I shall hope all through this evening that Lord Hugh will wire me, so that I can be in time for the last issues of this evening's papers.

If you could come down earlier to-morrow than you suggested last Saturday, I should be glad, for I am not quite clear as to the platform. You gave me a number of names that I have dealt with, and then you say you want 12 more. Does your 12 include Lord and Lady Lytton, &c or who? The platform will only hold 24, and I am fixed up already with about 10.

Yours very truly
J. MOORE BAYLEY

WSC to J. Moore Bayley

EXTRACT

13 November 1903   105 Mount Street
[Copy]

Dear Moore Bayley,
    I am very glad to have your letter.
    I do not know how Birmingham will regard the incident in the future, bu
I cannot believe that personally you will suffer for it. Nothing succeeds like
success, and taking it all round, I can well believe that the respectable people
are extremely glad that it is now known that their city is free from the
reproach of not being a place where free speech prevails.
    Everybody here seems very pleased with the Speeches. The postman who
brought me my letters – a perfect stranger – sent up by my servant to say
that, being a man on 24/– a week, he wished to thank me for what I had
said! I wonder what the working classes really do think at the back of their
heads about it all.

                                                    Yours sincerely
                                            WINSTON S. CHURCHILL

WSC to Lord Rosebery
(Rosebery Papers)

17 November 1903   105 Mount Street

Private

My dear Lord Rosebery,
    Hugh Cecil is worried about the seduction of papers like the *Birmingham
Daily Post* & has suggested my writing to you. Do you think it would be a
good idea to form a little private committee of (say) six or seven MPs
representative of all shades of opinion to survey and if possible to coordinate
the entire Free Trade Press of the country? Arthur Elliot,[1] myself, McKenna,[2]
E. Beckett, Edward Grey, & John Burns – would make the kind of body I
have in mind. They would have to find out all the papers on our side – get
into touch with them and consider how best to influence & assist them.
Ultimately I suppose we should have definite proposals to make involving

---

[1] Arthur Ralph Douglas Elliot (1846–1923), 2nd son of 3rd Earl of Minto; Financial
Secretary of the Treasury from April to September 1903; Liberal MP 1880–6; Liberal-
Unionist MP 1886–92, and 1898–1906; editor, *Edinburgh Review*, 1895–1912.
[2] Reginald McKENNA.

expenditure which could be put before the Liberal League, the Free Trade Union, & the Free Food League.

My own idea is that a Press Bureau should be formed on a large scale to circulate articles, gossipy newsletters, speeches etc all vy well done by good writers & sent out either in proof or stereo. We have attempted this on a vy small scale in the F.F. League; but I should like to see a really effective attempt made to sway & control the whole body of the Free Trade Press from some central point of view.

There are great & thorny difficulties to be surmounted, & hence my suggestion of a private committee to look into the subject.

Yours vy sincerely
WINSTON S. CHURCHILL

Beach is at this moment not at all satisfactory.

*   *   *   *   *

In the middle of these important fiscal controversies WSC was required to turn his attention to a tariff of a quite different nature, which had been imposed upon him while he was at camp with the Oxfordshire Yeomanry during the summer.

Lord Valentia[1] to WSC

18 November 1903   116 Park Street

Dear Winston,

Noble[2] tells me that you decline to pay the fines you owe to the Mess because they are not authorised by the King's Regulations. I am sure that on second thoughts you will conform to the custom of the Regiment & need hardly remind you that you must during your service have submitted to many charges for which there is no official authority except the decision of a Mess Meeting.

Yours as ever
VALENTIA

[1] Arthur Annesley, 11th Viscount Valentia (1843–1927), Lieutenant Colonel commanding Oxfordshire Imperial Yeomanry; succeeded his grandfather in the Irish Peerage 1863; Conservative MP for Oxford 1895–1917, when he was created Baron Annesley (in the United Kingdom peerage).

[2] Major (Hon Lieutenant-Colonel) Leonard Noble (1859–1943), of the Queen's Own Oxfordshire Hussars; he had served with the Imperial Yeomanry in South Africa.

WSC to Lord Valentia

20 November 1903   105 Mount Street

[Copy]

Dear Lord Valentia,

The fines you allude to are quite unauthorised and so high as to be a serious burden. I have never heard of any fines on such a scale in the army; and in any case they would be matters for ultimate reference to the General Commanding. If the GOC of the Army Corps to which your Regiment belongs approves of these fines I will pay them at once. Indeed if you will give me your personal assurance that the question shall be immediately submitted to higher authority, I will send you a cheque at once. But the Yeomanry is a great drain on officers possessing small private means and it scarcely seems desirable to levy charges of this kind in addition to all the other expense.

Yours vy truly
WSC

Lord Valentia to WSC

27 November 1903   116 Park Street

Dear Winston,

What a Barrack Lawyer you are. The fines to which you object were instituted at a Mess Meeting regularly held which I think is sufficient authority for this enforcement. The object of their institution was to prevent officers dining out in the days when the training was shorter & the numbers of Officers less than it now is. At a Mess meeting held last training which I suppose you did not attend the subject was reconsidered & the £5 was reduced to its present figure.

The GOC of the Army Corps I am sure does not want to be bothered to interfere with rules which officers pass at Mess Meetings for the regulation of their own mess. I can give you no personal assurance in the matter. If you object to the fine you had better bring your objection before the Mess Meeting held next training & move for its reduction or abolition. In the meantime you are as much liable for the amount charged against you as 'fines' as you are for your Mess Bill & I should recommend you to pay.

Yours as ever
VALENTIA

*   *   *   *   *

Lord Hugh Cecil to WSC

19 November 1903   24 Grafton Street

Secret & Confidential

My dear Winston,

I am in yr absence indulging in an orgy of intrigue: for I have written to George Wyndham asking him for an hour's interview to discuss the political situation wh I propose to spend mainly in denouncing AJB & explaining how badly & stupidly he has behaved. I am prompted to do this largely as a result of a conversation with my sister from wh I gather that AJB believes the more stalwart section of the Free Food L to be chiefly animated by malevolence against himself & his Govt & intent to wreck it on any pretence. This does us grave injustice. These cynics think of nothing but personal & party questions whereas what we care about is principle. What I want to do is to save Free Trade & annihilate Joe – & for that I will wreck (if I can) 20 Govts or none according as circumstances require. This I propose to explain to George. For I think it important that we should remove from the minds of the Balfourians the peculiar bitterness that is raised by a supposed conspiracy against a leader who excites much devotion. If we have to turn Arthur out I want him & his friends to understand that I do it on purely public grounds – just as I should have sent him to the stake in an earlier & more thorough age!

Beach is coming to the meeting: I wrote him a letter full of flattery and reproach. But I have not had an answer yet & don't know if I had anything to do with the result.

To continue, Gorst has fallen out with Murray Guthrie & George Hamilton[1] when I wasn't there & resigned in a rage from the meeting Comtee. It was about giving 200 tickets to a Socialist named Macdonald.[2] However we passed a resolution of confidence & compliment to Gorst & hope he will forgive us. There is certainly something about the fiscal controversy that makes people irritable. Meantime the Duke has given 200 tickets to the Liberal League – without consulting anybody! But that is a

[1] George Francis Hamilton (1845–1927), 3rd son of 1st Duke of Abercorn; Secretary of State for India, 1895–1903; Chairman of the Royal Commission upon Poor Law and Unemployment 1905–9; Conservative MP 1868–1906; Under Secretary of State for India, 1874–78; First Lord of the Admiralty 1885–6, 1886–92; Chairman of the Governors of Harrow School, 1913–24; PC 1878.

[2] James Ramsay MacDonald (1866–1937), Secretary of the Labour Representation Committee 1900–12; Labour MP for West Leicester 1906–18, Aberavon 1922–9, Seaham 1929–31, National Labour MP for Seaham 1931–5, Scottish Universities 1936–7; Chairman of ILP 1906–9; Treasurer of the Labour Party 1913–14; Prime Minister and Secretary of State for Foreign Affairs 1924; Prime Minister 1929–35; Lord President of the Council 1935–7.

dead secret which must be carefully kept from the knowledge of the League in general & Beach in particular. The demand for tickets is very good - already more than they have places for.

Yrs ever
HUGH CECIL

WSC to Lord Rosebery
(Rosebery Papers)

25 November 1903   105 Mount Street
Private

My dear Lord Rosebery,
    I am so sorry to miss you, but I could not be ready in time. I only wanted to wish you good fortune this evening, & tell you about the meeting last night. The duke was splendid. He is absolutely determined and in the end I feel sure you must come together. I am off to Oldham where there is every prospect of a lively row.

Yours vy sincerely
WINSTON S. CHURCHILL

Duke of Devonshire to WSC

27 November 1903   Devonshire House

My dear Churchill,
    I do not think that I can promise to go to Oldham without a little more consideration, and consulting from all the committee.
    I rather think that Manners-Sutton[1] has gone away, but I will try however to get into communication with Mr Humphreys who has gone to Liverpool and ascertain from him what are the prospects of forming a Branch there and holding a meeting. I will let you know again as soon as I can.

Yrs vy sinly
DEVONSHIRE

---

[1] F. H. Manners-Sutton, Secretary of the Unionist Free Food League.

Duke of Devonshire to WSC

1 December 1903   Devonshire House

My dear Churchill,

I have had a report this morning from Mr Humphreys who is at Liverpool and seems to be making good progress. I think there is no doubt that an active branch of the F.T. League will be formed there and that they will want me to attend a demonstration before long. This would probably be the best opportunity for me to speak in Lancashire, and I am afraid therefore I must give up the idea of going to Oldham.

Yrs vy sinly
DEVONSHIRE

William Finnemore[1] to Reginald McKenna

2 December 1903   Birmingham Liberal Association

Dear Mr McKenna,

I have heard some rumours that Mr Winston Churchill is inclined to try his luck at the General Election in the Central Divn of Birmingham where his father fought now so long ago. I have been wondering how I could find out whether there is anything in this but baseless rumour, & it occurs to me that in all probability you would have no difficulty in finding from Mr Churchill or his friends if any such move is contemplated. Of course the lamentable death of Mr Osler[2] has left an open place there & we shall have speedily to fix it up so that we should like to know what is in Mr Churchill's mind that no unnecessary complications may arise.

Our people – & of course our people practically filled the Hall – were very much struck with his speech here the other day. One of them observed to me 'that man may call himself what he likes but he's no more a Tory than I am'!

Forgive me troubling you but I'm sure you will help me if you can.

Yours faithfully
W. FINNEMORE

[1] Secretary of the Birmingham Liberal Association.
[2] Alfred Clarkson Osler (1847–1903), sometime President of the Birmingham Liberal Association; in May, 1903, he accepted an invitation to stand as Liberal Candidate for Central Birmingham at the next election; he had spoken strongly in opposition to Chamberlain's fiscal policies.

WSC to Lady Randolph
EXTRACT

4 December 1903   Canford Manor

Dearest Mamma,

... We have had a very pleasant week here with good shooting and all my friends. Much talk about Free Trade and politics, general conclusion in favour of much stronger and more decided action.

Beach has been here, very reticent and rather unsatisfactory. I think he desires to pose as the guardian angel of the Government which will be inconvenient from many points of view, though I do not blame him from his own.

Cardiff was a great success, I spoke nearly an hour and a half listened to with the closest attention by an immense audience. Nothing could exceed the gush of the Cardiff papers, they say no meeting in Cardiff for many years has produced such an impression and speaking for myself, I have never had a more friendly welcome.

Chelsea Town Hall is fixed for Thursday, the 10th. Do try and be there and make a supper party afterwards for friends. The meeting, I think, is going to be a very big one.

Best love
W

WSC to Hubert Carr-Gomm
(*Carr-Gomm Papers*)

5 December 1903   105 Mount Street

My dear Carr-Gomm,

Many thanks for your letter.

I hope you will let me know from time to time how you are going on in your candidature at Rotherhithe.

I have not the slightest idea what will happen to me at the next Election. I think it very improbable that I shall stand again for Oldham.

Everything is at present very obscure but I hope the air will clear as we go forward. Forward we shall certainly go.

I quite agree with what you say about the advantage to Chamberlain of keeping his proposals vague and uncertain. Very few people would pay for lottery tickets after the result has been declared.

The position at Oldham is very much complicated by the Labour candidature and I think indeed the problem of labour and labour representation is going to prove a very difficult one in the future for the Liberal party. I think myself that the Election will come before the Budget, so you ought to be prepared.

Come and see me sometime after the Meeting of Parliament. You will find me here every day and no doubt you have not yet forgotten the way upstairs!

Yours sincerely
WINSTON S. CHURCHILL

Harold Cox to WSC
EXTRACT

7 December 1903　　　　　　　　　　　　　　　　Cobden Club

Personal

Dear Mr Churchill,

I am told on sound authority that if you will stand [at West Birmingham] in any capacity the Liberals will welcome you. Some of them will support you openly; others silently: but they will abstain from asking you awkward questions about the Education Bill. There is as you know, a local Free Food League, and it is suggested that you should be brought out under its auspices.

I hope you will do this. It is the post of honour in the coming fight, and you ought not to refuse it.

Yours very truly
HAROLD COX

J. Moore Bayley to WSC

7 December 1903　　　　　　　　　　　　　　　47 Temple Row
　　　　　　　　　　　　　　　　　　　　　　　　　Birmingham

Dear Churchill,

Yours of the 4th inst to hand with Mr Finnemore's letter to Mr McKenna of the 2nd inst, which I herewith return. It would be utterly useless for you to attempt your luck, as matters at present stand, in the Central Division of Birmingham, or in any other Birmingham Division, otherwise than as a member of the Liberal Party, and as an officially adopted candidate. I do not think that an independent Unionist Free Trader would have a look in, for naturally the Liberals would put up a candidate, and between the

Chamberlainite and the Liberal the third man would soon find the ground. Of course, a great deal may happen between now and a General Election. It is to be hoped that the lessons the impending four bye-elections will teach will not be thrown away. Every day the position taken up by Mr Balfour as the leader of the Unionist Party becomes more contemptible, and involves the Unionist Party in fresh troubles and complications. A vote given for Mr Balfour at present is a vote given for Mr Chamberlain, and abstainers from voting for the Unionist candidate will, in my opinion, certainly in a bye-election, result in their votes being given for the Liberal. If Mr Balfour does not before long make his position clear and certain, the Free Trade Unionists will have to repudiate his Leadership, and follow the Duke of Devonshire. The present position of Unionist Free Trade Members of Parliament is deserving of every sympathy, and no Leader ought to place loyal members of his Party in such a predicament as they are now placed in.

I hear on very excellent authority from Mr Chamberlain's camp, that they have quite made up their minds to sustain a defeat upon Mr Chamberlain's proposals, in which Mr Balfour will be entangled and the Liberals will return to power.

The impression appears pretty general that you will not much longer be a member of the Conservative Party, and in this calculation I am being included. If I desired immediate Parliamentary honours I should probably justify this impression, but for the present I have decided to remain in the Unionist ranks, as I consider I can do more good there in supporting the principles I hold, than I should be able to do simply as an individual in the Liberal ranks. Chamberlain will not live for ever, and upon his departure from this sphere of labour there will be a big opportunity for those who have gained a reputation for ability to stand to their guns. I often come across the leaders of the Liberal Party in Birmingham, and I have more than once told them not to be in too great a hurry to fill up the vacancy in their ranks in the Central Division occasioned by the death of the late Mr Osler, nor in the South Division which is represented by Mr Powell Williams,[1] who I think if strongly opposed could be turned out. I certainly do think that if you did come out as a Liberal in the Central Division you would stand a better chance than any Liberal that the Party could bring forward, for you made a most favourable impression at the Town Hall Meeting, and Mr Ebenezer Parkes[2] is certainly a very weak candidate, and his hope of retaining his seat solely depends upon Mr Chamberlain's personal influence.

[1] Joseph Powell Williams (1840–1904), Liberal-Unionist MP for S. Birmingham, 1885–1904; Financial Secretary to the War Office, 1895–1900.

[2] Edward Ebenezer Parkes (1848–1919), Liberal Unionist MP for Birmingham Central 1895–1918; an iron-master; knighted 1917.

While dictating this I have been rung up on the telephone to know if there is any truth in a rumour that is recorded in the Birmingham *Daily Post* this morning – that you are being approached to fight Mr Chamberlain in the West Division. I have replied that I do not know anything about such a suggestion, neither do I credit it. Of course it would be useless for you in your position to take on a heroic task of that nature. Mr Chamberlain's influence might be beaten outside his own Division, but inside there no one on earth would have the slightest chance of a look in. You, of course, know your business best, but it looks to me as if it was not worth while your wasting much time at Oldham, and I think when it became known that you are looking out for another seat, you would very soon have several to select from.

Yours very truly

J. MOORE BAYLEY

WSC to J. T. Travis-Clegg

12 December 1903   105 Mount Street

[Copy]

Private & Confidential

Dear Travis-Clegg,

Unrecorded conversations are often the cause of misunderstandings and I think it as well to put my position – as I endeavoured to explain it – before you and the General Purposes Committee in writing.

It is unlikely that I shall stand for Oldham as the Conservative candidate at the next election. Unless I were supported by the whole Conservative vote the fight would be hopeless; and I do not think it probable – though it is not yet impossible – that my attitude on the fiscal question will command that unanimous support. I have not however only to think of myself. Other Conservative members are in the same position as I am. If I withdraw from my candidature just because it looks unpromising, or because the party organisation is hostile, I may compromise their position and discourage their efforts. Therefore I am not yet enabled to withdraw from the candidature, though I shall welcome any honourable opportunity of so doing.

Meanwhile I recognise the difficulties of the situation in Oldham & I regret especially the bitter feeling which this most unfortunate controversy is raising between old friends. But while I am the member for the Borough, I must preserve the right of addressing my constituents whenever I choose; for otherwise I should lose my connexion with the working class electors and degenerate into a mere creature of the organisation, to be dismissed ignominiously by a twist of the handles of the party machine. That is not a position I could ever consent to occupy – even for a year. I am quite sure the mass of the Conservative working men have not made up their minds on this grave question, and I think they are for the most part moved mainly by party feeling. If I were able and thought it necessary to make a complete tour of the Borough, aided by the speakers I can easily obtain, I might make a real impression upon them & obtain a personal following quite independent of the Executive or any existing party organisation. At any rate I shall not admit the contrary until I have tried and failed. And I fear that the attempt would greatly exacerbate feeling on both sides. I am anxious so far as possible to avoid any such unfortunate circumstances. The action of the majority – a bare majority only – of the General Purposes Committee on Wednesday night in censuring the honorary secretary does not make things easier; but in the hope of a friendly settlement of differences – which arise through no fault of ours – on either side – I make the following suggestion.

If I were assured formally by the representatives of the Conservative Association that during the life of the present Parliament I shall not be interfered with in any way, shall enjoy full liberty of action on the Fiscal question and cognate questions of finance and expenditure, shall not be assailed by hostile motions of censure or challenges to resign & submit myself to re-election, I would do all in my power to avoid disturbing the constituency. I would acquiesce in the selection of another Conservative candidate who would be an absolute supporter of Mr Balfour's Sheffield policy and be sympathetic to Mr Chamberlain.

I think there is a good deal of force in the claim of Mr Hilton that both sections of opinion should have their candidate. I presume that the best chance of the Conservative at the next election would be to run one candidate only: and I think it highly probable – though I decline to give any definite pledge – that if the Protectionist candidate seemed more fully to represent Conservative opinion than I did I should be willing gradually to withdraw more and more and leave the field clear for him.

If the Committee are able to give me the assurance for which I ask, I would propose that they should forthwith set about selecting a second candidate – not in antagonism to me – but to the Radical party; and that the motion respecting the honorary secretary shall be rescinded, his tenure being allowed to run its normal course till the next election of officers. Meanwhile I should not anticipate having to address many meetings in Oldham on the Fiscal question. I have an invitation to visit North Chadderton which it would be disrespectful to neglect, & I presume there must be an Annual meeting some time next spring; but otherwise I do not think I have any engagements or shall need to contract any before the Meeting of Parliament.

But in this respect I must preserve the fullest liberty and while I shall studiously endeavour to reciprocate any consideration which the Committee may show me, it may be desirable for me to offer the Duke of Devonshire a Lancashire platform and I do not know where he could find a better one than in Oldham. A few isolated meetings are however much less disturbing than a vigorous ward campaign & I desire at the same time to repeat my offer to convey an invitation to any prominent Protectionist speaker with whom I have influence.

Will you communicate this letter privately and in confidence to the General Purposes Committee?

Yours very sincerely
[WINSTON S. CHURCHILL]

Sir Michael Hicks Beach to WSC

13 December 1903   Coln St Aldwyns
                                                    Gloucestershire

My Dear Churchill,

I think the Duke's letter is the parting of the ways. Those who agree with it must necessarily go on – (and from their point of view, I should say, the sooner the better) – to discuss with the Liberal leaders terms of alliance, which must of course involve, not merely abstention from voting, but support of Liberal candidates by Unionist Free-fooders. To me this seems, to say the least, premature, while Chamberlain's policy is not the party ticket – but then, as you know, the new alliance would be odious to me, even if it were. I do not, however, propose to say or do anything at present, if I can possibly avoid it: and I don't the least care what the Protectionist or the Radical press may say about me. The *Daily News* telegraphed yesterday to ask whether I condoned the Duke's letter – to which of course I sent no reply. But my constituents may finally ask me what I think – and if they do, I must answer: though the answer will be as short as possible – probably only that I adhere to my Bristol speech, and cannot be held responsible for the Duke's letter.

If you join with the Radicals in an amendment to the address, the separation must come then, so far as I am concerned. But I rather doubt if you will – for it was clear that the Duke was decidedly against an amendment the other day.

I cannot tell you how much pain the whole business gives me. But I am grateful to you for your appreciation of my position: which, as you say, is essentially different from that of the Liberal Unionists, or the younger men.

Yours sincerely

M. HICKS BEACH

S. Smethurst to WSC

14 December 1903   Coldhurst House
                                                        Oldham

Dear Mr Churchill,

Mr Travis-Clegg asked me to go over this morning. He shewed me your letter, and said he thought it inadvisable to submit it in its present form, gave me one of his copies and ask[ed] me to carefully consider it and write you tonight.

I have read it *very* carefully, and I am of opinion that if you will make the alterations I suggest it will be for the best. I don't think that your proposals will be accepted even as altered, and to leave them as you have written them will give them sufficient excuse for rejecting them on the ground that by reserving your freedom to hold meetings other than the two named, you take away with one hand what you give with the other. Of course if they go on organising & holding meetings in the Clubs they will have broken the com-pact and you will be free to do as you like. The Duke of Devonshire's coming can be taken as [a] separate question. He will not want to come before Parliament meets, and then in my opinion the whole question will assume a different form. And we shall probably get some definite pronouncement on the one side or the other. In the meantime I think your offer should be as fair as possible so that your position will be all the stronger if they refuse it. I understand the meeting is fixed for Thursday night; *be sure* to write at once to Mr Travis-Clegg, saying what is to be submitted to Thursday's meeting.

Yours truly

S. SMETHURST

J. T. Travis-Clegg to WSC

11 pm   Shaw Lodge
16 December 1903

My dear Mr Churchill,

Hilton has just left. I have had a three hours conversation with him, & discussed the whole question at issue. To give you the result first – this is what he said he would accept, & what no doubt the majority on the Committee, the Executive, & the Party would accept.

'Supposing Mr Churchill found himself unable to support the government on the debate on the Address, he should write to the Chairman on the following day, or as soon as possible, definitely withdrawing from the candidature for the borough, under any circumstances, at the next General Election. The Association would then give him a free hand in Parliament, & in the Country to express his views & proceed *then* to select another Candidate if it was thought necessary or desirable. In the meantime till Parliament meets, if Mr Churchill will undertake not to address meetings in the borough the Association will not interfere with his carrying on his propaganda in the Country & will not hold meetings to further the Protectionist cause in the Constituency.' Hilton realises that you were a Free Trader when elected for Oldham & does not ask you to change your views, but if you seek to convert the electorate for the next election then he & those with him would feel bound to further their views to the best of their ability. If you should contest the seat at a by-election & not be opposed by the Labour or Liberal Parties the Protectionists would not contest the seat either.

If by any means you found it possible to vote for the Government on the Address the whole position would be discussed by the Association afresh.

If you accept these views the meeting of the Executive for the purpose of considering Brierley should be postponed till after Parliament meets.

In my opinion you will do well to accept these terms. I consider them reasonable & favourable to you, & I strongly urge you in the interests of the Party & yourself to accept them. Personally I am prepared to accept them & should feel myself compelled to reconsider my position as chairman if they were refused. I am calling the meeting of the Committee for next Wednesday. Will you write me as soon as you can? If you can wire me whether you accept these proposals or not it will considerably relieve my personal anxiety.

I am, Yours very sincerely
JAMES T. TRAVIS-CLEGG

PS In mentioning the fact of the Chairmanship I mean that I should have to consider if these proposals, by which I see a chance of retaining unity in the party, were refused whether or not I should be serving the best interests of the party in the borough by remaining at its head when there are so many other men qualified for the Chairmanship who are in sympathy with the majority of it.

WSC to Herbert Gladstone

17 December 1903   Chatsworth
Private

Dear Herbert Gladstone,
    I should like to have a talk with you some time before Parliament meets about politics. I could meet you in London almost any day in the first week of January. Perhaps you will send me a line to make an appointment.
                                               Yours vy sincerely
                                        WINSTON S CHURCHILL

WSC to F. Horne[1]

19 December 1903   105 Mount Street
[Copy]

My dear Sir,
    I cannot overlook your request for a letter on the Ludlow election, because I think that the time has now come for united action. Our system of Free Trade involves two conditions each of profound importance to those whose votes you are seeking – cheap food and honest government. Mr Chamberlain's victory would deprive the nation of both. I believe that an overwhelming majority of British electors are for Free Trade; but they are divided amongst themselves. The Unionist who is against Protection shrinks from recording a Liberal vote. The Liberal organiser is too often eager to score a point off a Conservative Free Trader in difficulties. It may now be right to consider whether the time is not approaching when these prejudices and jealousies ought to be smoothed away, and when Free Traders of all parties should form one long line of battle against a common foe.
    It is unlikely that farmers in Shropshire will benefit in any way by the proposed Fiscal changes; for what they gain through the Food Taxes they will lose in the increased cost of living, of clothing and necessaries, of agricultural implements & machinery. But it is absolutely certain that the labourers and quarrymen will lose. Sensible people find it difficult to see how taxing food is going to make it cheaper; & I myself heard Mr Chamberlain say in the House of Commons that the working classes would pay three-fourths of his new taxes. How many employers in the Ludlow division will undertake to raise wages accordingly?
    This is not however only a question of bread and butter politics. The

---

[1] Frederic Horne (1863–1927), Liberal candidate for Ludlow at by-election December 22 1903; farmer and writer on agricultural subjects; contested Ludlow 1906, Barkston 1910.

English people are shrewd but not selfish; and they will not overlook the moral and philanthropic conceptions of Free Trade. All these years we have held up among the nations the lamp of economic truth; and at this present time in spite of monopolies and all kinds of corruption, millions of Free Traders in Germany & America are struggling forward by various roads towards that liberty & justice we have so long enjoyed. We must not extinguish our beacon just when its light is most needed. All these years the good of England has meant the welfare of the world. It is to that inspiration that we owe our Empire & our fame. The triumph of Protection would set up instead a policy of brag and grab. The defeat of Protection – and perhaps you have it in your power to strike a smashing blow – will send forth to all the nations a message of peace & goodwill.

Yours faithfully
WINSTON S. CHURCHILL

Lord Tweedmouth to WSC

17 December 1903   Guisachan
Beauly

My dear Winston,

    A single line to ask you whether Sunderland would have any attractions to you. You might make some enquiries about it & let me know. It is open & should be a very good chance.

Yrs ever
T

Lord Hugh Cecil to WSC

December [1903]   British Agency
Cairo

My dear Winston,

    I have read with much annoyance yr letter to Horne & the speech about the Liberal Party. What is the use of settling elaborately with you what is to be done if at once you go & do just the opposite. How often have we not agreed that until Parlt met it was right to go on fighting the battle within the party!

    What object does your language serve? We want to win over the section of Unionists who are in doubt, who hesitate not much liking Joe & his plan but strong in their devotion to the party. Your language alienates them. We want to hold our heads high & drive a hard bargain for Liberal votes. You gratuitously assure the Liberal Party that they are the important people – precisely the opposite of what it is wise to say. The true tactics are (as we have over & over again agreed) to fight JC hard but at the same time to use the language of Conservatism. This does not at all interfere with your joining the Liberal Party. On the contrary it enhances your value. But your silly letter & speech – especially the speech – make you impossible as a Unionist. You have given away the 'life' you had as a member of the party – for nothing. Not choosing a memorable occasion, not with dignity but precisely in the manner of a ripe plum or a seduced woman which I have so often deprecated.

It is not only the folly of the proceeding that fills me with despair. It is your lamentable instability. We have gone into this question ten or twenty times. All the arguments have been considered; & you have assented – sometimes much more than assented – to the proposition that till Parlt met you not less than I ought to keep firm to the Unionist Party & fight the battle from inside. But now in one of your thousand foolish passing moods you wholly abandon this line & fling yourself into the arms of the Liberals. This instability makes you quite impossible to work with; & will unless you can cure it be a fatal danger to your career.

And now as to Worcester & Aberdeen I cannot shut my eyes to the fact that my plan, difficult in any case, is made more so by my association with you. We cannot very well, I suppose, break these engagements; but I hope you will not say anything wh will compromise me. I shall of course take care to emphasise my Conservatism very strongly – as I did at Oldham.

I shall not make any more such engagements. As you know it is a fixed principle with me not to allow personal considerations to interfere with a political design. To this rule I must keep & we must be separated. I have for some time foreseen that this would happen after the meeting of Parlt. You have only slightly accelerated what was inevitable.

The Duke's letter has turned out unfortunately. But I do not think we were wrong. It seemed as tho' we might give the Unionist party a salutary fright. We (the F.F.L.) must be very cautious for a bit. Cowper's[1] letter[2] shews this: tho' he does not see the whole of the problem.

All Free Traders here which is a comfort – except I believe the soldiers.

Yrs ever

HUGH CECIL

[1] Francis Thomas de Grey Cowper (1834–1905), 7th and last Earl Cowper; Lord Lieutenant of Ireland, 1880–2; KG 1861; PC 1871.

[2] In his letter to *The Times*, published on 23 December 1903, Lord Cowper urged free-food Unionists to support the Government, and to devote their energies to the important issues of Ireland, education and Army reform. He argued that the fiscal issue would cease to trouble political life after a year or two. *The Times* disagreed, asserting in a leading article that 'Mr Chamberlain's great campaign will leave an indelible impression on the mind of the British people'. Lord Cowper joined the Free Food League in October 1903.

WSC to Herbert Gladstone
(Herbert Gladstone Papers)

23 December 1903   Gopsall
Private   Leicestershire

My dear Gladstone,

I shall be near London all January & will propose a rendezvous after the 11th. I hope by that time it may be possible to discuss more cases than my own. I do not see why the Education difficulty should prove insurmountable. Certainly the majority of the Unionist free traders would not be uncompromising.

Yours sincerely
WINSTON S CHURCHILL

On December 23 the General Purposes Committee of the Oldham Conservative Registration Association met and passed the following resolution:
'That this meeting of the General Purposes Committee of the Oldham Registration Association intimates to Mr Winston S. Churchill, MP that he has forfeited their confidence in him as Unionist member for Oldham, and in the event of an election taking place he must no longer rely on the Conservative organization being used on his behalf.'
This resolution was to be submitted to a meeting of the General Executive on January 8 1904.

J. T. Travis-Clegg to WSC

24 December 1903   Shaw Lodge

My dear Mr Churchill,

The G. P. Committee last night would not accept the agreement after your 'Ludlow' telegram & your Halifax speech. They passed instead a resolution the exact wording of which you will no doubt see in today's papers, saying that you had no longer the confidence of the party & that you must not rely on the support of the Conservative Organisation. Do you intend to join the Liberal party? I am afraid after your Halifax speech you will find the Conservative gates shut against you.

Brierley comes out of this worse than anyone. He has done all his work for the party & unless he resigns will be thrown out at the meeting of the Executive on 8 January. If you can use your influence to find him some post it would be some small compensation to him. His chances for advancement from the Conservative party in Oldham are nil. I am afraid the blow has at last fallen. I did not endeavour last night to avert it. I could not pretend to defend your speech from a Conservative point of view.

With kind regards,

I am, Yours very sincerely
JAMES T. TRAVIS-CLEGG

WSC to W. Hilton

26 December 1903 Gopsall

Sir,

I beg to acknowledge the receipt of your letter of the 23rd instant enclosing a resolution which censures me for 'recent utterances and scurrilous statements delivered by me at Halifax on Monday Dec 21 against His Majesty King Edward VII.' This appears to me to be utter nonsense; & I challenge the members of your committee to produce the slightest shadow of foundation in any speech of mine ever delivered in Halifax or anywhere else for such a ridiculous & indeed abominable charge.

Yours faithfully
WINSTON S. CHURCHILL

J. T. Travis-Clegg to WSC

27 December 1903 Shaw Lodge
Private

My dear Churchill,

The most unfortunate part of the transaction is that you made your Halifax speech before the agreement was ratified by the G. P. Committee. If you had waited I have no doubt you would have had your freedom. They held that by your speech & telegram you had already declared against the Govt & there was no need therefore to wait till Parliament meets. I have been wondering myself if it is not possible that there will be a Devonshire Govt. The only thing to my mind is how many Liberal pills will have to be swallowed by Unionists to bring about a coalition. As I told you at the time of Lord Rosebery's Chesterfield speech, while I agreed with nearly all he said then, there were many points of policy which he left unsaid on which I could never agree. What would be the attitude of a coalition Government on the Education question, the House of Lords, the taxation of ground values, the licensing question, the suffrage question, foreign policy, to mention only a few? I think my position is infinitely stronger while I remain as I certainly feel, a Conservative who believes in Free Trade, than if I swallow Liberal doctrines for the sake of it. Everything to me seems to turn on the attitude of Mr Balfour. So far he has not accepted Mr Chamberlain's programme. Is he going to? So long as food & raw materials are untouched I am prepared to consider the question [of] taxing certain manufactured produce of foreign countries which place a prohibitive tax upon ours with a view to reduce or demolish the tax, though I am by no means sanguine of the results. I shall continue to labour for peace though it appears that both sides are preparing for battle.

I don't think anything you may do or say will affect the attitude of the party in the borough towards you. After all the choice of a candidate is in their hands, & they have a perfect right to select a candidate who holds the views of the majority of their party. I certainly think you should secure the option of another seat. With a labour candidate in the field as there is in Oldham your chances as an independent candidate are nil. The Liberals will vote for Emmott and Ashton who are free traders like yourself. You might get a few Liberal employers' votes & a few Conservative free traders, but party loyalty which is very strong in Oldham & personal inclination towards Protectionism will prevent your gaining any number of Conservative votes. I don't think a bitter campaign will help you. If after the debate on the Address, you resign I don't think you will be opposed by the Conservative party. Certainly not if the Labour & Liberals don't oppose you.

Then as you say, you would be free. I expect you will have seen Brierley who telephoned me that he was going to meet you Saturday. Please let me have your letter in plenty of time before the 8th. I think you are wise not to attend the meeting, it would only cause bitter speeches & widen the breach. They can't argue with, though they may argue about a letter.

Certainly I see no prospect of my changing my Conservative principles on account of the passing madness which has taken possession of the party, especially as the prime mover in it never was & never will be a Conservative.

I don't think you ever will be an 'Electioneerer'; though your principles are admirable, your tactics are more inclined to benefit your opponents than yourself. Still it is well we have some honest politicians. Meanwhile I will try my best to secure peace.

I am, Very sincerely yours
JAMES T. TRAVIS-CLEGG

WSC to Lord Hugh Cecil
(*Quickswood Papers*)

EXTRACT

27 December 1903   Gopsall

Private

My dear Linky,

It would for several reasons be a good thing if you were here; & in any case I hope you will return not later than the 23rd or 24th. I found at Chatsworth the duke vy determined. He has written to Rosebery on the lines of your Canford letter & has received a friendly reply. James has had a conference with Asquith by his authority about seats – the upshot of wh I do not yet know.

The Duke has also written Spencer & there is a movement among the Lib Imps to bring about a juncture of forces at the Guildhall meeting on the 8th of Feb. Lewisham[1] has produced a salutary effect upon the Liberal officials. They know they cannot be independent of the Irish without Unionist assistance, & yet – so curious & involved is the position – they cannot hope to keep their education pledges with Irish support. Therefore according to Massingham they want a Devonshire Government at any rate for a time.

Ivor is being approached by Cardiff Liberals who are quite ready to make concessions to his Conservative views (if he has any). *Voilà déjà quelque-chose.* But you will see how essential your presence is to any educational pact. The duke I believe takes the view that A. Balfour is the person mainly responsible for the Bill in its present form.

I have suggested & the duke is inclined to assent that a small committee from both sides should during Janr make a thorough examination of individual seats – to review the conditions of our arrangement. Meanwhile my letter to the Liberal candidate for Ludlow (which I wrote with the duke's sanction) has blown the lid off the Oldham volcano again. The Association has publicly repudiated me & I am at work to form another. My few poor friends are quite unflinching, but awfully bullied. What a dreadful thing it must be to be a local politician. The enclosed announcement from the *D.T.*

---

[1] At the by-election of December 15 1903, the Liberal party contested Lewisham for the first time since 1892. The result was:

Major E. F. Coates (C)	7,709
J. W. Cleland (L)	5,697

is I think the answer to any Ludlow moves. *Je m'en moque*: but I am now a 'heathen & publican' as the 39 Articles pithily puts it. The result of Ludlow was certainly encouraging. 1450 Unionists appear to have responded to the duke's appeal & voted the other way reducing the majority by 3000.[1]

A vy powerful Free Trade League of manufacturers & businessmen has been formed in Manchester irrespective of party. I am trying to get this into line with the duke's meeting at L'pool.

Aberdeen is to be on Saty 30th afternoon, not evening 29th as heretofore arranged. They have taken the big theatre there & all the country folk are to come in from the surrounding district.

You may be quite certain that the Joeites will do their utmost, quite regardless of by-electoral warnings or of party disaster. Their press hails even Ludlow as a great victory for Tariff Reform. Nothing but the scourge & flail will cure them.

With all good wishes
Always your sincere friend
W

WSC to (?)

28 December 1903   Gopsall
[Copy]

My dear Sir,

I do not believe that the Liberal party have any intention of introducing a Home Rule Bill for Ireland in the immediate future; nor do I think that the question of Home Rule can be in any degree at stake at the next general election. No doubt there is an immense number of people of both political parties who adhere to the general principle that countries should be governed by their own consent from within & not by other authority from without. But the objections to the Home Rule Bills of 1886 & 1893 were more effective against the details of that legislation than against the principles & aspirations by which it was supported. Much has happened in the intervening years to make the Irish question less acute & the Nationalist party who have accepted the alternative policy of the Unionists are more likely to find themselves in accord with Chamberlainite Protectionists than with Liberal & Unionist Free traders.

---

[1] WSC's analysis of the voting was incomplete. The Liberal candidate, Horne, polled 3,423 to the Liberal Unionist's 4,393. But the constituency had not been contested by the Liberal Party since 1892.

Time has brought us no practical or adequate solution of the four great problems of Irish self government *viz* the question of Irish representation at Westminster: the question of police: the question of Finance: & the question of Ulster; & I cannot bring myself to imagine a Liberal administration elected on a Free Trade basis plunging again into that thorny & perilous jungle. I notice as a curious proof of how little the politics of twenty or even of ten years ago bear upon the controversies of today – that the Unionist candidate for the Rye Division, the Hon T. A. Brassey,[1] is an avowed Home Ruler, while the Liberal (& *prima facie* Home Rule) candidate for the Bournemouth division[2] has declared that he will not if elected support a Home Rule Bill. We are surrounded by difficulties & I sympathise with your anxiety lest the vote you mean to give for Free Trade should imperil the vast substructure upon which the stability of these kingdoms depends. But you are now confronted with an immediate danger not less destructive to the material strength of the Empire & far more subversive of its moral forces than the separatist proposals of 1886. I conceive it is your duty without prejudice to your future action or your other political opinions to ward off this danger; and you may be perfectly certain that in following the Duke of Devonshire you will run no risk of being committed to such wild and dangerous schemes as may easily result from Mr Chamberlain's violence or Mr Balfour's weakness, or worst of all from a combination of both.

Yours faithfully

WSC

---

[1] Thomas Allnutt Brassey (1863–1919), eldest son of 1st Earl Brassey, whom he succeeded in 1918. He fought in 5 elections between 1892 and 1903, but was never successful.
[2] Probably a reference to A. A. Allen, the Liberal candidate for Christchurch.

5

Crossing the Floor

(*See Main Volume Chapter 2*)

J. T. Travis-Clegg to WSC

EXTRACT

29 December 1903   Shaw Lodge

Private

My dear Mr Churchill,

I am afraid I must have obscured my meaning in my last letter. Candidly, I thought & so did Smethurst that your Halifax speech foreshadowed your adherence to the Liberal Party. Particularly as Herbert Gladstone took you up the following day. My letter therefore was intended to convey to you that I could not follow you so far. That leaving out Free Trade my principles are entirely opposed to those of the Liberal party. Smethurst on the other hand is I believe prepared to leave the Conservative Party if you do so. I am bound from my position to have some regard to the local point of view; you can afford to ignore that for the sake of the national importance of the question & I have always agreed with you that you are justified in so doing.

That is why I recommend you to secure the option of another seat so that you may not lose your central platform, the House of Commons. With all due deference to your opinion I still think that you have played your cards very badly from a local point of view. If, as I continually asked you to do, you had come down at the beginning of the year & visited all the clubs in the constituency, not to make speeches & have them reported, but to talk with the members informally & explain your side of the case, you would have had a sympathetic reception & have prepared their minds for coming events. You will also remember that I have several times ventured to disagree on the tactics you were pursuing locally. In fact you have been so far carried away by the national importance of the Chamberlain proposals that you have altogether disregarded the local political aspect. There is also the very potent fact that this is by no means the first time that you have opposed the government. If it had been you would have received greater licence no doubt.

Politically as well as personally I hope our relations will remain unchanged. If the Association desire to pass any more discourteous resolutions I should not vote for them, any more than I voted for the last one – I did not (weakly perhaps) vote against it because as I have said I quite anticipated your joining the Liberals, & it was not quite correct to describe the resolution as being carried unanimously though it *was* carried *nem con.*

As to my urging them to adopt some more moderate course, that is what I have been doing all along, but the feeling is now so acute that I cannot hope to control it. If you place your resignation in their hands they will certainly not oppose you unless the other side do so. Therefore it is not likely that you will be opposed. In reference to any agreement, the Protectionists are quite as determined as yourself not to have any. Their first resolution at the meeting last Wed was that the proposed agreement which I had drafted be not entertained. Except Hilton, Smethurst & Brierley, none of them saw your 1st draft letter which remains in my possession. My course will be much clearer after Mr Balfour has spoken. I agree with the official policy as expounded by him. If he repudiates that policy then I shall have to consider afresh.

My fear about a coalition is this – supposing I leave my party & join a coalesced party which is bound to be chiefly composed of liberals to all intents & purposes I become a liberal. Now while a man who changes his politics once is welcomed by his new friends his return to the original fold ensures distrust of him by both parties. . . .

. . . I also agreed with the Duke of Devonshire's Queen's Hall speech, but he had not then advised Unionists to vote for Liberal candidates.

Whatever happens, whether you join the liberals or not I look on all your correspondence with me as absolutely private & confidential. You may have seen the resolution in the *Oldham Standard* which was passed by the G.P. Committee last Wed thanking me for my services. I replied at some length & asked them not to make it impossible for Conservative Free Traders to remain in the party. I told them I supported the official programme but was opposed to Chamberlain & advised moderation. I said if I found it impossible to hold my official position I should retire into privacy until such times as the Conservative party had recovered its head. I hope I have now made myself clear.

With kindest regards, I am Yours most sincerely
JAMES T. TRAVIS-CLEGG

F. Brierley to WSC

EXTRACT

30 December 1903   Oldham Conservative Association

Dear Mr Churchill,

I have just had a very long & pleasant talk with Mr Travis-Clegg & he has shown me in strict confidence all the correspondence which has passed between you during the past week and it is his desire that I should write you giving my opinion as to his true position between the Association & yourself. Your last letter to him was certainly to the point, I was glad you wrote it but *extremely* thankful you did not in any way imply how or when your fears had been aroused; the letter has certainly cleared the air and I think the following is Mr Travis-Clegg's present position:

1 Supposing the Oldham Conservative Association began a protectionist propaganda he would immediately retire from his position on the Executive.

2 He is a Free Trader with strong leanings towards Balfour, dead against Chamberlain.

3 You can rely upon him doing his very utmost to preserve peace between the Assoc & yourself in the interim between the present time & the general election.

4 He will do his utmost to prevent a by-election.

5 He feels his position most acutely, but the strong ties of the past prevent him from doing anything which would debar him from ever being a Member of the Conservative party in the future.

6 I think you can rely upon him being your friend and will always be ready to defend you, *but* (*this is my warning*) remember that the probability is, both Mr Smethurst & myself will be out of the way & there is no telling what great pressure this howling mob of protectionists will bring to bear upon him. Don't be *too* confidential, I mean with regards to any delicate scheme you may have for the near future.

7 He is strongly in favour of our proposed Unionist Free Trade Assoc: would probably join it (passive).

8 He thinks Mr Maclean[1] would be a great acquisition.

9 He also sees that the proposed Assoc would have to act in strong opposition to the Conservative Assoc which might to a certain extent be disadvantageous.

10 I talked rather large about your strong position supposing a by-election

---

[1] James Mackenzie Maclean (1835–1906), President of Oldham branch of Free Food League; newspaper editor and proprietor; Conservative MP for Oldham 1885–92, for Cardiff 1895–1900.

was forced upon us, about the arrangements already made supposing the protectionists forced your hand (which I don't think for one moment they will). I also said that if you were treated with consideration you would reciprocate. He said he was strongly of opinion that they would not ask you to resign but that they would allow you to go your way & that they would go theirs during the life of the present parliament.

11 Do you think it wise for the proposed Unionist Free Trade Ass to be affiliated with the *Liberal* Free Trade League?

When I get your reply relative to Mr Maclean & the kindred affiliated Free Trade & Free Food Association I will begin. . . .

I have secured all the various resolutions with dates, movers & seconders & in view of recent events they are very interesting reading. I am doing everything I possibly can to keep things going smoothly but at the same time I am preparing for *War*.

Yours very truly
FRED BRIERLEY

PS Your letter to Travis-Clegg re Executive Meeting anxiously awaited.

J. Moore Bayley to WSC

EXTRACT

30 December 1903   Château Diodato
                                   Callé-Roquebrune
                                   France

Dear Churchill,

I duly received your last letter re Central Division & have been hoping before now to have had a chat with Mr McKenna (quite on my own account & apart from you) who is in his new villa close to this place. Parkes the sitting member is personally a very weak man & under ordinary circumstances could easily be dislodged. The position so changes that it is impossible to make a forecast until it is known better when the election is probable & then the position of JC before the country at the moment . . . If you go over to the Libs so much will depend upon the exact circumstances in which you make the change, for of course so strong a Tory as you have been with your Father's record before you will require a great amount of care in selecting the opportune moment. Of course if you come out for a Birmingham Division as things stand today I should have to resign my official positions at once for I would not allow myself to stand in a possible false position between yourself & the Conservative Party. I will see you as soon as I am in a position to say how the land lies more definitely & in the meanwhile the Central Division must not be dealt with by the Libs.

I am having delightful weather here, just like English midsummer. With all good wishes for the New Year,

Yours very truly

J. MOORE BAYLEY

Edmund Robbins[1] to WSC

30 December 1903   The Press Association

London

Dear Sir

It is stated in today's *St James's Gazette* that it is generally believed in Oldham that you are about to resign, in order to make an appeal to the electors. Will you kindly inform us whether this statement is correct, and, at the same time forward us copy of any communication you may be about to send the electors of Oldham?

Yours faithfully

E. ROBBINS

PS Since the above was written, I have received yours of this day's date, and am communicating same to the newspapers tonight.

Charles Trevelyan[2] to WSC

31 December 1903   8 Grosvenor Crescent

Confidential

My dear Churchill,

I have been reading your letters and speeches with great interest. I should not write to you unless you had begun to speak of alliance with the Liberals in defence of free trade, which I have thought for some time was the necessary outcome for you, at least until protection has been so much smashed that your party gives it up as a bad job that won't pay. That won't be for

[1] Edmund Robbins (1847–1922), Manager of the Press Association 1880–1917; knighted 1917

[2] Charles Philips Trevelyan (1870–1958), Liberal MP for Elland 1899–1918; Labour MP for Central Newcastle 1922–31; Parliamentary Secretary to the Board of Education 1908–14; President of the Board of Education 1924, 1929–31; PC 1924; succeeded father as 3rd baronet 1928.

many years at any rate. I don't want to discuss free trade or to say how glad many of us will be to work with you on that. There is no difficulty on that score. The doubt lies in another direction. I am looking a little further ahead.

I am not speaking for anyone. I am writing merely of my own motion, in order to get your ideas if you care to give them to me.

The problem for most of us Liberals is not only Free Trade and never will be. The Liberal party is not situated like the Conservative party at the time of the introduction of Home Rule, only too glad to get any Liberals on the terms of their opposing Gladstone. They were content with that negative and had no more to ask of the Liberal Unionists.

Now no free trade government could hold office on a defensive policy alone. A cleavage of a hopeless kind would result in six months. The whole *raison d'être* of present day Liberalism is constructive reform. It may not appear so in Parliament. For our spokesmen are not very representative of the real party feeling. But whether it becomes apparent in the new type of advanced Liberal who will appear next election in much larger numbers in the house or in the vigour of the labour party, the next parliament will be shouting for economic and social reform. I have been going round a good deal lately, and there is a very general growl at our leaders for arguing against protection without talking of our counter policy.

If you will do me the honour to read my article in the *Independent Review* of January, which I am ordering Fisher Unwin[1] to send you, you will see better what I mean.

You are the most reforming spirit among Conservative Free Traders. And I should like to know your views as to the directions in which you think it would be possible to work together.

Economy of course is administrative rather than legislative. Bands of vigilant men on both sides will be able to do wonders. But it will never be a popular policy, though it may give certain men a great position. In reading Gladstone's *Life* one of the most striking things is that in the heyday of Liberal predominance he had less sympathy with his great economies from his cabinet colleagues or his party than with any other movement he led. Still combined with *Army Reform* it would stand more chance.

What I want to know is how much common ground can you find with reforming Liberals on economic and social questions?

Can you and your friends contemplate the alteration of the Education Act so as to put the schools under popular management, with any security you please for religious teaching except the present religious test for state-paid teachers?

Can you ally yourselves with Peel or any part of the movement against

[1] Thomas Fisher Unwin (1848–1935), publisher and Liberal politician.

the liquor monopoly? You were the first to speak about the political dangers of protection. I don't imagine you have much affection for the only great monied interest that at present plunges into politics.

Can you join with us at all to relieve local taxation by land value taxation? It is barely a party question, and all municipalities irrespective of party are with us in principle.

There is nothing in the tradition of Conservative democracy to prevent a common policy of state regulation of sweated industries. The extension of stringent factory laws to home workers would be some answer to Chamberlain's appeal to the proletariat.

The reform forces in the party are vastly stronger than ten years ago, and I am certain will never check themselves for the sake of a few Unionist votes. You may say – 'Oh! but we have ourselves to consider and we will not sell our Conservative opinions to save free trade.' I don't suggest it. I enquire whether many of you – the Seelys, Poynder, Lambton, Beckett etc – are not in fact as much inclined (at least in some directions) to economic change as most of us.

Well I leave it here, rather vaguely. But if the matter interests you I shall be glad to know your views. The danger comes after the next general election – Can the free traders work together at an alternative policy? The sooner we begin to discuss it the better.

I am to be married next Wednesday to Hugh Bell's youngest daughter. So I shall be away till the beginning of the session after that. But if you care to talk, I am pretty free till Monday at least.

I am glad you went to Halifax, which I partly represent, and glad they gave you so good a reception.

Yours v truly
CHARLES TREVELYAN

WSC to Lord Hugh Cecil
(Quickswood Papers)

1 January 1904   105 Mount Street

Private

My dear Linky,

I lunched yesterday privately with Lloyd George and had a very interesting and not altogether unsatisfactory conversation with him. He told me that the Duke had, he understood, opened negotiations with Spencer[1] for a

---

[1] Charles Robert Spencer (1857–1922), Liberal MP 1880–95, 1900–5. Son of 4th Earl Spencer by his second wife; succeeded his half-brother as 6th Earl 1910; married Margaret Baring, daughter of 1st Baron Revelstoke; KG 1913; PC 1892.

compromise in Education, the principle of this compromise he described to me as 'facilities for inside control' and he informed me that he had knocked it on the head as there was no use pretending he could carry his people where he could not. It is undoubtedly true that either you or he could blow up any arrangement which might be come to between the Leaders; but if you and he could reach any sort of understanding, all the educational dynamite would be safely damped. He is very anxious to meet you and have a talk and I would suggest that you and he should dine with me privately on the first night of the Session February 2nd in some quiet place.

I do not pretend to understand the passions of the Education controversy, and it seemed to me, talking to Lloyd George yesterday, that some of the differences were astonishingly small and petty. For instance LG says that his people will die rather than give 'facilities for inside control', that is to say they will not give right of entry into public elementary schools (so I take it) to any religion except the religion of Sir Henry Fowler[1] and Mr Perks[2] according to act of Parliament, or what I call 'the highest common factor' religion – 'neutral tint' – during school hours when compulsory attendance is required. But they are perfectly prepared to give facilities out of school hours to any religious denomination, and they are prepared to shorten school hours accordingly. In fact, a treaty has been concluded between Lloyd George and the Bishop of St Asaph[3] for Wales as follows:— School hours begin at nine o'clock four days a week with half an hour of neutral tint religion; but on two days a week, they begin at 9.30 and on these two days a week the School could be opened at nine o'clock to denominational teachers for the instruction of those children whose parents desire them to attend.

Now the difference between inside facilities which Nonconformists must resist as tyranny and outside facilities which no reasonable man could refuse appear to me simply to be whether the School hours officially begin at nine o'clock on the days that denominational teaching is appointed or at nine thirty. Now as the official hours can have nothing to do with the spiritual value of religious teaching, it is clear to me that if the Church people are determined to insist upon teaching within the official hours that is because they wish to avail themselves of the compulsory powers which Parliament has granted for educational purposes, and I don't think that is a tenable position.

[1] Henry Hartley Fowler (1830–1911), Liberal MP Wolverhampton 1880–1908. Secretary of State for India 1894–5; Chancellor of the Duchy of Lancaster 1905–8; Lord President of the Council 1908–10; created Viscount Wolverhampton 1908; PC 1886; the first Methodist Cabinet Minister.

[2] Robert William Perks (1849–1934), Liberal MP for Louth 1892–1910; businessman, lawyer; partner of Henry Fowler; treasurer of the Liberal League; prominent Methodist; baronet 1908.

[3] Alfred George Edwards (1848–1937), Bishop of St Asaph 1889–1934; Archbishop of Wales 1920–34.

I said to LG what do you propose to give the Church besides what you call 'outside facilities'? He said 'I would give them money.' I said 'how much?' He mentioned the figure of eleven millions and said that if the Church got eleven millions and spent it wisely on hostelries for teachers and so forth they would strengthen their position in a way that Nonconformists did not realise at all.

I was astonished to find that he is not at all a Secularist and insists upon compulsory religious instruction (neutral tint) in all state schools during certain hours in the week; and here he found himself in sharp difference with Massingham. I wish you had been there for I think I could have learnt a great deal if I could have heard your point of view put forward as tolerantly as he stated his.

I send you a cutting which explains my Oldham position very fairly well. I shall hear in two or three days from the Labour party whether they will oppose me in the event of my resigning, but I shall not come to any definite decision on this matter until your return.

I also enclose a spiteful letter about you and a pronunciamento of mine on Home Rule.

The Liberal party are not at all happy although they profess to have encouraging reports from the constituencies. Mr Dobbie,[1] the Liberal candidate for Ayr, has written me asking me to speak for him and he complains that the artisans are being 'captivated' by Mr Chamberlain's big wage proposals and he seems to write in very gloomy spirits. The Liberal candidate for the Lowestoft Division of Lincolnshire [sic] also writes asking for help and says that six months ago when he came forward as a candidate, he could easily have won the seat but that Lord Willoughby[2] has taken up Mr Chamberlain's case with an enthusiasm which he has never before shown on any other subject and has undoubtedly made a great impression on the minds of the farmers.

The Independent Labour Party have apparently broken all faith with the Liberals and in spite of immense concessions they now threaten to go to the poll both in Gateshead and in Norwich, thus in both cases securing the return of the Protectionist candidate.

I am sorry to say that Sir Samuel Hoare[3] has completely run away at Norwich and has declared that he will support the Government candidate in

[1] Joseph Dobbie (1862–1943), Liberal MP for Ayr Burghs 1904–6; Chairman Royal Scots Recruiting Committee 1914–16; knighted 1920.

[2] Gilbert Heathcoate-Drummond-Willoughby (1867–1951), Conservative MP Horncastle Division of Lincolnshire 1894–1910; succeeded his father 1910 as 2nd Earl of Ancaster.

[3] Samuel Hoare (1841–1915), Conservative MP for Norwich 1886–1906, partner in banking firm of Barnetts, Hoares and Company; baronet 1899. Father of Viscount Templewood.

order that 'in this European crisis the Prime Minister may be supported by the whole nation' or some rubbish of that kind.

Nothing could exceed the confidences of the Chamberlainites everywhere, and although I am perfectly sure that Free Trade forces are much the larger, we are so hopelessly divided and split up among ourselves that anything may happen.

Lloyd George spoke to me at length about a positive programme. He said unless we have something to promise as against Mr Chamberlain's promises where are we with the working men? He wants to promise three things which are arranged to deal with three different classes, namely, fixity of tenure to tenant farmers subject to payment of rent and good husbandry: taxation of site values to reduce the rates in the towns: and of course something in the nature of Shackleton's[1] Trade Disputes Bill for the Trade Unionists. Of course with regard to brewers, he would write 'no compensation out of public funds.' I was very careful not to commit myself on any of these points and I chaffed him as being as big a plunderer as Joe. But *entre nous* I cannot pretend to have been shocked. Altogether it was a very pleasant and instructive talk and after all Lloyd George represents three things:—Wales, English Radicalism and Nonconformists, and they are not three things which politicians can overlook.

To turn to another quarter of the field of perplexity and intrigue, I enclose you a copy of a letter which Harry Paulton[2] has written to Lord James of Hereford. Paulton is the secretary of the Liberal League and he is of course very well disposed to us. A great many of the official Liberals have lately become much more anxious for an arrangement. Herbert Gladstone much more accommodating, McArthur[3] (the Whip) very keen, and now I am told that Ripon[4] has also come out very strong for an arrangement. Nothing will persuade me that it is not worth while an effort in this direction.

The Wimbornes are giving a big political dinner to forty people on the evening of the 5th of February. The Duke is coming and lots of Liberals and

[1] David James Shackleton (1863–1938), Labour MP for Clitheroe 1902–10; Chairman of the Labour Party 1905; President TUC 1908–9; Senior Labour Adviser, Home Office 1910–11; National Health Insurance Commissioner 1911–16; Permanent Secretary Ministry of Labour 1915–21; Chief Labour Adviser 1921–5; KCB 1917.
[2] James Mellor Paulton (1857–1923), Liberal MP for Bishop Auckland 1885–1910; Assistant Private Secretary to H. H. Asquith 1893–5.
[3] William Alexander McArthur (1857–1922), Liberal MP for Buckrose 1886–7, St Austell 1887–1908; Junior Lord of the Treasury 1892–5.
[4] George Frederick Samuel, 1st and last Marquess of Ripon (1827–1909), Liberal MP 1852–9; Secretary of State for War 1863–6; Secretary of State for India 1866; Lord President of the Council 1868–73; Viceroy of India 1880–4; First Lord of the Admiralty 1886; Secretary of State for the Colonies 1892–5; Lord Privy Seal 1905–8; succeeded his father as 2nd Earl Ripon 1859; Marquess 1871.

Free Fooders. Afterwards there is to be a big party. They are very anxious that you should dine.

Now I have told you all the news and I fear it seems very petty and ephemeral on the broad flood of the Nile.

I hope you have profited by your rest and by the change of scene and occupation.

The newly excavated Temple at Carnac, the tombs of the Kings and the Temple of Dendera, are in my opinion, the best that Egypt has to show, but if you go to Sakkara, do not fail to see the Burying Place of the Bulls.

I wonder whether you have seen the battle field of Omdurman and the ditch into which we charged with such unfortunate results. But that seems a very long time ago.

The difficulties of the political situation depress me and it seems to me that whatever we may do at this next election, the Tory party will become permanently capitalist and Protectionist in character and the Liberal party will be smashed to pieces between organised capital on the one hand and organised labour on the other. However it is not much good trying to look too far ahead.

Yours ever
W

Thomas Ashton to Samuel Smethurst

2 January 1904   Oldham Operative Cotton
                                  Spinners & Provincial Association

[Copy]

Private

Dear Sir,

I read your letter of Dec 30th/03 to the Executive Committee at a special meeting held to-night, and taking into consideration the circumstances to which you refer, they have resolved that in the event of a by-election taking place and Mr W. S. Churchill stands as a candidate in defence of Free Trade, that the Labour Party won't oppose him by bringing out a Labour candidate. This decision is on the understanding that the promise made by you (that Mr Churchill won't stand as a Candidate at the next General Election) is strictly carried out.

With kind regards and wishing you a Happy and Prosperous Year.

I am, yours respectfully
THOMAS ASHTON

Samuel Smethurst to WSC

3 January 1904   Coldhurst House
                                                             Oldham

Dear Mr Churchill,

I am writing this at a friend's house to let you know that I received a letter
this morning from Tom Ashton in which he informs me that his Committee
agree not to contest a by-election. On the understanding of my letter – that
if they don't oppose you at a by-election you will not contest against them
at a General Election. I don't know whether your unopposed return at a by-
election would be considered as coming within the terms of the bargain.
Anyway I don't think I should attempt at this stage to get any further
definition attached to the arrangement as very likely your committee will
ask you to continue. I hope you will make no pledge to them (your committee) if they ask you as to your not standing at a General Election: and I
should, I think, make it clear in my letter to them for reaching on the 8th,
that they had by their action lost their right to expect pledges – or make
bargains. I have a very interesting letter from Travis-Clegg which I will
send you along with Ashton's letter tomorrow. I have written Maclean.
I think the Association that ought to be formed is a branch of the Free Trade
League Manchester. Can you ask the Secretary to communicate with me as
I don't know his address.

                                                         Yours Truly
                                                      SAM SMETHURST

Samuel Smethurst to WSC

4 January 1904   Coldhurst House

Dear Mr Churchill,

I enclose you letter I have received from Mr Ashton; please take a copy
& return. I have acknowledged it in the following terms:
   'Dr Mr Ashton,   4 December 1904
   I beg to acknowledge receipt of your letter of the 2nd inst which is very
satisfactory and for which I thank you. I take it the pledge which Mr
Churchill gives and to which you refer is the one contained in my letter
of the 30th of December last. Beyond that I have no power to go and it
must be understood that in the event of there not being a contest Mr
Churchill remains unpledged as to his action at the General Election.

Although it is exceedingly improbable, as far as I can see, that he will be a candidate for Oldham.

Yours truly
S. SMETHURST

The other letter I enclose is from Travis-Clegg which please also return – it is a reply to one from me – in which I asked him, presuming you were out of the way, if there was any chance of his standing as an official Balfourian Candidate – and suggesting he might satisfy the Protectionists. I think he would satisfy them as I don't think that Chamberlain carries them all.

The feeling against you is that they think you are not loyal to Balfour. You must let me know fully what you are going to do and let me have draft of your letter, which you propose to be read on Friday. Don't you agree with me that it is better to have Free Trade League than Unionist Free Food League? I think to have too many agencies at work only weakens our efforts. Besides when you appeal to all sections of politicians you can get so much stronger an association. I have written Maclean to that effect.

Yours Truly
SAM SMETHURST

WSC to J. T. Travis-Clegg[1]

January 1904   105 Mount Street

My dear Travis-Clegg,

I have received a copy of the resolution passed by the General Purposes Committee on the 23rd December. The character and terms of this resolution appear to render impossible any such agreement as you had hoped to effect. A new situation has been created locally, and I should be glad if you would invite the Executive Committee of the Conservative Association, at their meeting on the 7th inst, to let me know precisely what they want done. I may as well state that I have no intention of 'relying upon' the support of the Oldham Conservative Association, or indeed of any organisation definitely Protectionist in character, at the approaching general election; and in view of the possibility of my contesting the borough at a by-election, I shall take the necessary steps to form a Unionist Free Trade Association.

I have never left my constituents in much doubt about my opposition to Mr Chamberlain's new taxation, and in future I shall neglect nothing in my power to hinder him obtaining a majority in the next Parliament.

---

[1] Published in the *Oldham Standard*, 8 January 1904. There is a typescript draft of this letter, with alterations in WSC's hand, in the Chartwell papers. It differs only slightly from the published version.

When I undertook, at the urgent request of your Committee, to fight Oldham for the Conservative Party, it had been for many years a Free Trade party. When Mr Balfour succeeded Lord Salisbury in the leadership he solemnly pledged himself at the Carlton Club meeting that the policy of the party should be unchanged. And yet at Sheffield only a year afterwards he declared for 'a fundamental reversal of the policy of the last fifty years.' Therefore it is not against me that any charge of breaking pledges can be preferred. Before this question of Protection was raised I had criticised the Government policy in respect of the growth of public expenditure and of the cost and condition of the army; and I had ventured to predict that the high expenditure would lead to a depression of trade, and that the army scheme of 1901 would prove unworkable. My opinions on these subjects are entirely unaltered, except that I hold them more strongly than ever. Whether I was right or wrong does not arise now, for in both cases my action was approved and endorsed by the Association in formal resolutions and in their annual reports. Therefore the differences which unfortunately exist between us date from the introduction of the new policy. Upon that policy the Executive Committee have already formally accorded me by resolution full liberty of speech and action, and as it is a policy in reversal of the conditions under which I was elected, no obligation rests upon me to resign my seat and submit myself to re-election. At the same time, I need not say that I should treat any expression of the views of the Executive Committee with all possible respect, and should give to their wishes my most earnest consideration.

I regret profoundly the breach that has been opened in the Conservative party through Mr Chamberlain's campaign and the ill-feeling which it has caused among old friends and fellow-workers. It cannot fail to deprive the Association of several of its most valued and respected local leaders and of an unmeasured amount of working-class support. Six months ago the borough could have been won by a Conservative Free-trader; but now it is morally certain, whatever may happen to me that Protectionist candidates will be defeated – all as the result of the unrestrained ambition of a single man.

I confess myself disquieted at the levity with which party politicians embark on immense and uncalculated changes of policy at what they take to be the signal of their leaders. Eight months ago the doctrines to which the Association is about to bind itself irrevocably would have been laughed at by the majority of its members. When at our annual meeting in 1902 I – foreseeing what was coming – went out of my way to denounce the fallacies and follies of Protection, I received on all sides praise and support from my constituents, and no single protest of any kind was made. When at Whitsuntide, after Mr Chamberlain's first speeches, I had a prolonged conference with the General Purposes Committee, the whole body, with one or two exceptions, concurred with my Free Trade views.

I respect lifelong and convinced Protectionists. I hope they will credit me with being equally in earnest. I understand the politician who, thinking only of blue or red, says 'My party, right or wrong.' But I do not understand, and therefore cannot respect, the Free Trader who sees this great danger coming upon the country and yet hesitates to use the powers with which the Constitution has endowed him to ward it off. The government of nations is not a game of football, and when vast interests, involving the material comfort of millions of working people, and great truths quarried from the bed-rock by the toil and sacrifices of generations are assailed, those representative and responsible persons who sit by their firesides doing nothing are failing in their duty to the public.

The decision of all this must rest with the masses of the people. Nearly 13,000 electors gave me their votes at the last election. I am satisfied that the overwhelming majority of these have not yet arrived at any reasoned conviction upon this question. I know they wish to hear both sides of the case fully and fairly stated before making up their minds. It remains to be seen whether they will permit themselves to be manipulated by a party machine and marched this way and that way like a squad of recruits on a drill ground. It is perhaps premature to forecast the position at Oldham at the general election. You may be sure I should be perfectly willing to withdraw in favour of any Free Trader who possessed better claims to represent the borough; but while I remain its member I shall contrive to do my very best to oppose all Protectionist manoeuvres in Parliament, and to explain to the electors of Oldham how closely Free Trade and cheap food are interwoven with the welfare of the Lancashire artisan.

Yours sincerely
WINSTON S. CHURCHILL

WSC to J. T. Travis-Clegg

5 January 1904   105 Mount Street
[Copy]

Dear Travis-Clegg,

I am indeed sorry not to have had the advantage of talking matters over with you before the Meeting on the 7th; but I hope you will not mind my offering you my opinion as to the course you should pursue. I think both Brierley and Smethurst ought to be at the Meeting. I hope you will read my letter yourself and make it go as well as possible.

C II—PT. I—L

I do not think it necessary for you to divide against the proposed hostile resolution[1] unless you find unexpected support.

I should hope that you would find it possible to deprecate its aggressive tone, to point out that no other Conservative Association has attempted such a resolution, to remind the Committee that nobody but me would have won the last election and generally to deplore its violent spirit, which, whether displayed by the extremists of Free Traders or Protection, was equally calculated to injure the historic party etc.

I think you should say that frankly you do not approve of the resolution and that you would have thought the Committee would have been well advised to content themselves with affirming their confidence in the Government and with an expression of regret that their member could not give it a more effective support: you should declare yourself against the establishment of a general protective tariff, particularly the taxation of food, and announce that if such a programme becomes the policy of the party in the Borough, it would be impossible for you to take an active part in politics; you have no intention of joining the Liberal party now or at any future time but you think it monstrous that there should not be room in the Conservative party for those who have been loyal to it all their lives. You intend to continue to do your best to preserve the Free Trade character of the Conservative party, and although you feel much anxiety about the future, you do not yet abandon the hope that Mr Balfour's policy will be the most that the Conservative party will be asked to accept.

I trust you will not mind my making these suggestions which I offer you with all respect not for the purposes of making up your mind but only to show you my own.

I hope you will not allow discourteous personal attacks on me to pass without remonstrance; for you wish to establish in the mind of the Executive that you have a great deal of sympathy with the course I have adopted, and it is only out of loyalty to the party that you are continuing in office. This will give you a very strong position for they will try to consider you and make it easy for you. When the resolution is put to the Meeting you should I think say that you do not intend formally to resist it though you regret very much the course adopted. Smethurst and Brierley should do exactly what you do, only they should speak their mind as they feel inclined.

I am very glad to hear from Brierley to-day that you do not disapprove of the terms of my letter.

[1] 'That this Meeting of the General Purposes Committee of the Oldham Conservative Registration Association intimates to Mr Winston S. Churchill, MP, that he has forfeited their confidence in him as Unionist member for Oldham, and that, in the event of an Election taking place he must no longer rely upon the Conservative organisation being used on his behalf.'

Smethurst will have told you that the Labour party have undertaken not to oppose me. I am therefore in a very independent position. I do not mind the Committee passing any resolution but I do not want them to write me through you a long letter in reply to mine. Best of all I should like them to pass a resolution inviting me to continue to represent the Borough until the General Election and declaring that they do not want me to resign my seat. You will see by my letter that that is the conclusion to which it naturally leads. Write me a full account of what takes place.

With best wishes and many regrets at all the worry you are caused,

Believe me

[WINSTON S. CHURCHILL]

WSC to Samuel Smethurst

5 January 1904   105 Mount Street

[Copy]

Dear Mr Smethurst,

I have written to Mr Travis-Clegg explaining fully to him the line I should like him to take at the Meeting. Will you ask to see the letter and consult with him? I think both you and Brierley should attend and I should recommend that you should resign your position the next day. If you will write a letter putting forward your reasons, I think it would be an advantage. The Press Association will print it in every newspaper in the kingdom and firm action by individuals is a great example to other people. If you will draft a letter and put it in my hands, I will see that it is handed to the Press.

You have used to me a very strong argument about the gloomy prophesies of 20 years ago not having been fulfilled, and I wonder whether your letter would not be perhaps the best way of putting your argument on wheels so that it will be thought about all over the country.

As to the Free Trade League, I have communicated with the Free Food League and with the Free Trade League at Manchester, which latter I have put into communication with you, but you can use the name of the Free Food League in any way you like and they will supply you with any quantity of literature, a large part of it gratis.

We ought to have enough material to make a preliminary announcement to the newspapers early next week.

I will send you a cheque for £50 as a first subscription to the League whenever you let me know it is wanted. It is just as well this fifty pounds did not go to the Central Association as it might easily have done.

I quite agree with your idea of calling the League the Free Trade League. I would suggest Monday the 18th as the date for its first meeting if Maclean is able to come then.

I enclose you a letter which I have addressed to Mr Ashton which please read, and unless you think undesirable forward to him. My point is, no by-election, no agreement, in other words, in order to make our agreement operate it is necessary that I should apply for the Chiltern Hundreds and resign, but once having done that, I consider myself bound by the agreement whether there is an actual contest or unopposed return. You might also tell Ashton that I feel much obliged to him and to his friends for their courtesy.

Yours sincerely
[WINSTON S. CHURCHILL]

WSC to Thomas Ashton

5 January 1904   105 Mount Street

[Copy]

Confidential

Dear Mr Ashton,

Mr Smethurst has forwarded me your letter of the 2nd instant, for which I am much obliged to you.

Our understanding is that if I resign my seat and seek re-election at a by-election on the Free Trade issue I shall not be opposed by the Labour party; & in consequence of my not being opposed by them at such by-election, I shall not stand at the general election for the borough of Oldham.

Yours vy tly
WINSTON SC

Lord Tweedmouth to WSC

EXTRACT

5 January 1904   Brooks's
Secret   St James's Street

My dear Winston,

It was settled that Asquith & Herbert Gladstone should be authorised to confer with two of your party as to seats & possible conditions of an under-standing.

I think you will have to make up your minds definitely to a Free Trade amendment to the address and that voting for that amendment will be made the first condition of any understanding.

So far as I can gather the Duke is against such an amendment to the address & would like an enquiry resolution moved separately afterwards – That our people would never stand.

Yrs Ever

T

Duke of Devonshire to WSC

EXTRACT

6 January 1904   Chatsworth

My dear Churchill,

I do not think that I can say anything about attending meetings with Rosebery or any other Liberals until communications with them have progressed further. I have written to Spencer and he has promised to let me know what took place at a meeting of his friends which was about to be held when he received my letter.

A correspondence between Chamberlain and me will be published tomorrow or next day, which I expect will make some sensation.

One result of it is that I have resigned, or am about to resign, the Presidency of the L.U. Association; or perhaps rather that he has turned me out of it.

I suppose that C and his friends will claim it as a great triumph for them, but I think I had no alternative, and it will leave me more free than I have hitherto felt.

Manners Sutton has also written to me about the Norwich election and asked me whether you should be urged to go there. I cannot see sufficient reason for our interfering in elections when we cannot possibly do so with effect. . . .

Yrs very sincly

DEVONSHIRE

Samuel Smethurst to WSC

7 January 1904   Coldhurst House
                                                                       Oldham

Dear Mr Churchill,

I enclose copy of letter which I had forwarded to Travis-Clegg before I received yours. I had also sent copies to the Oldham & Manchester press.

I think Brierley rather overdoes things in his communication to the *Dispatch*. He is being attacked in the *Standard* – however that doesnt mean much. I suppose it will be my turn next. However I am indifferent. I am sorry I overlooked the point you name in my letter, but I am afraid it is too long as it is.

I think it better to withold the letter to Ashton for a few days. I intentionally put the word 'contest' in my last letter to him. I think it very inadvisable to let the protectionists know that you are bound by agreement not to contest at the General Election even though you have not the slightest intention of doing so. I think it will embarrass them if they are kept in the dark. If you send me a cheque I will open an account specially or place it to my account. I suppose we shall not get anything else – except what I may do. Are the Free Food League in need of money? I got an appeal the other day. I thought of sending them another £5.o.o. except you think it could be better used in Oldham.

Yours truly
SAM SMETHURST

PS I notice on reading your letter again that you propose the Subscription to go to the New League fund. Very good.

J. T. Travis-Clegg to WSC

8 January 1904   Shaw Lodge

My dear Mr Churchill,

I will not attempt to give you an account of the meeting last night. I am sending you an *Oldham Standard*, though you will probably have several, which contains a pretty correct account. I may say that my own speech is by no means fully reported. I got your letter suggesting the lines on which you thought I should go, & my notes already contained most of the points (I have just been interrupted by a *Manchester Guardian* representative who wanted to know if I thought there would be a by-election. I replied that I thought certainly not, I saw no reason for it.)

You will see that I declared for Mr Balfour's official policy. The resolution was carried against you last night with only one vote to the contrary, & he was a Chamberlainite who wished to confine the resolution to the fiscal question merely & not to say that you had forfeited confidence as Unionist member. There were perhaps half a dozen who did not vote at all. I hope the Association will let the matter rest where it is & pass no more resolutions.

I think it is their intention undoubtedly that you should continue as member during the present Parliament. I think the least they will do is to adopt a Balfourite Candidate or candidates with a favourable mind towards Chamberlain's policy. I don't see any reason why you should resign; it will only cause expense & accentuate bitter feeling in the party. I said last night that in choosing a candidate it should be one in opposition to the Liberal candidates, not to you. The position is still very difficult, I am sorry Smethurst has resigned.

I am, yours very sincerely
JAMES T. TRAVIS-CLEGG

Do you see that Kemp declared himself in favour of Balfour last night? I had several times difficulty in keeping out personalities among the speakers last night.

Earl of Dudley to WSC

9 January 1904   Vice Regal Lodge
                                                               Dublin

My dear Winston,
    A bed and 'Free Food' will be, as always, very much at your service in the house when you come over at the end of the month.
    I am afraid that I shall not be in Dublin myself but I will see that you are made comfortable and if you care to come on for a day or two to Rockingham and shoot woodcock we shall be delighted.
    It is a great regret to me that your views on this question are what they are but holding them so strongly you are of course right to fight it through to the end.

Yours sincerely
D

If you decide to do us the pleasure of coming here will you let us know exactly when you arrive.

WSC to Herbert Gladstone
(Herbert Gladstone Papers)

10 January 1904   105 Mount Street

Private
Dear Herbert Gladstone,
    I shall be in London on Tuesday & would call upon you – preferably

at your house – at any time after 12 wh may be convenient to you. Will you
kindly send a line to this address.

Yours vy sincerely
WINSTON S. CHURCHILL

WSC to Lord Hugh Cecil
(Quickswood Papers)

10 January 1904   105 Mount Street

Private

My dear Linky,
You cannot judge the rapidly changing situation here from a distance, &
it is not possible to refer everything to you while you are out of England.
I do not therefore propose to argue with you the question of my having
broken faith in writing to Mr Horne, further than to remind you that at
our last meeting in Gt George Street I asked the duke in your *presence*
whether I should accept invitations to speak at by-elections, & that he replied
that I was free to choose. To this you did not demur: & writing a letter is a
less serious step than making a speech.
The duke's letter to Lewisham has made a great change. He has just
written me that he has been forced to resign the presidency of the L.U. Assn;
& that he will now consider himself more free. My letter to Ludlow was
written with his sanction, & it & the Halifax speech were directly intended
to bring about that preliminary examination of seats which has now become
urgent & to wh your careful letter was directly designed to lead. I am
thankful to say that Tweedmouth has written me that the Liberal ex-
Ministers have authorised Asquith & H. Gladstone to meet the duke's
nominees in this matter, and I trust the discussion of individual seats will
begin this week. You will see by the newspapers how necessary it is that
negotiations should definitely begin. The opposition intend to force the
issue upon the address, & unless you have something better to offer your
people than destruction you will not get 10 men into the Lobby.
My language does not compromise you – & you are free to repudiate it if
you think it worth while. Neither does it separate me formally from the cons
party: tho that is a step wh cannot be long delayed. It does not present – but
indeed assists the driving of a bargain with the Liberals; for nothing is
better than that some of us should be vy friendly with them and on the best
of terms, that others should hold back vy stiff & proud, and that both
sections should declare they cannot desert each other.
I agree with you that it would be difficult to break off our engagements at

Aberdeen & Worcester. Anything like a public separation would excite ridicule. I believe there is no necessity for it & I hope that you will come to no decision until at least you are again in touch with the political situation here.

Yours ever
W

Lord James of Hereford to WSC

11 January 1904   Breamore
Confidential   Salisbury

My dear Winston Churchill,

It's strange you should have written to me – as I had arranged in my own mind to send you some words of congratulation by this evening's post.

You have been doing some splendid work and making a great name for yourself. Go on strenuously for the good cause. How I envy you your youth.

Very glad to receive your sanguine view of the position. I have always said that given time the commonsense of uninterested men would defeat J.Ch.

Might not there to be a systematic denunciation of these Tariff Reform Lecturers?

Throw discredit upon them as a class and they will be more than useless. Technically they may escape from the provisions of the Corrupt Practices Act but in all substance their expense ought to come within the Schedule. They are an ignorant unscrupulous set of mercenaries – and as I say ought to be denounced in every Constituency wherein they appear.

Well – The Liberal Unionist crash has come – JC has had a great weapon in his hands. The great majority of LU's agree with him – ¾ths at least – and he can carry any resolution he thinks fit. If the Duke had agreed to a meeting he would simply be expelled. As it is he and a few others will resign. I have no doubt but that Chamberlain will carry the association on – but it will be as a Protectionist Society.

Can you manage to come here for a day or two before you recommence your campaign? Do try. I think I could give you one or two topics for one of your many speeches.

Have you inquired at all about the Indian case? I would if I were you. It is a very good one for free-trade. The Indian Government here must be made to speak out – and tell the public what India thinks.

Yours
J of H

John Burns to WSC

12 January 1904   108 Lavender Hill
                                                             Battersea

Dear Mr Churchill,
    I would have liked very much for you to have taken the Bermondsey
meeting for me; but consider you were right in refusing especially when one
knows your friendship for Cust. I am temporarily only out of the fight
through tooth trouble which Robert Burns fitly described as the 'hell of a
disease'.
    I write however to express my gratitude to you for the fine stand you are
taking; I never lose an opportunity of expressing such and if I can some day
over Free Trade give you a help I will.
                    With best wishes for your tour and health, Yours sincerely
                                                             JOHN BURNS

Lord Hugh Cecil to WSC

13 January 1904   British Agency
                                                             Cairo

My dear Winston,
    I wired you today asking you to let the Aberdeen people know that I
cannot come as arranged. I had not their address at the time so had to
communicate thro' you. Since then a letter from them has arrived & I will
write to them – telegraphing is so frightfully expensive. My excuse – not
altogether untrue – is that I am not very well, that I am very anxious to
be well for the Session & that to go to Aberdeen just before Parlt meets will
be for me a great strain. But I have another reason. When it appeared that I
was to go to a meeting organised by young Scots & to stay with Lord & Lady
Aberdeen[1] & to speak in conjunction with you who had thanked God for a
Liberal Party & all this two days before the meeting of Parlt (a very important point; for politicians have very sharp memories) I felt the effect on
the mind of orthodox Conservatives would be precisely that which I wish to
avoid. Worcester is different: the audience is assembled by a body not less
respectable than a Chamber of Commerce. No one can be shocked at that.
    I am interested in your letter about Lloyd George. But tho' it is quite

    [1] John Campbell, 7th Earl of Aberdeen (1847–1934), Lord Lieutenant of Ireland 1886
and 1905-15; Governor General of Canada 1893-8; married 1877, Ishbel Maria, youngest
daughter of 1st Baron Tweedmouth; Marquess of Aberdeen and Temair 1916; KT 1906;
PC 1886.

right to be polite & amiable to everybody, I do not myself contemplate negotiating with him. I would not if I could help it touch any one except the Imperialists. But as the others have the machine it is necessary to deal with them. But I would keep to the officials – to Spencer, CB & H. Gladstone. And they ought to be content with an understanding limited to the fiscal question. The Lib Un in 1886 were left very free indeed on everything except Home Rule. Chamberlain (you will remember) attended the Round Table Conference wh tried to reunite the Liberal Party as late as the beginning of 1887 – & even so late as 1894 many L.U's including both Joe & the Duke took a line substantially opposed to the Conservatives over the Parish Councils Bill. Yet this bargain which seems so generous to the Lib Un was a splendid stroke of business for Conservatism. The Liberal Leaders will be great fools if they cannot point the moral.

The local noncons will no doubt be more exacting. But I think a great deal would be gained if we had an agreement with the central authority. Afterwards each individual could with the help & good offices of that authority make his own bargain with the locality. Very different degrees of assurance will probably be given by different Free Fooders on the education question. I shall myself be very stiff – I do not like bartering one important question for another & am indisposed to make more than slight concessions. Lloyd George's plan is quite impossible for it implies giving to undenm [undenominationalism] an advantage over denm [denominationalism]. There is something to be said for having no religious teaching at all in school during school hours & leaving every one to make their own arrangements outside – but to have 'neutral tint' to anyone inside at the public expense as a sort of state religion & the Church & RCs excluded would be quite intolerable. One must remember that 'neutral tint' may be anything – for it is only formularies that are forbidden. Unitarianism may be quite definitely taught for instance. – But you should read the late Canon Moberly's[1] 'Undenominationalism'. It is a pamphlet & will only take you 20 minutes. Then you will thoroughly understand the Church point of view – wh is mine.

LG's views on land are even more pernicious if possible. His idea seems to be that we should compete with Joe in appealing to the lowest predatory instincts of the electorate. Fixity of tenure has been ruinous in Ireland for it involves 'fair rent': & is very unfair in itself – I will not touch such a propaganda with a punt pole.

Yrs ever
HUGH CECIL

---

[1] Robert Campbell Moberly (1845–1903), Hon Canon of Chester 1890–3; Hon Chaplain to Queen Victoria 1898–1901.

PS I have written & sent to Manners Sutton a very confidential memo: to be shewn to the Ex-Cabinet Ministers perhaps later on to others. If you ask him he will shew it to you. Better not say anything about it to anyone till I come back wh will be about 23rd.

HC

WSC to Herbert Gladstone

13 January 1904   105 Mount Street
Confidential

Dear Herbert Gladstone,
    I send you herewith a completed list of the Members on our roll. Could you send me back the list of Liberal candidates opposed to them – for my private use.
    About B'ham – I do not want the initiative to seem to come from me; & I should not attempt such a struggle except on my own ground, & with general support. But I should like a cold-blooded report on the situation there, & I hope in any case the local leaders will not be in too much of a hurry to fill up the vacancies with candidates of their own – either in the Central or West Division. Kemp would make a splendid candidate against Chamberlain.
    I should also like to know about Oldham & what is the best Liberal opinion there. In any case there would be no contest till after the Address.
    I am sorry to hear that there is a difficulty about Guest for Cardiff. I do hope you will do what you can in this matter. He has I fear compromised himself with his own people at Plymouth.

Yours sincerely
WINSTON S. CHURCHILL

Sir Francis Mowatt to WSC

13 January 1904   35 Lennox Gardens

Dear Churchill,
    Yours just received. As we shall probably occupy adjoining cells in Hanwell we shall have many opportunities of fiscal discussion. I am full up this week for John Morley and Tweedmouth, who are just starting for the stump in Scotland, but I will try and let you have some notes on Ireland by Monday next.

You may certainly be thoroughly satisfied with the work you have done and are doing.

Yours very truly

FRANCIS MOWATT

Lord George Hamilton to WSC

15 January 1904   17 Montagu Street
Private

My dear Winston,

If you wish it I will leave the Cardiff meeting an open question, in the sense that if I can manage it I will go.

My vote is quite clear & I cannot go beyond it. I will oppose Protection & if the Radicals like to coalesce with Free Trade Unionists locally in opposition to Protection I do not object. But I cannot coalesce or combine with them in other matters.

Balfour's allusion to me was adroit. He did not deny my statement, but Rosebery's interpretation of what I said. My allegation can not be denied as I have possession of the document in question.

Believe me yrs very truly

GEORGE HAMILTON

Duke of Marlborough to E. Schofield[1]

15 January 1904   Colonial Office

Copy

Dear Mr Schofield,

I beg to thank you for your letter of 7th of January. I fear I do not see my way to accepting the position of honorary member of the Oldham Conservative Club. As you are aware, the reason of my connection with your Club was the fact that my kinsman, Mr Winston Churchill, was your representative in Parliament. Of late, circumstances have arisen which have caused him to find himself not in agreement with many of his former supporters, and I think I am right in saying that the harmony which existed between him and the members of the Club at the time when I was elected a member of it is not now so apparent.

I do not desire to make any comment upon a situation which concerns only Mr Churchill and the members of your Club, but as the conditions

[1] Edwin Schofield (b. 1835). JP 1896.

under which I became a member seem to have undergone a considerable change, I must, though with many regrets, sever my connection with an Association of which I shall retain pleasant recollections.

Believe me, yours sincerely
MARLBOROUGH

Lord James of Hereford to WSC

16 January 1904   Breamore
                                                     Salisbury

My dear W. Churchill,

I entirely share your view about Lytton. He is very able – and any matter however delicate may be its nature can safely be left to him – I am sure the Duke will be most pleased to utilise him. He is already recognised as one of those who must be consulted. Rest assured he *cannot* be overlooked.

It is all very well to say 'go down fighting'. It is singular how few Liberal Unionists are Free-traders. Nothing will give JC greater pleasure than to get the Duke to attend a meeting, attack him in every way and then take a vote of 20 to 1 against him. Will this 'going down' do us any good?

The fact is that Liberal Unionists for the most part are well-to-do men of the Producer class. But never mind our troubles. Everything is going well amongst the masses in the country. JC has had first run at them, and he must now see to it – that the *truth* is put before them. We *have* the TRUTH on our side, and have also the great advantage that we have nothing to construct, only to defend.

If Gateshead and Ayr follow this glorious Norwich result[1] surely Arthur Balfour will be really frightened and let his followers know that he does not wish them to support JC. The followers on the other hand will be glad enough to draw back from taxing food. But all depends upon the lessons they are taught by these elections.

Yours
J of H

[1] On the death of Sir Harry Bullard, one of the two unopposed Conservative candidates in 1900, a by-election was held on January 15 1904:

L. J. Tillett (L)	8,576
E. E. Wild (C)	6,756
G. H. Roberts (Lab)	2,440

A Labour candidate won at Gateshead and the Liberal won the Tory seat at Ayr.

WSC to Herbert Gladstone
(*Herbert Gladstone Papers*)
EXTRACT

16 January 1904   Brooke House
Confidential   Isle of Wight

Dear Gladstone,
. . . I hope you will keep Scarborough open for either Guest or me for the next few weeks at any rate. Liberals from Preston & also (curiously) Cardiff are making tender enquiries but I shall keep myself quite free, so that if after all we do fight in one line I can be employed where I am most useful.
I do wish you could settle the Isle of Wight situation. It would be a miserable business if the seat were captured by a 'Joeite' through a split free trade vote. Jack Seely has an immense personal following and without a Liberal opponent would be absolutely secure. In this case also there would be no difficulty in respect of education or temperance – provided a give-and-take mood prevailed. There are rumours here tonight that Godfrey Baring[1] will retire.
Norwich is really wonderful & may have far reaching effects. The reduction in the Unionist poll is the most striking feature & shows the influence of the Duke on the moderate folk. I hear he is to make a most determined speech at Liverpool.

Yours sincerely
WINSTON S. CHURCHILL

WSC to J. T. Travis-Clegg
[January 1904]
Copy/Draft/Secret

Dear Travis-Clegg,
The resolution passed by the Conservative Association on the 9th instant is of such a character that, although there is no moral obligation upon any Unionist Free Trader to seek re-election, I do not feel I should be treating the Executive with respect unless I placed my resignation in their hands. I have no desire to put the constituency to the trouble & myself to the expense of an electoral contest, but I shall leave the decision in their hands, and I shall be glad to know what it is within a reasonable time.

Yours vy sincerely
WINSTON S. CHURCHILL

---

[1] Godfrey Baring (1871–1957), prospective Liberal candidate for the Isle of Wight; Liberal MP for the Isle of Wight 1906–10, Barnstaple 1911–18; baronet 1911.

WSC to J. T. Travis-Clegg

20 January 1904   105 Mount Street

most private

[Copy]

Dear Travis-Clegg,

Although there is no obligation upon any Unionist Free Trader to seek re-election at the present time, the terms of the resolution passed by the Executive of the Oldham Conservative Association on the 9th instant, are such that – the decision shall rest with them; and I shall be glad to know before the meeting of Parliament what that decision is.

Yours sincerely

WINSTON S. CHURCHILL

J. T. Travis-Clegg to WSC

22 January 1904   Shaw Lodge

My dear Mr Churchill,

I return your letter herewith. I have made a slight alteration in it, as I don't think there is any necessity for you to assume a humble role. I should leave out the sentence I have erased & substitute something on the following lines – are such that 'they evidently desire to provoke my resignation. Personally if that *is* their desire I am perfectly willing to gratify it & to fight the constituency on a simple Free Trade issue. I should be pleased to know in plain & unequivocal language from the resolution.' The decision &c &c.

Brierley is here & agrees with me that this is an improvement. I don't think, though I have no official information, that the Association will fight, unless they are forced by the Tariff Reform League.

The Duke made a grand speech at Liverpool, though one of my friends here told me you had the best reception.

I am, Yours very sincerely

JAMES T. TRAVIS-CLEGG

PS As I am writing in a hurry I have not kept a copy of your letter.

WSC to A. J. Balfour

22 January 1904   Vice Regal Lodge
                                                        Dublin
[Copy]

Dear Mr Balfour,
   There is a statement in to-day's *Daily Telegraph* that I and some other
Unionist members are no longer to receive the Government whips, and as
the letter which I observe you have addressed to Unionist Members in view
of the Meeting of Parliament has not reached me, I write to ask whether the
statement is correct, and whether it is upon your authority that this step has
been taken.

                                         Believe me, yours very truly
                                         WINSTON S. CHURCHILL

Sir A. Acland-Hood to J. S. Sandars[1]
(Balfour Papers)

EXTRACT

24 January [1904]   St Audries
                                                     Bridgwater

. . . With regard to Winston Churchill and his 'Whip'. The Oldham
Conservative Association passed a resolution of want of confidence in him.
   He wrote a letter, copy of which I enclose[2], in which he distinctly stated
that he was against the Chief's policy (see marked passages). Under these
circumstances I think it absurd to send him the Chief's letter or the whip.
The rule I have laid down is that no whip should be sent when
   (a) a member has publicly stated that he is opposed to the Chief's policy.
   (b) a member has been repudiated by the recognised official local
Conservative organisation.
I think Winston's case comes under both heads.
   Of course if the Chief thinks my rule too stringent I will alter it in any way
he likes . . .
   Winston, who has squared the Oldham radicals will I think force a by-
election, and I am in communication with our leaders at Oldham as to
what steps we should take in that case. . . .

[1] John Satterfield Sandars (1853–1934), private secretary to A. J. Balfour 1892–1905.
[2] The enclosure could not be found among the Balfour papers.

Lord James of Hereford to WSC

24 January 1904   Breamore
                                                                   Salisbury

My dear Winston Churchill,

I only this morning received from Manners Sutton an account of the great success of your speech at Liverpool. He also tells me that you had a most remarkable reception. Well you have deserved it – and may you for your plucky good work receive much reward from the public.

What are you doing at Oldham? I see that crawly creature Wanklyn[1] has stated that you have 'reached the lowest depths of political ignominy.'

The brute has said worse things of me – and as I cannot make speeches I shall be very grateful to you if you will on my behalf as well as your own smash the wretched idiot to pieces.

Everything is going well – I see many signs that Chamberlain is losing ground.

I am coming to London tomorrow.

Yours
J of H

A. J. Balfour to WSC

TELEGRAM

25 January 1904   Whitehall

Have been making enquiries on subject matter of your letter and will write to you.

ARTHUR JAMES BALFOUR

Sir A. Acland-Hood to J. S. Sandars
(*Balfour Papers*)

EXTRACT

26 January [1904]   St Audries
                                                                   Bridgwater

. . . It seems to me that the answer to Winston lies in his own speech which I send you, especially in the marked passages which refer directly to the Prime Minister and his policy.

[1] James Leslie Wanklyn (1860–1919), Liberal Unionist MP for Bradford Central 1895–1906.

I think the Chief's proposed letter saying he gathered from his speeches that he was not prepared to give loyal, if independent, support to the Government is all right.

Unless I am completely misinformed W has already squared the Radicals not to oppose him at a by-election at Oldham. But I don't think it wise to let Winston know we have heard this. We must *not* oppose him at a by-election in any case, he will then look ridiculous. I don't like the idea of encouraging a Labour candidate.

I agree with the Chief's policy, that we should not drive out any member of the Party. . . .

It is really exactly in accordance with this that I have struck off J. Wilson,[1] J. W. Wilson,[2] Poynder and Winston (Bowles is a 3 yr old business). But if Winston is prepared to give loyal, though independent, support to the Government, by all means let him have our Whips.

I admit that G. Hamilton's case is difficult to distinguish from Winston's but he has been an old and tried Party servant and I rather think means retiring. While Winston is an active firebrand. . . .

W. Finnemore to Herbert Gladstone

25 January 1904   Birmingham Liberal Association
Copy

Dear Sir,

In your first letter you asked whether Mr W. Churchill would get 'the general support of the Liberals in the Division if he stood as a Free Trade Unionist with advanced views on Education and Temperance and I thought the correspondence would at any rate show that the Liberals had been anxious about him and would give him very considerable help.

Since getting your second letter I have carefully consulted different types of Liberals in the Division and others from whom we should expect to get valuable help in the fight and the feeling is unanimous that he would be far and away the very best candidate we could get. Once before the constituency he might rely on vigorous and enthusiastic support.

I have been asked to suggest whether Mr C could possibly stand as an

---

[1] John Wilson (1843–1918), Liberal Unionist MP for Falkirk Division of Burghs 1895–1906; baronet 1906.

[2] John William Wilson (1858–1932), Liberal Unionist MP for North Worcestershire 1895–1906; Liberal MP for N. Worcs 1906–22; PC 1911.

Independent Free Trader and I pass on the suggestion for what it is worth. I take it that if he stood as a 'Unionist' it would be necessary to get him brought before the constituency by some Committee of Unionists framed for the purpose as no Unionist organisation in Birmingham would as much as look at him.

As there seems not the slightest doubt as to the kind of support he would get from our people I shall be glad to know in what way you would like the promise of help to be made.

I am, Yours truly
W. FINNEMORE

WSC to Herbert Gladstone
(Herbert Gladstone Papers)

27 January 1904   105 Mount Street
Confidential

Dear Gladstone,
    I should like to know the result of your enquiries about Oldham. I have a letter ready written of resignation to the Chairman of the Conservative Association, & I should be stronger if they were compelled to invite me to continue. But I don't want to move till I am sure of my ground.

Yours sincerely
WINSTON S. CHURCHILL

Herbert Gladstone to WSC

28 January 1904   41 Parliament Street
Confidential

My dear Churchill,
    Emmott has not yet sent the report I asked for – I have written to him & will hurry it up.
    I send you a copy of a letter from Finnemore – it is clear you would have the hearty support of the Liberals.

Yours sincerely
H. J. GLADSTONE

Lord Hugh Cecil to WSC

31 January 1904   Hatfield

My dear Winston,

I don't take quite so gloomy a view. If we cannot win a division it matters only in a minor degree how many vote this way or that so long as (1) the Free Fooders remain really united against Joe (2) that whether by Balfourian or Liberal votes they get themselves back to Parlt at the election whenever it comes. These are the essential points.

Pray remember that conciliating pacific people is the proper sphere of tactics'. The thorough people will be right anyhow: management only helps with the others. I beseech you to say nothing 'disloyal' to the party at our F.F. meeting tomorrow – still less nothing friendly to Liberalism.

Yrs ever
HC

A. J. Balfour to WSC

1 February 1904   10 Downing Street

Dictated

My dr Winston Churchill,

I have enquired into the circumstances referred to in your letter of January 22nd, and I find that the authorities responsible for the issue of Circular Letters and Whips to Members of the Party were under the impression, derived apparently from some of your Speeches, that you did not desire any longer to count yourself as among the supporters of the present Government. I am delighted to gather from what you say that this is not the case.

This mistake, which has happily been remedied in time, appears not to have been without some plausible justification. A hasty reading, for example, of such a phrase as 'Thank God, we have an Opposition,' which occurs, I think, in one of your Speeches, is apt to lead to misunderstanding. It was rashly interpreted by some as meaning that the policy of the country would be safer in the hands of the Opposition than of the Government, a meaning clearly inconsistent with party loyalty. Obviously it is equally capable of a quite innocent construction. It might, for example, be a pious recognition of the fact that our heaviest trials are sometimes for our good. Or, again, it

might mean that a world in which everybody was agreed would be a
exceedingly tedious one: or, that an effective Opposition made party loyalty
burn more brightly.

There are, in short, countless interpretations, quite consistent with the
position which I understand to be yours, that, namely, of a loyal, though
independent supporter of the present Administration.

Exegesis is a harder task to perform in explaining, or explaining away, a
letter which you seem to have written to the electors of Ludlow, apparently
advising them to vote against the Unionist Candidate. But *you* are the best
judge of your own meanings; and I have therefore gladly given directions
that you are not to be deprived of the daily 'whip' which you desire to receive

Pray believe me, yours sincerely
ARTHUR JAMES BALFOUR

WSC to A. J. Balfour

2 February 1904   105 Mount Street

Dear Mr Balfour,

I expressed no desire in my letter of the 22nd to receive the Government
whips as you cannot fail to see if you read it through again. I neither invite
nor decline them. As a Unionist Free Trader I am opposed to what is
generally known as Home Rule & to Protection in every form. I canno
regard your administration as any satisfactory security against the latter &
on the whole the graver of these two dangers, & I am not quite sure that it
continuance is of any particular value to the cause of the Union. In these
circumstances I should leave you under a misconception if I offered you
assurances of support at the present time. My position is that of a whole
hearted opponent of Mr Chamberlain & his proposals & it is quite possible
that in such a position I may be forced into action which though no
necessarily contrary to the permanent interests of the Unionist party may be
incidentally hostile to the existing government. You must be the judge o
whether it is worthwhile to forward me the government whips & I shall
certainly not complain whatever your decision may be. But I thought the
Daily Telegraph newspaper rather an odd channel for such an announcement
and being curious to know whether this information was official I wrote to
you. I am only sorry you should have been troubled amid your other labour
to reply at such length.

Yours vy tly
WINSTON S. CHURCHILL

WSC to Sir A. Acland-Hood

4 February 1904   105 Mount Street

[Copy]

I forward you herewith (of course in confidence as I have not the Prime Minister's permission to make public his letter) a copy of the correspondence which I have had with Mr Balfour. Under these circumstances you will see that the enclosed announcement which has been widely copied by the Press, requires contradiction on your part.

Your very truly
[WINSTON S. CHURCHILL]

J. L. Wanklyn to WSC

5 February 1904   75 Chester Square

Sir,
    One of your friends opposite rudely interrupted Mr Wyndham in his speech yesterday afternoon and was told by the Speaker to resume his seat. When I called 'order, order', you had the impertinence to turn round and rebuke me for 'shouting people down'. Permit me to warn you that if I have any more impertinence from a young man like yourself, I shall know how to deal with it. Your conduct in using words like 'lie', 'quack', 'charlatan', 'weak', 'dangerous' of Mr Balfour and of Mr Chamberlain has disgusted most people, as, well as

Yours truly
JAMES LESLIE WANKLYN

J. S. Sandars to WSC

10 February 1904   10 Downing Street

Private

Dear Mr Churchill,
    Mr Balfour has no objection to the publication of the recent correspondence between you and himself.
    You will be glad to know that the doctor gives a rather better account of him this morning. Many thanks for yr kind enquiries.

Yrs very truly
J. S. SANDARS

PS I have asked for your letter of May last; but I rather think it was not filed. As you know, letters are received here in very large numbers and it is impossible to preserve them all.

Sir Bindon Blood to WSC

15 February 1904   Rawal Pindi
My dear Winston,
I see your name constantly in the papers, and I gather that you have more or less gone into opposition to Mr Chamberlain. I am afraid we in India are rather in the position of our friend Gallileo in regard to the 'Fiscal Controversy' – and perhaps, as far as I am concerned, it is my ignorance of the subject that leads me to think the fuss about it is a good deal a fuss about words – of about as much practical value as the famous quarrel as to the number of angels that could stand together on the point of a needle!
The 'Army of India' is still jogging along, and we have not had many reforms of late beyond a re-numbering of units that has not been a success, and the introduction of a new hat! I am afraid Lord K's schemes are too gaseous to be of much practical value, and meanwhile all steady progress is stopped pending the adoption (at the Greek Kalends I trust) of his counsels of perfection. The army of India is like a stout growing infant that wants its clothes altered progressively by people who understand it.
However, luckily the constitution of the infant is so sound that a little delay in the fitting, and even a little blundering, don't do much damage. . . .
Yours sincerely
B. Blood

Viscount Goschen to WSC

24 February 1904   38 Cadogan Square
Private

Dear Mr Churchill,
After the many months when we Free Fooders could not find platforms, there has come a time when the demand is so great that we can scarcely meet it. We old men cannot be so ubiquitous as you!
I have been very urgently approached by the Manchester Free Trade League to speak under their auspices, especially to the cotton [trade?] either in Manchester or in Blackburn, which they represent as specially important, and I have consented to give them the first chance, when I feel that the

time has come for me to be able to make another speech; so I fear I cannot undertake to speak at Oldham. It is capital that these non-party leagues seem to be springing up in so many directions.

From Rochdale John Bright's son[1] wrote to me that he had been elected president of a branch of the non-party Free Trade League in that town, and begged me to speak in a place which had been represented by Cobden and where John Bright had been born. But I had to plead my 'previous engagement'.

I am almost well again but my 'vocal chord' is not yet quite right. What a frightful mess in the H of C: almost incredible.

Yours sincerely
GOSCHEN

WSC to Sir Henry Campbell-Bannerman
(Campbell-Bannerman Papers)

3 March 1904   105 Mount Street

Dear Sir Henry Campbell-Bannerman,

I am vy much obliged to you for your friendly reference to my speech last night; & I particularly appreciate the high compliment you were good enough to pay it.[2]

Yours vy truly
WINSTON S. CHURCHILL

Lord James of Hereford to WSC
3 March 1904

My dear Winston Churchill,

Bravo – your speech was excellent last night. I always thought the Convention a most wanton sacrifice of the interests of the consumer. It was conceived in the interests of the West Indian people. They send us scarcely any sugar – and it would be a good bargain for us to pay them three times over for all they send rather than have the price raised all round.

You are doing magnificent work for Free-trade.

Yours
JAMES OF H

[1] John Albert Bright (1848–1924), Liberal Unionist MP for Central Birmingham 1889–95, Liberal MP for Oldham 1906–10.
[2] WSC had attacked the Brussels Sugar Convention in what Campbell-Bannerman called a 'brilliant' speech. 'The first part of that speech was the most sustained piece of irony I have ever heard in the House of Commons.'

Sir Frank Hollins[1] *to WSC*

5 March 1904   Greyfriars
                                                                Preston

Dear Mr Churchill,

While we thank you for letting us know so promptly the conclusion at which you have arrived we all regret very much that we are not to have you as our candidate.

It wd no doubt have proved a great advantage to us if we could have obtained your consent to stand for Preston but we are grateful for the consideration you have given to our wishes & we cordially hope that whatever constituency you decide to contest you may be successful.

Believe me to be
Yrs sincerely
FRANK HOLLINS

T. W. Killick[2] *to WSC*

8 March 1904   Free Trade League
                                                              Manchester

Dear Mr Churchill,

The people at Hyde are most anxious for you to address them on the Fiscal question. You have left such an impression upon them, that they say they want to hear you and nobody else. Knowing how hard you are working I really feel ashamed to pass on this request, but Lancashire regards you as the working leader of the Free Trade party and followers if troublesome are also a power.

Trusting you are recovering from your accident,

I am, yours very truly
T. W. KILLICK

The Hyde meeting would consist of about 2500 people.

---

[1] Frank Hollins (1843–1924), chairman of Horrockes, Crewdson and Company Limited, cotton spinners; baronet 1907.

[2] Thomas William Killick (b. 1849), member of Manchester Free Food League.

WSC to J. T. Travis-Clegg[1]

[11 March 1904]   105 Mount St

Dear Mr Travis-Clegg,
    I desire to draw your attention to the political situation revealed by the proceedings in the House of Commons last Wednesday. A Liberal member,[2] fortunate in the ballot, had placed the following motion upon the paper: – 'Fiscal policy – To call attention to the public utterances of Mr Chancellor of the Exchequer and other members of the Government on the fiscal question, and to move: That this House, noting the continued agitation in favour of preferential and Protective tariffs, which is encouraged by the language used by certain of his Majesty's Ministers, deems it necessary to express its condemnation of any such policy.'
    To this motion Mr Wharton,[3] a supporter of the Government and of Mr Balfour's Sheffield policy, proposed to move an amendment, the effect of which, if carried, would have made the resolution of the House read as follows: – 'That this House approves the explicit declarations of his Majesty's Ministers that their policy of fiscal reform does not include either a general system of Protection or preference based on the taxation of food.'
    When I read this amendment in Wednesday morning's newspapers, I frankly admit that I regarded it as a snare and a device. I noted especially that the words employed, 'A general system of Protection or preference based on the taxation of food,' were the very words that have figured in the speeches of Sir Michael Hicks-Beach and the Duke of Devonshire, and in the formal manifesto of the Unionist Free Food League, and I could not help thinking that they had been specially selected with the object of embarrassing and puzzling the members of that league, so that, if possible, they should be divided into an undecided flock, not able to agree on any course of action, and a few 'extremists,' whom it would be easy for the party Press and the party machine to discredit and destroy. I assumed that tariff reformers would be quite prepared to give a formal and verbal assent to a Parliamentary manœuvre, the tactical advantage of which was self-evident. Had I known then what I know now I would most certainly have undertaken to support Mr Wharton. It appears that his amendment was drawn up in consultation with the party officials, it was placed upon the notice paper with the consent and at the desire of the Prime Minister, and the Protectionists, so far from being parties to an elaborate strategem, were, in fact, affronted and dismayed by its terms.

[1] Published in the Eastern Daily Press, 12 March 1904.
[2] Duncan Vernon Pirie (1858–1931), Liberal MP for Aberdeen North 1896–1918.
[3] John Lloyd Wharton (1837–1912), Conservative MP for Ripon 1886–1906, Durham 1871–4; PC 1897.

So that we have it placed on record, for the very first time and in the clearest possible manner, that Mr Balfour is conscientiously opposed either to a 'general Protective tariff or to preference based upon taxation of food,' and we know that he desired that the House of Commons should deliberately approve his opposition to both these grave departures.

We know at last what are his own convictions in this great dispute, and what he would like the convictions of his party to be. When we look back on the political strife of the last eight months, on the resignations of Ministers, on the distractions of party organisations, on the separation from each other of old friends and not unworthy comrades, what is there more grim and melancholy than this belated declaration?

But I invite you to observe the consequences. The Protectionist party, to the number of 110, assembled, in the absence of Mr Chamberlain, under Mr Chaplin's leadership in a committee-room, and there and then, with the connivance – as I am prepared to assert – if not, indeed, at the instigation of the present Chancellor of the Exchequer, proceeded to dictate an ultimatum to the 'official' leader of the Conservative party. No compromise, no equivocation, was to be tolerated. The Wharton amendment must be withdrawn forthwith, or they would turn the Government out. No considerations of 'permanent interests of the party,' of 'personal loyalty to Mr Balfour, of 'the probable return of a Home Rule Government to power,' or of the duty of supporting the King's executive in the critical and momentous condition of foreign affairs, all of which we Free Traders are told daily in the newspapers ought to outweigh all fiscal opinions, at this juncture restrained these tariff gentlemen. So long as they had their way, their 'loyalty' would be an example to all, but let them be crossed!

The result is known to you. Face to face with immediate ruin, Mr Balfour surrendered. The Government, which at 4 pm was resolved to support a Free Trade declaration, opposed in words and spirit both to 'a general system of Protection or preference based on the taxation of food', was at 5.15 resolved to do nothing of the kind, and was at midnight appealing to its followers to meet with a direct negative Mr Pirie's proposal to condemn a policy of preferential or protective tariffs. And this last was solemnly rejected by a majority of 46.

I ask you to consider the conclusions which follow from all this.

(1) The Protectionist Party, although they vaunt their loyalty to Mr Balfour, are perfectly ready to turn him out – even at the risk of putting in a Home Rule Government, and all that sort of thing – the moment he fails to toe their line.

(2) The Chancellor of the Exchequer retains office in Mr Balfour's Administration, although he does not agree with its policy, and although willing

to acquiesce in the expulsion from Parliament of such uncompromising Conservatives as Lord George Hamilton and Lord Hugh Cecil, on the grounds of their 'disloyalty,' is himself ready, when occasion arises, to act against the Prime Minister, and to forward the interests and aspirations of another leader – not the leader of the Conservative party, and who has, in fact left the Government on account of disagreement with it.

(3) The Prime Minister, his chief Whip, and other official leaders of the party believe that 'a general Protective tariff and preference resting on the taxation of food' would be harmful to the public welfare, and they have publicly invited the House of Commons to join with them in the assertion of their belief.

But (4) they are not prepared to maintain their convictions at the peril of an adverse vote, and rather than incur one, they are willing deliberately to deny them.

And (5) under the stress of party exigencies the Prime Minister is prepared to exclude from his Cabinet, from the Conservative party – if possible from public life altogether – those whose Free Trade convictions he shared, in order to retain the support of those from whose Protectionist convictions he profoundly dissents.

When he had the power to combat Protection he had not the will. Now he has the will he has no longer the power.

I hope you will bring these facts to the notice of the Conservative Association. If in the next few months an unprecedented electoral disaster should overwhelm the Conservative party, a consideration of all these things will help to explain how that powerful confederation of men and ideas which the genius of Lord Beaconsfield, the energies of Lord Randolph Churchill, and the statecraft of Lord Salisbury laboriously created, was in eight months of folly negligently cast away.

Sincerely yours
WINSTON CHURCHILL

WSC to J. Kemp Welch[1]

15 March 1904   105 Mount Street

[Copy]

My dear Sir,

I am sorry not to be with you at Weybridge to-night to support Lord Hugh Cecil in the efforts he is making to preserve the Free Trade character of the

[1] James Kemp Welch (b. 1850), a leading liberal in Weybridge.

Conservative Party. Free Trade will not be safe unless both the great parties in the State are made to feel that Protection will be deeply injurious to their party fortunes as well as to the greater interests of the country. As a conservative of unimpeachable orthodoxy Lord Hugh Cecil naturally exerts a greater influence upon the present controversy than any Liberal however wholehearted. No one is better qualified to lift the minds of the people to the understanding of these great moral causes which underlie the doctrines of Free Exchange, & which strikingly contrast with the selfish, sordid materialism of the modern Protectionist. No one could bring more powerful aid to a League whose motto might well be 'Justice to all – Preference to none!'

Yours faithfully
WINSTON S. CHURCHILL

Reginald Lucas[1] to WSC

16 March 1904   House of Commons Library

My dear Churchill,

I dont think my position is quite as illogical as you think.

I agreed to support the present avowed policy of the Government: therefore I do so; (as Sir M Beach does).

But I foresee that this is not the end of the matter, & I do not intend to go further. At the same time I do not, upon other grounds, wish to break up the Party & I therefore prefer to be out of politics for the present. The difference between us seems to be that I would preserve the Party, if it be possible, in spite of fiscal affairs; & you would not.

Yrs sincerely
R. LUCAS

WSC to J. T. Travis-Clegg

17 March 1904   House of Commons

[Copy]

My dear Travis-Clegg,

The time is now approaching when I should hold my Annual meeting & I am anxious that a date should be fixed because I have several announcements of some importance to myself at least to make to my constituents. I would suggest that some day in the first fortnight after the Easter holidays might afford a convenient opportunity. I should be glad if you would

---

[1] Reginald Jaffray Lucas (1865–1914). Conservative MP for Portsmouth 1900–6.

preside at the meeting & although like all our meetings it must be open to the public generally, I hope it will be possible to make arrangements by ticket or otherwise to secure that any Unionist or conservative electors who may desire to attend shall be afforded special facilities.

Yours sincerely
WINSTON S. CHURCHILL

WSC to ?

23 March 1904   105 Mount Street
[Copy]

Dear Sir,
    I have to acknowledge the receipt of your letter.
    I thought it my duty to vote against the proposal of the Govt to introduce Chinese Labour into the Transvaal. 1st, because I think that the conditions prescribed by the Ordnance must inevitably make that debased labour, that is, labour with no hope of advance for skill or thrift, and no right to share in the general life of the country to whose welfare it contributes. 2ndly, because no case, to my mind, of real necessity has been shown. The shortage of black labour is largely due to the temporary dislocation of the war and to the unwise act of the mine owners in lowering wages. The cost of governing the country is now twice what it was under President Kruger. 3rdly, I am not satisfied that even the Transvaal is willing to approve of the experiment and it is quite clear that South Africa as a whole is hostile. If the Transvaal were a self-governing Colony we should have no locus to interfere but as it is, we are absolutely responsible; and it is a grave thing to commit the whole of South Africa to this strange and indefinite departure while they are, so to speak, in a tutelary state under our charge. Fourthly, when I think of the sacrifices which the working classes in this country and our Colonial fellow subjects in Australia and New Zealand have made, in the late war, I think that their opinion ought also to be taken into account.

Lord Hugh Cecil to WSC

24 March [1904]

My dear Winston
    Do write to me what is going on.
    I am all in favour of helping Jack; – if it were any use I would write him a

letter or even drag my infirm body to his lonely island to make a speech. But probably in view of Nonconformist feeling he is better without me – Moreover our disagreement over Chinese labour might be awkward. But pray write.

Yours

HC

WSC to Lord Hugh Cecil
(*Quickswood Papers*)

EXTRACT

26 March 1904   105 Mount Street

Private

My dear Linky,

I think on the whole everything is shaping satisfactorily as to the Isle of Wight election. We had a Meeting of the Executive on Wednesday. About fifteen attended. Yerburgh had written to say that he would resign if Seely were supported in any way by the League. Beach supported by Freddy Smith[1] and Bond,[2] were against helping him in any way. Fisher and Victor Lytton declined to express an opinion until they knew by what candidates he was opposed. Edgar Vincent was doubtful, but Ritchie in the chair, self, Elliot, Gorst, Austin Taylor[3] and one or two others were all for helping him in every way. We carried a resolution in favour of supporting him by about 10 to 5 and have referred it to a meeting of the whole League which was summoned for Tuesday but has since been declared 'off', because as the House rises on Tuesday, few members of Parliament would attend and probably only a few would turn up who did not know the whole facts of the case. I thought it very important while the question of candidates and opposition must be pending, that he should make a decided pronouncement and I therefore pressed that a statement should be made at once to the newspapers on these grounds. This was agreed to. I then urged that we should not meet again to consider the question until we had the whole facts of the Election before us, and had an opportunity of learning the opinion of the Duke of Devonshire. The object of this was to prevent the decision from being reversed until at any rate Jack had got as much good out of it

[1] William Frederick Danvers Smith (1868–1928), Conservative MP for Strand 1891–1910; son of W. H. Smith; succeeded as 2nd Viscount Hambleden 1913.
[2] Edward Bond (1844–1920), Conservative MP for East Nottingham, 1895–1906.
[3] Austin Taylor (1858–1953), Liberal MP for East Toxteth 1902–10; steamship owner.

as possible. This is why I am glad the meeting is cancelled as the Executive's decision holds good.

I do not think myself that the League will take any active *part*, and any attempt to force them to do so, would only result in disruption. Beach was very unhappy indeed and I think he finds his position more difficult every day.

I hope you liked Jack's address. He was very tractable in the matter. His own idea was to fight on Chinese Labour and make Free Trade quite a subsidiary issue. But he yielded very readily to representations, and in the end let me draw up the Address for him which he has adopted practically *en bloc*. I think you will probably approve of the phrasing of the first part, and perhaps the relegation of Chinese Labour to an admittedly subordinate place will remove some of the objections which the timid Leaguers entertained towards supporting him.

I was delighted to get your letter and to know you feel able to support him. Whether the Nonconformists would be offended is a matter which will have to be very carefully considered. I am writing to Jack by this post and he will let you know. I think in any case it would be a good thing to send him a letter. I am not sure that you need undertake the labour of journeying all down there. I think he wants me to go and address his opening meeting at Newport on Wednesday and I propose to stay there Thursday, returning to Blenheim for Easter. The Tuesday after Easter Monday I shall go to the Isle of Wight for three days and I would suggest that we should meet at Blenheim on Friday, the 8th April.

I think the Liberals have behaved very well about Seely. Lloyd George wrote a strong private letter to be read at their Meeting today and John Burns has promised to go and speak for him whatever the decision may be. Personally, I should not at all object to a Liberal split and from many points of view it would be much better that he should get in in spite of an extreme Tariff Reformer and a rabid Nonconformist. But the danger of such a situation would be very great.

I had a good Meeting last night at Huntingdon where there were three or four Liberal candidates for the Eastern counties. Three of these were extremely nice young gentlemen, very smart and sensible and outspoken Liberal Imperialists. They spoke of CB with undisguised contempt and seem to regard a Spencer-Bannerman administration as the greatest disaster that could overtake the country. They told me that there are 80 Liberal Leaguers standing at next election, and as they have so much of the money they have got an undue proportion of good seats.

What a struggle it will all be!

Lord R sent for me before he started and I found him very frank and more friendly than ever before. *Secret.* He told me positively that he would not join a CB – Spencer Govt: & that he had conveyed to the King his own inability to form one & had recommended HM to send for Spencer, & CB jointly in the event of a change. He thought the outlook vy obscure & said that nearly all the people who were worth anything were getting into impossible relations with either party – or words to that effect.

I think I shall have a go at Arthur Balfour on Tuesday on the adjournment and ask him a quantity of tiresome questions upon his fiscal views. I shall try to ridicule his retaliation plan and will ask him again and again whether he is in favour of a 10 per cent *ad valorem* duty.

I have practically made up my mind to accept an invitation which has reached me from Central Manchester. The chairman of the Association called upon me at the House of Commons last Wednesday and made me offers of a kind which it would be impossible to refuse. The proposal is that I should be brought forward as a special candidate of the Free Trade League. I am to call myself a Free Trader without any qualifications of party. The Liberal organisation, which is very well organised, will announce in the first instance that it will not oppose my candidature, but as the contest proceeds, they will range themselves more and more on my side and I am to have the full force of their machinery in the campaign. Mr Lamb[1] (the Chairman) pointed out to me that my return for the premier constituency or blue ribbon of Lancashire would be a great event and he has told me that the Liberals thought that the effect of my campaign would be felt in all the nine seats of Manchester and in the dozen constituencies which cluster round it.

They wanted someone to reply from day to day during the election to the speeches which AB would be making and when you consider that there is no Free Trade politician of the smallest eminence in Lancashire you will see for yourself the possibilities which it offers. Sir W. Houldsworth[2] has declared himself a 'whole hogger' and has consented to become President of the local Branch of the Tariff Reform League. But it is thought that he may retire at the election and accept a peerage. His majority is 1,200 odd, but it was won against a Roman Catholic who fought under depressing conditions. The seat costs little to fight and less to hold. Herbert Gladstone was most enthusiastic and implored me not to neglect this great chance and I am therefore dismissing Sheffield and I shall say 'No' to the Deputation from Central Birmingham which is coming here this afternoon. I am rather inclined to peeve at having so many suitors and I shall look forward to unfurling the banner of Cobden and Bright in the Free Trade Hall.

[1] Samuel Lamb, Chairman of Central Manchester Liberal Association.

[2] William Henry Houldsworth (1834–1917), Conservative MP for North-West Manchester 1883–1906; baronet 1887.

What a long letter! I met Cranborne today who said you were not to waste your strength addressing 'little potty meetings.'

Yours ever

W

Arthur D. Elliot to WSC

Friday [1904]   House of Commons

Private

My dear Churchill,

I hear a rumour that you are seriously thinking of taking your seat, perhaps even on Monday, on to the other side of the House. I do hope you will consider this step in all its aspects before you take it. It seems to me that by taking this line you give a victory to those who want to drive you out. In the country by declaring yourself a Free Trader, and that Free Trade is *the* question of the day, and that you will welcome support from whatever side it may come, you took firm ground. No one has a right to say that in so doing you have ceased to be a Conservative. If you transfer yourself across the floor, you shew not merely that you mean to assert independence but that you mean to follow Liberal leadership; and what this means at the present time no one can tell! At all events, if you ultimately do go over, why not wait till the end of the session, or the Parliament, and let things develop a little?

What I think is wanted more than anything else at present is a strong Free Trade Unionist body to take up the fighting which the F.F. League is too half-hearted to carry on. I know Gorst thinks as I do about the impolicy of the step of your crossing the floor. I have not talked about the thing at all except to him and H. Cecil.

Of course it is not my business to advise or urge you; but I should be very sorry if what seems to me to be a rash proceeding should injure your position in the Free Trade cause.

Believe me, Yours ever

ARTHUR D. ELLIOT

26 March 1904

WSC to Samuel Lamb

[Copy]   105 Mount Street

Dear Mr Lamb,

I have carefully considered the proposal which you were good enough to make to me on Wednesday and I have consulted with Mr Herbert Gladstone upon it. You have no doubt noticed that I have already given votes against Chinese Labour and in favour of the principles of Mr Trevelyan's Bill on Land Values and on Mr Shackleton's Bill on Trade Disputes. Upon the Licensing Question my position may be defined as follows: – I should oppose anything calculated to interfere with the discretion of the magistrates; but I am in favour of reasonable compensation being paid where deprivation occurs without fault committed, provided always that no charge is thrown upon public funds. The questions of Disestablishment and Disendowment to which you referred are not now before the country and cannot be among the issues at the next Election. I do not pretend to have arrived at any final opinions on these very grave subjects and I am not prepared to make any definite declaration upon them. The Education Question alone remains. I admit the urgent need of amending the Education Act and I should be prepared to recognise the principles of popular control in non-provided schools and the abolition of religious tests for teachers. How far and how thoroughly these principles should be applied must be determined by the new parliament. I do not expect that this question would cause me any serious difficulty in the conduct of such an election as you have suggested, provided there was a general disposition on the part of the Liberal leaders in the constituency to minimise points of difference and to discuss the matter with good will.

I shall endeavour myself to select the ground upon which the contest will be fought. Four main issues stand clearly out. First: Free Trade. Secondly: Retrenchment and the reorganisation of our finance upon strict Gladstonian principles. Thirdly: a definite reduction in the cost and size both of the Army and the Navy. Fourthly: a complete re-organisation of the Army System. Upon all these heads there is ample room not only for a positive policy of proposal and aspiration, but also for a comprehensive indictment of the conduct of the Government.

I have written these few lines at your request in order that you may place your colleagues in possession of the outline of our conversation on Wednesday last.

Yours very truly
[WINSTON S. CHURCHILL]

Lord Hugh Cecil to WSC

27 March 1904

My dear Winston,

I am afraid I think you made a mistake. In the abstract it is quite true I am in favour of the Free Food League supporting Jack. But I don't think it at all wise to have carried the matter by a majority in the teeth of a strong opposition led by Beach. There are many things in themselves desirable which are not desirable if they involve quarrelling with a large section of your supporters. And I do not see that the support of the League is of much – scarcely of any – help to Jack. If Ritchie would write a letter for him or speak for him that no doubt would be useful: but what influence has the League *as a body* in the Isle of Wight? Perhaps when the meeting was held it might have been awkward not to support Jack – for the Press might have got hold of the refusal, but you ought not to have had the meeting unless you were pretty sure of carrying everyone with you. You gained extremely little – for all the effective things could be done by individual members – & perhaps you risked a good deal. I think it may be laid down that the occasion must be a very rare & peculiar one for the Free Food League wisely to do anything by a majority. That is ro say if the minority are very strong & keen the majority should give way & nothing should be done. Of course this means the League can do very little – but that is a truth which I have long been ready to accept – & I thought you had too. It is mainly a 'bogey' – apart from the humble functions of literature & speakers. Perhaps in the next Parlt it may do more. But I incline to think the party will drop 'fiscal reform' after the election. They seem to me very sick of it now.

I will come to Blenheim on the 8th.

Yrs H C

Central Manchester sounds excellent. Don't be too violent on Tuesday. Take a reasonable position & argue it persistently.

WSC to Lord Hugh Cecil
(*Quickswood Papers*)

30 March 1904   105 Mount Street

My dear Linky,

No harm has been done; and in any case I did not intend to press the matter at the General Meeting to the verge of breaking up the League. But I thought it most important to declare ourselves upon his side formally while the selection of candidates was still uncertain, and in view of what has since occurred, I do not think that I was wrong. There is no possibility of a Government Candidate coming forward so all thorny questions connected with the attitude of the League automatically disappear. Beach himself said that he would be willing to use the League to support Seely against a Tariff Reformer should such a one come forward. But that too is unlikely.

I took your advice as to my speech in the House yesterday and couched it in a moderate and sorrowful vein, but as you have probably seen, I was the object of a very unpleasant and disconcerting demonstration. I would far rather have been rudely interrupted for I might have placated that kind of opposition, or at the worst, laughed at it. But the feeling of the whole audience melting behind one and being left with crowded Liberal Benches and an absolutely empty Government side was most disquieting, and it was only by a considerable effort that I forced myself to proceed to the end of my remarks. I was very sorry that A. Balfour went out the moment I had begun to speak, because my whole speech was intended to elicit information from him and of course it lost its point in his absence.

Banbury[1] made himself particularly forward, and with the aid of two or three of that kidney, cleared everybody out in a very short time. I have wondered very much whether this incident ought not to make me reconsider my position about resigning and I have been very nearly taking the plunge all the morning, but I have now decided to wait and see whether my people at Oldham take any action upon what is, after all, the very explicit statement I made last night. Brodrick was very indignant with what occurred and took occasion to come and express his regret to me. I thought it very nice of him.

I will tell Marlborough to expect you at Blenheim on the 8th.

Secret

G. Wyndham supped with me last night & was (in the course of three hours!) vy communicative. Evidently the Budget is a most critical affair. The want of money is imperative. What to do? Sinking Fund raiding destroys credit necessary to float Land Bill loans etc. Income Tax infuriates Tories. Nothing else will have higher [?] I should not be surprised if the Govt wd not propose Corn (as you were) or manufactured articles for revenue! This will be a crisis with a vengeance.

Yours ever
W

Don't I write you amiable letters?

On 29 March 1904 WSC, speaking in the House of Commons, said that the public had a right to know what public men thought on public questions. He had hardly begun speaking when A. J. Balfour rose and left the House, followed by all the other Conservative Ministers who were present. They in their turn were followed by seventy or eighty Conservative MPs, leaving WSC with an audience of less than a dozen Conservatives, mostly Free Traders like himself. At the end of his speech, which was listened to by an almost entirely Liberal House, Herbert Gladstone walked over to him and offered him reparation for the insult; and when he sat down he was loudly cheered by Liberal MPs.

---

[1] Frederick George Banbury (1850–1936), Conservative MP Peckham Division, Camberwell, 1892–1906, City of London 1906–24; baronet 1902; PC 1916; Baron Banbury of Southam 1924.

Master of Elibank[1] to WSC

EXTRACT

30 March 1904   House of Commons

Dear Churchill,
    One line to say how much I – in common with very many others –
resented the abominable rudeness with which you were treated in the House
yesterday. . . .
    Your speech was splendid & unanswerable.
    Don't trouble to answer this.

                                                Yours truly
                                    ALEXANDER O. MURRAY

WSC to Herbert Gladstone
(Herbert Gladstone Papers)

EXTRACT

30 March 1904   105 Mount Street
Confidential

My dear Gladstone,
    . . . I seriously considered resigning my seat after what happened last night;
but I have decided to leave the Oldham Conservatives to make up their
minds upon my vy explicit statements in the House.
    I hope you are having a pleasant holiday.

                                                Yours sincerely
                                    WINSTON S. CHURCHILL

WSC to Lord Hugh Cecil
(Quickswood Papers)

31 March 1904   Blenheim

My dear Linky,
    Marlborough expects you here on the 8th. Will you let him know your
train.

---

[1] Alexander William Charles Oliphant Murray (1870–1920), Liberal MP 1900–12;
Parliamentary Secretary to Treasury 1910–12; Scottish Liberal Whip 1906–10; Chief
Liberal Whip 1909–12; eldest son of 1st Viscount and 10th Baron Elibank; PC 1911; Baron
Murray of Elibank 1912.

I am much disturbed by the news from Tibet.[1] Surely it is vy wicked to do such things. Absolute contempt for the rights of others must be wrong. Are there any people in the world so mean-spirited as not to resist under the circumstances to which these poor Tibetans have been subjected. It has been their land for centuries, and although they are only Asiatics 'liberty' & 'home' mean something to them. That such an event should be greeted with a howl of ferocious triumph by Press & Party must be an evil portent.

I am still uncertain what to do about Oldham. Write to me.

Yours ever
W

Lord James of Hereford to WSC

31 March 1904   Breamore
                                                       Salisbury

My dear Winston Churchill

What a stupid lot these Protectionists are! Their treatment of you and Seely is not only contemptible – but has a strain of cowardly snobbishness in it. You certainly will find yourself more popular than ever in the country.

When the General Election comes these gentlemen will have a rough awakening.

Yours
JAMES OF H

T. W. Gibson Bowles to WSC

31 March 1904   Wilbury
                                                       Salisbury

My dear Churchill,

One word of sympathy – or perhaps it ought to be of congratulation – on the walking-out demonstration against you.

There seems to be a settled plan, on the part of the sons of Belial of the back benches, to browbeat all Free-Fooders and Free-Labourers – Four or

---

[1] A British mission, 3000 strong, under the command of Col F. E. Younghusband, had been sent by the Viceroy of India in 1903 to the Tibetan border to negotiate various boundary and trade disputes between Tibet & Sikkim. When the Tibetan and Chinese negotiators failed to appear, the mission moved on to Lhasa. When the mission reached the village of Guru on March 29, a clash occurred as a result of a misunderstanding, and over six hundred of the fifteen hundred Tibetan soldiers were killed. There were no British deaths. Younghusband himself described it as: 'a loathsome sight . . . I could not but be disgusted at the sight of those poor wretched peasants mowed down by our rifles and Maxims'.

five of the prize idiots walked out processionally during my little speech on the Address; then came the howling down of Seely; and now your adventure.

I really think we shall have to organize reprisals – not necessarily of the same kind. The rules of the House afford great resources to 3 or 4 who will attend and work together.

Faithfully yours
T. W. GIBSON BOWLES

Jack Seely to WSC

EXTRACT

1 April 1904

Totland Bay Hotel
Isle of Wight

My dear Winston

Many thanks for your letter.

Sheffield would certainly have merits – leave it open if you can until after Easter, when we can decide – of course it is possible Sheffield might not accept me, saying if they can't have you as a candidate they must have an out and out Radical. . . .

What asses these Tories are – walking out in a body when you began to speak has done them more harm than all their other follies put together – they spend their time in running away.

Some wag has billed the Isle of Wight with a placard 'Wanted a strong protectionist, in favour of Chinese Labour, to contest the Isle of Wight in the Conservative interest. Apply to the Head Quarters of the above party in London or at Ryde.' The same legend is displayed by Sandwich-men in different towns, Newport principally.

Of course, if there is no contest, as is probable though not certain, it will have certain merits – a saving of £1200 for one thing. It is very good of you to say you hold yourself ready to come and help if there is a fight – Wednesday is the nomination and I will telegraph to you at Blenheim in any case.

I have brought my wife here, because there is scarlet fever at Brooke village, and the drains are up at my house in Ryde – my wife is better, but she has been very ill – she sends you her kind regards.

Take care of yourself, and keep very fit – there is a great time coming.

Yours ever
JACK SEELY

Ivor Guest to WSC

EXTRACT

2 April 1904   Bedford House
                                                                        Brighton

Dear Winston,

... I don't suppose that you feel any special goodwill towards the Tory Party
just at present and how will that determine your attitude for election
purposes?

It was a most insulting discreditable 'lower boy' proceeding and only
indicates that noise and boycott comprises the whole of their argumentative
stock in trade.

Was AJB's exit intentional? Hugh Cecil's defence is fine and courageous
and will I think make them sick and ashamed.

This introduction of the personal attitude towards revered leaders is very
interesting. What have political convictions to do with personal relations or
vice versa.

The whole incident is nothing but an explosion of envy and malice and
that has always a boomerang tendency.

Anyhow it is proof that they recognise that it is you who has been mainly
instrumental in scotching their damned protection.

                                                                Yours ever
                                                                    IVOR

Let me know about next week.

WSC to J. T. Travis-Clegg[1]

3 April 1904   105 Mount Street

Dear Mr Travis-Clegg,

In accordance with my speech last October in the Unity-hall I have tried,
so far as greater considerations would allow, not to provoke division in the
Conservative party in Oldham or to impair the efficiency of its organization.
My private concern in the future representation of that borough is not large,
and I did not wish, if it could be avoided, to settle a difference of public
policy by a local quarrel which would probably leave party dissension and
lasting disagreements behind. I resolved, therefore, that unless my effective
action as a free-trader was impaired I would not upon my own initiative

[1] Published in *The Times* 9 April 1904.

force a by-election upon the constituency; I do not feel that that determination ought to be departed from for any reasons personal to me. But the general Parliamentary situation compels me pointedly to draw the attention of your committee to my statement in the House of Commons on March 29, when I declared myself ready to resign my seat and submit myself to re-election. I wish to deal fairly by the Oldham Conservative Association, neither thrusting a contest upon them against their will nor declining a contest if they desire one. The responsibility for decision shall rest with them, and I shall be glad to know within a reasonable time what that decision may be. If your committee wish for an appeal to the electors, may I venture to hope that they will let me know before Parliament reassembles in order that the necessary formalities may be complied with and the writ issued with all convenient speed?

Yours sincerely
WINSTON S. CHURCHILL

WSC to Lord Hugh Cecil
(Quickswood Papers)

3 April 1904　　　　　　　　　　　　　　　　　　　　　Blenheim

My dear Linky,

I appreciated your letter vy much not only because of its use to me publicly, but because I regard you as a person of whose good opinion I am ambitious. I am struck by the peculiar tactical strength of our combination, wh is greater because we differ than it would be if we were absolutely agreed. The Liberal party is anxious to get me. The Conservatives are anxious to retain you. I help to make the Unionist Free Traders popular with the Opposition. You preserve their claims upon the Government. If we can hold together notwithstanding we shall do more to upset Chamberlain than by any joint action of a simple character however vigorous.

I shall certainly take no part in the correspondence in *The Times*, & never thought of doing so.[1] I have written a temperate letter to my constituents pressing them to decide whether they will have an election or not. I expect they will say 'no'. The local conditions are now particularly favourable.

I hope you will come here on Friday. Marlborough will be disappointed if you don't. We are practically only family. The duchess' illness is not serious but the special treatment she is receiving from a French specialist could not be interrupted. She particularly desired the party to go on.

Yours ever
W

---

[1] Letters had been published expressing the view that WSC should resign.

F. Herbert Stead[1] to WSC

7 April 1904   29 Grosvenor Park

Sir,

As it was to you we owed the pleasure and honour of Major Seely's acquaintance, and as it was at Browning Hall that the first public protest was raised against the introduction of Chinese Labour into South Africa – on the evening when Major Seely was present – I trust you will permit me to offer you our sincerest congratulations on the unopposed return of Major Seely. It is a victory in which, I doubt not, you feel a very deep personal participation. The testing ordeal through which both of you have passed has marked you out more than ever conspicuously for leadership of the nation in times of strain and change. It is such a relief and strength to the people to find vertebrate statesmen.

Very sincerely yours
F. HERBERT STEAD

The Times

9 April 1904

Mr Churchill has, we understand, been approached by the Liberals of North-West Manchester with a view to his becoming their candidate in opposition to Sir William Houldsworth, MP, at the next election. . . . The leaders of the Liberal party in the division have been in communication with Mr Churchill for some time, but up to the present he has not given a definite answer. It is evident that the Liberals of the division are determined to confine their appeal to the electorate to the free trade and Chinese labour questions, as it is understood that Mr Churchill's attitude on these questions alone justify them in inviting him to become Sir William Houldsworth's opponent.

WSC to Sir Michael Hicks Beach
(St. Aldwyn Papers)

9 April 1904   Blenheim

My dear Sir Michael,

I feel I must write you a few lines to say with what profound regret & misgiving I have read of your intention to withdraw from public life. I do

---

[1] Francis Herbert Stead (1857–1928), Warden of the Robert Browning Settlement, Walworth; Assistant Editor, *Review of Reviews*; Congregational minister and campaigner for Old Age Pensions.

not doubt that you have most carefully considered the whole position &
that your decision to retire from what has, I fear, lately become a thankless
& ungrateful task is not lightly to be altered. But I shall still hope that the
course of public events between this & the general election may force you
to remain. I do not know who will fill your place & arrest Chamberlain's
influence from *inside* the Conservative party. Some of us have had to take a
different line & I don't think you will find it in your heart to blame us. But
I can assure you that I at any rate will always feel nothing but the most
sincere gratitude to you for the unvarying kindness you have shown me
during my first years in the House of Commons. If your influence had
prevailed in the councils of our party I might easily have continued an
active worker for it, instead of becoming a declared opponent; and I think
the same may be said of several other young men who are now altogether
alienated.

Yours vy sincerely
WINSTON S. CHURCHILL

Sir Michael Hicks Beach to WSC

12 April 1904   House of Commons

My dear Churchill,
    Many thanks for your kind letter. I did not arrive at the decision to retire
without long and careful reflection. My constituents would, I have no doubt,
have returned me again. But the fate of the Wharton amendment,[1] as well
as other things, convinced me that my party will, in the next House of
Commons, be a Protectionist party – and it would be odious to me to sit
here under such conditions. I am sorry that you, and others, are, as you say,
now altogether alienated: but I have never blamed you, and do not do so
now. Only I hope, for your own sake as well as your father's, that you will
remember that these things are essential to real Parliamentary success: first,
good health: second, sticking to one side or the other. A Tory may get on
admirably, who is more Tory than the Tories: or a Radical, who is more

---

[1] On 9 March Mr J. Wharton, Unionist Member for Ripon, put forward an amendment
'approving the explicit declaration of the Government that their policy of fiscal reform does
not include either a general system of Protection or Preference based on the taxation of food'.
Mr Wharton was under the impression that it had the support of the Treasury Bench, for its
phraseology, as *The Times* Lobby correspondent reported, 'was obviously chosen with the
object of putting the free-fooders in a quandary'. But it soon emerged that many of the Tariff
Reformers regarded it as an attack on Mr Chamberlain's policy; and at a hurried meeting of
112 Unionist members it was decided that the amendment should be withdrawn as it was
likely to 'seriously jeopardise the position of the Government'.

Radical than the Radicals: but Radical tendencies in a Tory, or Tory tendencies in a Radical, however agreeable to the conscience, handicap a man severely on the run.

Yours sincerely

M. HICKS BEACH

WSC to A. J. Balfour

12 April 1904   105 Mount Street

Not to go

Dear Mr Balfour,

I find it suggested that I had some objection to the publication of our correspondence at the beginning of the session. My real reason for not availing myself of your permission to print it was that you were ill & absent & could not read or receive the letter with which it closed. But I entirely sympathise with the desire of some of your official friends that your clever & amusing contribution should not be lost to the public eye; & if still agreeable to you I will send the correspondence to the newspapers without delay.

Yours vy truly

WINSTON S. CHURCHILL

Sir A. Acland-Hood to WSC

12 April 1904   12 Downing Street

Private

My dear Churchill,

I did not repeat our conversation of the 29th ult to the *Daily Telegraph* or any pressman, but I am well aware that it was criticised, as some of our men who were in the Aye Lobby at the time came to me afterwards and spoke about it. Nor did I comment to the Press one word about your correspondence with the Prime Minister earlier in the session.

I was very much occupied at that time with important business and though I saw the correspondence I should now say, from my recollection of it, that you were wise not to publish it.

But you may be assured that I never communicate any conversation I have with members either to the Press or to other members of the House, except when I am requested by members to convey their views to the Prime Minister.

Yours sincerely

A. ACLAND-HOOD

T. W. Killick to WSC

EXTRACT

13 April 1904   Free Trade League
Private   Manchester

Dear Mr Churchill,

Mr Garnett has sent me your letter of yesterday.

The Free Trade League are unanimous in the desire that you should be the Free Trade candidate for North West Manchester. But the League have to consider their influence in other constituencies, and this depends entirely on their strictly non-party character. . . . If you come to an understanding with the Association, the League will at once consult with you and the Assn as to the best way in which poll the Unionist and Labour votes for you. . . .

The Labour party welcomes your prospective candidature, but Kelley (candidate for SW M'chester) and Harker (candidate for NE M'chester) could not join the deputation, fearing trouble if they did so with some of their supporters on account of some position you once took up regarding Taff Vale, or some similar case. If you can now satisfy our Labour friends on this point they will be your enthusiastic supporters.[1] . . .

Yours very truly
T. W. KILLICK

Sir Henry Campbell-Bannerman to WSC

14 April 1904   6 Grosvenor Place

Dear Mr Churchill,

I see there is nothing on Wednesday evening to take me necessarily to the House of Commons, so I hope you will reserve that evening, if you can, for my proposed little dinner, at 8 o'clock.

Yours very truly
H. CAMPBELL-BANNERMAN

---

[1] G. D. Kelley, the Secretary of the Manchester and Salford Trades Council, was elected for South West Manchester in 1906. John Harker, Secretary of the Manchester and Salford Labour Representation Committee, resigned his candidature after the 1905 ILP conference had condemned people who attended Free Trade Union meetings.

General Sir Ian Hamilton to WSC

15 April 1904   Oriental Palace Hotel
                                                          Yokohama

My dear Winston,

Just a hurried line to tell you I am alive & kicking. Dead as mutton from
the WO point of view where I have not a friend now but if I survive the
Muscovite *obus* perhaps I may revive.[1] I have been pretty busy studying the
Army, sending K reports, making pals with the leading Jap Generals,
Admirals & Politicians. In this my French & German – combined with a
taste for saki & geisha girls – has helped me on considerably.

Dear Winston – note this which I have been writing home for 3 weeks
now: The Jap is the fighting man *par excellence* of the future. He has the
quick practical grasp of a situation; the initiative and the instinct of ground
& cover which are everything to the private soldier under the dispersed
conditions rendered necessary by modern fire. He is extraordinarily amenable
to discipline. He is intensely patriotic (there are no Pro Boers here – not
one!) He is hardy – quick on his feet – sound in his stomach and absolutely
fearless of death. What more do you want?

I admire the Generals immensely and they have the precious advantage
of recent war experience. If they get to Harbin they will exclude the Russians
from the fertile well stocked country between that place & Liao Tang & then
I do not see how the Russians could collect more than 50,000 men on the
Trans-Baikal Steppes. How could they feed them? The Japs are capable of
warm gratitude. At present we are prime favourites & no Yellow peril would
give *us* jaundice! But to retain this priceless advantage we must not attempt
to hedge, for if we do so & make ourselves safe by squaring Russia in any way
they will see they owe us nothing – then goodbye to China. Well dear boy –
God bless you. I am off next week – to hear the whizz & pick pock again.

Yours ever

IAN H

WSC to President of North-West Manchester Liberal Association[2]

18 April 1904   [105 Mount Street]

My dear Sir,

I have reflected carefully upon the conversation which I had on Friday
last with the deputation from the Liberal Association of North-West Manchester, and I have considered the proposals which these gentlemen put

---

[1] Sir Ian Hamilton had arrived in Japan a month before as the chief of the British Military
Mission with the Japanese forces in the field during the Russo-Japanese War. He recorded
his experiences in *A Staff Officer's Scrap Book* 1907.

[2] Printed in *Manchester Courier* 19 April 1904.

forward, together with the strong appeal which was made to me on the same day by Mr Tom Garnett[1] and the deputation appointed by the Free-trade League.

The plan which you have in contemplation is that I should become the Free-trade candidate for the North-West Division of Manchester, with the full and official support of the Liberal Association over which you preside. I am sensible of the peculiar honour which you have shown me by your invitation, and no political project could be more attractive personally to me than to seek the suffrages of the historic constituency which contains the Free-trade Hall, and which ought to be inseparably associated with the doctrines of Mr Cobden and Mr Bright. Any work I may have been able to do in resisting the tendencies of the party in power towards militarism and monopoly has lain mainly in Lancashire, and I feel that if I am to find a place in the long line of battle which Free-traders of all kinds are forming an invitation from the heart of Lancashire must, so far as I am concerned, take precedence of all others.

During the five years I have been associated with Oldham my views on current questions have been very fully set forth by the Manchester newspapers. Your Association, therefore, knows all about me, and is in a position to judge whether I should be likely to serve your cause with any advantage. I am not conscious of any reversal of my inward convictions on any of these subjects which I have been able to study. I remain of the opinion that the creation of a separate Parliament for Ireland would be dangerous and impracticable. I earnestly desire to see a broad and far-reaching policy of domestic and industrial reform, firmly, calmly, and patiently pursued. The necessary companion of any real schemes of social progress must be the re-organisation of our finances, now so lamentably strained and confused. That can only be achieved by brave and earnest efforts to reduce expenditure, particularly the expenditure upon armaments. I have always laboured to destroy the 'Army Corps Scheme,' which preserved in a permanent form all the excited expenditure of war-time, and to secure in its place a much smaller and cheaper Army. The time has now arrived when the growing cost and size of the Navy must also be averted. Such retrenchment will incidentally prevent purposeless and sanguinary excursions like those to which we are now committed in Somaliland and Thibet. It cannot fail to produce a corresponding restraint in the foreign and Colonial policy of Great Britain, and the restraint will be all in the interests of the workers at home and all in the interests of peace.

[1] Thomas ('Tom') Garnett (1857-1932), Mayor of Clitheroe 1903-7, Lancashire County Councillor and Alderman (1921), Member of the Dominions Royal Commission 1912-17; principal proprietor of Thomas Garnett and Sons, cotton spinners and manufacturers.

If you think that our country at this critical period in its history requires a decided change from the costly gaudy trappings of martial ambition to a more sober garb, a closer recurrence to first principles, a higher regard for the rights of others, a firmer reliance upon those moral forces of liberty and justice that have made her renowned, and if you desire that with all this Manchester should point the way, I should be proud to be of the smallest use. You explained to me on Friday that in the event of my accepting the suggestions of your committee you would proceed to submit more definite proposals to a general meeting of the Association. I regard this as an indispensable step, for unless I can appeal with confidence to the unstinted and unswerving support of every Liberal and every liberal-minded man in the division, not less than to those Unionists or non-party Free-traders who are embraced by the Free-trade League, it would be perfectly useless, or worse than useless, for me to undertake a long uphill battle against a member so widely and so deservedly respected as Sir William Houldsworth.

Yours very truly
WINSTON S. CHURCHILL

Sidney Low to WSC

23 April 1904   2 Durham Place
                                                  Chelsea

Dear Winston Churchill,
    I hope it is not too late to congratulate you on your letter to the North-West Manchester Liberals. It seems to me – if I may express an opinion – a most excellent, straightforward, and judicious manifesto, and will I am sure favourably impress all who value courage, ability and independence in public life, and who have been following with interest and appreciation, your conduct all through the trying and difficult transactions for the past few months. I don't think the House of Commons can spare you; so you must take care not to allow electoral, or any other causes, to deprive it of your assistance.

I am, Yours sincerely
SIDNEY LOW

On 22 April WSC hesitated during the course of a speech in the Commons, stopped speaking, fumbled in vain for his notes, sat down, and covering his face with his hands, muttered, 'I thank hon members for having listened to me'. Some younger Tories jeered but many MPs, with vivid memories of Lord Randolph's collapse, were aghast.

Jack Seely to WSC

EXTRACT

25 April 1904   23 Queen's Gate Gardens
Dictated

My Dear Winston,

I enclose a letter from one Dabbs[1] who used to be considered a great authority on the brain. . . . I send it principally because of the phrase I have marked with a cross which should relieve you of all anxiety.

At the same time I should take it easy for a few days if I were you for reasons given in the last sentence but one.

I am tempted to make a few sarcastic remarks about the Aliens Bill today.

If you stay away for one or two days let me know if there is anything I can do for you.

Yours ever
JOHN BERNARD SEELY

Do not trouble to return Dr Dabbs' letter.

Dr G. Dabbs to Jack Seely

EXTRACT

23 April 1904   Albany Chambers
                                                 Westminster

Dear Seely,

Many thanks for yr kindly remarks about me at the Vetensian Dinner. I hope to be at the next. Very sorry (but not surprised for I expect he has overdone his nervous system) to read of Mr W. Churchill's attack of defective cerebration: it comes to the readiest at times. . . . It is a strange experience to those who *have* experienced it. Luckily it hardly ever recurs. My view of it is that it is sudden brain anaemia: a sort of syncope of the memory cells. But it always spells overstrain and is not a symptom to neglect or pass by. After which unsolicited contribution to the literature of ephemeral oblivions, I will again thank you for remembering me.

Yrs ever
G. DABBS

[1] George Henry Roque Dabbs (1846–1913), medical practitioner, novelist, playwright and horsebreeder; practised in the Isle of Wight 1868–1903.

*   *   *   *   *

Samuel Lamb to WSC

25 April 1904   Highfield
                                                                         Heaton Mersey

Dear Mr Churchill,

I am pleased to report that the meeting of our Executive Committee was held this evening and that your Candidature was unanimously recommended to the General Committee which meets on Friday night next.

Whilst the vote was unanimous, all present did not vote, say 3 or 4 in a meeting of 40 preferring to wait for a fuller exposition of your views on Friday.

The Officers of the Association desire the pleasure of your Company to dinner on Friday, at 6 pm, at the Reform Club, afterwards meeting the Executive for conversation at 7.15 pm after which follows the meeting of the General Committee at 8.

The purpose of the 7.15 gathering is to give opportunity to a few of the Committee to hear your opinions on a few points privately. The Press will be represented at the 8 pm meeting and it is advisable to abate or take the edge off the questions in the reported meeting beforehand so that fewer divergences may be shown and greater unanimity characterise the meeting. I shall be pleased to hear that these arrangements are agreeable to yourself.

In haste,

Yours sincerely
SAMUEL LAMB

WSC to Lord Londonderry[1]

2 May 1904   105 Mount Street

[Copy]

My dear Londonderry,

You may perhaps have seen the announcement of my candidature for NW Manchester & the conditions under which it is to be conducted. Had I joined myself formally to the Liberal party I should have taken my name off the Carlton Club forthwith. That circumstance has not yet occurred. Whether it will occur or not depends on the future course of politics. But having regard to the general opposition I propose to offer to the present Government, I venture to ask you as a friend, a member of the Committee, a

---

[1] Charles Stewart Vane-Tempest-Stewart, 6th Marquess of Londonderry (1852–1915), President of the Board of Education 1902–5; Lord President of the Council 1903–5.

Minister, to look after my interests in the matter, to withdraw my name or not, entirely as you may think proper & fair towards the various interests concerned.

Yours vy sincerely

WINSTON S C

Lord Londonderry to WSC

EXTRACT

3 May 1904   Londonderry House

Park Lane

Private

My dear Winston,

I have your letter explaining your feelings with regard to your future action regarding the Carlton Club. I honestly confess that I feel some difficulty in giving you any advice on the subject without carefully thinking the matter over. I *should* like to consult one or two well known & fair minded men of the Party before tending you that advice.[1] . . . I am at your service any time tomorrow except from 12–2. Having lunch here at 1.45 or I shall be at P.C. [Privy Council] office in the afternoon. Thursday *afternoon* I go down to Frome & am at your service till Monday & any time Friday.

Whatever course you take politically will I hope never make any difference to our relations, & if the advice of one who was a sincere friend of your Father's is ever of use to you be sure to let me know.

Yrs

L

WSC to D. A. Thomas[2]

[4 May 1904]   105 Mount Street

[Copy]

Dear Mr Thomas,

I am I confess a little surprised to read in the newspapers of the opposition wh you felt it your duty to offer to Mr Guest's candidature at Cardiff. You

[1] It was not until 14 April 1905 that WSC formally resigned from the Carlton Club. He was reinstated in October 1925.

[2] David Alfred Thomas (1856–1918), Liberal MP for Merthyr Burghs 1888–1910, Cardiff 1910; President of Local Government Board 1916–17; Food Controller 1917–18; Managing Director of Cambrian Combine & other colliery companies; Baron Rhondda 1916; Viscount Rhondda 1918.

are reported to have said that 'you could not honestly & conscientiously support Mr Guest, because you did not believe that he would faithfully represent the progressive feeling in the metropolis of Radical Wales'. Now I am myself less advanced in my views in almost every particular than Mr Guest, & yet you were good enough to assure me that if I would come forward as a Free Trade candidate for Cardiff you would give me your full support. I do most respectfully submit to you that this is no time for mere personal preferences. We have been confronted with a vast new issue which cuts into existing party groupings on both sides. It would have been dishonouring to the Liberal party if their Unionist Free Traders who have been driven from their party because of their resistance to Mr Chamberlain had been simply allowed to be exterminated. The Liberal organisations in not a few of the greatest constituencies in England have risen to the occasion & have been found willing to make considerable sacrifices in order to secure the general welfare of the Free Trade cause; & I most earnestly hope that in view of the decision of the Cardiff Liberal association to adopt Mr Guest as their candidate you will regard the protest you have already made as sufficient, & will feel yourself able to extend to him the same measure of support you had promised to me, & thus secure what from the peculiar circumstances of the fight could not fail to be a striking & significant victory for Free Trade in 'the Metropolis' of Radical Wales!

Yours vy tly
WINSTON SC

D. A. Thomas to WSC

5 May 1904   House of Commons

Dear Mr Churchill,

I am obliged by your letter of yesterday prescribing the duty of the Liberal Party towards Unionist Free Traders.

When I expressed my willingness to support your candidature in the event of your coming forward for Cardiff, it was in the belief that you had abandoned the errors of your party, and were fully prepared to come over to our side. I fear, in my delight at the prospect of welcoming so distinguished a convert, I gave too ready credence to the rumours current at the time, and I now confess frankly my disappointment in observing the attitude you continue to adopt towards such cardinal principles of Liberal policy as those relating to Irish Home Rule, Disestablishment of the English Church and the House of Lords. It may be that Mr Guest is more 'advanced' than yourself, but that he falls very far short of what a Radical constituency is entitled to expect in its representative.

I cannot within the limits of this letter go fully into my objection to Mr Guest, but let me assure you that it is purely political, and in no way influenced by personal preference as you suggest.

Those who voted for the adoption of Mr Guest at the meeting to which you refer constitute only two or three per cent of the progressive vote in Cardiff, and time I think will show that they do not reflect the feeling in local Liberal and Labour Circles.

Cardiff virtually owes its Commercial existence to Free Trade, and there need be no alarm lest protectionist fallacies take serious root there. Under the circumstances, and with every desire to avoid embarrassment to those Unionist Free Traders who may have incurred the displeasure of Mr Chamberlain, I think it expecting too much to ask us to hand over a safe Liberal seat to the keeping of one who might at a critical moment prove a source of weakness rather than of strength.

Yours very faithfully
D. A. THOMAS

T. W. Killick to WSC

EXTRACT

17 May 1904   Memorial Hall
                                                   Manchester

Dear Mr Churchill,

We held a meeting here tonight at which we established a branch of the Free Trade League for the North West Parliamentary Division of Manchester. . . .

The Branch will canvass the Exchanges and the business community, and those names sent to it by your Liberal Assn.

The first thing we think we should do is to hold a meeting for you to address the business men of the City. . . .

Yours very truly
T. W. KILLICK

WSC to George Johnson

EXTRACT

19 May 1904   105 Mount Street
[Copy]

Dear Sir,

. . . Some conversation which I had with Mr Chamberlain in June 1902 convinced me that the tariff question would shortly pass out of the region of academic thought into that of action. I did not however come to any final decision until the autumn of that year. My prepossession in Mr Chamberlain's favour was strong; & I was not unaware that it would perhaps have been to my interest to support him. But after doing my best to consider the question from every point of view I came to the conclusion that the case for Protection was in theory unsound & would not bear sustained national scrutiny. I took occasion so to declare myself definitely to my constituents at Oldham in October 1902; so that when six months later Mr Chamberlain took the decisive steps I had no difficulty in knowing what to do. What has occurred since confirms my judgment both in regard to the abstract merits of the controversy & its practical & political bearings.

Yours faithfully
WINSTON S. CHURCHILL

Reginald Barnes[1] to WSC

25 May 1904

Snowdon
Simla

My dear old Winston,

I was most awfully sorry to see in the papers that you had to stop speaking in the middle of a speech in the House the other day. You must have overdone yourself & worked too hard, but I sincerely hope by now that you are all right again. Don't please be foolish & try yourself too high, there is a limit to everyone's capabilities & I am much afraid you don't quite realise where your limit is. It *can't* be right for you to strain yourself to the extent of suddenly losing your memory so please take it easy & get strong again. As regards your change of views & transferring yourself to the other party, I can only say I am sorry because I think you are wrong & are putting your weight on the wrong side; however I know it is no good my arguing with you about that, so shan't attempt it, and what is more, I feel in many ways in sympathy with you in your move, because from a distance, it looks to me very much as if the old-fashioned Tory asses in the House had not been giving you quite fair play & from this point of view, I can quite understand a pugnacious person like you telling them to go to the devil in words or rather actions to that effect. I *do* think that in consequence of your youth, abilities, & may I say your want of respect for elder people, you have made enemies who have not given you a fair hearing, or treated you quite fairly and I think they are 'swine', my dear Winston, of the deepest dye, but all the

---

[1] Reginald Walter Ralph Barnes (1871–1946), served with WSC in 4th Hussars and went with him to Cuba in 1895; Major General; KCB 1919.

same, on broad principles the Unionist side is the right one, and there are plenty of good sound men amongst them, who I think would be bound to be your friends in due time. Well, I hope you won't mind my saying all this, but I don't mind if you do! Because I feel that your affairs are mine as well, & whatever you do it won't harm our friendship I hope. I am regularly settled down as an ADC to Kitchener now and am having a pretty busy time up here at Simla – this job isn't quite a loaf. Well – *au revoir* dear old boy, keep fit, & let em all have it back as good as they give.

Yours ever
REGGIE

WSC to Lord Hugh Cecil
(*Quickswood Papers*)

EXTRACT

26 May 1904   105 Mount Street

My dear Linky,

... I have been thinking over your Black speech a good deal. The criticism I feel inclined to make is that you talked too much about the House of Commons aspect of the motion & amendment & not enough of the broad line issue & situation. And speaking generally you are prone to dwell over much on procedure. It is vy rarely that a point can be scored by an ingenious resolution. In a crisis men decide either to vote so as to help or so as to hurt the Government & no soothing arrangement of words will inspire frankness with the necessary decision.

I do not in the least regret 'Bob' [?]; & the immense authority you exerted on the House must impress you with the power & gifts you have received – for some purpose or other. Three times running you have been called by the clamour of the House. It must be long since a private member was so treated. I rejoice from the bottom of my heart.

... I lunched with A. Beit[1] last week who tells me that he & others subscribed £25,000 for J.C. at their dinner the other night, & seemed absolutely certain that the movement would be pushed for all it was worth.

Could you come to Blenheim. – if I make Sunny telegraph you? I go there tonight till Monday.

Yours always
W

---

[1] Alfred Beit (1853–1906), millionaire South African gold and diamond mine owner of German-Jewish origin; settled in London in 1888.

WSC to Lord Hugh Cecil
(*Quickswood Papers*)

2 June [1904]   105 Mount Street

My dear Linky,

Let me thank you very sincerely for the three books you have sent me. I will read them with the greatest care. I have much expanded & deepened my views as a result of the books you have sent me & in greater measure as result of our frequent talks. You are the only person who has any real influence on my mind.

I could not help thinking last night what a wrench it is to me to break with all that glittering hierarchy & how carefully one must organise one's system of thought to be utterly independent of it. The worst of it is that as the Free Trade issue subsides it leaves my personal ambitions naked & stranded on the beach – & they are an ugly & unsatisfactory spectacle by themselves, though nothing but an advantage when borne forward with the flood of a great outside cause.

Yours always
WINSTON SC

6

The Young Liberal

(*See Main Volume Chapter 3*)

(*See Main Volume Chapter 3*)

WSC to ?

9 June 1904   105 Mount Street
[Copy]

Dear Sir,
 It is my intention during the remainder of the present Parliament to vote
as far as possible according to the merits of the various questions upon which
divisions are taken. When I think that the government are in the right I shall
support them, when I think they are in the wrong I shall vote against them.
You will see therefore that it is not possible for me to answer definitely your
questions as to the 'arithmetical' effect upon the Government majority
which will result from my occupying a position on the Liberal benches.
That partly depends upon the conduct of the Government, & partly on the
conduct of the Opposition; but I should add that I am strongly of opinion
that a general election should take place at the earliest possible moment in
the interests both of Parliament & of the country & that this consideration
will necessarily weigh with me in deciding how to vote on any particular
occasion.

                                                           Yours faithfully
                                                   WINSTON S. CHURCHILL

Sir Henry Campbell-Bannerman to WSC

15 June 1904

Dear Mr Churchill,
 Irish votes are promised for the 23rd, so that the Colonial Office vote is
excluded. Besides this, all those interested in the subject whom I have been

able to consult agree that the discussion would be greatly spoiled if we had not the financial results of the year and the papers which Lyttelton has promised. These he now says can not be issued till next week at the earliest.

What a collapse of the Army Reform balloon! postponed *sine die* because (I am told) the new scheme so far from making a saving added to cost.

Yours very truly
H. CAMPBELL-BANNERMAN

T. W. Killick to WSC

20 June 1904   Townfield House
                                                Altrincham

Dear Mr Churchill,

The Labour people are disposed to join in a big demonstration in favour of Free Trade under the auspices of the Free Trade League. The idea is to have *all* the trade organizations represented. Nothing is yet fixed, but I have arranged to write a formal letter from the League to the Manchester Trades Council. The date at present suggested is Saturday August 6th, and I think the Labour organizations will agree to send you an invitation to address them. Mr Chamberlain in decrying the Labour leaders is making a big mistake and helping us greatly. Will you let me know privately if you would attend such a meeting and if the date would suit you? I need not tell you that it would be 'splendid business' if we can arrange it.

Yours very truly
T. W. KILLICK

WSC to S. H. Phillips[1]

27 June 1904

[Copy]

Dear Sir,

As I did not myself in the first instance seek the honour of membership of your club, but accepted it at the earnest invitation of your Committee, I do not feel bound in any way to relieve you of the full responsibility for any course you may think fit to take. I have for some time contended that all those who opposed Mr Chamberlain's Protectionist policy and resisted the changes which he is effecting in the aspirations and character of the

[1] Secretary of the Riverside Conservative Club, Cardiff.

Conservative Party would be driven from that party, and I shall not complain if the action on which your Committee may decide should make more plain to the Unionist Free Traders of Cardiff this bitter but obvious truth.

Yours very truly
WINSTON S. CHURCHILL

T. W. Killick to WSC

EXTRACT

30 June 1904   Townfield House

Dear Mr Churchill,

. . . That which may be really 'first class business' in the House of Commons is often regarded outside as mere flightiness. Lancashire is disposed to take you very seriously. The people are willing to regard you not only as the Free Trade candidate for North West Manchester, but as the fighting head of the Free Trade party, and as one of the Liberal leaders in the near future.

You asked me a question and I have replied to it frankly – as I am sure you would wish me to. Mind I am not expressing my own opinion.

The Manchester Trades Council have decided that it is not expedient to hold a labour demonstration in support of Free Trade just now. This decision, which I regret, has been come to for reasons connected with the Labour party, and has nothing to do with the Free Trade League or North West Manchester.

The Manchester [?Athenaeum] Committee think they ran some risk in asking you to address them, and considered they paid you a compliment, but they accept your refusal without any feeling of soreness.

Yours very truly
T. W. KILLICK

W. Bourke Cockran[1] to WSC

1 July 1904   31 Nassau Street
                     New York

My dear Winston,

Before leaving for St Louis I want to tell you how deeply I regret the change of plans which prevents you from being my guest at the Convention, and for the remainder of the summer at this quiet retreat.

---

[1] William Bourke Cockran (1854–1923), Irish-born American politician and lawyer; Democratic Member of Congress 1891–5, 1904–9. Campaigned for Republican President William McKinley 1896. Close friend of WSC and Lady Randolph.

Your explanation of the incident in the House of Commons is very re-assuring, not only to me but to a great many others who, though they are not acquainted with you personally, take a deep interest in your career.

While it is clear that the newspaper accounts were greatly exaggerated it is equally clear that the hard work of the last year must have told on you to some extent, and therefore it seems to me a rest is highly desirable, if not absolutely necessary now, as a precaution against graver trouble hereafter. The difficulty about a rest is not in finding a place where one can take it if he will but a place where he must take it. It is very difficult for an active mind to put itself entirely out of operation or activity and I think it would be quite impossible for you to stop thinking or working for any sensible period of time. What you can get is not a cessation but a change of employ-ment – a substitute of occupations which amuse the mind without affecting the nerve for those labors which wear both mind and nerves.

I cannot help thinking that this country is the place above all others where for the next four months you could be amused and interested without being fatigued for here you could watch a mighty struggle in the result of which you could have no personal concern.

Of course, the most interesting feature of the contest will be the convention to which I am about going, but since it is impossible for you to assist at the selection of a candidate or the adoption of a platform, the next best thing would be to see the electoral battle itself in progress. This you can do any time up to the eighth of November and I most earnestly hope you will come over and stay with me for as long a time as you can spare.

A chance to observe at close quarters a fight affecting the conditions under which a population of eighty millions must live for four years and in which all its male members are engaged should be well worth embracing, to a mind like yours. Moreover closer intercourse between all the great nations of the world is certain to be a feature of the new century and you would undoubtedly find it a great advantage to form acquaintance with men active in the political life of this country, and who are very likely to affect its course during the next generation. While you would be likely to meet in my establishment just now only the moving spirits in the Democratic party, matters could easily be arranged so that you would also come in contact with the leading Republicans, and thus see for yourself how both sides of the campaign are managed.

Think over this and let me have a line saying that I may expect you im-mediately after the adjournment of Parliament.

I am very curious to learn all about the conditions and prospects of the Free Trade fight in England. So far as we on this side can judge events on the other side of the Atlantic it would seem as if Chamberlain's plan has

wholly failed, while on the other hand the opposition is so divided and in-
coherent that the Government is likely to escape the defeat it so richly
deserves for recklessly countenancing and encouraging proposals which if
adopted would have imperilled the foundations of your own prosperity
and beclouded the whole prospects of civilized progress.

Pray give my cordial regards to your mother and believe me to be,

Yours very sincerely
W. BOURKE COCKRAN

The Master of Elibank to WSC

EXTRACT

2 July 1904   Brooks's

... You have infused a new spirit into the younger men of the opposition – as
last night witnesseth!

There are many of us, who manage to hold our own in our respective
constituencies, who are sick of the old weary round of lost opportunities, and
on these men you may most assuredly count.

I suppose it is heresy to mention it, but my limited observation of the H of
C tells me that for one who (like yrself) is hacking his way through an under-
growth of mediocrities, the most entangling obstacle he meets with is the
green-eyed jealousy amongst those who imagine they have an assured
position! But they whip in in the long run – and you will overcome it, & them.

There are many of your friends in the House who fear you are doing too
much. You must be careful of your strength. You will want it all in the
immediate struggle which is ahead.

Yours sincerely
ALEXANDER V. MURRAY

Jack Seely to WSC

17 July [1904]   Villa Adria
Langenschwalbach
Germany

My dear Winston,

I am assuming that the Colonial Vote is to be taken next Thursday, and
am coming back for that reason – I see however that Balfour gave a hesitating

answer, and can well imagine that he would like to put it off indefinitely on various pretexts – I hope you will not let him.

With joy I perceived in the papers that you have put down a resolution about the new Army Scheme which embodies certain views that I venture to share with you. These two year soldiers are designed to supplant the volunteers altogether, and since fewer men will receive any training or sense of patriotic obligation, the result will be to make small wars easier to begin, though perhaps not to finish, and great wars more disastrous.

It seems wrong of me to be away from the contest, but it could not be avoided, and I really believe this place may do my wife much good.

I have hired a horse, and ride all over these wooded mountains with the aid of a map and a compass – the inhabitants think I am a spy, but are very civil. Unless I hear from Runciman[1] that the Colonial Vote is postponed I shall be in London in Wednesday – will you dine with me at Willis's, that night and Linky too?

Yours ever
JACK SEELY

Lord Tweedmouth to WSC

21 July 1904   Guisachan
                                                       Beauly

My dear Winston,

Alas! that I should have to write an answer to your letter to Fanny but the hand of a mysterious providence has come down with an awful force upon us and poor dear she is not able to write for herself – I will not write you any of the ordinary formalities used in cases such as this – I can only tell you the bare truth. My darling is very ill, cannot get better – must more or less quickly get worse day by day till the end comes and all we can do is to make her comfortable and save her such trouble & sorrow as we can.

We must cloud the bitter present by the happy memories of the long years of happiness & good time we have had together. She sends you her love and bids me to say that you are by no means to put aside the idea of your visit to Guisachan whatever may be her case in the middle of September.

---

[1] Walter Runciman (1870–1949), Liberal MP for Dewsbury 1902–18, Oldham 1899–1900, Swansea West 1924–9, St Ives 1929–31; Liberal National MP for St Ives 1931–7; Parliamentary Secretary to the Local Government Board 1905–7; Financial Secretary to the Treasury 1907–8; President of the Board of Education 1908–11; of Agriculture 1911–14; President of the Board of Trade 1914–16, 1931–7; Head of Mission to Czechoslovakia 1938; Lord President of the Council 1938–9; shipowner; PC 1908; Viscount Runciman 1937.

I think your Glasgow and other Scottish meetings will go like wildfire. I shall not lose interest in them and shall take care that nothing is left undone that can make them a success, but alas to preside for you at St Andrew's Hall as I should have loved to do I'm afraid does not come within the range of possibilities. Perhaps Rosebery might do it but it would have to be as a Catholic Liberal not a Liberal Leaguer. If so much good might come of it.

I am very interested in what you say about LG's proposition. I should say go into it – but warily and under conditions – make your little party one of young Liberals and avoid the old hacks: Dilkes, Labbys, P. Stanhopes[1] *et hoc genus omne*, be vigorous but avoid much bitterness or sarcasm at the expense of our own molluscs on the front bench, be a cheering voice and a spur to them rather than a whip.

I think Cassel's Alpine Villa sounds too luxurious for you to get the highest benefit from a mountain life – May you convert him to sounder fiscal views.

All love & luck to you from both of us

Yrs ever

T

Lord Tweedmouth to WSC

29 July 1904   Guisachan

My dear Winston,

Both your letters have given very great pleasure to poor Fanny. She bids me tell you that she is very fond of you and takes the greatest interest in your career and hopes you will make a great name for yourself and your family.

She begs you not be too rampageous and aggressive & to remember there is truth in the old maxim *suaviter in modo fortiter in re*. She thinks that a sojourn in the Alpine retreat of Cassel will be very wholesome for you if you avoid too much champagne and too many cigarettes.

She would dearly have loved to see you once more but I fear it is too late. We can make her fairly comfortable and free from pain but that is all. She is very weak today and can take but little nourishment.

What a tragedy dear Winston but what an example of unflinching courage & unexampled self sacrifice.

God be with you

Yrs ever

T

[1] Arthur Philip Stanhope (1838–1905), Conservative MP 1868, 1870–5; Junior Lord of the Treasury 1874–6; succeeded father as 6th Earl Stanhope 1875.

W. St John Brodrick to WSC

Private and Personal

9 August 1904   House of Commons

My dear Churchill,

I listened to your Army speech last night with great interest, and I wonder if I may tell you how different I thought its tone from some you have delivered on the same subject? I am probably impartial as you still retain the imperfect appreciation of my schemes, which you have held from 1901! But, if I may say so, I think the line you took last night will stand you in stead. It is clear we are not yet at the end of changes, and you have such a thorough knowledge of the intricacies of the Army problem that you can really aid its solution.

Forgive my writing this – but I genuinely care for the future of the Army, and this consideration goes far beyond Governments or schemes, personal or political.

Yours very tly
St John Brodrick

*   *   *

On 29 March 1904 the Government introduced the first reading of the Aliens Bill, intended to prevent the spread of aliens within Britain and to enable undesirable aliens to be deported. Most of the newly arrived aliens were Russian and Polish Jews. The Jewish community in Manchester were opposed to the Bill and successfully enlisted WSC's support.

WSC to Nathan Laski[1]

[30] May 1904[2]   [105 Mount Street]

Dear Sir,

What has surprised me most in studying the papers you have been good enough to forward me is how few aliens there are in Great Britain. To judge by the talk there has been, one would have imagined we were being overrun by the swarming invasion and 'ousted' from our island through

---

[1] Nathan Laski (1863–1941), sometime Chairman of Manchester and Salford Jewish Council; Chairman Jewish Board of Guardians; father of Harold J. Laski (1893–1950), political scientist, author and pamphleteer.

[2] Published in the *Manchester Guardian* on 31 May 1904.

neglect of precautions which every foreign nation has adopted. But it now appears from the Board of Trade statistics that all the aliens in Great Britain do not amount to a one-hundred-and-fortieth part of the total population, that they are increasing only 7,000 a year on the average, and that, according to the report of the Alien Commission, Germany has twice as large and France four times as large a proportion of foreigners as we have. It does not appear, therefore, that there can be urgent or sufficient reasons, racial or social, for departing from the old tolerant and generous practice of free entry and asylum to which this country has so long adhered and from which it has so often greatly gained.

While good cause for such a change is wanting, the machinery of enforcement is both in principle and detail dangerous. Parliament has always declined to confer upon police or Customs officers, acting under the Executive Government the kind of powers accorded by clauses 1 and 2. No one can tell how much bullying and blackmail might result from their application, or what an instrument of oppression they would furnish to the hand of an intolerant or anti-Semitic Home Secretary. The custom in England has hitherto been to allow police and Customs officers to act and report on facts, not to be the judges of characters and credentials. The objections against the new procedure have been very clearly stated by Lord Rothschild,[1] a supporter of the present Government, in a recent speech. He said:—'The bill introduced into the House of Commons proposes to establish in this country a loathsome system of police interference and espionage, of passports and arbitrary power, exercised by police officers who in all probability will not understand the language of those upon whom they are called to sit in judgment. This is all contrary to the recommendations of the Royal Commission.'

The machinery, though highly objectionable in its character, is, according to Sir Kenelm Digby,[2] likely to prove largely unworkable in practice. As it is admittedly impossible to apply the provisions of the bill at all the ports of entry, the professional thief, Anarchist, and prostitute – often well supplied with money – have only to pick their route with caution and can pass in as easily as before. The simple immigrant, the political refugee, the helpless and the poor – these are the folk who will be caught in the trammels of the bill and may be harassed and hustled at the pleasure of petty officials without the smallest right of appeal to the broad justice of the English courts. When we come to such provisions as that contained in clause 2, sub-section 3, which provides for the banishment of an alien who is proved by

---

[1] Nathan Mayer Rothschild (1840–1915), Liberal MP for Aylesbury, 1865–85; succeeded uncle to baronetcy 1876; father was Austrian Baron 1879; Baron Rothschild (United Kingdom) 1885.

[2] Kenelm Edward Digby (1836–1916); barrister, Permanent Under-Secretary of State at Home Office 1895–1903; knighted 1898.

the testimony of the common informer – perhaps his private enemy or a trade rival – to have received parochial relief as late as one year after the relief has ceased, we can only wonder that an English gentleman should make such proposals to the House of Commons in the twentieth century.

The whole bill looks like an attempt, on the part of the Government to gratify a small but noisy section of their own supporters and to purchase a little popularity in the constituencies by dealing harshly with a number of unfortunate aliens who have no votes. It will commend itself to those who like patriotism at other people's expense and admire Imperialism on the Russian model. It is expected to appeal to insular prejudice against foreigners, to racial prejudice against Jews, and to labour prejudice against competition, and it will no doubt supply a variety of rhetorical phrases for the approaching election. The same men who are obstinate opponents of trade unionism will declaim about the rights of British labour. Those who champion the interests of slum landlords will dilate on the evils of overcrowding. Those who have been most forward in bringing Chinese into Africa will pose as the champions of racial purity at home.

I take leave to doubt the wisdom of this bill even as a political manoeuvre. In spite of militarism and false ideals about trade there is a growing spirit of fraternity between democracies. English working men are not so selfish as to be unsympathetic towards the victims of circumstances or oppression. They do not respond in any marked degree to the anti-Semitism which has darkened recent Continental history, and I for one believe that they disavow an attempt to shut out the stranger from our land because he is poor or in trouble, and will resent a measure which, without any proved necessity, smirches those ancient traditions of freedom and hospitality for which Britain has been so long renowned.

Yours very truly
WINSTON S. CHURCHILL

Nathan Laski to WSC

31 May 1904   M. Silverstone & Co
                                                        Manchester

Dear Mr Churchill,

Pray accept my personal thanks for your splendid letter received this morning – you have won the gratitude of the whole Jewish Community not alone of Manchester, but of the entire country.

Believe me, Yours very truly
NATHAN LASKI

Dr J. Dulberg[1] to WSC

29 June 1904   260 Oxford Road
                                                              Manchester

Dear Mr Churchill,
    Now that the meeting which you so eloquently and so forcibly addressed
last night is over, allow me, on behalf of Mr Belisha[2] and the other members
of the Committee as well as on my own, to thank you most heartily and
sincerely for the service which you have rendered to the cause and to the
Jewish community, a service which is not likely to be forgotten, and one
which will bring its own reward.

Believe me, yours faithfully
J. DULBERG

Nathan Laski to WSC

EXTRACT

14 July 1904   54 Princess Street
                                                              Manchester

Dear Mr Churchill,
    Though I have not written you ere this, yet my thanks are not less hearty
& sincere for the splendid victory you have won for freedom & religious
tolerance.
    You will doubtless be interested to know that I have got a body of splendid
workers together for you, & as far as our district is concerned – victory is
assured.
    Doubtless also, you would have learnt that Dr Dreyfus[3] – one of the princi-
pal supporters of Mr Balfour – will support your candidature – & as he is a
likely Lord Mayor – I know he refused the honour last year – he will prove a
valuable ally. . . . I have had over 20 years' experience in elections in Manchester – & without flattery I tell you candidly – there has not been a single
man able to arouse the interest that you have already done – thus I am sure
of your future success.

Believe me, Yours sincerely
N. LASKI

[1] Joseph Dulberg (1862–1925).   [2] Barrow I. Belisha (1853–1906).
[3] Charles Dreyfus (1848–1935), Managing Director of Clayton Aniline Company; Manchester City Councillor 1897–1905; President, East Manchester Conservative Association;
prominent Zionist.

WSC to ?[1]

23 November 1904   105 Mount Street

[Copy]

My dear Sir,

I am afraid it will be impossible for me to accept the invitation of the Reigate Liberal Association to address a Public Meeting at Redhill or Reigate at present, for I have already contracted as many engagements as I can profitably fulfil.

With regard to Captain Rawson's[2] references to the Aliens Bill, he should not, I think, repeat private conversation which he says he overheard when he 'happened to be staying in the same house' with me. The extensive adoption of such a practice would put an end altogether to the pleasant conditions which distinguish English political life from the politics of every other country. Passing from that, I do not in the least mind it being known that I opposed the Aliens Bill to the utmost of my power. I did so on the ground that it was vicious in principle and admittedly unworkable in practice, unless the Russian system of police espionage was established at our ports. But the opposition to the Bill would have been ineffective if it had been confined to the opponents of the present Government. Mr Balfour knows quite well how to force a Bill through Parliament when he is in earnest as the procedure adopted in regard to the Licensing Act and the Welsh Coercion Act last Session clearly proves. But the Government are not in earnest about the Aliens question. They have been fooling with it for nine years, and it is perfectly well known that the opposition of wealthy and influential Jews in their own party has always prevented, and probably always will prevent, their passing such a measure into law. That men like Lord Rothschild and others of his faith should earnestly strive to preserve a free asylum in England for their co-religionists who are driven out from foreign countries by religious persecution, although the expense must fall mainly upon themselves, is an honourable fact in thorough accordance with the traditions of the Jewish people. That a Government should yield to these gentlemen if they have a good case and are influential supporters of that government is also perfectly legitimate. But that this same government, having yielded to these representations and having refused all these years to take effective steps to legislate against the Aliens, should now go about the country trying to excite party cheers for having at length intro-

---

[1] Part of this letter was printed in the *Weston-super-Mare Gazette* 3 December 1904.

[2] Captain Rawson, the Conservative candidate for Reigate, claimed that WSC said 'Yes, I wrecked the [Aliens] Bill'.

duced a Bill which was never meant to pass, is a shabby hoax which is not likely to take in anybody.

Yours faithfully
[WINSTON S. CHURCHILL]

F. Blackwell to WSC

1 February 1905   2 Millfield Terrace
                                                    Normanton

Dear Sir,

The other evening a friend & I were talking over the withdrawal of the Aliens Bill of last Session by the Government. My friend maintained that the withdrawal was due to the Opposition wasting time by wilful obstruction, whilst I maintained that the discussion that took place was absolutely necessary so as to get the very best out of a bad bill, as had some gone through without being fully discussed, gross injustice would have been inflicted on hundreds of well-meaning foreigners, at the same time I said that in my opinion the measure was merely brought forward as a make believe. If I am not trespassing on your very valuable time I shall be obliged if you could give me a little information on the subject seeing that you are one of the members that took a leading part in the discussion of the measure.

Thanking you in anticipation

I remain, Yours faithfully
F. BLACKWELL

WSC to F. Blackwell

February 1905   105 Mount Street
[Copy]

Dear Sir,

You are perfectly right in believing that it was not the intention of those who opposed the Aliens Bill in Grand Committee to destroy the measure altogether. They were at every stage in the discussion willing to compromise with the Government. Had the objectionable features been removed from the Bill, the discussion could have been greatly accelerated and the measure would have now been the law of the land. The Government would however accept no compromise of any kind, being very glad to run the Bill on the

rocks so as to avoid offending their wealthy supporters. Under these circumstances and in the absence of any kind of compromise, we had no other
course open to us than to use to the full the advantage which the procedure
on Grand Committee gave to a minority.

Yours faithfully

[WINSTON S. CHURCHILL]

T. W. Killick to WSC

EXTRACT

19 September 1904   Free Trade League
                                                         Manchester

Dear Mr Churchill,

. . . Mr W. Joynson Hicks[1] is a fluent speaker and well enough liked in
Manchester, but he is not a politician, and you will have no difficulty in
dealing with him on the platform. His father-in-law's influence on which he
reckons is of little value. To badger him now would probably do more harm
than good. Many who are against him politically would feel a personal
sympathy with him. On the whole in my judgment you could not have well
had an opponent more favourable to your chance of securing the seat.

We send you tonight 50 copies of your second speech. I don't think it would
be of much use sending copies to the members of the Manchester Chamber
of Commerce – they get such a lot of literature that most of it goes into the
waste paper basket. About 2000 copies have been distributed by the can-
vassers of your own committee.

Acting on your letter I have written to Lord Hugh Cecil saying how glad
the League will be to arrange meetings for him. As to yourself will you
address any meetings for the League outside North West Manchester?
Throughout the area covered by the League you would be speaking to some
of your own constituents – men who have affairs in Manchester and works in
the country.

The only meeting arranged so far is that for the Duke of Devonshire.

I will write to Mr Guest about speaking for us.

---

[1] William Joynson Hicks (1865–1932), Unionist MP North West Manchester 1908–10,
Brentford 1911–18, Twickenham 1918–29; PMG and Paymaster General 1923; Minister of
Health 1923–4; Home Secretary 1924–9; PC 1923; baronet 1919; Viscount Brentford 1929.
He assumed the name of Joynson when he married Grace, daughter of Richard Joynson JP,
of Bowdon, in 1895.

Perhaps you might do much service to the League and yourself by speaking in the Manchester Divisions (other than North West) [and] in Stockport, Blackburn or Bury. But of course we would try to fall in with any wishes or views you have.

Yours very truly

T. W. KILLICK

WSC to James Southern[1]

23 September 1904   105 Mount Street

Dear Mr Southern,

The two points to which your letter refers show clearly that the existence of voting anomalies and the need of voting reform are not confined to the parliamentary franchise. It is of course only reasonable that as means of transit steadily improve, the limit of distance which regulates eligibility for municipal office should also be extended.

The other question is more complicated. As matters now stand a joint stock company is entered in the Rate Book as the 'occupier' of premises, if it is the occupier; but it has no vote as 'owner' or 'occupier', either for parliamentary or other purposes.

Down to the passing of the Local Govt Act of 1894 a Company had a vote for the purposes of Local Government. That act provided (Sec 44) that the Register of Parochial Electors is to be 'the Local Govt Register of Electors and the Parliamentary Register of Electors, so far as they relate to a Parish, taken together'.

And the 'Local Govt Register of Electors' is either (1) the County register, in the case of an administrative County, or (2) the Burgess role in the case of a County Borough, or other municipal Borough. The result is that the Co cannot vote either in the parish for the election of guardians, or for the election of a County Council, or for the election of a Member of Parliament. Companies are in fact in the unpleasant position of having duties without rights and suffering taxation without representation. The case is not one of the disfranchisement of property as property.

It is the disfranchisement of persons already holding property in a particular form; and it most frequently happens that a man loses his vote by transforming his private business into a limited Company. The man is the same; the business is the same yet the State views them in a different light while it enforces the same obligations. There is no doubt a real hardship in the present state of the law; and that it is a hardship extended year by year and already attaining striking dimensions the figures you quote clearly show.

[1] James Wilson Southern (d. 1909), Deputy Chairman, Manchester Ship Canal Co. Kt 1906.

The remedy would, of course, be to provide that a Co registered under the Joint Stock Companies Acts should be entitled to a vote as 'owner' or 'occupier', through its appointed officer in any case in which its qualification would entitle an individual with the same qualification to vote.

It might be objected against such a remedy that it would scarcely be possible to draw a distinction between the Parliamentary register and the register for Local Govt purposes; and I think it would be a strong measure to give a Company a Parliamentary vote. But I think that representation in respect of local govt may fairly be put on a different footing from representation in respect of Imperial affairs, if only from the fact that rating is so much more closely proportioned to the value of the property rated, than imperial taxation is proportioned to the wealth of the person taxed. And, as a matter of fact, there are already distinctions between the two Registers, for Peers and women are on one but not on the other.

One cannot however be blind to the fact that the present tendency is in the direction of their assimilation. Whether that tendancy should be arrested and to some extent reversed is a question the decision of which must rest largely with the Liberal Party. If the views which you have expressed represent the views of Manchester Liberals, I see myself no reason why we should not seriously consider an amendment to the law. That process of amendment could not however be limited to this particular point. I shall look forward to seeing the next Parliament deal boldly with Electoral Reform, Parliamentary as well as Municipal, and it is in connexion with some large measure which devolves the business of registration upon the local authority, which provides for the public discharge of Returning Officers' expenses, which simplifies and reduces the qualification necessary to obtain the franchise, and which sweeps away for ever the grotesque abuse of plural voting on national and Imperial questions that the reforms to which your letter draws attention would have the best chance of favourable treatment.

Yrs very truly
WINSTON S. CHURCHILL

T. W. Killick to WSC

26 September 1904   Townfield House
Private   Altrincham

Dear Mr Churchill,

I know you are working yourself very hard, but I think you should address one or two meetings in the Manchester suburbs early in the year. In such places as the Altrincham Division many NW voters live, who would never hear you speak in Manchester; and you want to attract fresh and more workers in NW. We are of course doing all we can in the Free Trade League to widen the area from which your active supporters are recruited.

I have written to ask Lord Hugh Cecil to speak at Preston after Mr Chamberlain.

Now in the *strictest confidence* let me express my firm conviction that Lord Rosebery's is not a name to conjure with in Lancashire. He has shaken the faith of the middle classes, and the working classes never did believe in him. It will be easy to arrange a demonstration for the Duke of Devonshire, but I should not like to be responsible for a Lancashire demonstration in honour of Lord Rosebery.

Yours very truly
T. W. KILLICK

T. W. Killick to WSC

4 October 1904   Townfield House
                                                 Altrincham

Dear Mr Churchill,

Mr Crawshay-Williams[1] writes to say that he wishes your promised visit to Chorley on Dec 7th to be under the auspices of the Liberal Association there. I am afraid he is making a mistake. He will want the support of Unionist and Labour votes, and these he will most easily get through the Free Trade League. You have now only one meeting to address this year for the League – that on Dec 2nd. The League recognise the enormous amount of work you are doing for Free Trade, but I think I ought to tell you that they are disappointed that you have so little part in their winter campaign. This is unfortunate because fully half the work in North West Manchester will have to be done by the League, and the more the League feel that you are identified with it the more work it will be possible to get out of it for NW M'chester. However a man can only do a certain amount of work, but I wish matters could have been arranged differently.

We had a most successful conference today between the League and its Branches.

Yours very truly
T. W. KILLICK

---

[1] Eliot Crawshay-Williams (1879–1963), prospective Liberal candidate for Chorley; Liberal MP for Leicester 1910–13; Assistant Private Secretary to WSC 1906–8; Parliamentary Private Secretary to David Lloyd George 1910–13; retired from political life because of a scandal involving the wife of another MP; author and playwright.

WSC to Lord Hugh Cecil
(Quickswood Papers)

EXTRACT

11 October 1904   105 Mount Street

My dear Linky,

I should much like to see you, as there have accumulated several things which it would be profitable as well as pleasant to discuss with you. Will you let me know your movements & plans. 'Superior persons' menaced by political extinctions must condescend to notice the more humble & more faithful & let me add more comfortably situated among their friends. I have been visiting Highbury![1] Have no sort of illusions as to any surrender or modification of purpose. . . .

Yours always
WINSTON SC

WSC to Lady Londonderry[2]
(Shane Leslie Papers)

EXTRACT

15 October 1904

I have not till now had time to thank you for your kind note and invitation. It was nice of you to express regret at my severance with the Conservative Party and as I said you and C [Charles] have a perfect right to express regret and even to formulate reproach. Had everyone adopted a tolerant line the present situation would be vastly different. I appreciate your attitude all the more because I had gathered from tales told that sometimes in the last few months you had commented upon my actions rather more severely than I had reason to expect from one who had known me all my life. But I was delighted to find at Blenheim that you still seemed to take a friendly interest in my fortunes. . . .

[1] The home of Joseph Chamberlain.
[2] Theresa Susan Helen Chetwynd-Talbot (1856–1919), eldest daughter of 19th Earl of Shrewsbury; married Charles Stewart Vane-Tempest-Stewart, 6th Marquess of Londonderry in 1875.

Charles Trevelyan to WSC

EXTRACT

17 October 1904   Cambo
                                                        Northumberland

Dear Winston

. . . I agree I think with your views about Devolution. There are two great
constitutional questions which a Liberal government will have to deal with
almost immediately. The first is the House of Lords which will arise first,
unless the Irish absolutely hold the balance and refuse to allow the machine
to work at all till something has been done for them. If so, I believe with you
the best Liberal policy to be some kind of administrative devolution, including Wales and Scotland in the offer, and basing it largely on the congested
state of public business. But if the Liberals have a clear majority they will for
the time bid the Irish be hanged and deal with finance, local and national,
and education. Then there is certain to be a row with the Lords. Before
three years are out both these questions must come up. I believe it would not
be policy to fight the election next year on either devolution or the H of L.
But the election after will be fought on both.

Hence I rather deprecate a very definite commit[ment] to any absolute
line of action in regard to either till after the election, though I think both
questions ought to be constantly discussed and I think we ought to try and
find common ground in both cases. I have written about the Lords in the
Independent for November.

I feel that we ought to put before the country this autumn the alternative
to Protection. The country has, after the campaign of last autumn, given its
decisive verdict against Chamberlainism for the present. It will be horribly
bored if we go on like Chamberlain talking on the old subject too much. It
wants to know now the positive policy of Liberalism. Let us decide to
emphasize:

Amendment of Education Act.
Rating of Land Values.
Economy.
Amendment of Licensing Act by Time Limit.
Taxation of Licenses for new National Revenue.
Reducing tea and sugar duties in order that Joe may have nothing to offer
to compensate for bread-tax.

I believe that hammering away at these, in whatever order we individually
prefer, interspersing it with lurid sketches of protection just to remind, and
gloating over Tory disruption, is the best line for this autumn.

Only one subject in connection with Joe wants really careful discussion. There is no hurry about it. But what attitude ought to be taken towards the colonies, who indubitably are flattered by Joe's offer? Balfour's talk about a Conference of course makes it more important. Liberal imperialists really ought to counter Joe with some general suggestions for regular colonial conferences, outline of Impl Federation. They ought at least to talk. If they won't, some of us who don't give ourselves such high-sounding names had better do it.

My wife joins in good wishes to you.

CHARLES TREVELYAN

WSC to J. Moore Bayley

17 October 1904   105 Mount Street
[Copy]

My dear Moore Bayley,

I was very glad to see your handwriting again. I certainly did not think that you had lost interest in my fortunes or politics. You know I do not change my mind when it is made up, and I have consistently pursued the course I indicated to you at the time of our meeting last year. I think Balfour is quite sincere in his opposition to Protection; but it is perfectly clear to me he will not take any effective steps to resist the certain evolution of his party. What use will it be to Free Traders when they find the whole party Protectionist, to know that the Prime Minister on whom they have counted, although unable to lead it any more, will nevertheless give it his hearty support from a private position?

I think the Government will try and step in next year and carry a Redistribution Bill and I think Chamberlain and the Protectionists will not agree to that long postponement. Mr Balfour's only chance of course is to kill Protection by a prolonged delay and it is hardly reasonable to expect the Protectionists to acquiesce in these amiable intentions.

I am at this present moment entirely isolated in politics – having no sort of connection with any group of politicians, but still I am not at all dissatisfied with the situation.

I am going to send you shortly my account in Lord Randolph's Life of the Birmingham affair. I hope you will keep it to yourself and let me have it back with any comments freely written over the proof which will be sent.

You will laugh when I tell you (secret) that I spent a very pleasant night at Highbury and had five or six hours very interesting and friendly conversation with the great Joe. My prognostication is that he and the Prime Minister will cut their own throats and bring their party to utter destruction between them, that the Liberals will gain a gigantic victory at the Election – far greater than anything even they imagine – and that they will break into fragments almost immediately afterwards.

Let me know anything that you hear from the Conservative side. Do you think it would be a good thing for me to write a polite letter of regretful parting to the Midland Conservative Club which could be published? I am meditating rather a nice epistle. I think perhaps it is rather open to criticism that I should remain on their list.

Yours sincerely
WINSTON S. CHURCHILL

Sidney Low to WSC

2 November 1904   2 Durham Place

Dear Winston Churchill,

I am afraid I cannot move in the matter you mention. I am not concerned at all in the business management of the *Standard* & really know nothing about it; & it would I think cause umbrage if I intervened in any way in the affairs of this Department.[1]

The *Standard* has been rather violent over the Baltic Fleet imbroglio.[2] But all the same the arrangement with Russia is an unsatisfactory one & so I notice everybody is saying today. And some of the very people who gushed over it on Saturday are now making the high-minded & honourable suggestion that we should try & get out of it! My publisher, Fisher Unwin, is sending you a copy of my book *The Governance of England*, which will be published on Monday next. If you have time to look at it I hope you will find some things of which you will approve.

Sincerely yours
SIDNEY LOW

Lord Hugh Cecil to WSC

7 November 1904   Hatfield

My dear Winston,

I am afraid I shall be in Northumberland on Wednesday as I am speaking at Newcastle that night. I am very much interested in Low's letter. But more

[1] C. A. Pearson (1866–1921), founder of the *Daily Express* and Vice-Chairman of the Tariff Reform League was buying the *Standard*, hitherto a Free Trade paper.

[2] On 22 October the Russian Baltic squadron had opened fire on the Hull fishing fleet in the North Sea, thinking that they were Japanese torpedo-boats. The Tzar apologized, his Government offered liberal compensation and agreed to the setting up of an international court of inquiry.

than money is wanted to start a newspaper. There must be some reason to think that people will read it, and I am not yet convinced upon that point. No doubt the *Standard* did very useful work, but I suspect most of its readers were those who liked its general tone and were accustomed to it, rather than people who deliberately preferred a Free Trade to a Protectionist newspaper. To what public then would the new paper appeal?

The loss of the *Standard* is grievous, but would have been far more serious a year ago than it is today. The influence of the press at the beginning of a struggle is very great; after every one has taken their part it sinks to a subordinate place. I think the purchase – if the amazing price be accurately put at £700,000 – is significant of a coming movement against AJB. The Free Food League is a great and distinguished body but I do not think anyone would value its extinction at £700,000. Nothing but the Prime-Ministership and the leadership of the Party is worth that stupendous sum.

I am going to Oxford on the 14th or 15th Nov, and could come over to luncheon at Blenheim any day if you were there. Do not encourage them to too much hospitality to me as I am really anxious to be at Oxford quietly, though I want to see you once in a way.

Yours ever
HUGH CECIL

Sidney Low to WSC

9 November 1904   2 Durham Place

Dear Winston Churchill,

Your letter, as it happens, only just 'meets my eye', & I am going to Oxford at once; back tomorrow evening. I can come & see you on Friday afternoon or will you come & dine with me that evening at the Garrick Club – a quiet place – where we can talk?

Thanks for your kind words about the *Standard*. The new proprietary have, very courteously, I must say, asked me to write as much as I like, & on anything I like, except the fiscal question & Mr Chamberlain: an exception I do not regret, for I am getting tired of both subjects.

No doubt your folks can carry elections just now; but can they afford to let the whole Press gradually pass under the control of a great Chamberlainized Trust? However let us talk of these things when we meet.

Will you send me a line here to say whether you will dine on Friday – at 8? Or if you are engaged, let me know whether I shall find you if I call between 4 & 5 that afternoon.

Yours sincerely
SIDNEY LOW

Charles Trevelyan to WSC

12 November 1904   Cambo
                                                   Northumberland

Dear Churchill,

I take blame to myself for not having replied to part of your letter to me
in which you asked me to post you up in the case for Rating of Land Values.
It is not very easy to do, because there is comparatively little in print about it.

For the quite general argument of the objection to rates and taxes on
industry and improvements, and the justice of land taxation as in its
nature harmless to and even productive of industry, you might read Judge
O'Connor's separate report to the Local Taxation Commission, which I
enclose. If you begin Page 9, you will avoid being offended by the more
polemical and rhetorical character of the earlier part of the report. Though
it is not necessary to go the length of believing in land nationalization with
Tolstoi and Henry George,[1] it is necessary to get hold of the fundamental
distinction between land and other kinds of property.

For your purposes in dealing with the proposals which are now before us,
I advise you to look at the cautious minority report of the Local Taxation
Commission on the Taxation of Site Values, the speeches by myself and others
in the enclosed pamphlet, the speech by me in Hansard this year March 11th.
But I am not sure that the yellow pamphlet reprinting Charles Booth's
endorsement of the policy from his great book on London is not the clearest
and strongest statement of all. He evidently thinks *all* rates ought to be on the
land value and quite certainly *none* on houses.

The real reason why I care about it politically at present is because I
believe it to be the only effective counter to Chamberlain. You don't end
trade depression by saying Joe would only make it worse, or stop overcrowding and physical deterioration by saying that a bread tax would make
the poor poorer. Putting the whole rates on the land value would have the
following results in answer to Joe's policy:

1. Force all land into the market directly wanted, so greatly lowering the
   first cost of production in starting an industry i.e. land price.
2. Relieve all buildings and commercial enterprises of taxation for local
   purposes. You would no longer tax the enterprising man higher in
   exact proportion to his expenditure of capital and success in business.
3. Make building cheap by abolishing house rate and forcing land into
   the market at just above its agricultural value. The fresh supply of

[1] Henry George (1839–97), American economist; best remembered for *Progress and Poverty*,
1879.

cheap houses would enable the overcrowded population either to get more rooms for same rent & consequently greater health, or to get same house-room cheaper and spend money on other things – so improving home trade.

Protection proposes to

favour a few trades and not necessarily those most fitted to survive; make everything dearer and so injure the home market; make the livelihood of the very poor harder by adding to the cost of prime necessities.

Relief of present rates by Land Value Taxation

makes all industries easier to commence and carry on, consequently favouring those most fitted to survive;

makes everything cheaper, especially houses and so improves the home market;

makes livelihood of very poor easier by cheapening a first necessity, houses.

Excuse my anxiety to get you to take up this subject. But your wise doctrines of economy apply in such a much smaller degree to local than to national taxation, and yet the local burden (being on industry & houses) is so much more severely felt than national taxes.

I hope I have not bored you.

I had a capital meeting in East Manchester the day before yesterday. All men speak well of your chances.

CHARLES TREVELYAN

Lord Hugh Cecil to WSC

12 November 1904   Hatfield

My dear Winston,

I had such a prostration of tiredness yesterday that I thought that Rawtenstall [Lancashire] & the really frightful journey that it involved was impossible. Were you there? I hope I am not thought to be weakening towards the Duke. I am full of gratitude & admiration for him.

As to the paper question I think something must be done. If you have any ideas let me know. I am told Harmsworth is much less Chamberlainite than Pearson & I thought he might be not indisposed to help mildly on Balfourian Free Trade lines – at any rate by advice. Can you put me in the way of making his acquaintance?

My brother wants me to remind you that he is expecting to hear from you about the publication of Ld Randolph's letters to my father – which you were to select from & send to him for his approval.

Ever yours

HUGH CECIL

I go to Oxford Monday or Tuesday

Lady Randolph to WSC

12 November [1904]   Sandringham

My dearest Winston,

I read your speech at Glasgow[1] with such interest – I did *not* discuss it with the King, you will be surprised to hear. I think it was rather a pity your Chairman attacked AB the way he did. I see the audience resented it – at least so the papers make out. Henri de Breteuil[2] tells me that in France they look upon you as the coming man. Here I am in a hot bed of protectionists. You have probably seen the party in the papers. We have been asked to stay on till Monday. It has been most pleasant nice weather – pleasant people & excellent sport. George shot very well & are both seen in good favour – so *that* is all right. Where shall you be next week? Salisbury Hall is at your disposal if you want to come. By the way, I have been so ill ever since I ate those oysters with you – I had to see the doctor here, & he told me I had been poisoned. I am all right now – we are thinking of going to Paris for Xmas. Why don't you come? The Breteuils would put you up – now goodbye.

Yr loving

MOTHER

WSC to Lord Hugh Cecil
(*Quickswood Papers*)

14 November 1904   105 Mount Street

Private

My dear Linky,

You will see from the papers that I am not at Blenheim this week. But from the 18th to 25th I shall be at Salisbury Hall & my mother would be delighted to entertain you to lunch or dinner any day you liked.

I could not go to Rawtenstall; but no one would have any suspicions of

---

[1] See Main Volume II, pp. 89–91.

[2] Henri Charles Joseph, Marquis de Breteuil (1848–1916), close friend of Lord and Lady Randolph Churchill. KCVO 1905; GCVO 1912.

you – ever. The Duke made a splendid speech; but I think it clear therefrom that he intends to make no concessions to Preference or Retaliation, that he intends to fight on the ultra-Cobdenite side & that it is not improbable that he will be called upon to lead the Liberal party. AB has let all his Free Trade allies depart. They will not return, however sorrowful his plight.

Did you observe how the Prot newspapers boycotted the speech? I thought it a sinister & significant demonstration; & *The Times* report was evidently a calculated insult. I will try to get into communication with Harmsworth when I return to London. But he & Pearson are largely amalgamated & own many newspapers in common – the *B'ham D. Gazette* for instance.

Sometimes when I think of the gigantic weight of prejudice & selfishness to be lifted, & the hopeless divisions which exist between so many of us, I am inclined to think that in the end Joe & his gang will triumph. Here in Scotland immense stolid audiences are comforting; & I am glad to feel I can do something. Nearly two hundred constituencies have asked me to speak. I want to talk to you.

I have written to your brother about the letters. He need not be apprehensive. I should not think of breaking faith.

Yours ever
W

Sir Alfred Harmsworth to WSC

14 November 1904   *The Daily Mail*

My dear Churchill,

I send you a cutting forwarded to me by a Press Agency, which, taken in conjunction with several remarks that I have heard, seems to imply that you were referring to my business.

The fabrication that I am engaged in running newspapers in various parts of the country advocating different political opinions is untrue.[1] The papers which I direct and am personally responsible for, are the *Daily Mail, Evening News, Daily Mirror,* and the *Weekly Dispatch* and no others. The other two are directed alone by my brother Harold[2] and owned by my brothers, and I

---

[1] *The Times,* reporting WSC's speech at Coatbridge, stated on 12 November 1904: 'He [WSC] thought there was not nearly enough of the personal element in journalism. The establishment of a mammoth newspaper trust which operated through five, ten, or a dozen newspapers at a time, and very often was managed by one management, and yet animated by totally different opinions in politics but which could turn its writers on this side or that at the caprice of some individual that was out of touch with the politics or the interests of the population affected, was to be deplored.'

[2] Harold Sidney Harmsworth, 1st Viscount Rothermere (1868–1940), the financial manager of the Harmsworth empire; Secretary of State for Air 1917–18.

am no more responsible for their opinions, than I am responsible for my brother Leicester,[1] the Liberal Member for Caithness.

Yours sincerely
ALF HARMSWORTH

WSC to Lady Randolph

EXTRACT

15 November 1904   Dalmeny

Dearest Mamma,

... Glasgow was a very great success, & there is no doubt that I have made a very distinct impression on the city. They all declared that no such speech had been delivered in the St Andrews Hall for many years. The whole audience stood up at the end, which is vy rare in Scotland. Cock-a-doodle-doo!!...
Times boycotting the old duke's speech. What blackguards the Protectionist Press are!

Marquess of Salisbury to WSC

EXTRACT

17 November 1904   20 Arlington Street

My dear Winston,

... Bother politics! But you will forgive me for saying that – though may we always remain personal friends – in politics as distinguished from personal matters I have to do, not with the people who have left us, but with those whom we still retain.

Yours ever
SALISBURY

Sir Alfred Harmsworth to WSC

17 November 1904   *The Daily Mail*

My dear Churchill,

A great many people thought your speech referred to me on account of the constant endeavour of my numerous enemies to suggest that my political conscience is even more elastic than it really is.

[1] Robert Leicester Harmsworth (1870–1937), Liberal MP 1900–22; baronet 1918.

Arthur Pearson has no brothers owning newspapers of divergent views, so they did not apply the speech to him.

Why not lunch with me to-morrow at the Parisienne Cafe, Savoy Hotel, at 1.25?

Yours sincerely
ALFRED H

C. A. Pearson to the Editor of the Spectator[1]

[?18] November 1904

Sir,

I feel that I can rely upon your courtesy and sense of fairness to allow me to reply to some aspects of the statements made and opinions expressed in your last issue with regard to my purchase of the *Standard*, and I trust that, if I am not encroaching too much on your space, you will permit me at the same time to reply briefly to some other assertions that have been made both in the Press and on the platform.

I do not complain in the least of the chagrin which has been felt and expressed at the fact that a newspaper which has latterly been a bold exponent of free-trade theories should pass under the control of one who has not shown marked enthusiasm for them; but I do feel that I have every right to protest against some of the assumptions made by yourself and others.

The notes which dealt with the matter in your last issue contained the following sentence: – 'Men feel that the saner and more moderate Conservative elements in the nation have been deprived of their one remaining representative in the London daily Press.' Mr Winston Churchill said in a recent speech: – 'The group of able writers who had exerted so much influence was scattered; their places were filled by the obedient scribes of a mammoth trust.' These statements are typical of many which have been made elsewhere. I venture to characterize that of the *Spectator* as being, to say the least of it, unfairly premature, while that of Mr Winston Churchill is a deliberate untruth.

It is my firm intention to preserve in every way the tone which has distinguished the *Standard* up to the present. My association with other publications does not prevent me from thoroughly appreciating the dignified *rôle* played by the *Standard* in the past, and I am determined to uphold the traditions of the paper in the future.

The assumption that it is my intention to lower the style and tone of the *Standard* is quite baseless. It is Utopian, I suppose, to hope that political opponents will believe this to be the case; but perhaps the fact that Mr

[1] This letter was also published in *The Times* on 19 November 1904.

Sidney Low and Mr Richardson Evans, who have been responsible for the leading articles for some 20 years, have entered into arrangements with me to remain on the staff for long terms, that Mr S. H. Jeyes, who has been with the paper for 13 years, and assistant editor for the last five, has agreed to retain that position with even larger responsibility than he has had in the past, and, finally, that so trusted and responsible a publicist as Mr H. A. Gwynne has accepted the editorship, will convince the public of my determination to adhere to old *Standard* traditions.

As for Mr Winston Churchill's misstatement, I wish to correct it, not because I attach any great importance to this or any other utterance of that eminent statesman, but because of the publicity which has been given to it by the Press. No writer on the *Standard* staff has left. Mr Curtis, the only member of the editorial staff who has gone, has not written in its columns for some 15 years. Then is it fair to talk or write of the creation of a 'newspaper trust'? My newspaper organization, to which the *Standard* is the latest addition, is no more a trust than is Lloyds Bank, the Gordon Hotels, Messrs Thomas Cook and Sons, or any other great business which has branches in different parts of the country. The fact that I have succeeded in extending my business rapidly seems for some occult reason to give serious offence to certain of my critics. If some of their assertions were true, I grant that there would be cause for adverse criticism. They say, for example, that my papers profess different principles in different parts of the country. This is not so. Every daily newspaper for which I am responsible – and I am connected with none for which I am not responsible in great issues – advocates the same views on subjects of national importance.

Finally, I should like to touch upon some purely personal matters. I trust that I may be excused an appearance of egotism. It is difficult to speak about oneself without this. I am not – as some people seem to think I ought to be – in the least ashamed of having been the manager of a great business, of which *Tit-Bits* was the principal production, when I was 19 years old, nor of having made an independent start by the production of *Pearson's Weekly* a few years later. Neither can I see that there is anything terrible in the fact that I am only 38 to-day. I know that to some minds it is almost a crime to attain success while one is young; but I believe that both in this respect and in that of having begun with comparatively small things I do not differ from many others who have arrived at some prominence both in our own and in former days. Will you allow me finally to say that I have neither the time nor the desire to reply to hostile criticism in detail, and that I trust those who have seen fit to express adverse views to my association with the *Standard* will think it fair to give publicity to this letter?

C. ARTHUR PEARSON

WSC to Lord Rosebery
(*Rosebery Papers*)

EXTRACT

19 November 1904   105 Mount Street

Private

My dear Lord Rosebery,

. . . I was delighted with your Glasgow telegram, wh it was kind of you to send, & also the chairman (who opened it while I was speaking) insisted on reading out. I was pleased with that meeting wh was in its way a triumph! Oh but what a labour & a battle to overturn this government, with our divided & undisciplined army!

Yours most sincerely
WINSTON S. CHURCHILL

Lord Salisbury to WSC

20 November 1904   Windsor Castle

My dear Winston,

My letter was impertinent and in it's implied rebuke not very just – for a man is right to change his Party if it does not suit his opinions. And I do not doubt that this was your case in many respects. So I am sorry. And yet in my heart I think it was not your act but your demeanour in so acting which led me to be rude. This I fear looks like another impertinence, but to a man for whom I have a great liking and regard I will risk saying it.

And so in spite of it and of the formality of your address I will still remain – with every apology

Ever yours
S

T. W. Killick to WSC
EXTRACT

20 November 1904   Townfield House
Private   Altrincham

Dear Mr Churchill,

. . . Taking the Irish as a whole they are – Home rulers, Protectionists and supporters of the Education Act; and I confess I don't see how they can be kept from following Chamberlain; who probably if the Redistribution dodge fails will adopt Home Rule.

I have been thinking what I should do if I were responsible for the organization of the NW Man Lib Assn. First I would get an active man who would do as he was told as agent, or sub-agent.

Then I would call Ward meetings by a circular addressed to *every* elector asking each one to attend if he were in sympathy with the objects of the meeting. I would also post bills in the Ward to invite the non-electors as well as the electors. At the meeting I would leave the candidate present to make a short speech. Then I would ask everyone present willing to work to put their names down as the Ward Committee, and also to get other men to work and to send in their names. Lastly I would ask the meeting to elect the representatives of the Ward on the Council. If possible the officers of the Ward should be elected by the whole Committee and not by the delegates to the Council only.

In this way the appeal would be made over the widest possible area. Fresh blood would be introduced, and there would be a reasonable chance of taking the control of affairs out of the hands of incompetent men.

The Candidate, the officers, and the workers would be in touch, and the best methods of working could be hammered out amongst them.

I hear Joynson Hicks is to address a meeting of business men in the Memorial Hall this week. If so his speech may be your last text at the meeting on the 30th.

Yours very truly
T. W. KILLICK

WSC to the Editor of The Times

21 November 1904   [105 Mount Street]

Sir,

Mr C. Arthur Pearson has used your columns to accuse me of 'deliberate untruth' in the comments I have made upon the purchase of the *Standard* newspaper. 'Deliberate' is an epithet necessarily founded only upon Mr Pearson's opinion of me, which I daresay is not good, and which I do not seek to alter. 'Untruth,' however, falls within the range of determinable facts, and may be profitably considered.

Why did Mr Pearson buy the *Standard?* No one has suggested, so far as I am aware, that it is his intention to lower the 'style and tone' of that paper. That would obviously be commercial folly; and I have no wish to accuse Mr Arthur Pearson of that. I am quite ready to credit him with 'thoroughly appreciating the dignified *rôle* played by the *Standard* in the past,' and to admit that his 'association with other publications' (presumably less dignified) does not necessarily prevent him from doing so. But I am prepared to assert that, quite apart from the commercial value of the *Standard* newspaper and the social influence its proprietor commands – both, no doubt, legitimate objects of desire – Mr Pearson's intention was to effect a change in the policy of the paper, to prevent it from continuing 'a bold exponent of free-trade theories' – to quote his own expression – and to make it the mouthpiece of the chairman of the Tariff Reform League. Mr Pearson's private objects do not concern the politician; but his public object is a matter of grave importance, and that object, I repeat, is diametrically to change the policy of the *Standard* newspaper upon the cardinal question of the day. And this Mr Pearson practically admits in his letter to the *Spectator*, which you, Sir, reprinted on Saturday, for he says that it is not true that papers under his control profess different principles in different parts of the country. 'Every daily newspaper for which I am responsible – and I am connected with none for which I am not responsible in great issues – advocates the same views on subjects of national importance.' Therefore it is quite clear on Mr Pearson's own admission that the *Standard* newspaper, hitherto 'a bold exponent of free-trade theories,' is now in policy to be brought into line, for instance, with the *Daily Express*. For the present, no doubt, there is a great difference between the political tone of the *Standard* and that of his other publications, and, while that difference lasts, it will be perfectly true to say, though Mr Pearson may not like it, that his papers 'profess different principles in different parts of the country.' But I readily admit that this is a passing phase, and that Mr Pearson's reason for making a gradual change instead of a sudden change in the policy of the *Standard* – though it involves a temporary inconsistency with his other newspapers – does not arise from any political insincerity on his part, but from his desire to carry with the *Standard* newspaper in its conversion as many of its old readers as possible; as a net is drawn in slowly to catch the greatest quantity of fish.

But, however slowly, none the less surely a complete reversal is to be made in the policy of the *Standard* on the question of tariff reform. Therefore it follows that either those writers who have previously expounded free-trade doctrines will be replaced by others, or they will be forced to adopt opinions entirely opposite to those they have hitherto professed. Charitably I had assumed the former, but Mr Pearson corrects me. The policy, he declares, is to be changed; but it is a 'deliberate untruth' to say that the writers will be changed. They will, according to him, be the same writers; but they will advocate a totally different policy. He has not changed them because he has been able to pervert them. I shall certainly not attribute deliberate untruthfulness to Mr Pearson; but it is difficult to reconcile his assertions with what is generally known of the character of the writers to whom he has referred. If it should after all be true (as, in spite of his denial, I certainly believe) that other men will have to be found to deal with the fiscal policy of the *Standard*, my statement which he has characterized as 'a deliberate untruth' will, quite apart from the literal proof afforded by the dismissal of Mr Curtis, be found substantially correct, and he himself will have been led into inaccurate assertion in matters upon which he is necessarily well informed.

Mr Pearson further complains that he should be described as creating 'a newspaper trust.' I have no wish to pry into his business, and I therefore write without actual certainty on this matter. But I believe that since the launching of Mr Chamberlain's policy, the proprietor of the *Daily Express* has acquired in addition the *Standard*, the *St James's Gazette*, the *Sun*, the *Birmingham Daily Gazette*, and a newspaper at Newcastle. I did not know what others he may have purchased, or may be planning to purchase, but, if the above list be mainly correct, it is at any rate a new and formidable feature – however it may be described – in the ever-extending operations of capital. Mr Pearson, in an illuminating sentence, likens it to the spread of a great hotel system. I do not know whether British working journalists will relish the comparison. There is nothing discreditable in keeping hotels, but it has usually been held that those who undertake to guide and influence the thought of the nation have a higher and more responsible function in the State than those who provide board and lodging.

Mr Pearson is, no doubt, within his rights in all he does; but Parliamentary representatives are also within their rights, and not without their duty, when they do their best to make sure that the change in the character of certain newspapers is not overlooked by the public.

I am, Sir, yours faithfully
. WINSTON S. CHURCHILL

WSC to Editor of The Times

23 November 1904   [105 Mount Street]

Sir,

When I attempted on Monday to make a list of the publications which Mr Pearson was believed to control, I was careful to state that it was a subject on which I could not pretend to complete or certain knowledge. Since then, however, a correspondent, upon whose accuracy I have reason to rely, has forwarded to me the necessary information. As his account both corrects and extends the list I had endeavoured to draw up, I may, perhaps, be allowed to present it to your readers. The complete list should read as follows: – The *Standard*, the *Evening Standard*, the *St James's Gazette*, the *Daily Express*, the *Birmingham Daily Gazette*, the *Birmingham Evening Dispatch*, the *Leicester Evening News*, the *North Mail*, the *Evening Mail*, and the *Newcastle Weekly Leader*. It will be observed that, although the tale is longer than I had believed, the *Sun* newspaper does not figure in it. The editor of the *Sun* is naturally indignant at the injustice I have done him. Although I might plead that the 'style' and tone of the *Sun* and its sudden change on fiscal policy a year ago made my mistake a very pardonable one, it is none the less a mistake; and, as it has caused pain and anger, I hasten to express regret for it.

But surely, Sir, this formidable list of allied publications scattered all over the country, assuming local character, professing unbounded independence, but all worked like marionettes by the chairman of the Tariff Reform League, will excite some disquieting reflections. Is it likely, for instance, to enhance the public respect for the editorial 'we'? Consider. The sonorous, patriotic, old-fashioned-fine-crusted-Tory 'we' in the *Standard* every morning is the same 'we' as 'the parrot' in the *Daily Express*. 'We' morning and evening at Newcastle, and 'we' also weekly in the same place, devoted to the prosperity of that port and city, ready to stand and fall by the welfare of the workers of the Tyne, are the same 'we's' who expatiate with authority, born, of course, of experience and interest, on the industrial condition of Leicester, and who 'announce with profound regret' the death of some local magnate whose public work in Birmingham 'we have long admired.' What tinselled humbug it all is! And where, I should like to know, is the vaunted freedom of the Press? A newspaper may have a quarrel with a Government; the newspaper may be wrong, and its action deeply injurious to public interest, but it is safe. The most miserable journal can defy the most magnificent Administration. Ministers of the Crown – except in times of great commotion – are powerless, and rightly powerless, to act against it. But now it is becoming increasingly clear that the same newspaper, so proud and bold towards the State, has a master whom it must obsequiously obey. The power of capital may undermine it; an ingenious speculator may buy it up at any moment, and one fine evening, just as its editor and its staff are about to begin their work in earnest, they may be told that the whole concern – office, plant, goodwill, reputation – has been acquired by the opposition party or by some unknown person; and, unless the conqueror graciously permits them to keep their situations by changing their opinions, they may be hustled out into the street with a celerity, a simplicity, and an absence of scandal which a Russian chief of police might enviously admire.

I have no personal illwill to Mr Pearson. Certainly I shall not assail him on the score of his youth. Politics apart, it is pleasant to see a young man getting on. But, knowing something of the resentment which working journalists feel at the ever-expanding growth of newspaper combinations, and the consequent decline in the individual responsibility of editors and writers, I would urge those who have influence upon public platforms to take every convenient occasion of drawing attention to the developments which are now taking place, and which, so far as they are effective, must inevitably degrade journalism from the *status* of an honoured profession like medicine or law to a sordid and irresponsible traffic in words and phrases.

I am, Sir, yours faithfully
WINSTON S. CHURCHILL

T. W. Killick to WSC

3 December 1904   Free Trade League
                                                                Manchester

Dear Mr Churchill,

Our friend Mr Lindsell[1] created the Unionist party in the Altrincham Division and is a most expert electioneerer. Today he came to me and said that the *first* thing required by the NW M Lib Assn, was a good man to devote his time to organization and work. I replied that you were of the same opinion, and asked if he knew of a man. He said he thought he might be able to put his hand on a good man. Further – and this is important – he said that he should never be an Election agent again for any party, but that he was so anxious for your success that if you got a suitable man he would help him with advice and suggestions and directions to the utmost of his ability. Now this is an offer which in my judgment should be accepted. I am not mentioning this to anyone but yourself so handle it as you think best. Lindsell's notion of a man is a young lawyer who is keen on the matter, and who has time, and requires to make himself known. Such a man with Lindsell's advice would be I think just what you want.

The Stalybridge election is vital to the Free Trade League, to Free Trade in the cotton districts and to Free Trade generally.

We have been discussing the matter and we think the best plan would be:
– For the Free Trade Union (Liberal) to distribute literature and to help

---

[1] Frederick Raymond Barber Lindsell, partner in firm of solicitors; Town Councillor; Mayor of the Court Leet of Altrincham 1896.

Liberal meetings. You see they have lots of money and plenty of literature, we are short of both. And for the League to organize nightly meetings of Unionist and Labour speakers. The Labour men cannot appear on Liberal platforms and the Unionists don't like it. What do you think? We should of course hold little as well as big meetings. Could you speak at a big League meeting?

Yours very truly
T. W. KILLICK

WSC to Editor, Manchester Guardian

9 December 1904   105 Mount Street

Sir,

Mr Joynson-Hicks is mistaken in supposing that I desire to depreciate his past services to the cause of Temperance or to throw any doubt upon the sincerity of his Temperance convictions. I was not aware that he was himself a teetotaller; nor should I have referred to any circumstance so purely personal and private. My criticisms were directed not to his private convictions, which are I daresay admirable, but to his public conduct. And I again ask is it not surprising that a man who has been, as he tells us himself, for 25 years engaged in active temperance work, and who feels so acutely on this question that he is a life long abstainer, should, because he wants to get into Parliament, affect to support a Licensing Act which has been variously opposed by such men as Sir William Houldsworth, Lord Peel, and the Archbishop of Canterbury[1] and which was notoriously repugnant to all sections – even the most moderate – of Temperance opinion?

Yours faithfully
WINSTON S. CHURCHILL

Lord Hugh Cecil to WSC

29 December 1904   Hatfield

My dear Winston,

Your psychical experience is very interesting.[2] It would seem that inanimate things can be charged with emotion as iron is charged with magnetism & as they approach a mind which is in a receptive state (as yours was – vacant

---

[1] Randall Thomas Davidson (1848–1930), 94th Archbishop of Canterbury 1903–28.

[2] It has not been possible to discover any letter from WSC bearing on this 'psychical experience'.

& fresh from sleep) that mind is affected – like a compass. If this be true it might also account for miracles of healing worked through relics & other inanimate things – such things being charged with vitality. Also for the ghost-stories in which a ghost is said to haunt the scene of his crime and the like. For the haunted room may be charged with emotion & stimulate the receptive mind until imagination is set to work & an hallucination is produced!

There! there's a theory for you.

Yours ever
HUGH CECIL

WSC to Lady Randolph

21 January 1905   105 Mount Street

Dearest Mama,

I have had this morning a long talk with Sunny about your affairs. He wants me to go into the whole matter with Lumley and to consider whether or not it would be desirable to transfer the business of looking after the property to some other lawyer. He tells me that both you and George [Cornwallis-West] have dwelt with emphasis upon my repeated refusal to take any interest in the matter. But you will allow me to say that I really have no right to interrogate Lumley without your authority. Will you therefore write me a letter authorising me to go into the whole matter and examine all the accounts. I will then endeavour to do that almost at once.

I am pestered by reporters who are fussing about this silly man at Preston.[1]

Ever your loving son
W

WSC to Edward Clarkson

24 January 1905   105 Mount Street

[Copy]

Sir,

I beg to acknowledge the receipt of your letter of the 18th instant. I cannot consent to recognise you as a principal in a matter which obviously

---

[1] After WSC had called the senior Member for Preston, Sir William Tomlinson, 'that miserable old man', he was challenged to a duel of fists by Mr Edward Clarkson, a veteran Conservative of that town.

concerns Sir William Tomlinson and myself. The advantages of settling political differences by the methods you suggest are not immediately apparent; but I feel that it would in any case be highly irregular for one of the principals to be represented in person, and the other by a champion. Such combats even if desirable should invariably be conducted either between principals on both sides or between champions on both sides. Several gentlemen whose qualifications seem unimpeachable have written to me offering their services in the latter capacity. I should not be unwilling to put you in communication with them on the chance of their being able to afford you the active exercise you desire.

Yours faithfully
[Winston S. Churchill]

WSC to Lady Randolph

EXTRACT

26 January 1905   105 Mount Street

Dearest Mamma,

Many thanks for your letter. I have appointed the 7th and 8th prox. as the days of Inquisition & have written accordingly to Lumley.

I have proposed myself to Bend'or[1] for Sunday & if he would like me to come, I could get to you for dinner Saty. Now do please read the *Manchester Guardian*. You will find such good reports of anything I say in it. Things are going vy well here. . . .

With best love, I remain, your loving son
W

WSC to Joseph Chamberlain

25 February 1905   105 Mount Street

[Copy]

Dear Mr Chamberlain,

For your information and convenience I enclose you a copy of the motion which I expect to make upon the 8th of March. May I ask you to use your influence with the Govt to secure a decision by the House of Commons, free from party bias upon a question, which you have repeatedly declared to

---

[1] Duke of Westminster.

be above party, and which the Prime Minister has stated is not within the scope of any policy which he will propose within the lifetime of the present Parliament.

Yours sincerely
WINSTON S. CHURCHILL

Joseph Chamberlain to WSC

27 February 1905   40 Prince's Gardens
Private

Dear Winston,

Thanks for your letter. I believe there is a question today asking for the terms of your motion.

As regards the request contained in your letter the matter is not one in which I see any reason to interfere.

Yours truly
J. CHAMBERLAIN

A. Akers-Douglas[1] to the King
(Royal Archives)

2 March 1905   House of Commons

Mr Akers-Douglas with his humble duty to Your Majesty begs leave to submit an account of the proceedings of the House of Commons this day.

The consideration of the Supplementary Estimate of £550,000 for Army Services occupied the whole day.

W. Bromley-Davenport[2] explained that the Expenditure was necessary to complete the payment for the operations in Somaliland – the total cost of the campaign had been £2,457,000. Reductions were moved in respect of the expenses for General staff but defeated by a majority of 49. A long discussion ensued in which Mr Winston Churchill complained of the expenditure on Staff & said he meant 'those gorgeous & gilded functionaries with brass

---

[1] Aretas Akers-Douglas (1851–1926), Secretary of State, Home Department 1902–6; Conservative MP for St Augustine's Division in Kent 1880–1911; Conservative Whip 1883–1895; Parliamentary Secretary to Treasury 1885–6, 1886–92, 1895; First Commissioner of Works 1895–1902; PC; Baron Douglas 1911; Viscount Chilston of Boughton Malherbe 1911.

[2] William Bromley-Davenport (1862–1949), Financial Secretary, War Office 1903–5; Conservative MP for Macclesfield 1886–1906; Brigadier-General 1916; knighted 1924.

hats & ornamental duties who multiplied so luxuriously on the plains of Aldershot & Salisbury.' This amendment was rejected by majority of 52. . . .

Note by the King in margin
What good words for a recent subaltern of Hussars!

ER

Lewis Harcourt to WSC

9 March 1905   14 Berkeley Square

My dear Winston,
    Though I am in bed here with pneumonia and was unable to hear you last night I must send you a line of warmest congratulation on what on reading it in the *Times* I thought was the best speech you ever made.[1] I suppose you were satisfied with the division; you must at least have been with the debate.

Yours very sincerely
LOULOU HARCOURT

H. H. Asquith to WSC

26 March 1905   Asquith House
                                                     Oakham

Dear Winston,
    The Walton motion[2] was put down in the form to which, I am told, everybody agreed on Thursday.
    It seems to me to be quite as clear a repudiation of Retaliation as the two former motions were of Protected food & the 10% Tariff.
    If you make it a direct note of censure on AJB he is quite capable of having a rally, in which he would be supported by many of the Free Fooders

---

[1] WSC was speaking on his own cleverly-worded motion on Imperial Preference.
[2] On 28 March, Mr J. Walton, Liberal MP for Barnsley, moved 'that in view of the declaration made by the Prime Minister this House thinks it necessary to record its condemnation of his policy of fiscal retaliation'. The Prime Minister, Mr Balfour, said it was his view that the Government ought not to exercise party discipline on private Members' Bills. For his part he said he would not join in future debates of this kind and suggested that his supporters would do well to follow his example. Although the motion was a direct attack on the Government's fiscal policies, the Prime Minister, his Ministers and most of his supporters were absent from the House during the debate. The Resolution was carried *nem con* but Balfour refused to treat it as a vote of censure.

and (as I believe) by not a few of the Chamberlainites – with the result that your motion might well be defeated.

If anyone likes to introduce (as can be done to-morrow) a little more pepper & mustard into the language I should be the last person to object.

Yrs sincerely

H. H. ASQUITH

C. H. P. Mayo[1] *to WSC*

4 April 1905   Garlands
                                                            Harrow-on-the-Hill

Dear Churchill,

During the Army debates in the House I do wish you could draw attention to a side of the work connected with the War Office, which is very important & only just touched upon – the most unsatisfactory way in which it has dealt with the Army Examns. Arnold-Forster[2] has lately made an attack upon the Schools & the boys sent up from them: he complains they are badly prepared & gets a hearing – it is so easy for a Cabinet Minister to get a hearing, – & probably after his 2 or 3 years of Office he knows very little about the facts.

The War Office has given us no chance. During the last few years they have had 3 or 4 schemes at least; we have never known what the Examiners thought they ought to examine in: at one time they seek for intellectual power, at another lay stress on the dullest mechanism. Another scheme, & in the opinion of many men qualified to express an opinion, the worst of all comes into operation next November; with reference to it I asked one of the leading Mathematicians at Cambridge – a Fellow of Trinity – to tell me what he thought of it, he wrote, 'the War Office has unwisely yielded to noisy clamour, & they at Cambridge would have nothing to do with such Mathematics.' Under such conditions the Schools have no chance & I do wish this unsatisfactory side of the many unsatisfactory sides of the work connected with the War Office could be mentioned during the Debates.

Yours sincerely

C. H. P. MAYO

[1] Charles Harry Powell Mayo (1859–1929), mathematics master at Harrow 1892–1919.

[2] Hugh Oakeley Arnold-Forster (1855–1909), Secretary of State for War 1903–6; Liberal Unionist MP for West Belfast 1892–1906, Unionist MP for Croydon 1906–9; son of William Delafield Arnold, Director of Public Instruction in Punjab; adopted son of Rt Hon W. E. Forster (1818–86); grandson of Thomas Arnold of Rugby.

WSC to Lady Randolph

EXTRACT

6 April 1905   105 Mount Street

Dearest Mama,

. . . Brighton is truly wonderful.[1] Never has there been such a landslide. I do not think the govt will go on much longer. I had a long talk with Lumley yesterday & am preparing a letter. I am going to spend the Sunday with Ivor at Ashby – with polo on Saty & Monday. I have begun electric treatment to tighten my dislocated shoulder. It is rather pleasant. We shall be together either at Blenheim or Salisbury Hall the whole of the Easter holiday.

With best love, Your loving son
W

WSC to ?

14 April 1905   105 Mount Street

[Copy]

Sir,

I have no desire to drag Mr Balfour's personal relations with Lord Randolph Churchill into current political controversy; but when Mr Joynson Hicks thinks it proper to assert that Mr Balfour was 'one of Lord Randolph Churchill's dearest friends' I feel bound to declare, after a study of the very extensive evidence which has been placed before me; that such a statement seems to me extravagant.

Yours faithfully
[WINSTON S. CHURCHILL]

---

[1] 'He [Mr Gerald Loder] was first returned at a by-election for Brighton, which was a two-Member Borough, in 1889, by a majority of more than 2,500 over a Gladstonian Liberal candidate, and at every subsequent election he had been at the head of the poll, the mean Conservative majority never falling below that handsome figure. Yet when the poll was declared on April 5, he was found to have been beaten, by a majority of 817, by Mr E. A. Villiers the Liberal candidate, who received 8,209 votes against 7,392 for Mr Loder. The Liberal poll was higher by some 2,750 than it had ever been before, and Mr Loder's total was less by several hundreds than any recorded for him since (and including) 1892'. *Annual Register* 1905.

WSC to Lord Londonderry

14 April 1905   105 Mount Street

[Copy]

My dear Londonderry,

I write you a line to tell you that I have now decided to leave the Carlton Club. The differences which drove me into opposition to the government have now developed into a total breach with the party. Old friendships have been snapped & on the other hand new obligations have been contracted wh I must endeavour faithfully to discharge. I no longer see that possibility of reunion in which when we last talked this matter over I honestly believed. I am moreover, in such constant conflict with the Conservative Party at all points that my membership of their club cannot be justified any longer & has become disagreeable to me.

I write this to you because of your kindness in the whole matter. If other conservative ministers had shown your tolerance the position of the party would have been far different today. I am vy grateful to you for assuming some responsibility for my continued membership & believe me, whatever may be the course of public affairs, always yours

most affectionately
[WINSTON S. C]

WSC to A. N. Streatfield[1]

14 April 1905   105 Mount Street

[Copy]

Mr Churchill presents his compliments to the Secretary of the Carlton Club and desires him to take the necessary steps to remove his name from the list of Members and to inform him when this has been done.

A. N. Streatfield to WSC

17 April 1905   Carlton Club

Dear Sir,

In accordance with your letter of the 14th inst, your name has been duly withdrawn from the list of Members of this Club.

Yours faithfully
A. N. STREATFIELD

[1] Secretary of Carlton Club 1887–1912.

WSC to Lord Rosebery
(*Rosebery Papers*)

25 April 1905   Blenheim

My dear Lord Rosebery,
   Please observe from the enclosed cartoon[1] how your sportive arrows are
deflected into the bosoms of your friends!
   You are well out of this weather which is all made up of rain & wind.
I have been toiling at my book – without much satisfaction. I think it is more
difficult the longer I try. Sunny returns today. I wonder whether you will
have seen him.
   Politics have stopped as though switched off by a handle. Only Brodrick
enlivens the recess. You are certainly well advised not to hasten your return.
When you do come back – this is the purpose of my letter – I hope you will
bring a small sheaf for me.

                                                      Yours always
                                          WINSTON S. CHURCHILL

Lord Rosebery to WSC

EXTRACT

4 May 1905   Villa Rosebery
                                                               Naples

Private

My dear Winston,
   I should have been glad today to get your letter, had it not been for the
poisonous insinuation that I was thinking of you or Lloyd George when I
made my last speech. No two people were further from my mind, for both,
I am sincerely convinced, possess high practical as well as high national

----

   [1] The Cartoon, from the *Pall Mall Gazette* of 18 April, was entitled THE MYSTERY EX-
PLAINED. It showed WSC and Lloyd George, with mud in their hands, being addressed by
Balfour. The caption read: –
   The Prime Minister: 'I'm afraid, gentlemen, that in this persistent mud-throwing you only
waste your time!' Messrs Lloyd George and Churchill: 'Not a bit of it, we're qualifying
for "high positions" in the next Liberal Government.'
   ('The man who may hope most to be appointed to a high position (in the Government) is
not the man who has given proof of the qualities of administration; it is the man who can
make the most active political campaign, *who can make the most speeches,* and who can apply
the most stinging epigrams to the tender places of a decadent Government.' Lord Rosebery
at the Liberal League Meeting.)

ability. In truth, I was thinking of no one, but rather of our strange but inevitable principle of distributing the great offices among orators and those who 'have deserved well of the party'. Of orators Bright and Sheridan were perhaps the greatest of the nineteenth century – both useless as ministers. And of the second class there are many whom I need not cite, who are neither orators nor administrators, but who go wherever the caucus bids them and deliver unreported speeches. These also have their reward. You cannot test administrative power in Parliament, and parties must be maintained – and fed. So, I say, the principle is inevitable. But it is not ideal.

I should like to see severe drafting (and offer myself as a prime example), and the largest admission of young talent into the vacancies thus caused. Neither you nor Lloyd George would suffer by this principle.

By the by tell LG that I did not quite like his last speech as reported. He said practically that the present Govt have pursued a Liberal foreign policy – they have surrendered the keys of the Mediterranean. Now I do not think that this is a Liberal foreign policy: it is foreign but not Liberal. But whether that be so or not, to say that the surrender of the keys of the Mediterranean is an essentially Liberal policy is to confirm a certain flouting view of Liberal foreign policy which does that party infinite harm in the country.

I doubt if I shall achieve anything for you. I have been ill ever since I left England and have thought more of cataplasms than biography. Write if there be news.

Yrs

R

WSC to Lord Rosebery
(*Rosebery Papers*)

EXTRACT

9 May 1905   105 Mount Street
Private

My dear Lord Rosebery,

Of course I never imagined that you *were* referring to LG & me. But I thought the cartoon would make you laugh. There is a good deal of truth in it. It is vy kind of you to write me such a long letter It will be carefully preserved among the Winstonian archives.

I am sorry you have been ill. So have I. Immediately after writing to you I was seized with the most villainous influenza, fever, head ache and sore throat – & it was a week before I could even crawl. Now I am better but at present the Statesman is in abeyance, and the Literary gent & the polo player are to the fore. . . .

. . . I will talk to LG about the key of the Mediterranean. It was certainly an unguarded & stupid remark. But I think *au fond* he has a strong element of jingoism in his nature. I should not be surprised to see that develop with the exercise of power.

I do hope that you will find time & inclination to write something about my father. When I consider how long, intimate & unbroken was your friendship, & how searchingly you measure the manner & character of those you know, I feel convinced that you have it in your power, as no other man, to preserve from the past a strong & vivid impression.

I will write again in case anything interesting comes to ear. Meanwhile I think you are very well situated at Naples. Such dullness never was in politics.

Yours ever
WINSTON SC

Sir Bindon Blood to WSC

EXTRACT

10 May 1905   Murree
                                                              Punjab

. . . We are all full of interest and amusement at your speeches and at your attacks on the Government – who, we quite see, want waking up – though we don't want them changed for your lot! I am looking forward with great interest to hearing from you next year why you changed over to the 'Liberals'. I fancy the enlightened class in England are not with the 'Liberal Party' as now constituted – a very different state of things from that of my young days. . . .

WSC to the Master of Elibank
(*Elibank Papers*)

25 May 1905   105 Mount Street
Private

My dear Murray,

It is vy kind of you to offer to forward my candidature at Brooks's Club.

I do not think while political animosities are so keen that I should care to expose myself to the petty malevolence of the ballot.

I was fortunate enough to be elected to a good many clubs while I was yet unknown. I am disinclined at present to put myself forward for others, though I should greatly like to be a member of Brooks's.

Yours sincerely
WINSTON S. CHURCHILL

Lady Wimborne[1] to WSC

EXTRACT

27 May 1905   Canford Manor

Dearest Winston,

I have been thinking a great deal about you, and so has Uncle Ivor. You know how much we care for you & your career not only for your dear father's sake, but also for yours, for you are always very dear to us & we want to be a little help to you. Now I know elections & Parliament in general all means a great deal of expense & so we want to enjoy the prerogative of standing in the relation of uncles & aunts to send a little present which we feel may be useful at any rate at the present time. When the heiress is found, I think the good fortune will not be only on your side.

Yrs affecly
CORNELIA WIMBORNE

WSC to the Master of Elibank
(Elibank Papers)

29 May 1905   105 Mount Street
Private

My dear Murray,

Since writing to you my caution in respect of Brooks's has received some justification. I foolishly allowed myself to be proposed for Hurlingham as a polo playing member; & was of course at once black-balled. This is almost without precedent in the history of the Club – as polo players are always welcomed. I do not think you & your Liberal friends realize the intense political bitterness which is felt against me on the other side.

Yours sincerely
WINSTON S. CHURCHILL

[1] Lady WIMBORNE.

W. *Bourke Cockran to WSC*

EXTRACT

12 June 1905   Dampfer *Scharnhorst*

Private and Confidential

... There is one idea in my head which will not down and which I fear will rob me of all rest unless it be given expression. Here then it is. It concerns you and I beg for it just such attention as you may deem it deserves after weighing it more or less carefully.

It arose from a paragraph in one of the newspapers which prompted a cartoon in the *Pall Mall Gazette* on Saturday last. This latter I saw on my way to Folkestone. It represented you as a mosquito or a fly or a wasp or some variety of winged irritant perched on the coach of Sir Henry Campbell-Bannerman whose repose you have evidently disturbed and are plainly striving to ruin. Under it is the paragraph to which I have referred and which states in substance that Mr Winston Churchill will not be given a place in the Liberal Cabinet if one should be formed after the next election. The cartoon was not particularly clever or funny but the idea conveyed by the paragraph has become a subject of extensive reflection with me.

To begin with it shows two things. First that your opponents believe you expect a seat in the Cabinet if a Liberal Government is to be formed and second that if you be not gratified in this expectation they count on your making trouble for the party which you have recently joined. Now this conception of your attitude presents you in rather a sordid character. It assumes that your sole object in politics is place and that to attain your ambition party success or party prospects would be sacrificed without scruple or hesitation. Of course we must realise that where a man changes sides, however lofty the motives which actually govern him, he is very likely to be accused by those whom he has left of being actuated by the very basest desires and ambitions. And the public – the vast masses of them absorbed in busy occupations have little time to sift and examine the evidence on which these personal assaults are supported. They can only see facts that are patent & so conspicuous that they cannot be overlooked. They know that you have changed sides. They vaguely feel that you have explained why you crossed the floor of the House and that your former associates have refused to accept the explanation, have assigned [other] motives for your conduct than you yourself would avow or admit. The public mind on this question in my judgment is not yet formed. Your career has been brilliant enough to arouse their interest, and so they have followed your movements as far as they are unmistakable. But when it comes to judging your motives I believe the majority of men who are not bigoted partisans are as yet of open minds – not at all convinced that the insinuations of your hostile critics are justified nor yet wholly satisfied that they are entirely baseless. The majority are waiting further developments before reaching their final conclusions. This then is very probably the crisis of your career. The judgment which men fairly un-biassed will form of you now is very likely the one that will follow you through life. For my part I don't think you could possibly desire a more favourable opportunity for confounding decisively and irretrievably your enemies and of vindicating your career to the full satisfaction of the friends who hold you dear. You have a chance now to take a position which will make it impossible for any one to question your motives for it will be so conspicuously unselfish that everyone must notice it and be impressed by it.

Every one has made up his mind that you are eagerly bent on being ad-mitted to the Cabinet. Under ordinary conditions this would be an ambition so natural that it would be praiseworthy. Indeed to acknowledge yourself without it would be to confess yourself unfitted for public life. But your cir-cumstances now are not normal. They are unusual. Your course then it seems to me should not be governed by usual principles of conduct. The thing above all others for you to do now is exactly the opposite of that which your enemies expect and which your lukewarm associates rather anticipate. All these are agreed that you will insist on entering the Cabinet or fight. Why not confound the hostile and surprise the indifferent by declaring now that you won't seek or even accept membership in a Liberal government if one is formed with the new parliament? Such a declaration would be in the nature of a bomb whose explosion would resound throughout the whole Empire but whose fragments would damage none but your critics. It would stamp as absolutely unselfish you whom all the Tory leaders and organs have com-bined to brand as self-seeking, self-centred, and self-conscious. It would not have one rag left of the garment which they have been laboriously trying to fit on your shoulders for the last two years and all the world would realize how baseless this conspiracy of slander has been.

What now would you sacrifice by such a declaration made at this moment?

First you will say that of course it involves renunciation of high office. That may be, but the renunciation would not be final. Indeed at the very worst it would be merely a brief adjournment. The man who has made your position in the House and in the Country can't keep out of office. If he refuse to seek it then office must in the nature of things seek him. Moreover the moment you cease to be a competitor all the men now watching you sus-piciously on your own side of the House will at once turn their jealousies in other directions – and you, no longer an object of their distrust, will very likely acquire their friendship. And if this be the result, as I believe it must

be, then you would be the only man prominent in your party without
personal animosities or rancour. Think what such a position would mean.
Conceive to what it must inevitably lead. Beyond any doubt it must result in
your becoming the unquestioned leader before the lapse of ten years.

It would be an attitude absolutely unique and so far as I know unprecedented in English public life – this of a young man furnishing to a political
party its most powerful support and yet declining to accept office under it –
giving it success and yet refusing to profit by the triumph to which he has
largely if not decisively contributed. Mind I don't mean that you should
remain aloof from both parties as Gladstone did after the fall of Peel for some
ten years I believe – on the contrary I think you should be the most active and
devoted partisan of the Liberal side – but a wholly unselfish one. Your word
in the House would thus acquire a weight that no other could possibly
possess. You would be the chief support of your party but not its beneficiary.
If Gladstone's isolation led to the Premiership merely because it freed him
from personal contentious concern [think] what the result must be of a
course which would keep you free from jealousies and competitions while at
the same time placing a whole party under a steadily growing burden of
obligation to you.

I beg you to weigh all this in the same spirit which inspires me to write it.
I have spoken with absolute frankness all that has come into my mind
through reflection on that paragraph re-printed in the *Pall Mall Gazette* and
whether you adopt these views or reject them I am sure you will realize that
they are the fruits of much solicitude for your future – I count on your reaching the highest place in your country – and this letter is sent in the hope that
it may serve to throw a ray of light, however faint, on your pathway.

Yours very sincerely
W. BOURKE COCKRAN

PS I have opened this long screed to add another word – I am not sure that
I have made clear the extent to which I think the renunciation suggested
should be carried. I don't mean that it should be permanent or absolute. The
fact that you are now a member of the Liberal party – not merely an
independent acting with it on one question but opposed to it on practically
all others – makes it incumbent on you to accept office if pressed upon you.
All that I think you should do now is to announce that you won't accept
office during the *next* parliament nor until you have earned it by service to
the Country *through* the Liberal party. If after such an announcement there
was an imperative demand that you take a place in the government or such
cabinet then a new situation would arise. It would present an entirely new
question – whether you would *accept* office at the demand of your party

differs widely from getting office under a threat or possibility that if refused you might make trouble.

Personally I should prefer that you kept out of office altogether for the present. A man who could support all party measures effectively and yet keep free from the differences and jealousies inherent in the most homogeneous cabinets would establish such a position, – in my judgment, that very soon he must be invited to join the govt on his own terms – even though these embraced the Premiership. Indeed I am not at all sure that the first place would not be forced on him for the simple reason that he would probably be the only means through whom all factions could unite for effective co-opera-tion. In fine my suggestion is to renounce the small merely to make sure of the great, to be slow about looking for a minor post in order to increase the chances of having the greatest placed at your feet. And this great result I would have you reach not by conduct that the most envious or hostile could criticise but by a course that the most scrupulous must praise. I have found through long experience that there is but one path to durable success and that is the straight & narrow one. To this I have never known an excep-tion.

WSC to Lady Randolph
EXTRACT

21 July 1905   105 Mount Street

Dearest Mamma,

I expect the Govt will resign & that a dissolution will follow from last night's division.[1] It was a great moment of satisfaction & excitement to all of us. . . .

Your loving son
WINSTON

George Wyndham to WSC

25 July 1905   44 Belgrave Square

My dear Winston,

I failed to find you today, what I wished to say is this.

The rule of pairing is that a pair cannot be broken except with the consent

---

[1] On Mr J. Redmond's amendment to reduce the Irish Land Commission supply vote by £100, which was carried by 200 to 196 at midnight on July 20. The Government did not resign.

of both parties to that pair. I have paired with you from the 27th instant to the end of the session.

But I am far from insisting that you shall *personally* abstain from voting on & after the 27th.

All that I ask is that you will either abstain from voting or, else, satisfy the Government whips that you have transferred your pair to a member of the opposition who can be fairly described as what we are, colloquially, a 'live pair'. That is the invariable rule which governs such arrangements.

Yours very sincerely
GEORGE WYNDHAM

George Wyndham to WSC

26 July 1905   44 Belgrave Square

My dear Winston,

I am much obliged to you for your letter. I am sorry that you shd be put to the inconvenience of seeking a substitute. But in this case I must consider my own obligations. I paired so that I might be free to carry them out: & I am bound to do so.

Yrs very sincerely
GEORGE WYNDHAM

WSC to Lord Hugh Cecil
(*Quickswood Papers*)

26 July 1905   105 Mount Street

My dear Linky,

You are always so just & to me so generous in your judgments that I am vy sorry indeed to get your letter. I value your good opinion and am most anxious to deserve it. But I cannot agree with the whole of what you say. I do not see where 'the pathos of failure' is to be found in the life of a man who although quite unsuited to Parliamentary life has passed so many years in great office which he still holds. You may know privately that Gerald Balfour is conscious that his abilities, distinguished as they are, undoubtedly are not suited to the House of Commons; that this has caused him pain, & also the Prime Minister. Except for some few sentences I remember to have heard you utter I do not feel that I have ever realised this forcibly. I have always thought of him as a successful man. I do now. It is because these Ministers are uplifted, guarded, served, praised that they excite my attacks. Any real misfortune to them would destroy all the superficial malevolence I allow myself to indulge. If I were to look through the House for 'the pattern of failure' I would find it in Bowles, or in Dilke – or in Hobhouse – or perhaps in Bartley[1] or Stuart Wortley.[2] I might find it even in Malcolm. I certainly find it – physical & political – in every page of the story I am writing. I say frankly I do not find failure in a reigning minister moving gradually yet prosperously to the close of ten years unbroken service.

But having said this much *truthfully* in my defence, let me also say that I do not acquit myself of having indulged spiteful feelings, & I should be really sorry if I had hurt any man's *private* feelings in consequence.

Yours ever
W

Master of Elibank to WSC

27 July 1905   The Automobile Club
                                                119 Piccadilly

My dear Churchill,

You must not mind my few words on the Terrace tonight, nor must you regard me as an 'impertinent meddler'! I am but a very ordinary 'rank & filer' with no political ambition or expectations.

As such, I may frankly say that although I have fought four elections in the last ten years, you are the sole Politician who has moved and attracted me. I speak from the point of view of 'leading'. Hence my reason for mentioning to you tonight for yr information, and guidance if you think fit, certain observations on the part of those who also, in public and in private, are your friends.

Personally, I like the fighting portion of your speeches in which you scourged the men who have treated you shamefully. At the same time, I cannot but feel that perhaps it is not wise entirely to lose sight of the more tender susceptibilities of that strong and silent element, who inevitably must rank amongst your backers in order ultimately to carry you and your policy to success in the Country. The feeling, then, amongst these men, is, I think, not so much that your reference to AJB is overdone, as that its continuance conceivably may detract, in the public estimation, from the

---

[1] George Christopher Trout Bartley (1842–1910), Conservative MP for North Islington, 1885–1906; established National Penny Bank, 1875; knighted 1902.

[2] Charles Beilby Stuart-Wortley (1851–1926), Conservative MP for Sheffield, 1880–1916; Under-Secretary of State for Home Department, 1885, 1886–92; Deputy Chairman of Committee of whole House 1895–1916; PC 1896; created Baron Stuart of Wortley 1916.

weight and general effect produced by the high level of your speeches on current problems.

Honestly, I am inclined to share that view.

You must forgive me for this note, but I know you will understand the spirit in which it is written, & please don't trouble to reply to it.

Whatever be your course, you will always find me your sincere well-wisher.

Yrs ever

ALEXANDER O. MURRAY

Sir Ian Hamilton to WSC

EXTRACT

4 August 1905

Tidworth House
Andover

My dear Winston,

About three weeks ago I met – one Saturday to Sunday – Arthur Balfour and two other Cabinet Ministers, and on my return I very nearly sat down and wrote to tell you of our conversation. I am sorry now I did not do so, for possibly the result might have been slightly to tone down some recent acerbities. Politicians were being discussed, and your name came upon the tapis. Everyone, male and female, in the smart party there assembled, were prepared to rend you to pieces, but Arthur Balfour spoke so exceedingly nicely about you, and expressed such generous hopes about your future, that no one raised a finger, and my customary mild protest was rendered superfluous. Had this been done with an air of false magnaminity, the effect on me would have been detestable, but I am fairly sensitive on such points and I can assure you it was not so, but the man was talking simply, naturally and genuinely from his heart. I really think that, in a way, he likes you, and rather admires you, at least he did then, and it is not a bad thing I think for you to bear in mind the next time you two have an encounter.

I am worked quite off my legs at present, but hope for more leisure after August. You will have to come down here someday and gallop over these Downs. I am in a palace, which runs Blenheim very close in mere dimensions and is ruining me to furnish. Goodbye for the present.

Believe me, Yours very sincerely

IAN HAMILTON

WSC to Lady Randolph

EXTRACT

31 August 1905   Ashby St Ledgers
Dearest Mamma,   Rugby

... Of course I am all for Curzon as against Kitchener, and for Constitutional Authority against military power. I cannot believe a Liberal Government will allow the Commander-in-Chief in India to engross to himself so much power. I am thinking of breaking into print upon the subject in the course of the next few days. I hope you found John Morley sound on this question. I should be greatly disconcerted if I thought the Liberal party were prepared to acquiesce in the handing over of the Indian Empire to an ambitious and indocile soldier. The military member in India is really in the same position as the Secretary of State for War in England. What has happened is that the Commander-in-Chief has not merely swallowed up his own War Minister but the Viceroy as well.

The appointment of Minto,[1] poor dear thing, is another piece of Arthurism *in excelsis*. For cynical disdain of public interests and contempt of public opinion, it exactly matches Brodrick's appointment to the India Office.

I must certainly see you before you go to Germany. Write & tell me when & where.

With best love, Always your loving son
W

WSC to Herbert Gladstone
(Herbert Gladstone Papers)

EXTRACT

19 September 1905   105 Mount Street
Private

My dear Gladstone,

... I have an immense deal of work in the Manchester district and I think I shall be more usefully employed there than in an indiscriminate campaign all over the country. I did a great many meetings last year – upwards I think of fifty – and until my book [*Lord Randolph Churchill*] is off my hands, I do not intend to undertake much this autumn.

---

[1] Gilbert John, 4th Earl of Minto (1845–1914), Governor-General of Canada 1898–1904; Viceroy of India 1905–10. Urged on by Morley, Minto became joint author of the 'Minto-Morley' reforms, which brought Indians for the first time on to the Viceregal Council, and is now considered to have been the first important official step towards eventual self-government.

I have been in the throes of proof reading, but it is now, thank goodness, very nearly finished and I hope to publish in January.

Yours sincerely
WINSTON S. CHURCHILL

* * * * *

WSC to Lord Hugh Cecil
(Quickswood Papers)

EXTRACT

8 October 1905   Blenheim

My dear Linky,

. . . . In my heart of hearts I have some doubt about this alliance, but for good or ill, we are committed to it.

Many thanks also for the quotation.

Yours ever
W

WSC to Sir Henry Campbell-Bannerman
(Campbell-Bannerman Papers)

28 October 1905   105 Mount Street
Private

My dear Sir Henry,

It was vy kind of you to write to me, & I am delighted to get your letter. I am sorry we could not clutch Hampstead;¹ but after all the turnover did not fall below the present average of by-elections.¹ You will certainly have an instrument of formidable power at your disposal after the Dissolution.

I wonder what your view is of the Kitchener-Curzon controversy. Of course the S of S must always control the Viceroy. Of course Brodrick & Curzon both exhibited characteristic tact & temper. But putting aside both these aspects, I am convinced that the new arrangement of duties in India gives excessive & improper powers to the Commander-in-Chief: & considering what has happened it seems to me that Kitchener is something very like a military Dictator in India. Unless you had other views on the question & how to raise it, I should propose to move an amendment to the Address condemning the new arrangement, & asserting the paramount importance of the civil power in India.

¹ A Conservative majority of 1715 had been reduced to 422.

Do not bother to write to me about this now; but when you return to England will you give me the pleasure of your company at dinner one night (which night?) for I should like to talk to you about it. It is a matter on wh I should be confident of convincing sober opinion in the H of C.

I am going to dine with John Morley tonight. I gathered from his last speech that he would share my views on the Indian Question. I abhor military tyrants!

I hope you & Lady Campbell-Bannerman are well. Vienna must be very interesting from a political point of view now.[1]

Yours vy truly
WINSTON S. CHURCHILL

Lord James of Hereford to WSC

EXTRACT

29 October 1905   Breamore
                                                       Salisbury

My dear Winston Churchill,

Of course nothing can be farther from my wish and intention than to do your candidature any harm and I hope that you will see that the facts do not justify your complaint of a personal slight.

The Free-Trade League is a mixed body composed of Liberals and Unionists. They have agreed to have nothing to do with any political action save the support of Free Trade. All differences on other subjects are kept out of sight. And so when these meetings have taken place great care has existed to show that no electioneering results were in view. Thus when the meetings of the League were held in Chelsea and Hampstead the Liberal candidates were excluded although of course Free-Traders. The Tories of the League in those constituencies would not submit to assist the Radical candidates for electioneering purposes.

Well, as to the coming meeting. It is a Lancashire County meeting. The Platform will hold an equal number of the representatives of Unionists and Liberals, from all parts of the county. You tell me that the Free-Trade Hall is in your Division – but, that fact does not get rid of the general character of the meeting.

Now if it be for a moment thought that your candidature is to be promoted through the agency of this meeting I am certain it will be a failure and probably will not be held.

[1] C-B had been at Marienbad since early August, returning to London, via Meran, Vienna and Paris on Nov 12. Austria was experiencing a major political and social crisis over the introduction of universal suffrage.

If you attend and make one of your rattling Radical speeches what effect will be produced on the 100 odd souls on the Platform? This rule goes far beyond your personal position. As I understand it no local – that is no Manchester – candidates will take part in the meeting.

But everything I can effect to show that the course pursued is in no way aimed at you shall be done. Full public intimation can be given of the general nature of the rule and of its application in relation to other constituencies. I hope the view I have thus presented will remove your sense of wrong. . . .

Yours
J OF H

Ivor Guest to WSC

EXTRACT

13 November 1905   Ashby St Ledgers
                                                              Rugby

Dear Winston,

. . . . I have been thinking a good deal lately about politics. I am much impressed with this development of the Unemployed problem.

It seems that a socialist doctrine is likely to take root in it and Labour will gradually disentangle itself from its connection with either party.

JC says truly, 'I have a remedy' (such as it is) and I notice Tariff Reform is coming to mean a great deal more than Imperialism, Economics or Party tactics and becoming a school of Social and Fiscal (I mean taxation) thought.

It is the means by which the social system is to be kept as it is for the benefit of all privileged members of society.

JC is also right when he says of the opposition 'You have no remedy' and therein lie the dangers and perhaps the opportunity.

Now I am not a socialist in the sense of believing that communistic effort can replace individual inducement although I have a great deal of sympathy for those who get crushed in the modern machine.

But it seems to me quite clear that unless Liberalism has a definite alternative to offer and unless that alternative is put forward before the socialistic ideas have taken shape there is no future for it and we may find ourselves after much vacillation and obloquy taking such places as we can in the Individualistic party of the future.

I don't know whether you may think that I make too much of this movement, but I would have you consider the growing mistrust of the Labour Party to ourselves. The influence too of the Russian revolution – as I am convinced it will be – may be far-reaching – first in Germany and then on ourselves and supply the needed impetus of example and experience.

Clearly the only way by which socialists can be combatted is by increasing the number of those who have profited by the present system and who therefore are content with it and hostile to any radical change.

I believe the main thing to do is to promote a policy for creating a great number of Freeholders in town and country. Leasehold Enfranchisement would create the former and State Credit for agricultural tenants to purchase, the other.

I think some inducement might be further provided to encourage sales by imposing a new Land Act of a Progressive character on landowners, its progressive character becoming automatically more sure with the lapse of years. Something should probably be done to create Smaller Holdings.

All this involves economy and the absence of Wars which swallow up National Credit. I think the Sinking Fund must be increased and military expenditure diminished until it bears a strict proportion to the National Revenue of the year, which proportion should not be capable of extension, except by Act of Parliament authorising this additional amount. This is rather awkward and artificial but it might provide a check on Tory profligacy in this direction.

I have been drawn into a long letter painful I fear to decypher. I should like to discuss this and many other kindred possibilities with you.

I believe the old liberal gang are quite hopeless. Not one of them goes further than criticism and amendment. I don't think they even see that anything else is needed whereas the march of events is I think bringing us towards a spot when a clear policy becomes essential.

Yours ever
IVOR

WSC to Lady Randolph

28 November 1905   Canford

Dearest Mamma,

I have cancelled all my meetings this week in order to have a good rest here. There is a wonderful rubber who has almost miraculous virtues & I am vy comfortable & peaceful. I shall be back in London Monday, & will try to come to you for a day or two next week. Cornelia talked of writing to you to come down. It is vy pleasant. I am practically restored, & am only resting to prepare myself for future labours.

Rosebery has I regret to say greatly injured himself by his reckless speech.

Parties do not forgive that kind of unnecessary quarrelsomeness at critical moments. Everyone knows there will be no Home Rule Bill in the next Parliament.[1]

Your loving son
WINSTON

John Morley to WSC

EXTRACT

29 November 1905   Flowermead
                                             Wimbledon Park

My dear Churchill,

... Your panegyric the other day on an eminent friend of ours has not proved quite opportune. You should have heard the strong words used to me yesterday by a powerful leaguer: 'Most disloyal thing ever done by a man to his own friends (i.e. L.L.)' – 'Not a hint of consultation beforehand' – 'Of course utterly impossible that the new govt can have anything to say to him' etc etc.

I listen with grim complacence. Now we shall go straight ahead. *There is no sort of doubt* as to their joining, and the lonely furrow will be lonely indeed. A pity!

Be sure not to commit yourself against acceptance of office, if Ministers resign. There will be no *rifiuto*, whatever random writers (not without a secret purpose) are now saying.

In all this I speak the things that I do know. And there is no question of forcing H.R. [Home Rule] to the point.

Take care of yourself. The less speaking the better for all of us.

Yrs
J. MORLEY

WSC to Lord Hugh Cecil
(*Quickswood Papers*)

30 November 1905   Canford Manor
Private

My dear Linky,

As I expect you are not out of touch with persons of mark, I mention for your edification this fact wh may be of interest *viz* that if one Scotchman wants to sell a pig, there is another who will most certainly buy it.

[1] In a speech at Bodmin Rosebery declared that he could not serve under the banner of Home Rule. He had misunderstood both Campbell-Bannerman's position and the views of Asquith and Grey.

Rosebery indeed has broken his own crockery. Was there ever such an unrelated, reckless & ill-judged pronouncement? How he could! Not one single friend was consulted with, & he has continued to irritate the whole party, by sticking it at a critical moment. I am really vy sorry about it; for you know how much I like him, & how kind he has always been to me. That he should stand apart from a Liberal Government is not serious – for that he always intended to do. But the purposeless sacrifice of his influence is a new & ugly feature in a situation already complex.

Please let me know if there is anything that we can do in Greenwich. I can always speak to McKenna, as if out of my own mind, if you whisper first in my ear. I *am* sorry about the money. What ruffians they are!

I hear a rumour that G. Curzon is to be put forward for Oxford University. You will no doubt be informed of this. Do make sure of the seat, if it is in your power.

The information at the beginning of this letter is serious & trustworthy. *Verbum sap* which means I suppose 'take my tip, but don't mention my name'. You will read in the papers that I am ill. Remain tranquil. I needed a rest, as my heart began to flag; but am swiftly recovering.

There is an American rubber, venerable God-fearing old lady – of sovereign virtue. Her healing powers are little short of miraculous. She has resuscitated Lord Wimborne: & cured his sister of a paralysed leg 10 years crippled. As for me in four rubbings, my circulation has become perfect, & my heart absolutely free from pressure of any kind. I would like her to cure you of your general debility. She can compel you to circulate and digest properly. You would then be certain of surviving Joe.

Yours always
W

H. O. Arnold-Forster to WSC

30 November 1905   War Office

Private

Dear Winston,

I am truly sorry to hear you are ill. Do take care of yourself. You know I don't agree with your politics but you are the only man on your side of the House who seems to me really to understand the Army problem. So from a purely selfish point of view I want you to be well again. May I add that from a personal view I entertain the same view and cherish the same life very strongly.

Believe me, Yours truly
H. O. ARNOLD-FORSTER

WSC to Lady Randolph

1 December 1905　　　　　　　　　　　　　　　　　Canford

Dearest Mamma,

I am vy sorry you will not come here next week. I am bound to stay here till next Thursday to finish my massage treatment, from wh I have so greatly benefited; so that unless you can come we shall not meet; for I go to Manchester on Thursday. Why don't you come? I have no doubt she could restore your circulation & digestion. She will say in a minute if she can't.

She also informs me I am tongue-tied. It is quite true. My tongue is restrained by a ligament which nobody else has. This is the true explanation of my speaking through my nose. I have made an appointment with Semon in London for Monday to consider the matter.

I think it probable that the Government will resign today. CB if sent for will certainly accept the commission. The newspapers are quite ignorant & stupid about his intentions. I daresay the new Administration will be formed by this time next week. But we have had so many falls, it is rash to prophesy.

I am bidden to North Mimms, I will try to go.

Your loving son
W

I shall look for the lampshades at Mount Street. 31 is vy old. Fancy I was 6 when my father was that age!

Duke of Marlborough to WSC

1 December [1905]　　　　　　　　　　　　　　　　Blenheim

My dear,

I was much concerned to see that you were unwell. Is it CB's speeches, old D's bad champagne, or the effects of too frequent visits to the vicinity of Marshall & Snelgrove? What ever the cause may be, I am concerned as to the result and I beg of you to take life easy. I am bored here hunting alone.

Yrs affet
SUNNY

Sir A. Acland-Hood to J. S. Sandars
(*Balfour Papers*)

EXTRACT

1 December [1905]　　　　　　　　　　　　　　　　St Audries
　　　　　　　　　　　　　　　　　　　　　　　　　Bridgwater

... Under no circumstances ought Hugh Cecil to be opposed. He is our best card amongst the young men against Winston Churchill. ...

Lord Knollys[1] to WSC

1 December 1905   Sandringham

My dear Churchill,

The King is very sorry to hear that you are 'laid up' & are not at all well, and he desires me to write and enquire after you & to say he hopes you will be able to give a good account of yourself.

Yours sincerely
KNOLLYS

WSC to Lady Randolph

4 December 1905   105 Mount Street

Dearest Mamma,

I am much better. Sir Felix Semon refused to cut off my tongue, so that is still 'tied'. I return to Canford tomorrow for two rubbings. Consuelo tells me she is going to bid you to Blenheim for Christmas. Do come. I am arranging to have the rubber. All our tummies will be put straight.

I suppose the new Government will be formed during the next few days. It is rather exciting, especially as a profound inactivity is the only course wh dignity & prudence alike enjoin.

The King wrote through Knollys to enquire about my health! What a change! I will not allow myself to make any speculations or anticipations about the future. I think the hour is fortunate & the combination of circumstances most favourable. But confident in myself, I await with composure the best or worst that Fortune has in hand.

I have accepted Burns' invitation to shoot at N. Mimms on 11th–14th. I speak at the City Liberal Club on that night (14th) perhaps with authority!

Your loving son
W

David Lloyd George to WSC

TELEGRAM

5 December 1905   Wandsworth Common

McKenna, Shaw[2] and self lunching Reform one. Join us.

LLOYD GEORGE

[1] Francis Knollys, 1st Baron Knollys (1837–1924), Private Secretary to King Edward VII 1870–1910; to King George V 1910–13; Lord-in-Waiting to Queen Alexandra 1910–24; PC 1910; Viscount 1911.
[2] Thomas Shaw (1850–1937), Liberal MP for Hawick Burghs 1892–1909; Solicitor-General for Scotland 1894–5, Lord Advocate for Scotland 1905–9; Lord of Appeal 1909–29; Baron Shaw of Dunfermline 1909 (Life Peerage); Baron Craigmyle 1929.

Sir Ernest Cassel to WSC

7 December 1905   Crichel
                                                                  Wimborne

My dear Winston,

I should have come to see you in London during the few days I was there if I had not been told you were in the country. Of course I shall be delighted to invest the £1000 and any further sums you may wish to send to the best of my ability when a good opportunity occurs. I trust that you have got rid of your indisposition and are fit for the fight that is to come. If you want a quiet Xmas and would like to come to Newmarket you will be most welcome. There is no party.

I trust that you will find satisfactory recognition in the arrangements now being made and with every good wish I remain

                                                                  Yours always
                                                                  E.C.

I expect to return Sunday.

Samuel Smethurst to WSC

1 December 1905   Coldhurst House
                                                             Oldham

Dear Mr Churchill,

I see from the *Manchester Courier* that you are recruiting at Canford Manor so am taking the liberty of addressing you there.

I am very sorry to know you have broken down in health and sincerely hope it is nothing serious. I do wish you would cease being so strenuous; I am thoroughly convinced if you would oftener give yourself a real rest you would lengthen your days and add to the effectiveness of your public work. I am quite sure that now you have established your position in the public mind you might with advantage appear less frequently; for I am persuaded it is the intense nervous strain occasioned by addressing large meetings which tells upon you most.

Perhaps you will know that Mr John Albert Bright has been selected as the Liberal candidate for Oldham, and Mr Crisp appears to be the elect of the Conservatives. The Labour elements (Socialist) seem determined to run a candidate; if they do it will make the position very interesting and will practically put the decision in the hands of the Irish vote, if it is solid for either party. I do think that Liberal statesmen should say definitely what they are prepared to do for the Irish. If it is to be Home Rule then the Conservatives will have another chance of power, if some more moderate and less dangerous scheme then I think they might with impunity risk what the Irish would do, for I am quite sure with Home Rule *not before them* the country would go for a Liberal Government. The time for a definite declaration has come and the game of finessing to end.

Yours very sincerely
SAMUEL SMETHURST

*   *   *   *   *

Sir H. Campbell-Bannerman to WSC

TELEGRAM

9 December 1905   29 Belgrave Square

Greatly obliged if you would come and see me here at six o'clock.

CAMPBELL-BANNERMAN

Sir Henry Campbell-Bannerman to WSC

9 December 1905   29 Belgrave Square

My dear Churchill,
    I am arranging for the Colonial Office. So that is all right.

Yours very truly
H. CAMPBELL-BANNERMAN

Of course this is secret until the Royal Pleasure is taken.

WSC to Lord Elgin[1]
(*Elgin Papers*)

9 December 1905   105 Mount Street

Private

My dear Lord,
    The Prime Minister has invited me to join his Government as Under-Secretary of State for the Colonies, & I learned from him that this was agreeable to you. In case you wish to see me I shall be in London on Monday during the middle part of the day & I would like vy much to call upon you, if you could find a moment to receive me.

---

[1] The Earl of ELGIN.

I had intended to go out of London for a day or two; but of course I can put this off if you wish it.

Believe me, Yours vy faithfully
WINSTON S. CHURCHILL

Lord Elgin to WSC

10 December 1905   29 Hyde Park Gate

Dear Mr Churchill,

Many thanks for your letter – I am sorry I missed your message – but my family is scattered about London at present.

We have rather a tough job before us – but with your assistance I hope & believe the Colonial Office will make a good show.

I shall be at 95 Eaton Terrace at 12 o'clock to-morrow and if quite convenient for you I should be very glad to have a few moments conversation. Of course I know nothing yet which renders this necessary.

I have to go to Scotland on Tuesday but am told I must be back on Thursday, and may put in a day or two then at the office to study a few details. I mention this simply to help your plans.

Yours sincerely
ELGIN

R. B. Haldane to WSC

8 December 1905   3 Whitehall Court

My dear Winston,

The suggestion of Jack Seely [as Under Secretary of State for War] is most agreeable to me & I have written at once to suggest his name. Press I dare not, for you know what the task of a Prime Minister is in adjusting offices. But I have put the case as thoroughly as I could in the way of suggestion.

Thank you for your kind letter about myself.

I wished for this business because I have no reputation to lose, & I do not mind failures. But it interests me intensely & I am grimly determined to get to the bottom of it. I shall probably have much occasion to seek your friendly counsel.

Always yours
R. B. HALDANE

R. B. Haldane to WSC

10 December 1905   3 Whitehall Court

My dear Winston,

As you will have heard I have not been able to carry Jack Seely's appointment. CB could not help himself, & one cannot press him in his difficulties beyond a certain point. I am genuinely sorry.

But my pleasure is great at thinking that we are to have the advantage of your debating power for Colonial affairs. It is splendid news.

I am full of ideas about the War Office & the Army & in a day or so shall be informed enough to be able to have a full consultation with you. I want your counsel.

Yours ever
R. B. HALDANE

Lord Elgin to WSC

13 December 1905   29 Hyde Park Gate

Dear Mr Churchill,

I had the pleasure this afternoon of signing the paper which I believe completes your appointment.

When I saw you I intended to have been in Scotland to-day but I was unable to go. I therefore go on Saturday for, if possible, an extended week-end. But I shall be in the office to-morrow afternoon and on Friday – and if you are able to look in I shall be glad to have a little more conversation.

Yours truly
ELGIN

Sir Walter Hely-Hutchinson[1] to WSC

EXTRACT

13 December 1905   Government House
                                                   Cape Town

. . A line to congratulate you on your first step on the ladder to the Cabinet. You will find the work at the CO interesting, especially as regards S. Africa, your knowledge of which will be of great use to you. . . .

[1] Walter Francis Hely-Hutchinson (1849–1913), Governor and C-in-C of Cape of Good Hope 1901–10; Lieutenant-Governor of Malta 1884–9; Governor and C-in-C of Natal and Zululand 1893–1901; GCMG 1897; PC 1909.

Dr J. E. C. Welldon to WSC

13 December 1905   Little Cloisters
                                                    Westminster Abbey

My dear Churchill,
    You will, I am sure, let me, as an old friend, congratulate you with all
my heart upon your happy entrance into official life. When I think of the
last words in which your father asked me, at my own door in Harrow, to
keep an interest in your future, it is with something of a pathetic feeling that
I look forward, in full confidence, to your making a noble use of the responsibility now laid upon you.
                        Believe me with all good wishes, Sincerely yours
                                              J. E. C. WELLDON

Walter Runciman to WSC

13 December 1905   Reform Club

My dear Winston,
    They still keep me dangling about here, more or less restless. Up till last
night & especially after I heard of some of the appointments yesterday morning which are out today, I was rather angry. The Home Office job is really
the most unpopular thing that has been done. I wonder if you know what led
to it? HJG [Herbert Gladstone] actually saw Samuel[1] & booked him without
consulting anybody, & when everybody else in the Cabinet objected he
claimed that it had gone too far & could not be recalled. He was thereupon
(at their dinner on Saturday night) asked why he had not taken me & left
Samuel alone, & he replied that Samuel had written a good deal about
Factory Legislation (Leaflets he meant) & was interested in Home Office
subjects. Thus he disposed of one post, & CB acquiesced. Samuel had already
been rejected by George Whiteley[2] for the Whips' Office.
    Today I have recovered from my anger, & the scramble – compared to
which cabinet making is child's play – has amused me immensely. There are

    [1] Herbert Louis Samuel (1870–1963), Parliamentary Under-Secretary Home Department
1905–09; Liberal MP 1902–18, 1929–35; Chancellor of the Duchy of Lancaster 1909–10,
1915–16; Postmaster-General 1910–14, 1915–16; President of the Local Government Board
1914–15; Secretary of State Home Affairs 1916, 1931–2; Chairman, Select Committee on
National Expenditure 1917–18; High Commissioner, Palestine 1910–25; Leader of Liberal
Parliamentary Party 1931–5; Liberal leader House of Lords 1944–55; PC 1908; Order of
Merit 1958; Viscount Samuel of Mount Carmel and Toxteth 1937.
    [2] George Whiteley (1855–1925), Patronage Secretary of the Treasury 1905–8; Conservative
MP for Stockport 1893–1900; Liberal MP for Pudsey Division of West Riding Yorkshire
1900–8; Privy Councillor 1907; Baron Marchamley of Hawkstone 1908.

some useful appointments however, Lloyd George is to have Kearley[1] under him, & that is well.

Jack Tennant[2] was offered to John Burns for the LGB, and Burns refused to have him. That post is still open.

Burghclere[3] is to be under secretary for Foreign Affairs.[4] The others are all out.

Today Reggie [McKenna] & I met John Morley by chance in St James's Park, when Morley asked me if I had yet been at Belgrave Square. He was surprised to hear that I had not received any message, for he said that it had all along been settled that I was to have one of the *under Sec of State* & on Saturday it had been decided that I was to go to the FO. On hearing who was to have that he said 'Damn Burghclere' rather warmly, & proceeded to say that the arrangement regarding myself & its reasons were given before him before he left CB; that I was to help Grey because foreign office receptions would sometimes keep Grey away from the early meetings of the House & he wanted someone on whom he could rely to answer questions. McKenna reminded JM that all the Unders were full up now & nothing remained except the LGB & the Civil Lordship. Morley said it was 'damnable' & he must see about it at once. McKenna rubbed it in most emphatically & said everybody spoke just as cordially as he did & all of them thought someone else was to have me. Morley replied that he would have had me for India, but that he thought I ought to have more chance of questions at all events, to say nothing of the work, in the House than the India Office with its solitary debate per annum could give me. Nothing could have exceeded his cordiality. He left us saying that he must write to CB at once; & no doubt he did so. I laughed at the repetition of the same yarn from each of these polite & fruitless Cabinet Ministers, & some day I shall write a little fable on 'The Good Young Man & the Seven stools'.

Emmott is to be Chairman of Committees, poor old chap.

I suppose I must hang on here & allow this waiting process to humiliate me to my true level.

If only a Lordship of The Treasury remains, I'll see CB damned first.

---

[1] Hudson Ewbanke Kearley (1856–1934), Parliamentary Secretary to the Board of Trade 1905–09; Liberal MP Devonport 1892–10; baronet 1908; Baron Devonport 1910; Viscount 1917.

[2] Harold John Tennant (1865–1935), Liberal MP for Berwickshire 1894–1918; private secretary to his brother-in-law H. H. Asquith 1892–5; Parliamentary Secretary, Board of Trade 1909–11; Financial Secretary to War Office 1911–12; Under-Secretary of State for War 1912–16; Secretary for Scotland 1916; PC 1914.

[3] Herbert Coulstoun Gardner, 1st Baron Burghclere (1846–1921), Liberal MP for North Essex 1885–95; President of the Board of Agriculture 1892–5; Baron Burghclere 1895.

[4] In fact, the Under-Secretaryship at the Foreign Office was given to Lord Edmund Fitzmaurice.

He certainly doesn't want me, and already I am armed with a prompt, practical, awkward question which shall ripen before Xmas. If necessary I shall have a weighty deputation of coal owners, miners & ship owners at the Exchequer next week quoting Liberal front bench speeches on the Coal tax. Urgency shall be the excuse for this early interview & it shall be a big affair, and dignity shall not be one of the least of its qualities. I shall organise & I shall introduce it. We shall see.

Yours ever
WALTER RUNCIMAN

Poor Jack takes his rejection good naturedly but I am very sorry for him. Apparently CB is marking his triumph over Grey & Haldane.

WSC to Lord Hugh Cecil
(Quickswood Papers)

16 December 1905

My dear Linky,

Many thanks for your kind congratulations. I chose it in preference to the Treasury. I had some difficulty in securing my wish as it involved considerable alteration in the other minor offices. However it is now settled. Was I right? I never knew that it was a complaint against me that I was incapable of working hard and I was not aware that I was capable of any great or prolonged period of lethargy. As to a 'solid reputation' I do not want other than will grow of its own accord. Nothing will please me less than that the Public should entertain a higher opinion of me than I deserve.

I am sorry that you considered my remarks gaseous. I thought I managed with extraordinary dexterity and almost ecclesiastical subtlety to deliver a controversial harangue without saying anything of the smallest definite meaning.

I am very sorry that Cameron Corbett[1] is to be opposed by a Liberal. I wrote particularly to them when they invited Freddie Guest[2] to stand and urged them not to oppose him. They replied that they had approached Cameron Corbett on several occasions asking for the most modest assurances and that they had been somewhat ungraciously repulsed. Cameron Corbett is however absolutely unassailable having given parks, mountains and other things to his beloved native town. Arthur Elliot is much more serious, and if there is any difficulty there, please let me know and I will myself exert any

[1] Archibald Cameron Corbett (1856–1933), MP for Tradeston Division of Glasgow 1885–1911 first as a Liberal, then as a Liberal Unionist until his secession from the Unionists in 1909; elected as an Independent Liberal January 1910; Baron Rowallan 1911.
[2] Frederick GUEST.

influence I may possess. You have certainly unfurled a very fine and gallant flag. I wish I could strike a blow in its defence, but I know that nothing is further from your wishes than that I should make any effort on your behalf.

I am speaking at Deptford on Tuesday night and shall deal only with the economic merits of Free Trade, and as you desire, ignore your existence altogether.

Yours ever
WINSTON SC

This seems rather a foolish letter. Burn it.

Lord Hugh Cecil to WSC

[?18 December 1905]   Junior Carlton Club

My dear Winston,

By 'gaseous' I mean that you have a reputation for shining on a platform & in the House – but as a firework. This has carried you well so far but the further steps require a reputation as a good administrator, a skilled & industrious official – the sort of reputation Edward Grey eminently has – you will remember your father greatly improved his position by his work at the India Office.

But still more important it is that you should stand well with & be liked by your colleagues. If a man's colleagues are all on his side he runs forward as easily as a bicyclist before the wind. Harcourt cd not be PM because he swore at his colleagues. AJB holds his position as leader almost entirely by the effect of his charm on his front bench – & in spite of enormous blunders & no popularity in the country. Hear the words of the sage!

Yrs
HUGH CECIL

J. B. Atkins to WSC

EXTRACT

17–21 December 1905   49 Rue des Belles Feuilles
                                       Paris
Private

My dear Winston,

I never see you now: though naturally I hear of you. This is just a line to send you the best of good wishes & hearty congratulations on your appointment at the Colonial Office. You certainly have beaten the record! How things have marched since we pitched our tent in the triangle of the railway station at Estcourt! [Natal].

I am corresponding for the *Standard* in Paris. I was glad of the opportunity to look into French politics. Don't forget I'm here when you pass through. . . .

Lord Elgin to WSC

27 December 1905   Broomhall

My dear Churchill,

I received your letter of yesterday by the last post tonight. I do not wish to suggest anything which you may think would weaken a material part of your address. But it seems to me that to say the Govt must do its utmost to *terminate* such a system will invite the retort, you are doing nothing to *terminate* it if your policy is to leave the question for the Transvaal Legislative Assembly to decide.

I think I will telegraph to-morrow the suggestion to insert after 'restrict' the words 'and limit the abuses of . . .' but you must judge which form of words is best.

Don't think, as I see you are rather inclined to do, that I like this system. I may not take the strong line agt it which those who have been engaged in the controversy not unnaturally assume: but in our conversations I have been led further in the other direction than my real sentiments from a desire to maintain the argument, and have the advantage of hearing your advocacy of the other side.

I suppose you are seeing the telegrams which are coming from SA. I do not think we differ much in our estimate of the situation except that considering the dates of the Licenses I find it difficult to see how we can differentiate sufficiently to keep many of the 14,000 out. But it occurred to me yesterday that if this happened it might give us an opportunity for the introduction of some measure of repatriation on the lines of Samuel's paper which you gave me.

I imagine I may use this paper – though perhaps I had better keep back the author's name. There would be great advantages in this. *The Times,* even, has offered to accept these coolies as sufficient for present purposes. We are therefore clear of all difficulties of compensation and if so we can the better afford to provide a moderate sum to assist repatriation. If Mr Samuel & those who think with him regard a measure of this kind as removing the chief blot, our policy becomes coherent & defensible.

That at any rate is how it strikes me–but I am writing it down now for the

first time, as is your due who suggested it to me. Only keep it to yourself till
we meet.

I rather think I shall be in London on Tuesday to get things ready for the
Cabinet on Wedy. I hope you have had a cheerful holiday before your
campaign.

With best wishes for it & the new Year,

Yours very truly
ELGIN

Thanks for telegram which I return.

WSC to Lord Elgin

29 December 1905   Blenheim

[Copy]

My dear Ld Elgin,

First let me thank you for the kindness of yr letter, wh enables me to
appreciate v exactly the view you take & enter into yr feelings on the
questions at issue.

I am glad you like the 'repatriation on demand' plan. I cd write a good
deal in support of it. I do not deny that there is a fighting case to be made
out on the line you suggest, viz the strict interpretation of the law – whether
favourable or not – to the mine owners or the Chinese. We cd say – we recognize existing licences even though we do not approve of them. We will
in no case upset traders' contracts based on the decisions of a previous Govt.
We will therefore allow the importn of all Chinese under existing licences
for whom bona fide preparations have been made & on a/c of whom ex-
tensions of mining industry have been contemplated. If, and in so far as, we
interfere with the importn, we recognize our liability for compensn for
genuine out of pocket expenses.

But we see a better way of employing our money than in merely shutting
out whole batches of Chinese, & that way is by enabling all Ch who are
dissatisfied or ill-treated or unhappy to be repatd at once. And in this course
also we shall be within the strict letter of the law as the Ordce prescribes it.
We shd say moreover that the exercise of this power to repatriate at Br
expense wd be a far better weapon of control over the whole area of the
mining district than any mere restriction of numbers. If I apprehend rightly,
this is what is in yr mind.

My only doubt abt it is whether it will be accepted as a sufficient action
by the Lib party, by the Cabinet, or by the H of C. I feel v strongly that the
spectacle of large importn of Chinamen being brought to SA, & large numbers being enlisted in China & embarked, wd appear to the public as

breach of the PM's declarn at the Albert Hall. It will be said – so far from stopping Ch labour, you are actively extending it, & are carrying it forward on a scale hitherto unexampled, & actually in excess of anything contemplated by Mr Lyttelton.

However I do not feel that an U.S. [Under Secretary] of Tory antecedents need become excited when a Libl cabinet with a strong Radl section remains calm; & if yr decision shd be as I have anticipated in this lr, I do not doubt my being able to make out a pretty good case, & I wd of course try my best.

I thought yr last tel to Ld Selborne[1] asking for full info abt the issue of the 13,199 licences very good. It contained no sort of imputation and yet it conveyed a rebuke wh wd be valid only if deserved. I must say I think Ld S is open to reproach. His silence in face of A.L.'s[2] Oct 27 telm, esp when he has such an item as the applicn of the Ch of Mines for 16,999 licences of the day before to report, is inexplicable. I have been told with some authority that the decision of the late PM to resign was come to some weeks before the announcement appeared simultaneously in the *Times* & the *DT*. The final publicn was on Nov 24. The licences were issued in a crop from Nov 12–18. It wd almost seem (tho' of course there may be an innocent expln) as if the Rand had even earlier infn than the *Times* of the impending change. Certainly I confess I have a hard heart abt these 13,199 licences.

The sentence in my address will read as follows: 'A Lib Govt, while it is forced to bear any part of the responsibility, is bound to do its utmost to restrict such a system & to put down its abuses'. I hope you will feel that this meets yr wishes.

I have to make a speech of some seriousness on the night of the 3rd. I shall not leave London till after the Cabinet, & if you think well I shd like to deal rather fully with the Ch labour question & defend the course pursued by HMG. In this view I am preparing a few remarks on wh I will consult you if you can spare the time. But I feel the matter shd be dealt with, for otherwise all sorts of wild statements will be made by Candidates committing us far beyond the line wh we intend to go.

I send you a speech of Burns' wh seems to me to go a good long way. By the bye I forgot to tell you that H. Samuel in a private letter to me said that he had forwarded his memo to the PM. I of course have told no-one of the proposal – nor shall I.

Yrs v truly
WSC

[1] William Waldegrave Palmer, 2nd Earl of Selborne (1859–1942), Governor of Transvaal and High Commissioner for South Africa 1905–10; Liberal MP for East Hampshire 1885–6, Liberal Unionist MP for East Hampshire 1886–92, West Edinburgh 1892–5; First Lord of the Admiralty 1900–5; President of the Board of Agriculture 1915–16; PC 1900; KG 1909.
[2] Alfred LYTTELTON.

Duke of Marlborough to WSC

? [December 1905]   Sunderland House
                                                      Curzon Street

My dear Winston,

I am truly glad. Henceforth you will be the most formidable of those whose duty it will be to defend the Colonial policy of your party. You don't realise yet what a position is now offered to you. Your speeches will be read throughout the Colonies and you alone will be the mouthpiece of the Govt in this particular policy.

Yrs affly
SUNNY

Edward Marsh¹ to Mrs Jack Leslie
(*Shane Leslie Papers*)

EXTRACT

[? December 1905]

. . . Such an excitement. I *must* tell you. Your nephew has asked me to be his private secretary for 6 months or so. It will be the most interesting thing I've ever done but I'm most terribly afraid of not being the right person and turning out a failure. I'm sure its your doing. When you come back in May I'll tell you whether I bless you or curse you! You'll find me a grey-haired skeleton in either case as he means to work me to death. It's funny that just after we were discussing the problem of what I should do to age myself this easy solution should have dashed [?] forth. I've just dined alone with Winston. He was most perfectly charming to me but made it quite clear what he would expect in the way of help and I almost *know* I can't do it – its awful!. . . .

WSC to the Electors of North-West Manchester

1 January 1906   Colonial Office

Gentlemen,

Two years ago, I promised a joint deputation of the Liberal Association and the Free Trade League to come forward at the general election in defence of the Free Trade cause in Manchester. The time has now arrived to fulfil that undertaking. I did not then imagine that I should present myself before you as a Liberal Minister; but remembering that this honourable responsibility has been placed upon me largely through the countenance

¹ Edward MARSH.

and support accorded me in the city of Manchester, I rely with confidence upon the active assistance of all those persons of repute and influence, irrespective of party, to whose invitation my candidature is due; and I call upon the Free Traders of Manchester to assert and testify to their economic convictions with courage and fidelity.

Free Trade. Whatever may be the precise relations, personal or fiscal, between Mr Balfour and Mr Chamberlain, it is certain that the victory of one is the victory of the other; that the victory of either is the victory of both; and that the victory of both involves the erection in one form or another, upon one pretext or another, of a retaliatory, preferential or protective tariff. Of all such plans I am the enemy. I do not accept a policy of Retaliation; for I believe with Sir Robert Peel 'in fighting hostile tariffs by free imports'. I am opposed to all devices to entangle the Empire in a net of differential duties; for I will not consent to hamper our freedom to purchase food and raw material in the markets of the world, and I do not believe in buying loyalty for cash. Most of all, I will resist any attempt to protect Home Industries from foreign competition; for I believe that such a system would prove a fertile source of national impoverishment and of political corruption, and far from relieving traders from their present embarrassments, or removing the evils of unemployment, would only aggravate both. Being convinced that all or any of these plans are founded upon essential fallacies, and would prove in practice injurious to the prosperity and honour of the British Empire, of the United Kingdom, and in particular of Lancashire, I think it right to declare my hostility to them with the utmost plainness, in order that no man may support me under any misconception.

Liberal Policy. My views on current questions have been freely laid before you. You will have noticed how closely they correspond to the statement of policy made last month at the Albert Hall by the Prime Minister. The more strict observance in our Educational system of the principles of Religious Equality, and Public Control; a reduction of expenditure upon armaments; the assured supremacy of the civil power in India; the development of inland waterways; the taxation of ground values; the amendment of the law relating to Licensing and to Trade Unions; all these I believe to be objects legitimate, definite, practical and urgent.

Ireland. I shall support no Irish legislation which I regard as likely to injure the effective integrity of the United Kingdom, or to lead, however indirectly, to Separation. I am persuaded that considerable administrative reforms are required in the government of Ireland, and I would gladly see the Irish people accorded the power to manage their own expenditure, their own education, and their own public works according to Irish ideas.

Chinese Labour. My opinions on the subject of Chinese Labour are un-

changed, except that having had access to official information I hold
them more strongly than ever. A Liberal Government, while it is forced to
bear any part of the responsibility, is bound to do its utmost to restrict such
a system, and to put down its abuses.

A Degenerate Parliament. I am glad that the Parliament elected in 1900 is
about to be dissolved. Few Parliaments in our modern experience have been
less deserving of respect. A majority elected under the spell of patriotic emotion, upon a national issue, in the stress of an anxious war, has been perverted
to crude and paltry purposes of party. It has spent public money with
careless, unexampled profusion. It has hurried to place retrograde legislation
upon the Statute Book. It has consented to every abrogation or infringement
of liberty, constitutional or personal, at home or abroad, that was suggested
to it. Under its hand the procedure of the House of Commons has been
mutilated, and respect for Parliamentary institutions has been notably and
notoriously diminished. Jealous of nothing, save the leisure of its members,
it has bartered Parliamentary rights for longer holidays and easier hours
of session, and shirked urgent public business at the promptings of personal
indolence. Viewy, intolerant, dilettante, lax, the tool of Whips and wirepullers, the lackey of private interests, the Parliament of 1900 has grudged
the freedom of speech, conspired against the freedom of trade, parodied the
freedom and the dignity of labour. Lastly, by accepting every humiliation,
and stooping to every artful manoeuvre that its master might require, it has
enabled a Minister to maintain in office himself and a small clique of
favourites – mostly incompetent – and to rule in default of national esteem,
and in defiance of popular authority for upwards of two whole years.

The Tory Record. The late Ministers were representatives of the Parliament that sustained them; their handiwork was worthy of themselves.
The Phantom Army Corps, the bullied Volunteers, the Sugar Bounties
Convention, the Education and Licensing Acts, the Aliens and Unemployed
farces, the warfare in Somaliland and Thibet, the scandal of the War Stores,
the Redistribution fiasco, the Cabinet intrigues, the Indian bickerings, the
Wyndham exposure, the Chinese experiment – all are milestones on a downward path. The altered condition of British finance in a season of good
expanding trade is a measure of the descent: the annual cost of governing
the country half as much again; formidable new taxes on coal, sugar and tea;
a shilling income tax; consols at 89! It is upon the strength of such performances and testimonials that Mr Balfour and Mr Chamberlain modestly
claim from you a renewal of their lease. Seven more years of dodge and dole
and dawdle! Seven years of tinker, tax and trifle! Seven years of shuffle,
shout, and sham! *Do not be taken in again.*

A National Cause. Is it wonderful that a Ministry with so ill a record, and such doubtful and divided aims should fear to present themselves at the bar of public judgment. They have slunk away in the hope that their deeds will be forgotten; and their place is filled by other men. The hour is propitious for a Liberal Administration. Not since 1868 has such a chance occurred. Many questions formerly disputed are settled. A lively sympathy with the Colonial Empire, a vigilant care for our vast Indian dependency, the maintenance of an undisputed and indisputable Naval Supremacy, loyalty to the Crown and to the Sovereign, are not to be claimed as the perquisites of any faction. They belong to all the people. In the defence of Free Trade, in the Temperance movement and many grave social questions connected with large cities, Liberal principles have gained and are gaining the support of moderate and reasonable men beyond the wide limits of our regular political organisation. After more than thirty years – as I read history – of chequered fortunes, the Liberal party advance once more as the true representatives of Great Britain. Our cause is more than a party cause. Our victory will not be merely a party victory. It will be a national victory; and if we are returned to power it must be as the guardians not of the special interests of class, or sect, or party, but of all that is precious in the life of the nation as a whole.

A Fair Chance. The new Government is deeply conscious of its responsibilities, of the generous and lofty expectations that have been formed of it, of the perplexing and unremitting labours that await it, of the grim social and Imperial problems that stand in the path. We are guided by the well-tried principles of Liberalism by which the history of Manchester is adorned. We appeal for a fair chance – for an opportunity as large and free as those which have been repeatedly offered in the last twenty years to our Conservative opponents. Time, confidence, zeal, and a solid working majority are all indispensable, if public affairs are to be transacted with advantage by the Liberal party, if any serious attempt is to be made to grapple with the physical and economic distresses of town and country, if any brave step onward and upward is to be achieved in the weary pilgrimage of man. We appeal to the electors solemnly; but we appeal in good hope; for we believe that by their votes they will restore the great governing instrument which Mr Gladstone wielded in the hey-day of his power; and we pledge ourselves to use it – if it should be granted to us – for the abiding glory of the British realm, and for the peace and progress of the world.

WINSTON S. CHURCHILL

Sidney Greville[1] to WSC

2 January [1906]   Chatsworth

Dear Winston,
    The King wishes me to send you the enclosed[2] as it refers to the con-
versation which His Majesty had with you at Newmarket especially the last
part.
                                                        Yrs ever
                                               SIDNEY GREVILLE

WSC to ?

8 January 1906   Midland Hotel
                                                       Manchester
[Copy]

Sir,
    The polling in North-West Manchester is fixed for Saturday next. We
have done & are doing everything in our power to secure the acceptance of
our principles, & we have good hopes of victory. As the contest has advanced
the one dominant decisive issue – Free Trade or Tariff Reform – has become
increasingly plain. It is certain that if Mr Balfour & Mr Chamberlain obtain
a majority they will at once proceed to erect a network of import duties for
other than revenue purposes, amounting in fact to a Preferential, Retaliatory, and Protective Tariff. In twenty years time nothing will be remembered
about this election except that it settled whether the Fiscal policy of Mr
Cobden & Sir Robert Peel was or was not to be repudiated. Being persuaded that cheap food & the power to purchase all things freely in the

[1] Sidney Robert Greville (1866–1927), Groom-in-Waiting to King Edward VII; Assistant
Private Secretary to Sir John Gorst 1887; Private Secretary to Marquess of Salisbury as
Prime Minister 1888–92, 1896–8, 1900–01; Equerry to Prince of Wales 1898–1901; Private
Secretary to Queen Alexandra 1901–10; Paymaster to H.M. Household 1911–15; Comptroller
and Treasurer to Prince of Wales, 1915–20; Groom-in-Waiting to King George V 1910–11,
1920–27; 4th son of 4th Earl of Warwick; unmarried; knighted 1912.
[2] An unidentified newspaper cutting which read as follows: 'Mr Winston Churchill's
address to the electors of North-west Manchester is interesting solely as an indication of
personal character and even in that capacity supplies nothing in the form of a new revelation.
It is, unfortunately, quite characteristic of the late Unionist member for Oldham that he
should do his best to exhaust his extensive and peculiar vocabulary of vituperation upon the
political leaders to whose patronage and goodwill he owed his introduction to parliamentary
life; and no one is likely to waste time and energy upon the hopelessly futile task of reproving
Mr Winston Churchill for that persistent defiance of the elementary canons of good taste
which has done more even than his undoubted ability to bring him into prominence. Otherwise, it might be worth while to suggest to him that hysterical violence of language is not
usually regarded as an evidence of statesmanlike qualities, and that the country expects
those who aspire to govern it to show some signs, at least, of their ability to govern themselves.'

markets of the world are vital to the industries & to the enterprise of Lanca-shire, & consequently to the prosperity of this city, I earnestly appeal to you to record your vote & exert your influence against the erection of a Tariff, and in favour of the Free Trade system we have upheld for sixty years.

Yours vy faithfully
WINSTON S. CHURCHILL

Ivor Guest to WSC

14 January 1906   Ashby St Ledgers

Dear Winston,

Bravo! You have given the pendulum such a swing as will be felt through-out the whole country. This seems likely to be the Tory Armageddon and the beginning of a new social era altogether. I am sorry to see so many Labour people returned. They are the salt but we may have too much of it.

At this rate it is impossible to speculate on results, but it is evident that Joe and his Protection have received the 'coup de grace'. I am delighted at Balfour's defeat and consider it a personal humiliation.

We expect you tomorrow by the train starting 3.30 from Paddington. There is a danger here that the Irish think things going too much one way and swing out at the last moment. This would seriously jeopardise my prospects.

An enormous crowd awaits you here. Don't give the time of your arrival. Bravo again, I hope you are not worn out?

Yours ever
IVOR

Sir Ian Hamilton to WSC

16 January 1906   The Coburg Hotel
                                                                                   Grosvenor Square

My dear Winston,

I was sadly disappointed to find you out of London today as I had been looking forward with the keenest anticipation of pleasure to congratulating you with all my heart & of telling you how I exult with you in your victory.

As to your deportment under these triumphant conditions, better read old Bacon's essay on envy. You will see there are two methods; – one to ride rough shod, the other to take your hat off & be unusually humble & polite.

I prefer the latter myself although I am aware it does not really blunt the eager fang of jealousy. Even greater than the political victory, & to my thinking more worth doing, is the book.

Well dear boy – goodbye for the present & good luck. Do not make me sorry I wrote by answering.

Yours ever
IAN HAMILTON

WSC to Lord Hugh Cecil
(Quickswood Papers)

17 January 1906   Wolverhampton

Secret

My dear Linky,

I am so sorry about your being jockeyed out. It hardens my heart against Joe, at a time when otherwise pity would be the only feeling. What a terrible catastrophe is this that he has brought upon the gt party that nourished him and his so long! But I blame A. Balfour even more. Never one finger did he lift to help forward talent, or even to defend truth as he saw them. All selfish & cynical – & this is the end: that the Tory Party is powerless. Remember that even in 1832 they were only delivered to the Whigs. Now it is to Radicalism. We give your only guarantee for the decent & orderly conduct of affairs in the personal integrity & moderation of those who have been so long insulted & despised. Their crowning & irretrievable disaster, wh my father always foresaw, always laboured to avert, is now upon you. More than that. There is a potent underslide sweeping us to new chores. Well! This is an odd letter for the full flush of victory. Alas what vanity it all is. Observe in your case and since the inversion of the story of the idle & industrious apprentice. All your fidelity & restraint count for nothing. Virtue must be its own reward – in a vile world.

Always your most sincere friend
WINSTON

Lord Hugh Cecil to WSC

19 January 1906   Hatfield

My dear Winston,

I did not notice your date for dinner was so soon. Apologies. I will try & come over on Sunday afternoon. But don't wait for me.

As to your letter read Belial in *Paradise Lost*.
'. . . This was at first resolv'd,
If we were wise, against so great a foe
Contending, and so doubtful what might fall.
I laugh, when those who at the Spear are bold
And vent'rous, if that fail them, shrink and fear
What yet they know must follow, to endure
Exile, or ignominy, or bonds or pain,
The sentence of their Conqueror.'[1]

But in Milton's day politics were more unpleasantly violent than now; & I don't admit that to lose one's seat is a great calamity – it isn't 'Exile, or ignominy, or bonds or pain'. But subject to that reservation Belial's observations seem to me to be just & in point. (But JC is not my conqueror: its the other way).

I don't quite like the tone of your letter. It reads bitter: & after your success you ought to be genial & forgiving to everyone – specially AJB. Pray don't be bitter: its both wicked & tiresome. Follow after charity – & you will attain to charm! There's an alliterative epigram quite impromptu! Nor do I think yr criticism of that afflicted gentleman just the right one. But he's muddled things shockingly.

Yrs
HUGH CECIL

Herbert Vivian[2] to WSC

31 January 1906   The Pleasaunce
Confidential   Woking

My dear Churchill,

I have seen Horatio Bottomley[3] (MP) today. He aspires to play the part which I intended to play in the House. Will you see him? I think he may be useful to you.

His immediate intention is to move an amendment to the address about

[1] *Paradise Lost* Book II, 201.
[2] Herbert Vivian (1865–1940), special correspondent for *Morning Post* 1898–9 and *Daily Express* 1899–1900; revived Dr Johnson's *Rambler* 1901; contested Deptford in 1906 election; published several books on his wide travels.
[3] Horatio William Bottomley (1860–1933), whose unscrupulous financial dealings several times led him into the courts, had been elected Liberal MP for South Hackney in the 1906 election. It was in 1906 that he founded *John Bull* which became an important propaganda organ in the 1914–18 war. He spent the years 1922–7 in prison and died in obscurity.

Chinese labour. He will point out that Campbell-Bannerman, Asquith etc have called it slavery. He will press for an assurance that it shall not be left to any colony to authorize what responsible ministers have condemned as slavery. Then he will say he is content to withdraw his amendment if he has your *personal* assurance that you will enquire into the matter. He is willing to submit his epigrams and repartees to your consideration beforehand, and he will play into your hands in the same spirit all through if only you give him a ha'p'orth of flattery. *I* think he might be useful. If you happen to think so too, can you spare half an hour to meet him at lunch or elsewhere early next week?

He is also ready to help me to run a weekly paper, which might be our organ. That might also be worth discussing with him, as he is certainly intelligent as well as ambitious.

If you don't like the idea, please don't hesitate to say so. But he is quite humble in soliciting your good graces.

Yours very sincerely
HERBERT VIVIAN

George Wyndham to WSC

7 February 1906　　　　　　　　　　　　　　　　Saighton Grange
Chester

Private

My dear Winston,

Many thanks for congratulations. I am immensely impressed by your writing in your own hand when you must be seriously taxed. I, in turn, congratulate you with emphasis & without one reservation on the life of your father. We will talk about it one of these days.

One word of advice – do not attempt to answer many letters yourself; dictate & train up a PS to deal with minor matters. You owe it to the country, the House of Commons, to yourself to give your mind, whole and fresh, to the Colonies.

You are the minister responsible to *us* in the House of Commons.

The only 'tip' I can give you is this: –

Your officials – excellent, I know – will supply you with facts correlated to the *form of the estimates*. But in order to interest & persuade the House, it is almost essential to group the same facts, so that you can tell us all about one Colony or all about subsidised steam-ship lines to all colonies, etc, as the case may be.

This entails a good deal of labour at the start. But when once you have the main facts & figures for each 'story' complete on a quarto sheet, & an index to these sheets, you can defy the accident of adjournments & sudden debates.

On personal grounds, I wish you Good Luck. Politically, I shall, probably, differ and collide.

Yrs ever
GEORGE WYNDHAM

G. B. Birdsall[1] to WSC

24 February 1906   Oakley
                                              Whalley Range

Dear Mr Churchill,

As chairman of your Literature Committee, I am pleased to say that, during the election, *not a poster or placard,* having any reference whatever, either directly or indirectly, to Chinese labour was issued by us in the North-West Division of Manchester. We purposely & assuredly refrained from doing anything of the kind, so that Mr Chamberlain's strictures are entirely out of place, & uncalled for so far as you personally are concerned.

I thought you perhaps might be glad to know this from an official source.

Yours faithfully
G. B. BIRDSALL

Jack Seely to WSC

25 February 1906   29 Chester Square

My dear Winston,

I have written out my recollection of our conversation with Percy the week before last, and enclose you the document of which I have taken a copy.

After seeing you I began to doubt whether you were the person principally aimed at, but, from conversations in my presence at Mitcham yesterday between H. Lonsdale and other members of the House of Commons I came to the conclusion that you were right, and that JC got his information from somebody with whom you had discussed the matter.

I need not assure you that I gave no hint of any knowledge in the matter. I shall be here tomorrow, Monday, until 12.15, and shall then walk to

[1] George Bradshaw Birdsall (b. 1850), JP 1907.

the House for lunch – all this in case you want to see me. In my view the matter will redound to your credit, but in any case I am at your disposal so far as my recollection of our interview has a bearing on the matter.

In haste, Yours ever

JACK

Don't think the account of the conversation was written 'in haste' – that only applies to this letter, for it is somewhat near post time.

Note by Jack Seely

29 Chester Square

The following is an account of the conversation between Lord Percy and Mr Churchill so far as my memory serves me.

About ten days ago I was walking with Mr Churchill from Pall Mall towards the House of Commons, at about 2.30 in the afternoon.

Between the Carlton and Reform Clubs we met Lord Percy, coming from Carlton House Terrace.

We discussed the recent election, the possibility of Lord Hugh Cecil's return to Parliament, and the probability of the passing of the Deceased Wife's Sister's Bill.

As we were about to pass on Lord Percy said words to this effect 'You are not going to do very much about Chinese Labour after all'. Mr Churchill said 'You'll see.' I think it was Lord Percy who suggested the repatriation of the Chinese who wished to go home, implying that it was a somewhat inadequate measure after the previous denunciations of the system. At any rate, whoever introduced the subject, it was discussed. Mr Churchill said words to this effect 'Well, it's true that the mine people don't seem particularly frightened at this proposal,' implying that in this respect Lord Percy's sarcasms might be justified to some extent.

Mr Churchill added that we should not stop there, and I said 'I should hope not' and the conversation ended, Lord Percy laughingly saying 'We shall see'.

JOHN BERNARD SEELY

PS The whole conversation lasted about five minutes.

Sir Henry Campbell-Bannerman to WSC

25 February [1906]   10 Downing Street

Dear Churchill,

I remain of opinion that it is better to leave this matter alone, unless the newspapers tomorrow revive it, or JC (or some one else of importance) attempts to raise it again. I do not think this likely.

As it is, he stands badly before the public, & we may leave it there safely.

Yours

HCB

WSC to Joseph Chamberlain

26 February 1906   Colonial Office

[Copy]

Dear Mr Chamberlain

In your speech on Friday last the following passage occurred.

'Mr Churchill: The words I used yesterday were almost word for word what I said to my own constituents in Manchester – (Ministerial cheers.)

Mr Chamberlain: But what you said in those words did not get you votes in Manchester. – (Ministerial laughter.) What did gain the Under Secretary votes were the production of those posters and the parading of every street in his constituency by gangs of men dressed as Chinamen and accompanied by an agent got up as a slave-driver. (Opposition cheers.)

Mr Churchill shook his head in dissent.'

I was sure at the moment that your statement was wholly without foundation, and I have confirmed my opinion by most careful inquiry at Manchester. In these circumstances I have no doubt you would wish to withdraw an assertion which is at once prejudicial and quite untrue.

Yours very truly

[WINSTON S. CHURCHILL]

Joseph Chamberlain to WSC

1 March 1906   40 Prince's Gardens

Dear Winston,

I have now received replies to the enquiries which I addressed to NW Manchester on the subject of your note of Feb 26.

I find that I was mis-informed as to the action taken in your Division in reference to the question of Chinese Labour, and that no mock Chinaman paraded in your constituency although they appear to have been present in some neighbouring Divisions.

As regards posters, Mr Gibbons, Hon Secretary of the Conservative Club, Cheetham Hill Road, states that a large placard representing a gang of Chinamen manacled was posted outside the Tower Liberal Club Cheetham, and also at the Committee Rooms, Cheetham Hill Road. This, however, does not justify the statements previously made to me & I unhesitatingly withdraw the answer which I made to your interruption in the House of Commons, and regret that I should have repeated a statement which now turns out to be without foundation.

Believe me, Yours very truly
J. CHAMBERLAIN

Marie Corelli[1] to WSC

20 April 1906   Mason Croft
                                                 Stratford-on-Avon

Private

Dear Mr Winston Churchill,
     Though I only know you slightly, having sat on your right hand just once at a dinner at the 'Whitefriars Club' – I resent very much the way in which you have been publicly *insulted* in this town, and forward you the papers herewith. I am amazed that Sir Albert Muntz,[2] whom I had occasionally met, and whom I thought to be a *gentleman*, should have used such disgraceful expressions concerning you.[3]
     This is not a 'Party' feeling on my part, even though I *am* entirely 'heart and soul', *with* the present Govmt – ; but I think that however high the tide of political differences may run; language such as Sir Albert has used, (especially among the rather 'boorish' electors down here) is most distinctly reprehensible.

Faithfully yours
MARIE CORELLI

---

[1] Marie Corelli (1855–1924), novelist, daughter of Charles Mackay, song-writer and *litterateur*; her books include *A Romance of Two Worlds* 1886, *Barabbas* 1893, *The Sorrows of Satan* 1895, *The Mighty Atom* 1896.
[2] Philip Albert Muntz (1839–1908), Conservative MP for North Warwickshire 1884–1908; baronet 1902.
[3] In a speech on 20 April 1906, to the S.W. Warwickshire Conservative Association, Sir Albert Muntz suggested that the Education Bill, which WSC supported, be called the 'Barabbas-Ananias Bill'. Sir Albert went on to describe WSC as 'a wretched rag of a thing.'

7

The Life of Lord Randolph

(*See Main Volume Chapter 5*)

Deed of Trust Regulating the Papers of
Lord Randolph Churchill[1]

I, THE RIGHT HONOURABLE RANDOLPH HENRY SPENCER-CHURCHILL, PC, MP, of 50 Grosvenor Square in the County of London by these Presents send Greeting WHEREAS I am possessed of various Political and State Documents Correspondence and Papers which are now contained in Tin boxes deposited in my name at the Westminster Branch of the London and Westminster Bank Limited and in Tin boxes and Drawers at No 50 Grosvenor Square aforesaid. NOW I BY THESE PRESENTS DO assign transfer and make over from and after the date of my decease the above mentioned political and State documents correspondence and papers unto George Richard Penn Viscount Curzon MP,[2] of 23 Upper Brook Street in the said County of London and Ernest William Beckett MP, of 138 Piccadilly in the said County of London. UPON TRUST that they the said George Richard Penn Viscount Curzon and Ernest William Beckett shall from and after the date of my decease deal with and use the said Political and State documents correspondence and papers for any purpose which they in their absolute discretion may think well   PROVIDED that no such Political or State documents correspondence or paper relating either to the Department of the India Office or the Department of the Foreign Office shall be printed published or used in any way either directly or indirectly without the written

[1] This deed was reproduced before the preface in WSC's *Lord Randolph Churchill*.

[2] Richard George Penn Curzon, 4th Earl Howe (1861–1929), Lord-in-Waiting to King Edward VII 1901–3; Conservative MP for Wycombe 1885–1900; Treasurer to HM Household 1896–1900; Lord in Waiting to Queen Victoria 1900–1, Lord Chamberlain to Queen Alexandra 1903–25; succeeded father 1900; married, first, Georgiana Elizabeth Spencer-Churchill (1860–1906) WSC's aunt; second, Flora, widow of 2nd Marquess of Dufferin and Ava; and third, his own cousin Katherine, widow of Captain Quintin Dick and daughter of Major Ernest Charles Penn Curzon.

consent of Her Majesty's Secretary of State for either of the said Departments for the time being   AND I HEREBY DECLARE that these presents are executed by me in triplicate one Copy whereof is deposited with the Right Honourable the Earl of Rosebery KG, PC, Her Majesty's Principal Secretary of State for Foreign Affairs, the second Copy is deposited at the Western Branch of the Bank of England, Burlington Gardens in the name of my Solicitor Mr Theodore Lumley and the third Copy is retained by me

As WITNESS my hand and seal this eighth day of March One thousand eight hundred and ninety-three.

Signed Sealed and Delivered⎫
  by the above named Randolph⎪
  Henry Spencer-Churchill in ⎬RANDOLPH S. CHURCHILL
  the presence of ⎭

THEODORE LUMLEY
Solicitor
37 Conduit Street, Bond Street, W.

WSC to Lord Rosebery
(Rosebery Papers)

EXTRACT

10 June 1902   105 Mount Street

My dear Lord Rosebery,

    I had some talk at Christmas with George Howe about my father's papers & that I should write his life. He was quite sympathetic and has promised to consult again with you and Hicks Beach. I hope in such an event that you will feel able to encourage the idea; for I should like very much to undertake the work and would approach it with reverence & industry. . . .

Yours vy sincerely
WINSTON S. CHURCHILL

WSC to Lord Rosebery
(Rosebery Papers)

8 August 1902   105 Mount Street

My dear Lord Rosebery,

    You did me a vy good turn in regard to George Howe; for I have yesterday been informed by him and Ernest Beckett that the papers of my father's life are at my disposal and that I can begin as soon as I like.

Is there any chance of our meeting at Dunrobin? I go thither on the 26th or 27th.

As for the Government, so far as I am informed, *'plus ça change, plus c'est la même chose'*!

Always your most sincerely
WINSTON SC

WSC to Lady Randolph

15 August 1902   Blenheim

My dearest Mamma,

I found Jack very busy the other day when I went to see him, with all the letters, and no doubt he has now reduced them to good order. If convenient and agreeable to you I will send Scrivings[1] for the box sometime next week. I have been wading through two of the eighteen boxes of papers and they are certainly most full of valuable and interesting material. There are here all your early letters which were most carefully put away. I have written to Howe suggesting that they should be sent to you for you to select from them anything that is likely to be of general interest for the purposes of the biography, after which they should I think become your personal property again.

There emerges from these dusty records a great and vivid drama, and I feel at each step growing confidence that I shall be able to write what many will care to read. But I do not mean to put pen to paper until the whole of the evidence is before me, and as there are six times as many papers as those I have looked through you will understand that my days are very fully occupied. It is very pleasant here and I do not in the least regret having abandoned my visit to Lowther. Lonsdale[2] sent me a very good-humoured telegram in answer to my letter and I do not think any offence was caused in that quarter. I do not think I shall go to Scotland until the end of the month and perhaps I shall come up to London before I do so.

Will you send me any scrap-book you have of my Father's newspaper-cuttings, and please keep turning over in your mind any way you can help me in collecting material; all is grist that comes to my mill and the more saturated I am with the subject before I begin to write the better the work will be.

Tell Jack that if he wants more work to do I can send him a great many

[1] George Scrivings (d 1907), WSC's manservant died of cholera and ptomaine poisoning in 1907 while accompanying WSC on his African journey; see Vol II, pp 235–6.

[2] Hugh Cecil Lowther, 5th Earl of Lonsdale (1857–1944), whose seat was at Lowther Castle in Westmorland.

letters of the old Duchess which require to be read in order to find out what there is in them of general interest, and which also require to be arranged in order, but which are written in a crabbed handwriting and make my eye, which I got knocked at Polo, smart too much to read. If he feels inclined I can oblige him with plenty of work in this direction.

There is no one here except Sunny and the Ivor Guests, but I apprehend that Bertha[1] is coming next week.

Always your loving son
WINSTON S. CHURCHILL

WSC to Joseph Chamberlain
(J. Chamberlain Papers)

2 September 1902   105 Mount Street

My dear Mr Chamberlain,

I have two things to write about. First: I am at work upon my father's biography, and I find among his papers many vy pleasant letters from you. Have you any of his which you could put your hand upon without too much trouble, and would you lend them to me for the purpose I have in hand? When I have covered the whole ground, I think I shall further trespass upon your kindness to ask some questions.

Secondly: I wonder whether you have ever considered Marlborough as a possible candidate for the post of Australian Governor-General. If he were asked – I think he would go. Blenheim would be a great sacrifice, but on the other hand to have held such an office with credit for three or four years confers a permanent rank in the Imperial hierarchy. Of course it might be difficult for future Governors to follow such a wealthy man; but if Liberal Governments cannot find suitable people for the big official posts, that is perhaps a reason for not indulging in too many Liberal Governments. Some years ago – at the Jeunes[2] – you put me a question in this connexion, and that is one reason why I write.[3]

[1] Marchioness of Blandford (1847–1932), former wife of the 8th Duke of Marlborough.
[2] Francis Henry Jeune (1843–1905), President of the Probate, Divorce and Admiralty Division and Judge Advocate-General 1892–1905; knighted 1901; Baron St Helier 1905; and his wife, Mary (1845–1931), a celebrated London hostess, and a great-aunt of Clementine Hozier.
[3] The 7th Earl of Hopetoun (and later 1st Marquess of Linlithgow) was first Governor-General of the newly federated Commonwealth which had come into existence on 1 January 1901. In May 1902 he announced his resignation after Parliament had reduced his allowance by £4,000 to £10,000 a year. He was succeeded in July by Lord Tennyson, Governor of South Australia, and son of the poet, who accepted the office for a year. Tennyson's successor was Lord Northcote, Governor of Bombay. In 1903 the Duke of Marlborough was appointed Under-Secretary of State for the Colonies.

I hope that your health and strength have quite returned. I am told that the loss of blood has been but slowly replaced. I hope you will find it possible to have an easy winter – comparatively at any rate. There was one thing in your B'ham speech over which I purred with approval.

Yours vy sincerely
WINSTON S. CHURCHILL

WSC to Lord Rosebery
(*Rosebery Papers*)

11 September 1902   [Dunrobin]

My dear Lord Rosebery,

I am to go to Invercauld on the 20th and should be in Oldham (to open a picture gallery!) on the 2nd October. I should like vy much to come to you on the 26th or 27th and stay until I go South. If this is convenient and agreeable to you I will bring with me my fat box of papers – amid wh I am now busy – and I am sure there are some you would like to see, and also several points on wh I want to ask your advice. The more I see of the material the more I like the task. The great difficulty seems to be the graceful weaving of numerous original documents into the regular narrative. But I think I see the way to do this. It is all most interesting to me – and melancholy too.

Neil [Primrose] is here & before him we had the King, the Royal Yacht, & a 1st Class Cruiser – as you foreshadowed to me in London.[1] Neil is vy political and talks about 'sweeping Cheshire' with a new League of Ladies organised at Crewe.

The duchess was rather seedy yesterday, but I am glad to say she is much better now. I have butchered two stags – right and left – and nothing shall tempt [me] to spoil my average this year. Fancy that ass Brodrick exposing himself to the German Army![2]

Yours most sincerely
WINSTON S. CHURCHILL

[1] After the Coronation on August 9 and the great naval review in the Solent on August 16, the King and Queen went on a yachting cruise during which they put in at Dunrobin among other places.
[2] At the invitation of the German Emperor the Secretary of State for War attended the German manoeuvres on September 6.

John Pemberton to Ernest Beckett

11 September 1902   30 Old Queen Street
[Copy]

Dear Mr Beckett,

I gather that you wish me to make any suggestions which occur to me on the draft agreement as to a biography of Lord Randolph Churchill.

(1) The first question is what is the scope of the Literary Executors' duty in the matter – Is their whole duty discharged when to the best of their judgment they have selected a suitable biographer, or must they take other precautions to guard against the ultimate publication of a biography which they may consider regrettable?

I do not propose to answer those questions, but rather to submit some points bearing upon them for you to consider, unless indeed you have already dealt with them.

When the biography is complete the Executors may be satisfied with it as a whole, but they may object to some particular statement, passage or phrase or to some quotation from a document. This difficulty is provided for by Clauses 2,3, and 4 of the draft agreement.

Again the Executors, although satisfied with the work in other respects, may consider that some political episode is not satisfactorily treated, as for example the history of the Fourth Party or Lord Randolph's resignation of the Office of Chancellor of the Exchequer.

There may be honesty of purpose and literary power, but in endeavouring to do justice to Lord Randolph other persons concerned may be unduly disparaged, or the Executors may consider that the episode as a whole is not presented in a manner which they could approve. The matter may not be capable of rectification by the alteration of any particular statement, passage or phrase, under Clause 3, but the entire chapter may require to be recast and rewritten. Under the draft agreement the Executors would appear to be powerless to interfere.

Or again, when the Executors have the entire biography before them, if they should be dissatisfied with it as a whole they would be powerless to prevent its publication.

In that case they would have provided the materials for a biography which they may consider to be marred by serious mistakes, arising it may be from filial bias or from lack of discrimination as to political relationships or many other possible causes.

The work too would be popularly supposed to be published with the Executors' sanction.

On the other hand the biographer may decline to undertake the task if he is liable to have the entire Work or even a whole chapter objected to.

He may however possibly agree to a Clause to the effect that any question of the fitness of the entire work or of any part or parts of it may be referred to the decision of some person or persons to be named in the agreement, with some provision for substituting another person or persons in the event of their deaths.

The following are other points which have occurred to me.

(1) Insert a Clause to the effect that before publication the entire work shall be submitted to the Executors who shall within a specified time state any objections which they may be entitled to raise under the agreement, and that the work shall not be published until such objections have been disposed of.

(2) The biographer not to make any use of the information derived from the Executors' documents except for the purpose of the biography in question.

(3) The biographer not to keep copies of or Extracts from the Executors' documents as other persons may get them in the event of the biographer's death &c.

For the same reason he should destroy all rough drafts and papers as they may contain (for example) a quotation or particular statement struck out of the completed copy by the Executors.

(4) The biographer not to publish any revised edition without first submitting the revised Life to the Executors who shall have the same rights as regards making objections as in respect of the original edition.

(5) Should some provision be made in the event of the death of the biographer before the biography is completed?

(6) The like as to Lord Rosebery's death.

(7) Should there be some specified limit of time within which the biography must be published, failing which the Executors may by notice terminate the agreement? In that case the biographer should deliver to the Executors or destroy all drafts and papers already written.

(8) It may perhaps be worth while to state expressly in the agreement that the Executors are not to pay any part of the cost of publication.

If you think that all or any of the above points should be provided for in the agreement and would like me to prepare clauses for that purpose I shall be pleased to do so.

Believe me, Yours very truly

[JOHN PEMBERTON]

WSC to Ernest Beckett

[September 1902]   105 Mount Street

[Copy]

My dear Ernest Beckett,

I incline strongly to the belief that the duty of the literary executors is discharged 'when to the best of their judgment they have selected a suitable biographer'. Questions of style, of literary taste, of the scope of the work, of the proportion of various incidents in the work, are all matters of opinion, and matters upon which opinion will very often be divided. A syndicate may compile an encyclopaedia, only a man can write a book. Once the human element in a book is destroyed by unsympathetic or foreign alterations, it cannot be of any real literary excellence and its only value is to be found in the facts it records. Therefore I am of opinion – and my opinion would be the same if I were an outside person advising you and not interested in any way myself – that the fullest discretion and liberty in the treatment of the subject must be accorded to the biographer; and I am quite certain that whatever arrangement, my strong personal feeling both of desire to write this work and of friendship to you might lead me to acquiesce in, no strange writer of any literary distinction and of financial independence would undertake the task if he were 'liable to have the entire work or even a whole chapter objected to'.

Now with this as a preliminary and without prejudice to any part of it, let me say that I am extremely grateful to you for your great kindness in allowing me to have the papers, and that I do not anticipate any real cause of difficulty between us, because I think we see eye to eye on a great many questions and most particularly upon questions connected with this Life. I am therefore willing now, as when I wrote last to you upon the subject, to agree to certain definite conditions which will enable the literary executors to reserve to themselves a very considerable measure of control.

First: The literary executors reserve to themselves the power of withholding from publication or from being recognisably quoted any documents which they may consider injurious to my Father's memory or disparaging to others.

Secondly: That the literary executors shall see the work from time to time as it progresses and shall see it in a completed form before it is published and that if they dislike the treatment of any particular incident or object to any phrase or passage, they shall (over and above the ordinary influence of their criticism) have the legal right of objection, which objection, in the event of the biographer still holding to his view, shall be settled by Lord Rosebery, or in the event of his death, by Sir Michael Hicks Beach, or some other person to be hereafter nominated.

I hope you will not underrate the control which these two provisions give to you, or overlook the fact that by using them to their fullest capacity, you could compel me against my will very largely to shape, extend, or curtail the work, or indeed assuming that a serious difference arose between us, perhaps bring it to a standstill altogether.

I need scarcely say that these are possibilities which seem to me beyond the bounds of reason.

Passing from this main aspect of the question to the various points of detail which Mr Pemberton raises, you will see that:

(1) is disposed of by the second condition of the main proposal stated above.

(2) is, I think, quite un-necessary to prescribe and impossible to fulfil; for it will be apparent to you that I must become possessed in the course of this work of a mass of valuable political information which no power on earth can prevent me using at my own proper discretion.

(3) I would agree to a clause that all papers in my possession, whether trust papers handed over to me by you or collected by myself from various sources, together with all notes, extracts, books, manuscript, proofs, connected with the biography, should, in the event of my death, be handed over to the literary executors at their absolute discretion: always provided that in regard to papers obtained from other sources, they shall themselves observe the conditions on which these papers have been lent to me.

I do not think it possible to put the following in a legal form but I may as well express here my earnest wish, that in the event of my dying, with the biography largely completed, every effort shall be made by the literary executors to make as much use as possible of any work I may have done.

(4) I agree to this.

(5) I have already dealt with.

(6) I think that in the event of Lord Rosebery's death, the two literary executors and the biographer shall, by a majority, appoint another referee in his place.

(7) I am of opinion that five years would be a fair and reasonable limit at the end of which time all the trust papers together with any extracts from or copies of them should revert to the literary executors, unless a new agreement is made.

(8) I agree to. The biographer in this agreement shall take all financial liability and all profits.

Furthermore I suggest insertion of a clause to the following effect: –

'After the biography is completed, all the trust papers shall revert to the possession of the literary executors who shall decide what course is to be taken in regard to them.' You will see that this practically enables you to make any new arrangement you may like in regard to a revised edition and largely removes the necessity for (4).

If you agree to have a legal agreement made out on these lines, I shall be very happy to sign it, and in the meanwhile, as the preparation of such agreement may take some time, this letter together with its references in Mr Pemberton's letter of the 11th September 1902, shall, so far as is legally possible, be binding upon me.

[WINSTON S. CHURCHILL]

WSC to Lady Randolph

19 September 1902   105 Mount Street

Dearest Mamma,

I enjoyed my Sunday very much indeed. It is always pleasant and interesting talking to you.

Chamberlain has sent me a large budget of interesting letters, upon which I am now hard at work.

Your loving son
WINSTON

PS Mrs Grenfell is at Assynt close to Lairg [Sutherlandshire].

WSC to Joseph Chamberlain
(*J. Chamberlain Papers*)

19 September 1902   105 Mount Street

My dear Mr Chamberlain,

Thank you for so promptly sending me the letters which I herewith return, registered. You will find them arranged in chronological order; for I could not quite make out how they were arranged by you & inadvertently mixed them up. I find it perfectly easy to understand the course of events, for I have so many papers here which connect with these letters of yours; but I hope you will let me have a talk with you sometime upon the subject.

I remember to have heard my father say in 1894 that he never had but one quarrel with you – Aston Park.

Yours vy sincerely
WINSTON S. CHURCHILL

A. J. Balfour to WSC

EXTRACT

8 October 1902   Whittingehame

My dear Winston,

I need not tell you that any letters I have from your father are entirely at your disposal. But alas I am a most disorderly person, and though I feel pretty confident that I have destroyed none, I may have some difficulty in laying my hands upon them. I ought to add that I do not think they are very numerous. We saw each other so constantly, sitting, indeed, side by side in the House of Commons, that communication by letter was hardly necessary. . .

WSC to Lady Randolph

9 October 1902   Canford

Dearest Mamma,

I have now been here two days and find very valuable material indeed for my work. Cornelia had kept Scrap Books of almost every incident of my Father's life, and with the letters which she also had, the material is now almost complete.

My secretary has gone away to India, (like a lot of other silly people)! so that I am very much stranded in regard to correspondence. Will you find out from Miss Anning whether she could come to me, two days a week let us say, and she could make what arrangement would be suitable to her. It is essential that I should have someone that could answer the simple letters that I receive.

I come back for Parlt on 15th. Dinner?

Your ever loving son
WINSTON SC

Lord James of Hereford to WSC

21 October 1902   Breamore
                                                         Salisbury

My dear Winston Churchill

I will have a try at the scene – but it is somewhat difficult to describe without being florid. Send me back Waldron's letter.

Do come here as soon as you can. As I told you the door is wide open.

Yours
JAMES OF H

WSC to Lord Rosebery
(Rosebery Papers)

23 October 1902   105 Mount Street

My dear Lord Rosebery,

I am off to make a speech at Oldham in support of the Education Bill – wh is a somewhat depressing prospect – Devonport notwithstanding. Thank you vy much about Lord Allerton.[1] I will come to see you next week – after these speeches – and it will be most kind of you to put me into communication with him. Of course he must know everything about December '86; for he was my father's financial secretary.

I send you a book which having survived for three years now reappears in a single volume.[2] When it was first published I thought that you viewed me with an eye of disapproval & so I did not venture to send you a copy. But now I shall boldly ask you to do me the honour of accepting it.

It is a vy good book!

Yours ever

WINSTON S. CHURCHILL

[1] William Lawies Jackson, 1st Baron Allerton (1840–1919), Conservative MP for Leeds North 1880–1902; Financial Secretary of the Treasury 1885–6 and 1886–91; Chief Secretary for Ireland 1891–2. His second son, Francis, was Governor of Bengal 1927–32.

[2] A thousand copies of this single-volume edition of *The River War* were published in London on 15 October 1902, and copies were exported to New York for American publication on 13 December. WSC had added a new chapter describing the ultimate destruction of the Khalifa and the end of the war. This volume was considerably revised. A large part of WSC's strong condemnation of Lord Kitchener was omitted, including the following controversial passage: 'His wonderful industry, his undisturbed patience, his noble perseverance, are qualities too valuable for a man to enjoy in this imperfect world without complementary defects. The General who never spared himself, cared little for others. He treated all men like machines – from the private soldiers whose salutes he disdained, to the superior officers he rigidly controlled. The comrade who had served with him and under him for many years in peace and peril was flung aside incontinently as soon as he ceased to be of use. . . . The wounded Egyptian, and latterly the wounded British soldier, did not excite his interest, and of all the departments of his army the one neglected was that concerned with the care of the sick and injured. . . . The stern and unpitying spirit of the commander was communicated to his troops, and the victories which marked the progress of the River War were accompanied by acts of barbarity not always justified even by the harsh customs of savage conflicts.'

Justice Gerald Fitzgibbon[1] to WSC

15 November 1902   His Majesty's Court of
                                                       Appeal in Ireland
                                                       Howth

Private

My dear Winston,

I send you an important letter from your father which I found today, dated January 13, 1892. I think that it will modify your view of his position and condition at that date – the end of your 'barren years'. It proves that his political prescience and the activity of his intellect, were often absolutely unimpaired; and it will also explain to you some of the reasons for my apprehension of the consequences of his undertaking the Irish Chief Secretaryship, then or at any other time. I should like to see my answer to this letter, but I shall be surprised if it does not disclose my distrust of the policy which he proposed. You must exercise your best judgement, and great caution, in deciding the effect which the publication of his views, as disclosed to an intimate friend, would have upon the public estimate of his statesmanship. The cynical, if not Machiavellian, tone of many of his letters to me needs to be discounted by my own propensity in the same direction. But this letter needs to be read in order to understand his dealings with the Irish Education Question, and you must follow that 'thread' from 1877 to the end. It was the first that he took up – first on the Erasmus Smith Endowment in the Commons – then the Commission of 1878, on which he worked hard for two years. Then he passed the Educational Endowments Act, 1885, by marvellous agility during the fag end of the 1885 Session.

He twice was on the point of settling the University question, and each time was 'headed off' by the precipitancy of the RC Hierarchs. You must look up all this in *Hansard* & the newspapers, and some of his letters to me explain the ever-changing situation. Do you want me to send you the 1885–7 letters *now*? I should prefer to see my own letter first, and also to complete my search for his letters, before I send you his, for I think more will turn up, and I don't fully understand all the references in those I have.

                                                       Very sincerely yours
                                                       GERALD FITZGIBBON

[1] Gerald Fitzgibbon (1837–1909), Lord Justice of Appeal in Ireland 1878–1909; Lord Randolph frequently spent Christmas with him at Howth; QC 1872.

Lord James of Hereford to WSC

16 November 1902   Breamore
                                                          Salisbury

My dear Winston Churchill,

I return all 'the copy' I have received.

The documents are *most* fascinating reading to me. The memo about Ashbourne[1] is very scathing. I hope its contents are somewhat exaggerated.

Is there any way in which I can help you *now*? It seems to me I can only be of use when you commence to construct. As I have told you I think many of the documents I have seen can be utilised only for the purpose of affording general knowledge to the biographer and cannot be quoted textually.

When shall you commence to construct?

Yours ever truly
JAMES OF HEREFORD

'The copy' shall be sent by tomorrow's post.

Sir Michael Hicks Beach to Lady Hicks Beach
(*St Aldwyn Papers*)

EXTRACT

15 July 1903   House of Commons

. . . Tomorrow I am going to see Salisbury at Hatfield: I want to see him about Winston's life of R. Churchill, and fear, from the accounts of his health, there may not be many more chances . . .[2]

WSC to Lord Rosebery
(*Rosebery Papers*)

27 October 1903   105 Mount Street

Private

My dear Lord Rosebery,

Do you remember my request for my father's letters? It would be vy kind of you to let me have those in your possession. There is of course no hurry, but I should like to get all the evidence before me.

We are still disturbed by 'mocking chance & wavering winds.' The position is one of astonishing difficulty, and these old ministers are weighed down

---

[1] Edward Gibson (1837–1913), MP for Dublin University 1875–85; Attorney-General for Ireland 1877–80; Lord Chancellor of Ireland 1885–92, 1895–1906; Baron Ashbourne 1885; he is best remembered for the Land Purchase Act of 1885 known as the Ashbourne Act.

[2] Lord Salisbury died on August 22.

by their sins. I hope you will not be drawn from your logical position to accommodate the programme of the F Food League. That cannot last as it is.

Yours vy sincerely
WINSTON S. CHURCHILL

WSC to Lord Salisbury
(*Hatfield Papers*)

27 October 1903   105 Mount Street

My dear Cranborne,
Your father was good enough to give me access to the letters he had received from Lord Randolph. He did not desire that they should go out of his possession, but he allowed me to study them, to make notes & extracts, and the question of what could be published was reserved for future consideration. The letters with my notes thereon are all in a small despatch box the whereabouts of which Linky knows. I am vy anxious to proceed with my work and these letters are essential to the most interesting period with wh it deals. I shall feel much obliged to you if you will let me see those letters again & make from them as many extracts as can properly be published.

I may add that Beach, Devonshire & Chamberlain have placed their whole . . . [?] of letters in my hands, and that as I possess the other half of the correspondence there are no new secrets to be learned, but only matter of interest to a biographer.

Yours vy sincerely
WINSTON S. CHURCHILL

WSC to Mrs Louis Jennings[1]

24 January 1904   Vice Regal Lodge
                                                       Dublin

[Copy]

Dear Madam,
I shall be very glad to give you my personal assurance that I will treat the relations which existed between the late Lord Randolph Churchill and the

---

[1] Widow of Louis John Jennings (1836–1893), journalist – he edited the *New York Times* after the American Civil War – and Conservative MP for Stockport 1885–93. Jennings rallied round Lord Randolph after his resignation in December 1886 and supported him until 1890. In that year Lord Randolph's bitter attack on the Government for the 'arbitrary and tyrannical character' of the Parnell Commission caused a breach in their friendship. See WSC's Life of Lord Randolph for details of the quarrel and the impartial way in which it is handled.

late Mr L. J. Jennings in a perfectly fair manner, and in a spirit sympathetic to both parties in the Biography which I have undertaken to write. But it was always my intention to do so, and I cannot conceive any more graceless and baneful task than to rake up and revive all sorts of bitterness which was certainly for the most part the result of misunderstanding. I do not doubt from the documents in my possession that an account could be given perfectly honourable to both parties of a quarrel in itself very regrettable, and which Lord Randolph Churchill would gladly have repaired.

With regard to the Memorandum which you inform me exists giving Mr Jennings' account of the Parnell Commission incident,[1] I will undertake that if it is quoted in any way, it shall be printed in extenso either in the Text or in the Appendix according to Literary exigencies.

> Yours truly
> WINSTON S. CHURCHILL

Lord Goschen to WSC

EXTRACT

1 Feb [1904]   Seacox Heath
                                               Hawkhurst

Dear Mr Churchill,

I am sorry to say that I cannot help you as regards the point on which you write. To my own regret I have scarcely ever kept any notes of conversations, and I have absolutely none of June 1885. Unhappily now my memory is very spasmodic. I do not, I think, have an inaccurate memory of events: I simply forget.

I recall distinctly matters you have reminded me: that there was an interview between your father and myself, that he came to see me at Portland Place and that we had a serious talk. I can even remember where he sat. But the important part, viz what passed between us, I cannot remember. I fancy we did not agree. As you know, I have always been a little shy of Tory Democracy & I expect that I did not meet Lord Randolph very cordially in the direction of such a fashion as you mention in your letter.

Lord Rosebery apparently has some recollection of what passed between your father and myself as he told you there had been an interesting interview. I will ask him when I see him for any further notes he may have as regards the purpose of the conversation to see if it tallies with the vague impressions which alone I have retained. . . .

> Yours sincerely
> GOSCHEN

---

[1] Reprinted as an appendix in WSC's Life of Lord Randolph.

Wilfrid Scawen Blunt[1] to WSC

30 July 1904   Newbuildings Place

Dear Churchill,

Before the Session is over & you have disappeared from London I write to remind you that I have not yet heard from you in regard to your father's letters to me which I left with you some weeks ago. If you think they may be of use to you, I shd like you to have them copied & then returned to me here. I have been looking through old journals of the years 1884 & 1885 & find a number of entries abt yr father which are more interesting than the letters.

Yours very truly
WILFRID SCAWEN BLUNT

WSC to Lady Randolph

EXTRACT

22 August 1904   Villa Cassel
                                                      Moerel
                                                      Valais Switzerland

Dearest Mamma,

I have waited a week so as to write with certainty about the effect wh this place produces. It is wholly good. I sleep like a top & have not ever felt in better health. Really it is a wonderful situation. A large comfortable 4 storied house – complete with baths, a French cook & private land & every luxury that would be expected in England – is perched on a gigantic mountain spur 7,000 feet high, and is the centre of a circle of the most glorious snow mountains in Switzerland. The air is buoyant and the weather has been delightful. Nearly every day clear and cool and bright, so that we can sleep with windows wide open & breakfast & lunch on the verandah. There are all kinds of beautiful walks and climbs from the modest 20 minutes on the flat to very formidable scrambles & exercises. Far below in the valleys which drop on both sides of the house, the clouds are drifting, & beneath and through these, green plains and tiny toy churches and towns. . . .

The days pass pleasantly & vy rapidly. I am astonished to think I have

---

[1] Wilfrid Scawen Blunt (1840–1922), served in the Diplomatic Service 1858–70, active in the Egyptian National Movement 1881–2. Unsuccessful Tory Home Rule candidate 1885. Unsuccessful Liberal Home Rule candidate 1886. Imprisoned in Ireland for calling a meeting in a proclaimed district 1888.

been here a week. It seems three days since we cleared the duck weed from
the Elizabethan moat [at Salisbury Hall].

I divide them into three parts. The morning when I read and write: the
afternoons when I walk – real long walks and climbs about these hills or
across the glacier: the evenings, of course 4 rubbers of bridge – then bed.
I shall stay here till Septr 1 & then to meet Sunny at Mont d'Or.

I thought a good deal over all you said to me about yourself & I feel sure
you are right to concentrate on and take pains with the few people you really
care about. But I have no doubt that when papa G. [Cornwallis-West]
is at length gathered to Abraham you will be able to renew your youth like
the eagle. . . . The newspaper cuttings are vy civil about my recent performances & have seen them in quite the right light.

Ever your loving son
WINSTON

WSC to Lady Randolph

EXTRACT

25 August 1904   Villa Cassel

Dearest Mama,

. . . I have been working away at my book and am slowly getting into the
stride. But the difficulty of the task impresses me as I proceed. What to
leave out, how to work this in – what line to take in regard to a whole series
of conflicting or contradictory letters? At present I am writing nearly everything. It will be easy to cut it down afterwards. I wonder whether J.M.
[Morley] wrote to you for the proofs. I get hardly any letters here: but masses
of quite civil press cuttings have arrived. Love to Jack,

Your affectionate son
WINSTON

John Morley to Lady Randolph

EXTRACT

26 August 1904   Flowermead
                                                     Wimbledon Park

. . . Will you now be so very kind as to send me the proofs of which
Winston wrote to me a fortnight ago? I shall read them with lively interest,
for I heartily wish him well.

Yours sincerely
JOHN MORLEY

A. J. Balfour to WSC

29 August 1904   Whittingehame
                                                           Prestonkirk

My dear Winston,

I had a hunt when you last wrote to me for your father's letters – a hunt which proved unsuccessful. This is curious, for it is very unlikely that I should have thrown them away, & though our correspondence was not large in amount, partly because I am the worst of letter-writers, & partly because most of our communications were oral, yet some letters there must have been. I will repeat my search, & I hope with better luck.

I am very glad the book is nearing completion.

Yrs very sincerely
ARTHUR JAMES BALFOUR

Lord George Hamilton to WSC

11 September 1904   Fenton
                                                          Northumberland

My dear Winston,

I will gladly send you the memorandum you want, & in such a shape as will enable you to make any public use of it which you may wish. I will let you have this in a few days. I will also look through my correspondence of 1885–1886. I think that I shall find something that will be of interest & of use to you. I am greatly enjoying freedom from the voluminous papers of the India Office, but I watched sadly the decadence & disintegration of the Unionist party. Balfour, even more than Chamberlain is responsible for this retrogression, & it is very difficult for any one, like myself who was trained under Dizzy, & Salisbury, to know what to do in the future, and the smash may come sooner than we anticipate.

Believe me, yrs very truly
GEORGE HAMILTON

WSC to Lady Randolph

14 September 1904   Salisbury Hall
Private

Dearest Mamma,

I have been making such good progress here – alone all day – that I cannot bring myself to cart all my traps to Scotland tonight. In any case I shall stay here till Saturday. If you thought it possible for me to stay on in the absence of the Waldens[1] with Scrivings & the kitchen maid – I would not leave at all. Here I can get my proofs day by day from the printers & all my material is at hand. This staying in one place – and such a nice place – without continual disturbances has comforted me vy much. JM whom I saw yesterday begged me to press on with the work – of which he held most encouraging opinions. He seems to think I shall make a great deal of money, 8 or 10 thousand pounds perhaps. It is worth making a sustained effort. I know how much time & energy is wasted in moving about. Will you explain all this to T [Tweedmouth] or must I write him a separate letter. It would be a great relief to me not to go to Scotland at all.

I daresay C is right in what he says, so far as party leaders & wirepullers are concerned. But the democratic view at election times is very powerful. If you are anxious you might talk to Edward about it. Telling him what C said. I never refer to such things except to you & Sunny.

Seven invitations to speak reached me yesterday.

Your loving son
W

Give my love to George.

WSC to Joseph Chamberlain
EXTRACT

15 September 1904   Salisbury Hall

[Copy]

Private

Dear Mr Chamberlain,

There are several points on which I am in perplexity with my father's papers relating to you. . . . On all these matters there are a good many of your letters some of which are vy important and also very private. Then in 1886 there are a number of letters from my father to Lord Salisbury giving detailed accounts of conversations with you before the Home Rule Government was formed, and during the great Home Rule debate.

I should like very much to have a talk with you about these papers. My own change of party is an additional reason for care on my part; & besides I

---

[1] Thomas Walden, Lord Randolph's devoted personal servant who accompanied him on his last voyage in 1894; went to South Africa in 1899–1900 as WSC's soldier servant.

should on personal grounds like to consult your wishes. On the other hand the more I can fairly publish the better for me & my book.

I see you are going abroad in October. I shall be here or at Blenheim until the middle of that month. I could call upon you in London almost at any time till then; & if agreeable to you I would send you your letters & copies of my father's letters to Lord S [Salisbury] a few days beforehand so that you could consider them.

Yours sincerely
WINSTON S. CHURCHILL

Joseph Chamberlain to WSC

16 September 1904   Highbury

Private

Dear Winston,

I shall probably not be in London again except for a few hours before I leave, but, as Birmingham is as near to Oxford as London, I propose that you should come here some day either to lunch or to dine and sleep, whichever may best suit your arrangements.

I am free from now to the end of the month, except on the following days – the 19th, 20th, 21st, 26th, 27th and 28th and shall be very glad to see you and talk over the question of the letters if you will send them to me a day or two beforehand.

Believe me, Yours truly
J. CHAMBERLAIN

WSC to W. St John Brodrick[1]

EXTRACT

21 September 1904   Blenheim

. . . You seem very contented with the political situation from your speech the other day. I have for the present abandoned politics for literature. . . .

[1] This letter was bought by Quaritch of Grafton Street at an auction held at Christie's on 21 November 1962.

W. St John Brodrick to WSC

22 September 1904   India Office

Private

My dear Churchill,

It will be a great pleasure to me to facilitate your analysis of the material for your father's life. I am sure you will find Sir Arthur Godley[1] a good adviser, and I should be disposed in nine cases out of ten to agree to anything he proposed. You may be quite sure that we will stretch a point wherever we can in your favour, as I should like to do anything I can to make the life a great success.

The best turn I could do you would be to write a short chapter comparing the Parliamentary career of the father and the son, so far as present advices go. Without being unduly pungent, I believe it would be more read than any chapter in the book, and I should expect a large royalty on the sale in the shape of a reconsideration on your part of some of those parts of my army scheme which you incontinently attacked.

As regards my speech, you will I think admit that it is the business of a Minister to seem contented on all occasions with his colleagues' performances, if not with his own, but I think it would have been of interest to the late Lord Salisbury, who told me about this day four years ago that he should be turned out after the election as every Prime Minister for fifty years had been within a year after dissolving, if he could see through what strange channels his party has had to travel in the four years which have elapsed.

Yours vy truly

ST JOHN BRODRICK

WSC to Lady Randolph

EXTRACT

24 September 1904   Blenheim

Dearest Mamma,

Jack departing for Blenheim on Saturday last, coupled with the flight of the Waldens, decided me to come too and I have moved a greater part of my tin boxes here and am now settled down in the Arcade Rooms which are most comfortable.

---

[1] Arthur Godley (1847–1932), Private Secretary to W. E. Gladstone 1872–4, 1880–2; Commissioner of Inland Revenue 1882–3; Under-Secretary of State for India 1883–1909; knighted 1893; created Baron Kilbracken of Killegar 1909.

Consuelo is quite alone here, and as you are not going to be at S.H. [Salisbury Hall] except for the Sunday, I don't think I will move until I go to Manchester which I do on the 30th for two days on political and semi-political work.

I have been working most assiduously at my book and the great thing to avoid is un-necessary movement. Of course if you find yourself alone at S.H. for four or five days, I should like to come. But failing that, I may as well remain here where I can ride each morning.

You will laugh when I tell you that I spent last Thursday night at High-bury and had five or six hours most pleasant and interesting conversation with Joe about old letters and old politics. I suggested an interview in London and he replied by an invitation to dine and sleep. He is, of course, tremendously partisan in his views both on me and things, but it was quite clear to me that we understood each other on lots of questions, and that my company was not at all unpleasant to him.

He got out the Cup which my father gave him on his third marriage and made great fuss about it and generally I preserve very pleasant recollections of a most interesting episode. . . .

I have done a quantity of work, another whole chapter since I have been here and I am incubating the material for the Home Rule chapter which is one of the most important of the book. I hope the next four or five days may see that launched if not completed.

Brodrick has written me a most gracious letter offering to give me every assistance through the India Office in dealing with that portion and George Hamilton has written me a memorandum setting forth the valuable departmental reforms which he was able to make in advance in consequence of the agitation my father raised for economies. I have also heard from Beach and Fitzgibbon. You see I am certainly bound up in the biography. Indeed I find it quite difficult now to turn my mind on to political speeches but it will be a change.

With best love
WINSTON S C

Joseph Chamberlain to WSC

29 September 1904   Highbury

Dear Winston,

I cannot believe that there was anything in the letters to the publication of which I agreed which would be mischievous, but as you are kind enough to give me the opportunity I had perhaps better see them again in the light of our conversation the other day, and of Morley's opinion, for which in such a matter I should have great respect.

I am very glad that you were able to come and talk over the matter with me. It revived old times and the memories of my pleasant associations with your father.

I hope the book will be a great success. I am sure that it will create a very great interest; but you must take care to keep the Government in until it is published, as the public cannot stand two sensations at the same time.

Believe me, Yours very truly

J. CHAMBERLAIN

WSC to Lord Rosebery
(*Rosebery Papers*)

19 January 1905   105 Mount Street

My dear Lord Rosebery,

Here are some proofs. They are vy rough and raw; but they will give you an idea of the stage which my work has reached. I shall be grateful for any comments or criticisms – still more for any suggestions either towards expansion or excision. You will see that Beach has minuted some of the sheets. I think it vy kind of you to wish to read them.

Yours ever

WINSTON S. CHURCHILL

WSC to Sir Michael Hicks Beach
(*St Aldwyn Papers*)

20 January 1905   105 Mount Street

My dear Sir Michael,

I sent Chamberlain all the passages about himself and have received from him a vy cordial letter & complete consent to their publication. I read with attention all your notes & your letter & I will in nearly every case alter the text accordingly. I will compose a paragraph to bring out the differences of temperament & personal habits between my father & Lord S wh you consider such an important factor in their final severance. But I don't want to base their splits too much on personal discordances when there were also such deep & wide chasms of political difference.

I am going to write to F. Smith to ask his leave to publish his father's[1]

---

[1] William Henry Smith (1835–1891), politician and newsagent; First Lord of the Admiralty 1877–80; Secretary of State for War 1885–6, 1886–7, First Lord of the Treasury and Leader of the House of Commons 1887–91; was responsible for developing his father's newspaper agency.

letters, & I propose to mention to him the fact that you have seen them & (subject to correction) thought no harm would result from such publication.

With regard to Foreign Affairs I am compelled by the Trust deed by wh I am bound to obtain the sanction of the S of S before publishing any document included in my father's papers relating thereto.

I have still got to do the chapter 'The Ministry of Caretakers' which covers the period when you led the House in a minority. After that the historical period is practically completed. I hope to publish in October, or if you do not dissolve till the Autumn – possibly in April.

I send you – 'The Abandoned Budget' 'The Parnell Commission' & the last chapter in the book (incomplete). I wonder what you will think of the Budget as regards 1. Finance and 2. will anybody take the trouble to read the account?

I need not say how much I value & appreciate your kindness in helping me.

I think the Chamberlainites mean to put the Govt in a minority. The long delay is killing them.

Yours vy sincerely
WINSTON S. CHURCHILL

WSC to Lord Rosebery
(*Rosebery Papers*)

24 January 1905   105 Mount Street

My dear Lord Rosebery,

I cannot resist writing while that recorded conversation is fresh in my mind, to ask you to let me use it subject to whatever suppressions you may think necessary on any grounds. It is a very vivid light, & will add greatly to the interest of my account.

I am vy conscious of the shortcomings of my work; & I shall certainly not let it out of my hands finally for some time.

Yours ever
W

WSC to Sir Michael Hicks Beach
(*St Aldwyn Papers*)

3 February 1905   Ashby St Ledger
My dear Sir Michael,

Your letter on the Abandoned Budget is vy interesting. No doubt it would have been a *tour-de-force*. And yet is it not true that sometimes a great measure passes through the House by its own momentum, where more modest proposals may come to grief? I will however make a short hedging paragraph out of your criticisms so as to show that I do not ignore the other side of the argument.

I am to see Cranborne on Wednesday about his father's letters. He has written to me in a most friendly spirit & I am full of confidence that he will be generous in permissions. I think perhaps it may be desirable that you & he should have a talk on the subject. You consulted Lord Salisbury in the last year of his life about the publication of these matters; & besides you were leader of the H of C or of the Opposition during the great part of the period in question. You can therefore advise with unequalled authority.

I will write again after I have seen him.

Mr Longman[1] is enthusiastic over the proofs & has offered me £4,000 on account of a 25% Royalty for the right to publish. I am reflecting upon this. It is a handsome offer.

I am vy greatly indebted to you for the help you have given me. I should never have secured the papers without your certificate of my fitness. If I could get 3 months clear the work would be finished. But politics are a sad distraction.

I am sorry not to meet you tonight at Lady Wimborne's.

Yours most sincerely
WINSTON SC

WSC to Lady Randolph

9 February 1905   105 Mount Street

Dearest Mamma,

Will you write for me three or four sheets of recollections about your life in London and in Ireland with my father from 1874 to 1880? You will remember how you first began in Charles Street I think – entertaining Mr Disraeli, hunting at Oakham, then the row, I suppose in 1877, then Ireland.

Do try and give me a few ideas about this. It does not matter how few they are as long as you really try and put me into possession of the personal aspect of his life in these days.

I have come to this part of the book now and I think I could very nearly write the chapter 'Member for Woodstock' if I had this blank filled in. I am counting upon coming down to you on Saturday the 18th and have marked it down in my book.

Your loving son
W

[1] Either Charles James Longman (1852–1934), member of Longmans, Green & Company 1877–1928; or Hubert Harry Longman (1856–1940), baronet 1909, also a member of Longmans, Green & Company 1880–1933. Both were sons of William Longman (1813–1877).

WSC to Lord Hugh Cecil
(*Quickswood Papers*)

21 April 1905   Blenheim

My dear Linky,

I have to thank you for the two volumes of your father's Essays wh have reached me. I have spent a delightful morning reading the first part of the review of Stanhope's Life of Pitt. My sympathies are divided. The two irretrievable mistakes which ruined Fox's life were his refusal to serve under Lord Shelburne on purely personal grounds & of course the disgraceful coalition. From that there could be no recovery. 'Never' being a much commoner word in politics than is often supposed. But it was a lucky thing for the world that the truths & hopes which Fox asserted were preserved by him through all the dark years which followed. Had he been in office the light might have been utterly quenched. So he too was perhaps an agent of high purposes, & there may be a deep meaning behind the phrase 'His Majesty's Opposition'!

I shall read the rest with keen interest. But now I am going to carry out my threat & cast upon you a bulky burden (following in a registered parcel). Do read it through for me & talk to me about it. Your mind is so full & mine is so empty, that it is a sad paradox that I should never have time to read, & you never the inclination to write. But you will see from this rough & scrappy work that these are valuable materials, if only I could do justice to them. I shall regard your criticism – above all your suggestion or creative criticism as an act of great friendship. I stay here for the next ten days, writing in the mornings & playing polo at Rugby in the afternoons.

Yours ever
W

WSC to Lady Randolph

EXTRACT

31 August 1905   Ashby St Ledgers

Dearest Mamma,

Your letter (which finds me here, where I have been for a week) makes me feel very guilty. It is very good of you to write, and I certainly do not deserve much consideration. My only excuse is that I have toiled at my book almost incessantly since I left England. It is now very nearly done: another ten days will, I think, complete all the heavy work in connection with it.

There will only remain a few checkings and revisings to be done before the pig may be taken to market. I can't tell you how delighted I am at the prospect of getting this off my hands; more than a thousand pages have really been a very serious undertaking, and nothing but a vigorous and sustained effort during this last month would have enabled me to carry it forward so far. Really, in the meantime, I have written to nobody. Miss Anning has buried herself in Scotland and this is the first time I have come in contact with shorthand, so do please forgive me.

Switzerland was peaceful. We did exactly the same every day, namely, bridge, writing, bridge, walking, dinner, bridge, bed. But the monotony was pleasant, and as I took a great deal of exercise every day I certainly benefited by the change of scene. Cassel was most amiable, and we had many a long and pleasant talk.

I led him to expect a letter from you giving an account of the Cowes celebrations; none arrived. However, he did not mind, and seemed to understand that you were very busy pursuing giddy occupations. I stayed three weeks all but two days, and returned here without stopping. We play polo here every day when the weather permits, and as I have got a small room to myself to write in, I labour undisturbed all of every morning. I am going to Blenheim for a night on Friday but shall return here the next day. Freddie is here and his wife. I think it possible that he will not go into Parliament as a Liberal. . . .

With best love, Always your loving son
W

WSC to Lord Rosebery
(Rosebery Papers)

2 September 1905   Ashby St Ledgers

My dear Lord Rosebery,

I have been thinking carefully about the notes you have so kindly written upon my father. Chronologically they should come at the end of the narrative. But I have got a brilliant idea. They are as they stand an Introduction. Nothing could be better than that this short sketch, covering as it does the whole ground, containing an appreciation from another pen, & upon an authority to wh I cannot pretend, yet so entirely in accordance with the general conception I have endeavoured to express, should come at the beginning & prepare the reader's mind in summary for the story that is to be told. I hope therefore that you will allow me to use them for this purpose in this manner. They will greatly add to the value & distinction of my book.

Secondly there is the 1885 conversation. The place for this is clearly marked. Lord James has given me some notes of a very remarkable demonstration by the Benchers of the Inns of Court of my father's popularity on June 10, 1885. It would be dramatic to contrast this evidence of outside triumph with your proof of inward doubt & almost despair. I should be greatly obliged if you would permit me to make such extracts as are necessary.

Thirdly would you now care to see the earlier chapters. The work is practically finished & scarcely anything remains to write. I am most anxious to get it off my hands, & I shall publish in November or January.

I passed a peaceful three weeks at Cassel's mountain retreat, & am now here for the end of the polo season. I wonder whether we are to be dissolved in October.

Yours vy sincerely
WINSTON S. CHURCHILL

WSC to Lord Rosebery
(*Rosebery Papers*)

11 September 1905   Ashby St Ledgers

Private

Dear Lord Rosebery,

I am vy sorry you have destroyed the notes, & I cannot admit that I 'rejected' them. On the contrary I remember that the last time we spoke of them at Epsom you said that writing them and talking them over had made you recollect much more about my father than you had set down, & I rather gathered that you thought of adding somewhat to them. At the same time I daresay I showed that I did not quite see at the moment where they would fit in; for at the end, where chronologically they should have come, they would have interrupted & forestalled my own plan – such as it is – for the closing pages. And it was with the intention of recasting & rearranging the text so as to fit this very desirable addition that I have allowed the delay of two months to occur.

I am particularly sorry that after I had pressed you so much, your trouble & your kindness should have been thrown away, & that a memoir of such importance should have perished.

As to the '85 conversation, I feel I cannot persist in view of your objections. And there again I am sorry; for it is a vivid gleam. I hope some day it may be published, although it will be separate from its proper place.

I will send you the earlier chapters in the course of a week. I am very glad you will read them.

My Edinburgh meeting has been postponed till January, before the meeting of Parliament as Asquith is to deliver an oration in October. I am going abroad for a fortnight at the end of this month to inspect chateaux on the Loire with Sunny. After that Blenheim.

Once more let me say how sorry I am about the destruction of the notes, & believe me,

Yours vy sincerely
WINSTON S. CHURCHILL

WSC to Lord Lansdowne
(Lansdowne Papers)

1 October 1905   105 Mount Street
Private

My dear Lord,

Mr Brodrick tells me he has forwarded to you some of my father's letters to the late Queen, wh I desire to publish in my biography of Lord Randolph Churchill. I have also to add to the budget wh must be submitted to you. The trust deed wh regulates the publication of my father's papers requires that all documents which concern directly or indirectly the Foreign Office or the India Office must be referred before publication to the respective Secretaries of State for those Departments. I therefore enclose such extracts from my book as may be included in that description for your opinion upon them. I should add that my purpose is biographical rather than historical, & that consequently the excision of any particular sentence or expression does not *necessarily* deprive any document of its usefulness to me. But I trust that you will find it possible to allow me to print the extracts now submitted without any substantial alterations or diminution.

Yours vy trly
WINSTON S. CHURCHILL

Lord Lansdowne to WSC
(Lansdowne Papers)

3 October 1905   Foreign Office
[Draft]

I am obliged to you for having allowed me to see your proofs, which I have read with great interest. My observations have, of course, reference only to the pages which came to me direct from yourself. Brodrick will no doubt write to you as to the passages which affect the India Office. I venture to make the following suggestions with reference to pages 39 to 59.

Page 42. Would it not be better to leave out the statement that the Chancellor of the Exchequer was 'left alone to deal with the Ambassadors'? Lord Iddesleigh was still Foreign Secretary, and unless some special arrangement was made with him and the Prime Minister, under which your father was deputed to take charge of FO business, the passage might be misinterpreted.

I suggest the omission of the words which I have enclosed in a bracket, and the insertion, after the word 'chief', of the words 'and freely imparted his views to the foreign Ambassadors'.

Page 43. I suggest the omission of the words 'who was our enemy almost as much as Russia'.

Page 44. I suggest the omission of the words in which Ld Salisbury describes himself as unable to make up his mind. The sentence might run – ' "If Russia attacked Constantinople", wrote the Prime Minister in a letter approving generally of this discourse, "and all the other Powers refused to intervene, I am rather disposed etc." '

Page 44 (bottom) and 45 (top). I suggest the omission of the words 'But England will be mad if she does not get something.'

Page 46. Might it not be better to omit the words, half-way down the page, 'That is the use of the Bulgarians for our purpose'?

These alterations would not, I think, substantially take away from the documents, while they would have the effect of getting rid of passages which, many people would, I cannot help thinking, prefer to leave unpublished.

WSC to Frank Harris[1]

2 October 1905   In the train

Private

[Copy]

My dear Harris,

While our conversation is fresh in my mind, let me put the gist of it on paper.

I authorise you as my friend to talk in confidence & privacy to publishers about my book. I reserve to myself the right to decide freely on every offer –

---

[1] Frank Harris (1856–1931), author and playwright; sometime Editor of *Fortnightly Review*, *Saturday Review*, and *Vanity Fair*. Author of *My Life and Loves* (1922), first published in the United Kingdom in 1964 by W. H. Allen & Company.

whether as regards whole world rights, or English, foreign or Colonial rights –
even to the extent of taking a lower one, if I choose. But if, as the result of
your negotiations, I make a bargain then I shall pay you 10% on the excess
net profit accruing to me from that bargain above £4000, as such profit
may be realised. Let me know if that is our agreement.

Many thanks for all your criticisms. I shall look forward greatly to the rest.
Write & let me know what passes with Murray.

Yours sincerely
WINSTON S. CHURCHILL

Frank Harris to WSC

TELEGRAM

5 October 1905   54 Acacia Road

Your letter perfectly correct. Have put all in train. Shall be ready meet
you with rest of suggestions any time after next Monday.

FRANK HARRIS

Frank Harris to WSC

7 October 1905   54 Acacia Road

My dear Winston Churchill,

I've finished the book: the last half of it is incomparably better than the
first. This is partly due, no doubt, to the natural heightening of the interest
as the tragedy swings to its climax; but also in no small degree to the increasing passion of the treatment. In these last ten chapters there is little to
criticise: we can run through my suggestions easily in a couple of hours:
when will you give me the time?

While still under the influence of the story I must assure you that you
have done a very fine & noble piece of work – out of sight better than
Rosebery's *Pitt* or Morley's *Gladstone*, a book which will be as Thucydides said
of his own history a κτῆμα ἐς ἀεί, 'a possession for ever,' something that even
this English public will not willingly forget.

I have written to Miss Anning acknowledging her letters & enclosures:
you may be certain that I shall deal with the publishers to the best of my
ability: I know the trade & the individuals & shall soon have things to report
to you.

Hill's proposal to run the book through *The Tribune* is quite absurd; but he might have a page of excerpts from it for his first issue, I trow, if he would pay £1000 for it. Don't laugh! I mean it. Properly worked this book shd bring you in £10,000 or I'm a Dutchman! And it's cheap at the price. There should be a shower of preliminary notices in the press & all should be paid for (no more must you let Harmsworth browse at ease on your pastures) but all this I will talk over with you when we meet.

By the way I'm uncertain about the advisability of an additional chapter since reading the last one: could this last one not be amplified? Or the added one should be short.

Ever Yours Sincerely
FRANK HARRIS

PS 'Well Played, Sir!' as we used to cry at school; by the by you could sign yourself with truth in Shelley's great phrase 'an inheritor of unfulfilled renown' – as yet.

FH

A. J. Balfour to WSC

9 October 1905   Whittingehame

Dictated

Private

Dear Winston Churchill,

Thanks for the two extracts from the forthcoming Biography of your father, on which you ask my opinion.

The one under the date 1893 is obviously unobjectionable from any point of view. As regards the one under the date 1885, I have no very deeply rooted dislike to its publication: but, on the whole, I would rather it were omitted because I foresee that its publication will drag me into a quite unnecessary and futile controversy.

Mr G at the end of 1885 was under the fixed impression that Lord Salisbury agreed with Lord Carnarvon, and would have been glad to carry through measures for Ireland, upon more or less Gladstonian lines, with Mr Gladstone's assistance in the House of Commons. Lord Salisbury was to play the part of Peel in '46, while Mr G occupied the more agreeable rôle of Lord John Russell.

Holding these views as to Lord Salisbury's opinions, Mr Gladstone was naturally disappointed at the result of the mission to my uncle, with which, when we met at Eaton, he entrusted me. He consequently put down the failure of that mission to the Ambassador, and not to the policy. But, in truth, Lord Salisbury profoundly disagreed with Mr G's views, and never for an instant entertained the thought of co-operating with him.

I forget in what form I conveyed this fact to Mr G; but, as the subject did not permit, in Lord S's opinion, of arguments, I have no doubt the form was concise, or, as Mr G describes it, 'curt'.

As, however, I have no desire to go into this matter in public, I should be glad if the passage in your father's *Life* could be omitted.

Yours very truly
ARTHUR JAMES BALFOUR

Frank Harris to William Heinemann,[1] *and to Sir Algernon Methuen*[2]

10 October 1905   *The Motorist & Traveller*
                                                  12 Henrietta Street

[Copy]

Dear Sir,

Mr Winston Churchill has asked me to negotiate for him in regard to the Life of *Lord Randolph Churchill* which is just completed and he has handed me your letter.

The book is already printed and makes about a thousand pages, or two volumes in quarto. It is as interesting as a great novel, partly because of the extraordinary vicissitudes and tragic end of Lord Randolph Churchill's life and partly because of the masterly treatment; it is of widest appeal more especially by reason of the number of letters it contains from the Queen, from Lord Salisbury, while Prime Minister, from Mr Gladstone, from Lord Hartington, Mr Balfour, Mr Chamberlain and other eminent persons, and the light which these letters throw on the secret workings of Cabinets and Governments in this country.

If you wish any further information or if you care to see me on the matter I shall be delighted to talk it over with you at any time.

Yours sincerely
FRANK HARRIS

Note by Harris to WSC
To show how I've written to the publishers.

F. HARRIS

[1] William Heinemann (1863–1920), founder of publishing company which bears his name, 1890. President of the Publishers' Association of Great Britain and Ireland 1909–11.
[2] Algernon Methuen Marshall Methuen (1856–1924), founder and Chairman of Methuen & Company Limited, publishers; 3rd son of J. B. Stedman; assumed surname of Methuen in 1899; baronet 1916.

WSC to Frank Harris

13 October 1905   105 Mount Street
[Copy]

Dear Frank Harris,

I shall be very glad if you will help me in negotiating with various publishers for the sale of my book. I shall avail myself of no other intermediary.
I hope you will put the publishing firms whom you approach on their guard
against persons who have no authority from me and apparently none from
them, but who, by running to and fro between the author and publisher,
represent themselves as charged with commissions from both.

Yours
WINSTON S. CHURCHILL

Frank Harris to WSC

EXTRACT

14 October 1905   12 Henrietta Street

My dear Winston Churchill,

As I think I told you, I wrote the letter to Beckett a few hours after leaving
you. I saw Cassell's[1] yesterday and had a long talk with them and put the
qualities of the book before them at some length: I hinted to them – not
unclearly, that nothing under £10,000 would be considered. They asked for
a copy of the book which they said they would return in three or four days.
I propose sending them my copy if you agree when I see you on Monday as
I hope to do.

I have also written to Macmillan[2] and I am now writing to Murray.[3] . . .

Heinemann writes to me that he 'would not, under any circumstances,
care to make a better offer than he has already made,' which did not
astonish me.

Yours sincerely
FRANK HARRIS

PS I hope to get a good offer from Cassells & one from Murray – for whom
you must bring me up another copy.

Yours
FR HARRIS

[1] Cassell & Company Limited, publishers.
[2] Macmillan & Company Limited, publishers.
[3] John Murray Limited, publishers.

Should like to see you Monday at lunch or later

Yours

F.H.

PS I have just seen Mr Morris Colles[1] and when I asked him whom he expected to be paid by, he said of course he expected to be paid by you, and when I rather ridiculed this he said that he held a letter from you asking him to submit any offer; 'but surely,' I said, 'you don't call this appointing you an agent and you can take it from me Mr Winston Churchill will pay you no commission.' Hereupon he said that he would go and see Mr Heinemann at once because he did not expect to work for nothing. Mr Massie, too, has written to me asking for an appointment. In view of these difficulties I want you to send me a formal letter which I can show these people: something to the following effect.

'My Dear Harris,

    I hereby appoint you my sole agent to negotiate terms for my life of *Lord Randolph Churchill*.'

Yours etc'

You see I cannot show them your private letter to me of the other day and I want something to satisfy Murray and the rest that I am authorised and alone.

The publishers are all asking for copies of the book; I think you ought to let me have two more sets at once – one set to give to Murray and one set, probably, to Cassell, whom I think most likely because they are the richest publishers.

Yours sincerely

FRANK HARRIS

Frank Harris to WSC

17 October 1905   12 Henrietta Street

My dear Winston Churchill,

    I got your telegram this morning and noted about the imprint which of course I shall remove before I send the copy to Cassells which I am now about to do. I send you herewith a copy of my letter to Cross which will accompany the MS.

    I saw to-day Mr Methuen and had a long and very interesting conversation with him. He is a Radical and a passionate supporter of yours: it appears that he went down to Manchester to hear you speak and believes in you as one of the future leaders of the Party. I rather astonished him by telling him

---

[1] William Morris Colles (d. 1926), founder and Managing Director of Authors' Syndicate 1890; member of Council, Society of Authors and of Copyright Association.

that you were already in fact a leader of the Party; but the talk was interesting because he is sympathetic.

So far in regard to the Radical supporter; but when I came to the publisher I found a great difference. He wanted me to put a price on the book and said he would try to give it if I put a price on it. I said 'I could not put a price on it; but four thousand had been offered for the English rights and six thousand for all rights. These offers were not considered.' And I think from what I saw of him that he is not rich enough to risk a sum like eight or ten thousand. I told him I would speak to you about his proposal; but I should want him to read the book before he determined that it was out of his reach and he said he would be delighted to read it.

Methuen kept me so late that I missed Edward Arnold[1]; but that does not matter much as I shall see him on Thursday instead.

By the way, I hope also to see George Macmillan,[2] to whom I have written. I have not heard from Murray yet. I am awaiting your copy and a half of the book. You will remember I have the first half and I want two whole copies besides – one for Cassells which I send now and one for Murray and one to send to Macmillan.

Next time I must ask you to lunch with me at the Café Royal and I will try to give you a rare bottle in a warm room.

Yours sincerely
FRANK HARRIS

PS I cannot find any imprint of Longman's on this copy.

Yours
F.H.

W. St John Brodrick to WSC

18 October 1905   India Office

Private

My dear Churchill,

I am very sorry to have detained your chapter so long. I sent it to Lord Lansdowne, and he agrees with me that the portions of the letters which have passed between Lord Randolph Churchill and the late Queen with

---

[1] Edward Augustus Arnold (1857–1942), publisher; founded the firm of Edward Arnold & Co in 1890.

[2] George Augustine Macmillan (1855–1936), publisher; director of Macmillan & Company Limited; Chairman of Stainer & Bell Limited, music publishers; son of Alexander Macmillan and nephew of Daniel Macmillan, founders of publishing house which bears their name; cousin of Harold Macmillan, Prime Minister 1957–63.

regard to the Amir must almost necessarily be deleted. I have made suggestions as to cutting them down, and hope they may commend themselves to you.

You have no doubt taken pains to ascertain whether the King would have any objection to the publication of letters between Lord Randolph and the late Queen. I believe it is necessary to get the Sovereign's permission in any case, and Lord Lansdowne asks the question whether the publication of letters between a Minister and the Sovereign, so soon as twenty years after their date, would not be an unusual proceeding.

Page 31. I quite realise that you desire to publish the Secret Correspondence with regard to the Duke of Connaught's appointment and Lord Randolph's resignation. This is probably one of the most interesting and one of the least known chapters of this history. Lord Lansdowne doubts whether this correspondence can well be published. I should not myself have thought that any objection would now be made, but I doubt whether I have any right to advise you in this particular matter. It really lies with Lord Salisbury and the King who, I suspect you may find, will take a view upon the matter. If he should in any way consult me, you may be quite sure I shall advise that all possible latitude should be given.

Page 43. Do you not think Beach should be consulted about his letter? Lord Lansdowne thinks he would resent its publication.

Page 46. Would it not be well to leave out the reference to the Queen's personal likes and dislikes? It is very interesting, but is it fit for publication?

Pages 50-1. The reference to the conduct of the French Government in the Burmese affair will probably give a certain amount of offence. On the other hand, you are not at present an official, and, as the question has so long passed away, it may be one of those cases in which it is desirable to run a risk, in order not to spoil the narrative.

I hope that what I have suggested will not have the effect of damaging the chapter materially. Nobody except you and those immediately concerned will know what portions of the letters to the Queen have been left out. But in any case I would suggest your getting the Sovereign's permission before you make use of the private correspondence.

I see you have not introduced any reference to private correspondence between Lord Dufferin[1] and Lord Randolph. I should have thought there might have been some questions of interest in the letters between two such men; and in the earlier lines of the chapter you do not, I think, point out how largely the business of India is carried on by the medium of private

---

[1] Frederick Temple Hamilton-Temple-Blackwood, Marquess of Dufferin and Ava (1826–1902), Viceroy of India 1884–8; Paymaster-General 1869–72; Governor-General of Canada 1872–8; Ambassador at St Petersburg 1879–81; created Marquess 1888.

correspondence, when there is a good understanding between the Secretary of State and the Viceroy. I only suggest this as being possibly worthy of your notice.

I have sent back the proofs with a few notes on it by Sir A. Godley, which I am sure you will keep, like my own, private.

Yours very trly
St John Brodrick

WSC to Lord Lansdowne
(*Lansdowne Papers*)

19 October 1905   Blenheim
Private

My dear Lord Lansdowne,

I am much obliged to you for the corrections you have made, & regret to be the cause of inroads upon your time.

The expression 'and freely imparted his views to the Foreign Ambassadors' wh you suggest should be inserted in the extract herewith enclosed, might it seems to me, be regarded by some as a reflection of officiousness with a flavour of presumption upon Lord Randolph Churchill. I should prefer merely to make the omission you have indicated.

All the other excisions which you think proper whether in this chapter or in that relating to the India Office will of course be made. I hope you will agree to this.

Believe me, Yours sincerely
Winston S Churchill

WSC to Lord Rosebery
(*Rosebery Papers*)

19 October 1905   Blenheim

Private

My dear Lord Rosebery,

After spoiling a deal of paper I have put this fragment down, wh I now send you. It embodies the points wh most attracted me in your fascinating record. But after all I only heard it read once & cannot remember with any accuracy or detail. Weak as it is, I should like to print it.

I have not sent you the early chapters, because I have been hoping to get them into 'last revise' before doing so, & there have been many delays.

Do let me know when you come to town & I will come & see you. I am looking forward with great interest to your speeches. There is much to be said.

Poor Lord Spencer.[1] It was rather like a ship sinking in sight of land.

Yours ever
W

Lord Rosebery to WSC

19 October 1905   Rosebery
Midlothian

My dear Winston,

You seem to have had a glowing week in Manchester. Consequently, I suppose, you have forgotten to send me Vol I of the *magnum opus*.

When last in London I found my paper of recollections in an obscure drawer, where I had chucked it; because I suppose there was no fire in June. They might just as well have been in the fire, for they would be quite out of place in an introduction.

Ever yrs
AR

WSC to Lord Rosebery
(*Rosebery Papers*)

20 October 1905   105 Mount Street

Private

My dear Lord Rosebery,

Our letters crossed. Please let me have those notes. I want them. If they will not make an introduction, I have another use for them. Let me quote them by extracts in the different places where they chronologically fit. I have done this with the memoranda Beach wrote for me – thus: – 'He was' writes Sir M. H. Beach 'deeply concerned at the increasing gravity of the dispute with the House of Lords . . . etc etc.' It is a vy convenient method & pleasant to read. Recollections scattered over a whole life, ought to come in where they actually occur. To print them *en bloc* at the beginning is perhaps–though I do not think so – to disconnect the story; to print them at the end is to repeat it. Will you not send them to me as if they were a private letter to me in answer to a request for your recollections of my father; & then allow me to use them

[1] J. Poyntz Spencer, 5th Earl Spencer (1835–1910), landowner and Liberal politician; Viceroy of Ireland 1869–74, 1882–5; First Lord of the Admiralty 1892; suffered a sudden cerebral attack in 1905 from which he never recovered.

as I like. Beach, Godley, James, G. Hamilton have written me similar memoranda as friends of my father, placing their knowledge at the disposal of his biographer. Don't think this an impudent request. But there are things in your notes that I want vy much – the quarrel with the Oxford tutor who had abused the 'silver-grey rabbit'; the Westminster Abbey story; the episode of the cigar in 1885; the meeting with you at Naples after resignation; & most of all the striking passage wh refers to his death – 'no curtain – no concealment.' There – I have put my case. I would not have pressed you, if you had not always treated me with so much kindness.

I have promised to speak at Hampstead on Monday night. Perhaps we shall win there.

When do you come to London? I have decided to send you the uncorrected proofs after all of the first volume – so that you may see the way in wh I have worked in memoranda from different people. But there are very considerable alterations to be made before the proofs go to press.

Yours ever
W

PS I have sent proofs registered to Dalmeny.

Lord Lansdowne to WSC
(Lansdowne Papers)

20 October 1905   Foreign Office
[Copy]

My dear Churchill,

I am much obliged for your note of yesterday, and for the considerate manner in which you have received my suggestions.

The passage of which you now send me a proof reads quite well with the omission which you propose.

Yours sincerely
LANSDOWNE

Frank Harris to WSC

24 October 1905   12 Henrietta Street

My dear Winston Churchill,

I am very sorry I was late to-night and found you gone; but I was on your business and I cannot make the publishers keep times exactly: I am extremely sorry.

Here is a letter of John Murray's which you should read. His two emendations are I think all right and it is disappointing that he will not make an offer for the book out-right. I think it shows his high opinion of the book that he offers to publish it on a ten per cent commission. I suppose he means a ten per cent commission on the published price; but it really looks, from this printed document of his, as if he meant ten per cent on the cost, which would be much less: in fact if that is what he means it would be very much less. Please send me his printed document back and I will see him upon it.

Cassells have written offering £2500 down on account of a thirty (30) per cent royalty which is in my opinion the best offer yet made; but by no means satisfactory. Still it was calculated on a basis of thirty-one shillings for the book and not on a basis of forty-two shillings, as it should have been. I have written to them about it.

Meanwhile I have sent copies of the book, one to Methuen, one to Spencer of Hutchinson's, and Macmillan has the other.

By the way, I have just heard from George Macmillan who wants to see me tomorrow about the book.

Both of his partners have read it and he says he has read it with great interest.

I am sorry to have missed you to-day; but I hope you will be up again soon.

By the way, I am drawing my bow at a venture in this address. The man of yours at 105, Mount Street told me 'Salisbury Hall' or else 'Salisbury House' I cannot remember which; so I shall put both unless I can get on the telephone to him. I have found it is Salisbury Hall.

Yours sincerely
FRANK HARRIS

PS I had written a great part of this to you; but my secretary held it for me to look through and forgot to post it on Sunday night.

Yours
FRANK HARRIS

John Murray to Frank Harris

21 October 1905   50 Albemarle Street

Dear Mr Harris,

I skimmed over the proofs of Lord Randolph Churchill's Life yesterday evening and recognize the interest of the work. I have noted what seem to me one or two errors – eg the Warden of Merton was Dr Marsham not Marshall and the fine for smoking in cap & gown was 10/- not £10: I was up at the same time as Lord Randolph & have paid the fine myself.

I am sorry to say we cannot entertain a proposal for the purchase of the work outright: no man can estimate even approximately the capital value of such a book, and any offer must be a pure leap in the dark – on which either the purchaser or the vendor will in all probability 'come off second best.'

We do not care about publishing books on commission but as we have proceeded my brother and I have much pleasure in making an exception, and offering you commission terms, on the supposition that we shall have to take over the printer's and other bills, and see to the passing of the book through the press.

Yrs vy trly
JOHN MURRAY

Lord Rosebery to WSC

24 October 1905 Madresfield Court
Malvern Link

My dear Winston,

I have altered the enclosed a little; mainly by striking out all mention of my name.

I suppose the volume in proof is at Dalmeny. I had to leave before it arrived. But I shall relish it on my return.

Do get that paper of mine out of your head. As I had told you I had burned it I thought it only truthful to tell you when I found I had not. But it is theoretically burned, and if you allude to it again, into the fire it shall go.

Yrs always
AR

G. A. Macmillan to Frank Harris

25 October 1905 St Martin's Street

Dear Mr Harris,

We have read with very great interest the sheets of Mr Winston Churchill's Life of his father and understanding that he wishes to sell the book outright we are prepared to pay the sum of £7000 for the entire copyright in this country and in the United States. We shall be glad to hear as soon as possible whether this offer meets Mr Churchill's views.

I am, Yours very truly
GEORGE A. MACMILLAN

Lord Rosebery to WSC

28 October 1905   Dalmeny

My dear Winston,

I arrived here this morning, after a grievous motor accident.

Many thanks for your letter which I will perpend.

I have at once clutched at your book which I cannot lay down. It is fascinating. I have read two chapters. I make the following observations. I do *not* like the opening about Blenheim, & should leave it out. Judging by my own experience, it is probably your favourite passage.

What excellent letters he wrote even from school!

I don't think he took any notice of the turf till after 1886.

I think 'Peace with Honour' was said on the journey from Berlin & not at the Knightsbridge Banquet. Verify.

I will write again as I proceed.

Yours

AR

WSC to Lord Rosebery
(*Rosebery Papers*)

30 October 1905   105 Mount Street

Dear Lord Rosebery,

I am most interested to think of you reading my book, & delighted that it pleases you. I shall pay the greatest attention to everything you say about it. The opening fanfaronade is dear to me – & to the Duke of Marlborough. But – I think I will send you the second volume too – for although you have read half of it you cannot judge the work without glancing through it in a connected form.

Please mark the proofs as you like; & show no mercy. There is still time to give effect even to extensive corrections.

'Peace with Honour' was *said* out of a railway carriage at Dover on the return of Disraeli from Berlin. But the banquet afterwards was called the 'Peace with Honour' banquet. Everything is being checked most carefully in the revised proof.

It would help me vy much indeed if you reviewed the book. There is unequalled material for an essay *à la* Macaulay. But I hope you won't dismiss the author so summarily!

Yours ever

W

How vy unpleasant that motor accident must have been. Poor woman. The *Westminster Gazette* recorded it under the heading 'Lord Rosebery's Mishap'.

Frederick Macmillan[1] to WSC

30 October 1905   St Martin's Street

Dear Mr Churchill,

My partners and I have discussed the proposal you made to us on Saturday, and I now write to say 'that we shall be glad to publish your *Life of Lord Randolph Churchill* on the terms suggested by you.

We understand these to be –

1. The exclusive right of publishing the book in the English language is to belong to us.

2. For this right we are to pay you the sum of £8,000 and no more until we ourselves shall have realised a net profit of £4,000. After that profit has been earned we are to hand over to you one half of all further profits derived from the sale of the book during the term of legal copyright.

As to the payment, we propose to send you a cheque for £1000 on receipt of your letter accepting this offer, £1000 when you have finally passed the proofs of the book for press and the balance (£6000) on the day of publication.

The terms are so simple that I do not think that any more formal document than this letter & your reply to it are necessary. These together constitute a binding agreement.

I hope very much that the book may have the success that you expect and that its intrinsic merits deserve. We will certainly do our best to bring about that result.

I am, yours truly
FREDERICK MACMILLAN

WSC to Lady Randolph

30 October 1905   105 Mount Street

[Dictated]

Dearest Mamma,

I am sorry we missed, but we shall meet at Newmarket on Wednesday. I go thither tomorrow to stay with Cassel.

His Majesty has been graciously pleased to signify his desire to meet me at dinner on Tuesday night and his determination to bring home to me the

---

[1] Frederick Macmillan (1851-1936), Chairman of Macmillan & Co. Ltd., President of Publishers' Association of Great Britain and Ireland 1900-1, 1911-12; son of Daniel Macmillan and nephew of Alexander Macmillan, founders of publishing house which bears their name; uncle of Harold Macmillan.

error of my ways. I settled this morning with Messrs Macmillan that they shall publish my book on the following terms:–

£8000 to be paid as follows:
£1000 now
£1000 when the proofs are corrected and
£6000 on the day of publication.

In addition to this after Macmillans have earned £4000 profit for themselves, we are to divide all further profits which may be realised during the period of legal copyright.[1] I think you will agree that I was right to close with this. Tempting as it was to 'run' the book myself, I do not think anyone can say I have not sold it wisely and well. I have paid Frank Harris £400 being 10 per cent commission on the excess £4000 he was able to get for me over and above the £4000 which Longman had offered originally. I think he has earned it well. I could certainly never have made such a bargain for myself.

It will be necessary now to push ahead with the business of publishing.

Will you please bring with you to Newmarket any photographs which you may think suitable, but particularly these two things. 1st the photograph in a fur coat taken at Belfast and 2ndly his diploma of Knighthood of the Primrose League which is No 1.

I think myself that the photograph of you with the star in your hair is the best and I have chosen that one but if you have any other choice, there may within the next few days still be time to alter it.

Have you a good photograph or reproduction of a picture of the old Duke? I have a picture of the old Duchess here.

With best love, Yours always
W

Lord Rosebery to WSC

31 October 1905   Dalmeny

My dear Winston,

I have finished your delightful volume, and shall bring it south with me tonight.

---

[1] An entry in the Author's Terms Book at Macmillans, dated October 30 1905 reads as follows:

'Exclusive Rights in English Language'.
'Pay £8,000 and when *our* profit reaches £4,000, then divide further profit. Of the £8,000 pay £1,000 on acceptance of these terms, £1,000 when book is passed for press and £6,000 on publication.
'N.Y. to pay £500 on account of 20% royalty.
Miss Hele paid £7. 7. 0 for Index.'

The only criticism I feel inclined to is that your father might speak a little more for himself in some chapters, which contain more historical narration – good as it is in itself – than is necessary for the biography.

The biography and the subject are the great things. Everything should be tested solely with reference to them. The biographer should be the unseen wire puller.

Yours
AR

WSC to Lord Rosebery
(Rosebery Papers)

1 November 1905
Moulton Paddocks
Newmarket

Dear Lord Rosebery,

You will I think have just missed the second volume of proofs wh I sent you yesterday to Dalmeny. There is however no hurry about them.

I recognise the justice of your criticism particularly as applied to Chapter IV. I fear there is a good deal in it that is irrelevant. I became so interested in the Irish situation as I studied it, that the temptation to put down my ideas proved too strong. Do you think it so much an error in literary art as to require excision? It would be a vy painful operation – more like a finger than a tooth.

The King consented to meet me last night for the first time for three years. He spoke most severely & even vehemently to me about my attacks on A. Balfour. I accepted it all with meekness. In the end he became most gracious & we talked one hour. So that episode may be considered at an end. I am glad of it.

It was cold & windy to-day at the races. I am endeavouring to console myself as you suggest, by recollecting that the unpleasant symptoms from wh I am suffering are a tribute to the efficiency of my red corpuscles.

Yours ever
WINSTON S C

Frederick Macmillan to WSC
(Macmillan and Company Papers)

2 November 1905
St. Martin's Street

Dear Mr Churchill,

I happened to see Mr Longman only yesterday afternoon, and he congratulated me on getting your book, but I am afraid he thinks we are going to pay too much for it; I hope that he may be wrong. By the way, we do not propose to tell the world at large what our arrangement with you is; it always seems to me that gossip of this kind serves no good end and is a little bit undignified.

I am, yours sincerely
FREDERICK MACMILLAN

C. J. Longman to WSC

EXTRACT

3 November 1905　　　　　　　　　　　　　　39 Paternoster Row

Dear Mr Churchill,

I must congratulate you on the splendid price you have got for your book. Naturally I am much disappointed that it is not to come out from Paternoster Row, but if I look at it from your point of view I cannot doubt that you were right to accept the offer. I must thank you for the very kind expressions in your letter, and I sincerely trust that the hope you are good enough to express that we may be associated in some other literary enterprise will be fulfilled at no very distant date. We will instruct Messrs Spottiswoode & Co to charge Messrs Macmillan with the printing expenses hitherto incurred. That I think is your wish. . . .

Believe me, Yours very truly
C. J. LONGMAN

Lord Knollys to WSC

6 November 1905　　　　　　　　　　　　　　Sandringham

My dear Churchill,

I have submitted to the King your letter & the enclosures which accompanied it, and he desires me to say he sees no reason whatever why the extracts from your Father's letters to the late Queen, which you have sent me, should not appear in your life of him.

I quite agree with you that these letters show that your Father obtained a wonderful mastery of the Indian situation in an extraordinary short time, but his insight into any matter of business and the quickness of perception which he displays in the most difficult questions of policy & statecraft were marvellous.

Yours sincerely
KNOLLYS

WSC to Frederick Macmillan
(*Macmillan and Company Papers*)

8 November 1905   105 Mount Street

Dear Mr Macmillan,

I send you herewith the preliminary matter and the first five chapters of the first volume. These can be put up at once into page proofs numbered consecutively from the beginning to the end. Only a word here or there may be altered in the future and there will be perhaps a few alterations in punctuation.

I hope the discretion of Mr Moy Thomas is to be implicitly relied upon. I gather from him that he proposes to correct the proofs at the National Liberal Club. If you know him well of course it will be all right, but I have rather hesitated sending the chapters to the National Liberal Club as I think great care should be taken in handling matter of such journalistic value, and I have asked Mr Thomas to call for them here; I only mention this as I know nothing of the gentleman in question.

Please let me have the last revises back from Spottiswoode as soon as they are printed. I will return them forthwith.

                                        WINSTON SPENCER CHURCHILL

WSC to Frederick Macmillan
(*Macmillan and Company Papers*)

13 November 1905

Dear Mr Macmillan,

I have been considering the punctuation of Mr Moy Thomas rather more carefully than I did hitherto and I am seriously disquieted by a growing feeling that it is permeated throughout by an absolute lack of system. I enclose the second chapter in which I draw your attention to two or three discrepancies in green pencil. I am very much concerned about this, as I am above all things anxious that the grammar and punctuation should be strictly correct. In these circumstances I suggest to you that the book should be read for punctuation solely once again before it goes to press. I am incompetent to do this, for I know the book nearly by heart and cannot concentrate my attention by reading.

I should have most confidence in my friend Mr Frank Harris, of whose scholarship and precision in such matters I entertain the highest opinion. I am sorry to cause a delay at the last minute and to add to the expense of the publication, but I hope you will meet my views on this point.

Feeling sure that you would oblige me in this matter and realizing that time is pressing, I have already seen Mr Frank Harris and I regret to say that he tells me that his time is fully occupied until Saturday, but that he would undertake to complete the entire revision by Monday morning.

I do not desire by this to reflect at all upon Mr Moy Thomas and I should especially regret if it ever came to his ears that I was not satisfied with his work. It has been painstaking and thorough, but as I say there has been a certain lack of any definite system. May I suggest therefore that Mr Moy Thomas should know nothing of any extra revision that we may make?

Will you send me word in the morning.

Yours sincerely
WINSTON S CHURCHILL

WSC to Frederick Macmillan
(*Macmillan and Company Papers*)

27 November 1905

Mr Frank Harris has now completed fully his revise of the proofs of my book. He has taken a great deal of trouble over them, and I now feel some confidence in submitting it to the public so far as grammar, construction and punctuation are concerned.

Lord Curzon to WSC

7 December 1905   Carlton Hotel

Dear Winston,

I forgot in the hurry of yesterday to say how interested I am to hear that your life of your father is about to appear & to learn from those who have seen the proofs that it is equally worthy of the father & the son.

Yours sincerely
CURZON

Frederick Macmillan to WSC

18 December 1905   St Martin's Street

Dear Mr Churchill,

We are strongly of opinion that it would be a mistake to alter the date arranged for the publication of your book. All the papers are keenly interested in it and there is not the least doubt that a number of very important reviews will appear on the day of publication. The chief injury that a General Election could do to a book would be to interfere with the reviews, but this will not be the case in the present instance. We shall, therefore, publish, as arranged, on January 5th.

I propose to send out early copies to the reviewers before Christmas, i.e. on Friday next. We will certainly send one to the *Westminster Gazette* and 5 copies to Sir Alfred Harmsworth. I will also send one to Sir Henry Wolff; can you kindly let me have his address?

I am, Yours sincerely
FREDERICK MACMILLAN

Frederick Macmillan to WSC

22 December 1905   22 Devonshire Place

Dear Mr Churchill,

I am sorry that I was unable to see you this afternoon particularly as I understand that you have been perturbed by Mr Frank Harris's ratiocinations with regard to the date fixed for the publication of your book.

I myself do not feel in the least alarmed. As I understand it the dissolution is not likely to take place before January 8 & the earliest election not before the 12th. This will give us a clear week to start the sale. The entire bookselling trade of the country is anxiously expecting its appearance: every important newspaper will publish a long review on the day the book comes out: they could not do more than publish one notice each if there were no election at all in progress. The mere fact that there is an Election & that you will be a prominent feature of it will do good rather than harm. When papers refer to you they will be constantly saying 'whose brilliant Biography of Lord Randolph Churchill has just appeared' etc etc. Besides which the book is not going to be dead in three weeks. It is absurd to talk about it as though it was going to be a mere flash in the pan. Mr Morley's *Life of Gladstone* went on selling enormously for months after it came out and the sales did not drop seriously for more than a year from the date of its appearance.

I refuse altogether to be frightened by what Mr Harris says although I have no doubt that he is speaking in perfect good faith & with the very best intentions. In any case I don't see how the publication could be postponed now for it has been advertised everywhere & the early copies have already gone out to the newspapers.

I am yours sincerely
FREDERICK MACMILLAN

Frederick Macmillan to WSC

28 December 1905   St Martin's Street

Dear Mr Churchill,

I write to say that we find it will be possible to bring out your book on Tuesday the 2nd prox instead of the following Friday, and as this will give us three extra clear days before the Election we have decided to do so. You will see the advertisements in to-morrow's and Saturday's papers. Will you kindly let us know how many copies you would like for yourself? We shall be prepared to give you any reasonable number, but of course it will be well for you not to make many presents of copies to people who ought naturally to buy them. I suppose you would like the copies sent to your rooms in town?

I am, Yours sincerely
FREDERICK MACMILLAN

Sidney Greville to WSC

1 January 1906   Chatsworth

My dear Winston,

The King has received your book and desires me to thank you for your kind thought in sending him an early copy on New Year's Day.

His Majesty is very pleased to have it – having been such an old friend of your father's. I am sending this tonight so that your messenger may take it back by a morning train.

Yrs sincerely
SIDNEY GREVILLE

J. A. Spender to WSC

2 January 1906   45 Sloane Street

My dear Churchill,

I came back on Sunday night to find your book awaiting me here but with an intimation that its day of publication was advanced to Jan 2. That was a catastrophe for me, & my W.G. [*Westminster Gazette*] notice which would otherwise have been a much more deliberate affair is, I am afraid, long, dull & inadequate. Much of it was written in the small hours of the morning. So I must add to it by a private word to say what a brilliant book I think it is, & how masterly in its grasp of forces & characters. But apart from that you have done what you chiefly set out to do – the son's part to the father as very seldom it has been done before. May I offer you my very warm congratulations?

You need nothing to better your 'situation', but a book of this kind does place you among the literary few – which is a great thing for a politician. I am sure you do wisely to make a modest beginning, but you must be in the innermost circle before the next Parliament is out.

I hope Manchester looks well.

Yours always

J. A. Spender

No answer to this on any account. You have other things to think of.

Joseph Chamberlain to WSC

3 January 1906   Highbury Moor Green
                                                  Birmingham

My dear Winston,

Pray accept my best thanks for your book. You have dared greatly in bringing it out at this time when we are all full of the current fight. But if you win I shall enjoy reading your book in such leisure as you allow me afterwards.

Yours very truly

J. Chamberlain

Mrs Jack Leslie to WSC

[4 January 1906]   Glaslough
                                                  County Monaghan

Winston dear,

It was more than kind of you sending me your book – & I am quite fascinated by it – and think you may indeed be proud of it. I would like to praise it in detail to you, but I know you are desperately busy at this moment, & I had better reserve my comments for another time!! But thank you again & again for giving me the book – & writing my name in it.

I heard of you through Mr Marsh and I am so glad you make *si bon ménage* together. He seems delighted to be with you – and already fond of you! Which is a good thing, as one can work so much better for anyone one cares for. What will happen to Ld Hugh? Good luck to you dear Winston in the New Year – & may some good Angel above watch over you.

Forgive this wave of an old aunt's pen.

Yr Aff
LEONIE

Duke of Marlborough to WSC

2 January 1905 [1906]   Blenheim

Winston,

The statement of the D.T. concerning your father, that he was dishonourable[1] and also untruthful, has made me angry. I do not recollect that a similar statement of this character during the last 20 years has ever been made against a public man, after his death, and I think that some notice and action should be taken in the matter. I propose tomorrow to send a letter to the D.T. which I shall expect them to publish and in which I shall ask for a withdrawal of the particular passage, and an ample and unqualified apology for having permitted themselves to use language which any fair-minded man would condemn.

The letter will be moderate and to the point. You can rely on me for that, but if you wd rather that I did not take the matter up I will not do so.

I think myself it is an unparalleled insult to the family in general and in my own judgment I am the proper person to administer a good and sound trouncing to that dirty little Hebrew.[2] I think I am on a good case and that I will force an adequate apology. Let me know your views by telephone.

Yrs
SUNNY

The Duke of Marlborough to the Editor, The Daily Telegraph[3]

3 January 1906   Blenheim

Sir,

I have read the article published in your paper on the life of the late Lord Randolph Churchill written by his son.

[1] In the course of an extremely hostile review the *Daily Telegraph*'s anonymous reviewer wrote of Lord Randolph: 'His treatment of his friends was often atrocious, sometimes even not honourable; he was very careless of the truth.' The reviewer described WSC's editing as possessing 'occasional lapses into execrable taste, which have not been wanting in his own career'.

[2] Harry Lawson Webster Levy-Lawson (1862–1933), manager of the *Daily Telegraph*, of which his father, 1st Baron Burnham (1833–1916) was proprietor; Liberal MP for W. St Pancras 1885–92, Mile End 1905–6, and as Unionist 1910–16; Viscount Burnham 1919. He was chairman of the committee which drew up the Burnham Scale for schoolteachers' salaries.

[3] Published on January 4.

I do not desire to express an opinion on the review which you make of Mr Churchill's book.

I wish, however, to remind you that you have permitted yourself the use of the following sentence in giving your own impression of the character of the late Lord Randolph Churchill: 'His treatment of his friends was often atrocious, sometimes even not honourable: he was very careless of the truth.' These are terms which you do not hesitate to employ against the character of a statesman who is dead, but which you would not have ventured to use if he had been alive.

I desire, therefore, to ask if you withdraw in unequivocal terms a statement which is unfounded in fact, and that you will offer an apology for the use of language which many will deplore.

In proportion to the frankness of your withdrawal and the extent of your apology, I shall recognise the good taste which you presumably possess yourself, since you censure so severely the lack of it in others.

Men in public life can defend themselves when their honour is impugned. But when the attack is delayed till after their demise they entrust the defence to those who share their name.

It is on behalf of Lord Randolph's family who loved him, his friends who esteemed him, and his political associates who honoured him that I desire to offer an uncompromising protest against an attack on the memory of a departed statesman the method of which appears to me to be essentially un-English.

I remain, Yours faithfully
MARLBOROUGH

Duke of Marlborough to WSC

Thursday

[3 January 1906]   Blenheim

My dear Winston,

I hope that the *D.T.* will publish my letter tomorrow and that you may approve of it. I trust the significance of the word 'un-English' may not be lost to the understanding of those who may read my letter. It was the sharpest thrust which my blunted pen was able to inflict. If the *D.T.* hide away my letter in back columns, I must rely on you to get it dug out by other papers and commented on.

I shall take the 1st opportunity of offering Levi Lawson a public affront. I don't allow Jews to say members of my family are dishonourable without giving them back more than they expected.

This performance of the *D.T.* is an unparalleled insult, and I shall not let the matter drop, unless they apologise.

I wonder if they will?

Yrs aff
SUNNY

Daily Telegraph[1]

5 January 1906

Having submitted the Duke of Marlborough's letter to our reviewer, we learn that he is not anxious to pursue the matter further. We consider, therefore, it our duty to express our deep regret that the particular passage complained of, which we unhesitatingly withdraw, should have appeared. For the rest we sincerely disclaim the intention of wounding the feelings of the members of the late Lord Randolph's family.

Duke of Marlborough to WSC

EXTRACT

7 January 1906   Sunderland House

My dear Winston,

Among the numerous engagements which require your attention it was good of you to devote a few moments to writing to me. My sleep during the last 3 nights has been curtailed owing to the hours which I have spent in reading your book. The story is told in an admirable manner, well condensed in the comparatively unimportant parts, carefully elaborated in the more eventful episodes. It is a great work, and compares favourably with Morley's Life which is too laboured. I doubt that many will criticise any passage in the book; you seem to have displayed great fairness throughout, and indeed your anxiety to be impartial to the main figure in your story has led you I think to lean towards the side of the stern critic. I wish I had looked through the mass of letters from which you have made your selection. I do not think that R C's letters are quite happily chosen. Some of them display too much the cynical and flippant frame of mind which characteristics were exceptional rather than permanent in him. The reader forms the idea that levity played too large a part in his nature. The omission of the word damn would have been preferable. It occurs in a meaningless way 3 or 4 times.

[1] Printed at the head of the Leader column.

The last chapters to my mind are the best of all. They are masterpieces of skilful writing. I regret rather that you did not include a short paragraph on the *état morale* of the old Duchess during and at the end of his illness. Their co-operation was an essential item in his political career; and I think a paragraph dealing with the melancholy yet outraged mother robbed of the darling of her hopes wd not have inappropriately balanced the elaborate part in the earlier volume where she figures prominently. In all this I feel like the apprentice criticising the craft of the master mason.

Levi has had his head rubbed in s – t & I am glad that my letter met with your approbation. I shrink from using my pen as you know, for I am conscious of lack of capacity in this acquirement. Fortunately I had Perkins[1] at Blenheim who I knew was a good English scholar and I submitted the draft copy to him in which he suggested some slight alterations. I was anxious to avoid the rejoinder from the *D.T.* 'that my knowledge of English was as deplorable as your capacity for good taste' etc etc.

The apology is satisfactory, for I did not anticipate that they wd give one. I do not think that a further letter from me wd be advisable. The climax was reached when the apology appeared, and anything subsequent is in the nature of anti-climax. Besides I think that from a tactical point of view, it is as well to leave Levi and Co in some doubt and apprehension whether to consider his repentance sufficient. Jews cannot be dealt with with that same good feeling that prompts the intercourse between Christians. I employed the word 'un-English' in my letter with the intention of conveying the idea that no one but a Foreign Jew wd have permitted himself to commit such an error, and any one of English birth wd have shrunk from such a course.

I feel that the phrase miscarried. I have received many letters in consequence of this fracas: – nearly all from those who are not members of the family. I enclose you three specimens which tear up when you have glanced through them. The Doggy Folk approved of my action and when the smell of the Tod was not apparent, it formed the chief topic of conversation.

I fear you will have a bitter and acrimonious struggle at Manchester, but G. Elections exist as a kind of political blood letting. T. Bowles' comments on J. C. [Joseph Chamberlain] appear to hold the field at present, for impertinent and vulgar recrimination. . . .

I shall indulge in amusements till Parliament meets.

Yrs tr
SUNNY

---

[1] William Turner Perkins (d. 1927), *The Times* Parliamentary staff 1892; Editor, Parliamentary debates for *The Times* 1895–8; special correspondent *Standard* 1900; Assistant Editor, House of Commons Official Report 1908–16, Editor 1917–27.

Lord Salisbury to WSC

8 January 1905 [1906]   Hatfield

My dear Winston,

I am so very much obliged for your most gratifying present.

I have not yet entered upon its perusal but it will be a comfort to pass away from the dust of present conflict to the serenity of the battles of the past.

With very many renewed thanks.

Yours very trly
SALISBURY

Wilfred Scawen Blunt to WSC

21 January 1906   37 Chapel Street

Dear Churchill,

I have been reading your life of your father. It is really admirable – a most clear history, truthful and proportionate. It has renewed vividly in me what I always had for him while he lived, a strong personal affection. I am glad you lay stress on his natural sympathy with the nobler ideas in politics. They were constantly in his mind though he often hid them & on some notable occasions acted contrary to them in a way that troubled me. In talking alone with me he had very little reserve about liberty either in Egypt or India or again in Ireland, nor do I think there was any great difference between his ideas and my own on these matters. He was far more of a Home Ruler than you seem to know, and I have always thought that, if the Election of 1885 had gone rather more favourably & Gladstone had not taken up the Irish cause when he did, your father would have persevered with it. His attitude abt Home Rule privately to me in 1884–1885, as about much else, was that he was educating his party to it and educating Lord Salisbury. But the fighting instinct in him was too strong when Gladstone changed his colours after the Election, and he could not resist going off to Ulster and waving the Orange flag. The open letter I wrote him just before the fall of Gladstone's govt in 1885 was written not only with his approval but with the correction of a phrase in it about Ireland which he himself suggested as a matter of policy, not of opinion.

I am of course delighted at your success at Manchester. It is a fine piece of poetical justice on the party which rejected his teaching and him.

'Moreover it is written that my race hewed Amon hip & thigh from Arser on Amon unto Minneth'

Yr very trly
WILFRED SCAWEN BLUNT

George Macmillan to WSC

5 February 1906   27 Queen's Gate Gardens

Dear Mr Churchill

Will you give Mrs Macmillan & myself the pleasure of your company to dinner here on Tuesday Feb. 27 at 8? Mr John Morley is coming & we are asking a few other political friends to join us in celebrating the Liberal victory.

You will be glad to hear that *The Times* has had 600 more copies of the book since I saw you last week & we are now not far short of 5000.

Yours very truly
GEORGE A. MACMILLAN

W. F. Monypenny[1] to WSC

14 February 1906   2 Queen Anne's Gate

Dear Mr Churchill,

Circumstances have so contrived that I have only now finished reading your book: but though rather late in the day I cannot refrain from telling you how much I have been delighted and from congratulating you on what seems to me a really great performance. Though I am not able to contemplate it from the summit of the mountain of achievement but only from half way up the slopes, still I am one of the small band of people who from practical experience can form some notion of the difficulties of such a task: and so you will perhaps not think it mere presumption if I say that alike in style and architecture and for its spirit, grasp and insight the book seems to me truly admirable. It might perhaps have gained in dramatic intensity by being a little shorter tho' I have not found a dull page in it. It has immensely clarified my views of the post-Dizzian epoch, and, what will probably please you most, immensely raised my conception of your father as a statesman.

---

[1] William Flavelle Monypenny (1866–1912), journalist on *The Times* 1893–9, 1903–12; Director of *The Times* 1908–12; Editor of Johannesburg *Star* 1899–1903; co-author with G. E. Buckle of *The Life of Benjamin Disraeli*.

If it is not too late may I also congratulate you with all the reserve be-fitting a partisan – though not a very strong one – on the other side on your victory at Manchester and without any reserve at all on the beginning of your official career? Tho' there is such an obvious opening just now for a Dizzy or a Randolph that I am half inclined to regret you are immured in Downing Street.

Yours sincerely
W. F. MONYPENNY

Joseph Chamberlain to WSC

EXTRACT

10 February 1906   Torquay

Private

My dear Winston,

... I have now nearly finished your book & must tell you that I think it is admirably done. It is extremely difficult for a son to write his father's life with sufficient impartiality & restraint, but you have succeeded & have allowed the facts & the letters to tell their own story while the necessary arguments are not open to any hostile criticism.

I notice one mistake in your references to the Kilmainham Treaty. The negotiations with Parnell were made known by me to Forster at an early period and I thought at the time that he did not disapprove. He certainly did not contemplate resignation in the first instance and he agreed to Parnell's release from prison.

But I have always thought that the appointment of Spencer over his head was too much for him and he rightly considered it as a sort of supersession.

The matter is only of comparatively small importance now, but I thought you would like to know the facts.

Believe me, Yours very truly
J. CHAMBERLAIN

WSC to Frederick Macmillan
(Macmillan and Company Papers)

6 June 1906   Blenheim

Dear Mr Macmillan,

I am very sorry to see by a cutting which has reached me from *The Publisher and Bookseller* that *The Times* have played you a shabby trick.[1]

---

[1] As a move in the 'book war' between *The Times* and the publishing trade, *The Times* Book Club was offering WSC's book as a 'loss-leader' at seven shillings.

I do hope you will find it will not cause any serious injury to the sale of the book. It certainly cannot in any way reflect upon your credit as a publisher.

I do not see how you can stop people selling things they have bought below the cost price, but I can quite understand the annoyance and derangement which it causes.

With good wishes, yours very sincerely
WINSTON S. CHURCHILL

C. H. P. Mayo to WSC

17 October 1906   Harrow on the Hill

My dear Churchill,

I have just put down your life of Lord Randolph Churchill, & should like to offer you my very warm & sincere congratulations upon it. I remember with some pleasure & pride that your first literary effort was made in the *Harrovian*. I think it was at my suggestion that you wrote a criticism of the School Concert. It was a small beginning, the proverbial mustard seed from which a great tree has sprung.

Your book has fascinated me. It was a wonderful life & struggle which you so well describe, so terribly full of incident that it is hard to remember that it was the life of a young man, many of whose colleagues are still living. This thought, that so many men with whom your Father worked & who could say with reference to much of what you describe, '*quorum pars magna fui*', made your work exceptionally difficult. You have, I am sure, been overwhelmed with letters of congratulation upon your success; I add mine with much sincerity, & not only upon the success of this book, but upon your triumph at Manchester & your position in the Government. If the dead are in any way conscious of our doings your Father must visit the scenes of his triumphs with no less sense of triumph now.

Yours sincerely
C. H. P. MAYO

8

Colonial Office 1

(See Main Volume Chapter 6)

A S Under-Secretary for the Colonial Office, WSC turned his
attention to resolving the two most important problems
which faced the Colonial Office in 1906: Chinese Labour in
South Africa and the establishment of a Constitution for the
Transvaal. Other problems of a less pressing nature sometimes
obtruded. No attempt has been made in these pages to explain
fully all the matters to which WSC and his correspondents
referred. Interested readers should turn to the detailed accounts
in the works of G. B. Pyrah, L. M. Thompson, G. H. L. Le
May, R. Hyam and Sir Keith Hancock.

WSC to Dr J. Dulberg

2 January 1906   Colonial Office
[Copy]

My dear Sir,
  I have delayed to answer your letter of the 26th of Dec until I have had an
opportunity of studying the documents in this office which relate to the
subject.
  You are no doubt aware of the numerous and serious difficulties which
present themselves to a scheme of establishing a self-governing Jewish colony
in British East Africa, of the differences of opinion among the Jews themselves, of the doubtful suitability of the territories in question, of the rapidly
extending settlements by British colonists in and about the area, & of the
large issues of general state policy which the scheme affects. Those difficulties
had powerfully impressed themselves upon Mr Lyttelton; & although Lord

Elgin will approach the consideration of this subject in a spirit of profound sympathy both for the aspirations of the Jewish race & for their recent terrible sufferings, I cannot believe that those difficulties will be absent from his mind. But I will own that I hope that they may be surmounted. I agree most heartily with the spirit of Mr Zangwill's[1] letter to *The Times* of Dec 12th 1905. I recognise the supreme attraction to a scattered & persecuted people of a safe & settled home under the flag of tolerance & freedom. Such a plan contains a soul, & enlists in its support energies, enthusiasms, & a driving power which no scheme of individual colonization can ever command. And although Lord Rothschild's contention that the immediate needs of Jewish refugees are best met by affording them opportunities of settling in Canada & the Argentine may be powerfully urged, I do not feel that the noble vision you behold so vividly ought to be allowed to fade, & I will do what I can to preserve it & fulfil it. There should be room within the world-wide limits of the British Empire, & within the generous scope of Liberal institutions, for the self-development & peculiar growth of many races, & of many traditions & of many creeds. And from an Imperial point of view, it is in the varied excellence of its parts, that there is most surely to be founded the wealth, the happiness & the higher unity of the whole.

Yours very truly
WINSTON S. CHURCHILL

Memorandum by WSC[2]

January 1906

Confidential

    1. As the question of the military vote may, and the multiplication of constituencies (if acceded to) must, involve amendments in the Letters Patent, the moment seems suitable (apart from political considerations here) to reconsider from the beginning the merits of the policy embodied in Mr Lyttelton's 'Constitution' despatch of the 31st March, 1905.

    2. The vital and fundamental issue is this: who is to govern the Transvaal Colony; are we to govern it through selected officers, or are the inhabitants of the Transvaal to govern it through elected representatives? The question is grave. There are many true things to be said for or against either course. Decision has however been taken. The late Government have determined definitely to abandon the policy of governing the Transvaal through selected

---

[1] Israel Zangwill (1864–1926), a leading Zionist; self-educated author, playwright and poet. His publications include: *Children of the Ghetto* 1892, *The Mantle of Elijah* 1900, and *The War for the World* 1916.
[2] Colonial Office Paper [African (South) No 804] on Transvaal Constitution.

officers as a Crown Colony. Mr Lyttelton's opinion is plainly declared. Lord Milner agrees to it 'as a concession which the restlessness of our own people under the present system forced upon us' (a significant sentence) (3263/S), 143 (41). Mr Chamberlain, the Conservative party, and Parliament as a whole have accepted the fact.

We have therefore abandoned one practical and defensible position, viz., Crown Colony Government. It will not be possible to return to it. We must now move on to another position which, while affording security to British interests, is capable of permanent defence. Mr Lyttelton's plan (despatch of the 31st March) does not appear to promise either permanence or stability. When one crest line is abandoned it is necessary to return to the next. Halting at a 'half-way house' mid-way in the valley is fatal. What is the next defensible position? I submit that it will not now be possible to deny the Transvaal a representative Assembly with an Executive responsible thereto.

3. Mr Lyttelton has proposed a Representative Assembly of 30 to 35 members, of whom 6 to 9 are to be nominated Ministers. What grounds of reason, of historical experience, are there for believing that such a plan will work? A solid Dutch party (probably half the elected members) demands responsible Government. The British are divided: some claim responsible Government as loudly as the Dutch; none resist it in principle. This movement will probably gain in strength with every decision, however wise, taken by the Home Government on South African affairs.

What will be the position of the 6 or 9 nominated Ministers in face of such a demand? They are altogether without trustworthy and effective support. They have not a majority nominated by the Crown; nor are they the representatives of an established and organized political party. Able administrators as they may be, it is admitted that they possess small, if any, Parliamentary abilities and experience. Moreover, if Lord Selborne's proposal to increase the number of constituencies to sixty, for which on its merits there is a good case, be agreed to, the official members (even though proportionately increased) will be in still greater numerical weakness.

In these circumstances, will not the 'risk' which Lord Milner foresees (3263/S) of a refusal of supplies producing a 'deadlock' be very real and great? But even without such an extreme step, shrewd politicians would have no difficulty in embarrassing, or even paralyzing the Transvaal Government, and of utterly discrediting the new Constitution.

4. All this time, while we have surrendered power, financial and legislative, and all that may follow therefrom, to a majority opposed to the very basis of representative Government, we shall continue to be responsible to the House of Commons for everything done under the nominal authority

of our officers. Many things will be done of which we disapprove, which we shall be powerless to prevent, but which we shall be forced to defend, to the intense dissatisfaction of our supporters. I do not myself believe that the next House of Commons will accept responsibility for the continuance of Chinese labour. But even if they were so persuaded, we must reckon with continued interferences by Parliament in the working of the Ordinance, and that constant supervision by the Colonial Office – which is clearly necessary to insure the strict and humane observance of its intricate provisions. This is only one of many vexing matters on all of which our action, however right, however honestly intended, will expose us to much Parliamentary danger, and cannot fail to cause perpetual irritation in the Colony.

Responsible Government will be demanded with ever-increasing vehemence by the Transvaal Assembly. They will be supported probably by the great mining interests which depend on Chinese labour, and certainly by the Radical, Socialist, and Nationalist forces in the House of Commons. We shall have already surrendered all that is necessary to enable the rest to be extorted. In the end, which may come quite soon, the Lyttelton Constitution will be recognized as unworkable, and we, or our successors, will be forced to concede full responsible self-government. The control of events will then have largely passed from our hands. We may not be able, without the employment of force, to prescribe the electoral basis of the new Constitution, or even to reserve the functions necessary to the maintenance of public order and the King's authority. What we might have given with courage and distinction both at home and in South Africa, upon our own terms, in the hour of our strength, will be jerked and twisted from our hands – without grace of any kind – not perhaps without humiliation – at a time when the Government may be greatly weakened and upon terms in the settlement of which we shall have only a nominal influence. It is a lively apprehension of these dangers which are inherent in the Lyttelton Constitution which induces me to write this Memorandum.

5. The reasons set forth by Mr Lyttelton in his despatch of the 31st March (p. 2) for choosing representative, rather than responsible, Government are hardly convincing even on paper:—

(a) That, having regard to the lately concluded war, 'the very existence of the Executive' should not be 'based upon the consent of a majority in the Legislative Chamber.' The power of the purse appears to enable the majority in the Legislative Chamber to terminate at any moment 'the very existence of the Executive' as a constitutional body. Nothing would then sustain it, but the military forces at the disposition of the High Commissioner. Such force would, even with responsible Government, be available to assert the authority of the Crown.

(b) That 'full self-government' will involve 'party government.' I hope it may. There is no other way of working a representative Assembly.

(c) That the party division would be upon racial lines. It is so at the Cape. Better far the alternation of two fairly equally balanced parties even though regrettably divided on racial lines, than a majority of pseudo-secessionists composed of the Boer vote plus a section of the Responsibles.

(d) Page 3. Mr Chamberlain's statements of policy. These may have appealed with great force to Mr Lyttelton. They are not *sacrosanct* to us.

(e) The Agreement made with the Boer leaders at Vereeniging. To proceed direct to responsible Government would be only a more punctual and more perfect fulfilment of that Agreement.

(f) That the presence of a large coloured population should enjoin 'greater caution in the direction of political change' in South Africa than in Canada. This remark reveals a complete misapprehension of the influence of 'the black peril' on South African politics. It may indeed be a grave danger, perhaps – though remote – the gravest of all. But so far as the possibility of a native rising operates on the questions under discussion, it is a unifying force, perhaps the only unifying force, drawing the two white races together for mutual protection in spite of their animosities, and leading them to turn gratefully to the military power of the Crown. In short, it appears to me that the reasons assigned in the despatch of the 31st March for the institution of representative, rather than responsible, Government have been collected to make some show of defending a decision already arrived at by an odd mixture of venturesomeness and timidity.

6. In the present situation there are two things which we should exert ourselves to secure:—

(1) The reservation to the High Commissioner of all that is necessary to public order.

(2) The building up of a powerful and well-organized British or non-Dutch party.

These are vital. To this end it is indispensable that we should ourselves prescribe the basis of the responsible Constitution whenever it does come, so shape our policy as to keep the British party well together, and so to frame the Constitution as to give it a fair chance of securing the balance of power. The importance of this is evident from Lord Milner's growing anxiety (see telegrams) to have certain electoral arrangements settled. One vote one value, single Member districts, and automatic redistribution, are devices unassailable on democratic grounds. They seem to have been, for the moment at least, generally accepted in South Africa, the Boers demurring mildly. It is not often that democratic principles are helpful in Imperial Administration. When they are they should be cherished.

7. But Mr Lyttelton's proposals will, if carried out, have the effect, first, of dividing the British party, already according to Lord Milner 'heterogeneous and fissiparous' (despatch 5th December), into Responsibles and Progressives; secondly, of putting the Transvaal Government into a large minority, and, thirdly, converting the Legislative Assembly into a kind of constituent body, which will begin by agitating the demand for responsible Government, and very possibly proceed to dictate its exact basis. In all this the *beau rôle* is assigned to the Boers, who, in their exertions for responsible Government, are admittedly voicing the opinions of men outside their own party organization, and appear as the champions of the Colony as a whole; while the Imperial Government can only fall back to that foundation of mere force from which we have laboriously endeavoured to raise it.

8. The points immediately at issue are small by comparison. The 'military vote,' computed at the highest at 500, but perhaps only 70, is a trifle, causing much annoyance to the Dutch, and not worth anything to the British. The increase of constituencies to 60 is, I think, desired by the Progressive party in the interests of minority representation, and also because, believing they will obtain a majority, they would like to double it.

9. Lastly, there is the question of language. In Canada, as in South Africa, the duality of language is inconvenient; but the difficulty is much more likely to persist in Canada than in South Africa, for in Canada the two races dwell separately in well-marked geographical areas, and local peculiarities are preserved; but in South Africa the two races are intermingled in every town, in every village, almost in every farm. The English language, with its literature and its flexibility, and, above all, its business convenience, must prevail in so universal a competition against a vulgar dialect. The only way in which the *taal* can be kept alive is by making it a prescribed language, which the Boers would cultivate as an easy method of defying their conquerors. Whatever may happen to South Africa in the future, it will certainly speak English. I am therefore of opinion that absolute duality of language in government and education may, so far as Imperial interests are concerned, be conceded in principle, as it has already been conceded in fact.

WINSTON S. CHURCHILL

Abe Bailey to WSC

8 January 1906   Johannesburg

My dear Winston,

Thank you for your cable. This place is in an awful state financially &
goodness knows when it will come right. If you good people do stop Chinese
in any way there will be a panic. This could extend through SA. I don't for
a moment think you will do anything to bring this about. I wish I had given
this place up years ago when you asked me to & settled & gone into Home
politics. However that is past & we must fight the battle here. Smuts[1] is a
very clever gentleman but I don't think he will deceive you with his greasy
loyalty. I wish you every success Winston & my prediction may come true
that one day you will be Prime Minister of England.

With kindest regards

Yours vy sincly
ABE BAILEY

J. C. Smuts to WSC

9 January 1906   Horrex's Hotel
                                                              Strand

Dear Mr Winston Churchill,

I have come from the Transvaal in the hope that I may have an opportunity to discuss with you the situation in the Transvaal and South Africa
generally. I have no desire to trouble you while you are busy with election
matters, but shall esteem it a great favour and honour if thereafter you
could find it convenient to receive me.

We Boers feel very deeply that, unless the main features of the Milner
policy are discarded, the Liberals will reap what their opponents have
sown in South Africa. The continuance of the policy which has been pursued
since the conclusion of hostilities can in our opinion only lead to an impossible situation sooner or later, while the reversal of that policy will clear
the way for a great Liberal reconstruction of South Africa.

[1] Jan Christian Smuts (1870–1950), barrister, politician and general; State Attorney,
South African Republic 1898; supreme commander of Republican Forces in Cape Colony
1901; Colonial Secretary, Transvaal 1907; Minister of Interior and Mines, Union of South
Africa 1910–12, of Defence 1910–20, Finance 1912–13; Prime Minister and Minister for
Native Affairs 1919–24; Minister of Justice 1933–9; Prime Minister and Minister of External
Affairs and Defence 1939–48; South African representative on Imperial War Cabinet
1917–18; Plenipotentiary at Paris Peace Conference 1919; PC 1917.

I am very anxious to discuss with you the various aspects of the whole question as they present themselves to us in the hope that the Government may see their way clear to the adoption of a policy which will not only heal old wounds but also pave the way to union and happiness in South Africa.

Whatever political knowledge or experience I have picked up in South Africa which might assist in the furtherance of this object I place unreservedly at your disposal.

I am, Yours very faithfully
J. C. SMUTS

Note by WSC: Ansd 11/1 promising further letter

Lord Elgin to WSC

14 January 1906   Broomhall

My dear Churchill,

I have not any returns but a rumour has come from the town that Manchester has covered itself with glory![1] On faith of it I send a line to congratulate you most heartily on fighting in the vanguard as you would wish to do. Your example in Manchester is sure to be contagious – and means I hope that our association in the CO will continue – and I have every confidence that we shall manage between us to put in some good work.

I am sending back a long telegram which Graham[2] is to show you. It so happened that I received to-day a letter from Selborne in which he again refers to our appointing a Commission, of course meaning on the general question. But he could scarcely object to one on the 'treatment' of the Chinese and it might be the best answer to Boland[3] & Co.

Yours sincerely
ELGIN

Lord Loreburn to WSC

24 January 1906   House of Lords

My dear Mr Churchill,

I am much obliged by your note and the enclosures as to the state of

[1] At the General Election on the previous day WSC in North-West Manchester received 5639 votes to his opponent's – W. Joynson-Hicks's – 4398, a majority of 1241; the Conservatives lost all eight seats they had held in Manchester and Salford, Balfour being defeated in Manchester East.

[2] Frederick Graham (1848–1923), Assistant Under-Secretary of State, Colonial Office. Served in Colonial Office 1870–1907; knighted 1907.

[3] F. C. Boland, a journalist who alleged in the *Morning Leader* that the Chinese labourers were ill-treated.

things in South Africa. I shall hope to talk to you about it. The perplexity
is that a constant stream of inaccurate information and foolish advice has
been coming from Lord Milner and others and you can't rely on anything.

At the same time it is very likely there is great discontent in Cape Colony
as well as the Transvaal though the idea of Germany operating against us
from their African possessions in the South West seems far fetched.

Anyhow we should, I think, be prepared for emergencies and the real
question is how to prepare. I am not a soldier but it seems to me that 20,000
men could do nothing against a rising in the N of the Cape Colony, a great
distance from the Transvaal, and could not be cut up into small detachments, in short would do no good and might be snapped up before relief
could come. In short, if you rely on bayonets you must have a huge force. A
small force merely exasperates. If you rely on freedom you had better do as
you do in Canada and Australia. Three or four thousand sufficed up to
1895 for all South Africa & would now suffice for the purposes of coast
defence & any sudden violence from the natives.

I think also you will find that our people here will object to paying for
20,000 men in S. Africa for a lengthened period.

I don't insist that it should be done hot foot within 2 or 3 months from
now; but reduce to 10,000 to begin with & then down to four.

The despatch of Lord Milner which you sent me is a curious revelation
of his notion of what exists and is to come. Dangerous insurrectionary spirit
all round, to be dealt with by a military occupation at our expense for an
indefinite time! It is his own unconscious comment on his own policy,
which to my mind has been one long record of folly, credulity & bad temper.

Yours sincerely
LOREBURN

J. C. Smuts to WSC

31 January 1906   Horrex's Hotel

Dear Mr Churchill,

Herewith I send you a statement[1] of the points I have urged before you[2]
in regard to the Transvaal constitution. I am sending copies also to the
Prime Minister, the Lord Chancellor, and Mr John Morley. I have some
copies left if you should wish to have any more.

Yours very faithfully
J. C. SMUTS

[1] A summary of this famous memorandum – which argued the case for the immediate
grant of self-government to the Transvaal and the Orange River Colony – can be found in
G. B. Pyrah, *Imperial Policy and South Africa* 1902–10 (Oxford, 1955).
[2] At their meeting on 26 January 1906.

WSC to J. C. Smuts
(*Smuts Archive*)

1 February 1906   Colonial Office

Private

Dear Mr Smuts,

Let me thank you for the memorandum on the Transvaal Constitution wh you have been good enough to send me. I will read it with attention. We shall I hope be able to come to a settlement accepted as fair to both parties in S Africa. In any event I shall always be glad to learn your views & hope you will not hesitate to communicate these frankly.

With good wishes for a pleasant voyage.

Believe me yours vy faithfully
WINSTON S. CHURCHILL

Memorandum by WSC[1]

30 January 1906

Confidential

1. In my last Memorandum [African No 804] I have endeavoured to set forth the reasons which, in my judgment, render the Lyttelton Constitution unworkable, and unsuited as a basis for Representative Government, and the reasons which support the conclusion that Imperial interests at home and in South Africa demand the transference of purely Transvaal affairs to a Representative Assembly with an Executive responsible thereto. I now wish to place on record a few observations upon the constructive aspect.

2. If it be admitted that the Transvaal is to govern itself under a Responsible Constitution, the next question which confronts His Majesty's Government is: Do we want to have a Boer or a British Ministry? There will be few elements of uncertainty about the Transvaal General Election. The lines of cleavage are too deep and clear-cut. The differences between town and country voters, plainly marked in every land, are nowhere half so crudely stamped as here. Differences of class and occupation, differences of religion, loyalty, and language, race hatred still red-hot from war, vital material interests, passionate national ambitions, divide parties and predetermine votes. Upon such moulding, ordinary political argument is mere

[1] Colonial Office Paper [African (South) No 817] on Transvaal Constitution.

varnish. We may talk airily of taking the sense of the inhabitants on this or that grave matter, but the only question that can in fact be decided by Transvaal electors will be which party has got most names on the register. Everything depends on the basis selected. His Majesty's Government are therefore in the position of Grand Elector. As they resolve, so will the balance of power be struck.

3. It must never be forgotten that the politics of the Transvaal are the politics of South Africa. Johannesburg is the railway, commercial, financial, and political nerve-centre of the whole. It is the arena in which all that is most militant in Boer and Briton meet and carry on their perennial duel. The British population of Johannesburg are the representatives and champions of the British authority in South Africa. The Transvaal Boers are the representatives and champions of the Dutch. Whatever is done for or against the one or the other is done for or against the whole race in the sub-continent. Cape Colony, Natal, Rhodesia, and the Orange River Colony form an audience of vehement and anxious partisans.

4. British authority in South Africa must stand on two legs. The inherent vice of Lord Milner's policy was that it stood only on one leg. Of Lord Milner's zeal and integrity in the public service, of his constancy through years of heartbreaking perplexity and peril, of his honourable poverty and voluntary self-effacement, it is not necessary to speak. But these considerations should not blind us to the fact that after the Peace of Vereeniging, no more unsuitable agent could have been chosen to discharge the functions of the High Commissioner. Being regarded after the war as the inveterate enemy of the Dutch and the prime author of all their miseries, he was condemned to fall back entirely on the support of the British; and of the British party the mining interest is, of course, the only formidable fighting part. The mining interest were, therefore, the only friends upon whom he could rely, and to preserve that allegiance scarcely any expedient seemed too desperate. But His Majesty's Government, coming fresh upon the scene, suffer from no such disability. They are at present independent, uncompromised, free to hold the scales even, cut off from neither race, able to work on terms of impartial justice with both. Let not that supreme advantage be thrown away. We cannot take either the one side or the other. We are free from the trammels of the mining interest. Do not let us throw ourselves into the arms of the Boers. Do not let us do anything which makes us the champion of one race, and consequently deprives us *for ever* of the confidence of the other.

5. The question of the Constitution ought not to be prejudiced by the desirability of terminating Chinese labour. It should be settled with reference to the general future of South Africa, and not with reference to any particular

question of South African politics. His Majesty's Government will no doubt be pressed so to frame the Constitution as to secure a verdict against Chinese labour. The demand is natural from those who see in South African politics only this one objectionable feature. But for His Majesty's Government to be led into such a policy would be to endanger the greater to obtain the less; and to regulate the whole for the sake of a part. My own opinion is clear that we ought not in any circumstances to allow any further importation of Chinese into South Africa under the conditions of the Labour Ordinance, whether the Transvaal 'Assembly' authorizes such importation or not. But it would be far better to prevent or hinder Chinese recruitments and embarkations boldly and plainly by Imperial power than to construct a local Assembly for that purpose. The first course would irritate temporarily the mining interest. The second would shatter irretrievably the British party.

6. We are not, of course, confined to any particular form of Responsible Government. 'Responsible Government' and 'Representative Government' are not specific prescriptions incapable of alteration, admixture, or dilution. They are only convenient labels used to describe certain processes familiar in Colonial administration. The conditions in the Transvaal are unprecedented and unique. We ought not, therefore, to be bound by any narrow interpretations of systems applied elsewhere, or prevented by any legal technicality from making whatever arrangements may, in the opinion of His Majesty's Government, best safeguard the interests of the Crown and deal even-handedly with both races in South Africa.

7. The Lyttelton Constitution rests upon a whole set of symmetrical and democratic principles easily defensible from any charge of gerrymandering, viz, one man one vote and no man more; one vote one value; equal electoral districts; automatic redistribution. Although the Boers are now asking for better terms, both races, utterly wearied of a costly and not too well-informed bureaucracy, were, until the change of Government in England, quite prepared to accept this basis for the purposes of Representative Government. Everyone in South Africa is familiar with the details of the scheme and has got used to the idea. Everything is in readiness, and it can be carried into effect with a minimum of novelty, delay or disturbance.

8. I admit, however, that Mr Duncan's[1] arguments in No 6995/S against the adoption of the 'one vote one value' basis are serious and substantial. I will not repeat them, or the answers by which they may be severally met.

[1] Patrick Duncan (1870–1943), Acting Lieutenant-Governor of the Transvaal 1906; Private Secretary to Sir Alfred Milner at Board of Inland Revenue; Treasurer of Transvaal 1901; Colonial Secretary of the Transvaal 1903–6; Minister of Interior, Public Health and Education, Union of South Africa 1921–4, of Mines 1933–6; Governor-General of Union of South Africa 1937–43; CMG 1904; GCMG 1937; PC 1937. Duncan was a founder member of Milner's 'Kindergarten'.

If the abandonment of this point would secure for the Constitution, in Mr Duncan's words, 'that both sides should accept it, not as being what either would like, but as a reasonably permanent settlement,' it should of course be abandoned. But will this be secured? 'One vote one value,' whatever may be its merits as compared with a population basis, has become the fighting position of the British party. Almost everything else has been conceded, or will be conceded, and this is their last and main line of resistance. As the controversy has developed the Boers have gained:—

(1) Abolition of the military vote.

(2) Sixty constituencies instead of thirty (for which they are not less eager than the British).

(3) Absolute equality of language recognized in the Letters Patent framing the Constitution.

(4) The first, and also the largest, of all their demands, 'Responsible' instead of 'Representative' Government.

To these concessions, which cover almost every request put forward by 'Het Volk,' it may be possible to add a somewhat larger margin, say, 10 per cent. instead of 5 per cent, in fixing the boundaries of constituencies, which would also please the Boers and meet to some extent the grievance of sparsely-populated districts formerly represented in the Volksraad. If, on the top of all this, the 'one vote one value' principle is thrown over, the British population will accuse the Imperial Government of having betrayed them, bound hand and foot, to their deadly foes, and will be able to cite in proof of this assertion that in no single point in dispute was their opinion allowed to prevail.

Such a temper will *ipso facto* destroy all prospect of that 'reasonable acceptance by both sides' which Mr Duncan desires. This is perhaps rather a 'Pull devil, pull baker' sort of argument; but it unfortunately happens to correspond very closely with the realities of Transvaal politics; and the difficulty of the problem to be settled consists largely in the fact that we have to discover principles which, while simple and symmetrical in themselves, will at the same time in their practical working effect a compromise acceptable to both parties. Such principles are few and far between.

9. On the basis 'one vote one value,' the elections (according to Mr Smuts, who takes, naturally enough at this juncture, the gloomiest view of Boer prospects) would send to a Transvaal Assembly of 30 Members, 18 British or non-Boer Members (namely, 15 for the Rand, and 3 out of 4 from Pretoria) and 12 Boer Members. In an Assembly of 60 the proportion would therefore be 36 to 24. This is a very convenient proportion for Government and Opposition.

It must not be forgotten, however, that while the 24 Boers forming the

'Country party' will be absolutely solid, the 36 non-Boer Members and constituencies will be divided by every question which in this country separates Conservative from Liberal and capitalist from miner. On the race question alone (also in a degree, be it remembered, the flag question) the British majority would be homogeneous. As against the special interests of the mining magnates, the Boers would certainly find support, both in the House and in the constituencies, outside the limits of their own party. Already there is a sharp division between the Progressive and Responsible sections of the British party, and no one can say with certainty in what way the white miners' vote will make itself felt, or what class of British representatives they will return. In fact, reviewing the forces which 'one vote one value' will send to the Assembly, it may be said that the British will have a working majority on paper, but every uncertainty against them; and that the Boers, though in an actual minority, will be sure of being in effect the strongest and most homogeneous party in the State. In these circumstances, it is idle to pretend that the Boers will not have full power to protect their own interests and to influence the course of legislation, even if they are not immediately in a position to form a purely Boer Government.

10. If 'population' be substituted for the basis of 'one vote one value,' the elections (again according to Mr Smuts) will send, to an Assembly of 30, 16 British or non-Boer (13 from the Rand and 3 out of 4 from Pretoria) and 14 Boer members. In an Assembly of 60, the proportion would be 32 to 28. But as every uncertain factor lies on the British side, and as, of course, this is the very lowest and most modest estimate of Boer chances, it may be assumed that, on a 'population' basis, the parties will be numerically equal. Having regard to the enormously superior strength and homogeneity of the Boer party, it would evidently be the duty of the Governor to send for General Botha. Is this what His Majesty's Government desire?

11. In considering so grave a question, we must think of the dynamics as well as the statics of the situation. If the country party represent the more stable and permanent elements in Transvaal life, the townsmen stand for the hope and possibilities of its future. Boer predominance, if secured, can shut the door upon expansion and fortify itself thereby. British predominance can only be obtained by keeping the door open. With every rise in the cost of living in the towns the influx of immigrants, especially women and children, is retarded, and the electoral prospects of the Boers, especially on a 'population' basis, are improved. Protective duties on food-stuffs would therefore increase at once their profits and their power. This is a single instance.

12. We must not endeavour by the gift of Responsible Government to rid ourselves of our South African responsibilities. It would be very pleasant to throw the reins on the horse's neck, and very easy. The conflicting dualities

in the character of the land and in the nature of its people, the solemn obligations we have contracted to both parties in South Africa and to our people at home, demand for years to come the constant watchfulness, guidance, and occasional intervention of the outside power. In granting Responsible Government we must reserve to ourselves the necessary facilities and checks.

I am inclined to agree with Mr Graham in his minute [African No 818] advocating a Second Chamber, and I think that the reasons he gives are good. But further, it is, in my judgment, essential that the control of all armed forces, military or military-police, should be in the sole hands of the Governor, with power to increase them, reduce them, or move them at his discretion, and that (*pace* the Colonial Laws Validity Act) the Letters Patent framing the Constitution should not be alterable at the pleasure of the Transvaal Legislature. I wish it were in our power to reserve railways also, but that is a matter on which the several Colonies of South Africa have a right to be wrong in their own way.

WINSTON S. CHURCHILL

Lord Selborne to WSC

2 March 1906   Government House
                                                              Johannesburg

Confidential

My dear Churchill,

I was very glad to get your letter of the 10th February, and am much obliged to you for sending me the enclosures [Colonial Office Papers, African (South) Nos 804 and 817].

If I can be of any help to you at any time write to me or ask me a question and I will either explain matters or tell you exactly what I think. I think the freest exchange of views between us may be useful to us both. For instance, I saw that in the House of Commons yesterday you attributed the native unrest in Natal partly to the effect of working in the mines on the Natal Kaffirs. Now this is not accurate. A good many Natal natives come to work in Johannesburg in domestic service and otherwise, but very few indeed in the mines, practically no number worth counting.

I will now make some remarks on your two Memoranda. In the first place, let me say that I congratulate you upon them as a most admirable exposition of your own views, and in the second place, let me say that with much of them I entirely agree. Where I differ I will say so. I will eliminate all controversy on the Chinese question. We must simply agree to differ on the merits. I would, however, like to ask you two questions. Why is it wrong to employ Chinese from China and right to employ Africans from Portuguese East Africa, both in the mines, and Indians from India in the Natal plantations? The principles on which they are engaged do not differ, though the details may. My other question is, How do you propose that the industry should be carried on if one-third of the labour is removed, that is all the Chinese, or even if the results of the policy of the Government are to reduce the Chinese labour by one-half?

Lord Elgin has alluded in one of his telegrams to labour-saving appliances, but says that HMG cannot admit that to remove all the Chinese would destroy the industry by one-third. I replied sympathetically as regards labour-saving appliances because it represents my view, and also that it looks so bad that we should always differ. But as a matter of fact I do not think there is anything to be done in the way of labour-saving appliances. It would be very odd if there were. The whole interest of the mines is in devising, and using, labour-saving appliances, and I am told that if a Commission were sent out here they would see that nowhere in the world was so much use made of labour-saving appliances. How then do you propose to fill the gap? And if the gap is not filled, what flaw can you find in my statement as to the consequences?

I now come to your arguments against Lyttelton's Constitution. You omit altogether one very important consideration, the educative effect of a period of Representative Government, however short. As I have said in my despatches and letters to Lord Elgin, the Boers have no conception of what Responsible Government means, and, with few exceptions, the British have no experience. I am perfectly certain that even two years of Representative Government would have been of very great value to the future of this country, nor, with a Unionist Government in power, should I have had any difficulty in working it. My plan was to add to the Executive Council advisory members drawn from Het Volk, Responsibles, and Progressives, without portfolio, as the foreign saying goes. And I have excellent reason for saying that the leaders of all parties would have been willing to serve under those circumstances. It is a mistake to suppose that the Boers really desire Responsible Government. They do nothing of the kind. It was they who instigated Hull[1] to come and see me to make the proposal, the history of which you will find filed in the Colonial Office. When your Government

---

[1] Henry Charles Hull (1860–1932), member of the Legislative Council, Transvaal Colony 1903-7; Minister of Finance, Union Cabinet 1910-12.

came into power, however, I admit that circumstances were changed, and I doubt if it would have been possible to have worked Representative Government even under my plan without great friction between the elected Legislature and the House of Commons and HMG. Under these circumstances, as I said to Lord Elgin, I would prefer Responsible Government at once to a serious conflict between the Transvaal and HMG.

Now I come to the first three paragraphs on page 5. Here I agree with every word, and the matter could not have been put better. I have not yet raised the question of the reservation to the High Commissioner of powers that are necessary to public order because I have been asked no questions and I do not want to seem to be raising fresh difficulties. You enlarge further on this point in your second Memorandum, and indeed you are right. If you want to know the mind of the Boers, as I have said over and over again till you must almost be sick of my remarks, put yourself into their place and consider what you would do if, four years after France had conquered England, the French gave you back the power of the sword and the power of the purse?

I see that I have omitted to make a point in respect of page 4, paragraph 5 (f). What you say about 'the black peril' is quite just. In my opinion the only way in which, under Responsible Government, HMG can provide for a wise and sympathetic, while firm, treatment of the natives and British Indians is through the medium of a nominated Upper House. That would be far more effective than any control the Colonial Office can exercise.

Now I come to your remarks about the Taal on page 6. With all that you say about the Taal I cordially agree, and you will see that my education policy has been based on your view. English has nothing eventually to fear from the Taal; but I should like to know what you mean by your last sentence. 'I am therefore of opinion that absolute duality of language in Government and education may, so far as material interests are concerned, be conceded in principle as it has already been conceded in fact.' I do earnestly hope that HMG will not touch the education question. I may say without conceit that I have settled that. The Boer leaders have absolutely accepted my decision, and are loyally doing all they can to get their people to agree to it. And their people do agree to it. It is only their pestilent predikants who do not agree to it. The British, who did not understand it at first, have now also thoroughly accepted it. Therefore, please do not touch the settlement. But what do you mean by 'absolute duality of language in Government'? At the present moment the official language of the Courts of Justice is English; but anybody may give evidence or speak in Dutch. As regards the new Legislature I have recommended that anybody may speak in either language. That is all the Boers have hitherto asked for, and it has absolutely satisfied them. But of course now they will ask for more. The more that they will ask for is that all records of proceedings and Bills be printed both in English and Dutch, and that all the official records of the Courts shall be in Dutch as well as in English. Now I earnestly beg that HMG will not accede to that. This proposal is on totally different grounds to the other. It has nothing to do with the Taal. If official records or proceedings of any kind are in Dutch, that Dutch will not be the Taal but high Dutch. Now high Dutch is to the whole Boer population, except for a sprinkling of educated men, a foreign language. Over and over again the Boers themselves have told me that they cannot understand a Hollander when he speaks to them. It is more a foreign language to them than English is. But the whole policy of the Bond Party and the predikants is to substitute high Dutch for the Taal, and nothing would help them to do so more than that we should recognise high Dutch as an official language alongside English. Now while the Taal never can be a rival to English, high Dutch may be a very formidable rival, and by conceding a place to high Dutch you will be undoing all the good you are doing by conceding a place to the Taal, and doing much additional harm.

I now pass to your second Memorandum.

It is difficult for me to too emphatically express my admiration and agreement with every word of your second and third paragraphs. HMG will be deciding nothing less than the fate of South Africa – whether it is to be Boer or British. And if they decide that it is to be Boer, then may I say, without any intentional offence, the whole of the British in South Africa will regard the act of HMG as a second Majuba surrender, and they will eventually do the same as the British did who fought for us during the first Boer War, when they found the country handed back to the Boers – they will shake the dust of England off their shoes. To summarise, if you want South Africa to remain British, the first majority in the elected Transvaal Legislature must be British, and the first Responsible Government must be a British Government. This is my opinion given with the deepest sense of responsibility and anxiety for the future. I have no doubt that Lord Milner would share that opinion; but I will not quote him because his opinion does not command the confidence of HMG. But when I tell you it is also the opinion of Lawley,[1] of Solomon[2] and of Goold-Adams,[3] and also of Hely-

[1] Arthur Lawley (1860–1932), Lieutenant-Governor of the Transvaal 1902–6; knighted 1901; succeeded brother as 6th Baron Wenlock 1931.

[2] Richard Solomon (1850–1913), Attorney-General of the Transvaal 1902–7; Acting Lieutenant-Governor of the Transvaal 1905–6; High Commissioner for Union of South Africa 1910–13; knighted 1901.

[3] Hamilton John Goold-Adams (1858–1920), Lieutenant-Governor Orange River Colony 1901–7; Governor 1907–10; High Commissioner Cyprus 1911–14; Governor of Queensland 1914–20; knighted 1902.

Hutchinson and of McCallum,[1] whom I have confidentially consulted, may I not plead that some weight should be attached to such a consensus of opinion of the most experienced and responsible servants of the Crown in South Africa?

I now pass to paragraph 5. You say that 'HMG will no doubt be pressed so to frame the Constitution as to secure a verdict against Chinese labour', and you go on very properly to dismiss that view as unworthy of HMG. But I would say much more. I would say that if your Radical friends think that a Boer majority and Government would ensure a verdict against Chinese labour they never made a worse mistake in their lives. With the Boers the question of Chinese labour is simply a question of bargain. I have told Lord Elgin so, and I know it from the Boers themselves. They would be perfectly willing on terms to continue Chinese labour. The opposition of the Boers to Chinese labour is simply good party business. But there are among the British some very determined opponents of Chinese labour. I have said, and I believe, that they are a small minority of the whole of the British, but I think that minority is larger than I thought it was three months ago. All depends on the miners, who are a very uncertain vote. All I can say is that the Political Labour League, which purports to speak for the miners, though I do not believe it speaks for them to so great an extent as it pretends, have, since I gave my opinion, pronounced against Chinese labour.

I now come to paragraph 6. I agree with every word of it. But let me turn your mind to an application of what you say, and that is the Constitution of the ORC [Orange River Colony]. If you have not done so, please read the despatch I sent to Lyttelton about the Constitution of the ORC. In my opinion the ordinary form of Responsible Government is totally unfitted to the circumstances of the ORC. What will suit the ORC is the nearest approximation you can get to the old Constitution of the Orange Free State. I think I have shown clearly how this can be done, and while giving them back their old Constitution with the mere substitution of the Lieutenant-Governor for the President, you will be doing what you cannot otherwise do, you will be protecting the Police Officers, the British School Teachers, and the British farmers, who naturally look to you for protection and to whom you owe protection, and you would also be giving as much protection as it is possible for you to give to the National Scouts, of whom there are some 3,000 in the ORC. I do not admire the National Scouts any more than I

---

[1] Henry Edward McCallum (1852–1919), Governor of Natal 1901–7; colonial administrator from 1874; knighted 1898.

admire Stead. I think Kitchener was utterly wrong to employ them. But he did employ them and we are in honour bound to give them what protection we can.

Again there is a class of Boers in the ORC, of which Fraser[1] is the most notable example (but there are many others), who were most loyal Burghers during the war, but who having sworn allegiance to the King, have done their best to help the Government since. Now under the form of Government which I propose these men will retain exactly the same influence in the new elected legislature of the ORC as they had in the old OFS [Orange Free State] Volksraad before the war. Those men were then in the minority, but their voice was heard and their influence was felt. Such would be the case under the Constitution I propose. But if you give the ORC the ordinary form of Responsible Government the influence of those men will be annihilated because there will never be any play of parties. You will be establishing a perpetual Hertzog[2]-Fischer[3] dictatorship, which will be used ruthlessly to squeeze out every British Police Officer, School Teacher or Settler, and to make life unbearable for the National Scouts, and any protests issued by Fraser and his friends in the Legislature would have far less effect than they did in the Volksraad of the OFS. The reason for this was that under the Constitution of the OFS, and under the Constitution which I propose, the Volksraad or Legislative Assembly had, and would have, much more influence over the Government than a Legislative Assembly would have over the Government under the ordinary Responsible Government system. You must remember how the Boer works politics. Once his leaders are elected they are dictators. And while with Anglo-Saxons the undefined relations of the Government of the day towards the Parliament it depends on tend to the control of the Government by that Parliament, with the Boers it would have the exactly opposite effect, while the defined powers of the Volksraad under the OFS. Constitution, which I wish to repeat, were formulated for the express purpose of giving it that control.

[1] John George Fraser (1840–1927), South African politician; represented Bloemfontein in Volksraad 1880–99; Member of Parliament and Leader of Opposition, Orange River Colony; knighted 1905.

[2] James Barry Munnik Hertzog (1866–1942), lawyer, farmer and politician; Judge of the High Court, Orange Free State 1899–1902; Assistant Chief Commandant, Orange Free State 1902; a founder of the 'Orangia Unie' Boer political party 1907; Minister of Justice, Union of South Africa 1910–12, Native Affairs 1924–9; Prime Minister 1924–39; Minister of External Affairs 1929–38.

[3] Abraham Fischer (1850–1913), lawyer and politician; Member of the Joint Republican Deputation to Europe 1906–10; Chairman of the Orangia Unie 1907–10; Prime Minister, Orange River Colony 1907–10; Minister of Lands, Union of South Africa 1910–12, Interior and Lands 1912–13; PC 1911.

It is on record that President Brand[1] left it as his opinion that the Cape Colony form of Government was utterly unsuited to the OFS; at least I am told so: I am having it hunted up.

Paragraph 7. You say 'The costly and not too well informed bureaucracy of the present Transvaal Government.' This is not fair. It is not a costly Government under the circumstances of the case. Of course it is costly compared with the Government of the old SAR [South African Republic], if you leave out every collateral consideration, *viz*, that the present Government of the Transvaal is a Government in the modern acceptation of the term, whereas the SAR Government performed no function of government except to repress the British, if that was a function of government. Again, if you compare salaries of the present officials and the corresponding officials of the SAR, no doubt the present salaries are higher; but is it fair to leave out the fact that many of the late Government officials were allowed private practice of every kind, which is debarred to present officials, e.g., the present Surveyor-General of the Transvaal was Assistant-Surveyor-General of the SAR; his salary is now about twice as big as that of his chief in the old days, but he tells me that even as Assistant-Surveyor-General in the old days he made much more money than he does now, because he was allowed private practice. Also I have learned that with a few honourable exceptions, the whole hierarchy of the SAR Government was corrupt, and public opinion expected it to be corrupt. Consequently, they made a far greater profit out of their posts then than the corresponding officials do now.

I say deliberately that any Commission that investigated the work of the Government of the Transvaal or of the ORC since the war would report with amazement as to the amount and excellence of the work of reconstruction and construction done since the war. Of course mistakes, and big mistakes, have been made, but you cannot produce the complex organisation of modern civilisation out of chaos and work only with such tools as you may find to hand without making mistakes. That fact does not alter the general truth of my statement.

Paragraph 8. I need not tell you that I agree.

Paragraph 9. First of all as to the characteristics of the Boer party and British party when elected. You are absolutely correct. Under all circumstances, no matter what the differences of private opinion may be, the Boers will vote solid. The British will never vote solid except on the question of the flag, and I am not too sure about that if they are tried too high. The idea

[1] Jan Hendrik Brand (1823–88), South African politician; President of Orange Free State, 1863; re-elected 1869, 1874, 1879, 1886; he remained neutral during war between Great Britain and Transvaal in 1880 and acted as mediator at the peace conference in 1881.

that the miners and artisans and middle class here in Johannesburg will be the tools of the capitalists is the most ridiculous proposition I have ever heard. They will be just as independent as the same class at home.

Now I come to Smuts' estimate. He says that on a Voters' basis the proportion of British members would be 36 to the Boer 24. This is, I think, approximately correct, though a little over-stating it. My estimate is 35 British to 25 Boers. But that is on the supposition that the British vote solid, and that is a very big supposition, especially when you remember that the Responsible Government Party and the Political Labour League are both now in open and avowed alliance with Het Volk. But when I come to Smuts' calculation in paragraph 10, as to what the results will be on a population basis, I can only characterise his statement, that the result will be 32 British and 28 Boer members, as an impudent attempt to deceive HMG. I have gone into the matter very carefully indeed over and over again, and the very best I can make out for the British is 26 against the Boer 34. Do not think that these figures are lightly arrived at or on inadequate information. I am prepared to stand by them. I would say that I could tell almost exactly what the results would be on any basis HMG chose to take.

Paragraph 11. May I point out that you have left out two very important considerations. The first is that the British pay, as near as I can estimate it, nine-tenths of the whole taxation paid by whites, and they certainly contain nine-tenths of the education of the country. I cannot too often repeat that the Boer farmer is absolutely uneducated and consequently entirely under the thumb of the predikants. The educated Boers, like Smuts, are but a fraction of the whole Boer population and are to be found only in the towns.

One last word. I am in deep anxiety as regards the effect of the period of suspense. As far as I can make out, if a Committee is to come out and investigate and there is to be a fresh Census and Registration of voters the earliest possible moment at which Responsible Government can be started is a year hence. Now what will happen in the interval Heaven only knows? The capitalists will suffer, but I do not care for them. But the population which I do care for and cherish, miners, artisans and trading and labouring classes, will suffer quite terribly. Already the Banks are calling in all overdrawn accounts and are everywhere pressing for money that is lent. Everywhere work is being shut down; building operations are being stopped, and artisans and clerks are every day being turned off. This is not a fancy picture; it is one of very real danger and distress. The reason is that capital is frightened; the future is unsettled, the people do not know whether there is going to be a Boer Government in the country a year hence; they do not know what supply of labour there is going to be for the mines.

Now the lot of the unemployed is far worse here than it is at home. A man with a family cannot hold out here because of the cost of living, and if the period of suspense lasts for a year it is only too probable that thousands of British will be driven out of the Transvaal. Some will go to other parts of South Africa, but most I believe, will go to Canada. Now what a terrible thing it is that just as we are building up a splendid British population this should happen! And nobody knows this better than the Boers. They are rubbing their hands and chuckling to see this. They say 'this depression and suspense hits our farmers badly, but they can pull through. Your people cannot pull through, and they must go. So, whatever basis HMG eventually choose, the year's suspense will do us good.'

Was there any real necessity for this year's suspense? The Registration of Voters will be completed within a fortnight. If you want a fresh Census, as I have told Lord Elgin, the officer who took the last Census says that from the information at his disposal he can give you the present Census with real accuracy for all practical purposes. And what is the Committee of Enquiry going to do? I honestly believe that there is no information which will be given to you but that I could not give you now. But I have not been asked a single question.

Believe me, Yours sincerely
SELBORNE

H. H. Asquith to WSC

1 February 1906   Treasury Chambers

Confidential

My dear Winston,

Would it not be a good thing if you could prepare a short reasoned statement, showing in each case the grounds on which the Committee[1] arrived at the four conclusions in our report of to-day?

It might be an effective aid to the discussion of the matter by the Cabinet.

You might perhaps ask Ld Elgin whether he concurs in this suggestion.

Yrs alwys
H. H. ASQUITH

[1] See Main Volume II, p. 147.

Memorandum by WSC[1]

4 February 1906

Secret

Lord Elgin has asked me to summarize for the information of the Cabinet the principal reasons which have guided the decision of the Cabinet Committee appointed to consider the Transvaal Constitution.

1. The question must be regarded as urgent. Both races and all parties in the Transvaal have now been looking forward for nearly a year to the privilege of electing a Representative Assembly, and this was originally conceded by Lord Milner and Mr Lyttelton in deference to strong and increasing local pressure. Had there been no change of Government here, the elections would have taken place in May and the Assembly would have been at work in June. But the Lyttelton Constitution (despatch 31st March, 1905) seems, apart from other objections, unworkable; for under it a nominated Executive of six to nine members, devoid of Parliamentary experience and not possessed of any ascertained Parliamentary capacity, would have had to face a dissatisfied Assembly without the support either of a nominated majority or of an organized political party. His Majesty's Government therefore resolve on granting full responsible self-government – namely, a Representative Assembly with an Executive responsible thereto.

It is important that that change should involve no delay in the date of the elections. First, because the people of the Transvaal are already impatient of a costly and none too efficient or well-informed bureaucratic régime. Secondly, because the difficulties of the House of Commons situation may be considerable, if His Majesty's Government are forced for a prolonged or indefinite period to be *responsible* for the day-to-day administration of the Chinese Labour Ordinance, with its various objectionable features and possible recurrence of improper incidents. Time is therefore a factor which must powerfully influence, if indeed it should not govern, Cabinet policy.

2. A Constituencies Delimitation Commission has already started for South Africa, and should be at work not later than the end of February if the elections are to be held in June and the new Assembly to meet in July. Even so the first Session will be somewhat cramped; for the South African winter will already be far spent, and the hot weather in Pretoria is severe. If certain essential points in the basis of the Constitution can be settled forthwith, preliminary Letters Patent can be issued, enabling the Commission

---

[1] Cabinet Paper [African (South) No. 823] on the Transvaal Constitution.

to undertake its survey without delay. Meanwhile, the detailed and complete
Letters Patent can be sent in draft to the High Commissioner and adapted,
if desirable, to local opinion.

3. The points which immediately press for settlement are these:—

(a) Whether the basis of representation should be population or voters,
commonly called 'one vote, one value.'

(b) The number of constituencies.

(c) Whether single-member constituencies or double- or treble- member
constituencies.

(d) The margin on one side or the other to be allowed to the Delimitation
Commission in fixing the boundaries of constituencies.

(e) Whether soldiers of His Majesty's regular army should be allowed to
vote, if qualified.

To these may be added—

(f) Whether English or Dutch, or both, shall be recognized in the
proceedings of the Assembly.

4. Of these, (a), though not perhaps the most important, has become the
most controversial. No objection can be taken on grounds of principle to
either a basis of voters, or a basis of population. 'Population' is, no doubt,
more usual, but sufficient precedents exist in our Colonial system for 'voters.'
Both plans are simple, symmetrical, and democratic. But to substitute a
basis of population for the basis of voters proposed by the Lyttelton Constitution would involve, unless we proceed upon a census alleged to be
obsolete and misleading, the taking of a new one and would thus make it impossible for the elections to be held this year and for the new Assembly to
meet till April 1907. This consideration is important in view of the urgency
by which the whole question is pervaded.

The basis of voters has, in the process of discussion, become the last and
main fighting position of the British party in the Transvaal and consequently
throughout South Africa. On almost all other points at issue the wishes of
their opponents will be gratified and their view overborne. On the principle
of 'one vote, one value,' the British community, fiercely divided in much
else, is solid. The abandonment of this principle by His Majesty's Government will certainly be regarded by them as a mortal injury; and although
their view of its actual importance is no doubt extravagant, the mere fact
that nearly half the population of the Transvaal will *think,* however unjustifiably, they have been betrayed will in itself prevent the resulting
settlement from being accepted as fair and even-handed dealing between the
two conflicting races. It should be added that Lord Selborne seems to have
committed himself so strongly in favour of the existing basis, that he might
find it difficult to recede.

It is quite true that a basis of voters is more to the advantage of the British as against the Dutch, and of the town as against the country, than a population basis. But after all the result is to make the vote of the adult white male exactly equal all over the Transvaal irrespective of race or condition – a proposition not in itself indefensible – whereas a basis of population, on the other hand, makes the vote of the adult country Boer of considerably higher value than the vote of the adult British voter, who is hindered from marrying or bringing in his family by the very high cost of living in the towns. Further, the British in the towns pay not less than nine-tenths of the whole taxation of the Transvaal; and although this may not prove that they should therefore have more voting power, it certainly does not prove that they should have less.

Upon the basis of 'one vote, one value' a working British, or, to speak correctly, 'non-Dutch,' majority will probably be secured. But the Boer country party will be the most formidable homogeneous body in the State. Although in an actual minority, they will be united, while their opponents are already divided by every question which in this country separates capitalist from miner, and Liberal from Tory; and, except upon a naked race issue, the Boers will obtain powerful support outside the limits of their party organization, both in the new Assembly and in the constituencies which elect it. Reviewing, therefore, the urgency of the matter, the delay and disturbance involved in alteration, the certain resentment of the British population, and believing that 'one vote, one value' will be, if not ideally the best settlement, probably upon the whole the best practical settlement now open to us, and regarding it as in itself fair, legitimate, and even-handed as between the two races, the Cabinet Committee have come to the conclusion that the existing basis of voters should be retained.

5. (b) Although thirty constituencies is the number originally contemplated by the Lyttelton Constitution, an increase to sixty involves no delay, and the Delimitation Commission can proceed at once on either hypothesis. Sixty members are certainly needed for the effective working of Responsible Government. The greater number of seats favours the representation of local minorities – otherwise likely to be swamped – and is in itself, a partial safeguard against corruption. Oddly enough, this increase appears to be desired by both parties in the Transvaal, and is one of the very few points on which they are agreed. Sixty seats are therefore recommended.

6. (c) Single-member constituencies seem to be the only plan which has been seriously considered in the Transvaal. In a country where the distances are so great and means of communication poor, it is already a matter of difficulty for candidates to present themselves to their electorates. To adopt two-member or three-member seats is to double or treble this difficulty.

The experience of the Cape Colony, particularly in the Worcester district, a three-barrelled constituency returning three Bond members in spite of a strong Progressive majority in Worcester town, seems to show that these intricate and attractive devices for securing minority representation do not in all cases command the success that their merits deserve and their inventors claim. The decision of the Cabinet Committee was therefore to recommend single-member districts. But it is thought that the margin in delimitation (d) – 5 per cent both ways – proposed by Mr Lyttelton and favoured with a slight discretionary power by Lord Selborne does not give sufficient elasticity. 10 per cent both ways, that is to say, a total variation of 20 per cent, will give adequate discretion to the Delimitation Commissioners*, who can be thoroughly trusted to use their power impartially, and may, to some extent, enable them to meet the grievances of large sparsely populated districts formerly represented in the Volksraad. This latitude will, it is believed, be agreeable to the Boers, as correcting in a measure any arbitrary incidence of 'one vote, one value,' in particular cases. (e). Further, the Boers have always protested vehemently against the military vote. The British party are, on the other hand, determined to poll all soldiers whose qualifications place them on the register (800). Mr Lyttelton himself did not approve of this; but unless the Letters Patent are altered, the question would be one for the Courts of the Transvaal, and high legal opinion suggests that the right of qualified soldiers to vote could be sustained in law. It is proposed forthwith to amend the Letters Patent to prevent what would be evidently an anomaly and an abuse.

7. The language question has been much disputed. The British party wish to make English the only recognized language, and while not refusing to allow members to speak in Dutch, contend, variously, that permission should in each case be asked from the Speaker of the Assembly or that speeches made in Dutch should be afterwards interpreted. Lord Selborne and his Executive Council, while recognizing the right of members to address the House in either language, think that the records of Parliamentary proceedings should be kept only in English. The Cabinet Committee recommends that absolute lingual equality should be formally established in the Letters Patent, that members should be allowed to speak indifferently in Dutch or English, and that records and Minutes of the House should be kept in both languages. As a matter of fact there is every probability that English will in practice prevail, and that the best way to keep the Dutch language – or, rather, the 'Taal' dialect – alive would be to proscribe it. But the admission of lingual equality is one which is precious to a small people, and the concession, if made at all, should be made frankly and generously.

* Colonel Johnston, RE, Sir W. Smith, a Judge of the Transvaal, and Mr Justice Lawrence, a Judge of the Cape Colony.

8. Two other most important matters must be determined before the fundamentals of the Transvaal Constitution can be considered settled, viz., the provision or omission of a second Chamber, nominated or elective; and the continued existence, position, functions, and character of the Inter-Colonial Council. There is also the question of the Constitution of the Orange River Colony. But none of these are affected by the same degree of urgency, for they do not interpose delay in the proceedings of the Delimitation Commission.

WSC

Leo Amery[1] to WSC

7 February 1906   2 Temple Gardens

My dear Churchill,

I hope you won't think I am pressing if I write to you about this South African franchise business, but I have been getting a good many letters from people out there and there can be no doubt that they are getting very excited at the idea of what the Government may do. I don't want to go into the merits of the case – I expect you know them well enough – but only into just this point, namely that the British Transvaalers there have come to consider the existing scheme as the charter of their liberties, & that if it is altered nothing will persuade them that it was not done for the sake of the *'beaux yeux'* of Mr Smuts. I cannot see myself why on earth anybody should want to alter the Lyttelton scheme (barring the change to full responsible Government). It is quite democratic; it met with no serious criticism when A. Lyttelton formulated it; you can take all the credit you like for giving responsible government.

On the other hand if you make a change, Smuts' gratitude will take no very tangible form, whereas Johannesburg's – or rather British South Africa's – indignation will lead to a pretty vigorous explosion out there, & I expect to something of the same kind here at home. These things won't upset a Government with so mighty a majority: still if you are going to be in for a good many years it would be a pity to start off with a fixed feud between you and all the loyalist element in South Africa, & with a general reawaken-

---

[1] Leopold Stennett Amery (1873–1955), member of the Editorial staff of *The Times* 1899–1909; he organised *The Times* war correspondents in S. Africa (1898–1900), and wrote *The Times History of the S. African War* (7 vols), which was completed in 1909; at Harrow with WSC. Unionist MP for Sparkbrook 1911–45; Assistant Secretary War Cabinet and Imperial War Cabinet 1917; Parliamentary Under-Secretary for the Colonies 1919–21; Parliamentary and Financial Secretary to the Admiralty 1921–2; First Lord of the Admiralty 1922–4; Secretary of State for Dominion Affairs 1925–9, for India and Burma 1940–5; PC 1922; CH 1945.

ing of distrust on the part of all sorts of people in this country who had in the last year or two got very tired of your predecessors. Of course, for all I may know, as distinguished from rumours and alarms, you may never have been intending any change whatever. In any case it would be an excellent thing if you could stop the excitement out there – and the beginnings of excitement here – by declaring that all this alarm is groundless & making clear exactly what you do intend doing.

> Yours sincerely
> L. S. AMERY

Memorandum by WSC[1]

24 February 1906

Since taking office I have, with Lord Elgin's full consent, made it my business to see persons representative of every class, section, and interest in South Africa, who either desired to lay their views before the Government, or who I considered might have information of a useful character to impart. Thus I have had conversations with Mr Smuts, Mr Creswell,[2] Mr Massingham, Mr S. Evans,[3] Sir Somers Vine,[4] and many others.

The question of repatriating those coolies who wished to return to China has always attracted my personal interest in a special degree. I desired particularly to find out what proportion of coolies would be likely to avail themselves of the boon which it was proposed to offer them; and apart from the official enquiries which were made of Lord Selborne and are published in the Blue Book (Cd 2819), I put the suggestion, hypothetically, to the two most prominent representatives on either side of the Chinese question, whom I knew personally, Mr Creswell and Mr Beit.

Mr Creswell expressed the opinion that the plan was a dangerous one, for that so many coolies would claim repatriation that an economic collapse might easily ensue in Johannesburg. Mr Beit also disapproved of the project: but for quite a different reason. He thought the coolies were very well treated and quite contented with their lot, and that, therefore, very few of

[1] This memorandum was prepared by WSC after Joseph Chamberlain had alleged in the House of Commons that, before deciding on the repatriation of Chinese labourers, Ministers had consulted with ' "Magnates" who are not creditable acquaintances and who live in palaces, usually in Park Lane.'
[2] Frederick Hugh Page Creswell (1866–1948), South African businessman, soldier, and politician. One of the leaders of movement to abolish Chinese Labour. Member of Union Parliament 1910–38; Minister of Defence 1924–33; Minister of Labour 1924–5, 1929–33.
[3] Superintendent of Foreign Labour in the Transvaal.
[4] John Richard Somers Vine (1847–1929), superintending editor for Messrs. Waterlow and Sons 1876–86; official Agent to Fisheries, Health, Inventions and Exhibitions 1883–6; Assistant Secretary Imperial Institute 1886–97; knighted 1886.

them would wish to return; but he thought that the option which was extended to them, would be likely to lead to insubordination, and make the task of mine managers more difficult. Both these views appear to me to be perfectly sincere, though I do not, myself, agree with either, believing the probability to lie between the two extremes.

These inquiries which I made were of course private inquiries to find out as nearly as possible what was the truth of the matter, and to guide me in forming an opinion. The Cabinet which decided in favour of repatriation knew nothing of such inquiries, or of the answers to them.

I do not know how the Right Honourable Member for West Birmingham [Joseph Chamberlain] was led to the belief that 'the terms of this alteration were submitted to the magnates before they were submitted to the House of Commons.' I presume he must have overheard some private conversation, have learned in confidence that I had made such an inquiry, or in some way caught the tail-end of some drifting gossip about a plan for repatriation which was being considered by the Government; and that thereupon he thought it proper to assert that the Government had submitted their proposals to the mining magnates; and that he hoped to gain some advantage by making the allegation on the verge of an important division.

WSC

Sir Walter Hely-Hutchinson to WSC

28 February 1906   Cape Town

Dear Winston,

I have been reading your father's life: & I hope you will let me say that I think the work is most admirably done. You have managed just to find the golden mean between bald chronicle and superabundant comment – the book is interesting throughout; and whilst nothing is neglected or omitted which is necessary to complete the picture with all its lights & shades, there is no unnecessary elaboration – nothing to indicate the personality of the artist – nothing, except the evident pleasure which he takes in his work, to show the deep affection & regard which he feels towards his subject. I have bought the book & shall read it again.

The Natal native disturbance seems to have simmered down: but we have still to hear how things go in the Mapumulo district. There has been a rather rowdy meeting in Cape Town on the subject of free trade vs protection – the free traders were howled down. The free traders say the meeting was packed. I don't know how this may be but think it quite possible. 'Free trader', here, means a man who does not wish to see additional duties, especially on food. Few people wish to take off any of the existing duties, which are high.

Yours sincerely
WALTER HELY-HUTCHINSON

J. Keir Hardie[1] to WSC

8 March 1906 House of Commons

Dear Mr Churchill,

Several attempts have been made to induce the Colonial Office to inquire into the circumstances of the great cattle sweep which took place in the northern district of Natal after the Boers had been driven back into their own country in the early stages of the War.

The facts as submitted to me are that the farmers – Dutch and British alike – in the district were quite loyal and intended remaining so until they were *forced by the Boer invaders to enlist in their ranks*. In the absence of any protection whatever they had no option whatever but to yield to the pressure which they allege was put upon them. Subsequently they returned to their homes and it was understood that they were again under British Protection and it was whilst they were in this frame of mind that the whole of their cattle were taken from them, not, it appears, for the use of the troops but simply as a form of punishment.

Doubtless you are aware of the whole facts of the case which I need not go into at greater length but would suggest that some inquiry be made into the circumstances. The people feel that they have been very badly treated and now that an effort is being made to set up peaceful relations all round it would be a pity if this corner of Natal were left with a rankling of injustice in the minds of its people.

I should be glad to hear from you on the point and meanwhile I am,

Yours very truly
J. KEIR HARDIE

WSC to Lord Selborne

11 March 1906 Colonial Office

[Copy]

Personal and Secret

My dear Lord Selborne,

I share your anxiety at the protracted delay in effecting a settlement; and so far as I am able to exert any influence upon events, I have tried to

---

[1] James Keir Hardie (1856–1915), Labour MP for S. West Ham 1892–5, Merthyr 1900–15; chairman of newly formed Independent Labour Party 1893–1900 and 1913–15; first leader of Labour Party in Parliament 1906–7.

end it. I expect we shall get the cabinet to agree to one vote one value with manhood suffrage as the basis; and I hope that this can be declared – with if possible, without if necessary, the assent of Het Volk – before this letter reaches you. The committee – three shrewd and trusty persons – can then proceed to investigate at their leisure (a) minor points connected with the Transvaal constitution (b) ICC [Inter Colonial Council] (c) 2nd Chamber and (d) Orange River Colony constitution. But I feel that for public convenience and commercial security the 'fundamentals' of the Transvaal constitution must be settled first and placed above the reach of eager factions. These are of course my own private views; but I have now hopes of seeing them become effective.

I am anxious, as I cabled to you, about Repatriation. It is a plan in which I have always taken particular interest, and I feel that from a H of Coms point of view it is of high and real value. I hope that not more than 3,000 and not less than 1500 coolies will take advantage of it. I do not want to see a collapse of industry; but on the other hand the mine owners will be great fools if they try to bring this scheme into ridicule by making it inoperative. We have already suffered embarrassment in the House by being reproached from the Conservative benches with not taking sufficiently drastic action against the Chinese. I do not at all complain of such party attacks which are quite fair and perhaps not undeserved. But the only result is to provoke the extremists of our party still further – to the excessive sorrow of the mining interest. This has now I think been realized in the City.

I must tell you that I think this H of C will insist *coute que coute* upon the expulsion of the Chinese and the complete ending of the experiment. All reasonable and even generous time will be secured by the Government for a gradual change, but I should mislead you if I pretended that there is any chance whatever of the question being allowed to drop. If the Transvaal Assembly re-enact the Ordinance, it will certainly be vetoed here, unless the objectionable features are removed. As these cannot be removed – without the Chinese overrunning the country, to which SA will never consent – there can, as I foresee things, be only one end.

In these circumstances surely it would be wiser to look abroad for substitutes. Why has the Indian coolie been ruled summarily out of the problem? Could not some concessions be made to the Indian Government in respect of the general status of Indians in the Transvaal as a quid pro quo for a supply of coolies? I think John Morley would be willing to reopen the question; and I am trying to raise it again from this end.

I have ventured to write to you with candour and I hope you will understand that I feel a very real and lively sympathy with the difficulties of your task and appreciate the anxieties and vexations by which you must be harassed. Everyone who knows is grateful to you for the efforts you are making to serve strange masters, and I myself believe that all will come right at the end of a long and dangerous journey.

With all good wishes

Believe me, Yours sincerely
WINSTON S. CHURCHILL

Letter to a Correspondent

WSC addressed this letter to a correspondent who had drawn his attention to the fall in the price of South African shares. Copies were sent to the Press on the following day, and widely published.

15 March 1906   Downing Street

Dear Sir,

Any depreciation in South African securities which may have followed from the debate in the House of Commons on Wednesday last is due far less to the statements of Government policy than to the lugubrious and pessimistic orations of Mr Balfour and Mr Chamberlain. The policy of the Government, though more elaborately explained, was in no way extended beyond the limits assigned to it in the previous speeches of Mr Asquith and Lord Elgin. But every effort was made by the leaders of the Opposition to create a feeling of despondency and apprehension: and, as they are aided in these mischievous endeavours by a vast newspaper organisation here and in the South African Colonies, it is no great wonder that they should attain some measure of success, which is of course accurately and immediately reflected in the share markets.

Mr Chamberlain's course through these South African debates seems to me to have been especially deplorable. I cannot recognise that he has even attempted to restrain his partisanship in dealing with matters of grave concern to everyone, of peculiar significance to him. In the debate on the Address he was at such pains to prove that the policy of the Government in regard to Chinese Labour was an unreal policy, and amounted practically to nothing, that he even asserted that it was a policy upon which the mine-owners had been consulted and with which they were perfectly satisfied. This having failed to sow dissension among the supporters of the Ministry, Mr Chamberlain entirely shifted his ground; and on Wednesday last he dwelt with portentous solemnity upon what he represented to be an approaching conflict between the Mother Country and South Africa.

Yet if His Majesty's Government had announced an intention of leaving the whole question of Chinese Labour to the unfettered and final decision of a Transvaal assembly, Mr Chamberlain would have been the first to exclaim, as he exclaimed last sesssion, 'What! Slavery under the Union Jack!' Such tactics are no doubt not unusual among irresponsible politicians on the look-out in Opposition for a chance to embarrass a Ministry; but they ill become the statesman at whose bidding this country has squandered upon South Africa blood and treasure inestimable.

Yours faithfully
[WINSTON S. CHURCHILL]

Lord Elgin to WSC

15 March 1906   76 Eaton Square

My dear Churchill,

It is not from any want of sympathy that I should prefer not to send out this Minute to-night. The Cabinet is for another purpose to-morrow & the introduction of a discussion on this – which must be prolonged – would cause much inconvenience. Moreover if we submit it (and I should like time to consider that carefully and to discuss with you) it will come with more effect if this is done together with the Terms of Reference next Wedy. In the interval I might sound some others.

I must however add that I fear from what I have heard said that it would be difficult to get an agreement.

Excuse haste in writing – but I feel my opinion on the case is deliberate enough, for I have had something of the kind in my mind.

Sorry you are to have a late night. I shall hope to get away from Cabinet in time to see you to-morrow.

Yours v truly
ELGIN

I kept the Memo to study this evening

WSC to Lord Elgin

15 March 1906   [Colonial Office]

Secret

Lord Elgin,

An increasing disquietude about South African affairs induces me to submit this Minute to you.

1. I fear the effects of delay in deciding the fundamentals of the Transvaal Constitution. It causes uncertainty to pervade all classes and both races, not only in the Transvaal, but throughout South Africa. This uncertainty is at once economic and political. It excites the fiercest racial passions. It makes everybody lose their money. In Johannesburg itself there is produced a practical suspension of credit. The enormous depreciation of shares and fall in values is accompanied by an increasing want of employment, without any apparatus of relief. Physical suffering is therefore one of the results of the prevailing political instability. And the vexation, and, indeed, exasperation which is produced in an arrogant, highly excitable population by the feeling that their most vital interests are held in suspense from day to day, and even from month to month, may provoke a bitter hatred against His Majesty's Government.

2. Who are to be our friends in the Transvaal? I would do strict justice to the Boers; but when we remember that 20,000 of their women and children perished in our concentration camps in the year 1901–1902, is it wise to count too much upon their good offices in 1906? And if we are to consider at all as one of the pillars of our power the loyalty of the British, are we not subjecting them to a terrible strain? I am certain that the House of Commons will insist – and, I think, rightly insist – upon the ultimate repatriation of all the Chinese. But I believe that this policy – severe in itself – to which we are committed, would prove far less detrimental to material interests if it were not aggravated by a paralysing uncertainty as to the political future of the country.

Certain I am that while this uncertainty continues everything that goes wrong in the Transvaal, and much must necessarily go wrong, will be ascribed to His Majesty's Government and to the interference or to the hesitation of the outside power. Remember that the worst possible construction is always placed on our motives and our words. The most extreme and sinister intentions are attributed to us, and the whole British population are taught by lying newspapers to regard us with resentment and distrust. It is idle to answer that it serves them right for believing such things. We have to deal with the facts as they are. And the fact which glares me in the face is that a six months' delay in settling the fundamentals of the Constitution will, through economic pressure and political uncertainty, drive many British voters from the Transvaal, and alienate from the Mother Country the affections of the rest.

3. I cannot think that this is altogether unnatural. It is only four years ago that we – the Imperial Government – exhorted the British population, by every appeal to honour and allegiance, to take our side in a savage war. Now the very root issue of the war seems to them held in suspense, a matter

to be discussed with composure, a matter even of indifference to His Majesty's Government. And yet in response to our appeals individuals have run great risks to life and lands, and have incurred deadly animosities. *They* do not know that the Cabinet, while anxious to do what is fair and right between both races, while resolved not to lend themselves to anything like a trick, are absolutely determined to maintain, in the words of Lord Durham's Report, 'a numerical majority of a loyal and English population.' *They* only hear the worst of us. And every debate which necessarily takes place in the House of Commons increases their apprehension and their anger. If, after a thorough alienation of the British population through months of uncertainty, we are on top of all to demand repatriation of the Chinese (as we certainly must), what will be left to us of the already precarious basis of British power?

Will not both races join together in common repudiation of an authority which has (as they will believe) been exercised without regard to their sentiments, and with disastrous effects upon their welfare? I was always in my heart against the annexation of the Republics. But it would be far better to give the country back to the Boers as a great act of renunciation and of justice than to fritter it away piecemeal.

4. What to do? I urge most earnestly the following plan:— Appoint the Committee. Solemnly declare in its reference that the principle of one vote one value, *plus* manhood suffrage, must be regarded as the fundamental basis of the Transvaal Constitution. With these two guard rails firmly fixed let them proceed to their work. Let them examine (1) whether constituencies should be single member or treble member; (2) what means can be taken to secure some labour representation in Johannesburg; (3) Second Chamber; (4) Intercolonial Council; and (5) (which does not press) constitution of the Orange River Colony. Instruct them to furnish their report on these matters (or at any rate on (1), (2), and (3)) at the earliest moment; and, in the meanwhile, let Lord Selborne at once set to work to prepare the new register on the basis of manhood suffrage.

I would not write so strongly on this subject if I did not know that these opinions are not opposed to your own, and if I did not feel a darkening anxiety about our immediate policy.

WSC

T. W. Gibson Bowles to WSC

16 March 1906   25 Lowndes Square

My dear Churchill,

I am not sure, that, in the absence of any Report of a Commission or of a House of Commons Committee bringing Lord Milner's conduct officially before the House there may not arise a technical default of evidence to support a vote of censure.[1] His admission in the Lords cannot be brought to the official & formal knowledge of the Commons without some difficulty.

I conceive he might be examined at the Bar. But I am not sure he could be examined as to what passed in the Lords without a Lords' leave.

In short I rather lean to the view that, before censuring any man, but especially a member of the other House, some firmer or more formal foundation should be laid than at present exists.

I have no opportunity at present of referring to precedents – nor have I indeed referred to the despatches – which I presume were laid by *command* (not an unimportant circumstance) and am therefore not so soaked with the facts as I always try to be before coming to any conclusion.

I should suggest, for instance, reference to Lord Melville's case in 1805 & to the Mrs Clarke & Duke of York's case in, I think, 1809.

It is essential that the accused should have fair & customary 'law'.

Apart from this, I can conceive nothing that more urgently demands the censure of Parliament than the conduct of a High Commissioner who tricks the laws of his country, violates a Treaty with another country, & whether by act or by neglect, deceives the King's Ministers to whom he owes his commission.

Whether such a censure should be followed by other action is another matter. '*Hay tiempo.*' One step at a time.

The argument that because he was in a high position he ought not to be attacked for misdeeds is really an argument the other way. The highly placed misdoer should come up first for punishment.

But to revert. Do be sure that the ground on which the first step is to be taken is made quite good.

Faithfully yours

T. W. GIBSON BOWLES

---

[1] On 27 February 1906 Lord Milner had admitted in the House of Lords that, while he was High Commissioner for South Africa – 1897–1905 – he had sanctioned the flogging of Chinese labourers in breach of the law. He said that the canings were inflicted only for acts of violence and disturbances which it was thought necessary to repress in the interests of the coolies themselves. He added that, in the light of subsequent events, such punishment was wrong and that had he continued on as High Commissioner after 1905 he would have put a stop to it. But William Byles, Radical MP for Salford North, put down a motion in the House of Commons censuring Lord Milner's conduct; this was debated on 21 March.

WSC to Lord Selborne

17 March 1906

[Copy]

Most Private

My dear Ld Selborne,

Let me thank you for the interesting telegram which you sent me about manhood suffrage and High Dutch. I have done & am doing my utmost to secure immediate declaration in favour of the principles of one vote one value plus manhood suffrage – I think if this were made there would be less uncertainty & apprehension among the British. But you will understand how likely a Cabinet is to incline to the 'safer' course of awaiting the report of a Committee on all the aspects of the question.

The position in the H of C is difficult because no Ministry will quarrel with even a section of its supporters until the last moment is reached; and until this week this difficulty has been aggravated by repeated tauntings from the opposition benches that we were not fulfilling our Chinese pledges. Since Mr Balfour has returned however a much more sober line has been and I think will be taken. Further there is this difficulty that the Labour Party & the advanced Radicals would avoid all danger of conflict between HMG and the Transvaal Assembly by making sure that that assembly was so constituted as to terminate Chinese Labour of its own accord, even if to secure this they had utterly & irretrievably to smash the British party. Now I – who hate Chinese labour as much as I honour the Flag – am most anxious to keep these two things separate. I am certain that one vote one value would perish if it had also to bear the weight of the final decision on Chinese Labour. It would be said 'you have packed the Transvaal Assembly to suit the magnates and you have virtually perpetuated Chinese labour by a trick.' Therefore I dwell upon the veto which reserves the Chinese question to the Crown and leaves us free to constitute the Assembly on a just and equal basis.

I am afraid you only get the worst reports of us in S. Africa, and every word is made to look as menacing & hostile as possible by the enormous power of the metropolitan press and all its ramifications – & hitherto we have had no words of real comfort to speak. But I trust this period will not be prolonged & that perhaps before this reaches you something may have been said to allay the anxiety and I must say to improve the temper of our excitable British friends.

Such an occasion may perhaps arise on Wednesday night when a motion is to be brought forward censuring Ld Milner for the sanction of illegal flogging. I have I believe persuaded the Govt to allow me to meet this resolution by an amendment deprecating any formal censure of individuals in the interests of peace and reconciliation in SA. It will be a difficult job to persuade the House but I hope I shall be allowed to try.

I don't write all this to you in order to excite your sympathy with the various vexations of a Liberal Ministry – but I think you ought to understand the difficulties as they present themselves in the House of Commons; & I feel that perhaps a knowledge of those difficulties may make your mind easier about Parliamentary incidents & utterances.

Don't forget the Indian coolie – much may depend on him.

Yours sincerely
WSC

Lord Loreburn to WSC

18 March 1906   8 Eaton Square

My dear Mr Churchill,

Let me add a word to what was said at the Prime Minister's yesterday. I do not wish to be unjust to Milner and I wholly agree with the view you indicated that this country is too great & our success at the election too overwhelming and the situation in S. Africa too critical to warrant our engaging in the task of making martyrs. And therefore I heartily concur in the course you suggested. What I feel I did not quite express is that those whom Milner and his friends have habitually insulted and those who have suffered by the war in this country would be profoundly irritated by anything like *commendation* of Milner. I believe they will be quite willing to refrain from censure, but I am certain they would be restive if they were asked to endorse praise. It is one of the best features of our public life that we are disposed to be generous to opponents. On the other hand there are many of us who believe after close study that Milner has not only been rash but also deceitful and that the more the thing is investigated the more it will appear that he has engineered the war by forcing the hands of foolish ministers. If we lose South Africa it will be almost wholly his doing and his folly or worse has led to the postponement of social reform for our own poor people at home. He has received honours and incense while ruining South Africa.

Under these circumstances (and my view is very widely held) I would submit to you that he is very well treated and very generously if he is simply exempted from attack. I am told no one in S. Africa believes in him now.

Will you excuse my writing in an abridged form, giving conclusions & not reasons, for you know the story & no doubt have judged it all for yourself. You will I know say exactly the right thing & if you don't accept my views

I shall feel sure that there is more to be said against them than I have myself perceived. Will you tell Lord Elgin?

Vy sincerely yours
LOREBURN

In the House of Commons on March 21, WSC defended the government's position on Chinese labour. He also attacked Joseph Chamberlain for his conduct in the matter, claiming that he had aggravated the situation by his emotional speeches.

WSC then turned his attention to the motion of William Byles[1] to censure Lord Milner. Although he sympathized with the motion, he felt that in the interests of peace and conciliation in South Africa Members should refrain from passing censure upon individuals. He therefore added an amendment to the motion condemning only in general terms the flogging of Chinese coolies.

Byles' motion was negatived and WSC's amendment was carried by 355 votes against 135.

Sir William Anson[2] to J. G. Talbot
(*Talbot Papers*)

EXTRACT

23 March 1906   St Raphael-Valescure
France

... What a wretched figure the Government made over the Milner debate. They ought surely not to have left this matter in the hands of Winston Churchill who seems to have been both pompous and impertinent.

It is terrible to think what harm that young jackanapes may do with a big majority behind him and an incompetent Prime Minister to look after him. . . .

WSC to Lord Selborne

24 March 1906

[Copy]

Dear Lord Selborne,

I daresay the reference to the Committee will disappoint those who had

---

[1] William Pollard Byles (1839–1917), Radical MP for Shipley 1892–5, for Salford North 1906–17; knighted 1911.
[2] William Reynell Anson (1843–1914), Unionist MP for Oxford University 1899–1914; Parliamentary Secretary to the Board of Education 1902–5; Warden of All Souls' 1881–1914; succeeded father as 3rd baronet 1873; PC 1911.

hoped for some decided pronouncement in favour of one vote, one value. I laboured to that end as hard as I could, and I enclose you a Minute which I wrote on the question, but this somewhat colourless document was the best that could be obtained. Still if you read between the lines you will see that it tacitly presupposes that the Voters basis will be maintained, and if the British party are clever, they will read that construction into it, and force it to take that colour. At any rate, you may be quite easy in your mind about the final result so far as the Cabinet is concerned. Indeed I think the decision will ultimately be reached without any difficulty or division.

Asquith showed me your letter to him about the Constitution. I think you are very wise to correspond with Ministers. It helps very much to solidify opinion.

I am still hankering after Indians, even if we could get 10,000 looming in the distance that would prevent the feeling of apprehension which the prospect of contraction in the Labour supply no doubt excites. But there seem to be many difficulties, principally this, that there are no Indians to spare of the hardy Hill type that alone can work the Mines.

I had an anxious day in the House on Wednesday but in the result no harm seems to have been done either to the markets or to the party. That at least is something. I think the South African papers are very ill natured about the Govt. After all, no other course but the one adopted by me would have prevented Lord Milner from being censured formally by the House of Commons. We interfered to parry the blow and did parry it, much to the disgust of many of our supporters. Surely that fact ought to have received the recognition of South African observers: instead nothing appears but the (angry comments) of the (great) political organisation of the Metropolitan dailies.

I write this not because I personally mind criticism, but because I think it is a dangerous thing for the whole loyal British press in South Africa to go on howling at a Government, which for good or ill, is a concrete fact and likely to remain so for a considerable time.

Note on WSC's copy: There was no time to copy the remainder before posting. It was mostly about Sir Francis Hopwood's[1] appointment to the Commission.

[WINSTON S. CHURCHILL]

---

[1] Francis John Stephen Hopwood (1860–1947), Permanent Secretary, Board of Trade 1901–7; member of the West Ridgeway Commission to South Africa 1906; Permanent Secretary, Colonial Office 1907–12; Additional Civil Lord of the Admiralty 1910–12; Secretary to the Irish Convention 1917–18; President of the Reform Commission to India 1918–19; Baron Southborough 1919.

J. C. Smuts to Margaret Clark[1]
(Smuts Archive)

EXTRACT

25 March 1906   Pretoria

... I see our friend Winston is occupying the stage under the full limelight and that his pity for the Chinese-flogging Milner is no less Olympian than for the benighted radical who thought the Chinese indentures partook of the nature of slavery. ....

WSC to Lord Selborne

TELEGRAM

4 April 1906

Personal & Secret

Your proposals Chinese repatriation sound quite good but protracted delay may deprive concession virtue & effect. Surely you can so draft & work regulations as to cut off slice of right thickness say one thousand. So long as substantial attempt fulfil pledges Parliament I can defend even if extremists not satisfied. At present Commons believe we are dealing fairly with them and consequently things much easier but disastrous forfeit confidence.

Lord Selborne to WSC

8 April 1906   Kimberley

Private

My dear Churchill,

Many thanks for your most interesting letter of the 17th March. It is a great help to me to know the inside of things.

I fasten naturally on this sentence in your letter:—

'Further, there is this difficulty, that the Labour Party and the advanced Radicals will avoid all danger of a conflict between HMG and the Transvaal Assembly by making sure that that Assembly was so constituted as to terminate Chinese labour of its own accord, even if to secure this they utterly and irretrievably smash the British Party.'

---

[1] Margaret Clark (1878–1962), grand-daughter of John Bright; a Quaker, suffragist, and supporter of the Liberal Party; visited South Africa with Emily Hobhouse in 1905 and began a life-long friendship with Smuts.

Now I say to you with the most absolute conviction of truth, as earnestly and sincerely as I can, that, if these advanced gentlemen really think by utterly and irretrievably smashing the British party, they would have secured the termination of Chinese labour by giving the Boers the majority, I cannot imagine a more amazing case of self-deception. The Boers have not an ounce of principle in their composition against Chinese labour. Their only real objection to Chinese labour in its present form is that it is not servile enough, that is, that the Chinese are not shut up in compounds. The comparatively few Boer farmers who live close to the Witwatersrand of course dislike the Chinese labourers because their women folk have been frightened, and naturally frightened, by the outrages of a few Chinese ruffians. But even these very farmers realise the great value of the market which the Chinese have given them.

And do you seriously suppose that the enormous majority of Boers in the country, who suffer nothing, not even fright, from these outrages, desire to get rid of this source of so much Revenue which they can spend upon themselves, and of a market where they do sell their produce so profitably? No, the Boers have passed as opponents of the Chinese only because they are such good party politicians. They knew that to do so would please the Radicals, who are their friends, and they saw at once the immense value of the question to them as a matter of bargain. It is only in the spirit of bargain that they would use the question if they got the power. They would laugh at the Radicals who had given them the power. They would use the power for themselves. They would say to the mining industry: 'You want your Chinese labour, what will you give us in return?' It would simply be a bargain, as a result of which Chinese labour would remain; but the British Flag would have been sold, first, by your advanced friends at home, and secondly, by a certain section of the British population in the Transvaal. The short-sightedness of your advanced friends is amazing. I am not speculating on the Boer attitude. The leaders do not conceal it in confidential conversation, as I have told Ld E.

There is only one section in the Transvaal who are really opposed on principle to Chinese labour, and that is a section of the British miners. These are the very men whom your advanced friends propose to tie hand and foot by giving the country over to the Boers, who, although they have once more shown their astuteness by making an open alliance with the Labour Party at the present moment, would simply swallow them once they had full power. Politically there is in the whole world no two people so absolutely incompatible as the British Labour man and the Boer farmer.

No, amongst the British Labour Party there is a real body of opinion against Chinese labour. How big it is I cannot tell you.

I do not think, to be honest, that it embraces the majority of the white miners; but it embraces a larger proportion of them than I thought four months ago. I think what has happened in England has distinctly reacted upon them, and that what I said at that time was not inaccurate then.

Now, if anybody tells you that these white miners are going to be the tools of the capitalists, he is simply telling you an absurd falsehood. The Colonial miner and workman is not less but more independent than his fellow who has never left the United Kingdom, and in this matter, though I shall not be believed, my interests and those of the Labour Party and the advanced Radicals are identical. I want to give the fullest measure of political power possible to the British in the Transvaal in order to preserve the Flag. For those who want to see the greatest amount of power given to those who would oppose Chinese labour, the only possible policy is to give it to the British and not to the Boers.

You again tell me not to forget the Indian coolie. I have told you in a previous letter where the essence of the matter lies. There really is no use in beginning to think about them unless I know the views of the Indian Government and of John Morley.

Believe me Yours sincerely
SELBORNE

WSC to Alfred Lyttelton

10 April 1906   Colonial Office

[Copy]

My dear Lyttelton,

If I may judge from your letter in this morning's *Times*, you seem very completely to have misunderstood the argument of my speech on Thursday. I have just consulted the Hansard verbatim report and I cannot find in it any grounds for the conclusions you have formed. I did not say – still less did I intend to say – that the basis of your Constitution was intentionally unfair. I examined it at length for the purpose of approving the principle of one vote one value. I showed that that principle could in the Transvaal only be obtained upon a Voter's basis. I was forced to own that a Voter's basis was unusual in British Colonies and foreign states, and that it was not the basis of this country; but I sought to explain that this singularity was not due to any denial of the principle of one vote one value, because in almost every other state except the Transvaal, the differences between a distribution of seats on the basis of voters and a distribution of seats on the basis of population were inconsiderable. That is what I meant when I said that in every other country for the purpose of distribution of seats 'population is the same as the electorate and the electorate the same as population.' This is certainly a generalisation; but how is it absurd?

I proceeded to examine your franchise. I was careful to make it clear that while £100 annual value is an artificial franchise, I did not condemn it in the case of the Transvaal as an undemocratic franchise; and of this you must be aware as I observe the terms of your letter upon this point follow almost word for word the argument which I employed. Indeed after carefully reading your letter, I frankly do not understand what your quarrel is with this part of my reasoning.

Having thus examined the two main propositions in your Constitutional system, I argued that though one was desirable and both were defensible, yet the basis of voters could not escape the epithet 'unusual' and that the franchise deserved that of 'artificial.' Upon this I find myself reported to have said: 'Taking these two points together, the unusual basis of distribution with the apparently artificial franchise acting and reacting as they must one upon another – there is sufficient ground to favour the suspicion, at any rate, that something was intended in the nature of a trick artificially to depress the balance in one direction and to tilt it in the other. . . .

'The Government are concerned in South Africa not only to do what is fair, but to do what South Africa will accept as fair – not merely to choose a balance which will deal evenly between the races but which will secure the acceptance of both races.'

This statement taken by itself – still more taken in its context – certainly does not amount to an accusation of gerrymandering. It merely points out the foot-holds for misconception which exist and the grave injury which would arise if this misconception were to possess the Boer people.

I have now unfolded to you in other words the argument of my speech in the hopes that if you should find the time to study the passages in question again and preferably in the verbatim report, you will see in the light of this exegesis what my meaning was and what I believe everybody who heard the speech and most of those who read it understood it to be.

I am still more puzzled to know to what passage you are referring when you speak of 'slanders against one of the races concerned', or what information can lead you to suggest as you do in your last sentence that I am guilty of misrepresenting the views of the Secretary of State; but my object in intruding upon your good nature at such length is only to remove so far as possible from your mind any misunderstanding which may have arisen and certainly not to make complaints about the ordinary, and indeed, rather hackneyed, recriminations and insinuations of political warfare.

[WINSTON S. CHURCHILL]

J. C. Smuts to WSC

15 April 1906   Pretoria

Dear Mr Churchill,

The enclosed cutting with reports of speeches by Genl Botha and myself may perhaps interest you. I direct your attention especially to what I said in reference to the probability of an artificial crisis at the mines as the mine-owners' answer to Liberal policy on the Chinese question. There is no doubt that such a crisis is in contemplation.

Yours faithfully

J. C. SMUTS

Lord Selborne to WSC

15 April 1906   In train near Mafeking

Private

My dear Churchill,

I was very glad to get your letter of the 24th March, with its enclosure.

Let me say at once how cordially I welcome the plan of frank and constant correspondence between us. You can help me thereby, and I know you will; I can help you and I will with pleasure.

Your letter explains how the reference to the Committee was not prefaced with a definite pronouncement in favour of the principle of one vote one value; but as you have, since you wrote to me, formally announced this basis in the House of Commons on the Colonial Office Vote just before the adjournment for the Easter holidays, the pronouncement has in fact been made well in advance of the arrival of the Committee. For this my profound and grateful thanks to HMG, and my warm thanks to you for the part you have played in securing this pronouncement.

As regards the Milner debate, I fully realised that your intention was to parry the blow aimed at him by his enemies; but if you put yourself in the place of South African Britishers, as in your dispassionate critical nature you can, you will not be surprised at their attitude towards HMG. It is true to say that the South African British as a whole idolize Milner, and to them it is absolutely impossible to conceive how any man can propose anything in the nature of a vote of censure on him unless he is a traitor. After all, men's minds are made by their own history, not by the history and experience of their relations 6,000 miles away. And the great misfortune of HMG is that they have tied to their tail a tin can of the metal of Byles and Herbert Paul,[1] without sense and without taste. The South African Englishman does not understand English party politics and he resents the Herbert Pauls' and and Byles' venom more than words can say.

I think the danger of a really serious breach of sentiment between the Liberal Party and the South African British is a very real one, and one which exercises me deeply. I have omitted, and shall omit, no occasion to fill that breach; but Ministers themselves can do a great deal. I would not advise any attempt being made until after the new Constitution is settled; but after that I think that a great deal can be done by wise and sympathetic words. You who are in such close touch with public opinion at home would be the first to scoff at anybody who suggested that the great Liberal majority at the last election was not the result of a wonderful solidarity of public opinion from Land's End to John o'Groats; but when you find South African Englishmen and Scotchmen, and British Colonials saying the same thing from the Zambesi to the Cape of Good Hope, you will also recognise that that public opinion and sentiment is as much a concrete fact as is the public opinion at home, which has put your Government into power for six years.

Quite another point. You say that the distinct danger that you foresee is that perhaps the Boers may try to wreck the whole plan (that is, a constitution based on one vote one value) by refusing to participate in such a Constitution. Don't you worry your head about that. There is no more chance of the Boers refusing to participate in the elections and not trying to gain a majority under any Constitution which HMG may give, than there is of HMG gratuitously advising His Majesty to dissolve Parliament while they have a majority of 200 or 300. Why, but bless you, the Boers had no intention of standing out under the Lyttelton Constitution. Their hesitation was only a part of a very astute move in their political tactics.

I have not said anything about the Cabinet paper you enclosed to me. It did not bear fruit at the moment, but it has since. It is a thousand pities however that the Cabinet have not yet 'let Selborne at once set to work to prepare a new Register on the basis of manhood suffrage.' It would save so much time!

Believe me Yours sincerely
SELBORNE

---

[1] Herbert Woodfield Paul (1853–1935), Liberal MP for South Edinburgh 1892–9, for Northampton 1906–9; Second Civil Service Commissioner 1909–18.

WSC to J. C. Smuts

12 May 1906   Colonial Office
Copy

Private   Dictated

Dear Mr Smuts,

Many thanks for your letter of the 15th April and its enclosures which I have read with interest. I have no doubt that by this time you will have had some opportunity of laying your views before the Commission and I feel convinced that you have expressed yourself to them with your usual force and fluency. You will, I daresay, also have followed the course of affairs in the House of Commons, and the regular developments of Government policy which have taken place. From all this, I trust, you will have concluded that it is the desire and intention of those who now advise the Sovereign to do their best to strike a fair and just balance between the Dutch and British races in South Africa, to secure either race from danger of oppression by the other, and then while preserving at all risks and at all costs the authority of the British Crown to leave South Africa as much master of its own fortunes as the Australian Commonwealth or the Dominion of Canada. If we are enabled to carry this policy to its conclusion, I am not without hopes that the darkest days of South African history may have drawn to their close. The power of the Government has greatly strengthened as the session has advanced, and our great majority is proving every day a much more stable foundation than many people had at first supposed. I am very sorry to hear of the distress which prevails not only on the Rand but among the farmers. It is my hope that when the period of uncertainty which our deliberations upon the Constitution have rendered necessary shall have come to an end, business and industry will revive.

If there should be any matter on which you wish to write to me, I shall always be very glad indeed to hear from you, though it will not always be possible for me to reply with unfettered freedom while I continue to occupy my present post.

[WINSTON S. CHURCHILL]

WSC to Sir Walter Hely-Hutchinson   —

19 May 1906

[Copy]

My dear Sir Walter,

I must thank you for your long and most interesting letter. Please always write to me exactly what you think. I should never mind hearing disagreeable things when they were said in good faith, even if they were not true and what you wrote was neither disagreeable nor untrue.

I am afraid there is no doubt that the dominant and articulate element in the self-governing Colonies hate the Liberal party and will do their best to injure the present govt. It is a great pity that this should be so in view of the fact that we probably have five years of power before us but there is no good complaining against the inevitable, and we must just do our duty and make the best of their ill humour.

With regard to your private affairs, I have had your letter by me for such a long time that I fear you will think me very remiss in correspondence. Even now that I am able to deal with it, I am afraid I cannot give you any precise information such as you naturally desire. I find from the enquiries I have made that the Colonial Office generally have a very high opinion of your services and claims and that this opinion is fully and frankly accepted by Lord Elgin. I cannot of course write with any certainty or authority upon the subject, but I am sure there will be every disposition to press further employment of a character which I should suppose you would regard as suitable upon you when your present tenure expires. You may in any case rely upon my doing all in my power to further your wishes, and perhaps it might be a good thing if you will let me know privately and for my own information precisely what those wishes are.

I daresay you will have read my various utterances on South African matters and the answers to questions which I have to give almost daily in the House of Commons. I hope you will feel that the policy of the Govt has been sober and moderate from the beginning, and although I may have said (amid the difficulties of debates in which I have had to cope single handed with opposition and attack from every quarter of the House) certain things which perhaps I would not repeat were the occasion to return, yet I believe sincerely that any aggravation of South African conditions which may have taken place in the last six or seven months has been due not to the policy of the Govt or to the speeches of its spokesmen but to the prejudice and un-worthy interpretations and inferences which have been founded thereon.

After all, if people spend their time & their money in impressing upon the public that the country is ruled by fools and traitors who are seeking to ruin South Africa and sacrifice the results of the war by handing the Transvaal back to the Boers, it is very likely that the public will wish to sell their South Africa shares. I have greatly regretted to see the decline in market prices which has taken place during our administration. To some extent, no doubt, the measures which we have taken in regard to Chinese labour must be considered a cause, but I fear the root of the matter lies much deeper. The truth is that the Witwatersrand Gold Fields are hopelessly over-capitalized.

Since Peace was declared, the shares have declined almost 60 per cent in nominal value, forty per cent under the late and twenty per cent under the present Govt, and I cannot conceal from myself, judging by all I am able to gather from financial circles, that a further deterioration in price is inevitable before a true relation is established between capital and earning power.

I earnestly hope that no trouble with the natives will arise in the Cape Colony – the growth of this great population is indeed a dark cloud spreading over the future of South Africa.

I cannot think that the Natal people have been very wise in their treatment of the race problem. I am told that the magistrates upon whose tact, judgment and personal qualities everything in regard to the management of the natives depend, have during the last few years, been allowed increasingly to fall in status and standard, and that mere attorneys rather than capable men of character and position have had the handling of the very gravest issues in native affairs. I trust the Colony will find means to repress the revolt. The heavy expenditure thrown upon them will impose very serious considerations when future native policy is considered. I do not think the House would consent readily to Imperial intervention even were it requested. Indeed the utmost I have been able to do has been to secure the Colony freedom to conduct the operations in its own way and upon its own responsibility. Do please write to me and let me know your views.

What are the prospects of the Jameson[1] Ministry in the near future? I gathered from him when he was in this country that he did not rate his chances very high. He is a very good fellow and I personally like him very much but I was amused at his fervid protestations against Imperial interference with the rights of a self-governing Colony when I remember that only three years ago he and his friends were besieging Mr Chamberlain not merely to interfere with the Cape Colony but to abrogate his constitution altogether.

How circumstances alter cases!

With all good wishes

Believe me Yours very sincerely
WSC

---

[1] Leander Starr Jameson (1853–1917), Premier, Cape Colony 1904–8; led raid on Transvaal 1895–6; surrendered to Boers, tried in London and sentenced to 10 months' imprisonment 1896; served only seven months due to ill health; elected member of Cape Legislative Assembly 1900; MP Harbour Division, Capetown 1910–12; Director of De Beers Consolidated Company 1900; M.D. 1877; PC 1907; baronet 1911.

Lord Elgin to WSC

EXTRACT

25 May 1906
Private

My dear Churchill,

... I hope you will excuse my saying a word about two points in regard to the case of the Ceylon guard.[1]

(1) Whatever the merits, I do hope you will agree to remove at least part of your last Minute from the record. I am not personally touchy in these matters, but you know that my successor in India was eloquent as to the inconvenience of notes by junior officers – and Kitchener upset the Army system on the same question. Thus whatever force there may be in these objections there is certainly as much in sending through an office like this, for the perusal of successive relays of juniors, Minutes which reflect so severely as yours does on the conduct of a Governor of a Colony. In the interests of discipline I hold very distinctly that, while of course *I* should desire to hear your opinion without reserve, it is not expedient to record all & every opinion, strongly expressed.

(2) On the merits I cannot pretend myself to follow your argument.

I cannot see why a servant employed on State Railways should be in so essentially different a position from a servant in the employment of a Company or individual that he can only be dismissed if actually convicted of crime. There is no doubt in my mind that this guard was an inefficient and unsatisfactory servant – and I cannot condemn the Governor for getting rid of him: just as when I was a member of the Board of a Railway Co I should have concurred in a similar dismissal. The right of summary dismissal is, I think, a necessity.

I want above all things to avoid any record of a difference of opinion between us – and I should hope therefore that it may be possible to substitute a Minute which while not abandoning your contention (I do not ask that) would not compel me to do more than indicate my preference for the Orders which in my judgement are desirable.

I am keeping the case back till I see you. I hope you are not feeling worse – but I once more beg you not to hurry back before your doctor quite concurs. Nothing much doing here.

Yours very truly
ELGIN

---

[1] See pp. 575-9.

WSC to Lord Selborne

TELEGRAM

12 June [1906]   [Colonial Office]

Copy

Private & Personal

Much obliged to you for your letter wh enables me more fully appreciate your position in recent negotiations constitution. Have shown it Asquith. I agree futility of self denying ordinances in election times & will do my best ensure your other arguments understood but expect report of committee will appeal strongly to cabinet. Fitzpatrick's malevolent speech will offend.[1] Further as I warned you since repatriation fiasco opinion Commons much aggravated on Chinese question. Friday's debate prelude to organised Parliamentary agitation. I shall have greatest difficulty in maintaining even present *modus vivendi* and am quite sure fencing precautions impossible arrange.

J. B. Robinson[2] provoked by refusal allow equal recruiting facilities TMLA [Transvaal Mines Labour Association] as to WNLA [Witwatersrand Native Labour Association] in Portuguese territory. Have read all your papers on this matter. Robinson will soon say publicly through several channels that WNLA under Beit-Eckstein[3] influence is curtailing black labour supply to force Chinese on independent mine owners and that you & consequently we are upholding monopoly & therefore responsible. This is an ugly prospect. On other hand if Robinson could get independent recruiting for TMLA I could persuade him give Creswell good mine to try 50 per cent white labour plus kaffir experiment irrespective of cost. Please realise how advantageous this would be from every point of view. It would keep Creswell quiet & busy & pacify his friends here, would greatly please and interest Labourists & Commons. Even if experiment failed result valuable as proof positive of

---

[1] Sir Percy FitzPatrick (1862–1931), a leader of the British settlers in South Africa, in a speech on June 3 in Johannesburg, objected to what he called the Boers being made the arbiters of the fate of the British people 'just as in the time of President Kruger'. Every proposal put forward so far, he added, was conducive to undermining that which they held above every other consideration – namely, British supremacy. He went on to say that a compromising of their principles, a giving away of their rights to a vanquished foe and putting him on an equal footing with themselves was not moderation, but folly.

[2] Joseph Benjamin Robinson (1840–1929), discovered and owned gold and diamond mines in South Africa; Chairman, Robinson South African Banking Co; baronet 1908; through his TMLA he was trying to break the Chamber of Mines' WNLA labour recruiting monopoly.

[3] Frederick Eckstein (1857–1930), German businessman, represented for many years the firm of Wernher Beit & Company in Johannesburg, Transvaal; Chairman for many years of Sudan Plantations Syndicate; baronet 1929.

economic impossibility. Will you consider question tolerating TMLA from
this point of view? Would any changes and if so what in personnel TMLA
remove your objections? Surely room for two responsible recruiting agencies.
    All this most secret.

                                                    WINSTON CHURCHILL

                            WSC to Lord Selborne

16 June 1906   12 Bolton Street

Private & Confidential

Copy

[Dear Lord Selborne]
    Although I rejoice at the very great measure of agreement which has been
recorded in the course of the Constitutional discussions, I cannot help
feeling that South African affairs have rather clouded over again since I
last wrote to you.
    The fiasco which has attended repatriation has been deeply injurious to
the interests you have at heart. I accept frankly all you say about the *bona
fide* manner in which the Chinese were informed of the offer of the Govt and
I understand – and even to some extent shared – your apprehension as to
the effect of the notices. But the unfortunate result remains. If 1500 or 2000
coolies had applied for repatriation, the whole edge and sting would have
been taken out of the parliamentary agitation, and I think it probable that
you would have been left entirely alone until the grant of self-government
was completed. Had the notices been issued in terse clear terms and had only
a dozen coolies taken advantage of it, the contentions which you have always
made would have been enormously strengthened, if not indeed admitted as
proved; and though the willingness of the coolies to carry out their contracts
is by no means the whole question at issue, it is a good part of it. This advantage has been lost; the elaborate conditions and verbiage of the proclamation have rendered it ridiculous; the opponents of Chinese labour will
not admit that the contentment of the coolies is established, and opinion in
the House of Commons is only divided as to whether you are fooling us or
whether we are fooling them.
    In fact ever since the announcement of the terms of the proclamation there
has been a marked deterioration in the feelings of our supporters towards
us and the trust, hitherto my chief support, has been largely destroyed.
As a consequence I think you must recognise that the Chinese question will

enter on a new phase, and I cannot myself at the present attempt to forecast its character.

I have to thank you very much for your telegram about Robinson and the TMLA. Robinson complains to me privately that the WNLA will not recruit Kaffirs properly because they wish to force Chinese Labour upon all mine owners. He declares that there are plenty more Kaffirs to be got if greater freedom in recruiting were allowed, for instance, that he would not require to import 3,000 Chinese which he at present holds. What he says tallies with much that I hear from South Africa from Dutch Labour sources. Your knowledge of the House of Commons will easily enable you to perceive difficulties which would wait on a Minister who had to defend the maintenance of the recruiting monopoly in the hands of the hated ring of financiers against an attack of such a character. Further I do not myself see what justification there is on the merits for denying equal treatment to another substantial and responsible agency.

Your telegram enables me perfectly to appreciate your position. Your objections are involved. First you think the TMLA is not a reputable or respectable body and secondly you do not want yourself to have to decide upon the claims of a swarm of would-be recruiters.

The first objection seems to me to be a serious one and, unless it can be removed, I would certainly not desire to go further. I have talked this over with Lord Elgin and we agreed yesterday that Robinson should be told that he must first of all remove your objections to the *personnel* of the TMLA. You must be satisfied that it is a responsible body of respectable people who will not tell lies to the natives and reproduce the scandals of earlier days. If and when you are able to inform us that you are satisfied on this point, we will relieve you of the invidious task of interfering on behalf of the TMLA by using the machinery of the Foreign Office at Lisbon. The whole matter will therefore turn in the first instance upon whether you are satisfied with a reformed TMLA or not. If you choose to judge them by an unduly high standard, having regard to the general character of persons engaged in the gold mining industry, nothing further will be done by us. We shall inform Robinson accordingly and he will begin his attack in Parliament and in the Press upon the WNLA. I do not see how I can undertake the defence of that body in the House of Commons and I should think that the controversy which will follow will be lively and unedifying.

In the course of my conversation with Robinson on the question of the TMLA I have tried to induce him to give Creswell one of his mines and let him begin again his 40 p.c. white-labour-cum-Kaffir experiments. This he is ready to do – not at all as part of a bargain but because I think he realises the popularity and honour which would accrue to any man in

England who exerted himself to restore the status of white labour on the Rand. He offers to deposit £70,000 with trustees in this country to cover increase in cost of production which may in practice result from the white labour experiment. He would himself go to South Africa to work the experiment and to see that Creswell does nothing impracticable. The effect of this plan would be advantageous from every point of view. If it succeeded you would I am sure rejoice at the prospect of a white working class community in Johannesburg settling as it would once and for all the question of British supremacy. If it could be conclusively shown by figures to have failed the argument for the importation of Chinese Labour would have at any rate an economic justification. Meanwhile Creswell would be kept quiet and busy, and the country interested and pleased. This plan, although originally entirely independent of the fortunes of the TMLA will obviously fall through if we become engaged in a public dispute with Robinson; so that your decision upon the TMLA involves not merely the creation of new dangers but a sacrifice of benefits almost within reach.

I send you also a telegram about another scheme which has been weighing with me for some time. I have been impressed by Milner's arguments in favour of Land Settlement, and I frankly add touched by the disinterested earnestness of people like Lovat[1] & Westminster. I should greatly desire if it were possible to secure the permanent operations of the Land Settlement fund in the Transvaal and in the Orange River Colony, but how is this to be done in the latter Colony without the acquiescence of the future Government, and how is the acquiescence of that Govt to be obtained? I do not think it would be practicable to arrange some plan whereby the Land Board was entirely independent of the responsible government of the OR Colony unless by consent. It seems to me that, however carefully your arrangements had been made, the new Govt could, if its malevolence were excited, easily smash them up. Nor could I look for any parliamentary support against them in this country.

How then to procure their consent? This brings me to the other part of the plan. I have been going into the papers about compensation for war losses, and I think there is no doubt we have behaved with great injustice, and even in some cases with dishonesty towards persons who hold military receipts. That I find is the opinion expressed in Minutes by the majority of the permanent officials in the South African department at the Colonial Office. It is clear to me that the gravest doubts have assailed both Mr

---

[1] Simon Joseph Fraser (1871–1933), succeeded father as 14th Baron Lovat 1887; served in Boer War as commander of Lovat's Scouts which he raised himself; on his return he raised two yeomanry regiments which formed part of the Highland Mounted Brigade; KCVO 1908; KT 1915; KCMG 1919; GCVO 1932.

Lyttelton and Sir Hamilton Goold-Adams and that more than one proposal has been examined for paying some larger sum, at any rate in cases of special and peculiar hardship. I believe that an immense amount of bitterness is being preserved in South Africa which the expenditure of a sum of money, large perhaps in itself but trifling compared to the sums we have disbursed, would wholly or largely allay. Now why cannot we make both these horses pull together? The £30,000,000 war contribution presents itself.

I have always myself doubted the wisdom of requiring any payment from the Colony to the mother country. I am quite sure that there is no more certain way to arraying all Colonial forces against us, and of course the informal meeting of mine owners from whom Chamberlain obtained a promise had no right or power to commit the future Govt of the Transvaal, but at the same time the war contribution is a real factor in the game because until we withdraw our claim it would be very difficult, if not indeed impossible, for the Transvaal to borrow money. Therefore the forgiveness of that debt by the British Government would be a real act of benevolence. I would forgive it frankly as part of the general constitutional settlement, but I should like in its place to see the underwriters come forward to support not only ten million, but such similar sum as might be necessary (1) to place land settlement upon a permanent footing and (2) to pay outstanding military receipts. Surely this plan if presented as a whole – incapable of sub-division – might command the support and agreement of both races. The Boer leaders would find it almost impossible to refuse a relief so vehemently demanded by their own people, the British would secure an unrestricted fairway for immigration. Of course I see the element of unreality which lurks in the proposal, and also the rejoinders which can be made against it; yet when you reflect upon the immense importance in national settlement of appealing to the imagination and the compulsive power of large and generous conceptions, I think you will be indisposed to brush the idea aside without friendly and sympathetic consideration.

[WINSTON S. CHURCHILL]

WSC to Lord Selborne

TELEGRAM

6 July [1906]   [Colonial Office]

Secret private & personal

Draft

Your private personal of 5 July. A limited company cannot indulge in sentimental experiments at shareholder's risk but if controlling director chooses to guarantee any increase in cost of working which may result from trial of white labour, no one can complain. Result of course can only be judged by commercial standards fairly applied, but experiment most desirable whatever result may be. Hope you will carefully consider my letter of 16 June now reaching you.

Loan composition scheme must soon be considered and if you can make concrete constructive proposals I am sure Lord Elgin will study with every desire help. But essence of my proposal was parity of advantage to Boers & British. Your private personal 18 June seems rather one-sided. If honest & practicable repayments of military receipts & settlement [of] hard cases do not balance expenditure necessary to secure permanence Land Settlement could we not throw something else into scales?

How about your land bank plans? It is not necessary or even desirable that loan should be raised forthwith. Substantial agreement by real leaders both races upon composition of the war contribution involving certain future ear-marked expenditure upon specific objects is all that is requisite. Once get that & we might perhaps say with truth that Land Settlement funds were vested in private trustees forming Land Board by general consent. Worth trying anything. Thus perilous interval would be bridged safely & colony could choose its own time float reduced loan necessary fulfil bargain.

Lord Elgin was gratified & I am very much obliged to you for your complaisance in amendments to the proclamation which makes my task in Commons easier. All extremists now agree pledges [about] repatriation fairly carried out. About Portuguese labour recruiting I do not see your insuperable difficulty. Why may not we persuade Lisbon allow all who hold certificates of respectability from Transvaal Government to recruit on equal terms & to hinder all others? If your issue of certificates has hitherto been merely formal & indiscriminate why not issue new certificates all round to which real significance can be attached?

This last question in all its details will shortly become subject of debate [in] both houses as both Robinson & his rivals are inclined appeal Caesar & are talking freely.

It is of course with Lord Elgin's knowledge & consent that I exercise privilege of private telegraphic correspondence with you but I know you will understand that my telegrams are only in the nature of intimate informal conversations such as might pass between us if by any happy dispensation we could meet now & then for a quarter of an hour.

CHURCHILL

Major-General R. Baden-Powell[1] to WSC

13 July 1906   Horse Guards
                                               Whitehall

My dear Winston,

I send you rather an interesting pamphlet, in case you may not have seen it, on the Native question in Natal, by John Shepstone[2] whom you probably know. I had a very interesting time this spring in S. Africa, Rhodesia, East Africa and Uganda.

What a country East Africa could make with a good go-ahead Governor. Couldn't you put Garstin (or me!) in there when the present wise old gentleman gets smothered under his reports!

Don't bother to reply to this as you must be more than busy enough as it is. With best wishes,

Yours sinly
R. BADEN-POWELL

WSC to Israel Zangwill

13 July 1906   12 Bolton Street

[Copy]

Dear Mr Zangwill,

I have reflected carefully on your letter of July 4th and have also discussed it with Lord Elgin.[3] My views upon this question remain what they were when I wrote to you in December last, and I should gladly help forward any practicable scheme. But the more I examine the question the more oppressed I am by consciousness of the serious, and in some cases, growing obstacles, which stand in the path of action. Since the Colonial Office offer was first made to your people, much land has been occupied in the East African Protectorate and the Guasau Gishu plateau is no longer an unoccupied table land. Other enquiries I have made of local feeling fill me with apprehension at the violence of the local opposition which will certainly

---

[1] Robert Stephenson Smyth Baden-Powell (1857–1941), Inspector-General of Cavalry 1903–07. Military tactician; hero of siege of Mafeking; founder of Boy Scouts and Girl Guides 1908; author of many books on military strategy and history, scouting, art, and sports. Lieutenant-General 1907; knighted 1909; baronet 1922, Baron 1929; OM 1937.

[2] John Wesley Shepstone (1827–1916), South African civil servant, 1842–82; British Commissioner Native Reserve, Zululand 1882.

[3] Zangwill had written to WSC urging him to persuade the Government to declare its intentions regarding the establishment of a Jewish National Home. In the letter he talked of 'this moment of massacre and panic', a reference to the pogrom of Kishinëv, a town in Bessarabia where several hundred Jews were massacred in 1903.

be offered by the existing settlers and by the whole official world. Further, there is undoubted division among the Jews themselves, which seems to have impressed itself even upon some of those, who, like Lord Percy, were strenuous in your support. Lord Elgin is quite resolute in his decision that he can do nothing until and unless you are able to present him with a definite scheme, adequately supported by persons of wealth and influence in the Jewish world. Surely this is not an unreasonable position for the head of a Public Department to assume. If you were able to come to us with a long list of powerful names guaranteeing a great sum of money, I would do my very best to further your wishes, though, even then, I cannot command success. But it seems to me that nothing else than a definite detailed plan sustained by ample funds and personalities, would have any chance against the obstacles to which I have referred.

Believe me, your letter touches responsive chords. If you think any good would come of another conference, I should be very glad to receive you at the Colonial Office, and I will keep an appointment for you on Wednesday, the 18th at 12 (noon) unless I hear from you to the contrary.

Yours sincerely
WINSTON S. CHURCHILL

WSC to Sir Frederick Lugard[1]

18 July 1906

[Copy]

Private

Dear Sir Frederick Lugard,

I am very much obliged to you for the Memorandum and its addendum which have reached me and which I have read carefully. I enclose you herewith a few notes I have made myself on the subject which will show you the conclusion to which I have up to the present arrived. I think you will make a mistake in changing your plan at this stage, and I should strongly recommend you not to send the Secretary of State your addendum. I must confess I was rather disquieted to find you apparently ready to relinquish so lightly the very serious arguments which you had pressed upon me against the construction of a 3′ 6″ railway in Northern Nigeria. I cannot believe that the British Cotton Growing Assocn can have presented you

[1] Frederick John Dealtry Lugard (1858–1945), British soldier and colonial administrator, High Commissioner and Commander-in-Chief of Northern Nigeria 1900–06; was severely wounded when commanding expedition against Arab slave traders on L. Nyasa, 1888; Governor of Hong Kong 1907–12; Governor-General of Nigeria 1914–19; author of *The Dual Mandate in British Tropical Africa*, 1922; KCMG 1901, GCMG 1911; Baron 1928.

with any new facts sufficient to justify such a modification of view. In any case, I am not myself prepared – as at present informed – to advocate the building of a railway in Northern Nigeria other than the train upon which I thought we had agreed, and I think it might easily jeopardise the whole of your project if any serious changes were proposed by you. Remember the fate of the young officer who endeavoured to advance his square when the enemy were already committed to the assault.

I hope upon reflection you will find yourself able generally to agree with the policy indicated by me in my memorandum. I have striven very hard to give full effect to the Sec of State's views, and also to safeguard the Exchequer here from any rash expenditure. Mr Antrobus[1] has signified his general concurrence with what I have written, and I should hope that it would be found also to satisfy you, Lord Scarbrough[2] and the British Cotton Growing Assocn.

I am so busy with the Transvaal constitution and South African matters generally this week and the next that I cannot at present fix a day for another talk but we must have one before Parliament disperses on its holidays.

Please give my respects to Lady Lugard.

[Winston S. Churchill]

Sir Frederick Lugard to WSC

19 July 1906

Little Parkhurst
Surrey

Private

Dear Mr Churchill,

Thank you for your letter & the *excellent* Memo on the railway position You apparently think me open to a charge of inconsistency & ready to 'lightly relinquish' my own serious arguments. I have never adopted the line of 'trying to squeeze all I can out of the Govt' & urging the expenditure of imperial funds upon N. Nigeria because I happened to be High Commr there. I feel that if a man has the larger interests in view it is his duty to place before the Secy of State with absolute impartiality his considered judgment of what is absolutely essential, & likely to be remunerative & I

---

[1] Reginald Laurence Antrobus (1853–1942), Assistant Under Secretary of State, Colonial Office 1898–1909. KCMG 1911.

[2] Aldred Frederick George Beresford Lumley, 10th Earl of Scarbrough (1857–1945), ADC to King Edward VII 1902; Director-General Territorial and Volunteer Forces 1917–21; Major-General 1917; succeeded father 1884.

have never wavered in the opinion I have expressed regarding the essential for Nigeria, even though I should be apparently opposing the expenditure of a larger sum for the development of Nigeria. When I met the Cotton people the other day, there was an almost heated discussion in this sense. They assured me that they had figures in proof of the certainty of an extraordinary cotton development. They pledged themselves to large expenditure for this purpose & they were unanimous that the 2′ 6″ tramway could not carry the stuff & they said they were certain of getting sanction for the broader gauge railway if I did not oppose it. In my 'Addendum' I admit that in such circumstances it may be advisable to make the Baro-Zunguru Section on the 3′ 6″ gauge if the statements & promises are sound. I also understand Lord Elgin to favour the project. The main thing – the tramway & *not a railway* from Zunguru to Kano & its connection with the water transport at Baro & not the aggrandisement of an impracticable port at Lagos were safeguarded. Those are the essential points, & it seems to me to matter little, or at least to be a point of secondary importance, whether the short section (96 miles) from Baro is a 3′ 6″ rail or a 2′ 6″ tram.

Sincerely yours
F. LUGARD

On July 31, the House of Commons debated the Government's proposals for a new Transvaal Constitution. They were approved by 316 votes to 83.

Lord Ripon to WSC

1 August 1906   9 Chelsea Embankment

My dear Churchill,

I have been reading with great interest your excellent speech last night on the new Transvaal Constitution. It is an admirable exposition and vindication of the policy of the Government. Accept my warm congratulations.

Yours sincerely
RIPON

Sir Ian Hamilton to WSC

2 August 1906   Head Quarters, Southern Command
                                                      Andover

Private

My dear Winston,

I cannot let you off a letter of congratulation (which however I beg you
on no account to think of answering) on the occasion of your brilliant and
moving speech on Tuesday night. No other thing that has happened lately
has given me so much pleasure for, as a staunch upholder of your genius,
I have, during the last two months had to begin again my arguments with
numerous people supposed to be more or less your friends, as to the possibilities of your failure. I feel now that the last bad corner has been turned,
and that those who a week ago were busy shaking their heads over your
supposed decline will now be amongst the most eager to applaud.

As to the subject matter of the Debate, I am absolutely certain that those
who try to press some analogy between Boers and British in their way of
looking at such questions as are involved in the grant of a Constitution, are
profoundly mistaken. It is of course possible to put the idea into the heads
of Boers that it is a manly and fine thing to do to make use of the Constitution to defeat the legal peace terms to which they had put their names,
but such I am sure is not a natural Dutch way of looking at a binding
engagement. My only regret is, as you well know, that this Constitution was
not given directly the rifles were handed over after the Vereeniging terms
had been signed. Both the country as a whole, and the Anglo-Saxons as a
race, would have had a better chance than now, but it is equally certain
that, from the political point of view, *now* is just by so much better than four
years hence.

                                                      Yours very sincerely
                                                      IAN HAMILTON

WSC to Lord Elgin
(Elgin Papers)
EXTRACT

8 August 1906   Blenheim

Secret

My dear Lord Elgin,

The enclosed from Selborne is in answer to one from me telling him of L.
[Law] Officer's convenient opinion & also asking him whether Solomon
would not be gravely injured politically by public pension. In view of the

movements wh he contemplates in Sept & Oct, I am having a draft telegram prepared in the Office for submission to you in the regular course,
authorising him to make the inquiries among the SA parties upon the
Land Settlement – War Contribution scheme. It will reach you in the course
of the week: & I do hope you will feel able to approve it.

At present Selborne holds three good cards. First the ORC Boers want
their constitution & will be vy civil & obliging in the hopes of accelerating it.
Second, the LO opinion which seems likely to deprive the Colony of all
funds repaid by settlers unless devoted to original purpose of loan; & they
can never borrow so cheap again. Third, the War Contribution lever such
as it is. Now all these three cards if played soon ought to be able to take the
trick viz the establishment of a Land Board by tacit consent. But if we wait
too long two out of the three will simply become valueless. So I trust you
will be willing to proceed by telegram instead of despatch as you had
contemplated. . .

I am off to Deauville on Saturday. But all letters sent to the CO will
reach me.

I hope you are enjoying your rest.

Yours vy sincerely
WINSTON S. CHURCHILL

Marlborough thinks we have won all along the line, & is full of rueful
admiration for our 'statecraft'.

Count F. von der Schulenberg[1] to WSC

11 August 1906   German Embassy
                                                         London

My dear Winston Churchill,

I am so sorry to miss you yesterday when you called at the Embassy. You
have been invited by the Emperor, and during the whole time of your stay
at Breslau you will be his guest, and the Hofmarschallamt will provide
accommodation for you. You have nothing to do but to write to the German
Embassy here the exact time when you will arrive at Breslau on the afternoon
of the 6th of September. You will be met at the station by an officer and will
find everything arranged for you.

In my opinion it would not be suitable to wear your diplomatic uniform, for
on these military occasions military uniform is always worn in Germany,
even at dinner to which you will certainly be invited. From your military
uniform you want the Levée Dress for the Review at Breslau and for a State
Dinner, which will be given, I believe, the same day.

---

[1] Freidrich Werner von der Schulenberg (1875–1944), German Military Attaché; German
Ambassador to Moscow 1934–41.

During the manoeuvres you will have to wear Undress Field Service Uniform with the sword. There will not be any objection that Captain Guest of the 1. Life Guards attends our manœuvres *privately*. But he must write to your Military Attaché at Berlin to provide him with a passport, and he must procure a horse himself. The manœuvres, I suppose, will be far away from Breslau, and you will run down daily by a special train which conveys only the official guests of the Emperor. I add this because I do not believe that Breslau will be the right place for Captain Guest to stay during the manœuvres. I am sure Colonel Trench[1] will tell him also the places where it will be the best for him to stay.

Very sincerely yours
F. VON DER SCHULENBERG

Lord Knollys to WSC

HM Yacht *Victoria & Albert*
Cannes

11 August 1906

My Dear Churchill,

I have shown your letter to the King, & he desires me to say that he thinks you will be quite right to wear your yeomanry at the German manœuvres.

HM will be very glad to hear from you on the S African situation.

Yrs very sincerely
KNOLLYS

WSC to King Edward VII[2]
(*Royal Archives*)

Honor
Off Deauville

15 August 1906

Sir,

It is vy kind of your Majesty to allow me to write to you about South African affairs. I remember that at the beginning of the Session I had the honour of a conversation with your Majesty, & now that Parliament has risen, I am grateful for an opportunity of setting forth some considerations wh could not well be stated in a public or formal manner.

The form of the Transvaal constitution has I think on the whole met with a vy decided measure of approval. No one denies that it is a grave and adventurous step. But on the other hand I feel most profoundly convinced

---

[1] Colonel Frederick John Arthur Trench (1857–1942), Military Attaché, Berlin 1906–10; attached to German Headquarters during operations in German South-west Africa 1905–06.
[2] This letter ran to 35 hand-written octavo pages.

that it is the only practicable step; & also the safest. Even before the change
of Ministry here, the colony was fretful & impatient under government from
England. The Boers always pressed their claim to a Free constitution, &
they were being strengthened every day by defections from the British party.
Any intelligent community will much rather govern itself ill, than be well
governed by some other community: & we, whatever our intentions, have
not the knowledge of their problems to enable us to give even good government. All this restiveness & these difficulties, wh had led to the production
of the Lyttelton constitution, were aggravated & probably doubled with
the advent of the new House of Commons. It was certain that Boer aspirations towards self-government would rise upon the assumption of office
by Liberal Ministers. It was certain that the British party would be suspicious
& resentful of our policy. It was certain that the new Parliament would take
a close & even morbid interest in Transvaal politics, & would insist from
time to time on interfering from a wholly detached point of view in native
and labour questions. The continuance of such a state of things was fraught
with vy real dangers to British supremacy.

In South Africa we ran an ever increasing risk of throwing all parties into
combination against the Imperial connexion. In the House of Commons
we could not really plead that the Transvaal Govt must be left to itself, &
that we were not responsible, because it was perfectly well known that under
Your Majesty's authority the Transvaal Government was wholly in the
control of Ministers here & that responsibility for its actions did actually
devolve on us & could not by any means be avoided.

The Lyttelton constitution would have given us no relief from any of these
difficulties. I daresay Your Majesty has realised that Mr Chamberlain never
contemplated any intermediate stage between representative Government
resting upon a nominated official majority & direct Responsible Government.
Under the Lyttelton constitution we should still have borne the direct
responsibility for Transvaal policy, since we chose the Transvaal Ministers.
Under it we should have parted with all effective power, since these ministers
would have been without the support either of a nominated majority or of a
regular organised party.

I have never doubted therefore that the grant of Responsible Government
was enforced upon us by necessity & was in short the only way open. But
although that is no doubt a sufficient reason I should be sorry to think we
had no better. There are among the Boers disloyal men who would rise in
arms against the British authority if they had the opportunity. But I do not
think they are a great number. The majority & their leaders regard the
Treaty of Vereeniging as a vy solemn undertaking on their part. They have
taken the oath of allegiance to Your Majesty, & I believe they mean to keep

it faithfully. They are a strong rough-hewn race, & they think in regular steps. I believe they have definitely renounced their old ideal of a United States of South Africa, & have adopted instead the ideal of the Australian Commonwealth or the Dominion of Canada.

If they find under the British flag that they can live their own lives freely & take their rightful share in the Government of their country, I believe that the formal allegiance wh they have professed after a terrible struggle, will grow into a lively personal loyalty to the Throne & to Your Majesty and it is a vy lucky thing that they should regard the Liberal party as their friends & wish to put themselves in good relations with a government chosen from it during the years of this critical transition stage.

But my principal object in writing to Your Majesty is to explain that while the grant of the constitution is in principle susceptible of both negative & positive defence, we have in practice not neglected various important precautions. First it would have been an error in policy as well as a breach of trust for us to have attempted to win the good will of the Boers at the cost of doing injustice to the British population. The constitution is admitted by the Boers themselves to be perfectly fair & straightforward; but none the less at every point we have been most careful to secure every advantage to the British which could rightly be claimed.

Your Majesty impressed upon me in February the importance of the principle of 'one vote one value' involving a distribution of seats according to electors & not according to population. I have always felt that the British population would have felt themselves deserted if that point had been abandoned. Yet the arguments against it were not easy to meet. When Parliament met certainly the prevailing opinion in the Liberal party was for the population basis; & that opinion was reflected in the Cabinet. With Lord Elgin's permission, however, I took it upon myself to make a speech in May in the House of Commons affirming the principle of 'one vote one value' & explaining all the arguments in its favour; & this was vy well received by the House & confirmed next day by the Prime Minister. The principle was never subsequently in dispute.

It is true however that to procure a general acquiescence in this basis of one vote, one value & to avoid all appearance of unfairness we had to adopt Manhood Suffrage instead of the Lyttelton franchise of £160 annual value. Much has been made of that; & I am glad that people on both sides should think it important. But, as Your Majesty is no doubt aware, the difference between the Lyttelton franchise & manhood suffrage is almost insignificant. It looks ponderous. It is in fact a featherweight. Such is the distribution of population in the Transvaal that in practice the extension of the franchise to manhood suffrage only means that Boer majorities will be rather more overwhelming in constituencies where they would in any case win by overwhelming majorities; that British majorities will be large in perfectly safe British seats; & that perhaps in *two* doubtful constituencies out of sixty-nine, the Boers will gain an advantage. This is a vy small thing compared to the effect of one vote, one value.

Another point of mark was whether the constituencies should all be single-membered or whether double or treble barrelled. On the occasion of Your Majesty's Birthday dinner at the Colonial office, I had the advantage of some conversation with Lord Milner; & I was much struck by the great importance which he attached to single-member seats, wh he said, if adopted, would enable a few moderate British members to be returned by country towns, who would otherwise be swamped by the Dutch in the surrounding districts. I have no means of judging with any certainty of exactness how far this view is correct; but the constitution provides for single-member districts.

Lord Selborne, with whom I have had very pleasant regular & intimate correspondence, attached great weight to a six months residential qualification instead of twelve months. The shorter period is all to the advantage of the British urban population which is a new & I hope will be an increasing population; & it has been adopted. Every man will therefore have the right to vote who has lived six months in the Transvaal. Further – a still shorter period regulates the transfer of voters from one district within the Transvaal to another. All that is required is a *bona fide* residential qualification (term not actually fixed); so that the miners who have to move about from one district to another as the conditions of their work require will not thereby become disfranchised. Your Majesty will no doubt have attached due weight to the vy important addition of a nominated second chamber. I do not, as I have said, anticipate difficulties or dangers in bringing this constitution into operation. But if difficulties & dangers there should be, here is a safeguard substantial, effective & direct.

The policy adopted in dealing with the Inter-Colonial Council affords further security – not perhaps much appreciated except by those who know the subject thoroughly. It is proposed that the responsible government of either colony may withdraw from the Inter-Colonial Council on giving 12 months notice. I think it probable that both will certainly withdraw. But I do not [expect] this can take effect for nearly two years from now. Meanwhile the powerful & costly constabulary force will be practically under the control of the High Commissioner – that is to say during the period of transition & uncertainty.

These are pregnant facts. It would have been of course perfectly easy to introduce precautions & restrictions into the constitution which would have been more obvious, & which in consequence would have excited deep resentment among the Boers, & have robbed our policy of self Government of all that grace, trust & courage upon which it largely depends for its success. But when we survey the vy general goodwill and acquiescence with which the constitution – safeguarded as it is – has been received, I cannot help feeling considerable satisfaction at the course we have threaded through so many conflicting difficulties.

The Orange River Colony which still remains to be settled is quite a different case from that of the Transvaal. In the Transvaal we had to hold the scales even between the rival races & parties, & to try to reconcile the differences of interest & feeling between the new population & the old. In the Orange River Colony we want to restore as faithfully as possible the old government of the Orange Free State as it was when inspired by the wisdom of President Brand. I do not think the Orange River Colony presents serious or anxious features. I think it may be possible to make an arrangement whereby the towns have a third of the whole representation, & thus secure at the outset something like two parties & minority representation. But it is a good simple agricultural community & there is vy little for them to quarrel about – with each other or with us – even if they are so minded.

But while it is the declared intention of Your Majesty's Government not to adopt a dilatory policy in granting Responsible Government to the Orange Colony, it seems to me that there is no reason for extravagant or extraordinary haste. Further, certain delays are inevitable. The Letters Patent for the Transvaal Constitution will not be ready till October. The Orange Colony constitution cannot conveniently be settled until these are out of the way. A statement thereupon might perhaps (though this is doubtful) be made to Parliament during the autumn session. Then there will be the register of voters to make & the delimitation of constituencies. This cannnot take less than 8 or 9 or perhaps 10 months. I do not therefore think it possible that the Assembly can meet in Bloemfontein before the last months of next year; & perhaps not till early in 1908. Meanwhile the desire of the Boers both in the Transvaal & Orange River Colony for the extension of responsible institutions to the latter Colony, & for the acceleration of the process will be a valuable and convenient lever in our hands & will make their leaders vy anxious to stand well with the British Government & win its confidence. This is in itself a salutary mood. Before therefore the OR Colony Constitution can come into being we shall know the result of the Transvaal elections & be able fully to judge the temper & the complexion of the Transvaal Assembly. Sir West Ridgeway[1] asserts with much confidence

[1] Joseph West Ridgeway (1844–1930), Chairman of Committee on the Constitution of the Transvaal and Orange River Colonies; soldier, civil servant and diplomat; Governor of Isle of Man 1893–5; Governor of Ceylon 1896–1903; knighted 1885.

that there will be a British majority of possibly 9 & certainly 5. The rather ingenious device which we have introduced of making the Speaker vacate his seat upon election, means that the party wh has the majority will not have to sacrifice one of their members to fill the Speaker's chair; & it is regarded by the British party as almost equal to the gift of another seat. Colonial majorities are often vy small according to our ideas without being unstable. In the Cape Dr Jameson has been able for nearly 3 years to carry on the government with a majority of 2 or 3; so that if Sir West Ridgeway is right in his forecast, there should be no difficulty in bringing into & maintaining in power during the first Parliament a Government, wh although, as I hope, including in its cabinet representatives of both races, will nevertheless depend for its main support upon a distinctively British majority: and I should suppose that Sir Richard Solomon (the present Lieutenant Governor) would be the first Prime Minister.

I cannot however dismiss without submission to Your Majesty the other less likely alternatives. The divisions in the British party are numerous & serious. Whereas Het Volk is united & solid, the British colonists are divided by all these political social & economic cleavages which we see here at home; and it is possible that although the British would return a substantial British majority, a goodly number will prefer to vote for or act with the Boer leaders. In that case again I should expect Sir Richard Solomon to be the Prime Minister, but he would be forced to rest for his support much more upon the Boers than in the event of the British voting solidly.

The third alternative – namely a clear racial Boer majority – is outside the bounds of possibility. The balance of representation is such that neither extreme faction – Het Volk nor Progressive – can dominate without winning and keeping the support of the moderate members who will be returned from Pretoria & from several country towns & Rand constituencies. This will be the great preventive against a violent or harsh partisan policy either way. In fact it seems to me that whichever complexion the Solomon Government may wear, it will be drawn by self-interest to mollify & conciliate its opponents, & thus the racial bitterness will be sensibly diminished & union promoted on the basis of working for the common prosperity.

Although, however, I believe that a distinctive Boer Administration is an utter impossibility, I should like to tell Your Majesty that, even in that impossible contingency – there seems no reason to apprehend evil consequences. Such an administration would be subject to too many restraints from an opposition united & almost equal to it in strength, from the second chamber, from the general power of the High Commissioner, & from the powerful currents of public opinion in England to embark on any dangerous or revolutionary course. They would be on their best behaviour & would probably merely disappoint any extremists among their followers. It is not perhaps worth while to dwell upon these purely hypothetical aspects; but I should not like to pass from them without repeating my firm conviction that if treated chivalrously & fairly & above all not interfered with unduly in native matters from this country, the Transvaal & Orange Colony Boers will become increasingly a pillar of the Imperial power in South Africa.

There were other matters connected with securing the position of the settlers placed on the land under Land Settlement & also with the war contribution on which I had intended to write to Your Majesty; but I fear this letter has already trespassed unduly upon Your Majesty's kindness and patience. I hope however I may venture to say that the session that is now over has been full of difficulties to me. All S. African business in the House of Commons has been left entirely in my hands. I have had to speak more than any other minister except Mr Birrell[1], & to answer something like 500 questions, besides a great number of supplementary questions put & answered on the spur of the moment. I have had no previous experience in this kind of work. I have had a new & unfathomed House of Commons to deal with in respect of subjects upon which it is strangely excited; & at least four perfectly separate currents of opinion to consider. If therefore I have from time to time turned phrases awkwardly, or not judged quite the right time or tone, I feel certain that Your Majesty will have put the most favourable construction upon my words & will have credited me throughout with loyal & grave intentions.

One never can tell what will happen in SA, but I do not think that any difficulties in the Parliamentary conduct of S. African affairs in this Parliament will be so perplexing as those that are past. Greater knowledge is producing more moderate opinions. The extreme people have weakened their position through being allowed full licence to disclose it. The Government & its ministers are seated more firmly in the saddle. Finally when we have in existence a real honest representative Transvaal Parliament, I do not think that anyone could force us to interfere with it, or hold us responsible for its actions so long as it confines itself to matters proper to its own jurisdiction.

We are having a pleasant week on this comfortable yacht, though the rainy weather has somewhat spoiled racing & polo. Next week I am going to stay with Sir Ernest Cassel at his mountain villa, & after that I go to the German manoeuvres.

Let me once more thank Your Majesty for allowing me to write directly

---

[1] Augustine Birrell (1850–1933), President of Board of Education 1905–7; Chief Secretary to Lord Lieutenant of Ireland 1907–16; Liberal MP for West Fifeshire 1889–1900, for Bristol North 1906–18.

and personally on these South African matters; & I have the honour to remain Your Majesty's faithful & devoted servant

WINSTON S. CHURCHILL

Frederick Ponsonby[1] to WSC

20 August 1906   Hotel Weimar
                                                  Marienbad

My dear Churchill,

The King desires me to thank you for your letter which he read with the greatest interest and to tell you that he is glad to see what importance you attach to matters relating to South Africa.

His Majesty sincerely hopes that the sanguine views you express with reference to the future of South Africa may be realised, but at the same time he trusts that in dealing with all abstract questions regarding the self government of a mixed community, you will never lose sight of the fact that the Transvaal is a recently conquered country. The King quite understands that the granting of self government to the Transvaal was unavoidable but in solving the many difficult problems in South Africa, it might be dangerous to assume that it is simply a colony desirous of self govt like any other in His Majesty's dominions and the King knows you will agree with him that it would be deplorable to run the risk of another war in South Africa or of losing this colony when we have spent so much blood and money.

It is impossible for the King to enter into details on all the points you raise in your letter but so long as you bear this in mind and are careful to maintain British preponderance,[2] you may rest assured that any measures His Government may take for the welfare of South Africa will receive His Majesty's approval.

The King was glad to see that the Government had decided to postpone the granting of self government to the Orange River Colony until the end of next year and considers it most desirable that we should first see how the Transvaal constitution works before embarking on another venture.

There is one point which the King would be glad to hear about and that is what will be the eventual outcome of the Transvaal constitution. Will the English majority increase or diminish? Will the measures now adopted tend to increase the immigration from England or will they have the effect of choking off would-be immigrants? The King can well understand that the onus of all these discussions in Parliament was thrown upon your shoulders

---

[1] Frederick Edward Grey Ponsonby (1867–1935), Assistant Private Secretary to King Edward VII 1901–10; to Queen Victoria 1894–1901; to George V 1910–12; knighted 1910; created Baron Sysonby of Wonersh 1935.

[2] 'Supremacy' in the typed draft in the Royal Archives.

and no doubt severe criticisms were made from both extremes but his Majesty is glad to see that you are becoming a *reliable* Minister and above all a *serious* politician. *Which can only be obtained by putting country before Party*[1].

Yours very truly

F. E. G. PONSONBY

WSC to King Edward VII
(*Royal Archives*)

20 August 1906   Villa Cassel

Sir,

I have had the honour to receive Your Majesty's gracious letter of the 20th instant, for which I am most grateful & which will be a guide & encouragement to me.

Your Majesty has noticed an omission in the argument of my last letter, which I made in order to reduce its length, but which is of high & essential importance. 'What will be the outcome of the Transvaal constitution? Will the English majority increase or diminish? Will the measures now adopted tend to increase the immigration from England or will these have the effect of choking off would-be immigrants?'

Let me say first of all that I believe the transition from crown colony government to Responsible government will be favourable to British immigrants from the fact that English people of enterprise such as would naturally be attracted to a new country hate being governed by officials without having any say in the matter themselves; and that I believe the Transvaal would never really go ahead until it obtained free institutions. But that is of course a sentimental view, & I would submit more material considerations to Your Majesty.

The growth of a non-Dutch population in the Transvaal must mainly depend upon the prosperity of the gold mines. That does not mean feverish or purely speculative expansion, but steady development & above all no violent set back. I cannot conceive that any party which will be powerful in Transvaal politics would deliberately set itself to injure the gold-mining industry upon which all sections of the British population live, & from which the Boer farmers have already derived & will continue to derive increasingly substantial benefits. Whatever Government is placed in power in the Transvaal will find their credit, their services, the whole fabric of their administration & public service, all projects of rural development – Land

[1] The last sentence was added to the draft in the King's own hand.

Banks, Irrigation & Railways – absolutely dependent upon & interwoven with the economic prosperity of the gold mines. And we have recently seen from the pronouncement of General Botha & of Mr E. P. Solomon,[1] the leader of the 'so-called' Responsible party, that these leaders vie with the Progressives in asserting their intention to sustain the staple industry of the country, & to secure it a proper & sufficient supply of labour. Self-interest may not be a vy noble motive, but it is a vy trustworthy motive, & Your Majesty may, I think, count with confidence upon the earnest desire of a Transvaal Parliament to get as much money out of the gold mines as it possibly can & to use at any rate a vy large proportion of that money for the development of the country generally. Certainly a local Assembly, all of whose members are personally & through their constituents certain to become poorer or richer as the gold industry wanes & waxes is, from a material point of view at least, much better qualified to deal with the complicated questions of Mining & Labour, than the House of Commons, which has no interest one way or the other, & which can therefore indulge sentimental views, not always based upon the most accurate information, without any consequential disadvantage to themselves. In this all important respect the measures now adopted should be favourable to the prosperity of the gold industry, & therefore to the growth of British immigration; & the improvement in Kaffir prices which has been the consequence of the recent Parliamentary statements seems to show that this is fully realised by those most naturally concerned.

A local government will further be in a much better position to settle the labour problem than Your Majesty's Ministers in Downing Street. They will I feel assured be vy anxious to get rid of Chinese labour, some of the moral consequences of which Lord Elgin tells me have already excited Your Majesty's concern; but they will take their time about it, & although difficulties will no doubt arise in the House of Commons I am confident that they can by tact & patience be surmounted without any serious collision between the two governments. Meanwhile the local Labour supply will no doubt be reorganised with the force & authority of the new government & a more effective system of recruiting of Kaffirs established. All such matters – so long as they did not involve anything in the nature of slavery or apprenticeship partaking of slavery – would be fully within the competence of the Transvaal Assembly.

The second point (after the prosperity of the mining industry) which would affect immigration, is a reduction in the high cost of living on the Wit-

[1] Edward Philip Solomon (*ca* 1845–1914), founder and President of the Responsible Government Association, Transvaal; Member of Transvaal Parliament and Minister of Public Works 1907–10; Senator in the Union Parliament 1910–14; KCMG 1911.

watersrand. So long as it costs more than twice as much to keep a family in Johannesburg as it does in England, the very class of British settlers whom we specially desire to see in the Transvaal, namely those who will make it their permanent home, are discouraged & impeded. An oppressive customs Tariff, high railway rates, many unhealthy conditions in the tenure & taxation of urban land, await the consideration of the new ministers. In respect of food prices there is evidently a divergence of interest between the Boer agriculturists & the British miners. That must be faced. But I am convinced that the majority in the first Parliament will be favourable to reducing the cost of living in Johannesburg, that they will succeed in doing this & that even if they do not effect a positive improvement, the conditions will in no case & at no time be more oppressive than at present. With regard moreover to the vy high rents which prevail – both ground and house rents – it is possible that a little Radical legislation, as is not at all unlikely, would produce a distinct public advantage.

The question of reducing the high freights to S. Africa, which are maintained by Shipping rings & which incidentally operate positively to the disadvantage of British trade, is engaging the attention of Your Majesty's Government. It is proposed almost immediately to ask Your Majesty to assent to a Royal Commission on this subject, & perhaps some improvement may be effected as the outcome of their deliberations. The President of the Board of Trade has thought of asking the Duke of Marlborough to become the chairman of this commission; but I do not know whether he will accept.

The third element in the increase of the British population lies in Land Settlement. This is of more importance in the Orange River Colony than in the Transvaal, because first Land Settlement has been made more successful in the former, & secondly because in the latter a natural British preponderance already exists & will continue. Under the existing Land Settlement schemes about 700 heads of families have been planted in the Transvaal & about 800 in the Orange River Colony; & a sum of 3 millions (of which $2\frac{1}{2}$ millions have already been spent) was specially earmarked to that purpose out of the 35 millions guaranteed loan. The Law Officers of the Crown have given their opinion that all sums of money repaid by settlers must either be reemployed in the original purpose of Land Settlement or be devoted to the extinction of the Debt. That is vy important; because it makes it easier for us to continue this process of settling people on the land gradually but perpetually. The Cabinet have fully recognised their responsibility towards the settlers who are already planted, & that they are entitled not only to a sympathetic administration, but to full security for such administration. This can best be obtained through the creation of a Land Board under the High Commissioner but quite independent of the Local

Government, as if it were a private corporation – thus interposing a screen between mortgagor & mortgagee. But the cabinet are not yet convinced that (apart from the security of the existing settlers) it would be wise to provide for the continuance of this artificial process, at the expense of the local Government, but beyond their control, unless we are assured beforehand that such provision would not arouse antagonism & resentments which would be positively harmful.

In the hopes of procuring a general acquiescence both here & in South Africa, I have therefore proposed some months ago the following plan, which Lord Elgin has accepted & which he allowed me personally to bring before the Cabinet:—That we should forgive the 30 millions war contribution for which Mr Chamberlain obtained a sort of promise, in consideration of a new loan of a much smaller sum being raised to be spent not in relief of the British taxpayer but upon certain Colonial objects agreeable to both races in S. Africa, & in which the Imperial Government takes a lively interest – namely Land Settlement & rural development generally & also the payment of certain vy hard cases of war compensation for which the Boers have clamoured. Lord Selborne is strongly in favour of some such arrangement, & he has been authorised to open negotiations with the leaders of the various parties in the two colonies to that end. He has begun by suggesting that a permanent Land Board should be appointed to Your Majesty's Government in which should be vested all the assets derived from the $2\frac{1}{2}$ millions spent on Land Settlement & an additional $1\frac{1}{2}$ millions. To balance this he has proposed spending another $2\frac{1}{2}$ millions on compensation for hard cases, a Transvaal Land Bank (to enable the farmers to borrow at less exorbitant rates of interest), & a short railway earnestly desired by the Orange River Colony farmers from Sanna's Post to Wepener: a total new loan of 4 millions, subject of course to the approval of the new legislature, & in consideration of which we will waive our claim – which we had scarcely any chance of recovering – to the 30 millions war contribution.

There are great difficulties in the way of this plan & I do not know whether Lord Selborne will succeed. But I am sure Your Majesty will agree that it is worth trying. If it fails, we must be content with something more modest & less attractive; but I will in any case fight tenaciously for the creation of a Land Board to administer the existing funds & safeguard the existing settlers.

The proper time for establishing this will be when the Letters Patent for the Orange River Colony are issued, & if necessary we might let it be supposed that we shall be more inclined to accelerate our labours upon the Orange River Colony constitution, if we are agreeably met in this respect. There will thus be kept open a sort of doorway, through which year by year as opportunity offers & suitable candidates present themselves, a slow but steady trickle of British settlers may be placed upon the soil.

These are puny ways to influence the destinies of vast territories, & I do not want to seem to exaggerate their importance. But I have written this in order that Your Majesty may see that Lord Elgin & those who work with him are far from ignoring the immense importance of facilitating British immigration into S. Africa by every reasonable and legitimate means in our power, & that we will neglect nothing that may seem to promote that object.

As to the possibility of restrictive legislation being introduced & an attempt being made to shut up the country & choke off newcomers, I do not believe that the Boers would be so blind to their own interests, now that they have no longer a threatened autonomy to preserve. But the provision of a nominated second chamber which will certainly be made in the Orange Constitution as well as in that of the Transvaal will be an effective bulwark & in any case vy restrictive tendencies will be resisted by us with all the many influences at our disposal.

But speaking generally of the future, I believe that it is in vain to expect anything like a homogeneous British-type population within periods which this generation can usefully consider. Although the British & non-Dutch elements will undoubtedly increase steadily with the development of the colonies, with every improvement in communication, with every expansion in the population of European countries, the Dutch will never be swamped, & we have got to reckon as a certainty upon a continuing racial duality, though not I hope a continuing racial antagonism, in the politics of South Africa. That is why it is indispensable that the Imperial Power should be made to rest jointly upon both races, & why our policy must, even against the dearest promptings of our hearts, wear an aspect of lofty impartiality.

As I see S. Africa in the years that are immediately to come, it will be racially a piebald country. Dutch & British will have to live together side by side – neither race being sufficiently preponderant to enforce its character & ideals upon the other, & every consideration of prudence & self-interest deterring both from anything in the nature of another violent wrench or appeal to arms. There will be two states almost equally divided – the one the Transvaal with a British preponderance; the other the Cape Colony with a slight Dutch preponderance. In both of these there will be from time to time alternative governments of a more or less distinctive racial complexion. There will first be two states of decided & overwhelming colour – a British Natal with a small Dutch minority; a Dutch Orangia with a moderate British minority. That is the grand equipoise. But what will in the end, I believe, swing the balance upon the British side in a Federal South African Parliament, will be the weight of a growing & developing British Rhodesia cast decisively into the scale. I need not say that we will do our best with all the means & opportunities that the years may bring to work towards a conclusion so necessary to the glory & solidarity of the British Empire.

Let me, in thanking Your Majesty for permitting me to write thus unreservedly, say what an immense relief it is to me to do so. I trust Your Majesty will have been benefitted by the cure at Marienbad, & will have found that place pleasant as well as health giving. Here we have beautiful weather, although the season is advancing, & Sir Ernest Cassel & I propose long walks over the glacier & mountains. Sir Vincent Corbett,[1] the Financial adviser in Egypt is here, & Lord Revelstoke comes this afternoon. I go to Breslau for the German manœuvres on the 6th & afterwards to Eichhorn[2].

I remain Your Majesty's faithful & devoted servant

WINSTON S. CHURCHILL

Frederick Ponsonby to WSC

2 September 1906   Marienbad

Dear Churchill,

The King desires me to just thank you for your letter in which you have fully answered His Majesty's enquiries. The King still fears however that you are somewhat sanguine in your prognostications. There will inevitably be mistakes and failures. The machinery which the Government are now starting may at first prove disappointing, and it will take some time before the whole Govt of the Transvaal is in working order.

Yrs very truly

F. PONSONBY

WSC to Edward Marsh
(Marsh Papers)

EXTRACT

21 August 1906   Deauville

... I have been vy idle here & vy dissipated – gambling every night till 5 in the morning. I have made a little money – had made a lot.

I hope you are frisking & the British Empire slumbering in the calm sunlight of the Parliamentary recess.

Yours ever

W

[1] Vincent Edwin Henry Corbett (1861–1936), Financial Adviser to Egyptian Government 1904–7; Minister Resident to Venezuela 1907–10; to Bavaria and Würtemberg 1910–14; KCVO 1905.
[2] Baron de Forest's place in Moravia.

Jack Churchill to WSC

EXTRACT

23 August 1906   12 Bolton Street

My dear Winston,

We have had a very exciting fortnight, the history of which is well worth knowing. I must confess I did not know a month ago that Union would go up 20 points in an afternoon. But I have some consolation in knowing that all the big dealers over here shared my ignorance, and have consequently made very large losses in the last few days. About a year ago, it was known that the South Pacific & Unions had made enormous profits – and that there was a possibility of a dividend being declared on S. Pacs & an increase being made on Unions. A large 'pool' was formed by people who expected this dividend to be made. The directors of these lines, I believe, finding that this 'pool' had been made, and that the parties in it were not their friends announced no dividend or increased dividend. The stocks did not go up. The 'pool' was useless and the shares sold at, I think, a loss. This year however the directors got it all into their own hands – and when they had got hold of as many shares as possible – they declared dividends 1 & 2 per cent above the most sanguine anticipations – and reaped a harvest worth many millions.

The Union directors met and decided their dividends last Tuesday week. On that day we received orders from New York to give for the call of an enormous number of shares – in the evening these orders were doubled and we found all the other option dealers trying to do the same thing. No dividend announcement was made on Tuesday or Wednesday or Thursday. During these three days the option dealers here were giving for the call all the time. At last they could do no more, the option prices became very dear, and it was evident no more calls could be bought. The directors declared a 10% dividend on Union instead of a 7% sanguine expectation, and a 5% div on S. Pac instead of a 4% sanguine expectation. Union went at once from 166½ to 185 and S. Pacific from 84 to 90. All the option dealers found they had promised to deliver large amounts of shares, which they had not got, at from 5 to 15 points below the price of the shares.

Lord Natty R. [Rothschild] told me he received an official cable saying that an increase of dividend on the Unions – although warranted by the earnings – had been postponed by the directors for 6 months. He received this on Thursday and when he had had time to sell his shares and to take for the call of shares the directors then declared their dividend – and the market soared away up.

It was almost a certainty after the dealings I saw, at the beginning of last week, to predict a big rise in Unions – although no one, I think, thought they would go up in one night.

Sir E. C. [Ernest Cassel] told you, you had bought Unions to go to 200 – but you did want to 'job' on the market – and having a 10 point profit you sold in the hope of buying back lower down. Had there been no increase of dividend declared, Unions would certainly have gone down again. Lord R – after the directors had met and one day before any announcement – believed there would be no increase and sold his.

It was a great 'coup' and the net result here is that the option dealers have lost heavily. However we win so often over options—that one must not grumble if they go wrong once in a way. Yes £1000 would have been most acceptable – as it is, I think it will take a lot of work to make this half year look nice and to enable me to get stamps put on my bills at Xmas!

London is very hot – and I have had a fortnight in the city from 10 am to 8 pm every day – so that I am tired out – and shan't write any more. . . .

WSC to Jack Churchill

EXTRACT

26 August 1906   Villa Cassel

My dear Jack,

Vy many thanks for your most lucid & interesting letter[1] wh I showed to Cassel. He has railed at me a good deal for selling my Unions. I wish you had sent me a telegram about these when it was clear that great changes were taking place. Even if I had bought after the dividend had been declared there would have been a splendid profit. Alas, it was a vy unlucky combination of events that prompted me to go out of my way to lose the fruit which was within my grasp.

I took away £260 from the Deauville Casino, some of which I spent in Paris on more beautiful French editions – wh you might arrange provisionally in the French shelf near the window – & some of which I spent in other directions.

We have had good weather here so far & I really think it would be worth your while to come next Friday arriving here early Saturday morning & returning by the night train on Monday. If this strikes your fancy, send Cassel a wire proposing yourself & me one to warn me. . . .

[1] In which his brother had explained how option dealers in London had been caught short by the Union directors who had postponed the declaration of an increased dividend until the situation was advantageous to themselves. WSC, anticipating a fall and against the advice of Sir Ernest Cassel, had sold his shares when they showed a 10 point profit in the hope of buying them back at a lower price.

... The Kaffir circus seems increasingly to like the look of the Transvaal constitution! I have had an active and gracious correspondence with the King, & I think have put everything on a much better footing in that quarter. This is secret. Do write to me. Marsh always knows my address. ...

Your loving brother
WINSTON SC

Sir Henry Campbell-Bannerman to WSC

25 August 1906   Hotel Klinger
                                                      Marienbad

My dear Churchill,

This morning brought your letter from Paris which I was very glad to receive. You are with your usual energy making good use of the holidays.

I saw nothing wrong in what you said about the Labour Party. Our own people are singularly long-suffering but there is a great deal of smouldering indignation, and Cockermouth was an especially flagrant case, the local Liberals being ready to support a local working man.[1] I was sorry also that Smillie was for the second time made the instrument of malicious interference, for anything I have seen of him impressed me most favourably. I return Shackleton's letter; he always does the right thing.

Personally I have always favoured the second ballot. There are inconveniences in it, but these are as nothing to the advantages, so far as I can judge. And I agree that we must contemplate a comprehensive scheme of reform in a year or two, embracing registration as well as voting. Our local agents were found when registration was tackled before, to be essentially antipathetic to the Scotch public, official, automatic plan – which works admirably – & they will put a spoke in the wheel if they can.

A day or two ago the K told me you were going to the manoeuvres, and asked me to warn you against being too communicative and frank with his nephew. I have no doubt you will, as the penny-a-liners say, 'Exercise a wise discretion'.

HM is taking things very quietly here, and last year's round of feasting is not being repeated. The English Kurguests are not very numerous, nor very [?].

---

[1] The by-election on August 3 for the Cockermouth Division of Cumberland resulted in a gain for the Conservatives: Sir John Randles (Unionist) 4593 votes; Captain Frederick Guest (Liberal) 3903; R. Smillie (Labour) 1436.

Thanks for your reference to my wife: she got over the journey without damage, but has not made much progress in improvement yet.

Get all the enjoyment and lay in all the health you can.

Yours always
HCB

Ridgeway is here: and on Monday the Great God of War, RBH [Haldane] appears, positively for one night only, en route for Berlin.

*   *   *   *   *

WSC to Sir Henry Blake[1]

27 August 1906   Villa Cassel

[Copy]

Private

Dear Sir Hy Blake,

Altho' I have not yet had the pleasure of making yr acquaintance, I venture to presume on our official relation to write to you directly & privately upon the subject of the reinstatement of Guard David, in the hopes of explaining to you the views wh I hold most strongly on this & similar cases.

I do not at all dispute the right of yr Govt to dismiss its employees because they are found to be inefficient, superfluous, or personally undesirable, so far as that right is accorded under Colonial Regulations. Personally I think that the Rly servants of the Ceylon Govt Rly are in justice entitled to exactly the same protection *pro rata* as other Govt servants; but I recognize that a different practice has hitherto prevailed, & I waive all objections on that head to the procedure adopted.

But I hold that when a man is suspended on grounds of inefficiency, those grounds shd be the real or bona fide grounds of his suspension; and that this immense discretionary power shd not be used as a sort of bypath for avoiding the trial of issues wh form the proper subject of judicial processes. In the existing case, so far as I can judge from the pp, Guard D was suspended not really because he was inefficient but because he was suspected of stealing a mailbag: & the charge of inefficiency was only brought forward against him because of the difficulties of proving the real & grave charge of theft.

This is to my mind a dangerous and undesirable procedure. Under it Guard D was given no opportunity of meeting the charge of theft, nor was that accusation ever tested by a Court of Law. Yet it is for stealing & not for

[1] Henry Arthur Blake (1840–1918), Governor of Ceylon 1903–07; colonial administrator 1859–1907; knighted 1888.

inefficiency that he has been punished. Further the punishment inflicted is too severe in my opinion for the specific acts of inefficiency alleged against him, but not nearly severe enough for the real charge which lay behind. I really do not understand how such a case if raised as it easily might have been in the H of C wd be capable of defence. In short my view is that while power of summary dismissal must be retained, it is indispensable that that power shd only be used for the express purposes for wh it is reserved, namely of dealing with cases wh are not within the cognizance of Criminal Courts, & never in substitution for regular criminal procedure.

I observe further that in yr desp of Ap 25 '06 para 5 you state that a charge of theft was 'clearly brought home' to Postmaster Kiriatuduwa upon 'circumstantial evidence'. Now if this meant that K has been found guilty by a Court of Law I shd have nothing to say. But it does not mean this. All that it means, so far as I can tell, is that you or your advisers *think* him guilty, *think* the circumstantial evidence conclusive, *think* the charge 'clearly brought home'. But if you are so positive on these points, I cannot understand why you did not take steps to have this conclusive evidence submitted to a Court of Law in order that a thief might be punished as he deserved. And if on the other hand you refrain from doing this because I presume you do not feel that the Court wd agree with you, I can only say that there is no just ground for saying that the charge has been 'clearly brought home' & that the Gov himself assumes the responsibility of arriving at a verdict wh he does not think wd be concurred in by a Court, & then acting as if this personal decision carried with it the authority of a Court. That appears to me to be the assumption of duties for wh no individual however earnestly desirous of doing justice is competent & for wh he is certainly not authorized.

I recognize vy fully the difficulty & delicacy of many of these cases & the embarrassment wh they cause. But I feel it is better that I shd put these arguments before you as they occur to me in a private letter than that one of these days they shd appear garnished with every suggestion of prejudice & malice in the columns of a Parly debate: & believe me

Yrs v fly
WSC

Sir Henry Blake to WSC

25 September 1906
King's Pavilion
Kandy

Dear Mr Churchill,

It was very good of you to write to me so fully on the question of the suspension of Guard David, and to give me your views on the general principles that should guide the action of Colonial Governments in the suspension or dismissal of public servants.

As regards David the grounds of his suspension were fully shown in the charge made against him, which was copied in paragraph 2 of my despatch No 63 of 23 Feby 1905. Of that charge he was clearly guilty, and the question as to the action to be taken was considered and advised upon by the Attorney General, the Treasurer, the Auditor General, the General Officer Commanding troops, and the Lt Governor & Colonial Secretary, all officers of long experience who had separately and independently examined all the papers. In their opinion I entirely concurred.

Your view is, I take it, that in the consideration of this action the Government should have put aside every fact other than that David had failed to deliver a mail bag the receipt of which he had acknowledged, and that we should not have contemplated any circumstances that might have formed part of a criminal charge, except a charge had been made in a Court of Justice. I may say at once that the adoption of such a view would save the Governor and the members of his Executive Council a great deal of trouble: but it would be a reversal of the principles on which charges against public officers have hitherto been dealt with in all the Crown Colonies.

There are cases frequently occurring where though dishonesty is practically certain the Law Officers do not consider it desirable to take the case before a Jury; and where unsuccessful prosecutions have been instituted the Colonial regulation No 96 (a) clearly points out that the action of the Governor should not be determined by the action of the Court. Now, if a Governor may, notwithstanding an acquittal by a Court, proceed to the suspension of an official, he must be equally justified in dealing with an official even on a charge involving a criminal offence where the responsible Law Officer though convinced of his guilt advises that it would not be expedient to send the case for trial. If this be so, in considering the general question of a man's reputation, based on facts brought within the knowledge of the Governor and the members of Executive Council they ought not to exclude facts because they might form an ingredient in a criminal charge. In David's case there were not alone facts of this kind but his general reputation for efficiency was unsatisfactory as shown by the report of the General Manager of the Railway. One may have very strong grounds for belief in the dishonesty of his steward, butler or coachman, but not sufficient evidence to ensure his conviction and punishment. Will he therefore retain him in his service? The State is equally entitled to protect itself by terminating the employment of an undesirable servant.

On the question of the retention of the special power of summary dismissal of railway servants there is much to be said on both sides; but in dealing with such a service in a country where a sense of public responsibility is not high, the moral standard deplorably low, and criminal combinations are formed with a cunning that I have never known exceeded, the power is necessary if the officials responsible for the conduct of the railway operations are not to be rendered practically helpless.

The passage in par 5 of my despatch of 25 April with reference to the postmaster was, as the paragraph shows, the opinion of the members of the Executive Council and of myself. I hardly think that the House of Commons would hold that a jury of seven men drawn by ballot from the Ceylonese panel was more capable of forming a sound judgment on a very intricate case than the Governor with his Executive Council, including the principal Law Officer of the Crown, who inquired into it with very great care and considered fully the defence made by the offending official. However the Postmaster's petition has now come in and will be forwarded in due course, as will no doubt the petitions of most of those whose services have been dispensed with for some years past.

After all, the ultimate appeal is practically to the Secretary of State who advises the King, and save for the inevitable local effect upon the public service I see no reason to complain of the exercise to the fullest extent of the duty of revision imposed upon him under our Colonial system.

But, as I have said, the general principle that you advocate is very far reaching and it ought if adopted to be formally promulgated by circular despatch from the Secretary of State for the Colonies.

Again I thank you for the kindness with which you have informed me so freely and fully of your views, and remain

Very faithfully yours
HENRY A. BLAKE

*   *   *   *   *

WSC to Lady Randolph

EXTRACT

1 September 1906   Villa Cassel

Dearest Mamma,

. . . I am delighted to hear of George's good fortune. Really I think he might have a better opinion of the Govt. Even Kaffirs have improved since the Transvaal Constitution was announced; & I observe leaders in *The Times* on 'The Improvements in Business'. I trust it may continue. I am still vy sad about my Unions. It seems predestined that money is to avoid me except in such driblets that it cannot be enjoyed without feelings of uncertainty & anxiety.

I received a gracious reply to my long letter to HM with a request for more. I sent another vy carefully considered screed, the result of which I have not yet learned. CB also wrote me an amiable letter, mentioning incidentally that the King had asked him to warn me not to be too frank with 'his nephew' at the manœuvres. I expect I will have to mind my P's & Q's, so as to appear entirely candid & yet say nothing either platitudinous or indiscreet. I go to Berlin from here on Tuesday. If you write to the Embassy, Berlin, it will find me till the 6th. But I think the CO or B [Bolton] Street better. This place has been very pleasantly dull; & in spite of it being late in the year, the weather has been simply perfect. Not a cloud in the sky & delicious warm sun with glacier air. Cassel & I climbed the Eggishorn[1] yesterday. A vy long pull & I should never have got home without the aid of a mule. Le vieillard tramped it all out like a bird. Rather discreditable to me, I think. I cannot say how I hate losing money at Bridge. It is a wretched game when you are a bad player & hold the worst of cards....

Always believe me, your affectionate son

W

WSC to Lord Elgin
(*Elgin Papers*)

EXTRACT

14 September 1906   Vienna

Private

My dear Lord Elgin,

I don't disagree with your minute on Nigerian Railways, & I shared your misgivings as to Lugard's estimate & our relations with the Treasury thereupon. But I recast the draft letter entirely in accordance as I believed with the letter & spirit of your minute of Aug 3, a quotation from wh I enclose. So many people are raising obstacles that I cannot usefully contribute to the number. There are more ways than one of pushing this project forward & I thought that in the interests of action it would be best for me to support that way which your minute indicated. Had I to bear the final responsibility, I would have sent for Eaglesome[2] to England (as I think I suggested to you) & would have given him and Lugard full opportunity

---

[1] 9,625 feet above sea level, the highest peak of a ridge which separates the Great Aletsch Glacier, the largest in Europe, from the Rhone Valley.

[2] John Eaglesome (1868–1950), Director of Public Works Northern Nigeria 1900–06; Manager of Baro-Kano Railway 1907; Director of Railways and Works, Nigeria 1912–19. Served Ministry of Munitions 1916; knighted 1916.

to make out their case to the satisfaction & with the assistance of high expert authority *sympathetically disposed*. I am therefore quite content with your decision & think it a nice one.

Further I have always opposed the Lokoja-Baro extension. It is an intrusion of the office, & was never maturely considered by either of us. It enabled Sir M. O. [Montagu Ommanney[1]] to say that '70 miles' of the proposed line 'had not even been surveyed'. The plan of local construction will excite fierce opposition in that quarter, & you will require to exert all your authority to obtain the services of friendly experts. If you employ the Crown Agents the proposal is doomed & it will not be worth while to worry about it any more at present.

Sir A. Jones[2] & his cotton folk are prodding me a good deal for some statement of our policy in the matter; but I think we may fairly take another two months before deciding.

I am vy sorry that you have bolted the door against Lugard. It was his personal plan & his personal effort was an essential factor – in my judgement. In view of the ultimate & perhaps not distant unification of N. & S. Nigeria, it seems to me not vy important to introduce another temporary & artificial adjustment of territory, finances & administration by carrying S. Nigeria to the Niger. It is making two bites at a cherry; & I do not think the necessity of this step sufficiently proved to get rid of Lugard at once on its account. However as you have decided against Lugard, there may be immediate conveniences in parting his raiment with Egerton.[3] In the main question we are so completely agreed, that I will do my best to bring my ideas into conformity with yours on all subsidiary points.

I have had piteous letters from Hindlip[4] about the Nairobi-Fort Hall railway. As the result of your last minute on this question (concerning wh I wrote you privately a long letter) the office hung the whole thing up for two months while they inquired whether an electric railway was possible *in principle;* although we had already offered the company the opportunity of paying for the survey of such a railway & although their plan was for an electric railway or nothing. The Engineers having now expressed the opinion that an electric railway is possible in principle, the office write the snuffiest letter to the company that can be justified on your minute.

[1] Montagu Frederick Ommanney (1842–1925), Permanent Under-Secretary of State for Colonies 1900–7; Crown Agent for Colonies 1877–1900; KCMG 1890; KCB 1901; GCMG 1904.
[2] Alfred Lewis Jones (1846–1909), shipowner; supporter of the British Cotton Growing Association; tariff reformer and admirer of Joseph Chamberlain; knighted 1901.
[3] Walter Egerton (1858–1947), Governor Southern Nigeria 1906–12; of British Guiana 1912–17; knighted 1905.
[4] Charles Allsopp, 3rd Baron Hindlip (1877–1931), an old friend of WSC, he was seeking a concession to build a railway in Kenya from Nairobi to Fort Hall.

We refused them the permission to send an independent engineer with the Government survey party; & we even go the length of saying that their money will not be returned if we choose to offer them terms which they cannot accept. This means that we force them to come entirely within our power. Suppose the railway seems to be such a good business that we feel bound in the public interest to make it a government line, it will be open to us to make stiff terms & then when these are refused we shall have got our survey for nothing. I am so sure that you would not think that fair, that I wonder why you will not accept the simple principle of no railway concession, no payment: 'pas de succes, pas d'argent.' I am astonished that the company accept. I did not think they would. If they do, it is because they count on gaining a greater advantage from your magnanimity & sense of justice towards people who place themselves in your power, than from an ordinary business proposition. They have sent me a copy of their answer. It seems to me that the assumption on p.2 wh I have marked is more to the prejudice of public interests than would be a simple arrangement involving no moral obligations, & giving us power at any moment to undertake the work on handing back the Survey money. I think you will find that the correspondence on this proposal has lasted a good long time & I suppose it will be another two years before a sod is cut. . .

I wish you could have seen your way to make the Pearls[1] the subject of a Parliamentary Enquiry. That would be a course which would win for you & the Government a great measure of public respect & approval & wh would put a stop once & for all to the innuendos & suspicion of which the action of the Colonial office – believe me – is vy widely the object.

I am sorry that disconnected accounts of the Land Settlement plan have obtained such wide publicity. I daresay the Selborne proposal will fail in its existing form to win acceptance. If it does we must try something less attractive & more modest. We might for instance say that we had reason to believe from the negotiations attendant on the larger plan that the formation of an independent Land Settlement Board to administer only the existing $2\frac{1}{2}$ millions would be agreeable to the majority of moderate men of all parties as the quid pro quo wh the Imperial Govt should take in return for forgiving the 30 millions; & this said we might clap the Land Settlement article into the Letters Patent for ORC. I think I could defend it easily in the H of C if you could get it through the Cabinet. There would then be no new loan.

Reading over what I have written I feel this is rather a graceless letter of grumblings for me to write from a holiday jaunt to you who have been

---

[1] Ceylon Company of Pearl Fisheries Limited. Some MPs scented a scandal over a lease given to this company under the late Government. WSC denied the existence of any impropriety.

toiling through daily pouches. But the Nigerian Railways & Hindlip's business have been in my mind a good deal in these last few weeks & seem to have produced a rather acid fermentation.

I have had a most interesting & varied excursion. At Trouville where I stayed for ten days we defeated the French so utterly at polo that it was difficult to persuade them to continue the match. We were however beaten by the other English team by a goal in the final. Then I went to Sir E. Cassel's Swiss villa & climbed about those wonderful mountains for a fortnight in perfectly glorious weather – bright warm sunshine & glacier air – greatly to the advantage of my health. Then I went to Breslau for the manoeuvres wh were indeed impressive. There is a massive simplicity & force about German military arrangements which grows upon the observer; and although I do not think they have appreciated the terrible power of the weapons they hold & modern fire conditions, and have in that & in minor respects much to learn from our army, yet numbers, quality, discipline & organisation are four good roads to victory.

I had about 20 minutes talk with the HIM at the Parade dinner. He was vy friendly & is certainly a most fascinating personality. He was pleased to be sarcastic about 'his design of flying across the deserts to seize Cape Town' wh he suggested we attributed to him; & he said that if a native rising took place all over SA 'those people (in Cape Town) would by vy glad of my troops'. He enlarged on the fighting qualities of the Hereros[1], & I said in reply that in Natal on the contrary our chief difficulty had not been to kill the rebellious natives, but to prevent our Colonists (*who so thoroughly understood native war*) from killing too many of them.

Trench of the Intelligence reports was with us at Breslau. He is a vy fussy fellow & I don't think I should attach too much importance to his reports in the future. I gathered from the Embassy that our inquiries through FO about well-boring & violations of Cape territory had exposed them to a good deal of difficulty with the German FO & that they thought we had not given them vy good cases. It was interesting seeing this aspect of our minutes from the other end!

Indeed I should like to come & stay with you for a night in my visit to Glasgow on the 10th: & it is most kind of you to ask me. I will write to you later and propose myself either for the day before or the day after when my plans are a little more formed. I go to Venice tonight for a week or so & then to Eichhorn in Austria to shoot partridges.

Believe me, Yours vy sincerely
WINSTON S. CHURCHILL

---

[1] Bantu-speaking people of SW Africa and Angola. In the Hereros war of 1904–6 they were reduced by the Germans with great brutality from at least 100,000 to about 25,000.

PS I am delighted that you have sent old Gorst[1] to NZ. It will give him immense pleasure & I am sure he will do it well.

WSC

WSC to Lord Elgin
(*Elgin Papers*)

17 September 1906   Hotel Danieli
                                                          Venice

Private

My dear Lord Elgin,

The enclosed from Robinson seems to me vy serious. Evidently by a low quibble the freedom to recruit which we have *pledged* ourselves to secure for him has been destroyed. When we gave a licence to Holmes[2] we meant that he was to be the responsible head of a recruiting agency & not that he was personally to recruit every Kaffir himself & delegate this function to no subordinate. The latter position would obviously have been absurd. I must say I think Selborne has been strangely silent upon the development of what has evidently been a sharp trick to thwart the declared intentions of HMG.

There will certainly be a great row about this unless it is put right before Parlt meets. The whole Cresswell experiment is meanwhile hung up, & I feel personally that our position with regard to Robinson is extremely awkward. I do trust you will put your foot down at once. The FO should be instructed to press Soveral[3] & Lisbon to carry out their promise in a bona fide manner: & I think Selborne ought to be asked to report what he knows of the case. Is it possible that when he urged us not to grant licences to anybody else but Holmes until an inquiry had been held he *meant* to make the freedom to recruit wh we were granting practically a dead letter? We have always construed 'anybody else' as meaning other firms or agencies, never as meaning individual recruiters. It is clear that to adopt the second meaning throughout the official correspondence would utterly foil & overturn the whole of our policy.

[1] Sir John Eldon Gorst (1835–1916), Lord Randolph's old Fourth Party colleague, had been sent by the Colonial Office to the opening of the International Exhibition in Christchurch, New Zealand. Gorst had spent three years in New Zealand 1860–3.

[2] George John Holmes (1874–1937), financial journalist, businessman, and Member of the Hackney Borough Council 1900–26; author of *The Transvaal Mines*; employed by J. B. Robinson to recruit native labour.

[3] Luiz Maria Pinto, Marquis de Soveral (1853–1922), Portuguese Minister to London 1897–1910. Portuguese Foreign Minister 1895–7.

Is it conceivable that Selborne has allowed this obvious misunderstanding to work itself out in facts, so that the policy of the Govt while apparently strictly executed in the letter has in the spirit & in the practical result been brought to nothing? That would seem to me to be a profoundly disquieting conclusion.

But action is the important thing; & action I do implore you to take even with asperity. I say 'with asperity' because there is an air of impudent humbug about this business, wh I think requires some sharp assertion of your authority to correct.

I enclose you a couple of press cuttings which I have picked from a good many similar ones. It will be disastrous if Parliament meets & we have no effective position to occupy.

Yours vy sincerely
WINSTON S. CHURCHILL

Lord Elgin to WSC

21 September 1906 Broomhall

Private

My dear Churchill,

I received your letter of 17th yesterday evening on my return from London: and I may say at once that I found Robinson's letter there & dealt with it without a moment's delay. I thought it best to telegraph to Selborne because I do not see that any further reference to Lisbon can be necessary. I pointed out that our intention was quite clear i.e. that the Robinson Group should have the same facilities for recruiting as the Witwatersrand Assocn. They did not know in the Office what the precise arrangements were. It is possible there is only one principal License & subordinate authorisation for subordinate agents. But Selborne must know – and I hope he may be able to clear the matter up with the Portuguese Governor. If there is any difficulty or delay I will certainly ask Grey to move at Lisbon.

I really do not think we need suspect Selborne of anything underhand – it is quite unlike him: and my impression is that he was well satisfied with the outcome of the former discussion.

I had to go up to see Jameson with whom I had two interviews. I telegraphed his proposals to S & to my mind they were reasonable. Moreover they were intended by J and might I think in fact become a contribution towards federation both railway & political.

I also went thoroughly into the Singapore matter with Sir W. Matthews[1] & Blake.[2] I had from Anderson[3] an opportunity of reconsidering his decision to proceed but he adhered & I did not see how I could do otherwise than allow the contract to stand.

I find that the man in the Office who worked this case was Fiddes[4] – not Lucas,[5] who really could not speak at first hand to the details: and as Fiddes was away there are things I should still like to get at – but I cannot agree that a parliamentary enquiry would be desirable. There may have been some muddling – but I see no trace of anything corrupt or underhand.

I also looked into Lugard's railway schemes – dealt with the Newfoundland crisis – broken telegraphs etc. etc. for two busy days – and just escaped the Grantham accident on my way home.[6]

Be assured I will stick up for our engagement with JBR and continue to enjoy your holiday.

Yours very sincerely
ELGIN

Just heard that Solomon will sail for England on Oct 3. I was anxious to arrange this.

PS Sept 22. Since I wrote the above last night or rather in the early hours of today, I have received the enclosed which shows that my intervention has not been ineffective. I do not withdraw anything I said of Selborne, but as a matter of fact I suppose Solomon is the author of this telegram in the absence of S in Swaziland. Hopwood sent me a letter in which he expressed himself as much interested in Robinson's experiments.

[1] William Matthews (1844–1922), civil engineer; consulting engineer to the government for harbour and dock works; KCMG 1906.

[2] Herbert Acton Blake (1857–1926), member of Departmental Committee of the Board of Trade on Mercantile Marine; Member of the Port of London Authority 1906–7; KCVO 1914, KCMG 1918.

[3] Kenneth Skelton Anderson (1866–1943), Managing Director of Orient Steam Navigation Company; KCMG 1909; baronet 1919.

[4] George Vandeleur Fiddes (1858–1936), Colonial Office Official; Permanent Under-Secretary 1916–21; KCMG 1912.

[5] Charles Prestwood Lucas (1853–1931), Assistant Under-Secretary of State at the Colonial Office 1897–1907; Head of Dominions Department 1907–11; Fellow of All Souls 1920–7; historian of the British Empire; KCMG 1907; KCB 1912.

[6] On September 19 the Scots Night Express which had left Kings Cross at 8.45 pm ran through Grantham Station on to the Nottingham Branch, left the rails, turned over, and caught fire. Twelve people were killed and sixteen injured, two of whom died later.

WSC to Lord Elgin

(*Elgin Papers*)

EXTRACT

28 September 1906   Siena

Private

My dear Lord Elgin,

What a providential escape you have had from that fearful accident! I felt when I read of it that you must have been within a few trains one way or the other of the catastrophe. It is a vy suggestive experience – like standing not far from a bursting shell, wh leaves one quite untouched & tranquil, while only a few yards away a dozen people are destroyed.

I am vy glad that you have taken such prompt action about J.B.R. Do you not think *you* might ask him when he proposes to begin the *Cresswell* experiment. Once we have done our part, we may fairly put the screw on him to make good his promises. I will tackle him as soon as I return: but a hint from you would be most efficacious.

I enclose you a lot of letters from Dewdney Drew.[1] We must take him as being the real out & out Boer partisan: & I don't wonder the local Govt is not inclined to smile upon him. But is it not good cogent stuff that he writes? I confess to all sorts of misgivings about my Land Settlement aspirations when I read his letters & articles. If it be true that many of these settlers have been placed on overacred & overvalued holdings that can *never* pay, it would be a hard thing for us to say that they are never to be evicted & that the loss is to be borne by the local Boer Govt wh *naturally* loathes the whole process. On the other hand what a row there will be in England, if the eviction of settlers on a considerable scale should be a feature of the first few months of the new régime! . . .

Lord Arran[2] writes about the Isle of Man. But surely this is not in any of our archipelagoes? I only send the letter on in case the appt may be in your gift. *He* is a vy good fellow & would do it quite well.

Did I seem to cast a base aspersion on Selborne? All I meant was that he might have put the telescope to his blind eye. But *that* I should resent in view of our great effort to keep a good cordial understanding with him.

[1] Dewdney William Drew (1864–1929), journalist; Congregational minister and politician; editor of the *Friend* 1902–8; member of the Legislative Council of Orange River Colony 1907–8; member of Union House of Assembly 1915–20.

[2] Arthur Jocelyn Charles Gore, 6th Earl of Arran (1868–1958), Lieutenant-Colonel commanding 15th battery County of London Regiment 1904–8; succeeded his father 1901; KP 1909; PC, Ireland 1917.

I shall be home on the 8th: after having been vy idle for two months!

> With good wishes Believe me
> Yours vy sincerely
> WINSTON S. CHURCHILL

PS will you kindly send my enclosures to Mr Butler,[1] Colonial Office, who is looking after me in Marsh's absence.

WSC to Lady Randolph

29 September 1906   Siena

Dearest Mama,

Your letters all three reached me here yesterday after perfectly idiotic peregrinations in Colonial Office bags. Always write to Bolton Street when you have any doubt of my address.

I am glad to hear your account of George's affairs; & that he has weathered the storm. In certain circumstances I might have been able to help him to a limited extent. But I'm glad those circumstances have not arisen.

I must tell you all about the German manœuvres and my meetings with the Emperor when I return. It would take too long to write. But everything I saw in Germany was most instructive & indeed my whole holiday has been full of varied interest. After Breslau I travelled with Bully Oliphant to Vienna & so to Venice, where I luckily just missed Consuelo's yachting expedition. I then came on in Lionel Rothschild's motor car with Lady Helen (Vincent) and Muriel (Wilson)[2] on what has been a vy delightful tour. Forty miles an hour across Italy: Bologna, Ravenna, Rimini, Urbino, San Martino, Perugia, Siena. Such a lot of churches we have seen and saints and pictures 'galore'. Today is the *Atonement* and our Jehu is fasting in solitude. Tomorrow we return in one fell swoop of 330 kilometres to Venice, & I go on by the night train to Vienna and Eichorn. It has been vy pleasant. Nothing could exceed the tranquil *banalité* of my relations with M. But I am glad I came.

As I told you I do not desire . . . were they called upon to do so.

The situation in New York is most interesting. B. Cockran is working for Hearst,[3] & Jerome denounces him and all his backers as 'a gang of dis-

---

[1] Frederick George Augustus Butler (1873–1961), Colonial Office official; Private Secretary to Duke of Marlborough and to WSC when they were Under-Secretary of State for Colonies 1904–6; Finance Officer, Foreign Office, 1922–38; Assistant Under-Secretary of State 1933–8; KCMG 1920.

[2] Muriel Wilson (1875–1964), later Mrs Warde; WSC once proposed to her.

[3] William Randolph Hearst (1863–1951), American newspaper magnate, ran unsuccessfully for Governor of New York State with the support of the Democrats in 1906; popularized sensational journalism, the 'Yellow Kid', a comic strip in one of the Hearst newspapers, giving rise to the expression 'Yellow Journalism'; was instrumental in involving America in the Spanish-American war of 1898: Democratic Congressman for New York City 1905; later pursued independent line in politics, often supporting Republican candidates.

reputable crooks'. The papers wilfully misrepresent the situation in the interests of the Republican party. I don't pretend to know; but I have a sort of feeling that the Democrats will sweep the board in spite of everything & that Hearst will be Governor. This is a piece of quite gratuitous prophesying, & vy likely you will be able to rebuke me for it when the result is known.

Lord Elgin was vy nearly in the Grantham Railway accident. Poor old boy – what a Providential escape! He writes me most friendly letters & is doing all the work! while I remain

Your loving son
WINSTON SC

* * * * *

WSC to Lady Randolph

13 October 1906   Blenheim
Secret

Dearest Mamma,

Sunny has definitely separated from Consuelo, who is in London at Sunderland House. Her father returns to Paris on Monday. I have suggested to her that you would be vy willing to go and stay with her for a while, as I cannot bear to think of her being all alone during these dark days. If she should send for you, I hope you will put aside other things & go to her. I know how you always are a prop to lean on in bad times.

We are vy miserable here. It is an awful business.

Your loving son
WINSTON SC

Lord Hugh Cecil to WSC

[October 1906]   20 Arlington Street

My dear Winston,

I am satisfied after hearing much talk that Sunny is in danger of falling between two stools. What I said to you is evidently true: what he is doing pleases neither the Christians nor the fast set. The Christians feel that whatever his wife may have done, at any rate he is to blame as himself unfaithful: the fast set do not like a fuss made about such a matter & the implied rebuke at their own lives. His position, that his wife is unfit to live with him because she went wrong before he did & because the standard for women in these things is higher than for men, is not defensible either before the Church or the World. I am sure he will do himself harm.

This is the low point of view. A much higher consideration is his children: to break up the home is ruinous to them — sooner or later it will dawn on them what it means – & there will be a third generation of shame.

I do feel this very strongly: the children are the only people concerned who are innocent – their well-being ought to be the dominant consideration.

Yrs
HC

This is I fear rather an excitable letter in appearance – but I have plunged into the matter without preamble since I know you will not expect ceremony.

*   *   *   *   *

WSC to Lord Elgin
(Elgin Papers)

15 October 1906

Private

My dear Lord Elgin,

I have been considering the Railway dispute. First let me say with what astonishment I read the resolution of the 13th August by the Ry Committee. I cannot understand how such language can be tolerated from a body largely if not mainly official in its character or how the HC can make himself the channel of its communication to you.

I disagree with the Railway Committee on the merits. It seems to me to be clear that the obligations of the CSAR [Central South African Railways] to Natal was fully discharged when most favoured rates over the CSAR mileage were granted; & that it is purely gratuitous & partisan for the CSAR to attempt to intervene in disputes quite outside their scope either of interest or authority. The proper course for the Railway Committee & it seems to me for the HC & the S of S as they were successively appealed to was to use the immense powers of the CSAR position only in so far as was necessary to safeguard the '*modus vivendi*' area.

Instead of this the Ry C are evidently well disposed towards Natal, to whom they conceive themselves under an obligation almost of a sentimental character, & prejudiced towards the Cape who they think, I daresay rightly, have been mean & grasping in the past. It is evident that such considerations & emotions however natural & creditable should play no part in what is essentially a business proposition & a matter of figures.

If these arguments are of weight in respect to the Ry Committee, it seems to me that they press themselves with added force upon the HC & upon S of S.

The hand controlling the potent levers of the CSAR must have no favourites & no scapegoats. As it is we are undoubtedly in my opinion using the power we possess to aid Natal in a railway dispute with the Cape. That power is of course overwhelming. The mere imposition of countervailing surcharges at once deflects the trade to the cheaper Natal route, & in addition enables the CSAR to rake in as profit the whole money value of the rebates which the Cape have given & are giving *vainly* to assert their rights or their view of their rights. I therefore agree with your opinion upon the merits of the question.

But I also agree that there is nothing to be done at the present except to propose the *interim* Conference here. If it is accepted we will be able to thrash the whole matter out. If it is refused by Natal (who, having got her whole claim, is naturally not eager to discuss the matter further), then it seems to me you have got another card in your hand, with which you can equalize matters & compensate the Cape. The Bethlehem & Modderport line will be completed in a few months (before Resp Govt) & I suggest that we should give the Cape the balance of advantage on that line. It is a vy valuable trade with Maseru & Basutoland. Hitherto it has been Cape trade. But the completion of the Bethlehem & Modderport will make it dependent entirely on the rates fixed whether everything goes via Durban or East London. This is Sir H. G. Adams' idea – or rather it is the idea he put into my head.

We have telegraphed today in accordance with your instructions.

I had a fine meeting at Glasgow, & I trust you will not have disapproved vy strongly of the tone, the tact, the taste, or the temper of any part of my discourse.

The 'massacre' of rabbits did not reach our expectations – 1200 alone fell: but as in the Natal case, we are going to have the others tried later.

Yours vy sincerely
WINSTON S. CHURCHILL

WSC to Lord Elgin
(*Elgin Papers*)

16 October 1906

My dear Lord Elgin,

J. B. Robinson came to see me this morning. He is in a hole. The WNLA are about to fling him out unless he undertakes to abandon his projects of independent recruiting. He is quite willing to go out, & will do so voluntarily; but at the present moment he is falling between two stools. The Portuguese are apparently still recalcitrant & every time that Holmes journeys to Delagoa Bay, he returns empty handed, being met at each point with stolid official refusals no doubt prompted by *douceurs* from the 'reserve fund' of £200,000 wh he declares the WNLA have amassed. I told him that we regarded ourselves as pledged to secure for him equal effective facilities with the WNLA & that we would keep our word strictly; & I am bound to say that he seemed vy good tempered & calm. But I do feel we must exert ourselves. I am sure to be attacked on this question when Parlt meets: for JBR will not & cannot begin the Cresswell experiment till he gets Kaffirs from somewhere. He has decided now to resign from WNLA: & will thus be cut off after this week from everything.

Grey is dining with me tonight & I will explain to him the position of affairs in such a manner that it will only be necessary for you to give permission for him to see Soveral & settle the matter. I think we have been taken in by the wily oily Portuguese. They keep their promise to the letter & break it in the spirit.

Will you allow this matter to go forward through the FO, if it is ascertained that Selborne has done all he can do or means to do!

JBR seems vy pleased about SA generally. He said the Boers would agree willingly to contribute 5% on 35 millions (viz something like the extra advantage they got for borrowing on our credit) towards Land Settlement.

> Yours vy sincerely
> WINSTON S. CHURCHILL

*   *   *   *   *

The Duke of Westminster to WSC

EXTRACT

19 August 1906

My dear Winston,

... What I want to do now is to help in some small way the difficulties that have fallen to George West in losing £8,000. I hear you & your brother Jack have between you come to his aid. I would have helped before I left, if there hadn't been some misunderstanding between us. I send you enclosed cheque to be used on condition that George should not know of this transaction till I choose, if ever, to let him know. I think it very hard that you & Jack should bear the brunt, when it should have come on me, as his brother-in-law. I hope you will take this letter in all confidence. ...

... I don't want this to GO BEYOND JACK – & if you deem cheque unnecessary tear it up.

Yours always

BEND'OR

The Club, Bulawayo, Rhodesia will find me.

WSC to George Cornwallis-West

18 October 1906   12 Bolton Street
[Copy]
Confidential

My dear George,

I send you herewith a cheque for £3,000 to be devoted to the repayment of the sums of wh you were robbed by your solicitor, & wh I understand you have now borrowed from Cox's Bank. The transaction is personal between us & the money is a loan to be repaid at any time at three months notice on my request. Meanwhile you should pay interest at 2½% per annum into my account at Cox's. Perhaps you will write me a letter confirming this in precise detail.

Yours ever

WINSTON S. CHURCHILL

WSC to The Duke of Westminster

Private & Confidential
18 October 1906   12 Bolton Street

[Copy]

My dear Bendor,

I could not carry out your commission satisfactorily until I returned to England & cld see George personally & find out the exact state of his affairs. I have now succeeded in doing what you wish. I have sent him the £3,000 at 2½% & out of it he has repaid me the smaller sum with wh I had been able to assist him. The interest will be paid into my Bankers each year & will be forwarded by them to you. The principal is of course a loan wh I can reclaim at any time on your behalf.

George knows perfectly well that £3,000 is a sum far greater than I could spare to help him out of any embarrassment however grave, so that I had to practise a pious fraud in order to prevent him guessing or inquiring too closely about the source whence this money was derived. I therefore impressed upon him that in no circumstances was he to speak to Sir Ernest Cassel about the matter; & I am satisfied that he is persuaded that in some sort of way Cassel has come to his assistance, & that he has no suspicions that you were in any way concerned. I have therefore I hope complied with your wishes in every respect. But will you let me say that I shall hope most sincerely that the day will come in the future when you will allow me to make the truth known to George; for then your £3,000 will not merely help him out of his pecuniary difficulties; but will do what is really more important, remove all clouds between two honest-hearted men who are so nearly connected by family ties.

Let me say in conclusion that it gives me a vy warm feeling of pleasure to read your generous letter, & I think it vy kind of you to express so much sympathy with my mother. I hope you are enjoying yourself in SA, & that your Land Settlement schemes are prospering finely.

Yours most sincerely
WINSTON S. CHURCHILL

George Cornwallis-West to WSC

EXTRACT

20 October 1906   Salisbury Hall

My dear Winston,

Many thanks for your letter & enclosure. I enclose a formal receipt. I thank you also, my dear Winston, for your great kindness of heart, as I feel convinced that this welcome contribution towards my financial losses is more or less, if not entirely, due to your influence. One thing I must ask you is not to reveal to a soul who the person was who originally helped me through this difficulty. If perchance you have done so please make certain that the name is not repeated. Poor little Consuelo is here. I do pity her with all my heart, what a tragedy. The whole thing reminds me of Hogarth's series of satyr [sic], '*Marriage à la mode*'. Take my advice & if ever you do marry, do it from motives of affection & none other. No riches in the world can compensate for anything else. . . .

Do come down here soon; I am sure you want a rest, or soon will.

Yours ever
GEORGE CORNWALLIS-WEST

RECEIPT

20 October 1906   Salisbury Hall

Received this day from Winston Spencer Churchill the sum of £3000 (three thousand pounds) repayable on demand at 3 months notice, & bearing interest at the rate of 2½% per ann payable half yearly.

GEORGE CORNWALLIS-WEST

*   *   *   *   *

Duke of Westminster to WSC

14 December 1906   Grosvenor House

My Dear Winston,
   Would it be too much to write a line to George patching up matters? I honestly think the whole thing so absurd now. I must thank you for all you have already done in the matter. So no more about it.
   Can you let me have names of promoters and money that we can put up for Mombasa show tomorrow? Hope it will be alright.

Yrs in haste
BEND'OR

George Cornwallis-West to WSC

16 December 1906   Salisbury Hall

My Dear Winston,
   Many thanks for your letter. I at once rang up Bendor and we made it up through the telephone, but of course have written as well. I am very grateful to you for the part you have played in the matter.

Yours ever
GEORGE C-W

Memorandum by WSC

EXTRACT

25 October 1906

   His Majesty's Government have declared that the conditions under which Chinese coolies are employed on the Witwatersrand are 'tainted with slavery',[1] and are therefore resolved to determine such a system, irrespective of the material loss which may be involved. But the conditions prescribed in the various Ordinances regulating the employment of Chinese on the Witwatersrand, evil though they be, are nevertheless superior to any conditions hitherto prescribed by foreign countries in such cases. If therefore His Majesty's Government consider themselves bound to terminate the existing system of Chinese labour in South Africa, and to forgo themselves, or to deprive the Transvaal of, any profit resulting therefrom, all the more are they bound to abstain themselves from any participation in the profits arising from the conveyance of coolies to conditions of servitude not less and possibly more 'tainted with slavery' than those which have been denounced upon the Witwatersrand. It appears to be enjoined upon His Majesty's Government, if they are to maintain a consistent and defensible policy, that they shall in no case allow Chinese coolies to be carried to foreign countries in British ships, without assuring themselves beforehand that the conditions under which those coolies will be employed are so far superior to the Witwatersrand conditions as to be wholly unobjectionable. Is this likely to be the case? Is Mexico for instance likely to practice a greater strictness in the conditions of her indentured labour than Parliamentary vigilance and pressure has enforced upon the Transvaal? And how are we to satisfy ourselves? Would Mexico in its present state of development consent to be thus judged by the agents of a foreign Power upon a question of humanity and morals? Would the United States submit to such an inquisition? And even so what probability is there of a favourable result?

It is therefore submitted that this traffic – lucrative though it may be – cannot be carried on by British subjects under the authority of the British Government. Still less is it desirable that His Majesty's Government, casting aside the restraints which their predecessors have observed for more than fifty years, should themselves take positive action by repealing the existing Ordinance, to facilitate and encourage such a traffic. Least of all should they select this particular moment for such a departure.

WSC

[1] Minute on Coolie Emigration from Hong Kong and China ports. Although the Liberals made much of 'Chinese Slavery' during the General Election campaign, WSC soon after admitted that the term 'slavery' was not really an apt description of the Chinese labourers' condition in South Africa. On February 22, he had said that such a term could not be used without 'risk of terminological inexactitude'. This remark was greeted with cries of derision by the Conservatives.

WSC to W. T. Stead
(*Baylen Papers*)

31 October 1906   12 Bolton Street

Private

Dear Mr Stead,

I am much obliged to you for sending me the extract from a private letter written to you by Mr Steyn. You are quite justified in reassuring him as to the intentions of the Government in the matter of the Orange River Colony constitution. It is the fundamental principle of our policy that the burden and responsibility of the Government of that Colony shall be frankly thrust upon the shoulders of those who live in it. Mr Steyn is however in error in supposing that the Upper Chamber will be nominated by Lord Selborne. He has only to read the text of the speeches in which the Constitution of the Transvaal was described, to see that it will be nominated by the Crown i.e. the Liberal Government upon the advice of such persons as they may choose to consult.

The native question is, no doubt, primarily a South African question, and so far as I am concerned, I should certainly not be forward in pressing upon the South African Colonies views in regard to native franchise which they are at present not ready to accept. But our responsibility to the native races remains a real one, and we cannot divest ourselves of it until at least a Federal South African Government shall have placed the whole treatment of native races upon a broad and secure platform beyond the range of local panics.

As to what Mr Steyn says about 'distrust', I can only say that it is not altogether to be wondered at that there are a good many persons who cannot bring themselves to regard him as the best friend England ever had. But the policy of this Government is based not upon nice calculations of the amount of trust which may be reposed in this or that prominent individual, but on a sincere conviction of the efficacy and solvent powers of free and representative institutions.

If Mr Steyn does his duty by his country and by its poor people, in the years that are to come, he may yet live to see the Orange River Colony as free and as tranquil as the Orange Free State, and even more prosperous.

Yours vy try

WINSTON S. CHURCHILL

WSC to the King

2 November 1906

[Copy]

Sir,

Sir Richard Solomon, the Acting Lieutenant Governor of the Transvaal, is now in England. As I wrote to Your Majesty a few weeks ago he is almost certain to be the first Prime Minister of the new Transvaal Assembly. No one possesses in a similar way the confidences of all parties. No one can more easily reconcile or at any rate alleviate the racial differences that prevail. No one has the same grip of the actual and practical details of the administration of that country, & I think we are fortunate in finding such a good, capable, loyal man to tide over a period & a transition not free from anxiety.

It has occurred to me that perhaps Your Majesty would be interested by a conversation with him before he returns to South Africa about the 24th instant; & I know he would embark greatly encouraged upon his responsible duties if Your Majesty felt inclined to accord him an audience of a private character one of these days.

I trust Your Majesty will not think me presumptuous in making this suggestion.

I am Sir
Your Majesty's faithful servant
WINSTON S. CHURCHILL

WSC to Lord Elgin
(*Elgin Papers*)

1 November 1906

Private

Dear Lord Elgin,

The natural course in regard to the distribution of honours for military operations under the Colonial Office is for them to be considered by the Rewards Council, at wh the representatives of the Colonial Office meet the high officers of the Army. It is the custom – & I have hitherto observed it – for the Under-Secretary of State to attend the meetings of that Council, & when he attends, he of course presides. If the usual procedure is to be varied in this case & the matter is to be settled by an appeal to the Army Council, the result will be to prevent my taking part in the discussion of this question, & I am sure that you would not wish such a thing to happen in view of the

strong opinions I hold upon the matter & the obligation that rests upon me
to defend any decisions that may be taken.

Yours vy sincerely
WINSTON S. CHURCHILL

Lord Elgin to WSC

1 November 1906

My Dear Churchill,

I am sure you will admit that I have never wished to curtail your functions. At the same time the responsibility of the S of S imposes on me the
necessity of sometimes varying what may be the regular procedure in
ordinary course.

I think this is one of those cases, I mean the Natal Honours on which you
have written. I have consulted the Prime Minister and with his consent and
approval am consulting the Army Council. I did this before I got your letter
or I should have spoken to you.

But after all I have not in any way diminished your real opportunity. The
recommendations must go from me to the PM, and whatever the Rewards
Council had said it would have been the same. I do not intend this to go to
the PM until I have seen the case on my return to Office on Monday, and
before I decide I hope to have your counsel.

Yours very truly
ELGIN

WSC to Lord Elgin
(Elgin Papers)

3 November 1906   Colonial Office

Private

My dear Lord Elgin,

I hope you will not think that I do not fully appreciate the kindness of
your letter, when I point out to you that *no reason* has ever been assigned to
me for the change in procedure you have now ordered. The Rewards
Council was already summoned to meet at noon on Thursday, & it was only
when you fixed that hour for our talk about the Letters Patent that I directed
it to be postponed in order that I might wait on you. I am left at a loss to
imagine what other cause there can be for the change, wh of course you have
a perfect right to make, than a conviction that the less I have to do with the
matter the better. That is not a vy satisfactory conclusion. I do not feel that
it will be any use my intruding further in the discussion of the Natal Honours;

for you will have the advice of the Army Council to guide you, & no doubt Mr Haldane will be able & willing to deal with any Parliamentary difficulties that may arise. I do not see why one should anticipate them, now that the special medal is, as I hear from Sir M. Ommanney, to be abandoned.

You will I am sure be shocked to hear that the Lord Chancellor nearly died from heart failure on Thursday night; & is at present, though better, utterly unable to attend to the smallest kind of even private business.[1]

Yours vy sincerely
WINSTON S. CHURCHILL

Lord Elgin to WSC

3 November 1906
Personal

My dear Churchill,

I put out my hand for a quarto – but withdrew it for this more moderate sheet. For you will only get it as I am approaching the office. And the main point I wish to state does not require much detail.

There are a number of questions at this moment e.g. Natal Honours, Nigerian Railways, pensions & other points in the Constitution on which you have written Minutes and if you will allow me to say so Minutes of weight. But I have a difficulty in dealing with them in the ordinary way.

In most, if not all of them, we, you & I, as members of the Govt are compelled to judge of them from a different standpoint from the Office Staff. *We* must take political considerations into account. *They* are bound not to do so.

I want to put it to you that where the political element comes in the less *we* write the better. I hope I may say that we know each other well enough now not to scruple to say what we think if we confer, or to hesitate to compromise if that becomes necessary. But I feel very strongly that nothing of that ought to appear on the Minutes, if it can be avoided.

Under these circumstances I am keeping back some of these papers till I see you on Monday. Do not think I am preparing for an onslaught on your opinions – quite the contrary – but there are some things which I must criticize, if I am to act up to my responsibility.

Yours very truly
ELGIN

PS Just got your letter – Believe me I had no idea you had personally arranged for the Rewards Council meeting or I should certainly have communicated with you.

[1] Lord Loreburn remained Lord Chancellor until 1911 and died in 1923 at the age of 77.

I found the soldiers were agt it (the Rewards Council). Haldane told me the Adj Gen had come to him about it. So I said I was quite willing to have the opinion of the Army Council & he promised me he would get them to give it. I told him frankly that I considered the Natal proposals impossible. If they will give us the few *Military* Honours we suggest they will be so mixed up that they may escape detection.

But these Honours are – abominable. It was bad enough in India, but there one was at least Master in one's own house. In the Colonies Premiers & Chief Justices fight for stars & ribbons like little boys for toys – & scream at us if we slap them!

I am indeed distressed about the Ld Chancellor.

On August 4, WSC promised the House that he would inquire into the alleged prevalence of unnatural vice among the Chinese in South Africa. However, on November 15, WSC told the House that, because of the unprintable, confidential and markedly conflicting evidence that had been uncovered, the report could not be published. Some of the information, purporting to be a summary of the report, was published in various Liberal papers three days previously, and tended to confirm the worst fears entertained in 1904. WSC went on to say, however, that all persons suspected of practicing 'unnatural vices' would be repatriated at once and that, furthermore, the machinery for recruiting coolies in China would be broken up.

Lord Elgin to Lady Elgin
(*Elgin Papers*)
EXTRACT

15 November 1906   House of Lords

. . . I have to make a statement on the disagreeable subject at 9 tonight. Churchill has just been here and has carried off my speech to copy! He has to speak to-night on the same subject and wants to use my phrases! . . .

WSC to J. B. Robinson
EXTRACT

17 November 1906
[Copy]
Confidential

Dear Mr Robinson,

I am very sorry your son was unable to utilise his ticket for admission to the House of Commons the other night, but there was, as I know, an unusual crowd and my own brother who was similarly provided was also shut out.

Everything however went off very well and I think the HC is generally satisfied with the development of our South African policy. The conclusion is growing more solidly in the mind of the English people as a whole that Chinese Labour will certainly have to go, and I do hope you will try to use your influence as much in the future as you have in the past to bring this home to the mind of the great mine owners.

With regard to your affairs, I must tell you that the Portuguese are showing themselves very stiff and contrary, and Sir E. Grey is pressing the views of the Government upon them both by written communications and in oral interviews with the Portuguese Minister. I must be very guarded in what I say about these Foreign Office affairs but you may take it from me that nothing is being neglected to procure the fulfilment of the intentions of His Majesty's Government which remains quite unchanged. I will let you know as soon as any result is reached. . . .

Yours very truly
[WINSTON S. CHURCHILL]

J. W. S. Langerman to J. C. Smuts
(Smuts Archive)

27 November 1906   Johannesburg

EXTRACT

. . . . I cabled to Robinson on the 20 to inform Churchill about your views on Compensation and Land Settlement 'if war contribution were withdrawn and no reservation made in Constitution with regard to Land Settlement which people would deeply resent being reflection on their loyalty, sense of justice and humanity. Leaders are anxious to prove their good faith and prevent friction and misunderstanding between two governments which will result from Reservation, besides feeling of resentment which will be created among people. Cannot too strongly impress upon Churchill it is of the greatest importance' . . . I also wrote to Churchill by the mail which left here on the 19 in the same strain and perhaps more strongly. I got the following reply from Robinson 'Churchill has begged me to thank you for information and request you to thank and to inform the two Leaders' (you and Botha) 'that government is considering the matter referred to.'

I hope it will have the effect of making them pause and consider the matter more seriously than they would appear to have done hitherto. I think that when they do issue the Letters Patent for this country the covering dispatch will express the pious hope that trusting to the good sense of the people they confidently leave the matter in their hands, and reserving to the

British government the right at any time to intervene if those pious hopes are not fulfilled – or they might even reserve the question in the Letters Patent on the lines we discussed and in accordance with Churchill's views which we could agree with. . . .

WSC to General Louis Botha

24 November 1906   Colonial Office

[Copy]

Private and Confidential

Dear General Botha,

I am sorry that your message which reached me through Mr Langerman[1] and for which I thank you did not arrive sooner: for the proposals which you and General Smuts make are perfectly satisfactory to me. But our plans are now at last complete and to reopen any question connected with the Letters Patent would involve a very serious delay affecting not only their issue – which has depended on the sittings of the Cabinet and the holding of the necessary Privy Councils – but also in the announcement of the Orange River Colony Constitution which is to be made at the same time. I have been so anxious that both these grave matters should be satisfactorily discharged before Christmas that I could not myself take any step which might tend at the last moment to retard them.

I have never doubted that the Land Settlers would receive just and humane treatment from any Government of which you were a member. But there is a good deal of genuine anxiety not confined to our political opponents which it is a matter of high policy to allay. Our obligation to these people is an obligation of honour; and such obligations are not easily transferable. Further I think the new Governments in the Transvaal and Orange River Colonies would be put in a very difficult position, if they were forced to evict a number of settlers in the first few years of their Office. They might be thoroughly justified in each case and the tenant evicted might be a person quite unworthy of sympathy; but that would not prevent a storm of prejudice being excited by the Conservative Party and its powerful press, and the smooth and peaceful development of S. African affairs being in consequence disturbed by a series of controversies as bitter as they would be petty.

[1] Jan Willem Stuckeris Langerman (1853–1931), South African businessman and politician. President of Rand Chamber of Mines; Member House of Assembly, Union of South Africa 1910–15; knighted 1912.

The Government proposals when they are made public will be found to lie well within the limits of those put forward by you and General Smuts. No new settlers can be introduced except upon lands already occupied. The provisions are operative only for a less period than you yourself have suggested; and power is given to the Transvaal Assembly to terminate the system at any moment by coming to an agreement with the Imperial Government for affecting the objects aimed at in a different way.

There remains only the question on which Mr Langerman dwells of a 'slur' upon the good faith and humanity of your people. Believe me that is entirely illusory. There is no greater mistake than in seeing offence, where none is meant: and I am quite sure no one in the world will think of such a thing, unless you yourselves proclaim it.

Let me say in conclusion that the prestige and strength of this Government in any conflict which may arise with the House of Lords in the near future, will very largely depend upon the success of its South African policy towards which you can so powerfully contribute.

And with earnest good wishes for the future peace and prosperity of your people and the land they live in.

Believe me Yours very truly
WSC

WSC to J. Keir Hardie

3 December 1906   Colonial Office

Private

[Copy]

Dear Mr Keir Hardie,

I am obliged to you for your courtesy in giving me private notice of the question you propose to ask in the HC about the removal of the Hausas line, and for the enclosures which you have sent me for my information. We have been in telegraphic communication with the Governor Sir Walter Egerton since you last put a question on the paper, and I will give you in reply in the House a statement of the position. While I feel that the removal of the line is very desirably on sanitary and other public grounds, I agree with you that vigilance is required to prevent hardship or injustice to poor people. I have done and will do my best to see that they are treated with the same measure of compassion usually so generously extended to the slum landlord. I think the question you have asked and Lord Elgin's action in telegraphing will produce considerable effect. I should add that the news-paper whence you have received your information is a violently partisan organ which attacks the Administration with great bitterness, and some caution is in my opinion needed in regard to its presentation of the case.

I will return the extracts to you when I have shown them to the S of S.

[WINSTON S. CHURCHILL]

J. Keir Hardie to WSC

3 December 1906   House of Commons

Dear Mr Churchill,

Thanks for your sympathetic letter re the Hausas Lines. I note what you say about the newspaper. The information came direct from some of the people affected and the parts of letter which I sent you were merely supple-mentary and confirmatory of the information itself. I ought to have made it clear in my letter that I meant to put the question down today for reply on Wednesday & it was good of you to let me have such full reply on such short notice.

Faithfully

J. KEIR HARDIE

WSC to Herbert Samuel

7 December 1906   Colonial Office

[Copy]

My dear Samuel,

British citizenship is a privilege well worth an earnest effort to win. It is not and ought never to be a mere formality, but rather the solemn acceptance of duties & dignities. But I quarrel with our present regulations because they impose a wholly unreasonable & untrustworthy test which capriciously disregards the merits & the character of the applicant, and bars only the poor. Five pounds ten shillings is a very serious disbursement for a working man however thrifty he may be, & to many men of good record & conduct, who have laboured industriously & have faithfully performed all the duties of a British citizen for many years, so great a sum is often in fact an absolute impediment. This is another instance of that same odious principle of a poverty test which we stigmatised in the Aliens Act, which accords the truest enfranchisement to a well-to-do person however undesirable he may be, & shuts the door with a slam in the face of a poor man however honestly &

high-mindedly he may have lived. I am therefore strongly of opinion that whatever other tests may be prescribed, the naturalisation fee should be reduced. I think such a reform would come appropriately from a Liberal Government & with special grace from one who bears a name honoured throughout the world wherever counsels of sympathy & tolerance are in the ascendant.

Yours vy tly

WINSTON S. CHURCHILL

Lord Elgin to WSC

EXTRACT

27 December 1906   Broomhall

Private

My dear Churchill,

...I have been dreading every post to find the rumours true and that I was to lose your help. You might think it unkind if I said I 'hoped' not to hear – but however it may turn out I shall always look back on our cooperation during this year of toil & strife with peculiar satisfaction – and with real gratitude to you not only for the courage & ability with which you have fought our cause – but for the invariable consideration you have shown for me & my opinions.

With every good wish of the season.

Yours very sincerely

ELGIN

WSC to Lord Elgin
(Elgin Papers)

30 December 1906   Blenheim

Private

Dear Lord Elgin,

I have explained the financial position of Land Settlement to Marlborough. Of course there will be plenty of money; but I think it would be wise to telegraph and find out the exact income & outgoings that may be expected; & I am sending you on a draft in this intention. At present it seems to me that we place at the disposal of the Board £2,500,000 worth of capital – *interest free*. This money, ill-invested from a commercial point of view tho it may be, yielded last year, *after* sympathetic administration had been accorded – something like £50,000 from the two colonies. Such is the income of the Board *after* it has discharged its main function. I cannot see what other objects will require expense, except the administrative charges, now that no new settlers are to be planted. But for whatever may be discovered the funds are ample. From the standpoint of the new Governments the Land Boards are invested with 2½ millions of capital on wh the new Govts will have to pay £100,000 annually in interest. Originally it was intended that the moneys allocated to Land Settlement should (1) sustain the settlers (2) plant new ones & (3) pay interest & sinking fund on the whole sum. It will be strange indeed if the Boards cannot pay their way when relieved of the two last most important duties.

I enclose you a letter I have extracted with some difficulty from Basil Blackwood.[1] This man deserves your care. Goold-Adams' last request was that his services should be recognised; & I am sure you will feel that the State owes some consideration to a son of Lord Dufferin who shows so many good qualities and has done much responsible work at an early age with success. I should most deeply regret if the career wh he has by much enterprise opened out to himself were to be abruptly cut short: & I am sure the Colonial service will have lost a vy good officer. If you are able to secure him further employment, it will give me a great deal of pleasure.

I have not heard a word of Cabinet changes, except from the newspapers. Of course I should like to come into the Cabinet, so as to be able to take my proper part in national as apart from departmental politics. But I can easily imagine that no vacancy wh would suit me will be created in the near future, & I shall be quite content & happy to go on working under you in the Colonial Office for another year, if events should so shape themselves.

It is vy kind of you to write such generous things about our association. No one could ever have had a more trustful & indulgent chief than I have been most lucky to find on first joining a Government; & I have learned a vy great deal in the conduct of official business from your instruction and example which I should all my life have remained completely ignorant of, if I had gone elsewhere. Believe me I value vy highly the words of approval you have bestowed.

With all good wishes Yours vy sincerely
WINSTON S. CHURCHILL

[1] Ian Basil Gawaine Temple Hamilton-Temple-Blackwood (1870–1917), 3rd son of 1st Marquis of Dufferin and Ava (1826–1902); Assistant Colonial Secretary, Orange River Colony 1903–7; Colonial Secretary, Barbados 1907–9; member of the Development Commission 1910–17; killed in action.

9
Colonial Office 2

(See Main Volume Chapter 7, pp. 202–21)

I N early 1907, WSC learned that a larger number of Chinese coolies than had been anticipated were being shipped into the Transvaal.

WSC to Lord Elgin
(Elgin Papers)

3 January 1907

Private

My dear Lord Elgin,

I must most strongly & earnestly appeal to you to enable me to keep faith with the House of Commons on this point. First the office allowed me to say that the last shipload had gone in. Then when another shipload was discovered on the high seas, I was informed that only 1000 coolies were aboard. Then finally it turned out there were 2129 coolies aboard; & I had to promise that if any had been shipped beyond the licensed number they should be repatriated at once.

I never dreamed that such would prove the case; & I am quite sure you never intended it to happen. But it has; & we ought to act up to our words – unless the currency of Colonial Office pledges is to be seriously depreciated.

Yours vy sincerely
WINSTON S. CHURCHILL

Lord Elgin to WSC

4 January 1907　　　　　　　　　　　　　　Broomhall

Private

My dear Churchill,

On two bundles today I must write personally. (i) The extra number of coolies imported – (and I was sorry not to return this to-day – but I had a meeting of my Church Commission in Edinburgh & had only just time to open my bag.) I entirely sympathise with you in annoyance at this stupid blunder – and I have added words to the telegram, which as it stood seemed to me to accept the excuses. But when we come to the action to be now taken I am not so clear. By all means, if we can, let us repatriate. But I cannot see that you personally – or I, through you, break faith with the House if this has happened without our knowledge & we cannot redress it: or cannot do so except at extravagant cost. The House after all is a practical Assembly. We engaged to abide by the Licenses issued, then 259 coolies have been admitted in excess – we cannot send them back without consider-able expense, prob to the British taxpayer, – and at the same time raising doubts about contracts which it is in our interests to avoid. The House I think would accept an argument of that kind – when after all the *end had arrived*.

I have put nothing on the Minutes of this & have let the telegram go with my strengthening addition. But I hope we may agree on some such course of action before the reply comes. It is clear that if the cost of repatriation has to be met from British funds the Ch of the Ex must be consulted but, as I have hinted on the papers, I should certainly not have acted without reference to the Cabinet as a whole, had Parliament been sitting.

The second paper which troubles me I enclose with this. I do not at all understand how the proposed telegram throws you over: it was no desire of mine to do so.

On Dec 20 you said that a formal ackt was sufficient. It seemed to me that as S [Selborne] directly asked what he should reply, this would be scarcely polite. But I suggested nothing – & so far as I see there is nothing in the draft reply – which has not been said before either in the Houses or in telegrams. Now you propose a long & argumentative reply. I think that in-judicious, at any rate till we have got the Portuguese Govt really hooked. I don't quite like their delay. I must just add one word: I have loyally done all I could for Robinson. What has he done? He has given up the 3000 coolies – but by no means enthusiastically. As to white labour &c – *nothing*. I will not throw him over – but I distrust him – & would rather not see him in our front rank.

You wont mind my writing frankly for your eye only.

Yours very truly
ELGIN

The Morning Leader

8 January 1907

On 10 Dec Mr Churchill stated, in the House of Commons, that the steamship *Cranley* had left China for South Africa with 1,000 coolies on board. He explained that these coolies

> do not amount to a complete shipload, and are the remainder of those for whom licenses had been issued. But I am quite free to admit to the House that the figures at my disposal had led me to believe that the total number of coolies licensed to be imported had already been accomplished without this last shipment, albeit incomplete, and the information contained in the newspapers was to me as unexpected as it was unwelcome.

WSC to Lord Elgin
(Elgin Papers)

EXTRACT

8 January 1907   [Brooke, Isle of Wight]

Private

My dear Lord Elgin,

I do not want to be unreasonable about the 259 extra Chinese, & if great difficulties are encountered in repatriating them, I suppose they will have to stop. But it is important that we should have a try. I daresay the H of L will be content with that, & will recognise that the mistake was pure accident.

What I disliked in the Robinson telegram was the flat contradictions of what I had said in the House, wh is not emphasised by your minute but comes out vy strongly in the draft. I said that if reputable firms applied we would try to get them equal facilities, but that would take time. The draft says distinctly that we will not until after the enquiry. The difference is verbal merely, for we are quite agreed upon the policy. But having regard to the fact that Selborne's telegram refers specifically to my statement, I should prefer that the reply avoided what looks like contradiction. After all our position has been for the last three months that we would not refuse to consider similar applications. If these are made now I think the answer should be – that we have not yet secured any facilities for Robinson, but that when we do the applications of other firms will also be considered.

This seems to me to be a soft answer & not disagreeable to my words such as they were. Further I think the charge ofi nvidious treatment of Robinson would be awkward. It is much better to declare that our intentions are to deal evenhandedly with all. We shall of course do nothing – as the time is now so short.

I send you two letters wh have been sent me by Mr Ramsay Macdonald. I fear they will vex you; but you ought to see them. I think your defensive position 'The [Colonial] Conference must be master of its own procedure' is quite strong: but as you know I regret that we are occupying it. The question of Asiatic labour & Immigration would certainly affect State Premiers. I would certainly have allowed them to come, & would have let Laurier[1] bring three of his ministers. Total seven extra. Deakin[2] is the most hostile to our Government of all the Australians, & will simply be turned into a demonstration of the Tariff Reform League. The State Premiers would ipso facto have gone the other way. *Divide et impera!*

We ought soon to begin to consider vy carefully how to give these visitors, whoever they may be, a good show. Don't you think Haldane might review his Army at Aldershot, & the N L Club might give a grand 'swarree'! Then I would, if you agree, ask the Duke of Westminster – or will you – better still – to give a garden party & an evening party at Grosvenor House. He will do it like a shot. I feel we have not got the plant that the Tories had for sprinkling champagne, & must take thought accordingly. . . .

I shall be at the office on Thursday. At present I am staying with Seely at a nice old house in the Isle of Wight. Unluckily the sea has been dead calm, so that there are no great waves which I could watch for hours.

It was close to this place (Brooke) that Seely swam out six hundred yards to the wreck, when the life boats could not be launched owing to the fury of the storm, and carried a life line to the survivors of the crew: an action of almost miraculous good fortune & devotion.

Yours vy sincerely
WINSTON S. CHURCHILL

---

[1] Wilfrid Laurier (1841–1919), Premier of Canada 1896–1911; PC 1897; knighted 1897.
[2] Alfred Deakin (1856–1919), Prime Minister of Australia 1903–4, 1905–8, 1909–10.

Ramsay MacDonald to WSC

                                                    RMS *Ophir*
6 December 1906   off Adelaide

My dear Churchill,

I am venturing to write to you on the subject of the representation of the Australian States at the Colonial Conference in spring, and to urge upon you the desirability of their Premiers receiving invitations. There is considerable feeling here *in official circles* on this subject, & as there are one or two matters outstanding between the States and ourselves & others which though nominally on the whole Federal & not State, can be settled satisfactorily only by the cooperation of both. In view of the trouble ahead regarding anti-Asiatic immigration, I also think that this Government will be wise to have the State Premiers over to discuss what is to be done.

Further, I do not think we quite understand at home how the State authorities are as yet determined to keep their sovereign status & to regard the Federal Parliament as a subordinate authority. That cannot last, but the action of Mr Lyttelton & Lord Elgin in not inviting the State Premiers appears at this end as an attempt to take sides on a matter which will have to be fought out in Australia.

But above all, you cannot overestimate the importance of getting as many Premiers as you conveniently can to come and meet Liberal Officials & a Liberal Government. The cable & press conspiracy against you here is abominable. I have been trying to do something to make people touch Liberal & Labour Parties, & have gone bald headed for Deakin & Natal. But you have a tremendous task in front of you to break down the fears entertained about you & your party.

If you would like to see me at once on my return, drop me a line to 3 Lincolns Inn Fields. I expect to be in London again on the 12th or 13th of January. (I return by the *Moldavia* not by the *Ophir*) I am now leaving for Western Australia where I shall be for a week and then home. I have got so interested in Colonial questions that when you go to the House of Lords I shall put in for your job!

                                                    Yours very sincerely
                                                    RAMSAY MACDONALD

WSC to Lord Elgin

(*Elgin Papers*)

10 January 1907

Private

My dear Lord Elgin,

1: I have sent you on today a suggested answer to Selborne's telegram about Robinson's license, on wh I have bestowed some thought. If you agree, will you send me a telegram to say so, as owing I fear to my interference, there has been a great deal of delay in replying. I have arranged with Ommanney to keep a copy of the draft, so that it can go off at once.

2: Acting on your note authorizing me to accelerate the fixing of the Anglo-Portuguese Commission of Inquiry, I consulted with Ommanney & we sent a telegram asking Selborne for his views about it. I also sent him a private message explaining how the passage of time had altered the situation, & urging him to let us have his proposals about the joint enquiry as quickly as possible. He has responded at once with what I think are vy sensible proposals. They are now being minuted & will go to you to-morrow. Meanwhile I have seen Grey, who has done nothing since we last met, & have shown him Selborne's answer. He is quite willing to arrange with the Portuguese via Soveral & Lisbon; & has left full instructions (as he was going away) at the FO which will prevent any unnecessary delay as soon as your decision on the papers has been taken.

I hope that you will decide to work through the FO instead of *via* Selborne & Mozambique. Evidently Selborne would prefer it (see his telegram) and I am further convinced that Lisbon is the only road by wh HMG can approach the Gov Gen of Mozambique.

The Transvaal road is already blocked with Rand shekels. As soon as the papers come back from you, I will go over to FO & have the matter pushed forward.

3: How vy ill natured the press have been about the New Hebrides. I am making the office look up the numberless detailed communications wh in the last five years we have had with the Australian Govts on this subject.[1]

4: I send you a cutting which shows that I have been betrayed into an inaccuracy. It was not altogether my fault: but I need not say that I am much vexed at it on my own account & yours. Many thanks for the stiff telegram about the 259 extra coolies. The last words were vy necessary.

From all I hear – though I *know* nothing – Birrell goes to Ireland &

[1] For a discussion of the points at issue between the British and Australian governments, see J. A. La Nange *Alfred Deakin*, 2 vols, Melbourne 1965, Vol 2, Chapter 19.

McKenna to Education. Then I suppose Runciman will go to the Treasury as Financial Secretary, perhaps Buchanan[1] to India Office under Morley. *I* remain with you, I expect, & thus will take you vy much at your word in respect of all those kind things you said about wishing to keep me.

Yours vy sincerely
WINSTON S. CHURCHILL

PS I shall be here a good deal during the next week & am trying to get abreast of my work.

Lord Elgin to WSC

10 January 1907   Broomhall

My dear Churchill,

Thanks for your letter received yesterday evening. I meant to have replied this morning but was interrupted. I am glad to see that, as I expected, there is not much real difference of opinion on the two cases which I had mentioned. I am not quite sure what you have done with the 'Robinson' telegram. I sent it to you without an initial so that it might be quite open to you. Of course my object was not to give away anything to the WNLA: I had not done so in the House and I was simply sticking to my position with the hope that by so doing I should prevent the break up of the Assoc at an inconvenient moment. I agree that when it does break up we must treat them fairly & give the same measure as we do to Robinson. (By the way I see it reported that that worthy has sailed.)

Thanks for sending Ramsay Macdonald's letter – but I do not suppose you expect me to climb down now? I have great respect for him – he seems certainly one of the best of the Labour men – but he cannot any more than other men, in a rapid tour round the world get at the bottom of big questions. I do not believe there is much backing to this Australian demand.

Northcote[2] assures me that there is not: it is chiefly a personal question and the men who make the demand (the States Premiers) are in some cases by no means high class.

But believe me I am not simply blundering along (as the *Daily News* politely hints). On the contrary I think it necessary to abide by the constitution as it was defined – and above all not to increase the numbers. It is

---

[1] Thomas Ryburn Buchanan (1846–1911), Financial Secretary to War Office 1906–8; Under Secretary of State, India Office 1908–9; Liberal MP Edinburgh 1881–1885, West Edinburgh 1885–92, East Aberdeenshire 1892–1900, East Perthshire 1903–11.

[2] Henry Stafford Northcote (1846–1911), Governor-General of Australia 1903–8; Conservative MP for Exeter 1880–99; Financial Secretary to War Office 1885–6; Governor of Bombay 1899–1903; PC 1909; baronet 1887; Baron 1900; son of 1st Earl of Iddesleigh.

a simple lie that I am 'restricting' numbers – because in my humble judgment that would be to forestall the decision on the most important question that will come before the Conference. I do not myself think there is much fear of our getting tied up in preferential Tariffs: but unless we take great care a resolution might be carried, or powers claimed for the Conference or for some Council representing it, which might seriously hamper us in our international arrangements. This is a matter on which I have been meditating a letter to Grey – and I cannot do more than hint at it here. I shall at any rate have to bring it, & other points, before the Cabinet.

As you know, from something I once said to you of a possible reform of the House of Lords, I have no wish to stand aloof from Colonials, but the great difficulty is not the giving authority but the corresponding responsibility.

May I trouble you on a personal question. I enclose two letters from Mackarness.[1] I wrote in reply to the first pointing out that his quotation was unfair – it was taken out of the middle of my statement of the subject, that just before it I definitely declared that 'we forbid renewals' – and the lines which follow the quotation describe how the withdrawal of the coolies is to be practically effected & ends with a declaration of my personal opinion that 'the system as a permanency was impossible'. Further I referred him to *Hansard* on a point raised by Courtney,[2] that I gave 'an unrestricted discretion to the new Legislature' & showed that in my reply (which did not appear in the newspapers) I accepted entirely the view that any new Ordinance must be 'reserved'.

I think it is a bit strong that I should have to write to the papers because Mackarness has not got *Hansard* at Eastbourne! But my real reason is that while I think it would be easy for me to show that I have been absolutely staunch on the Chinese Coolie question, I could never satisfy the fanatics without using language which would be taken up by the other side – and it seems to me that I must face the abuse of the *Daily News* clique rather than do anything of that kind before the Elections.

You know these men better than I do – do you agree?

11th. I have yours of yesterday. I have telegraphed approval of the 'Robinson' telegram – though personally I do not think this is a 'Robinson' case. It is the Assocn licenses only that are in question.

I quite agree that the FO should work out an arrangement with Lisbon

[1] Frederic Coleridge Mackarness (1854–1920), Liberal MP for Newbury 1906–10; Advocate of Cape Supreme Court 1882; County Court Judge, Sussex Circuit 1911–20.
[2] Leonard Henry Courtney (1835–1918), Liberal MP for Liskeard 1875–85; Unionist MP for Bodmin 1886–1900; Under-Secretary of State for Home Office 1880–1; for Colonial Office 1881–2; Chairman of Committees and Deputy Speaker 1886–92; advocate of 'forbearance and conciliation' during South African War; Baron Courtney of Penwith 1906.

as to enquiry. My doubt of Selborne's proposals was whether they did not go further than the Portuguese would ever agree to. But we shall see.

I am a little afraid that Keir Hardie will make mischief about the Railway men. Mr Bell[1] has also written asking to see me as he is going out there soon. I have answered very civilly & told him to apply freely to Holland[2] – but perhaps you might see him. On the Railway men's case – if they have got the same as the Post Office – and as the men on the Cape & Natal Rys I really think we must support the H.C.

Poor Birrell – he deserved a little more of a rest after last session! As to . . . . . [?] I stand absolutely by what I said.

Yours very sincerely
ELGIN

Lord Selborne to Lord Elgin

(*Elgin Papers*)

TELEGRAM

(Received Colonial Office, 10.5 p.m. 10th January 1907)

[Copy]

10 January 1907, No 1.

Matter most urgent. Your telegram No 2, 7th January, I do not think that any incident of my administration has caused me more annoyance or regret than this unfortunate blunder made by my officers so long ago as 10th June 1905, and which is producing its consequences now. It was a perfectly bona fide slip such as all men are liable to. The Labour Importation Agency acting equally bona fide on mistaken information supplied by the Foreign Labour Department cannot reasonably be made to share responsibility. I quite understand that His Majesty's Government consider it very desirable that in view of pledges given 259 men of the new arrivals should not have licences issued to them or be allowed to proceed to the Rand but I am most grateful for being allowed to state extraordinary difficulty of Transvaal Government in the matter. If I am compelled to send back 259 of the coolies who have just arrived by the *Cranley* and are now in the

---

[1] Richard Bell (1859–1930), Labour MP for Derby 1900–10; General Secretary of Amalgamated Society of Railway Servants 1897–1910; Chairman TUC 1903; Officer of Employment Exchanges 1910–24.

[2] Bernard Henry Holland (1856–1926), Private Secretary to Secretary of State for the Colonies 1903–8; Private Secretary to the Duke of Devonshire 1892–4; author of *Life of The Duke of Devonshire*, 1911; CB 1904.

depôt at Durban and my officers succeed in explaining position to them without producing a riot whole expense will have to fall on Transvaal Government and from the point of view of the Transvaal tax-payer Government's position will be indefensible. Government will have to pay to the Labour Importation Agency same sum for each of the 259 as is charged to His Majesty's Government with respect to state-aided repatriated namely £25 per head. We must also pay coolies reasonable compensation for loss of advantages they expect under their contract I put this at £20 a head being very least sum which Jamieson[1] estimates that a reasonably hard working and economical coolie could save in the 3 years for which these men think they have come. Total £11,655 or say £12,000.

This is an estimate of minimum sum on which in opinion of Superintendent of Foreign Labour he can hope to persuade the men to return willingly. He says that none of them will return willingly without it. Says that it is more than possible that when they appreciate position they will stand out for more liberal compensation for breach of contract than £20 a head. We shall thus be involved in an absolute waste of public money to the extent of £12,000 at a moment when Government is in sore straits for money (and) is obliged to starve most necessary works in an effort to hand over the administration to the new Government without a deficit on the budget in spite of the very serious falling off in the revenue. For instance, a programme of new school buildings urgently required to replace existing insanitary accommodation has had to be postponed and it is pointed out to me that merely on account of a clerical error Government will have to throw away a sum which would provide school accommodation for 800 children. I would remind you that total number of licences which have been issued is 63,043 and total number of coolies in the country including all those brought by the *Cranley* is only 55,018, the difference being accounted for by the number who have been repatriated in one way or another or who have died. I am not in any degree whatever responsible for what has happened though I wish no one else to share with me responsibility for its consequences. I can only say that if His Majesty's Government can spare me this additional strain on Transvaal finances at a moment to me of extreme administrative difficulty and allow me to pass this extra 259 men into the Transvaal I shall be sincerely grateful. May I beg for an immediate reply to this telegram. In ordinary course last of the coolies who arrived by the *Cranley* would leave Durban for the Rand on 12th January and *Cranley* is due to start on return journey on 17th January. Heavy charges

---

[1] James William Jamieson (1867–1946), Superintendent of Chinese Labour in the Transvaal 1905–8 (seconded); commercial attaché to British Legation in China 1899–1909; Consul-General, Canton 1909–26, Tientsin 1926–30; KCMG 1923.

for demurrage and consequently further expense to Transvaal Government will be incurred if it is delayed.

WSC to Lord Elgin
(*Elgin Papers*)

11 January 1907

Private

My dear Lord Elgin,

I sent a private telegram to Selborne after consultation with Ommanney telling him that in view of his vy strong reasons against repatriation of the 259 he might assume that we would not press our request; & that an official answer would follow on Monday. I did this as time is of importance & trust you will approve. It follows out your wishes as expressed to me in your last letter.

I only hope that the guilty 259 will pass undetected. But if they are spotted, I will do my best & I think that the telegrams that have passed will be a very good protection.

Hopwood is here, & is on the best of terms with Ommanney who is helping him in every way in his power. I am so glad you were able to get Graham his KCB. I wrote to congratulate him.

Yours vy sincerely
WINSTON S. CHURCHILL

WSC to Lord Elgin
(*Elgin Papers*)

12 January 1907

Private

My dear Lord Elgin,

I recognise that your decision about State Premiers must stand & though I am sorry for it, I will of course accept it loyally & unreservedly.

I am of opinion that Selborne's line about the Railwaymen is quite correct & that he should be supported. No one can quarrel with us effectively, for imitating Post Office practices here & Railway practice in Cape & Natal, based as it is upon the minute of so respectable a First Lord of the Treasury as Mr Gladstone. Therefore I would give a short plain answer to Mr Keir Hardie on these lines. I have asked Mr Bell to come & see me here next week. I suppose you would wish him shown the usual courtesies, if he visits SA. He is a good honest fellow & personally I have a great deal of respect for him.

Mackarness. I think you should say that you will no doubt be called upon to speak on the question of Chinese Labour when Parliament meets, & that you think that any statement would be more conveniently made from your place in the House of Lords than by isolated letters to the newspapers. He presumes too much upon good nature & upon the ample consideration we have always shown to his views. It would be a pity to spoil the 'Kaffir boom' wh is now in full swing by an unnecessary bucket of cold water.

We are quite agreed that the whole matter must be brought to a settlement with the new Assembly. At present only one thing can be predicated about that settlement viz. that no more Chinese will be imported under existing conditions. That ought to be realised; but I see no use in detailed consideration of the time & manner of the winding up process. I think therefore you are quite right to shut Mackarness up. But I should mark my letter doing so 'private' in view of our past experiences.

I am *dead against* anything like a Colonial Council to interfere in our Foreign Relations, & am delighted to read what you say about it. I think it vy wise to approach Grey early.

Sadler[1] has returned. I am to have a talk with him next week. He looks younger than I thought.

Yours vy sincerely
WINSTON S. CHURCHILL

WSC to Lord Selborne

12 January 1907 [Colonial Office]
[Copy]

I am much obliged to you for your kindness in dealing so promptly with my telegram about the Anglo-Portuguese Labour Commission. You are quite right to remind me of your warnings and of how you said we should certainly burn our fingers if we touched this question, but pray believe me unrepentant. It was always impossible, and will always be impossible for the present Government to stand forward in the House of Commons as the supporters and champions of the WNLA in its present private and

[1] James Hayes Sadler (1851–1922), Governor British East Africa Protectorate 1905–9; Consul Muscat 1892–6; Consul-General Somali Protectorate 1898; Commissioner in Uganda 1901–5; Governor and Commander-in-Chief Windward Islands 1909–14; knighted 1907.

monopoly form. I regret extremely that we have not been able to secure for Robinson the effective facilities which we had promised to seek on his behalf. No one could forsee the interminable labyrinth of Portuguese prevarication in which we have been led. We might perhaps have bombarded Lisbon and made the war of 'Robinson's Licenses' as famous as that of 'Jenkins' Ear'; but the Foreign Office cannot bring their strongest pressure to bear upon Portugal, for fear that she, becoming sulky, should give coaling stations and other tit-bits to Germany. And while months have slipped away, we have been brought nearer to that blessed time when these questions will only very indirectly affect the Colonial Office. The situation has been materially changed from the fact that even if the secret agreement between the Government of Mozambique and the WNLA is denounced before this letter reaches you the three months notice which must necessarily precede its expiration, will carry us into the period of responsible Government.

Meanwhile no violent collision of opinion has arisen in the House of Commons, a succession of effective parries have been provided against direct attacks, and after all, we are 3000 licences to the good. I confess I have been rather puzzled to find how quietly Robinson has accepted the later development. The situation I had always pictured him as starving for labour, being excluded from the privileges of the WLNA and not yet possessed of any means of independent recruiting in Mozambique. But he seems to me composed though rueful and I observe in the papers that Langerman has stated – I think at Randfontein – that since the Robinson group had left the WNLA they had been able to recruit more Kaffirs than they could take. Now what is the explanation of that?

I had many long talks with Solomon when he was over here, and I am sure I hope most earnestly that the course of events will place him at the head of the new Government. I could not presume to advise what his course should be, because it seems to me that an enlightened opportunism is imposed upon him by the many uncertainties of the situation.

I say frankly that I should regard a Progressive Government as a very great danger and disaster at the present time.

From all I hear I do not think that there is much probability of such a thing. Indeed according to some rather knowing people twenty is the top limit to which that party will attain. I am sure it will be much better for South Africa in the long run, and be better for the relations between South Africa and Gt Britain at the present time if effective coalition can be formed between the non-capitalist section of the British population and that old agricultural Conservative party called the Het Volk. I therefore hope that Solomon's influence will be directed to that end, and I gathered from him that such was certainly the trend of his mind. But I agree with you that it would be a great pity if he were to come out in violent opposition to the Progressive party, and for that reason I greatly regret Fitzpatrick's candidature against him in Pretoria. However it is not much use speculating about these affairs until we get into the flood of the election.

Looking back over the past year, I feel relieved to think how many parliamentary difficulties lie back behind us; but still we must not conceal from ourselves that the great decision on Chinese Labour lies ahead. A succession of postponements has allowed the temperature greatly to cool down, and I think that a much more instructed and tolerant opinion prevails.

It is no good trying to make up our mind upon detail until we know what is the character and composition of the new Assembly; what its opinion is upon Chinese Labour and thirdly, by how large a majority that opinion, one way or the other, is expressed. I hope that the new Parliament will be found to be opposed in principle to the continuance of Chinese Labour and will declare its opinion unmistakably; that in consequence of those views it will of its own accord forbid all further importation, and having done this, will make proposals to us as to the best means of repatriating the coolies now in South Africa. The House of Commons would certainly judge with the utmost hostility any proposals which came from a Progressive Govt favourable to the principle of Chinese Labour. But if the new Parliament is unfavourable to that system, and if the Progressive party are in a minority, then it seems to me that a much more friendly and tolerant attitude will be assumed. We shall all be agreed upon the principle, and the only questions at issue will be questions of manner and time. In these respects, I should expect the House of Commons to be generous; the matter must of course be settled as a whole. It is indispensable that in no circumstances whatever shall any more Chinese be allowed to come in, it is necessary that a programme of extinction should be provided showing an immediate decrease, a constant dimunition, and a complete ultimate clearance.

Of course I think the sooner they are gone the better, but still I will myself endeavour to secure as easy conditions as possible for the winding-up of the system, although these conditions may imply the temporary re-enactment of the existing Ordinance, and even possibly – though on this I express only a very tentative and purely personal opinion – a certain proportion of renewals.

But believe me there is one point upon which there will be no yielding; whatever is demanded, whatever is proposed or by whomsoever it is demanded or proposed, we will not allow any more Chinese coolies, under indenture, to enter South Africa. Everyone is resolved on that, the most moderate members of the Government, equally with the most extreme members of their party; and the resources of the Foreign Office and, if necessary, of the Admiralty will be ruthlessly used to enforce that determination. Do not, I pray you, allow those people with whom you come in contact to nourish illusions on this subject. Of course it is conceivable that this Govt may be overthrown, but that will not happen for two or three years at least and when it does happen, do you suppose that the Conservative party are going to deprive themselves of all chance of regaining power by announcing [that] their return to office means the renewal of Chinese importation? Already no Conservative speaker attempts to justify the policy.

It is absolutely discredited, it is outside the area of practical politics, even by those who care about it and have suffered most for it. Therefore it behoves the Rand industry to face facts as they are, and to fill the constantly widening gap which the Chinese shrinkage will produce, by a reorganisation of native labour and still more by those attractive Gordon drills of which we are beginning to hear a good deal.

Do not suppose that I do not recognise the gravity and perils of any sharp collision between the House of Commons and the new Assembly in South Africa. I have done and will do my best to moderate and adjust and stave off any violent differences. When the new Parliament is erected, I will do all in my power to protect it from interference on any question, land, native, Indian, which may arise. I recognise that the native question must be settled by South Africa, and like you, I look forward to the speedy erection of a Federal system which will supply a platform for the more elevated and comprehensive view of native policy. I think it highly desirable that any restrictions to which they now object, would necessarily be modified – if not entirely removed – if we had an august Federal authority to deal with instead of a group of petty Governments pursuing local and selfish aims.

But Chinese labour is an exception to all this. It was introduced while the Transvaal was inarticulate, in opposition, as I shall always believe, to the wishes of the majority of the people, by oversea authority. The British people have made great sacrifices for the South African Colonies. On no subject have they ever developed or expressed so strong or persistent a resolve, and if Sovereignty means anything, they will most certainly get their way.

WSC

WSC to Lord Elgin
(*Elgin Papers*)

15 January 1907

Private

Dear Lord Elgin,

Don't abuse me for reopening a *chose jugée*. It reopens itself. That is the difficulty.

Ramsay Macdonald called here today. He is in earnest about the State Premiers & means to move an amendment to the Address on the subject. He has seen them all, & all are furious. Further I hear the Prince of Wales is much excited, & has been to the King to urge that they should be invited to attend. Thirdly these potentates themselves have today sent in official protests, & we are no longer confronted with Carruthers[1] alone but with the whole lot.

In these circumstances are we not making a great deal of trouble for ourselves? Will there not be endless abuse in the papers & a vy awkward debate in the House? I have said that I will do my best to defend your decision, & to that I stand. But surely a matter of this complexity & controversial importance ought really to be submitted to the Cabinet. At any rate the Prime Minister ought to know – & to know both sides.

I saw Bell today & reassured him about the Railway Circular. I have promised to write him a letter for the information of the Railwaymen in this country. An official answer is being sent to Keir Hardie in accordance with your minute.

Yours vy sincerely
WINSTON S. CHURCHILL

Lord Elgin to WSC

10 January 1907   Broomhall

By this morning's Bag Holland sent me the *Speaker* with Mackarness' Article: and I think under these circumstances I had better not write to *The Times*.

I had not time to finish my letter before coming in here for a meeting of my Church Commission – and I take an interval now to ack your letter which I got on my way to the station.

I am the very last person not to refer matters of importance to the Cabinet – but as the question stood when we left London I thought the case for refusing the States Premiers conclusive. Personally I think so still – and I have the Gov Gen – and I suppose his Govt – with me. But I shall certainly write to CB immediately – indeed I had already intended a letter on another point connected with the Conference.

The King made an enquiry, possibly inspired by the Prince (?) – and I sent him a Memo since which I have heard nothing more.

I am glad you did not come in for Jamaica[2]! I have no details yet except the newspapers.

[1] Joseph Hector McNeil Carruthers (1857–1932), Premier of New South Wales 1904–7; Member of NSW Legislature 1887–1908; knighted 1908.
[2] See pp. 634 et seq.

It may be that Ommanney's winding up has sent me more paper[1] – but as for a holiday!! On the contrary I am feeling a bit done up.

Yours very truly

ELGIN

The Scotch papers to-day declare that you are packing up your papers. [This letter formed the postscript to Lord Elgin's letter on p. 613.]

WSC to Lord Elgin
(*Elgin Papers*)

EXTRACT

17 January 1907

Private

My dear Lord Elgin,

Many thanks for your letter & I am vy glad that you are going to write to 'CB' about the State Premiers. The question is a difficult one, & I have discovered a good many arguments in favour of your views wh I will bring forward if the need arises. Yet it seems to me that a *via media* might be found wh would enable these six Premiers to receive the invitations they desire, without infringing upon your main position that the Conference must be master of its own procedure. You have always taken the view that one of the most important duties of this Conference is to decide its future composition – i.e. whether the State premiers shall be in or out. Surely they might be parties to that discussion. This I understand is one of their contentions. Further other questions of Immigration (Asiatic) & recognition of the status of British & Colonial professional men have now been formally raised by the colonies attending, & both these matters do undoubtedly affect the jurisdiction of the State Premiers. Would it not be a possible means of soothing their susceptibilities & meeting their wishes, if we were to invite them to attend to take part in such discussions as affect them in their State authorities, without too precisely defining what those discussions will be? I fear our refusal to invite them, no matter what reasons we assign, will be under the reproach of being ungracious, & that it will be made a great stick to beat us with, by our numerous enemies.

It is hard to measure the importance of such matters when they first appear on the horizon. Some turn out to be cockle-shells & others Cunarders.

I have discussed Mackarness with Holland. We both think that you

[1] Sir Montagu Ommanney retired from his position as Permanent Under-Secretary of State for the Colonies in 1907.

would pay him too much attention if you were to reply specially in *The Times*. I therefore return your draft letter.

Yours vy sincerely

WINSTON S. CHURCHILL

PS That impudent paragraph about 'packing up' has nettled me. It is a scandalous thing that persons in this office should impart to the Press information about what goes on in my room. I had ordered boxes – 3 months ago – to put away the papers of the year. I have asked Sir WBM to inquire of the messenger how such leakages occur.

WSC

Sir H. Campbell-Bannerman to WSC

22 January 1907   Belmont Castle
                                                                Scotland
Private

My dear Churchill,

I will bear in mind what you say regarding an invitation to the State Premiers of Australia, & will see that the Cabinet has both views before it when it decides. But what do you say to Canada with its Provincial Premiers?

Many people in the Press have been making free with your name, and your position and your success in it justify their very obvious speculation. But I am sure that it is better both for yourself and for the Government that you should continue to represent, and help in administering, the Colonial Office especially in a year so full of events – I particularly name three: viz (i) the introduction of new blood into the Office. (ii) the application of the new Constitution in S. Africa, and (iii) the Colonial Conference. We want your help at the CO for each of them, and they will be full of interest & of lessons applicable in other Departments. I am sure therefore that you gain by your continuance at the CO whatever might be the charms of change![1]

Yours vy truly

H. CAMPBELL-BANNERMAN

[1] In Campbell-Bannerman's first Cabinet changes, announced on January 24, Augustine Birrell was appointed Chief Secretary for Ireland; he was succeeded at the Board of Education by Reginald McKenna.

Lord Elgin to WSC

31 January 1907   Colonial Office
Private

My dear Churchill,

I am sorry not to at once accept any proposal from you but I really
cannot circulate this Memo on the Premiers. *I* know that it does *not* mean
that you & I are at daggers drawn on this subject – or any other. But this
is a direct negation to the reasoned proposal which I am putting forward on
behalf of the CO – and no one would ever believe me if said that behind
that blast of defiance there was the calm which prevails.

I will take it with me and shall not fail to mention that you take a different
view – but you will I hope forgive me if I cannot do more.

Yours v. truly
ELGIN

Memorandum by WSC

30 January 1907
Confidential

1. The main reason for inviting the State Premiers of Australia to the
Colonial Conference is that they want to come. In point of serious business
the Conference is not likely to lead to large practical results. His Majesty's
Government is not able or disposed to meet, except by a reasoned and decisive
refusal, the wishes of the Colonial Representatives for a system of Imperial
preference based upon the protective taxation of food. The Colonial Representatives have not hitherto given us any indication of a desire on their part
to contribute in substantial proportion to the cost of the Imperial fleets and
armies. It seems scarcely possible that any convenient machinery can, in
present circumstances, be devised for enabling a permanent Council of
Colonial Representatives to assist and restrain the Secretary of State for
Foreign Affairs in his conduct of European negotiations. Of the variety of
smaller matters which may also be discussed, some few may possibly be
advanced towards a settlement. But these are not in themselves sufficient
reason for collecting persons of consequence from the four corners of the
world. Unless some other, extra, serious, public advantage were to be hoped
for from the Conference, the utility of its expensive proceedings would not
be obvious.

2. But there is one set of benefits of immense practical convenience and
solid value which we hope this Conference may secure or help to secure, to
wit, the establishing of good personal relations between the new Liberal

Ministry and the leading men in the various Colonies; the friendly discussion of difficulties mutually comprehensible if frankly stated; and, above all, the object lesson that the affections of the British people for the Colonies are not a matter of party at all, but proceed on a plane above the ebb and flow of domestic politics.

It ought not to be forgotten that a Liberal Government has to encounter in Colonial affairs the steady and malignant detraction of a most powerful press service. Every action or inaction is represented in the Colonies – and, I think, particularly in Australia – in the most odious light by the press telegrams. The worst excesses of partisan opponents at home are cabled to the newspapers of every Colony as the opinion of patriotic England upon this or that particular event. By these agencies a great volume of prejudice has been excited in the past, and is still being aggravated. But His Majesty's Government have now a fine opportunity of dispersing these unhealthy vapours, which, however contemptible in origin, are a positive hindrance to the smooth working of the Colonial Office. We have the chance, and perhaps it will not recur, of meeting face to face, in circumstances of hospitality and friendship, many of the principal persons with whom we have to deal; of doing them honour, which they court, and according them recognition for which they are eager.

3. It is therefore submitted that it is an object of State policy good in itself to invite as many of the Colonial Premiers as possible, and to make the amenities of British hospitality effective throughout the widest possible circle. Arguments should be sought not to exclude but to include within reasonable limits prominent Colonial Representatives, even if, as is disputed, a severe logic or some strict rule of precedent or etiquette appeared to stand in the way. But still less should Colonial Representatives be excluded when their exclusion means not only the not securing of an advantage, but an actual cause of offence: for that would make our Conference positively harmful – a costly and elaborate function resulting in a net balance of ill-temper and misunderstanding.

4. The political situation in Australia has altered considerably since the Commonwealth Act. However desirable that measure may have been in principle, it was plainly premature. A reaction – natural and inevitable, serious, yet not probably lasting – is in full progress against Federation. Amid other cleavages in Australian politics, and cutting transversely through them, is the growing controversy of State rights against Federal authority. I cannot pretend to measure the force or direction of this dispute; but no one can read the Australian despatches from the State Governments without observing the bitter jealousy with which they regard anything in the nature of an encroachment by the Federal Power on their residuary prerogative.

5. It is obvious that the position of the Australian State Governments is fundamentally different from that of the Canadian provinces; for whereas the Canadian Provincial Parliaments only enjoy their powers in virtue of devolutions from the Federal Government, the exact reverse is true in Australia, and the powers of the Commonwealth are composed only of those functions of which its various Sovereign States have voluntarily divested themselves. Without entering into an elaborate argument upon the exact constitutional position occupied by an Australian State at the present time, or attempting to measure whether that position reaches the status of a self-governing Colony, or, if not, by how far it falls short, it must be conceded that appearances strongly favour the State claim. Especially is this the case in all matters of ceremonial usage, where, indeed, the distinction between the Australian States and the Canadian Provinces is strikingly marked. Governors, chosen often from the lesser nobility, are appointed by the Crown to the Australian States; Lieutenant-Governors of local origin are selected by the Governor-General in Council for the Canadian Provinces. The former enjoy the privilege – if privilege it be – of direct correspondence with the Colonial Office; the latter have no relations with this country. Thirdly, the laws passed by the Canadian Provincial Parliaments are assented to by the Governor-General, and are not referred, as is the legislation of the Australian States, to the Secretary of State for the approval of the Sovereign. These important distinctions, in themselves of a ceremonial character, apply with especial force to the Colonial Conference, the ceremonial aspects of which are so important.

6. It may pertinently be asked why, since these things are so, did the Australian States not protest against their exclusion from the Conference of 1902? To this they reply that the invitations in this case were to the Coronation of the King, and not to a Conference; that they had no right to demand invitations to the Coronation, and that such a request might have been misunderstood had it been preferred; further, that the Conference held on that occasion was one which fortuitously arose out of the presence of so many Colonial Premiers in London; that, however convenient and important it may have been, it was not a formal and authoritative Conference as the earlier ones had been, and that certainly, above all, it had no right to regulate the character and composition of future Conferences. Such reasoning may be good or bad. A more practical explanation of any inconsistency in the attitude of the States is to be found in the growing cleavage upon the question of State rights *versus* Federal authority.

7. It is not the business of the Imperial Government to take sides in a purely Australian controversy. The federation of groups of separate Colonies into single Governments of wider resources and more august authority is doubtless a desirable object. But the relations of the Colonial Office with the

individual Colonies, as well as with the Federal Power, require to be very carefully adjusted during the transition period, or we may run the risk of substituting for the policy of 'divide and rule' the practice 'unify and estrange'. A certain degree of enlightened opportunism must influence our action. Whether in Australia or South Africa, the creation of a new Central Government ought not to be allowed to alienate the loyalties of the subordinate or contributory Governments, so long, at any rate, as they retain in any effective degree their identity and power. Still less should we, at a time when so much is uncertain in Australia, pronounce decisively upon a disputed Australian question, stake our whole influence upon the side of the Federal Government, and so incur the resentment of six Governments with whom we have continual relations for the sake of gratifying a single Government, which, whatever its parchments, has less direct and natural force. Such a course, it is suggested, would be injurious to the conduct of Colonial affairs, and prejudice the settlement of many difficulties which crop up from day to day. It would, further, fail altogether to help the Commonwealth to worry through this difficult period, would only, on the contrary, stimulate the controversy, aggravate the jealousies, and embroil the Imperial Government in their midst. The best way to dispose our own affairs and gradually fortify the position of the Commonwealth is by remaining neutral in this quarrel, bringing both parties together, inculcating forbearance, soothing ruffled susceptibilities, and showing to both an equal measure of courtesy and respect.

8. If it be objected that the scope of this argument is altogether too wide and serious for such a light matter as the giving or not giving of a semi-social invitation to half-a-dozen gentlemen from Australia, I would direct attention to the protests of the Australian States themselves especially to that of South Australia, and to the evidence of their resentment, which has already accumulated on other matters. Mr Ramsay Macdonald, who has just returned from a visit to Australia, fully confirms the strength of the feeling which has been excited, and proposes himself to move an amendment to the Address upon the subject.

9. It is not denied that reasons may be found to make a good debating case against the inviting of the State Premiers; but it is submitted that these are only good reasons for doing an impolitic and an unpopular thing. No real difficulties lie in the way of their inclusion. There are solid and numerous grounds for distinguishing between the Premiers of the Australian States and those of the Canadian Provinces; and as Sir W. Laurier has already obtained permission to bring a number of his Federal Ministers, it would not seem that any protest is to be looked for from that quarter. Logic cannot be pleaded as a bar, for what logic is there in a system which freely accords two Representatives to Natal and Newfoundland, and will deny any representation to

New South Wales with five times their aggregate population? No embarrassment is to be looked for at the Conference Board, for hardly anything is settled by votes, and no decision is binding. The State Premiers would take their seats upon the same terms as other members of the Conference; but their position and *status* would have to be borne in mind in considering the weight to be attached to any opinions they might express upon subjects which, formally at any rate, have been vested in the Federal Government.

10. It is necessary, however, that the State Premiers should be invited for some specific act of business of which their competence to judge is beyond dispute. One of the most important acts of the Conference will be to decide upon its future composition – that is to say, among other matters, and first among such matters, whether the State Premiers are to attend future Conferences or not. It cannot be denied that this at least is a question which directly concerns them, and at the decision of which they have a right to be present; and this should be the reason assigned for their invitation to the Conference.

By taking this path we may even at the eleventh hour avoid the difficulties in which a decided pronouncement either on the one side or the other will involve us, and may gratify the desires of the State Premiers without derogating from the status of the Commonwealth Government.

*   *   *   *   *

Lord Elgin to WSC
(Elgin Papers)

17 January 1907   [Colonial Office]

My dear Churchill,

I enclose letters which Lucas handed on to me without remark – but Ommanney said – 'Lucas is sending you a letter from Sir H. Blake which, making every allowance for his Irish impulsiveness, calls for serious consideration. I think these reversals of the Governor's decisions in matters of discipline are dangerous everywhere, specially so in the East.'

I take some blame to myself for I have had the experience of the East – but I also had considerable sympathy with your championship of the Law. But I must say that I do not think a Colony like Ceylon is in a state in which we can say that no Govt servant is to be dismissed on a suspicion of dishonesty or the like – unless the charge can be proved in a court of law. Any person so dismissed, after, say, a departmental enquiry, ought to have the right, if he likes, to bring an action for wrongful dismissal; but that is enough to protect him. To go further & to allow appeals such as those we have had lately would make the whole system unworkable: & the result would be corruption unabashed.

In my opinion we ought to accept the decision of the Governor's despatch in this case. I have no doubt in my own mind that it is *just:* and you admit it is probably merciful. But I am not inclined to give the offender any option. Please return with the papers that I may Minute.

Yours truly
ELGIN

WSC to Lord Elgin
(Elgin Papers)

19 January 1907   [Colonial Office]

Private

Dear Lord Elgin,

Apart from the case now in point the Governor's decision has been reversed in only two instances. On others he has been asked to explain; but wherever the explanation was even plausible his view has prevailed; & in at least twenty cases in the last year it has been accepted without challenge. There is therefore no justification for the complaints in his letter & still less for his tone. Even this office have commented severely upon the vy unsatisfactory manner in which personal cases are disposed of in Ceylon; & you yourself have in more than one minute assented to this view.

In this particular case I have nothing to add to my minute. I do not see what connexion there can be between the irritation of Sir Henry Blake and an abstract question of law & justice affecting a humble person who has appealed to you. Nothing could well be more indefensible than the impropriety committed in this instance: & to offer the man the option of a criminal trial in open court is in my view the only step that can safeguard our position without injuring that of the Governor. The right course would have been to say that the acquittal of the Supreme Court was final in respect of the charges of peculation against Mr Serasingka; & that if the Governor had not taken the trouble to present his case to the Court in its full strength, he had only himself to blame for the consequences. But I was anxious to find a middle course which would, I thought, harmonise with your administrative methods in these sort of disciplinary questions & so I proposed the option.

You now inform me that you intend to brush aside altogether the argument wh I have set out in the paper & to confirm with your approval the shocking violation of elementary principles of law & justice which has occurred. And you send me the Governor's letter, as if I ought to agree to this man being treated with wanton illegality & flat injustice, in order to save Sir Henry Blake's face & to satisfy his impatience under correction. I cannot think you mean this.

I do not know what to do. You can of course over-rule me *with* reasons or *without* them. But any of these cases may at any moment be brought before the House of Commons. If Mr S chooses to write to any Member of Parliament – Liberal or Tory – & point out that he has been dismissed by a Departmental Inquiry for frauds on wh he was acquitted in the High Court, the brickbats will be about *my* ears; & let me say most solemnly that the Liberal party cares vy much for the rights of individuals to just & lawful treatment, & vy little for the petty pride of a Colonial Governor.

I can only say that a determination not to consent to such improprieties which are cruel to individuals & fatal to good Government has always actuated me, & that I will never depart from it because it is expedient in the supposed interests of discipline. I am quite sure that if this file of papers were submitted to the Lord Chancellor, to Mr Morley, to Mr Asquith or to any of your principal colleagues their opinion would be that a protest against such methods of administration was necessary. If Sir H. Blake dislikes his decisions being over-ruled he has a simple remedy. He can avoid breaking rules which even a schoolboy would understand, & committing errors in procedure which in any court in the British Empire – civil or military – would invalidate proceedings.

As to Ashmore[1] – I do not wish to criticise a dead man. But I am sending you a newspaper extract wh Mr Morley sent me from the India Office, wh throws an odd gleam of light upon the tone & temper wh high officers of the Ceylon Govt observe towards the amiable, civilised & cultivated people whom they are set to govern.

Yours vy sincerely
WINSTON S. CHURCHILL

WSC to Lord Elgin
(*Elgin Papers*)

23 January 1907   [Colonial Office]

Private

My dear Lord Elgin,

This is the charge which we should have to meet if the Serasingka case were raised in Parliament: – that he was falsely & perhaps maliciously

---

[1] Alexander Murray Ashmore (1855–1906), Lieutenant Governor and Colonial Secretary to Ceylon 1904–6; served also in Cyprus, Transvaal, Gold Coast and British Guiana; knighted 1905.

accused; that upon lawful trial he was acquitted by the High Court; that conscious of his innocence he confronted his accusers with the decision of that court & demanded further inquiry; that these accusers thereupon constituted themselves into a new & wholly non-legal court; that they retried the case & decided that he was guilty of the frauds for wh he had been acquitted by law; that thereupon they dismissed him from the service *for fraud;* that upon the improprieties of this procedure being pointed out by S of S the accusers for the first time explained that the cases of fraud of wh they had found him guilty *departmentally,* although they belonged to the same series of defalcations, were different from, though similar to, the counts rejected by the High Court; that although these new charges are described by the accusers as so conclusive that there can be no doubt what the verdict of the High Court would be upon them, they are not to be submitted to a judicial test; & the ground to be assigned for not so doing is – (& surely it is the climax) – consideration for the interests of the accused!

I have never attempted to pronounce upon the guilt or innocence of the accused, nor do I assert or impugn the integrity of the accusers. The case stands 'Rex v. Serasingka'; & both parties must conform to the ordinary customs of law. But if you ask me whether I think S guilty or not, I say that I find in his charges against his superiors after his acquittal vy strong grounds indeed for believing him innocent.

A man who had escaped by the skin of his teeth, by a legal quibble, by the chance failure of a witness for the prosecution, & who knew that there lay behind him a long & indefensible series of frauds on many of wh no charges had yet been preferred, would in my opinion not be likely to press for further inquiry into his conduct.

In minuting I was content to put the case at its lowest; for the argument is to my mind the same whether S is guilty or innocent. We have no right to jump to conclusions on that point. We are face to face with a flagrant impropriety, which if it were detected would be universally condemned. The only course wh in my opinion would extricate the Ceylon authorities from their difficulty would be to offer the man another criminal prosecution; & then if he declined it & prepared to accept his dismissal in silence they could at least point to that significant fact. It would not excuse their conduct; but it would afford some assurance that justice had not been perverted by gross errors in procedure.

May I say further that when I wrote my minute I had no reason to suppose that you would differ from it as the action proposed was essentially moderate & in the nature of a compromise. Indeed I was at pains to re-write the whole minute in order to state my vy strong view in terms of sufficient restraint. I could not foresee that Mr Lucas would after consultation with Sir M.

Ommanney append to my minute private letters from the Governor of
Ceylon & expressions of their own opinion upon them. Had I been allowed
to see these letters I would have communicated my minute to you privately
instead of putting it on the papers in the ordinary way.

As to the passage wh you now propose to write to Sir H. Blake privately, I
do not see how it can help matters: for unless Mr S is informed that he can
have a trial if he wants it, he will only know that his memorial to you has
been rejected *sans phrase*. Why should he petition again? What more can he
say?

I have now said all that I can on this subject. Your letter to me is very
kind & considerate; & I am most grateful to you for the patience with wh
[you] treat me on all occasions. I did not mean to write bitterly, & certainly
I have always written in a spirit of profound respect; but I do most deeply
regret the view you take of these questions, & that matters, in themselves of
vy small importance relatively, should make such inroads upon our time &
strength.

I will write later in the day about Jamaica & one or two other matters
wh are not yet quite clear.

Yours vy sincerely
WINSTON S. CHURCHILL

WSC to Lord Elgin
(*Elgin Papers*)

26 January 1907 [Colonial Office]

Private

Dear Lord Elgin,

Your decision in the Ceylon case causes me the most profound disquietude.
In over-ruling me you do not assign any reasons, nor attempt to do justice
to the vy grave arguments I have so earnestly submitted to you. You give
me no indication of the line of defence you would expect me to adopt, if this
matter were to become, as it easily might, the subject of a debate in the
House of Commons. As the matter stands I do not see how I could possibly
defend it. Of course these sort of questions fall so largely within the legal zone
that I recognise that a lay opinion like my own may be at fault. I would
suggest therefore that I may at least be fortified with the opinion of the Law
officers upon the legal aspects of the procedure adopted, before action is
taken which commits the Colonial Office to approving it.

Yours vy sincerely
WINSTON S. CHURCHILL

Lord Elgin to WSC

28 January 1907   Broomhall

My dear Churchill,

I think you have not been quite so fair to me as usual on the Ceylon case. You write rather bitterly of my over-ruling you. What have I done? I deliberately abstained from doing anything of the kind, for instead of re- cording any minute I sent the papers back to you with a private letter telling you how the case presented itself to me. May I take the opportunity of saying once more – what I have said previously – that I think it is of some consequence that any difference of opinion between us should not appear on the minutes circulated in the Office if that can be avoided. When we are both in London it is comparatively easy for you have only to mention the matter – but even in holiday-time I should greatly prefer to have notice beforehand of your views on debatable cases. I can promise, I think, in no way to prejudice your position.

Now as to this case. It seems to me that the real difference between us is not as to the merits but as to the procedure. I understand your last Minute to amount to an admission that Serasingka was presumably guilty of frauds. But your point is that he had not been convicted by a Court. My view may be coloured by the fact that I also had been a 'man on the spot' – but I cannot see why conviction by a Court should be a *sine qua non* for this class of servant. The Governor's despatch seems to me to state fairly the reasons why he did not appeal a second time to a Court, (and observe he also frankly admitted the justice of the first acquittal).

I do not think it is fair, in this case, to allege the 'petty pride' of a Colonial Governor. No doubt petty pride exists among them as amongst other men and even in the House of Commons. Nor do I overlook what Ommanney says of Blake's 'Irish impetuousness'. But I am not convinced by the letter, which I return, that the Ceylon Govt intends anything less than just & lawful treatment: I agree that in the case of a dead man we must anyhow be silent.

Will you accept a decision that we do not interfere in this case, if I write a private letter in the terms of the enclosed?

Yours vy truly
ELGIN

*   *   *   *   *

In 1906, the United States Government was embroiled in an argument with the Governor of Jamaica, Sir Alexander Swettenham,[1] over the pro-

[1] Alexander Swettenham (1846–1933), Captain-General and Governor-in-Chief, Jamaica 1904–7; Acting Governor, Straits Settlements 1898 and 1900; Governor and Commander-in-Chief, British Guiana 1901–4; KCMG 1898. He was the brother of Sir Frank Swettenham, Governor of Straits Settlements 1901–4, who gave his name to Port Swettenham.

curement of labourers to build the Panama Canal. Relations were further strained after an earthquake in the island on 14 January 1907 which partially destroyed the town of Kingston and which took the lives of 800 people. Rear Admiral Charles Davis, USN, (1845–1921), landed armed troops from his warship in the harbour to assist in clearing the town's streets, justifying his move on the grounds of 'common humanity'. Swettenham, however, felt that Davis' action reflected on his ability to maintain law and order. He sent a sarcastic letter to Davis, later published in the newspapers, in which he said, by way of example, that the recent ransacking of a New York millionaire's home did not justify a British Admiral in landing an armed party to assist the local police.

Arthur Lee to WSC

13 December 1906

Private

My dear Churchill,

With reference to our conversation of this afternoon the complaint made to me (privately on Nov 5) by President Roosevelt was (i) that the Governor of Jamaica has been 'deliberately and quite needlessly' trying to impede the efforts of the American authorities to procure labourers for the Panama Canal works and (ii) that, when interviewed on the subject by one of the American Canal officials, he used language of a very derogatory, and even insulting, nature about the US Govt, and the Secretary of War in particular.

I must add that President Roosevelt was most anxious that no official action should be taken by the US Govt in connection with this matter – but it would perhaps be possible to improve the situation by a private hint to the Governor.

In any case I trust that you will consider this expression of the President's views as strictly private and confidential.

Yours sincerely
ARTHUR LEE

WSC to Lord Elgin

TELEGRAM

[Copy]

January 1907   Colonial Office

Clear the line

Swettenham's letter to American Admiral published in today's papers Hopwood & I both think letter plainly indefensible & wantonly insulting.

We consider it of highest importance that your action in relation to Governor's conduct should precede any demand for apology from United States. Sir Charles Hardinge[1] fully concurs and thinks that incident is especially unfortunate in view of Root's mission to Canada.[2] We have telegraphed to Governor asking for text of his letter & if verified hope you will authorise instructions being sent forthwith to him to withdraw letter & express regret for having written it. In event refusal we ought to recall him at once

CHURCHILL

Lord Elgin to WSC

TELEGRAM

22 January 1907

Regret absence delayed reply to your telegram lamentable incident at Jamaica. Approve enquiry made. Entirely agree that if text of letter verified it must be promptly and unreservedly withdrawn.

Refusal to obey surely impossible: it would mean complete collapse and must involve immediate recall.

ELGIN

Lord Elgin to WSC

22 January 1907

This Jamaica business is a nuisance – One does not want to sack a good man for a bad manner – but sometimes a blunder becomes a crime. I sincerely hope there may be a compromise of some kind.

If Swettenham had really to go it occurred to me that perhaps Macgregor[3] might be sent. He is very hopeful to move from Newfd to a warmer climate and he has tact & firmness. But I only mention this to *you* & I hope there will be no occasion.

E.

---

[1] Charles Hardinge (1858–1944), Permanent Under-Secretary of State for Foreign Affairs 1906–10, 1916–20; Ambassador to St Petersburg 1904–6; Viceroy of India 1910–16; Ambassador to Paris 1920–23; knighted 1904; Baron Hardinge of Penshurst 1910; KG 1916.

[2] On January 19 Mr Elihu Root, the American Secretary of State, paid a private visit to Earl Grey in Ottawa apparently to see if there were any grounds for settlement of the off-shore fishery disputes. His visit was cut short by the grave—and eventually fatal—illness of Earl Grey's daughter, Victoria Grenfell.

[3] William Macgregor (1847–1919), Governor of Newfoundland 1904–9; of Lagos 1899–1904; of Queensland 1909–14; knighted 1889; PC 1914.

Lord Knollys to WSC

23 January 1907   Windsor Castle

My dear Churchill,

I have submitted to the King your letter about the unfortunate incident which occurred at Kingston the other day, & he desires me to thank you for having been so good as to inform him as to the situation.

I have no doubt that you or Mr Holland will kindly acquaint HM with Sir A. Swettenham's answer to Lord Elgin's telegram as soon as it arrives.

Yrs sincerely
KNOLLYS

WSC to Lord Knollys

24 January 1907

[Copy]

Private

Dear Lord Knollys,

I am sending by special messenger the telegram wh: Ld Elgin authorized me to send on Tuesday to Sir A. Swettenham, together with the 3 telegrams wh he has sent in answer thereto & to an earlier inquiry. It wd seem on the first view difficult to resist the Gov's desire to retire, more especially as this is not the first occasion when trouble has arisen between him & the subjects of foreign powers. But I am writing to Ld Elgin to suggest that now that the regrettable letter of Sir AS is out of the way,[1] we might with propriety ask the FO to ascertain the circs in wh armed parties were landed in a Br Colony from a foreign warship. We have no wish to dwell on the incident; but questions will certainly be asked abt it when Parlt meets. We have already addressed an enquiry to the Gov in this sense.

Yrs v. sincerely
WSC

PS Enclosing 2 FO telegrams.

Lord Elgin to WSC

25 January 1907

Private

My dear Churchill,

I am sorry I have not been on the spot these last days – but felt you would carry things through. I rather wish we could have let the Governor down a

[1] Under pressure from the Colonial Office, Swettenham expressed his regret to the United States Government that such a letter had been sent. His apology was accepted.

little more gently, but it is really his own fault. He ought to have reported his difficulties with the Americans, if these existed, when they arose, or at any rate as soon as he resolved to take action. Had he done this the quarrel, so far as we were concerned, would have been entirely as to mode of expression – a serious one I admit: but capable of treatment.

I should like to save the man, I confess. For though rather rough, I think he has been a good officer.

I was going away with my Commission yesterday – but I did not think you expected any reply to your cypher telegram, when I got it. I have got a bit of a cold but intend to be up on Monday for this Australian dinner.

One word about our Ceylon friends (tho' I agree we ought not to spend so much time over them) as my draft letter to Blake did not please you I have said nothing about it in accepting the suspension – which I cannot honestly refuse to do. We shall soon have a new Governor & Co Secy in Ceylon and we ought to be able to introduce reforms.

Yours very truly
ELGIN

Lord Knollys to WSC

25 January 1907   Windsor Castle

My dear Churchill,

The King desires me to thank you for your letter of yesterday & its enclosures.

He thinks the proposal that the FO should, now that Sir A. Swettenham's letter is out of the way, make enquiries as to the circumstances relating to the landing of armed foreign sailors without permission is a very good & proper one.

I see in some of the papers today that the feeling in Jamaica against the Governor is running rather strongly at present.

Yrs sincerely
KNOLLYS

WSC to Lord Elgin

TELEGRAM

25 January 1907   Colonial Office

Secret

Hopwood has shown me yr letter & suggested telegram to Swettenham. We both feel that circs now render it inapplicable. The point outstanding is to decide as to method of dealing with resignation. This you can settle on Monday. Probably you will write kindly letter dealing with past services. I think we shd treat it that resignation is on ground of age. Swettenham is evidently overtaxed. See telegram in *Times* today as to his behaviour & feeling in Jamaica. Sir C. Hardinge has been here. The Americans are pressing to know whether HMG have any ground of complaint. We told him we had telegraphed for the facts & until then nothing cd be said.

CHURCHILL

* * * * *

WSC to the Adjutant, Queen's Own Oxfordshire Hussars

5 December 1906   12 Bolton Street

[Copy]

Sir,

I should be very glad if you would inform me what is the nature of the course of instruction which I should attend in order to become qualified for Field Rank; and I would certainly make every exertion in my power to comply with the regulations. But my official work is at the present time very heavy and has been so the whole of this year, and it would be quite impossible for me to be absent from London while Parliament is sitting and very difficult for me to attend satisfactorily to any course of instruction which required daily attendance. I would be glad if you would submit to the General Officer Commanding on my behalf, that my case is a special one and differs from that of many other Yeomanry Officers, both because of my Ministerial office and also because of the thorough training which I received at Sandhurst and in the Army as a regular soldier and on account of War Service. If it were possible for the General Officer commanding to relieve me from the necessity of attending any definite course of instruction I would undertake to prepare myself privately in such leisure as I could find for the necessary examination. If this could be done I think I should have no difficulty in obtaining the necessary qualification and of course I could attend anywhere and almost any day of the week for the purpose of being examined either in writing or practically in the field. Otherwise I fear I shall have to ask that the period of grace may be extended until such time as my official duties have come to an end.

[WINSTON S. CHURCHILL]

*Lieut-Colonel Sir Robert Hermon-Hodge[1] to the Assistant Military Secretary, Southern
Command*

12 January 1907   Queen's Own Oxfordshire Hussars
                                             St Thomas' House
                                             Oxford

Copy

With reference to your letter asking for a report on the cases of Major
Winston Churchill MP and Major the Hon Eustace Fiennes MP[2] and their
failure to present themselves for examination for Field Rank on promotion.
I recommend that these Officers be excused this examination for the following reasons: –

Both these Officers have exceptionally long and meritorious experience
on active service, particulars of which are sent herewith. Both Officers are
occupied with Parliamentary duties. Major Churchill has also to attend to
official duties, and Major Fiennes has a City business to look after. Both
Officers are natural leaders and thoroughly competent in every way. In
reporting on the Regiment in 1905 the GOC remarks 'I thought the Squadron Commanders exceptionally well qualified for their positions.' and in 1906
he remarks, 'The Squadron Commanders are all good, indeed I may say they
are distinctly above the average.' Copy of reports of 1905 and 1906 are
enclosed herewith.

                                             ROBERT HERMON-HODGE

Lieut-Colonel Sir Robert Hermon-Hodge to WSC

20 January 1907   Wyfold Grange
                                             Nr Reading

Private

Dear Winston,

Some correspondence has been taking place as you know with reference
to your passing for Promotion to Field Rank. I wrote last week as strongly
as I could recommending that you should be excused on the grounds of

---

[1] Robert Trotter Hermon-Hodge (1851–1937), Lt Colonel and honorary Colonel Oxfordshire Yeomanry. Conservative MP 1886–92, 1895–1906, 1909–10, 1917–18; baronet 1902;
Baron Wyfold of Accrington 1919.
[2] Eustace Edward Twisleton-Wykeham-Fiennes (1864–1943), Later Lt Colonel Oxfordshire Hussars. WSC's Parliamentary Private Secretary at Admiralty 1912–14; Liberal MP
for Banbury 1906–10, 1910–18; Governor and Commander-in-Chief Seychelles Islands 1918–
1921, Leeward Islands 1921–9; baronet 1916.

your varied and meritorious active service, your natural capacity as Leader, and the very complimentary reports on the Squadron Leaders of the Regiment by the inspecting Officer in 1905 and 1906, and also of course the difficulties of your Parliamentary and official position. I am pleased to tell you that Sir Ian Hamilton has forwarded my recommendation to the Army Council for favourable consideration on the same grounds as those above mentioned. I am at the same time requested not to make use of his letter in any official correspondence or in any other way outside the Regiment.

I sincerely hope the result may be to your convenience; but if it is I must ask you to be extremely guarded in making reference to it. I am sure you will agree that while the class of man which provides the Yeomanry with officers must often present 'special cases' such as yours, it would never do to make them precedents.

I am yours sincerely
ROBERT HERMON-HODGE

PS I shall try and spend a week or two at the school myself in April. If you could come in the same way at the same time it would be nice – but I fear you will be tied.

WSC to Lieut-Colonel Sir Robert Hermon-Hodge

22 January 1907   12 Bolton Street

[Copy]

My dear Colonel,

Thank you very much indeed for your kind letter and for the testimony which you have been so good as to bear on my behalf. I hope that your efforts will be successful. I spoke to Mr Haldane on the subject and he was certainly sympathetic. I should, of course, like to compete for the examination, and I am quite sure, if notice were given, I should be able to prepare myself privately to pass it.

I have been studying Mr Haldane's schemes with much care lately and I think he certainly has great ideas about the Auxiliary forces. We will have, however, to keep a vigilant eye upon the interests of the Yeomanry.

With all good wishes,

Yours very sincerely
[WINSTON S. CHURCHILL]

Sir Edward Ward[1] to General Officer Commanding-in-Chief, Southern Command

31 January 1907   War Office

Copy

Sir,

With reference to your letter of the 17th instant no. 91/309, I am commanded by the Army Council to express approval, as a special case, of your recommendation that Major the Honourable E. E. Twisleton-Wykeham-Fiennes and Major W. L. S. Churchill, Oxfordshire Imperial Yeomanry, be exempted from qualifying for promotion to their present rank in consequence of the war services and varied military experience of each officer.

I am Sir, Your obedient Servant

E. W. D. WARD

*   *   *   *   *

Frederic Mackarness to WSC

24 January 1907   6 Crown Office Row

Dear Mr Churchill,

I have been asked to send you the enclosed letter: and I wish to tell you that about three weeks ago I wrote to Lord Elgin on the same subject, but could not persuade him to do what we are now begging you to use your influence with him to sanction.

It occurred to us that, as you had made known the views of the Colonial Office in the Railway vote, so Lord Elgin might have no objection to you writing something which would clear up the doubts which have been raised with regard to the meaning of his speech.

I need hardly add that the signatures to the letter have been attached by me at the request of the signatories who have each written to me on the subject.

Yours vy truly

FREDERIC MACKARNESS

[1] Edward Willis Duncan Ward (1853–1928), Permanent Under-Secretary of State, War Office, 1901–14; AAG Ladysmith 1899–1900; Director of Supplies South African Field Force 1900; KCB 1900; KCVO 1907; baronet 1914.

G. P. Gooch[1] *& others to WSC*

24 January 1907

Dear Mr Churchill,

In his speech on the Transvaal Constitution on the 17th December the Secretary of State used these words:—'The contracts under the Ordinance are for three years, but there is the power of renewal. We respect them for three years, but we forbid renewals . . . . The new Transvaal Government may do one of two things. It may propose a new Ordinance, or it may not. *If it does, and acts with reasonable promptitude, I do not think any serious question will arise about renewals.*'

This last sentence, which has been published in the Transvaal by order of the Government in a summary of Lord Elgin's speech, has created much perplexity as to what is the real mind of the Imperial Government.

In the 'Letters Patent and Instructions relating to the Transvaal', it is stated to be the Royal will and pleasure 'that all persons within our dominions shall be free from any conditions of employment or residence of a servile character,' and that 'upon the termination of the period of one year from the date of the first meeting of the Legislature the . . . Labour Importation Ordinance 1904 . . . and all Rules and Regulations made under the authority of the said Ordinance shall be repealed . . . . *and the system of labour deriving effect from the said Ordinance, Rules, and Regulations shall accordingly be determined*'.

On the 23rd February last the Chancellor of the Exchequer, after declaring that the Government would repeal the Ordinance and then leave it to the Transvaal to say whether it would have Chinese labour or not, explained his meaning in these words:—

"Do not let the House misunderstand me: I say Chinese labour. It will be for the Colonists themselves to determine whether or not they will allow Yellowmen to go on labouring in their midst, *either in the mines, on farms, or exercising any trade in any way.*'

And he added:—

'Any legislation corresponding to that of this Ordinance and inconsistent with our best traditions would unquestionably be vetoed by the Government on behalf of the Crown.'

We have understood from the above passages, especially the parts we have underlined, that it is the policy of the Imperial Government not to sanction Chinese labourers in the Transvaal, after the expiration of the existing contracts, except as free men and potential citizens. We cannot doubt that

[1] George Peabody Gooch (1873–1968), historian; Liberal MP for Bath 1906–10; CH 1939; OM 1963.

this is the policy to which His Majesty's Government adheres. Since, however, misapprehension has arisen in the Transvaal, and at a time when it is all important that the electors should be in no doubt, we earnestly hope that Lord Elgin will allow some explanation of his meaning to be published with the same authority as that which accompanied the publication of his speech on the 17th December by the Government of the Transvaal.

We beg to remain, Yours faithfully

G. P. GOOCH   R. C. LEHMANN[1]   FREDERIC MACKARNESS
GEORGE GREENWOOD[2]   C. F. G. MASTERMAN[3]   PHILIP MORRELL[4]
HERBERT PAUL
J. B. SEELY

PS We enclose cablegram from *Daily News* Special Correspondent.

WSC to F. Mackarness

25 January 1907
Private   [Colonial Office]
[Copy]

Dear Mackarness,

There is nothing in Lord Elgin's speech in the House of Lords wh is inconsistent with the policy of the Government as he & I have often explained it to Parliament. He considers, & I am bound to say I most heartily agree with him, that his statements of policy upon important matters are much better made from his place in Parliament, than by isolated & fortuitous letters to *The Times* newspaper upon the challenge of individuals.

But I agree with you in thinking that the determination of His Majesty's Government to put an end to the existing system of Chinese Labour requires emphasising at the present time in view of the Transvaal elections, & I will take advantage of my meeting at Manchester on the 4th Feb to make that clear.

Yours vy try
WINSTON S. CHURCHILL

[1] Rudolph Chambers Lehmann (1856–1929), Liberal MP for Harborough 1906–11; member of Staff of *Punch* 1890–1919; Editor *Daily News* 1901.

[2] Granville George Greenwood (1850–1928), Liberal MP for Peterborough 1906–18; knighted 1916.

[3] Charles Frederick Gurney Masterman (1873–1927), Liberal MP North West Ham 1906–1911, South West Bethnal Green 1911–14, Rusholme 1923–4; Under Secretary of State, Home Office under WSC 1909–12; Financial Secretary to Treasury 1912–14; Chancellor of Duchy of Lancaster 1914–15; PC 1912.

[4] Philip Morrell (1870–1943), Liberal MP South Oxfordshire 1906–10, Burnley 1910–18; married Ottoline Bentinck, half-sister of 6th Duke of Portland.

WSC to F. Mackarness

30 January 1907   [Colonial Office]

[Copy]

Dear Mackarness,

Ld Elgin has written me the enclosed letter which I may forward to you for the infn of yourself & the other gentlemen who signed yr letter to me.

I do not think you have any grounds for supposing that the policy of the Govt in respect of the winding up of the Chinese Labour experiment has undergone any modification. All the pledges wh have been given to Pt will be carefully respected & fulfilled in their regular course.

Yrs v truly

WSC

Lord Elgin to WSC

29 January 1907

My dear Churchill,

I am very sorry that you have been troubled abt my speech in the H of L. I have always endeavoured to give a courteous attention to any representations from our friends in the H of C – and I shall much regret it if I do not continue to have opportunities of personal intercourse.

On this subject, when Mr Mackarness first wrote to me, I ventured to say that I thought it unfair to quote from a summary wh was incomplete, when the full report of what I said in the debate in the H of L was available in *Hansard*. It is true that I, by inadvertence, omitted to refer to the veto reserved in the case of any new Ordinance at the point in my speech to wh the quotation belongs – tho' it certainly was in my mind.

My omission having been noticed by Ld Courtney, I expressly corrected it in my reply.

I am prepared to stand by my declarations on that occasion as being entirely in accord with the pledges given for the Govt by myself – or other members of the Govt, & I think my friends ought to accept that assurance. I think that any challenge or development of that position ought to be raised where the declarations were made, i.e. in Parlt.

Yours v sincerely

ELGIN

F. Mackarness to WSC

31 January 1907   6 Crown Office Row

Dear Mr Churchill,

Many thanks for your letter with its enclosure from Lord Elgin. I will show them both to the co-signatories of the letter we sent to you, & tell you what they say.

In the meantime may I ask you whether your letter may be published? It is not marked private, and I think might do good in the Transvaal. Would you look at the marked part of the enclosed cablegram in today's *Morning Leader*?

Yours vy truly
FREDERIC MACKARNESS

PS As you may not have kept a copy of your letter to me, I return it to you in case you do not recall its exact terms. May I, please, have it back?
FM

*   *   *   *   *

WSC to Herbert Gladstone
(*Herbert Gladstone Papers*)

8 February 1907   Colonial Office
Private

My dear Gladstone,

I enclose you some cuttings from the Manchester papers upon the working of the Aliens Act.

I was concerned to find the other day how vy bitter & disappointed the Jewish Community have become in consequence of the continuance of this very harsh & quite indefensible measure. I am sorry to trouble you on such a matter, but I should think your own people at Leeds were equally offended. I hope you will be able to do something to allay the feeling wh is rife. I am sure the Liberal party would support the Repeal of such a foolish piece of legislation.

Believe me, Yours vy sincerely
WINSTON S CHURCHILL

4 February 1907

The recent blue-book on the first year's working of the Aliens Act shows that those who refrained from welcoming the measure as a heaven-inspired piece of legislation had time and facts on their side. The Act was for the purpose ostensibly of keeping out undesirable aliens. Every man, be he patriotic in the largest sense or in the narrowest sense, is fully convinced that Great Britain should not show the height of hospitality to undesirable people.

But the question is, what constitutes the objectionable and ejectionable degree of undesirability? The Act does not prevent a Witzoff from coming into England and marring and 'marrying' as many English women as will believe in his vows; it does not prevent the entrance of all sorts of swindlers, rogues, vagabonds, thieves, of both sexes, so long as they can afford (with stolen money!) to come first or second class. But it does prevent poor but honest people from coming in. It makes poverty a crime, but not a preventable one.

During 1906, 49,017 immigrants came to us, and of these 489 (less than one per cent) were rejected. And it cost £24,000 or £50 each to keep them out. No fewer than 792 appealed against their ejection, and 442 appeals were successful. All those who were turned back from the land of promise to the regions of despair – from England to Russia – were so treated because they had not sufficient means, not because they were undesirable in the sense that the dishonest and the depraved are undesirable.

Figures show that the officials have attempted to justify the Act and their own salaries by vexatious examinations and inspections. Children were parted from parents, and people have been sent back to their own country and thence returned here at the expense of charitable institutions, as first-class passengers. That shows the grotesque value of the Act. As long as a foreigner can beg, borrow, or steal the price of a first-class passage, he is welcome. Let him save his money and come third class, and he will be rejected, unless that money happens to be a certain sum, alterable at the whim of the Home Secretary.

The Act calls for amendment, because it is useless and vexatious. If it did what it was intended to do, it would undoubtedly justify the expenditure on its administration.

*   *   *   *   *

Lord Selborne to WSC
TELEGRAM

10 February [1907]
Private Personal

See Telegram from S of S for Colonies No 3 Feb 8th. Do you admire it? I am asked if the men I have recommended are of good character professionally and personally. The power of comment fails me. Is that telegram compatible with any confidence in me and what answer would you give in my place? I have divided the council in my recommendations in answer as nearly as possible between the Boers & British but from the native point of view I should have preferred to have another British or two because you cannot find among the Boers men wisely sympathetic to natives and I make the greatest point of including such men in the council because we shall find none of them in the Assembly. Even Solomon has greatly disappointed me by the line he has taken about natives in his speeches. I lay great stress on getting nominations out on the 20th or 21st as I see now that it will save a world of future trouble if we do. See my telegram Feb 9th A.

SELBORNE

WSC to Lord Selborne

TELEGRAM

EXTRACT

12 February 1907   Colonial Office

Private & Personal

You quite misunderstand telegram No 3 of Feb 8th. Of course we do not doubt for a moment the propriety of your recommendations for second chamber or the care & impartiality with wh they are made but every name is liable to challenge in Parliament. We have deliberately assumed direct responsibility for approving selections & what would be said if I were cross questioned about age professions & characters of selected candidates? . . . We must have full details so that our personal responsibility may effectively support your judgement. I will do what I can to hasten decisive reply and expect it will reach you in ample time but it would seem to me good policy to keep a few vacancies till after elections. I will study your Federation paper with greatest care.

CHURCHILL

WSC to Lord Selborne

TELEGRAM

14 February [1907]

Private & Personal

It would of course be improper to pack second chamber with rejected candidates but nevertheless I do not see why a man who has received votes of perhaps thousand electors should be less eligible than one who has never presented himself to popular election. We are so much to the good over

Constitution and have played so fairly throughout that we have a right to ask for full confidence from all parties in the Transvaal & I do not think you are under necessity of taking any notice of protests to wh your telegram refers. They must just wait till you are ready announce decision.

*   *   *   *   *

WSC to Lord Elgin
(Elgin Papers)

14 February [1907]   Colonial Office

Lord Elgin,

Of course you must decide. But Parliament is sitting now & I am quite sure there will be a row if we are committed to participation with Natal in this ugly business.

I claim nothing: but I should be glad if you would mention to the Cabinet my opinion – that it will be a vy awkward matter to defend & may easily involve us in serious embarrassments. The unscrupulous action of the opposition on the New Hebrides Convention shows the sort of help we shall get from them.[1] I earnestly hope that you will *yourself* decide to tell Natal that as there seems no prospect of improving sensibly the condition & status of the prisoners in question we do not see our way to intervene.

I will do my best to defend the policy determined, but we shall greatly add to the burdens of the CO in Parliament, if, without any real justification, we make ourselves responsible for the misconduct of Natal.

WSC

WSC to Lord Elgin
(Elgin Papers)

16 February 1907   Colonial Office

Please add to my minute the following:—

I have nothing to add to my minute of October 25, except that the conduct of the Opposition upon the New Hebrides Convention shows vy clearly the sort of use that will be made of the action to wh we are asked to commit ourselves; & whereas in the case of the New Hebrides Convention there were no real grounds for a charge of inconsistency, there appears to me to be considerable ground in this matter, of wh full advantage will be taken in the House & in the country.

WSC

[1] In a speech in reply to the Address on February 12, Balfour attacked the Government for tactless and ill-judged dealings with the Australian and New Zealand Governments.

Sir Edward Grey to WSC

7 March 1907　　　　　　　　　　　　　　　Foreign Office

Private

My dear Churchill,

I have looked into the question of the Swettenham papers, and I am more than ever strongly of opinion that nothing ought to be published.

Roosevelt has resisted the pressure of the press on his side, and we were told last month that he was determined not to publish if he could avoid doing so, as he wished the incident to be closed and done with.

Our publication, even of the papers you have sent, means re-opening the whole matter, and surely our case is quite strong as it is. The only censure passed upon Swettenham has been in connection with his letter, which he was asked to withdraw. After that, he resigned, his resignation was not accepted, and he was given an opportunity of withdrawing it. It was only when his resignation was sent in a second time that it was accepted. Therefore, there is nothing in question between him and the Government but the letter. I am inclined to think, now, that he made a mess of other things too. But the only possible complaint he could have against the Government is in connection with the letter. And all we need say is that the Government remain of opinion that the letter was not a proper one to have been written under the circumstances; and that they have so far confined their disapproval to this one point, which is absolutely clear, and which could not be further elucidated by the publication of papers, since the letter itself is already public property.

If Swettenham chooses to launch out into the press and drag in other matters, I do not think he will gain by the controversy, and if it does become necessary to publish papers the reason will be apparent, and the case will have been re-opened not by us but by Swettenham.

But until something of that kind happens and creates a new situation, I am strongly of opinion that we should keep the whole controversy to the subject of the letter, and refuse papers.

Yours sincerely

E. GREY

WSC to Lord Elgin
(*Elgin Papers*)

7 March 1907

Lord Elgin,

I talked this [the above letter] over with Sir E. Grey. He is willing to consult the American Embassy about publication. I am sure that you will suffer if it can be stated that we dare not publish the papers that Swettenham demands, & if he states, as he will do, to all & sundry, that he has been unjustly treated & would be justified if the facts were not concealed. (See *Globe*). I think FO are unhandy about this. It only shows how well *we* have behaved to Swettenham & to USA. Please let me have the letter back.

WSC

Lord Elgin to WSC
(*Elgin Papers*)

8 March 1907

My dear Churchill,

I am not sure if you wrote before or after you received the enclosed from Grey. But my duty is clear. If the FO on their responsibility declare that publication of any document will prejudice relations with the U.S. I cannot urge publication because *I* shall suffer.

I agree with Grey that our defence is really good as he puts it – but even he admits the possibility of Swettenham forcing our hand: and if it had been possible in any way to publish enough to stop that move on his part, without exciting American rejoinder it would be advisable. I must confess however that to my mind the selection as proposed must be followed by publication in America.

I will speak to Grey at the Cabinet tomorrow.

Yours
E

WSC to Sir Edward Grey

EXTRACT

9 March 1907   Colonial Office

[Copy]

My dear Grey,

I have been thinking over your letter to me about Swettenham and our conversation thereupon. It may be because I do not understand your foreign combinations, but I really cannot see how the publication of the papers I sent you should cause annoyance to the American Government. For what do the papers show? They show that Swettenham was an ass, that he was wrong at every point, that he wrote an indefensible letter which he was made to withdraw, and that afterwards on being invited to state any circumstances of provocation known to him, he utterly failed to do so, and furnished us with no information that would have justified for a moment diplomatic representation. They show us as a Government perfectly fair to Swettenham, prompt in our respect for international courtesy and frankly recognising the generous and humane motives which prompted their action. How the publication of facts like these could be supposed to embroil us with the United States is to me incomprehensible.

On the other hand, I foresee the possibility of considerable embarrassments if we persist in complete refusal to publish papers. . . . I don't see how a debate cd possibly be conducted without a clear explanation of the circs which led to his resign. & I am very doubtful whether that explann can be given without reference to the telegrams which have passed which would necessitate their publication.

In any case, so soon as Swettenham returns home, he will be bombarded by reporters, politicians and friends. He has expressed the opinion that he has been unfairly treated in his official despatches to us, and he has demanded the publication of papers. If we refuse, he has only to say to all and sundry who resort to him that he has been unjustly served as would be proved if the papers were published, but the Govt dare not publish the papers, so his lips are sealed. The result of this will certainly be a debate in the HC in which either the Govt will be forced to disclose the correspondence or else to bear the offensive imputations which will certainly be made that it can be asserted they have something to conceal. In the latter event 'the unjust treatment of Sir Alexander Swettenham' will form the subject of another taunt for service on party platforms.

Of course your view must prevail but I gathered from our conversation the other day that you were not disinclined to send the correspondence to the American Embassy, to point out to them the pressure to which we shall be subjected in consequence of Swettenham's resignation and to ascertain in their view what is the line of least resistance. I hope you will still find it possible to do this.

Yours very sincerely
[WINSTON S. CHURCHILL]

WSC to Lord Elgin
(Elgin Papers)

27 March 1907   Chateau Bellefontaine
                                                        Biarritz

Private

My dear Lord Elgin,

I am glad you have decided to relieve Swettenham forthwith.[1] His conduct was rapidly degenerating. I hope Olivier[2] will do well. He certainly is keen & capable. The King dines or lunches here *daily!* & seems vy well disposed to us. He is much reassured by the beginnings of self-government in the Transvaal & by Botha's attitude and speeches. He grumbled a little about the State Premiers. I said that personally I would have liked them to come; but that the arguments against were vy serious; that possibly Deakin would have refused & that in any case it was now too late. He accepted this last with regret, & the matter is at an end I think so far as he is concerned.

I hope there is no danger of Laurier throwing us over. It would be a shocking cold *douche*. Surely some private representation might be made to him. Could not you or the PM send him a 'private & personal' urging him not to fail us. I should be so sorry if he did not come. Really it would be a disaster.

The weather here is glorious & there are a great many people I have known a long time – all Tories! I get a good deal of chaff & prodding, especially from high quarters – endeavouring always to frame suitable replies.

I think my holiday will do me a lot of good.

Alack I have undertaken to address the Land Reformers in Drury Lane Theatre on the 20th Ap & the speech involves a good deal of work in unfamiliar ground. As however I possess no land, I approach the subject of its redistribution with serenity & an impartial mind. Loulou Harcourt writes me that he is about to join the Cabinet. But this is to be secret till after Easter.

With good wishes, Yours vy sincerely
WINSTON S. CHURCHILL

[1] His resignation was announced on April 1.

[2] Sydney Olivier (1859–1943), Colonial administrator; succeeded Sir Alexander Swettenham as Governor of Jamaica 1907–13; previously served in British Honduras, Leeward Islands, and West Africa; Secretary for India 1924; knighted 1907; PC 1924; Baron Olivier of Ramsden 1924.

Sir Arthur Davidson[1] *to Lord Elgin*
(*Elgin Papers*)

28 March 1907   Biarritz

Dear Lord Elgin,

The King desires me to thank you for you letter of the 25th and to say that he perfectly understands the situation with regard to the Jamaica Governorship.

His Majesty has signed the submission, and feels sure that the choice of Mr Olivier which you have made is a good one.

The King has also had the opportunity of hearing details of the situation, and of Mr Olivier's capacity for dealing with the work in hand, from Mr W. Churchill who is here.

I remain, dear Lord Elgin, Yours very truly
ARTHUR DAVIDSON

Sir Francis Hopwood to WSC

EXTRACT

30 March 1907   Colonial Office

My dear Churchill,

Hexham was good enough for you. I had seen Lloyd George & Burns the day before & both seemed to fear that the Govt would lose the seat.[2] Causton[3] told me that there are a great many out voters in the Division, – at a by-election they can get in to vote & no doubt did so pulling down the majority. There is no official news. Lady Elgin has been ill and the S of S could not leave town but I think he got off to Scotland last night. The King wrote him a very clear & able letter stating the arguments for not excluding the State Premiers but the letter did not press for any reconsideration on this occasion – I wish I had been brought face to face with that question six months earlier, with your help we should have got them united on some terms & on some pretext. . . .

Yrs sincerely
FRANCIS HOPWOOD

---

[1] Arthur Davidson (1856–1922), Equerry and Assistant Keeper of the Privy Purse and Assistant Private Secretary to King Edward VII 1901–10; Groom-in-Waiting to Queen Victoria 1895–6; knighted 1906.

[2] At a by-election the Liberal majority only dropped from 2,085 to 1,157.

[2] Richard Knight Causton (1843–1929), Paymaster-General 1905–10; a Liberal Whip 1892–1905; Liberal MP Colchester 1880–5, Southwark 1888–1910; PC 1906; Baron Southwark 1910.

Lord Elgin to WSC

2 April 1907   Broomhall

Private

My dear Churchill,

Thanks for your letter of 27th and for your support in high quarters. Nothing in our collaboration is more gratifying to me than the confidence with which I can reckon on your support for any act done – even if in the earlier stages there may have been some difference of opinion. Pray believe that I never act without your concurrence if I can see my way to do otherwise and above all I keep ever in view that you in the House of Commons have the labouring oar in the defence of our policy.

So far as Olivier is concerned I was afraid a figurehead might be suggested which would have been a calamity. I think that knowing O so well we shall be able to keep him at hand and the only letter I have yet seen welcomes the appointment.

You will have seen it is all right about Laurier coming – I agree his abstention would have been a disaster – so would have been Deakin!

I am delighted to hear you are having a good time. I was kept in town till Sunday by Lady Elgin's health. She had a sharp attack of influenza. Yesterday I had a busy day on Scotch Churches & have two more in prospect. But I hope to benefit by the change.

Yours very sincerely
ELGIN

King Edward VII to WSC

6 April 1907   HM Yacht *Victoria & Albert*
                                                               Toulon

My dear Winston,

Many thanks for your kind letter which I received yesterday just before my departure from Biarritz.

I was very glad to have the opportunity of having several conversations with you on various interesting subjects.

It is quite true that we have known your parents for many years (even before their marriage) & you & your brother since your childhood. Knowing the great abilities which you possess – I am watching your political career with great interest. My one wish is that the great qualities you possess may be turned to good account & that your services to the State may be appreciated.

Believe, me, Very sincerely yours

EDWARD R

Lord Knollys to WSC

24 April 1907   Buckingham Palace

Confidential

My dear Churchill,

Perhaps you will allow me to say that I do not think if I were you, I would bring forward your proposal to the King about General Botha[1] – I mention this to you purely from friendly motives as the PM wrote to him on the subject, and the King, judging from a letter which I received from him today, viewed the suggestion with great disfavour. In fact, he has told me to let Haldane know privately that he could not agree to it.

Pray do not trouble to answer this.

Yrs sincerely
KNOLLYS

Miss Muriel Wilson to WSC

[2 May 1907]   Maryland
                                                St Jean sur Mer
                                                       France

My dear Winston,

I hear you are engaged to Miss Botha – is this true? But this is not the only matter of congratulation on which I am writing you. I was so pleased to hear you had been made Privy Councillor & meant to write to you the moment I heard it – & then this place with its lotus-eating propensities prevented me – ah it is such a divine spot – & the roses & honeysuckle smell almost too strong when we sit out after dinner – it is a world of profusion of the most georgeous flowers & I look forward to a peaceful old age here in the sun & surrounded by the blue sea, & *you* I hope – & Miss Botha, & all the little Bothas will come & see me & my garden (I shall be like Alice Rothschild) & I will have a luncheon party to meet you – other old crocks like ourselves – & the Prime Minister will write his name in our visitors' book & we will talk of wisteria in Lady Brougham's garden of prehistoric times.

... Alas! Alas!

Yours ever
MURIEL WILSON

[1] General Botha of the Transvaal was most eager to present the then uncut Cullinan Diamond to the King as a token of Transvaal loyalty. He spent the early part of 1907 assessing the King's reaction to such a move.

General Botha[1] to WSC

9 May 1907   London

Private

My dear Mr Churchill,

Before I leave it is my pleasant duty to write and thank you most heartily for the way in which you have received and helped me in the discussion of the most burning questions of the Transvaal. It has been indeed a pleasure to have been here and to have strengthened our acquaintance.

I know how glad my Government will be when I tell them of what assistance you have been to them, and what a thorough grip you have of all matters relating to the Transvaal.

I am well aware of the fact that you and the other members of the Government have as it were staked your reputation on the Transvaal, and I can assure you that my colleagues and I and the important section of the public who support us will see to it that your reputation is not imperilled and that the splendid confidence reposed by you in us all will prove a source of strength, nay more a great victory to you.

May I also wish you every success and say that I soon hope to see you at the top of the ladder?

Believe me to be, Yours very sincerely
LOUIS BOTHA

* * * * *

On May 15, the day after the Conference ended, the *Daily Mail* published a sensational account of the close of proceedings, representing that Sir Robert Bond,[2] the Premier of Newfoundland, had pleaded with Lord Elgin for revision of the Newfoundland fishery treaties, and, receiving the reply, 'We can give you nothing,' had jumped to his feet, denounced Newfoundland's treatment as 'a gross humiliation' and a deliberate neglect of the Colony for the sake of American interests, and walked out of the room. Bond denied that such an incident had occurred. In the House of Commons, WSC labelled the report 'a baseless and impudent fabrication' and expressed surprise that a 'person lately created a Peer [Lord Northcliffe] should allow newspapers under his control to employ methods of such transparent mendacity for political ends'.

[1] Against all predictions, the Het Volk had won the greatest number of seats in the Transvaal elections the previous February and Botha became the first Prime Minister.

[2] Robert Bond (1857–1927), Premier and Colonial Secretary, Newfoundland 1900–9; PC 1902; knighted 1901.

Baron Herbert de Reuter[1] to WSC

Reuter's Telegram Company Ltd

17 May 1907   24 Old Jewry

Private

My dear Sir,

We beg to acknowledge receipt of your letter of yesterday's date.

In dealing with a particular matter such as that which formed the subject of your statement in the House of Commons on Wednesday last, we have considerations both public and private to take into account. With regard to the *Daily Mail* report, we venture to maintain that we discharged our public duty in cabling to South Africa that you, at question time, most vehemently and absolutely contradicted the story told by that paper respecting the alleged episode at the Colonial Conference. The original report was a sensational one which was not likely to attract over-much attention in South Africa and accordingly, when we telegraphed that you had officially denied it in the most plain, the most complete and the most emphatic manner, the whole thing was disposed of once for all. Had we given your reply at greater length and touched upon your remarks with reference to the proprietor of the *Daily Mail*, we should, in our view, have involved ourselves in controversial questions which our private interests imperatively require us to eschew. A Minister is well entitled to pursue an attack and direct it against an individual person or newspaper and his statements in Parliament are privileged, but we have had some experience of the laws of South Africa which obliges us to observe the greatest caution in the wording of the despatches which we cable to the Colonial papers.

We fully believe that, on reflection, you will concur in the view which we have put forward that your absolute contradictions of the statement of the *Daily Mail* has crushed it once for all and that nothing more remains to be said about it.

Believe me to be, Yours very faithfully

HERBERT DE REUTER

[WSC's note: Ack & thank for their reply. 'Still I should have thought the full text of my answer wd have been protected by Parly privilege, & should have been cabled.' WSC.]

---

[1] Auguste Julius Clemens Herbert, 2nd Baron de Reuter of the Duchy of Saxe-Coburg-Gotha (1852–1915), Managing Director of Reuter's Telegram Company; granted permission by Royal Licence 1891 to use title in United Kingdom.

WSC to Sir Robert Bond

[Copy]

6 June 1907　　　　　　　　　　　　　　　　Downing Street

Dear Sir Robert Bond,

It did not seem necessary to publish your correspondence with Sir Francis Hopwood for two reasons: first because while you dissociated yourself from the account of the discussion upon Newfoundland questions published in the *Daily Mail* newspaper and denied the statement subsequently attributed to you by that paper to the effect that their account was 'substantially correct' you at the same time referred to other matters, which if I may say so without disrespect, were irrelevant to the point at issue and tended only to broaden the circle of controversy; and secondly, because the statement which I made with the concurrence of Lord Elgin and Sir Edward Grey as to the utter untruthfulness of the *Daily Mail* report seemed to have been accepted without challenge or dispute by the House of Commons, and to have stripped that newspaper of any claim in this matter at any rate upon public credence. Had further questions been put to me in Parliament it was my intention to avail myself of the letters which you had been good enough to write. In the absence of such questions, I was content to let the matter rest. I cannot however allow your speech at the West India Club to pass without a full acknowledgement of the frankness and integrity which you have shown in coming forward yourself to deny the untruthful reports which have been put into circulation and above all to repudiate the unwarranted and dishonest use of your name and authority in support of such reports.

Opinions may no doubt legitimately differ as to the merits or demerits of the various *précis* which were given from day to day of the proceedings of the Conference. All I know is that they were prepared with the greatest care by officers of high character and ability wholly removed from party or partisan influences and without any interference from political chiefs; and I am sure you will readily believe that Lord Elgin and I have quite enough work to occupy us without busying ourselves in cooking up versions of the Conference proceedings. But so far as the verbatim report of the Newfoundland discussion is concerned it was agreed that with the exception of your speech nothing should be published. This decision, to which you were a party, was come to unanimously by the Conference at the instance of the Secretary of State for Foreign Affairs, not because of any interest of His Majesty's Government which was involved, but solely because of the interests of Newfoundland and of Canada.

Yours sincerely

WINSTON S. CHURCHILL

Sir R. Bond to WSC

The Hotel Metropole

7 June 1907   London

Dear Mr Churchill,

I am in receipt of a note from your Private Secretary, covering a letter addressed by you to me under the date 6th instant, in which he intimates you propose to publish together with previous correspondence with Sir Francis Hopwood in the matter of the Colonial Conference.

I am much obliged for your kind reference to my remarks at the West Indian Club Banquet. I was hopeful that those remarks would have terminated all discussion, but I can, of course, have no objection to your publishing the correspondence, if you deem it necessary to do so at this date.

You will appreciate, I am sure, the impropriety of my entering into a discussion of the conduct of either the Colonial Office or of the English Press, except in so far as it directly affects my Colony, but, since you have mentioned that I was a party to the decision 'that with the exception of my speech nothing should be published', I feel it my duty to the Colony to put on record the fact that I was reluctantly compelled to become an unwilling party to that decision, in order to secure any mention whatsoever of the case of Newfoundland in the Proceedings of the Colonial Conference.

I shall feel much obliged if you can see your way to include this letter in the publication of previous correspondence.

Yours sincerely

R. BOND

*   *   *   *   *

WSC to Sir Percy Girouard[1]

TELEGRAM

5 June [1907]   Colonial Office

[Copy]

Private & Personal

I recommend your confining railway report to general policy & basing yourself upon existing surveys & estimates. These cannot be departed from without risk of delay so that grave convictions are needed to justify large changes. At the same time let us be on right lines at all costs. Report should

[1] Edouard Percy Cranwill Girouard (1867–1932), High Commissioner Northern Nigeria Protectorate 1907–08; entered Army 1888, served on the Nile Expedition 1897; Director Soudan Railways 1896–98; Commissioner of Railways Transvaal and Orange River Colony 1902–04; Governor of East Africa Protectorate 1909–12; Director-General Munitions Supply 1915. WSC wrote an account of Girouard's work in the Soudan in *The River War*.

be decisive upon policy dealing clearly *inter alia* with navigability Niger, proposed rate of construction, cotton production & possibilities of Kano & Zaria districts. It should further specify with full argument how much money could usefully be spent this year upon all work preliminary to actual track-laying assuming favourable decision reached upon main policy. When may we expect report? Pray continue to write fully hope you are keeping well.

CHURCHILL

Lord Elgin to WSC

5 June 1907   Colonial Office

My dear Churchill,

The last time we spoke of the subject of your plans for the autumn you expressed a wish that I should write you a few lines about your proposal to visit East Africa. I can only repeat that if it is convenient & appeals to you to undertake that expedition, it will I am sure be of the greatest advantage that you should have seen the country – where we have so many difficult problems to deal with.

I can only hope that it will be a pleasant as well as an interesting trip.

Yours ever
ELGIN

Lord Elgin to WSC

17 June 1907   Colonial Office

My dear Churchill,

I have passed the East Africa (Nairobi) draft without comment: as I see you want it early. But I notice that you gave directions for its preparation 'at once' though the despatch to which it is a reply was marked by Hopwood, quite properly, to me as well as yourself. I do not think this is a convenient course and I notice it now because it might have been very inconvenient to me – since Hindlip is attacking me in the H of L.

Yours v truly
ELGIN

WSC to Lord Elgin
(*Elgin Papers*)

18 June 1907

Dear Lord Elgin,

The Nairobi papers raised no question of policy not obviously determined by you already. No new issue of any kind was presented – except the preparation of a Blue book to wh a terminal despatch is the usual, recognised & almost inevitable conclusion. It seemed to me perfectly natural that the proposed Blue book should be presented for your approval or disapproval as a whole: & I do not see how such a procedure can be said to infringe in the slightest possible manner – direct or indirect upon your authority & effective control. So much a matter of form did I regard the drafting of the despatch – so clearly marked were the lines upon wh it should proceed – & marked by your decisions – that I gave no instructions of any kind verbal or written as to its tenor; nor did I alter a single word. The only decision I took upon myself was to direct that a despatch should be drafted for your approval in accordance with what I understand are in fact your views. This practice is adopted every day in the office by Assistant Secretaries & even by junior clerks. Where the policy is clearly decided it is unquestionably convenient. It saves time to the public, & to yourself the labour of reading the same file on the same point twice; & your decision is awaited as to whether the draft shall be altered, amended, suppressed, or replaced; or whether no despatch at all should be written, or no publication made. Over & over again Davis,[1] Lucas, Antrobus, Hopwood & others have adopted the course of sending on the draft for consideration with the minutes. But if you do not wish me to exercise such a discretion, I am most ready to defer to your instructions.

Let me only add that I am quite unable to understand how you could have been inconvenienced in any debate wh might have arisen in the Lords. You would have sent for the papers. You would have found a complete statement as well as the various telegrams & despatches. This I should have thought would have been a help & not a hindrance.

But in any case it could easily have been destroyed or put aside unread.

Yours vy trly

WINSTON S. CHURCHILL

Lord Elgin to WSC

20 June 1907   Colonial Office

My dear Churchill,

I am sorry I gave you the trouble of writing at length about the Nairobi despatch. We had not been quite at one at one stage but I admit we were at the end – & I had nothing to object to in the despatch. The difficulty is that I sometimes don't see the papers & get out of date with my information if they go back for drafting from you.

[1] Charles Thomas Davis (1873–1938), served in Colonial Office 1897–1930. Permanent Under-Secretary of State for Dominion Affairs 1925–30.

The cases where they stop lower down are different, for it is only you & I who have to fight in the open.

I have sent Hindlip a message to ask if he minds telling what papers he is going to ask for – but I rather think he may run up agt the Army Bill next week.

You may like to see enclosed from Sadler.

Yours v truly
ELGIN

*　　*　　*　　*　　*

WSC to Aylmer Haldane

(*Aylmer Haldane Papers*)

EXTRACT

11 June 1907   Colonial Office

My dear Haldane

... I am afraid there are a good many ugly versions of the events of that exciting night lurking about in the background of controversy, & fostered by very natural political antagonism. But I have a conscience absolutely clear. When I took my courage in both hands and climbed the wall, I had no idea that you had abandoned the attempt for that night, and still less did I know that you would be prevented by the vigilance of the sentry from following me. Once over – return was impossible. But I waited in imminent risk of detection for nearly an hour in the hopes you would be able to join me, & it was not until you yourself told me this was impossible, that I plunged out alone upon what seemed as desperate & forlorn an adventure as ever I have dreamed of.

I do not forget of course that when I first purposed to join in your plans of escape, you were embarrassed; because you knew that I was not strong enough to face the fatigues of such long marches & privation & because numbers multiplied dangers. But if I persisted in my desire to join you, it was because I felt that our comradeship on the 15th Nov, and my refusal to escape with the engine in strict and punctual execution of that comradeship, & my return to what I believed to be an utterly hopeless struggle – rather than leave you – constituted a solid claim. And you most loyally recognised this.

Deeply did I feel for you when at last I found myself safe in Lorenzo Marques. But in my heart I felt no shadow of reproach, and it [is] to that fact that I attribute the absence of emotion with wh I have heard of such imputations as are contained in your friend's letter.

All was well that ended well – for you too: for your own dramatic and wonderful escape was the most effectual re-establishment of your military reputation (after a surrender) wh could be conceived; & has most notably aided the steady course of your career.

With good wishes,

Believe me Yours vy sincerely
WINSTON S. CHURCHILL

Sir P. Girouard to WSC

TELEGRAM

7 August 1907   Government House
Zungeru
Northern Nigeria

Earnestly impress on you that question of amalgamation of Nigerias not clearly understood at Colonial Office, certainly not in S. Nigeria. It would be of inestimable value if you could come here instead of visiting East Africa. Best time to see our countries and place yourself in ideal position to know greatness of this little India. Arbitrary merging under existing conditions will be highly dangerous & hinder laying real foundation of West African progress.

[GIROUARD]

Lord Selborne to WSC

TELEGRAM

EXTRACT

22 August 1907

. . . My opinion has throughout been in favour of gift of Diamond to His Majesty. I am writing fully officially about it. . . .

WSC to Lord Knollys
(*Royal Archives*)

22 August 1907

Private

My dear Lord Knollys,

I enclose you a telegram I have received from Lord Selborne. I do trust no final decision will be taken by His Majesty in regard to it until the whole facts arrive officially together with the opinion of the High Commissioner which is on its way. Believe me it is a genuine & disinterested expression of loyalty & comes from the heart of this strange & formidable people. The Cabinet takes a vy unimaginative view wh in my opinion does not do full justice either to the significance or to the importance of the event. The feeling of loyalty to the King & of gratitude for the liberties which have been restored to them in His Majesty's name, are the strongest links between this country & the Transvaal.

I write this to you privately; but pray do not hesitate to show the letter to the King if you think that course would be proper.

Yours vy sincerely
WINSTON S. CHURCHILL

Note on letter: Seen ER

WSC to Lord Knollys
(*Royal Archives*)

27 August 1907

Private

My dear Lord Knollys,

Many thanks for your letter & I appreciate fully the force of all you say. But please read the enclosed from Selborne which expresses a vy strong opinion. I agree with every word of it; & I earnestly trust that it may commend itself to the King.

I understand the Cabinet this morning was inclined to think that the Diamond should after all be accepted, & that in any case His Majesty should be advised to await the full despatch of the High Commissioner & the formal offer of the Transvaal Government.

It is a great pity that Botha did not defer his presentation till he was sure of a unanimous vote: but the fact is that he did not, & if there are disadvantages in the King's accepting the gift, they must be pronounced altogether less serious & grave than those wh would result from a refusal however graciously expressed.

> Believe me, my dear Lord Knollys, Yours sincerely
>
> WINSTON S. CHURCHILL

Note on letter: I agree with this letter and after High Commissioner's telegram feel bound to agree with his advice. E R

WSC to Lord Elgin
(*Elgin Papers*)

1 September 1907   Colonial Office

Private

My dear Lord Elgin,

I wrote a sour Minute on Gallwey's[1] despatch about the Zulu prisoners in St Helena; but knowing your views in these matters, I have had it pasted all over.

I do not like his tone at all. It is quite clear that he has no sympathy with these unfortunate men. We seem to have the spirit of Sir Hudson Lowe[2] revived again in a most petty and prosaic form over these dusky captives. I do not look upon them as murderers, although no doubt that is their legal status. It has always been understood that they should be treated more like political *détenus* than common convicts. I do not think that the House of Commons would be impressed by their dietary. If they are to have no other groceries than salt, it is clear that their confinement will be most rigorous in this respect. I do not accept the easy assurance of the Governor that Zulus do not eat other groceries except salt, for I remember that he himself telegraphed to the Government of Natal saying that the Zulu prisoners who were in St Helena some years ago were allowed to have any groceries they liked. (See official papers.)

I do not think that stone-breaking ought to be their only employment. They ought to have a moderate task upon the roads each day; but after they have done their allotted task, they should be allowed to cultivate a small patch of land on which they could grow vegetables for their own use or for sale.

---

[1] Henry Lionel Gallwey (1859–1949), Governor of St Helena 1902–11; of Gambia 1911–14; of South Australia 1914–20; changed surname to Galway 1911; knighted 1910. The Zulu prisoners were gaoled after a rebellion in 1906.

[2] Sir Hudson Lowe (1769–1844), Governor of St Helena 1815–21, during confinement of Napoleon Bonaparte; was the object of an attack in 1822 by Barry Edward O'Meara, Napoleon's medical attendant at St Helena, who claimed that the distinguished prisoner had been maltreated by the Governor.

I do not see why they should not be taught to make baskets or carve wood, or make shoes, or some other simple form of light work, and I think that if any profit be made from the sale of these articles, the money should be given to them to buy any extra comforts they may wish.

I think that the Governor ought to be impressed by the fact that you are in earnest about the pledges which have been given to the House of Commons and that you will hold him responsible if he does not exert himself to make the lot of these unhappy Zulu exiles as little miserable as is compatible with their safe custody.

Pray forgive my writing this by another hand, but I am in the throes of packing up and am off in a few hours.

I had a most successful visit to Manchester and succeeded in settling the cap strike which had caused so much trouble and loss in my constituency. It was a great *coup* and will be of solid advantage if and when an election should become necessary.

With all good wishes, I remain, Yours vy sincerely

WINSTON S. CHURCHILL

Sir H. Campbell-Bannerman to WSC

9 September 1907

Belmont Castle
Scotland

Private

My dear Churchill,

Now that we have had a little breathing time, I feel impelled, on looking back over the Session, to send you a special line of congratulation and recognition of the large part you have had in our success. There cannot be two opinions on one point, viz. that the most conspicuous event in the year is the creation of a self-governing state in the Transvaal and in the Orange Colony. It is not only the greatest achievement of this Government (which is a comparatively small matter) but it is the finest & noblest work of the British power in modern times. And you have so identified yourself with this courageous & righteous policy, and so greatly contributed to its successful enforcement that a large part of the credit of it must be always attributed to you.

I cannot thank you too greatly for the help you have given in this and in other matters, and the constant readiness and effectiveness with which you have upheld true principles of government amid the debris and wreckage left by the blunders and crimes of recent years.

Take a good holiday and mind your health in this pilgrimage you are undertaking. Don't overdo it.

Your sincere friend and grateful colleague
H. CAMPBELL-BANNERMAN

Sir Francis Hopwood to Lord Elgin
(Elgin Papers)

EXTRACT

12 September 1907   Horswell House
                                                         S. Devon

... I return Gallwey's despatch ... The wording of the despatch evidently affected Churchill's temper but I cannot think he would press his 'remedies'. ... Churchill writes from the Continent in good spirits about his trip. I have begged him to be careful in Malta & Cyprus! ...

*   *   *   *   *

Lady Randolph to WSC

                                                         Rhifail Lodge
12 August [1907]   Thurso

Dearest Winston,

It was very good of you to read my 3rd chapter.[1] I have noted what you say about Blenheim. I only hope that my material will hold out to the extent of 100,000 words! I have left three chapters with Eddie Marsh and I *do* hope that you will be able to read them before you leave. The 5th chapter is political and I daresay you will not like some of the things I have said. In the 4th I have left a space for some Irish political notes – I do not know exactly where I can get my information. Perhaps you can help in this? Darling boy – I know I am asking a great deal – but I have such confidence in your judgement that I cannot do without it.

Now about yr house – I went to see Mabbett and Edge, who live in Mount St and made the man come with me and go over it. He is going to do his best to let it for you – for 6 months if possible. I went into all the particulars which I will not trouble you with. An inventory will be taken of everything including the books. This will not cost more than a few pounds. They charge a guinea a day. 2 days shd do the library. I hope you are enjoying yourself and are feeling fit.

[1] Lady Randolph was writing her *Reminiscences*, which were published the following year.

It is glorious here as regards air – one feels so fit, doubts on any subjects are impossible – I feel *everything* must succeed that I undertake. I hope it will turn out so. I can hardly realize that I shall not see you again for 6 months. Write to me before you go. Bless you darling I envy you your trip. Think of me sometimes. I love you very dearly.

Your
MOTHER

WSC to Lady Randolph

21 August 1907   Colonial Office

My dearest Mamma,

I have not had a moment till now to answer your letter. You will see the reason in *The Times* of yesterday. That Transvaal Loan took me a long time to prepare & consider & I really had no leisure to put pen to paper in other directions.

I am worried about the letting of the house. No Inventory has yet been taken & I wonder whether there is any real prospect of finding a satisfactory tenant. Also Miss Anning. I wish you could manage to board her out for me during my absence. It is deplorable to think of all the expenses that will be mounting steadily up in my absence. I do rely upon you dear Mamma to help me in arranging these affairs; for wh I am not at all suited by disposition or knowledge.

I spent a very peaceful Sunday with Jack at SH[1] and am going there again on Saturday when I return from Lancashire. Last night we had an all night sitting & I did not get to bed till 8 am!! Imagine how gummy I feel to-day.

The session drags on its belly to an end: not I fear before Thursday next. But these vy late sittings are making a great impression on Government business, & I think we shall have a very fair catch of fish to show for our pains in the end.

Nothing could be more poisonous than the behaviour of the Tories over the Transvaal Loan & the Diamond. Sneers & snarls of disappointed spite. I don't know why they wanted to drag these wretched Boers inside the British Empire, if they will not accept even their loyalty so generously tendered. Late lt night I replied again on the debate & walloped them well.

I have just come back from a long walk & talk with Rosebery, very pleasant & friendly. I am glad again to have seen him after such a long gap in our conversations. He seems to me to follow politics vy closely for all his

[1] Salisbury Hall, Lady Randolph's house near St Albans.

protestations to the contrary. But it is difficult to see how the future can help him – esp as he will not help himself.

I am settling up everything here as well as I can. I think I shall go to Paris on Sat or Sunday 31st or 1st & on straight to the manoeuvres with 'FE.'[1] Then we shall motor about through France & N Italy till we meet Sunny near Venice & so Vienna (22nd).

Freddie [Guest] has chucked me for my journey. His wife began to fuss about her accouchement & he had vy little choice. I expect he was wrong ever to contemplate going.

Gordon Wilson[2] comes with me instead. This is in some ways an advantage as he is an older man, vy sensible, & high in the Army. He will be just the man to deal with the soldiers. Wingate[3] proposes to send me a special steamer to Gondokoro, as I wished.

With best love, Mamma, ever your loving son
W

I will read your chapter before I go.

Lady Randolph to WSC

EXTRACT

22 August [1907]
Glenmuick House
Ballater

Dearest Winston,

The inventory of your house will only be taken when it is let. Don't worry about it – I shall be back the 28th of Sept and if it is not let by then, I will do my best to find you a tenant. Sept is not a good month, as people are away – October wd be more likely. Miss Anning will be back next month, and I will write to her about getting some work. She is away for her holidays but I know she means to try and find something on her return.

I am so glad you went to SH and are going again this Sunday. I had hoped to hear from Jack, but he hasn't written – I have been *au bout du monde* at Rhifail, letters taking 3 or 4 days on the way, but I have followed the H of C debates – and Eddie wrote to me of your all-night sitting.

---

[1] F. E. SMITH.

[2] Gordon Chesney Wilson (1865–1914), husband of Lady Sarah Spencer-Churchill, WSC's aunt; Lieutenant-Colonel Royal Horse Guards; served on General Baden-Powell's staff during the defence of Mafeking; killed in action on Western Front November 1914.

[3] Francis Reginald Wingate (1861–1953), Governor-General of Sudan 1899–1916; High Commissioner, Egypt 1917–19; knighted 1898; General of Artillery 1913.

You will be glad to get away from speeches – I thought the Govt wd have to practically drop the Scotch bill – I hear nothing but abuse of it. I don't pretend to know anything about it – but that dual ownership business has been tried in Ireland and has been found more than wanting! I liked yr Transvaal speech and quite agree with you that the Conservatives are odious and rude about the diamond. Of course it is rather awkward for the King, if the gift is not unanimous. Honestly I think Gordon Wilson is a good substitute for FG. He is very resourceful and when 'on his own' a very pleasant companion. There is a fund of dry humour in him which few people know.

Do try and read my chapters at SH. The 3 will only take you an hour – if as much – I want you to add to the 5th chapt that story of yr father and Goschen and the Exchequer. If told at all it must be well told – and I feel diffident – also make a little note in the 4th as to where I can get some Irish data – that chap is too short. I am still hankering after the letter about the pictures. Sunny denied having it – and yet you showed it to him.

I hate to think of your going off for so long – and that I shall not see you again before your departure. But you will enjoy it, and it will be a great rest and change. I still think you need not have offered to pay for your journey – *c'est magnifique mais ce n'est pas la guerre* – and no one will thank you for it. Mind you get Trevelyan's *Garibaldi* to read en route – also *Memories and Impressions* of George Brodrick. . . .

Goodbye my darling boy. I ramble on out of all bounds. Bless you – Do write again before you go. Walden knows where to forward letters. Scrivings can telephone and find out.

Your loving Mother
JCW

Lady Randolph to WSC

27 August 1907   Glenmuick House

Dearest Winston,

I hear from Jack that perhaps you go off tomorrow to Paris. I read with interest your speech at Manchester. I liked it all but the part referring to the land – but then – perhaps I do not understand it. George thinks that it does not matter about yr House & the trust. He certainly does not mean to have anything more to do with it, & you wd not like to take steps to force him to. You had better let Jack settle with George in what the money of St James's Square is to be invested in. Jack is quite competent to look after it, & you had better lease him a power of attorney to act for you. We cannot afford to let the money lie idle in the bank – & it might be months not to say years before Lumley disgorges those accounts. I hope you went to SH for Sunday. I have no news. My book & golf take up most of the time. It is very comfortable here & one can please oneself. George has gone stalking. I'm afraid poor Jack will be very dull without you or anyone – we do not return to SH till the end of next month. Write to me when you have a moment. Bless you. I have written to Leonie about yr house.

Your loving
MOTHER

Lady Gwendeline Bertie[1] to WSC

27 August 1907   Wytham Abbey
                                                          Oxford

Dear Mr Winston,

It is positively cruel of Fate to determine that we should not say good bye, not to allow us the opportunity of bidding each other a friendly farewell, for it is a long time to lose sight of someone, five months, it is five months that you will be away, five is it not, & that is a long time, & I really do think it might have been allowed us – I can not help rebelling against fate, for how entirely unreasonable it can be, considering what pleasure it would have given us, I made the assertion in the plural; why I can not think, but all the same you would have liked me to have wined & dined & I would have liked to have done so, & what I call fate is a chain of impossibilities which prevented me from coming up to London, & which was of no use my trying to free myself from; so I must content myself by wishing you from here a very pleasant, happy & delightful journey, which I feel sure it will be, it will be wildly interesting, & you will be wildly interested, but please don't become converted to Islam; I have noticed in your disposition a tendency to orientalism, pasha-like tendencies I really have; you are not cross my writing this, so if you come in contact with Islam, your conversion might be effected with greater ease than you might have supposed, call of the blood, don't you know what I mean, do do fight against it!

I am just off to the manoeuvres on the Downs, where what *Punch* calls the flower of the British Cavalry [are] mounting dashing chargers.

Goodbye, Yours sincly
GOONIE BERTIE

[1] Gwendeline Theresa Mary Towneley-Bertie (1885–1941), daughter of 7th Earl of Abingdon.

Lady Gwendeline Bertie to WSC

EXTRACT

28 August 1907   Wytham Abbey

Dear Mr Winston,

I wish I could go with you to Paris on Sunday – I have not been there for two whole years, and I do love it so, but I don't expect I know much of your Paris, it is the other Paris, the *jeune fille* Paris that I am better acquainted with.

It always sounds so, what shall I call it, 'radish', to say one likes Paris, going on a trip to Paris, but anything more prosaic, *comme il faut,* elevating and educating than the *jeune fille Pari* can not be found any where, that I am quite sure of; & now with motor cars & quick modes of conveyance one can get out so so easily to those wonderful earthly paradices such as Versailles & Fontainbleau & Chantilly; I remember as a child been taken there to see the Duc D'Aumale, but what a day's expedition it was in a carriage, & the dust or the mud, whichever the case may be according to the time of year, & I also remember the head gardener's little boy being eaten by one of those enormous carps in the moat there; have you ever been there? There are some huge carps, man eating animals, & that child disappearing down one of those creatures throats formed the foundation for ever after, of all my most nightmarish nightmares; they always have something to do with carps now. It was a pity you were not manoeuvring on the downs here this week – they would have interested you. You like manoeuvres & soldiers & war things, don't you? and I would have seen you, if you had been there, which would have been very nice, for I was out nearly every day; I do not profess to understand anything about it whatsoever, but I am bound to say I was rather disappointed with the whole show, of course I know it was not meant to be a show, and I must have been very much in the way, as I was twice removed from the middle of a charge, but I am sorry I am not more impressed with our soldiers, and not at all with the British officer that is to say the Home Cavalry ones – those were the only ones I saw.

I actually heard one of them, having come down with his squadron down the hill before he ought to have done so, & having discovered his mistake when he had got there, not wanting to have the trouble of going up again, exclaim he would now hook it back to camp for tea, & he did, he & his squadron; now I think that is a disgrace; just fancy thinking about tea in the middle of manoeuvres & showing so little keeness. Perhaps he is a rare exception, he must be I think . . . I do so admire your hostess of tomorrow,

Lady Crewe,[1] I think she is so handsome, a 'jolie laide' really, I do not know her, but I am sure she is clever & interesting.

I have written, written such a lot of rubbish, all ill spelt, ill composed, uninteresting & unpunctuated. I write, but you need not read! but I had a lot to tell you for tonight, I do not know why, but I had to tell you all this, it amused me, though it bored you. I am sorry!

Yours sincerely
GOONIE BERTIE

Lady Randolph to WSC

EXTRACT

30 August 1907   Glenmuick House

Dearest Winston,

I am glad that you are going to have 4 months respite from all enemies. Make the most of it. You have done splendidly & I hope this next move in the Cabinet will be to take you in. When does Eddie Marsh leave to join you? I want to send him a little present. . . . I wonder if you will approve of the 3 chapters you have to read. I sometimes feel disheartened about the book – & think it is not going to be good. . . . Bless you darling – take care of yourself – & do write. Any scrawl however short. Send the chapters *here* – if you send them not later than Sat 31st.

With best love yr loving
MOTHER

Lady Gwendeline Bertie to WSC

7 September 1907   Wytham Abbey

My dear Mr Winston,

Where are you? Where have you been? Where are you going to? What are you going to do? I have lost you for a whole week, I want to find you again – you have effaced yourself from my horizon – you know, you have never told me anything at all about your expedition to Africa – I should like to know what are your plans. I hope you are not going to Uganda are you? I have just been reading a book all about it; it is a country of fevers, man killing country, full of pestilentious insects and poisonous marshes, you really must not go there – I have sat down to write to you a letter, and

[1] Margaret Etrenne Hannah, second wife of 1st and last Marquess of Crewe, and daughter of 5th Earl of Rosebery.